REAL WORLD LABOR

SECOND EDITION

A READER IN ECONOMICS, POLITICS, AND SOCIAL POLICY FROM
DOLLARS&SENSE

EDITED BY IMMANUEL NESS, AMY OFFNER, CHRIS STURR,

AND THE *DOLLARS & SENSE* COLLECTIVE

REAL WORLD LABOR, 2nd edition

ISBN: 978-1-878585-78-3

Published by:
Economic Affairs Bureau, Inc. d/b/a *Dollars & Sense*
29 Winter Street, Boston, MA 02108
617-447-2177; dollars@dollarsandsense.org.
For order information, contact Economic Affairs Bureau or visit: www.dollarsandsense.org.

Real World Labor is edited by the *Dollars & Sense* Collective, which also publishes *Dollars & Sense* magazine and the classroom books *Real World Macro*, *Real World Micro*, *Current Economic Issues*, *Real World Globalization*, *Real World Latin America*, *Real World Banking and Finance*, *The Wealth Inequality Reader*, *The Environment in Crisis*, *Introduction to Political Economy*, *Unlevel Playing Fields: Understanding Wage Inequality and Discrimination*, *Striking a Balance: Work, Family, Life*, and *Grassroots Journalism*.

The 2011 *Dollars & Sense* Collective:
Arpita Banerjee, Ben Collins, Katharine Davies, Amy Gluckman, Ben Greenberg, Vera Kelsey-Watts, James McBride, John Miller, Larry Peterson, Linda Pinkow, Paul Piwko, Smriti Rao, Alejandro Reuss, Bryan Snyder, Chris Sturr, and Jeanne Winner.

Co-editors of this volume: Immanuel Ness, Amy Offner, Chris Sturr
Editorial Assistant: Katharine Davies
Editorial assistance: Hallie Acton, Jared Eisenberg, Amy Gluckman, Christopher Hearse, John Miller, Linda Pinkow, Alejandro Reuss, and Bryan Snyder.

Cover design: Chris Sturr, based on a design by David Garrett, dgcommunications.com.
Cover photo: Copyright © Jim West, jimwestphoto.com.
Production: Chris Sturr and Katharine Davies.

Printed in U.S.A.

CONTENTS

CHAPTER 10 • LABOR AND MILITARISM

Chapter 1

LABOR LAW, POLICY, AND REGULATION

Article 1.1

ANOTHER WORLD IS POSSIBLE
Reviving the labor movement requires returning to solidarity unionism.

BY STAUGHTON LYND
March 2008—WorkingUSA

The new worldwide movement against "globalization"—meaning U.S. imperialism—and for a better day, has come up with a defining slogan: Another World Is Possible. The words remind us that a social movement is unlikely to bring about what it does not even try to achieve. Current efforts to revive the labor movement in the United States define their objectives so narrowly that even if successful, they would not change anything fundamental.

One such proposal is to *increase the amount of money spent on "organizing"* to increase the percentage of the labor force that belongs to unions. Such an increase in union "density" might maximize the influence of existing unions, but would not change their entanglement in the management prerogative and no-strike clauses that exist in almost all collective bargaining agreements. These two clauses give profit-maximizing management the right to make the fundamental decisions and take away from workers the ability to do anything about it.

Another widely endorsed strategy is *card-check elections*. If enacted into law, that procedure would very likely increase the number of bargaining units represented by existing unions. It would do nothing to change the top-down, bureaucratic character of those organizations. Indeed, in the absence of prolonged election campaigns and vigorous public controversy, card-check elections might very well cause unions to become even less democratic than they now are. Moreover, experience suggests that in the absence of legislation, in order to obtain card-check elections, unions often make significant concessions (about which the affected workers have no say) as to what will be in the contract after the union is recognized.

A third widely articulated strategy is *minority or members-only unionism*. The idea is that an employer should be required to bargain with any group of employees who request it, even if those workers are not a majority of the workforce. This is much the best mainstream formulation for improving the labor movement because it requires a union to prove its value through actions, not promises. However, the idea has significant drawbacks.

Those who favor minority unionism see it as an intermediate step toward majority support and recognition of the union as exclusive bargaining agent. Moreover, like so many other notions of labor law reform, it seems to require legitimation by some arm of government (such as Congress or the National Labor Relations Board) before it becomes real.

Better than any of these strategic visions would be a deliberate return to the essential principle of the labor movement: the principle of solidarity. The Knights of Labor and the IWW articulated this principle of solidarity for all time in the words, "an injury to one is an injury to all." Certain applications of this principle are self-evident. For example, it would finally preclude the creation of separate wage tiers for workers who do essentially the same jobs and differ only with respect to their dates of hire. Again, it would require the labor movement to seek solutions that benefit *both* workers who seek to enter the U.S. *and* workers who are already here.

In order to develop such solidarity unionism in practice, workers, labor historians, trade union officials, and labor lawyers must affirm the underlying idea that answers to the miseries presently experienced by workers in the U.S. (and elsewhere) will develop from the bottom-up, not from the top-down.

We need to go back to the experience of workers in this country in the early 1930s who were unable to get help from either national unions or the national government, and who, therefore, turned to each other, improvising new central labor bodies to coordinate their local general strikes. Rather than seek assistance from the courts, they sought to get the judges off their backs, through the anti-injunction provisions of the federal Norris-LaGuardia Act and the little Norris-LaGuardia laws of a number of states. The indispensable precondition for a new bottom-up labor movement is to give up the quest for a magical new leader of the existing trade union movement who will make all well again.

Intellectuals associated with the labor movement have a special responsibility. In 1995, two labor historians circulated an Open Letter to President-elect John Sweeney, which greeted Sweeney's elevation as "the most heartening development in our nation's political life since the heyday of the civil rights movement," assessed his election as "promis[ing] to once again make the house of labor a social movement around which we can rally" and pledged "to play our part in helping realize the promise of October."

When Andrew Stern later denounced Sweeney and led several major unions into a new organization, Barbara Ehrenreich declared that "the future of the American dream" was now "in the hands of Andrew Stern" possessing a "vital agenda for change" and "a bold vision for reform." This was presumably before Stern's coalition with Wal-Mart.

The foregoing makes clear why it is so important to look again at John L. Lewis, to move beyond Saul Alinsky, Melvyn Dubofsky, David Brody, and Robert Zieger, indeed beyond the consensus of labor historians, concerning this paradigmatic figure. Here, the research of Jim Pope is the gateway to understanding the importance of rank-and-file activity as central to labor movement growth. As Pope states:

> According to the standard story, section 7[a] of the National Industrial Recovery Act [made possible] a brilliant organizing campaign that reestablished the mine workers' union in the soft coalfields. The story begins in late May 1933, when UMW President John L. Lewis—anticipating the enactment of section 7(a)—commits the union's entire treasury. . . . One hundred organizers fan out into the coalfields . . . claiming "the President" wants the miners to join the union. . . . [W]ithin weeks of section 7(a)'s signing, the union enrolls the overwhelming majority of miners in the soft coalfields.

In this standard story, Pope rightly observes, "coal miners rarely appear and strikes—if they enter the story at all—play a subsidiary role," and are said to have been masterminded by Lewis.

Pope tells us that he began his research when the *New York Times* headline "Coal Men tell Roosevelt Code will be Signed Today: 16 Shot in Riots at Mines" caught his attention. Inquiry revealed that strike activity in the summer of 1933 involved 100,000 miners spread out over 1,000 miles of mountainous terrain. The self-activity of coal miners in southwestern Pennsylvania and West Virginia began before any initiative by Lewis and without his assistance. In Pope's words, they "brought their common law of solidarity into the realm of public struggle." Section 7(a) "neither sparked the movement nor shaped its demands." By May 17, 1933, when the NIRA was presented to Congress, "the organizing upsurge in garment and coal was already in full swing."

From self-organization, the miners moved on, according to Pope, to enforcement from below. Lewis advised miners not to strike because the real action would be in Washington and announced that strike activity was unauthorized. When President Roosevelt intervened personally to broker a truce, striking miners refused to return to work. UMW Vice President Philip Murray then entered into an agreement with the owners that banned all mass picketing. The strikers, however, viewed picketing "not as a form of communication, but as an enforcement device."

Space does not permit a full summary of Pope's marvelously detailed narrative. The miners stayed out despite wage cuts and promised wage increases because Pope says what they wanted was "structural change" and a "new industrial order." The strikers organized themselves through pit committees that superseded the official UMW apparatus. Pope concludes:

> Throughout the struggle, John L. Lewis had been a step behind the local union activists. His celebrated organizing campaign was not launched until after rank-and-file miners had already rejuvenated the union. Once deployed, his organizers worked persistently to undermine the strike movement. . . . Thus, the sensational recovery of the UMW union—later touted by Lewis as a product of centralized discipline and federal government lawmaking—was in fact brought

about by a democratic movement of local activists enforcing their own vision of the right to organize.

We must demythologize not only John L. Lewis, but also all such leaders including Philip Murray, Walter Reuther, Cesar Chavez, Arnold Miller, Ed Sadlowksi, Ron Carey, John Sweeney, and Andrew Stern, and we must reconceptualize rank-and-file movements as something more than caucuses to elect new bureaucratic union leaders.

The rank-and-file movements of the early 1930s ran candidates for office, but they also refused to accept collective bargaining agreements negotiated behind closed doors; initiated wildcat strikes, local general strikes, and a national textile strike; and did not shy away from the option of seceding to start new unions.

They believed, in the language of the antiglobalization movement, that another world is possible, and in the language of Karl Marx and Friedrich Engels, that they had a world to win. ❏

Sources: "The Rise of the House of Labor," *In These Times*, December 25, 1995; Steve Early, review of John Sweeney, *America Needs a Raise*, and Andrew Stern, *A Country That Works*, in *WorkingUSA: The Journal of Labor and Society*, March 2007; James G. Pope, "The Western Pennsylvania Coal Strike of 1933, Part I: Lawmaking from Below and the Revival of the United Mine Workers," *Labor History*, May 2003.

The Short Run: Labor Rights Begin at Home
September/October 2007

The National Labor Relations Board "guarantees the right of employees to organize and to bargain collectively with their employers," according to its mission statement. But not if the employer is the NRLB itself, apparently. Created by Congress in 1935 to administer the National Labor Relations Act, the seminal law that gave U.S. workers the legal right to form unions, the board is now refusing to bargain with the union representing its own field attorneys, field examiners, and support staff, *Labor Notes* reports. On June 8 the Federal Labor Relations Authority (FLRA), which oversees federal employees, certified the workers, formerly covered by four separate contracts, as a single bargaining unit. But the NLRB is challenging the FLRA decision. "The decision," claims NRLB General Counsel Ronald Meisburg, "places the independence of the General Counsel at risk." What about the independence of NLRB employees to determine the composition of their bargaining unit and the selection of a union to represent them?   —*Sudeep Bhatia*

Article 1.2

BEFORE AND AFTER TAFT-HARTLEY

BY HARRIS FREEMAN
March 2008—WorkingUSA

In June of 1947, the U.S. had a new labor policy when both houses of Congress handily overrode Harry Truman's presidential veto to pass the Taft-Hartley Act amending the National Labor Relations Act of 1935 (NLRA). Future amendments to federal labor law have not mitigated the fundamental anti-labor impact of Taft-Hartley. Despite tumultuous shifts in the U.S. and world economies and the precipitous decline in private-sector union membership, Taft-Hartley's amendments to the NLRA remain integral to the legal framework for 21st-century labor relations.

The Taft-Hartley Act was an explicit governmental rebuke of the mass working-class movement set in motion by the Great Depression that spearheaded the unionization of basic industry in the 1930s and compelled Congress to enact the NLRA in 1935. The NLRA granted American workers what the Supreme Court famously labeled the *fundamental right* to organize unions, strike, and bargain collectively. By 1941, when the U.S. entered World War II, union membership had spiked to nine million workers; by 1945, union membership soared to fifteen million. Most of basic industry was 80–100% organized and a third of the civilian workforce belonged to unions.

A decade later, at the close of World War II, the world witnessed American labor's greatest upsurge. Pent-up demand for consumer goods, the erosion of purchasing power, soaring corporate war profits, and the massive layoff of two million defense industry workers eroded rank-and-file support for the wartime wage freeze and no-strike pledge adopted by the AFL and CIO leadership. On top of this, tens of thousands of soldiers, many of whom were schooled in the militant tactics of the 1930's union drive, were organizing to demand that that the eight million GIs be brought "home now" and be provided with jobs. An organized American working class appeared well positioned to address these and other challenges facing workers in the postwar economic and social order. Indeed, between 1945 and 1946, U.S. workers engaged in unprecedented mass demonstrations, carried out the sequential shutdown of almost all basic industry and, in many cities, launched general strikes. In the year following V-J day, more than five million workers participated in the largest strike wave ever in an advanced capitalist nation, surpassing the scope and size of the often-heralded 1926 British general strike. Importantly, these strikes advanced broad political and social demands to sustain working-class purchasing power and direct postwar economic growth. Calls for full employment, 30% wage increases and a shorter workweek with no cut in pay echoed on picket lines. It was during this time that United Auto Workers president, Walter Reuther, famously called for a 30% wage hike at General Motors with no increase in car prices.

While the strike wave brought advances in wages and benefits, labor uniformly failed to win its broader social and economic demands. Moreover, draconian measures to restrain labor's power were advanced by all branches of the federal government. President Truman threatened to conscript strikers. Truman also won a victory at the Supreme Court permitting him to ignore the anti-injunction provisions of the Norris-La Guardia Act and invoke presidential commander-in-chief powers to enjoin coal-field labor strikes. Given the state's assault on labor, it is not surprising that millions of workers shunned the 1946 midterm elections and that Republicans won a majority in Congress. Following the Republican victory, Truman called for cooling-off periods before strikes, bans on secondary boycotts, and other restrictions on labor rights in his 1947 State of the Union address. The stage was set for the passage of the Labor Management Relations (Taft-Hartley) Act.

The following provisions are among the Taft-Hartley Act's most significant revisions to labor law:

1. The NLRA's preamble was conspicuously revised. No longer was the employing class a denier of labor rights. The preamble now stated that only "some" employers were anti-union. Strikes and other forms of concerted action sanctioned by the NLRA were being utilized by "some" union leaders and members to impair commerce and, as such, federal policy required that such practices be "eliminated" to ensure the public's economic interests.

2. Accordingly, the right to engage in concerted activity, to join unions and bargain collectively codified in Section 7 was offset by a new labor "right" that protected a worker's right "to refrain" from concerted activity.

3. The NLRA's coverage, already excluding agricultural, domestic, and public sector workers, was further narrowed. Independent contractors were placed outside the Act's definition of employee, denying them protection of federal labor law. Foreman and supervisors were also excised from the definition of employees, shutting down a burgeoning unionization wave among frontline shop floor supervisors.

4. A new class of unfair labor practices committed by labor organizations was added for which individual workers and employers could seek redress. Section 8 was enlarged to include a barely intelligible thicket of statutory text that banned workplace picketing, strikes, and concerted activity if intended to promote secondary boycotts and refusals to handle "hot cargo." In addition, a union strike to compel industry-wide collective bargaining agreements was made an unfair labor practice, limiting strike activity that reaches beyond the level of the firm.

5. Under the original NLRA, union elections were strictly an employee affair; deciding which union, if any, to join was a debate among employees. Under Taft-Hartley, elections soon became a forum for the boss's anti-union diatribe. Under § 8(c), the right of an employer "to express any views, argument or opinion" to employees was immunized from any claim of unfair labor practice under as long as the speech does not contain a "threat of reprisal or promise of

benefit." This so-called "free-speech" clause opened the door for the sophisticated employer campaigns widely used to oppose unionization.

6. Individual states could now outlaw mandatory membership under union shop provisions, allowing workers to opt out of paying union dues while reaping the benefits of collective bargaining. By 1953, seventeen southern and western states passed so called "right-to-work laws."

7. The President of the United States was authorized to declare a national emergency, circumvent the anti-injunction provisions of the Norris-LaGuardia Act and order the Attorney General to seek a federal court injunction to halt any industry-wide strike or lockout, if, in the President's opinion, the strike or lockout "imperil[s] the national health or safety." A mandatory 60-day cooling-off follows such an injunction during which any strike action is prohibited.

Taft-Hartley, branded by the union movement as a "slave-labor bill," revamped the official policy driving federal labor law and reworked key statutory provisions governing labor organizing, strikes and boycotts, collective bargaining and the relationship between the state and the unions. But Taft-Hartley was not an overnight sea change in American labor-relations policy. Major portions of the bill had been developing in Congress since at least 1940. Moreover, judicial rulings and National Labor Relations Board (NLRB) policy had by the early 1940s reflected the federal government's policy of subordinating worker rights to the goal of achieving economic stability and industrial peace. Nevertheless, the enactment of Taft-Hartley codified an important shift in labor policy. ❏

The Short Run: Forced into Scabbery
November/December 2005

A temp agency in San Francisco placed twelve Hurricane Katrina survivors as scabs at the California Pacific Medical Center, *Labor Notes* reported in October. Eight hundred workers, represented by the SEIU, have been on strike at the hospital since September 13. So the time-tested antiunion strategy of pitting workers against one another provides yet another way for the bosses to exploit natural disasters!

—*Amy Gluckman*

Article 1.3

U.S. LABOR LAW—STACKED AGAINST WORKERS

How the United States' stacked labor laws make it nearly impossible for workers to gain union representation.

BY ANDREW STROM
September/October 2003

Ever wish you had a union at work? Surveys show that half of all non-union workers do. Still, less than 10% of private sector workers in this country enjoy the benefits of union representation. How is this possible? U.S. labor laws that are stacked against workers can take much of the blame.

Under the National Labor Relations Act (NLRA)—the law that governs labor relations for most of the private sector—to obtain bargaining rights a union must represent a majority of the employees in an appropriate "bargaining unit." So, first you and your co-workers have to figure out who counts as an "employee." According to the NLRA, supervisors—anyone who uses "independent judgment" to "responsibly direct" the work of others—are not "employees." This excludes millions of workers who would qualify as workers under any common sense definition and leaves millions more unsure if they have a legal right to unionize.

Let's say there are 60 people at your workplace; five are clearly supervisors, five more are borderline supervisors, and 35 of the remaining 50 workers want a union. You should be home free, right?

Not so fast. Your employer is not required to bargain with your chosen union just because all or a majority of workers sign a petition. Instead, your employer can demand a secret ballot election held by the National Labor Relations Board (NLRB, the federal agency that administers the NLRA). The law gives employers any number of ploys they can use to drag out the election process and to craft a bargaining unit where they'll win the vote. Before the election, your employer can insist on a hearing about whether the bargaining unit the workers have selected is "appropriate." For instance, if workers at a retail chain store want a union, the company will argue that the bargaining unit must include every store in the metropolitan area. The employer may also demand a hearing about the borderline supervisors, trying to exclude them from the union if they are pro-union and insisting on their right to vote if they are anti-union.

If you clear these hurdles, your employer will almost certainly wage an anti-union campaign in the months before the election. When the NLRA was first passed in 1935, the NLRB held that employers were prohibited from interfering in union elections, but the 1947 Taft-Hartley Act allowed employers to express anti-union views as long as they do not make threats or promises.

Now, employers may require workers to attend anti-union meetings without providing equal time to pro-union workers. (By contrast, under federal election law, if an employer invites one candidate to address employees, it must give the same opportunity to all other candidates.) Supervisors can meet individually with workers and ask them to vote against the union. (Compare this with sexual harassment law, which recognizes that it can be inherently coercive for a supervisor to ask a subordinate for a date.) The company may also post and distribute anti-union propaganda while simultaneously prohibiting workers from distributing union literature in work areas. (Imagine a political election where only the incumbent is allowed to advertise.) And thanks to a 1992 Supreme Court decision, non-employee union organizers have no right to campaign on the employer's private property, even if the property includes a large parking lot open to the public.

If you work in the airline industry you are covered by the Railway Labor Act (RLA), and a different set of rules applies. The National Mediation Board, which regulates elections under the RLA, has found that it is inherently coercive for employers to hold small group or one-on-one meetings to campaign against the union. But in other ways, the RLA makes obtaining union representation especially difficult for those it covers. Under the RLA, for example, you must organize as part of a nationwide bargaining unit, making it highly impractical for workers to organize at large, geographically dispersed companies. This is why Federal Express got Congress to amend the RLA in 1996 so that it would be covered.

Some anti-union tactics are illegal. But even where the law does place limits on employers' actions during an organizing drive, it fails to provide meaningful remedies or deterrents. You may think that if you were fired for trying to organize a union, a clear violation of the NLRA, you could sue and win a multi-million dollar verdict. But unlike laws that protect workers from other forms of discrimination, there is no private right to sue under the NLRA. Your only recourse is to file a charge with the NLRB. The Regional Director will conduct an investigation, but won't give you access to the information it gets from your employer. Your chances aren't good; Regional Directors dismiss almost two-thirds of all cases without a hearing. Even if the Regional Director decides to take your case, the only remedy is an order of reinstatement and back wages, less any wages you earned in the interim. There are no fines, no penalties, and no punitive damages. And reinstatement only comes at the end of a lengthy legal process—a hearing before an Administrative Law Judge, an appeal to the five-member NLRB in Washington, followed by an appeal to the U.S. Court of Appeals. The process routinely takes five years. No wonder companies regularly fire workers for trying to organize.

What if, despite your employer's anti-union campaign, you and your co-workers stick together and vote for union representation? Your employer has one more chance to contest the result, by claiming (again) that the bargaining unit was inappropriate, or that workers were threatened by union organizers, or any of a dozen other reasons to invalidate the election. Whether or not the arguments succeed, the employer can usually buy two more years of delay until the U.S. Court of Appeals orders it to bargain.

Once bargaining finally begins, your employer's only obligation is to bargain in "good faith." One-third of the time, workers who vote to unionize never even get a first contract. Why? If your employer fails to bargain in good faith, the only remedy is ... an order requiring it to bargain in good faith. Workers cannot recover damages for the deprivation of their right to bargain.

Suppose your employer does negotiate in good faith. Getting a good contract is still hardly a given. Traditionally, workers would strike if their employer refused to give in to their demands. But strikes rarely succeed these days. Your employer can't fire you for striking, but it can hire "permanent replacements." When strikers try to return to work, the employer does not have to take them back, it merely has to place them on a preferential hiring list in case any of the permanent replacements quit.

Of course, any strike would be more effective if you could expand it beyond your own employer. But the Taft-Hartley Act made it illegal for workers to strike or picket one employer in order to put pressure on another. This prohibition against "secondary" strikes applies even to strikes against another subsidiary owned by the same company. It also prohibits actions that go one step up the corporate food chain; for example, janitors who work for a cleaning contractor cannot picket the building owner. And workers at Ford or GM are prohibited from striking to support workers at a parts supplier.

Nevertheless, there are still some workers who have enough power to wage an effective strike by themselves. But once again Taft-Hartley is there to keep the workers in check. The law allows the President to enjoin any strike that poses a threat to "health and safety"—a provision courts have interpreted broadly to include threats to the nation's economic well-being.

Unions grew rapidly after the NLRA was passed in 1935, but the percentage of unionized workers has declined steadily since the passage of Taft-Hartley in 1947, when over 40% of private sector workers belonged to unions. A comprehensive labor law reform bill was introduced during the Carter administration that would have given unions equal time when employers hold anti-union meetings, strengthened the remedies for violations of the law, and speeded up the enforcement process. The bill was filibustered to death by Republicans. During the Clinton administration, there was a proposal to limit the ability of employers to hire permanent replacements for strikers, but again it didn't get the backing of the 60 Senators necessary to prevent a filibuster. Since that defeat, unions have virtually given up on achieving labor law reform.

In a few instances workers have, with union backing, waged successful campaigns that get around one-sided labor laws by using shareholder activism, marches and rallies, reaching out to elected officials, handbilling, and the Internet. But with labor law so stacked against workers, it's a miracle that any workers manage to gain union representation at all. ❑

Article 1.4

UNREGULATED WORK
Is enforcement the next battle in the fight for workers' rights?

BY SIOBHÁN McGRATH AND NINA MARTIN
September/October 2005

Guillermo* regularly puts in 70-hour weeks as a prep cook in a New York City restaurant. He came to the United States from Ecuador six years ago because he heard that "you can earn something for your family." But these aspirations soured after he wasn't paid for three weeks. Small sums of money and continued promises from the boss keep Guillermo returning to work each day for his 12-hour shifts.

Non-payment of wages plagues Guillermo and his co-workers, but their employer uses other tactics to reduce labor costs as well. Guillermo explains, "Workers have to punch out as if they had worked eight hours. So after eight hours, they punch out and then work four more hours. It is almost like a threat that if you don't punch the card, you're fired." With an average wage of about $300 per week, these long hours translate into just over $4 per hour. Some of Guillermo's co-workers have left the restaurant for other jobs, usually at food establishments, but often the working conditions they face are frustratingly similar.

Brenda, an African-American grandmother, is a child care worker in Brooklyn. Formerly a home health care worker, Brenda's own health no longer permits her to make the long commute to her patients' homes. Caring for children in her home seemed like a good way to replace this lost income. The parents of the children she cares for receive subsidized child care as they move from welfare to work. Brenda has no sick days or vacation days, and she only has health insurance through her husband's job.

Worse, her pay often dips below minimum wage. But the city's Human Resources Administration, which cuts her check, maintains that this does not break the law. Even though the city effectively sets her pay, it classifies her as an "independent contractor," rather than an employee. So Brenda doesn't have the same rights as a regular employee, such as the minimum wage, overtime, or paid leave.

Unfortunately, the experiences of Guillermo and Brenda are far from unique. Violations of employment and labor laws are a growing problem in U.S. workplaces. Employers in many sectors of the economy are breaking the law in order to cut costs, gain a competitive edge, and boost profits, and workers are suffering the consequences. In some industries, the abuses have become so common that they are now routine practice. And enforcement by the government has steadily declined, so that more and more workers are facing abusive and unsafe conditions at work. Anyone who pays attention knows that U.S. workers in certain industries and occupations have long been vulnerable to employer abuses. But today, illegal and abusive practices are becoming common in a far larger swath of the economy, and the will and resources to enforce worker-protection laws are shrinking.

We are part of a large research team working out of three universities that

---

* The names of the workers have been changed.

is studying this phenomenon—what we call "unregulated work"—in New York City and Chicago. Over the past two years we have conducted in-depth interviews with over 400 workers, employers, government officials, community groups, union staff, and policy advocates. The next phase of our project will be a survey of workers in unregulated jobs, in order to estimate the size of this hidden zone of the economy. To date, we have found unregulated work in 14 industries. While many people are familiar with the conditions faced by garment workers and construction day laborers, the tentacles of unregulated work stretch into many other sectors of the economy, including workplaces as diverse as restaurants, grocery stores, security companies, nail salons, laundries, warehouses, manufacturers, building services firms, and home health care agencies.

We have documented considerable variety in how employers violate laws. They pay their workers less than minimum wage, fail to pay them overtime, refuse to pay them for all hours worked, or simply don't pay them at all. They disregard health and safety regulations by imposing unsafe conditions, forcing employees to work without providing necessary safety equipment, and failing to give training and information. The list of ways employers break the law goes on: they refuse to pay Unemployment Insurance or Workers' Compensation; they discriminate against workers on the basis of race, gender and immigration status; they retaliate against attempts to organize; they refuse medical leaves.

Such stories of substandard working conditions may sound familiar—they carry strong echoes of the experiences of workers at the beginning of the last century. At that time, the solution was to pass laws to create wage minimum standards, protect workers who speak up for their rights, and eventually, guarantee workplace safety and outlaw discrimination. That these very laws are now being so widely violated poses new challenges. While efforts to pass new laws raising workplace standards are still critical, a new battle has emerged to ensure that existing laws are enforced.

What Explains Unregulated Work?

The rise of unregulated work is closely tied to many of the same factors that are thought to be responsible for declining wages and job security in key sectors of the economy. Over the last 30 years, for example, global economic competition has been extinguishing the prospects of workers in manufacturing. Local manufacturers struggle to drive down their costs in order to compete against firms located in Asian or Latin American countries where wages and safety standards are lower.

Yet unregulated work cannot be explained simply as a byproduct of globalization. It's true that the competitive pressure felt in manufacturing may ripple through other parts of the economy, as wage floors are lowered and the power of labor against capital is diminished. But we found businesses that serve distinctly local markets—such as home cleaning companies, grocery stores, and nail salons—engaging in a range of illegal work practices, even though they are insulated from global competition.

Declining unionization rates since the 1970s also contribute to the spread of unregulated labor. One effect has been a general rise in inequality accompanied by lower wages and workplace standards: a weaker labor movement has less influence on the labor market as a whole, and offers less protection for both unionized and non-union workers. More directly, union members are more likely to report workplace violations to the relevant government authority than non-union workers, as a number of studies have shown. So it makes sense that employers are increasingly committing such violations in the wake of a long-term decline in the percentage of workers in unions.

But even the powerful one-two punch of globalization and de-unionization provides only a partial explanation. Government policy is also instrumental in shaping unregulated work—not only employment policies per se, but also immigration, criminal justice, and welfare "reform" policies that create pools of vulnerable workers. In this environment employers can use a variety of illegal and abusive cost-cutting strategies. Perhaps most significantly, they are deciding whether or not to break the law in an era of declining enforcement, when they are likely to face mild penalties or no penalties at all.

Immigration Policy

The deeply flawed immigration policy in the United States creates a labor supply that is vulnerable at work. For example, employers often convince undocumented workers that they have no rights at the workplace. If undocumented workers demand to be paid the minimum wage, their employers threaten not just to fire them, but also to "call immigration." Armed with such threats, employers break the law with little fear of being held accountable. Yet this strategy is only possible because U.S. immigration policy currently denies an estimated 10 million undocumented immigrants legal recognition, thereby ensuring a steady stream of vulnerable workers. In spite of the protections they have on paper, undocumented workers consistently report feeling that government assistance is off-limits because of their immigration status.

The victims of unregulated work are not, however, limited to undocumented immigrants. Immigrants who are authorized to work are also a significant part of this workforce. Employers sometimes simply assume that people from certain countries are undocumented. Some workers are hampered by a lack of proficiency in English. Many new arrivals also lack knowledge of U.S. labor and employment laws and employers can, and do, exploit this ignorance.

For example, the newly arrived Polish women we interviewed who work at A-1 Cleaning in Chicago are usually very pleased to have quickly found work that does not require a full command of English. A Polish immigrant founded the home cleaning company, using his ties in the community to find new workers. But this is not a story of ethnic solidarity. This employer often fails in his duty to inform these workers that their rights under U.S. law include such novel concepts as a minimum wage and overtime pay, and routinely violates these rights. If employees don't fully understand workplace regulations and their rights under the law, an unscrupulous employer can get them to work for less than minimum wage.

Prison, Welfare, and Discrimination

Immigrants are not the only workers made more vulnerable to workplace exploitation by government policies. Many workers, like Brenda, were born and raised in the United States but face barriers to employment in the more regulated part of the labor market. Predictably, race, ethnicity, and gender play a role in determining who ends up in the unregulated workforce. In addition, people leaving the welfare rolls or coming out of prison are especially vulnerable: they are pushed to find work as soon as possible, yet the stigma attached to having been on welfare or in prison limits the options available to them. For "ex-offenders," this is compounded by the fact that they are legally barred from certain jobs. Similarly, some features of welfare reform policies, such as abrupt or arbitrary benefit cutoffs, or "work first" policies that force people to take the first job offered, only make it more difficult to find a satisfactory job. Ironically, the only stable employment history some workers are able to build is in unregulated work, but because they are "off the books" this does not translate into better prospects in formal jobs, so they stay mired in exploitative jobs.

Employers also keep workers trapped in unregulated jobs through illegal discrimination. In New York City's restaurant industry, for example, a white college student applying for a job will be given a front-of-the-house job such as waiting tables, seating people, or operating the cash register. A Mexican worker, regardless of language skills or immigration status, will instead be funneled into a back-of-the-house job such as dishwashing, cooking, or janitorial work. These behind-the-scenes workers are then more vulnerable to violations and extremely unlikely to be promoted to better positions.

Externalization and Exclusion from Legal Protection

New business strategies in recent decades have produced a clear shift towards the "externalization" of work. Various forms of subcontracting and outsourcing are now widespread, and allow employers to evade responsibility for mistreating workers. When workers complain about abusive or illegal practices, the firm and its subcontractor can always point fingers at each other. Overall, the growth of outsourcing has driven many jobs into spaces where the reach of regulation is weak or nonexistent.

Employers also insulate themselves from workers' demands for improved working conditions by hiring temporary workers or using subcontractors. Some use placement agencies to do their dirty work, routinely asking them to screen workers on the basis of gender, race, age and other characteristics. In one of the most egregious examples we discovered, some employment agencies in New York demand sensitive health information from job seekers. A group of workers explained to us that these agencies also post signs refusing job applications from western Africans or South Africans. In this way, they seem to believe that they are screening out potentially HIV-positive candidates for their clients. One of the main services these agencies provide, then, is to discriminate simultaneously on the basis of national origin and disability.

Tapping into a contingent workforce of day laborers allows many employers to keep their costs to an absolute minimum. The emergence of day labor corners in many cities is one of the most visible examples of unregulated work. Day laborers are hired for a variety of jobs, including construction, cleaning, and moving. Besides the often dangerous and difficult working conditions they face, day laborers may work for employers who scrimp on promised wages or fail to pay them at all.

Chicago's largest day labor corner is on the city's northwest side, in the parking lot of a gas station. Known colloquially as the "slave station," the corner is the morning destination for large numbers of men who hope to find a day's work. Many of the men are Polish; others are Mexican, Ecuadorian, Guatemalan, and Ukrainian. They have often just arrived in the city and have large debts incurred while traveling to the United States. Contractors actively try to bid down wages of workers by playing them off against one another. While the going wage in the area for these jobs is between $8 and $10 per hour, day laborers are sometimes forced to accept as little as $4 per hour rather than go without work.

Some workers are especially vulnerable to employers' abuses because they are located outside the reach of some, or even all, legal protections. For example, although domestic workers are covered by minimum-wage laws and other protections, they are not covered by the National Labor Relations Act, and so they don't have the right to organize. This means that their employers are effectively given free reign to fire them for complaining about their jobs or demanding better treatment. Farm workers are similarly vulnerable, since they are exempt from protection of many labor laws.

Employers are increasingly misclassifying their workers as "independent contractors" in order to evade workplace regulations. The problem, as Cathy Ruckelshaus of the National Employment Law Project points out, is that this classification is only supposed to be applied to independent businesspersons. "You have to ask yourself, especially in the case of some of the low-wage workers," she says, "whether these people are actually running their own businesses or not." Child care workers, construction day laborers, janitors, street vendors, delivery people and bathroom attendants have been placed into this category, when in fact they were dependent upon their employer for scheduling, job assignments, equipment and training—signaling their status as traditional employees.

The Enforcement Problem

Our fieldwork indicates that unregulated work is a growing feature of business strategies at the bottom of the labor market. Very few attempts have been made to estimate the prevalence of workplace violations, but our preliminary findings are in line with evidence gathered by other researchers. For example, in the late 1990s the U.S. Department of Labor (DOL) carried out several surveys to assess compliance with the Fair Labor Standards Act (FLSA)—the law that regulates the minimum wage, overtime, and the use of child labor. Among their results: in 1999, only 42% of restaurants in Chicago and only 35% of garment shops in New York City were in compliance with FLSA.

Unfortunately, just as employer violations appear to be increasing, the resources allocated to enforcement are waning. Data we recently received from the Department of Labor shows that while the number of workplaces in the United States more than doubled between 1975 and 2004, the number of compliance actions by the DOL's Wage and Hour Division (WHD) declined by more than a third. As Howard Wial, a senior researcher at the Brookings Institution, writes, "The general picture that emerges … is that there has been a long-term decline in the adequacy of enforcement resources, which has probably resulted in a long-term decline in the amount of attention that the WHD pays to low-wage workers."

So employers are unlikely to be the target of WHD inspections, and if they are, penalties are unlikely to be high enough to provide a deterrent. An unprincipled employer may find that it is cheaper to break the law—and run the slight risk of getting caught—than it is to comply. David Weil, an economist at Boston University, conducted a cost-benefit analysis of compliance in the garment industry, including data on the annual likelihood of inspection, the average underpayment per worker, and the median civil penalty. He found that for an apparel contractor with 35 workers, "the potential cost of not complying [with minimum-wage requirements] is $121 versus a benefit of $12,205, implying that an apparel employer should clearly choose not to comply."

The problem of unregulated work is not just a "race to the bottom." It is a race that is taking place below the bottom. The legal floors on wages and working conditions are increasingly irrelevant to American employers. For the workers who populate this segment of the labor market, there is no guarantee that workplace laws will protect them.

Workers Push Back

The good news is that on the ground, community groups and other advocates are taking action. Workers are protesting for the wages owed them even as they are filing complaints with the Department of Labor or filing suits in court. In New York, workers have also collaborated with the state Attorney General's office, which has undertaken a number of initiatives to bring law-breaking employers into compliance. Immigrant workers in particular are organizing, either with unions or through Worker Centers, on the basis of industry and occupation. Day-labor groups across the country are creating "job centers," where wage rates and rules for hiring are collectively set and enforced by workers.

Advocates are also using legislation to pressure the relevant government agencies to enforce the law to protect workers. Campaigns are also underway to pass state legislation that would tie businesses' operating licenses to their compliance with labor and employment laws. In 2003, a new law in California increased employers' responsibility for violations carried out by their subcontractors. And a local law passed the same year in New York City increased the responsibility of employment agencies for the actions of their clients who hire domestic workers.

Clearly, a greater commitment to workplace enforcement, backed up by sufficient resources, will be necessary to combat the increasing number of violations of workers' rights. Yet more enforcement alone will not be enough. A deeply flawed immigration policy also needs to be fundamentally changed, so that all workers enjoy the minimum standards under the law, regardless of their citizenship status. In practice, our current immigration system accepts people into the country but then effectively denies them rights in the workplace. This creates a steady stream of vulnerable workers. Comprehensive immigration reform, with a sound path to legalization, is an essential component of efforts to guarantee workers' rights. Similarly, comprehensive changes to welfare and penal policies would make people returning to the workforce less vulnerable to exploitation in the unregulated workforce.

The growth of unregulated jobs has created a new terrain in the battle for workers' rights. While continuing efforts to raise the minimum wage and improve workplace standards are critical, in practice employers are routinely violating the standards that already exist. A greater commitment to enforcement, comprehensive reform in a range of areas of government policy (including immigration, penal, and welfare policy), and efforts to close the loopholes employers are currently taking advantage of, will all be necessary to fulfill the promise of protective labor legislation. ❑

The Short Run: The Smelly American
September/October 2007

Are the inexorable laws of global capitalism causing corporations to export their manufacturing and service operations to low-wage countries, or is it just that U.S. workers are boorish, lazy slobs? Secretary of Labor Elaine Chao says it's the latter. A recent article in *Parade* magazine entitled "How safe is your job?" quotes Chao as expressing her concern for the competitiveness of the U.S. workforce. "American employees must be punctual, dress appropriately, and have good personal hygiene," Chao said. "They need anger-management and conflict-resolution skills, and they have to be able to accept direction. Too many young people bristle when a supervisor asks them to do something."

Chao has since claimed that her comments were taken out of context, *Labor Notes* reports. Evidently, she thinks that in addition to all their other flaws, U.S. workers are too stupid to recognize an insult when they hear one.

—Allison MacDonald

Article 1.5

TAKING CARE OF THEMSELVES

BY JULIE HERLIHY
September/October 2010

After years of struggle and debate, the state of New York has taken a big step toward improving working conditions for domestic workers. The law, which passed the state's legislature on July 1, guarantees domestic workers time-and-a-half pay for overtime, one day off per week, and the protection of anti-discrimination laws and standards.

Political compromise left other rights and protections, including paid vacation, advance notice of termination, severance pay, and paid sick days, on the cutting room floor. The new law also side-steps the question of collective bargaining rights, promising only to study the issue. Nonetheless, the domestic workers of New York are now the only ones in the country with even the most basic legal protections.

Domestic workers, responsible for the care of the elderly, of children, and of homes, are not protected by modern labor regulation; they were specifically excluded from the purview of the 1935 National Labor Relations Act. An estimated 93% of domestic workers are women, many of them migrants. Working in unregulated household settings, they are particularly vulnerable to exploitation and abuse.

The movement to develop and pass the bill was largely spearheaded by Domestic Workers United, an advocacy organization for New York City's estimated 200,000 domestic workers. Members drafted the first version of the New York Domestic Workers Bill of Rights in 2004, then kept up the pressure throughout the painstaking six-year legislative process. They developed relationships with state legislators, made contacts with powerful feminist leaders such as Gloria Steinem, and testified about their own work experiences in numerous appearances at the statehouse in Albany.

Now, activists in fourteen other states who are working toward the same goal hope the victory in New York will be just the first of many. ❑

Article 1.6

HARD WORK AT AN ADVANCED AGE

BY AMY GLUCKMAN
September/October 2010

Among the many proposals that the Social-Security-is-in-crisis crowd is tout-ing is an increase in the retirement age. The Social Security "full retire-ment age" was 65 from the program's inception until 1983, when Congress leg-islated a gradual increase, based on year of birth, to 67. The 1983 amendments did not change the age of earliest eligibility for Social Security retirement ben-efits, which remains 62. However, those who opt to start receiving benefits before they reach the full retirement age for their cohort face a lifetime cut in their monthly payment.

At first glance, it seems reasonable to push the retirement age upward in line with average life expectancy, which rose rapidly in the United States during the 20th century. But that rise in life expectancy owes a great deal to sharp drops in infant

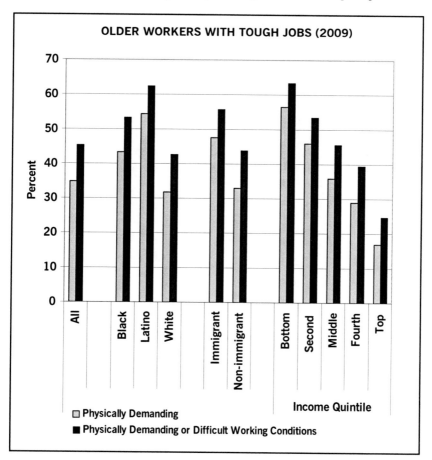

and child mortality. For those who survive to adulthood and especially to old age, the change is far less dramatic. People who turned 65 in 1940, the first year monthly Social Security retirement benefits were paid out, could expect to live to nearly 79; those who turned 65 in 1990 had a life expectancy only about four years longer.

What would it mean to ratchet up the full retirement age further? The answer is: It depends. Some 60- and 70-somethings can readily continue working and postpone receiving Social Security benefits; a few have sufficient personal savings and/or private pensions that they will never need to rely on Social Security at all. But for the millions of older custodians, cooks, cashiers, construction workers, and others who do physically demanding work, having to put in even a few more years on the job before they can receive their full Social Security benefits is a different story.

A surprising number of older workers have these kinds of jobs, as a study by Hye Jin Rho of the Center for Economic and Policy Research shows. Following the classifications used in the U.S. Labor Department's Occupational Information Network database, the study defines "physically demanding" jobs as those that require significant time standing or walking, repetitive motions, or handling and moving objects. "Difficult working conditions" include outdoor work, use of hazardous equipment, and exposure to contaminants. Of the 18.8 million U.S. workers who are 58 or older, over 45% have physically demanding jobs and/or difficult working conditions. The rate is even higher for the 5.2 million workers 66 and up (48.2%).

Certain groups of older workers—in particular, non-white, immigrant, and lower-income workers—perform these tough jobs at disproportionate rates (see figure). Not surprisingly, the workers who can least afford to take an early-retirement penalty in their monthly Social Security check are often those who are most likely to reach their mid-60s saying, "Time to quit!" ❑

Sources: Hye Jin Rho, "Hard Work? Patterns in Physically Demanding Labor Among Older Workers," Center for Economic and Policy Research, August 2010; U.S. Social Security Administration, "Life Expectancy for Social Security"; Laura Shrestha, "Life Expectancy in the United States," Congressional Research Service, August 2006.

Article 1.7

WHAT'S BEHIND UNION DECLINE IN THE UNITED STATES?
Questions and answers about industry trends, the "employer offensive," declining enforcement of labor law, and "business unionism."

BY ALEJANDRO REUSS
March 2011

I understand that union membership has been going down in the United States since the 1980s. How much have unions shrunk?

The total number of union members in the United States peaked in the late 1970s and early 1980s, at over 20 million. As of 2010, it remained near 15 million. The story of union decline in the United States, however, does not begin in the 1980s, nor is it as modest as these figures would suggest.

Union density (or the "unionization rate"), the number of workers who are members of unions as a percentage of total employment, has been declining in the United States for over half a century. The share of U.S. workers in unions peaked in 1954, at just over one fourth of employed workers. For nonagricultural workers, the high-water mark—at more than one third of employed workers—came even earlier, in 1945. It would reach nearly the same percentage again in the early 1950s, before beginning a long and virtually uninterrupted decline (see Figure 1).

By 2010, the unionization rate for employed workers was less than 12%. The percentage would be even lower were it not for increasing unionization among public-sector workers since the 1960s. For employed private-sector workers, the unionization rate is now less than 7%.

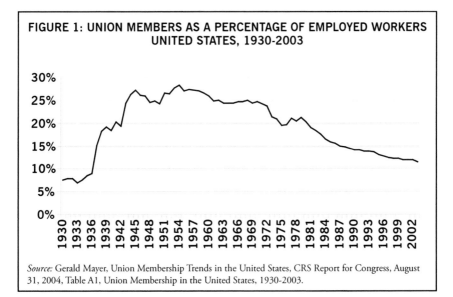

FIGURE 1: UNION MEMBERS AS A PERCENTAGE OF EMPLOYED WORKERS UNITED STATES, 1930-2003

Source: Gerald Mayer, Union Membership Trends in the United States, CRS Report for Congress, August 31, 2004, Table A1, Union Membership in the United States, 1930-2003.

What are the main reasons for union decline? Is it just that there are no manufacturing jobs anymore?

There are multiple reasons for union decline, including declines in employment in highly unionized industries, declines in unionization rates within these traditional bastions of unionism, and failures to unionize in new, growing sectors.

In the heyday of U.S. unions, from the 1940s through the 1960s, union membership was concentrated in the "core" sectors of manufacturing, construction, mining, and transportation. In the early 1950s, unions included over 40% of workers in manufacturing, over 60% in mining, and over 80% in both construction and transportation/communications/utilities.

Total employment levels in manufacturing, mining, and utilities have declined dramatically in recent decades. Employment in manufacturing was much larger, at its peak, than in these other sectors. Its decline, from over 19 million workers in the late 1970s to less than 12 million today, is paralleled by smaller absolute declines in mining and utilities. Increasing mechanization and automation are a big part of the reason for the long-term employment declines in manufacturing and other former core sectors. Increased imports and "offshoring" of production are also factors.

Figure 2 shows the difference, for selected industries, between actual union membership in 2010 and what it would have been if total employment and industry unionization rates were as in 2010, but the distribution of employment among different industries was as in 1983. (A comparison with the early 1950s would have been preferable, but consistent data are not available going back that far.) As the graph shows, union membership

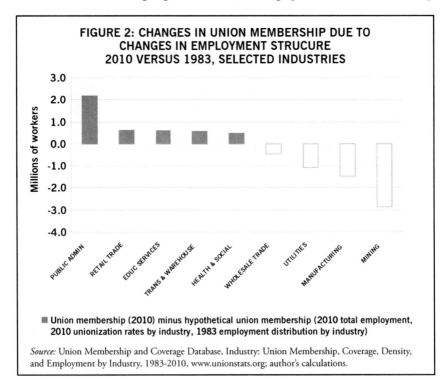

FIGURE 2: CHANGES IN UNION MEMBERSHIP DUE TO CHANGES IN EMPLOYMENT STRUCURE 2010 VERSUS 1983, SELECTED INDUSTRIES

■ Union membership (2010) minus hypothetical union membership (2010 total employment, 2010 unionization rates by industry, 1983 employment distribution by industry)

Source: Union Membership and Coverage Database, Industry: Union Membership, Coverage, Density, and Employment by Industry, 1983-2010, www.unionstats.org; author's calculations.

is lower now than it would have been in sectors with declining employment, with the largest "losses" in manufacturing, mining, utilities, and wholesale trade.

Meanwhile, however, union membership is higher now that it would have been in sectors with increasing employment, with the largest "gains" in public administration, retail, education, transportation, and health care. The losses in the declining-employment sectors are partly offset by gains in the increasing-employment sectors. (Remember that "gains" and "losses" refer to the difference between actual union membership and *hypothetical* levels, if the employment structure had remained as in 1983.) While the losses in the main losing sectors are greater than the gains in the main gaining sectors, and much larger if we look only at the private sector, the changes in employment structure only explain a fraction of the decline in union membership.

If it's not the loss of manufacturing jobs, what are the main causes of union decline?

Unionization rates have declined dramatically across most industries, including in what were traditionally highly unionized sectors. In manufacturing and transportation/communications/utilities, the unionization rates in 2000 were less than one third what they had been a half century before; in construction, less than one fourth; in mining, barely one sixth.

Declining unionization rates account for much of the overall decline in union membership. Figure 3 shows the difference, for selected industries, between union membership now and what it would have been, with total employment and the

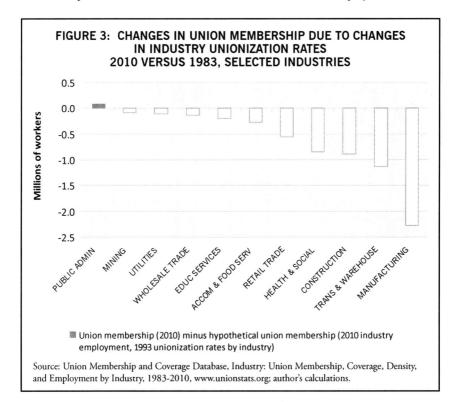

FIGURE 3: CHANGES IN UNION MEMBERSHIP DUE TO CHANGES IN INDUSTRY UNIONIZATION RATES 2010 VERSUS 1983, SELECTED INDUSTRIES

■ Union membership (2010) minus hypothetical union membership (2010 industry employment, 1993 unionization rates by industry)

Source: Union Membership and Coverage Database, Industry: Union Membership, Coverage, Density, and Employment by Industry, 1983-2010, www.unionstats.org; author's calculations.

employment structure as they are now, but with industry unionization rates from 1983. Since unionization rates have declined in almost all industries, we see union "losses" running across nearly all the industries shown, with the only exception being public administration. The largest losses come in traditional union strong-holds: manufacturing, transportation, and construction. Notice, however, that there are also losses in growing industries: health care, retail, hotels and restaurants, and education. (Remember, again, that "losses" here compare actual union membership to what it would have been, given current industry employment, but 1983 union-ization rates. In fact, total union memberships in health care, education, and hotels and restaurants have increased, due to increasing employment in these sectors.)

Why have unionization rates declined?

Employers' determination to rid themselves of unions has certainly played a major role in declining unionization rates. Where employers could not break unions by frontal assault, they were determined to find ways around them. Unionized companies estab-lished parallel non-union operations, a practice sometimes known as "double breast-ing," gradually shifting production and employment away from their unionized facili-ties. Some employers began contracting out work, formerly done by union employees, to non-union subcontractors (the original meaning for "outsourcing"). Some estab-lished new operations far from their traditional production centers, especially in less unionized and lower-wage areas. Many companies based in the Northeast and Upper Midwest, for example, set up new production sites in the U.S. South and West, and eventually in other countries. (For a great historical account on one company, see Jefferson Cowie's *Capital Moves: RCA's 70-Year Quest for Cheap Labor.*) Finally, new employers entered highly unionized sectors, but most often remained non-union. The auto industry is a good example. So-called "transplants" (factories owned by non-U.S. headquartered companies) have accounted for an increasing share of the industry's shrinking labor force, and have remained largely non-union.

You also mentioned failures to organize unions in industries where employment is growing. Why is that?

Historically, union growth has come primarily in short spurts when unions expand into new industries. Since the 1940s, however, U.S. unions have failed to organize in growing industries to compensate for the declines in employment and union-ization rates in traditional union strongholds. The one major exception has been unionization, since the 1960s, among public-sector employees. Since the early 1970s, union density for public-sector workers has increased from about 20% to over 35%. This has not been nearly enough, however, to counteract the decline among private-sector workers. To maintain the overall unionization rates of the 1950s or 1960s, unions would have had to enlist millions more workers in the private sector, espe-cially in services.

   We should not assume that the explanation for the lack of new organization in growing private-sector industries is simply that workers do not want unions. In fact, poll-ing data from 1984 to 2004 show an increasing percentage of non-union workers would have voted to form a union, if given the opportunity to vote in a secret-ballot election. In 1984, less than one third of non-union workers would have "definitely or probably" voted to form a union. Two decades later, more than half of non-union workers would have. Meanwhile, the percentage that would have "definitely or probably" voted against a union declined from nearly two thirds to a little more than one third.

It is clear, on the other hand, that *employers* have turned sharply against unions. In the 1930s and 1940s, many employers accepted unions, grudgingly, as a way to ease labor unrest. As much as employers might dislike unions and collective bargaining, they were preferable to strikes or even factory occupations (or "sit downs"). Since the 1970s, however, employers have fought unions and unionization drives with increasing aggressiveness, as part of what labor historian Michael Goldfield calls the "employer offensive." In the early 1970s, Goldfield notes, about 15% of National Labor Relations Board (NLRB)-supervised union elections were so-called "consent elections," in which employers had come to a prior agreement with the union(s) on the terms of the election. Historically, unions are more likely to win consent elections than elections in which the employer formally disputes the terms of the election, such as the group of workers (or "bargaining unit") that has the right to vote and will have union representation if the union wins. By the early 1980s, only about 3% of NLRB elections were consent elections.

In addition, employers increasingly sought to delay union elections. Goldfield shows that, the longer the delay between an organizing campaign and election, the lower the likelihood of union victory. Partly, this may be due to a predictable decline in enthusiasm, with the passage of time since the beginning of a unionization campaign. It is also due, however, to employer intimidation of union supporters in the time between unionization campaigns and elections. In many unionization campaigns, employers fire vocal union supporters, both eliminating pro-union campaigners and making other workers afraid of being fired as well. Researchers at the Center for Economic and Policy Research (CEPR) have found that, between 2001 and 2005, pro-union workers were illegally fired in around one fourth of all union election campaigns. Meanwhile, in many campaigns, employers threaten that, if the union wins, the workplace will be shut down (at least in part) and workers will lose their jobs. Labor researcher Kate Bronfenbrenner reports, in a study from the mid 1990s, that employers threatened plant closings in more than half of all unionization campaigns, and that such threats cut the union victory rate (compared to those in which no such threat was made) by about 30%.

Aren't there labor laws that protect workers' rights—to join unions, bargain collectively, and even go out on strike? Are employers really allowed to engage in these kinds of intimidation tactics?

There are labor laws, but these protections are not always strong enough, and they are not always enforced. The employer offensive has unfolded, especially since the 1980s, against a backdrop of government hostility towards unions. Unions and pro-union commentators have argued that, since the 1980s, the federal government has often turned a blind eye to illegal tactics (or "unfair labor practices") routinely used by employers to fight unionization drives. Employer retaliation against workers (by

firing or otherwise) for union membership, union activity, or support for unionization is illegal. An employer threat to close a specific plant, in response to a unionization drive, is also illegal. However, union supporters argue, the government agencies
tasked with enforcing labor law have ignored such practices, imposed only "slap on
the wrist" punishments, or delayed judgment, sometimes for years, long after the
unionization campaign is over and done with.

Many labor historians point to the Reagan administration's mass firing of striking
air-traffic controllers (members of the Professional Air Traffic Controllers Organization,
or PATCO) in 1981 as a signal to private employers that the federal government approved
of their own "union-busting" activities. Before the PATCO strike, it was relatively rare
for employers to fire striking workers and hire "permanent replacements." (Sometimes,
employers would bring in replacements during a strike, but striking workers would
get their jobs back after a settlement was reached.) After PATCO, private employers
responded to strikes, with increased frequency, by firing the strikers and bringing in permanent replacements—a practice that is illegal in many countries, but not in the United
States. The number of large strikes, already in sharp decline during the preceding few
years (possibly due to the employer offensive, rising unemployment, and other factors),
has since declined to microscopic proportions. (see Figure 4).

*But employers and the government have opposed unions in the past, too, and still unions
have had periods of growth. Are unions doing something wrong now that explains the
failure to organize new workers?*

Pro-labor and pro-union commentators have been among those *most* critical of
U.S. unions and their leaderships for not devoting themselves sufficiently to new
organizing. Union leaderships, they argue, have been largely content to mark the
time between one bargaining period and the next, collecting dues from their existing memberships, even as the number of union members dwindled. Moreover, the

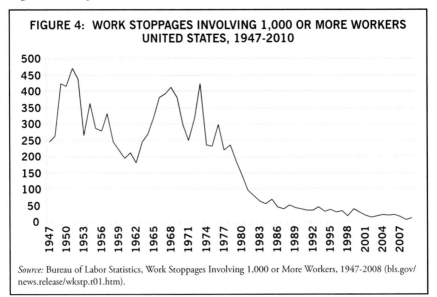

FIGURE 4: WORK STOPPAGES INVOLVING 1,000 OR MORE WORKERS UNITED STATES, 1947-2010

Source: Bureau of Labor Statistics, Work Stoppages Involving 1,000 or More Workers, 1947-2008 (bls.gov/
news.release/wkstp.t01.htm).

whole spirit of the labor movement changed in ways that made new organizing more difficult.

Unions were built, economic historian Gerald Friedman argues, primarily through mass upsurges by workers themselves. They grew the most during waves of strikes and other dramatic bursts of collective action. They were mass social movements. Over time, however, this spirit waned. Union members became less active in the unions, and unions played smaller and smaller roles in the lives of their members. Union leaderships usually did not seek to encourage members' active involvement, which they saw as a threat to their authority. Leaders embraced "business" or "service" models of unionism: Workers hired a union to represent them at the bargaining table and get them a better deal, or to argue their side in disputes with management, much as one would hire a lawyer or an insurance company. That is hardly a vision to inspire great movements of people.

Well, are there any prospects for a union revival?

Union decline is not a uniquely U.S. phenomenon. Union densities, Friedman notes, have declined in almost all rich capitalist countries. In some countries, however, unions have been relatively successful in new organizing, and the declines have been modest. The decline has been greater in the United States than almost anywhere else (see Figure 5). Partly this is due to an especially negative environment for both existing unions and new organizing, and partly to the weaknesses of organized labor itself. Changes in labor law, or even in the enforcement of existing labor law, could make the organizing environment more favorable.

The weakness of the organized labor movement as a political force and the absence of a major labor-based, social democratic, or socialist political party (unlike in most rich capitalist countries), however, makes these kinds of public policy changes less likely. The failure of the U.S. union movement to win labor-

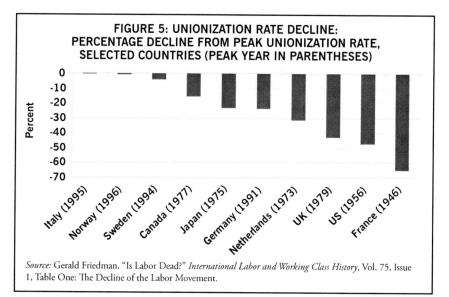

FIGURE 5: UNIONIZATION RATE DECLINE: PERCENTAGE DECLINE FROM PEAK UNIONIZATION RATE, SELECTED COUNTRIES (PEAK YEAR IN PARENTHESES)

Source: Gerald Friedman, "Is Labor Dead?" *International Labor and Working Class History*, Vol. 75, Issue 1, Table One: The Decline of the Labor Movement.

law reforms during the current administration, especially long-sought legislation that would have required employers to bargain with a union as soon as a majority of the workers signed union cards (known as the Employee Free Choice Act), reflects this weakness. Meanwhile, several state administrations have launched a new wave of attacks on labor rights, particularly the collective-bargaining rights of public-sector workers.

At this point, unions in the United States—including less than a tenth of private-sector workers—are almost back down to the level they were at the beginning of the Great Depression. The 1930s turned out to be the greatest period of union growth in U.S. history, with substantial additional growth in the 1940s and 1950s largely an aftershock of that earlier explosion. There is no guarantee, however, that history will repeat itself, and that the weakness of organized labor today will give way to a new burst of energy. In the midst of a deep recession, and now the beginnings of a halting recovery, there have been few signs of a labor revival. Ironically, only the recent attacks on public-sector workers and unions have provoked a mass-movement fight-back. Labor supporters, however, should understand this, soberly, as coming from a very defensive position. ❏

Sources: Bureau of Labor Statistics, Table 1. Union affiliation of employed wage and salary workers by selected characteristics (www.bls.gov/webapps/legacy/cpslutab1.htm); Gerald Friedman, "Labor Unions in the United States" (eh.net/encyclopedia/article/friedman.unions.us); Bureau of Labor Statistics, Employees on nonfarm payrolls by industry sector and selected industry detail (www.bls.gov/ces/cesbtabs.htm); Bureau of Labor Statistics, Table 3. Union affiliation of employed wage and salary workers by occupation and industry (www.bls.gov/cps/cpslutabs. htm); Union Membership and Coverage Database, U.S. Historical Tables: Union Membership, Coverage, Density and Employment, 1973-2010 (www.unionstats.org); Michael Goldfield, "Labor in American Politics—Its Current Weakness," *The Journal of Politics,* Vol. 48, No. 1. (Feb., 1986), pp. 2-29; Kate Bronfenbrenner, "Final Report: The Effects of Plant Closing or Threat of Plant Closing on the Right of Workers to Organize," *International Publications,* Paper 1, 1996; Gerald Friedman, *Reigniting the Labor Movement: Restoring Means to Ends in a Democratic Labor Movement* (New York: Routledge, 2008); Gerald Mayer, Union Membership Trends in the United States, CRS Report for Congress, August 31, 2004, Table A1, Union Membership in the United States, 1930-2003; Bureau of Labor Statistics, Work Stoppages Involving 1,000 or More Workers, 1947-2008 (www.bls.gov/news.release/wkstp.t01.htm); Richard B. Freeman, "Do Workers Still Want Unions? More than Ever," Economic Policy Institute, EPI Briefing Paper #182, February 22, 2007 (www.sharedprosperity.org/bp182.html); John Schmitt and Ben Zipperer, "Dropping the Ax: Illegal Firings During Union Election Campaigns," Center for Economic and Policy Research, January 2007 (www.cepr.net/documents/publications/unions_2007_01.pdf), Gerald Friedman, "Is Labor Dead?" *International Labor and Working Class History,* Vol. 75, Issue 1, Table One: The Decline of the Labor Movement.

Article 1.8

WHAT WISCONSIN MEANS

BY ROGER BYBEE
May/June 2011

When Wisconsin Gov. Scott Walker addressed the Milwaukee Press Club on Friday Feb. 11 about public-sector union rights, he sounded less like a rookie governor floating a legislative proposal than a uniformed *generalissimo* issuing a demand for total capitulation.

Citing a $137 million state budget "crisis," Walker called for the legislature to act immediately on a bill that would effectively gut the union rights of state and local public employees (except for police and firefighters) by, among other things, prohibiting collective bargaining over any issue besides wages, limiting contracts to one year, eliminating dues check-off, and forcing unions to win annual re-certification votes. His address was followed by a carefully timed barrage of radio and TV ads funded by the right-wing lobby group Club for Growth. Highlighting recent concessions made by workers at several private-sector companies in the state, the ads called for sacrifices from supposedly overpaid public workers in the name of "fairness."

Then, as everyone knows, all hell broke loose.

The dramatic events of the month that followed—from the massive daily demonstrations, to the self-imposed exile of Democratic state senators to an Illinois hotel, to Gov. Walker's revealing 20-minute phone conversation with an activist impersonating one of his wealthiest patrons—inspired labor activists across the nation and captured international headlines. The state capital was under a non-violent siege for some six weeks. Outdoor rallies drew as many as 100,000 people despite frigid weather, while inside, the ornate Capitol was occupied by protesters who held sleep-ins and organized clean-up patrols to keep the halls neat. The protests drew a mixture of public employees (including firefighters, police, and state troopers whose unions were exempt from Walker's proposal), private-sector union members, high school students who had walked out of their classes, university students, and a 50-strong "tractor-cade" of farmers. Smaller but equally diverse groups of protesters staged rallies in cities and towns across Wisconsin.

In a narrow sense the protests failed: the new law passed in the early morning hours of March 9 following questionable procedural maneuvers that will likely keep it tied up in the courts for months. Now, some of the progressive energy evident in February and March has been channeled into recall campaigns against several Republican legislators. In a closely watched election, a pro-labor challenger unexpectedly took on an incumbent conservative for a seat on the state supreme court. How the state's unions of teachers and other public-sector workers will carry on if the new law is upheld is an open question.

In the meantime, Walker's eroding popularity testifies to at least some weakness in a corporate-Right coalition effort to target hapless public employees as a means of crippling labor, weakening the Democrats' electoral chances, and preventing public resentment over widespread economic insecurity from turning upward.

The Right Pushes Its Luck

The massive outburst of labor-based protest exploded in Wisconsin just three months after this Democratic-leaning state (e.g., Wisconsin has voted for every Democratic presidential candidate since 1988, giving Barack Obama a 14-point edge) went through the nation's sharpest turn to the right in the mid-term elections last November. The Democrats lost a U.S. Senate seat, two U.S. House seats, and the governor's chair, and both houses of the state legislature flipped to big Republican majorities.

Nonetheless, Walker was taking a big chance when he pushed not only to force significant wage and benefit cuts on the state's public employees but also to go after their rights to collective bargaining. But the stakes were high, and Walker was not acting alone. His election last November and his policy agenda as governor owe much to networks of right-wing and pro-corporate lobbies, think tanks,

---

MAKING UNION REPRESENTATION FUTILE

In 1959, Wisconsin, under Democratic Gov. Gaylord Nelson, was the first state to legalize collective bargaining by local public employees. In 1967, Republican Gov. Warren Knowles expanded these rights to state employees. Today, the state's new law on public-employee unions would make it nearly impossible for them to function. Among its provisions:

- Public-employee unions would be restricted to bargaining only over wages.

- Public-employee contracts would be restricted to a length of one year.

- Unions would be required to hold an annual re-certification election.

- Unions would no longer be allowed to collect dues via dues checkoff, nor could they assess non-members "agency fees" for the costs of representing them.

- Wage increases above the inflation rate could be granted only with the passage of a local referendum.

- State and local public employees would pay 12.6% of their health costs, a doubling of their present share. Pension payments for public employees would rise to 5.6%. This would amount to a pay cut of approximately 8%.

- Limited-term employees would lose all health-care benefits.

- University of Wisconsin faculty, granted collective-bargaining rights for the first time in 2009, would again be deprived of any union rights.

- Graduate teaching and research students would be required to pay about 20% of their income to cover health-care benefits.

and individuals, from the billionaire Koch brothers to organizations like the Club for Growth, Americans for Prosperity, FreedomWorks, and the American Legislative Exchange Council. In Wisconsin and around the country, the offensive against public-sector unions has the potential to accomplish many of the aims of these networks.

Billionaire David Koch, with his brother Charles, gave $43,000 in direct contributions to Walker's campaign and another $1 million to the Republican Governors Association, which spent $3.4 million on negative ads targeting Walker's Democratic opponent last fall. The Koch brothers have been major funders of a national crusade to essentially extinguish unionism as a force on the U.S. landscape, as Judith Davidoff described in a Feb. 23 *Capital Times* article. Koch Industries, the largest privately held corporation in the United States, has 3,000 employees in Wisconsin at facilities including a Georgia-Pacific toilet-paper plant, several power plants, and numerous pipelines. (Interestingly, Walker's budget-repair bill would give the governor the power to sell state-owned power plants under no-bid procedures.)

In this vein, Walker's effort would have provided a model, showing other Republican governors how to crush what is now the last bastion of union strength in the United States. In the private sector, union density nationally has fallen to 6.9%, compared to 36.2% in the public sector. In some states, public employees make up more than half of all union members.

Walker did not openly characterize his bill as aimed at sacking unions. Instead he focused his public statements on the need for severe spending cuts to balance the state's budget.

On one level this strategy backfired when the major public unions, the 23,000-member Wisconsin State Employees Union and the Wisconsin Education Association Council, representing 98,000 teachers and other school employees, agreed to the economic concessions but declared that their union rights were sacrosanct. Walker was left sputtering, "There is no room to compromise. We are broke." By refusing to take "Yes" for an answer, Walker's aim of destroying public-sector unions was unmasked.

MORE DRACONIAN THAN TAFT-HARTLEY

Wisconsin's new law on public-employee unions "goes further than anything since the Taft-Hartley Act of 1947," according to labor historian Stephen Meyer of UW-Milwaukee. Taft-Hartley was the law that brought the New Deal-era expansion of collective-bargaining rights to a sudden halt. Among other provisions, it allowed states to adopt "right-to-work" laws which ban union shops yet mandate unions to undertake the cost and responsibility of representing members and non-members alike.

"In fact," says Meyer, "Walker's plan is worse than the 'right-to-work' laws because it requires that unions get certified by their members yearly, at the same time that the unions are prevented from accomplishing anything for their members."

"Right-to-work" laws alone make it hard for unions to first get established and then to survive over the long haul. The shift of much U.S. industry to the South, where right-to-work laws are ubiquitous, has helped to drive private-sector unionization in the entire nation to 6.9%, down from about 35% in the mid-1950s.

In the long run, strong public-employee unions do raise their members' pay and benefits, with consequences for state and municipal budgets, as Jane Slaughter of *Labor Notes* has pointed out. But those effects do not constitute a crisis; for Walker, the real crisis was not a budget problem to be solved, rather an opportunity to be seized. Besides inspiring his fellow Republican governors, a quick "shock therapy" success against public unions would have set the stage for further shifting Wisconsin from its generally progressive traditions toward a low-wage, de-unionized, Southern-style model where the undisputed first priority of state government is to subsidize large corporations.

Weakening public-employee unions would confer political benefits as well, depriving the Democrats of a key on-the-ground organizational asset and a major source of funds. The *Capital Times*'s Davidoff summarized labor's vital electoral role: "As the 2010 elections showed, public sector unions were the only groups with enough cash and people power to counter the corporate money that flowed to Republicans once spending restrictions were lifted by the U.S. Supreme Court ruling in the Citizens United case."

State Senate Majority Leader Scott Fitzgerald offered a blunt admission of the GOP's political motives on Fox-TV: "If we win this battle, and the money is not there under the auspices of the unions, certainly what you're going to find is President Obama is going to have a much difficult, much more difficult time getting [re-]elected and winning the state of Wisconsin."

Labor Pushes Back

Walker and his advisers no doubt miscalculated. They evidently believed that a recent round of painful concessions endured by private-sector union workers— for instance, at Mercury Marine, Harley-Davidson, and Kohler, where profitable firms had extorted massive wage cuts via two-tier wage structures, using the threat of relocating the jobs—would serve to justify an all-out attack on public-sector workers in the name of "fairness" and "shared sacrifice."

During the campaign, Walker depicted public-sector workers as a pampered, privileged class shielded from the free-market solution to excessive wage costs. "We can no longer live in a society where the public employees are the haves and taxpayers who foot the bills are the have-nots," he declared.

In reality, public employees are implausible villains: studies show they earn less than their peers in the private sector for comparable work. (See "State Workers Face a Compensation Penalty," *D&S*, March/April 2011.) An Economic Policy Institute study of Wisconsin wages found a private-sector pay and benefit advantage of 4.2% to 8.4% when educational differences are taken into account. And the allegedly high-end pension benefits public employees receive actually average just $19,000 nationally.

This time, divide-and-conquer did not work so well. Instead of blaming their own and the state's fiscal troubles on teachers and highway workers, a broad swath of Wisconsinites seemed to recognize Walker's action as a concerted effort to drive down wages for working people generally, and his manufactured budget crisis as a ploy to compensate for the non-payment of taxes by Wisconsin corporations. Somehow, perhaps because of their over-the-top arrogance, the new governor's tactics quickly re-ignited Wisconsin's still-smoldering pro-labor tradition. As observed by political scientist and sociologist Frances Fox Piven, author of numerous works on social movements like *Poor People's Movements* and *Challenging Authority*, "The Wisconsin uprising was largely unpredictable. It's always hard to assess when people are going to be able to see beyond the clichés and fabrications of politically powerful."

"In Wisconsin, maybe this maneuver was just too obvious, maybe the elites have tried it too many times," Piven reflected. "When it becomes this transparent, when we are told that we must have cuts in rights and earnings for public sector workers, food and health while taxes are being cut for corporations, it becomes clear that it is a manufactured crisis."

The Wisconsin protests are crucial to build upon, says Piven, because they have reflected a profound rejection of the elite notion that state and federal deficits necessitate more sacrifices for working people but continued incentives and tax cuts for corporations and the wealthy.

Other observers agree that the Wisconsin uprising revealed a major progressive opening in the state. The level of support for labor and against corporate domination of state government was evident not just in major rallies in Madison and Milwaukee, but also in unprecedented crowds of 2,000 showing up in tiny hamlets like Burnett. On a single day, pro-labor rallies were held in 19 different cities, showing a much greater reach than past protest movements.

The strength of the pro-labor, anti-Walker movement reflects a growing awareness that middle-class jobs are under systematic attack. As Mike Imbrogno, a cook at UW-Madison who makes $28,000 a year, put it: "[Walker's] basically trying to smash the last remaining organized upward pressure on wages and benefits in Wisconsin." This message clearly resonated with thousands of non-union members around the state.

The issue of tax fairness is also emerging with a new force, as evidenced by the proliferation of protest signs denouncing corporate tax loopholes. "I'm pleased with recent polls saying that nearly 70% of Wisconsinites support higher taxes as part of a balanced solution to the budget challenges. People are always much more favorable toward taxes when they know the money will go to something important that matters to them, such as public education, services for the frail elderly or severely disabled, or garbage collection," says Jack Norman, research director of the Institute for Wisconsin's Future.

Labor attorney and former gubernatorial candidate Ed Garvey sees the recent uprising as a turning point for labor and progressives after years of defeats. "Labor had lacked the confidence that it could win the middle class to its side until the Wisconsin eruption. But the now the movement really has the confidence that it will win in the recall elections and frustrate Walker's efforts to obliterate unions."

Labor's rebellion in Wisconsin has created a large group of new leaders with the potential for building a very broad movement to challenge corporate power, in the view of Michael Rosen, president of American Federation of Teachers Local 212. "Right now, there's enormous potential for a genuine workers movement that is broader than just labor, incorporating low-wage immigrant workers, environmentalists, church and neighborhood groups," says Rosen. "Labor brings organizational strength and resources while the new movements bring energy, passion, courage, and numbers."

While Walker's anti-union moves are on hold in the courts, labor and progressives have a chance to do something even more important than recalling Republican state legislators: to build a durable coalition that will support union rights and oppose draconian budget cuts. ❑

Sources: Judith Davidoff, "Walker's Plan to End Bargaining Has Deep Roots in GOP," *The Capital Times*, February 23, 2011; Ethan Pollack, "State Workers Face a Compensation Penalty," *Dollars & Sense*, March/April 2011; William P. Jones, "Public employees: Low-wage workers would be the hardest hit," *Milwaukee Journal Sentinel*, February 14, 2011; Roger Bybee, "Class War Heats Up in Wisconsin," *Z Magazine*, April 2011; Les Leopold, *The Looting of America*, Chelsea Green Publishing, 2009; David Kocieniewski, "G.E.'s Strategies Let It Avoid Taxes Altogether," *The New York Times*, March 24, 2011, Jane Slaughter, "Collective Bargaining Rights: A Money Issue," *Labor Notes*, March 19, 2011.

Chapter 2

WAGES AND THE LABOR MARKET

Article 2.1

THE CRISIS OF WAGE THEFT

Billions of dollars in wages are being illegally stolen from millions of workers each and every year.

BY KIM BOBO
February 2009

A few years ago, I heard about a garment factory near my house where workers weren't making the minimum wage, or so I was told. I couldn't believe that such a place operated four blocks from where I live. I didn't even know it existed.

I'd heard about this place because some workers had visited the Chicago Interfaith Workers Center and told their stories. In addition, I'd heard that this place was an exclusive subcontractor for a leading national company. I wanted to know what was going on.

With the help of Interfaith Worker Justice colleagues, we organized a fact-finding delegation of religious leaders to investigate what was going on. One cold Chicago morning, twenty-five of us dropped in at the factory. The place was located in a largely residential neighborhood in a small turn-of-the-century industrial building that faces the Metra train stop. There was no sign outside identifying the facility. The front door was unlocked, so we marched on up to the second floor.

Sure enough, when we opened the second door at the top of the stairs, we stepped into a small entryway, which then had a door opening to a large high-ceilinged room full of Latina immigrant women huddled over sewing machines. Despite twenty-five folks, including some in clerical collars, dropping in unexpectedly, no one looked up from their machines. (I can't believe it was because they were accustomed to regular visitors.)

Despite the cold outside, the workroom was quite warm. We all imagined how hot the room would be in August. Such Chicago buildings have impressive boilers, but no air conditioning.

We scoured the place looking for the manager. Once the manager got over the shock of seeing us in her place, she quickly tried to shoo us back into the lobby area. I must confess, we were not the most cooperative crowd. It took us a while to get back to the lobby.

Once back and contained, we began peppering her with questions.

"What do you pay these workers?"

"I pay them the minimum wage, $5.15 per hour."

"But this is Illinois; the minimum wage is $6.15, not $5.15."

Slapping her forehead, "Why didn't they tell me!"

"Do you provide any health insurance for the workers?"

"Well, I asked them if they wanted health insurance, but none of them did. They all get it through their husbands. Oh, and these workers are like my family. We celebrate birthdays and babies."

Meanwhile, one of our colleagues went to use the bathroom. A worker jumped up to give her a few sections of toilet paper.

So we asked the manager, "What's the deal on the toilet paper?"

"Oh, I used to provide it, but the workers would steal it, so now they prefer to bring their own." Right.

But this manager was not the only culprit here. The workers claimed this garment sweatshop was sewing exclusively for Cintas, the nation's largest industrial laundry. Cintas is not a mom-and-pop shop that doesn't know any better. It is a leading national company. The Cintas website describes itself as follows:

> Cintas is a publicly held company traded over the Nasdaq Global Select Market under the symbol CTAS, and is a Nasdaq-100 company and component of the Standard & Poor's 500 Index. Cintas designs, manufactures and implements corporate identity uniform programs, and provides entrance mats, restroom cleaning and supplies, promotional products, first aid and safety products, fire protection services and document management services for approximately 800,000 businesses.

> Cintas operates more than 400 facilities in the U.S. and Canada, including 11 manufacturing plants and seven distribution centers that employ more than 34,000 people.

> Cintas has grown for 38 consecutive years, with fiscal 2007 sales of $3.71 billion, an increase of 8.9% from 2006. Net income of $334.5 million increased 3.4% from $323.4 million last year, and earnings per diluted share increased 8.9% from $1.92 last year to $2.09 this year. Cintas was founded by Richard T. Farmer, Chairman of the Board. Scott Farmer was appointed Chief Executive Officer in 2003 and Bob Kohlhepp serves as Vice Chairman.

Several months after our call at the factory, Interfaith Worker Justice (IWJ) published a report called "Airing Dirty Laundry" based on the delegations and other interviews; as a result, Cintas threatened to sue IWJ and all its affiliates. When I called to talk with the attorney representing the company, he told me Farmer and Kohlhepp were willing to meet with some religious leaders. At the meeting, we came with stories we had gathered from workers around the country. Farmer and Kohlhepp were prepared with their power points, their directors of contracting and diversity and health and safety, and so on. Our spokespeople included a guy who had taught Kohlhepp's children in confirmation classes, a Methodist bishop, a Baptist pastor, a nun, and a few others. We brought no real expertise, just a concern for workers.

The Cintas officials assured us they had excellent subcontracting guidelines in place. We assured them that the subcontracting guidelines weren't working.

On a personal level, Farmer and Kohlhepp and their staff were all very nice and pleasant. They give generously to their churches and the community. I'm sure they are great with their own families. I'm sure they are very nice people. Oh ... and did I mention that Farmer is one of the richest men in the state of Ohio?

Still, Cintas is a part of the crisis of wage theft in the nation.

The Chicago Interfaith Workers Center helped Cintas's subcontractor's workers file complaints for the lost wages, for the sub-minimum wages they received, with the Illinois Department of Labor. Eventually, the workers recovered $209,867.82 in back wages and penalties.

Cintas, as the ultimate employer of these workers, had essentially stolen over $100,000 from poverty wage workers with no benefits by allowing them to receive less than the minimum wage, the lowest amount that workers can legally be paid. This is what I mean by wage theft. And Cintas and its subcontractor are not alone. Not by a long shot.

Billions of dollars in wages are being illegally stolen from millions of workers each and every year. The employers range from small neighborhood businesses to some of the nation's largest employers—Wal-Mart, Tyson, McDonald's, Target, Pulte Homes, federal, state, and local governments and many more.

Wage theft occurs when workers are not paid all their wages, workers are denied overtime when they should be paid it, or workers aren't paid at all for work they've performed. Wage theft is when an employer violates the law and deprives a worker of legally mandated wages. Wage theft is widespread and pervasive across all types of companies. Various surveys have found that:

- 60% of nursing homes stole workers' wages.
- 89% of nonmonitored garment factories in Los Angeles and 67% of nonmonitored garment factories in New York City stole workers' wages.
- 25% of tomato producers, 35% of lettuce producers, 51% of cucumber producers, 58% of onion producers, and 62% of garlic producers hiring farm workers stole workers' wages.
- 78% of restaurants in New Orleans stole workers' wages.
- Almost half of day laborers, who tend to focus on construction work, have had their wages stolen.
- 100% of poultry plants steal workers' wages.

Although wage theft is the most pernicious when employers steal money from workers earning low wages, wage theft affects many middle-income workers too, including construction workers, nurses, dieticians, writers, bookkeepers, and many more. Wage theft affects young workers, mid-career workers, and older workers. Although some of the worst wage theft occurs when immigrant workers aren't paid minimum wage or aren't paid at all, the largest dollar amounts are stolen from native-born white and black workers in unpaid overtime.

Millions of workers are having their wages stolen. Two million, possibly as many as three million, workers aren't being paid the minimum wage. More than three million workers are misclassified by their employers as independent contractors when they are really employees, which means their employers aren't paying their share of payroll taxes and many workers are being illegally denied overtime pay. Untold millions more aren't being paid overtime because their employers claim they are exempt from the overtime laws, when they really aren't. Several million more aren't being paid for their breaks or have illegal deductions made from paychecks. The scope of these abuses is staggering.

The Economic Policy Foundation, a business-funded think tank, estimated that companies annually steal $19 billion in unpaid overtime. Labor lawyer colleagues suggest the number is far higher.

Cases of unethical employers stealing wages have reached epidemic proportions. As a nation we are facing a crisis of wage theft.

Private Lawsuits Explode

There is perhaps no better evidence of the breadth of the crisis than the explosion of private lawsuits seeking to recover unpaid wages. The Fair Labor Standards Act, which covers minimum wage and overtime issues, provides workers the "private right to sue," which means they can take their cases to private attorneys. They are doing so in record numbers.

Current business magazine headlines, including a *BusinessWeek* cover story and management-side law firms' articles tell the story:

Wage Wars: Workers—From Truck Drivers to Stockbrokers—Are Winning Huge Overtime Lawsuits

Wage and Hour Violations: An Employer's Single Greatest Uninsured Risk

Time Bomb Waiting to Explode: Wage and Hour Claims over Exempt Employees

Wage and Hour Audits: Wage and Hour Laws Are Violated More Often than any Other Employment Law

According to the Administrative Office of the U.S. Courts, there were 7,310 Fair Labor Standards Act (FLSA) lawsuits filed in 2007, compared to only 1,633 in 1997. In ten years, the FLSA suits have more than quadrupled. In just one year, from 2006 to 2007, the number of FLSA cases filed increased by 73%. These figures account for only the federal lawsuits and do not include wage cases filed under state wage laws. Most of those lawsuits were filed for groups of workers, which means that these cases are recovering wages for several hundred thousand workers. The number of workers recovering wages would be much higher if workers didn't have to "opt-in" to the suits. "Lawyers on both sides estimate that over the last few years companies have collectively paid out more than $1 billion annually to resolve these claims."

Most of the big wage and hour lawsuits deal with overtime pay. The Fair Labor Standards Act has been clear since 1938 that all workers, except those exempt from the law, are eligible for overtime pay (1.5 times the FLSA "regular rate") for hours worked over 40. The real issue is who is exempt and who isn't. Thousands of workers and their attorneys claim they are "nonexempt" workers and thus due overtime pay. But many of the employers claim the workers are exempt and thus not due overtime. The crux of the matter is the classification of workers—whether they are really exempt or nonexempt. In an effort to clarify and streamline the overtime provisions, the Department of Labor issued new overtime regulations in 2004. Unfortunately, the regulations are still complicated, and employers continue to break the laws. Whether out of ignorance or willfulness, employers who illegally deny workers overtime are stealing wages.

Workers Centers and Wage Theft

Wage theft is acutely felt at the nation's workers centers where workers whose wages have been stolen seek help. Jeffrey Steele is one such worker who sought help in New Orleans.

Steele, an African American from Atlanta, wanted to be part of history in rebuilding New Orleans after Hurricane Katrina. Responding to a flyer advertising "Free Room and Board, Free Food, Pay $10/hour," he signed up with Workforce Development Corp., Inc., run by Carroll Harrison Braddy, and boarded a van to New Orleans in mid-October 2005. As it turned out, Braddy reneged on his flyers' promises. Steele's first few days were particularly miserable: he received no food, he had to sleep in the van, and he was made to work long hours. A few weeks after arriving in New Orleans, he was finally fitted for an aspirator, a critical piece of health and safety equipment for all those involved in the cleanup and exposed to dangerous contaminants.

When Steele's first paycheck was due, he calculated he was owed $1,400, not even assuming any overtime pay (1.5 times the regular rate over 40 hours per week). But Braddy only paid him $230. By mid-November, Steele left Braddy's employment and went to work for another cleanup firm called JNE where he was promised $18 per hour. After four weeks of very long hours (almost 100 hours per week), Steele estimated he was owed about $7,000. He was initially paid $300 and then got another $1,000.

In January 2006, he started working for a third employer, with whom he stayed for nine months. This third employer paid him as an "exempt" salaried employee, even though he was probably legally eligible for overtime coverage (more on this issue later), which means he probably had wages stolen with this employee too.

At the last New Orleans job he worked, Steele injured his hand, which then required surgery. He received no workers' compensation for his injury, nor did his employer provide any medical insurance. In all, Steele had four employers in New Orleans—and all of them stole wages or workers' compensation from him. In testimony before the Domestic Policy Subcommittee of the House Oversight and Government Reform Committee on June 26, 2007, in New Orleans, Steele said,

> I went to New Orleans to help and to be part of history. I did the dirty, hard work that was needed. Yet, I was exploited by contractor after contractor who crammed us into filthy living spaces, provided next to nothing to eat, offered practically no safety precautions or equipment and paid workers late and so much less than even promised. If this is how this country allows employers to get away with treating hard working citizens while companies make a profit—then shame on us. I've worked hard all my life and I pay taxes. I'm a United States citizen. I've been working since I was 9 years old. I've never been to jail and I've never asked the government for nothing. If another catastrophe happens in this country, I hope you never let any one else treat workers and the people they are trying to help like they did in New Orleans.

Although wage theft was particularly bad in New Orleans immediately after Katrina, workers centers throughout the nation help thousands of workers annually who have had their wages stolen.

Many of the examples of wage theft involve immigrants. This makes sense because the examples come from many of the IWJ workers centers that work with immigrants. Although the centers work with all workers in low-wage jobs, it is undocumented immigrants—who are most fearful of approaching government agencies—who flood the workers centers seeking help. Nonetheless, most of the workers whose wages are stolen are U.S. citizens. Perhaps the worst exploitation occurs among immigrants, but the crisis of wage theft would exist even if there were no immigrant workers in the society.

Wage theft affects all American workers by lowering the nation's workplace standards, but especially those in middle- and low-income jobs. Stealing wages hurts workers and their families. Workers who aren't paid their wages still have to pay their rent or their child care. Workers who are required to work long hours without overtime compensation are deprived of the opportunity to get another job or spend time with their families. Workers who are cheated of wages can't save for their kids' college tuition or for a home. For some earning the lowest wages, not getting paid means their families go hungry or become homeless. As a society, when we allow employers to steal wages from some workers, it drives down wages and standards for all workers.

Wage theft places ethical employers at a competitive disadvantage, thus undermining ethical businesses. Those businesses that pay workers legally and fairly and pay all their taxes as required are undercut by businesses that steal from workers and don't pay taxes and insurance as required. In addition, wage theft steals from public coffers and denies communities the economic stimulus generated when workers spend their wages. ❏

Article 2.2

INSIDER EXPLOITATION

*The informant in a high-profile insider-trading case had
run afoul of the law before—by ripping off her housekeeper.*

BY ESTHER CERVANTES
January/February 2010

You would think that with all the money she gained from insider trading for Galleon Group, Roomy Khan could have afforded to pay her help—but apparently Khan didn't think so. Just a day before she was outed as the informant who brought down Galleon, the New York-based hedge fund management firm, and its founder Raj Rajaratnam, Khan settled a lawsuit for unpaid wages with her former housekeeper and nanny, Vilma Serralta.

For four years, Serralta worked six 14-hour days each week cleaning Khan's $17 million, 9,700-square-foot home in Atherton, Calif., and caring for Khan's daughter. Although California's minimum wage is $6.75, the Khan family paid Serralta less than four dollars an hour. Despite Serralta's long hours, they never paid her overtime.

When the Khans dismissed her abruptly, Serralta turned to San Francisco's La Raza Centro Legal (LRCL) and Legal Aid Society Employment Law Center. "I didn't do this for revenge, I simply wanted justice," Serralta said of her decision to take legal action.

In October [2009], after two years of litigation, the Khans settled with Serralta after her lawyers revealed that the Khans had forged key documents for their defense.

The Khans' exploitation of Serralta is not unusual. "Her isolation and lack of familiarity with her legal rights," which are typical of immigrant domestic workers, according to her attorney Hillary Ronen, "made her particularly vulnerable."

But Serralta and others are working to change that. She now belongs to LRCL's La Colectiva de Mujeres, a member-run domestic workers' organization for Latina women that offers a living wage, job training, and education about legal rights. La Colectiva recently launched a social-marketing campaign aimed at attracting employers who will respect domestic workers' rights and at recruiting domestic workers to join the organization and enjoy its protections.

La Colectiva is also part of a larger movement. La Colectiva members and domestic workers from throughout the western United States met in November to draft and plan their state-level legislative strategy for enacting a Domestic Workers' Bill of Rights.

Like farm laborers, domestic workers have been excluded from the protections of U.S. labor law since the New Deal, when Southern Democrats out to preserve Jim Crow made their support for minimum wage legislation and the National Labor Relations Act contingent on leaving out those two (then largely black) sectors.

Activists pushing for the new Domestic Workers' Bill of Rights, and groups organizing domestic workers elsewhere in the United States, hope to finally end that exclusion so that workers like Vilma Serralta will no longer face exploitation at the hands of the likes of Roomy Khan. ❏

Resources: La Raza Centro Legal (techforpeople.net/~lrcl); Legal Aid Society Employment Law Center (las-elc.org).

Article 2.3

DON'T BLAME THE MINIMUM WAGE
Does raising the minimum wage cause layoffs? An economist says no.

BY PADDY QUICK
January/February 2008

When businesses organize production, they figure out what different people they need to employ and in what numbers. A restaurant, for example, needs cooks, waiters/waitresses, dishwashers, cashiers and, sometimes, after-hours cleaning staff. It needs managers to keep track of who is doing what and when. Some of these people are paid a lot more than others, but they are all necessary. The lower-paid workers are as important as the higher-paid workers. Although the restaurant owner would like to pay them all less so that his profits would be higher, he needs them all.

This is important to understand. A bicycle needs two wheels, two pedals, a seat, a set of gears, and any number of parts that connect them all together. Which is most important? The front wheel? The rear wheel? The seat? The pedals? The fact that a pedal costs less than a wheel doesn't make it any less important. Similarly, all of the people who work in a restaurant play their part in the production of the meals, even though they "cost" their employer different amounts. If the pedal of a bicycle cost a bit more, it wouldn't be eliminated. Why then do people think their job would be eliminated if they had to be paid a little more?

People are laid off for many reasons. One possibility is that employers just want to shuffle people around so that everyone feels under pressure. There are always a lot of people unemployed, and it is pretty easy to lay one person off and hire another to replace her. The new person is now likely to work harder, even if the previous employee was doing a great job. There are also changes in the number of customers in different locations, and competition from other restaurants for these customers.

When the minimum wage increases, employers have to pay higher wages not only to those who received the old minimum, but also to those whose positions paid an extra dollar or more above that. If they decide to reorganize production, they may well decide to lay off these workers rather than the ones at the very bottom of the pay scale. Information technology, for example, may displace more highly paid workers who are responsible for inventory management at corporate headquarters, rather than the people who have direct contact with customers.

Corporations are, of course, always "crunching the numbers," figuring out whether they can save money by changing the combination of people and things they purchase in order to produce the pizzas and other things they sell. Sometimes they may be able to do so, but other times it may not be possible.

So let's look specifically at the fast-food restaurant business to see the effect on employment of an increase in the minimum wage. It turns out that there isn't much that fast-food restaurants can do when wages go up—other than hand over a small portion of their huge profits to their workforce!

Fast-food corporations, such as McDonald's, spend millions lobbying Congress in opposition to a raise in the minimum wage, pretending that their opposition has nothing to do with its effect on their profits. Instead they argue that it would break their hearts to have to lay off some of the poor people they employ. (Their employees are poor, of course, because of the low wages they receive!)

A famous study by two well-known economists, Alan Krueger of Princeton University and David Card of the University of California, Berkeley, looked very carefully at what happened to fast food employment in New Jersey in 1992 after that state raised its minimum wage. (This study is summarized in their 1997 book, *Myth and Measurement: The New Economics of the Minimum Wage*.) They compared New Jersey with its neighboring state, Pennsylvania, which did not raise its minimum wage. Fast food industry executives had argued that they would be "forced" to lay off workers if New Jersey raised its minimum wage, but the facts proved otherwise. New Jersey workers got higher wages, but they did *not* lose their jobs. So although it is *possible* that an increase in the minimum wage could lead restaurants to lay off workers, it turns out that this doesn't actually happen in the fast food industry.

After they studied minimum wages in the fast food industry, Krueger and Card went on to prove that increasing the minimum wage across the country as a whole has little or no effect on unemployment. This position was supported by a total of 650 economists, including five Nobel prize-winners, in a 2006 letter supporting the bill to raise the federal minimum wage to $7.15 an hour.

Production requires workers. Workers use tools and machinery, and businesses have the capital that is needed to buy these, but it is workers who turn the ovens, pizza dough, and tables into meals for their customers, and it is workers who make the computers that increasingly "mechanize" production. The big question, according to Adam Smith and other classical economists such as David Ricardo and Karl Marx, is how income is distributed, and in particular, how much of it goes to wage-earners.

Adam Smith, for example, believed that the level of wages depends on workers' bargaining power, and thought it obvious that the government was on the side of the employers. He did, however, think that if the rate of unemployment was low, wages could increase. Today, one part of the government, the Federal Reserve Board, takes this piece of theory very seriously, and makes sure that it keeps the rate of unemployment high enough to prevent wages from increasing! Smith's theory implies that we need to organize, both at the workplace and within the political system, to strengthen the power of labor against the power of capital.

Adam Smith also believed that wages could not sink below the minimum needed for workers to survive and bring up children. But unfortunately, when there is a lot of unemployment, workers find themselves in a "race to the bottom": "I'll work for whatever you're willing to pay me." "No, take me. I'll work for $1 less." "Please, please, I'll work for food." During the Great Depression, massive unemployment made this a terrifying possibility, and led to the enactment of minimum wage legislation. This was an important victory for an organized working class. But it is an ongoing struggle. With a decent minimum wage and low unemployment, we can get the higher wages that our hard work entitles us to. ❑

Sources: David Card & Alan B. Krueger, *Myth and Measurement: The New Economics of the Minimum Wage*, Princeton University Press, 1997; Adam Smith, *Wealth of Nations*, 1776 (Part I, Ch. 8).

Article 2.4

WHAT'S GOOD FOR WAL-MART ...

BY JOHN MILLER
January/February 2006

> "Is Wal-Mart Good for America?"
>
> It is a testament to the public relations of the anti-Wal-Mart campaign that the question above is even being asked.
>
> By any normal measure, Wal-Mart's business ought to be noncontroversial. It sells at low costs, albeit in mind-boggling quantities. ...
>
> The company's success and size ... do not rest on monopoly profits or price-gouging behavior. It simply sells things people will buy at small markups and, as in the old saw, makes it up on volume. ... You may believe, as do service-workers unions and a clutch of coastal elites—many of whom, we'd wager, have never set foot in Wal-Mart—that Wal-Mart "exploits" workers who can't say no to low wages and poor benefits. You might accept the canard that it drives good local businesses into the ground, although both of these allegations are more myth than reality.
>
> But even if you buy into the myths, there's no getting around the fact that somewhere out there, millions of people are spending billions of dollars on what Wal-Mart puts on its shelves. No one is making them do it. ... Wal-Mart can't make mom and pop shut down the shop anymore than it can make customers walk through the doors or pull out their wallets.
>
> What about the workers? ... Wal-Mart's average starting wage is already nearly double the national minimum of $5.15 an hour. The company has also recently increased its health-care for employees on the bottom rungs of the corporate ladder.
>
> —*Wall Street Journal* editorial, December 3, 2005

"Who's Number One? The Customer! Always!" The last line of Wal-Mart's company cheer just about sums up the *Wall Street Journal* editors' benign view of the behemoth corporation. But a more honest answer would be Wal-Mart itself: not the customer, and surely not the worker.

The first retail corporation to top the Fortune 500, Wal-Mart trailed only Exxon-Mobil in total revenues last year. With 1.6 million workers, 1.3 million in the United States and 300,000 offshore, Wal-Mart is the largest private employer in the nation and the world's largest retailer.

Being number one has paid off handsomely for the family of Wal-Mart founder Sam Walton. The family's combined fortune is now an estimated $90 billion, equal to the net worth of Bill Gates and Warren Buffett combined.

But is what's good for the Walton family good for America? Should we believe the editors that Wal-Mart's unprecedented size and market power have redounded not only to the Walton family's benefit but to ours as well?

Low Wages and Meager Benefits

Working for the world's largest employer sure hasn't paid off for Wal-Mart's employees. True, they have a job, and others without jobs line up to apply for theirs. But that says more about the sad state of today's labor market than the quality of Wal-Mart jobs. After all, less than half of Wal-Mart workers last a year, and turnover at the company is twice that at comparable retailers.

Why? Wal-Mart's oppressive working conditions surely have something to do with it. Wal-Mart has admitted to using minors to operate hazardous machinery, has been sued in six states for forcing employees to work off the books (i.e., unpaid) and without breaks, and is currently facing a suit brought by 1.6 million current and former female employees accusing Wal-Mart of gender discrimination. At the same time, Wal-Mart workers are paid less and receive fewer benefits than other retail workers.

Wal-Mart, according to its own reports, pays an average of $9.68 an hour. That is 12.4% below the average wage for retail workers even after adjusting for geography, according to a recent study by Arindrajit Dube and Steve Wertheim, economists at the University of California's Institute of Industrial Relations and long-time Wal-Mart researchers. Wal-Mart's wages are nearly 15% below the average wage of workers at large retailers and about 30% below the average wage of unionized grocery workers. The average U.S. wage is $17.80 an hour; Costco, a direct competitor of Wal-Mart's Sam's Club warehouse stores, pays an average wage of $16 an hour (see sidebar).

Wal-Mart may be improving its benefits, as the *Journal*'s editors report, but it needs to. Other retailers provide health care coverage to over 53% of their workers, while Wal-Mart covers just 48% of its workers. Costco, once again, does far better, covering 82% of its employees. Moreover, Wal-Mart's coverage is far less comprehensive than the plans offered by other large retailers. Dube reports that according to 2003 IRS data, Wal-Mart paid 59% of the health care costs of its workers and dependents, compared to the 77% of health care costs for individuals and 68% for families the average retailer picks up.

A recent internal Wal-Mart memo leaked to the *New York Times* confirmed the large gaps in Wal-Mart's health care coverage and exposed the high costs those gaps impose on government programs. According to the memo, "Five percent of our Associates are on Medicaid compared to an average for national employees of 4 percent. Twenty-seven percent of Associates' children are on such programs, compared to a national average of 22 percent. In total, 46 percent of Associates' children are either on Medicaid or are uninsured."

A considerably lower 29% of children of all large-retail workers are on Medicaid or are uninsured. Some 7% of the children of employees of large retailers go uninsured, compared to the 19% reported by Wal-Mart.

Wal-Mart's low wages drag down the wages of other retail workers and shutter downtown retail businesses. A 2005 study by David Neumark, Junfu Zhang, and Stephen Ciccarella, economists at the University of California at Irvine, found that Wal-Mart adversely affects employment and wages. Retail workers in a community with a Wal-Mart earned 3.5% less because Wal-Mart's low prices force other businesses to lower prices, and hence their wages, according to the Neumark study. The same study also found that Wal-Mart's presence reduces retail employment by 2% to 4%. While other studies have not found this negative employment effect, Dube's research also reports fewer retail jobs and lower wages for retail workers in metropolitan counties with a Wal-Mart. (Fully 85% of Wal-Mart stores are in metropolitan counties.) Dube figures that Wal-Mart's presence costs retail workers, at Wal-Mart and elsewhere, $4.7 billion a year in lost earnings.

In short, Wal-Mart's "everyday low prices" come at the expense of the compensation of Wal-Mart's own employees and lower wages and fewer jobs for retail workers in the surrounding area. That much remains true no matter what weight we assign to each of the measures that Wal-Mart uses to keep its costs down: a just-in-time inventory strategy, its ability to use its size to pressure suppliers for large discounts, a routinized work environment that requires minimal training, and meager wages and benefits.

How Low Are Wal-Mart's Everyday Low Prices?

Even if one doesn't subscribe to the editors' position that it is consumers, not Wal-Mart, who cause job losses at downtown retailers, it is possible to argue that the benefit of Wal-Mart's low prices to consumers, especially low-income consumers, outweighs the cost endured by workers at Wal-Mart and other retailers. Jason Furman, New York University economist and director of economic policy for the 2004 Kerry-Edwards campaign, makes just such an argument. Wal-Mart's "staggering" low prices are 8% to 40% lower than people would pay elsewhere, according to Furman. He calculates that those low prices on average boost low-income families' buying power by 3% and more than offset the loss of earnings to retail workers. For Furman, that makes Wal-Mart "a progressive success story."

But exactly how much savings Wal-Mart affords consumers is far from clear. Estimates vary widely. At one extreme is a study Wal-Mart itself commissioned by Global Insight, an economic forecasting firm. Global Insight estimates Wal-Mart created a stunning savings of $263 billion, or $2,329 per U.S. household, in 2004 alone.

At the other extreme, statisticians at the U.S. Bureau of Labor Statistics found no price savings at Wal-Mart. Relying on Consumer Price Index data, the BLS found that Wal-Mart's prices largely matched those of its rivals, and that instances of lower prices at Wal-Mart could be attributed to lower quality products.

Both studies, which rely on the Consumer Price Index and aggregate data, have their critics. Furman himself allows that the Global Insight study is "overly simplistic" and says he "doesn't place as much weight on that one." Jerry Hausman, the M.I.T. economist who has looked closely at Wal-Mart's grocery stores, maintains that the CPI data that the Bureau of Labor Statistics relies on systematically miss the savings offered by "supercenters" such as Wal-Mart. To show the difference between prices at Wal-Mart and at other grocers, Hausman, along with Ephraim Leibtag, USDA Economic Research Service economist, used supermarket scanner data to examine the purchasing patterns of a national sample of 61,500 consumers from 1988 to 2001. Hausman and Leibtag found that Wal-Mart offers many identical food items at an average price about 15%-25% lower than traditional supermarkets.

The Costco Alternative?

Wall Street Prefers Wal-Mart

In an April 2004 online commentary, *BusinessWeek* praised Costco's business model but pointed out that Costco's wages cause Wall Street to worry that the company's "operating expenses could get out of hand." How does Costco compare to low-wage Wal-Mart on overhead expenses? At Costco, overhead is 9.8% of revenue; at Wal-Mart, it is 17%. Part of Costco's secret is that its better paid workers are also more efficient: Costco's operating profit per hourly employee is $13,647; each Wal-Mart employee only nets the company $11,039. Wal-Mart also spends more than Costco on hiring and training new employees: each one, according to Rutgers economist Eileen Appelbaum, costs the company $2,500 to $3,500. Appelbaum estimates that Wal-Mart's relatively high turnover costs the company $1.5 to $2 million per year.

Despite Costco's higher efficiency, Wall Street analysts like Deutsche Bank's Bill Dreher complain that "Costco's corporate philosophy is to put its customers first, then its employees, then its vendors, and finally its shareholders. Shareholders get the short end of the stick." Wall Street prefers Wal-Mart's philosophy: executives first, then shareholders, then customers, then vendors, and finally employees.

Average Hourly Wage		Percentage of U.S. Workforce in Unions		Employees Covered by Company Health Insurance		Employees Who Leave After One Year	
Wal-Mart	Costco	Wal-Mart	Costco	Wal-Mart	Costco	Sam's Club*	Costco
$9.68	$16.00	0.0%	17.9%	48%	82%	21%	6%
* Sam's Club is the Wal-Mart unit that competes directly with Costco.							

In 2004, Wal-Mart paid CEO Lee Scott $5.3 million, while a full-time employee making the average wage would have received $20,134. Costco's CEO Jim Senegal received $350,000, while a full-time average employee got $33,280. And *BusinessWeek* intimates that the top job at Costco may be tougher than at Wal-Mart. "Management has to hustle to make the high-wage strategy work. It's constantly looking for ways to repackage goods into bulk items, which reduces labor, speeds up Costco's just-in-time inventory, and boosts sales per square foot. Costco is also savvier … about catering to small shop owners and more affluent customers, who are more likely to buy in bulk and purchase higher-margin goods."

Costco's allegedly more affluent clientele may be another reason that its profit per employee is higher than Wal-Mart's and its overhead costs a lower percentage of revenue. However, Costco pays its employees enough that they could afford to shop there. As the *BusinessWeek* commentary noted, "the low-wage approach cuts into consumer spending and, potentially, economic growth."

—Esther Cervantes

While Hausman and Leibtag report substantial savings from shopping at Wal-Mart, they fall far short of the savings alleged in the Global Insight study. The Hausman and Leibtag study suggests a savings of around $550 per household per year, or about $56 billion in 2004, not $263 billion. Still, that is considerably more than the $4.7 billion a year in lost earnings to retail workers that Dube attributes to Wal-Mart.

But if "Wal-Mart hurts wages, not so much in retail, but across the whole country," as economist Neumark told *BusinessWeek*, then the savings to consumers from Wal-Mart's everyday low prices might not outweigh the lost wages to all workers. (Retail workers make up just 11.6% of U.S. employment.)

Nor do these findings say anything about the sweatshop conditions and wages in Wal-Mart's overseas subcontractors. One example: A recent Canadian Broadcasting Corporation investigative report found that workers in Bangladesh were being paid less than $50 a month (below even the United Nation's $2 a day measure of poverty) to make clothes for the Wal-Mart private label, Simply Basic. Those workers included ten- to thirteen-year-old children forced to work long hours in dimly lit and dirty conditions sewing "I Love My Wal-Mart" t-shirts.

Making Wal-Mart Do Better

Nonetheless, as Arindrajit Dube points out, the relevant question is not whether Wal-Mart creates more savings for consumers than losses for workers, but whether the corporation can afford to pay better wages and benefits.

Dube reasons that if the true price gap between Wal-Mart and its retail competitors is small, then Wal-Mart might not be in a position to do better—to make up its wage and benefit gap and still maintain its price advantage. But if Wal-Mart offers consumers only minor price savings, then its lower wages and benefits hardly constitute a progressive success story that's good for the nation.

If Wal-Mart's true price gap is large (say, the 25% price advantage estimated by Hausman), then Wal-Mart surely is in a position to do better. For instance, Dube calculates that closing Wal-Mart's 16% overall compensation gap with other large retailers would cost the company less than 2% of sales. Raising prices by two cents on the dollar to cover those increased compensation costs would be "eminently absorbable," according to Dube, without eating away much of the company's mind-boggling $10 billion profit (2004).

Measures that set standards to force Wal-Mart and all big-box retailers to pay decent wages and provide benefits are beginning to catch on. Chicago, New York City, and the state of Maryland have considered or passed laws that would require big-box retailers to pay a "living wage" or to spend a minimum amount per worker-hour for health benefits. The Republican board of Nassau County on Long Island passed an ordinance requiring that all big-box retailers pay $3 per hour toward health care. Wal-Mart's stake in making sure that such proposals don't become law or spread nationwide goes a long way toward explaining why 80% of Wal-Mart's $2 million in political contributions in 2004 went to Republicans.

Henry Ford sought to pay his workers enough so they could buy the cars they produced. Sam Walton sought to pay his workers so little that they could afford to shop nowhere else. And while what was good for the big automakers was probably never good for the nation, what is good for Wal-Mart, today's largest employer, is undoubtedly bad for economic justice. ❑

Sources: "Is Wal-Mart Good for America?" *Wall Street Journal,* 12/3/05; "Gauging the Wal-Mart Effect," *WSJ,* 12/03/05; Arindrajit Dube & Steve Wertheim, "Wal-Mart and Job Quality—What Do We Know, and Should We Care?" 10/05; Jason Furman, "Wal-Mart: A Progressive Success Story," 10/05; Leo Hindery Jr., "Wal-Mart's Giant Sucking Sound," 10/05; A. Bernstein, "Some Uncomfortable Findings for Wal-Mart," *BusinessWeek* online, 10/26/05, and "Wal-Mart: A Case for the Defense, Sort of," *BusinessWeek* online, 11/7/05; Dube, Jacobs, and Wertheim, "The Impact of Wal-Mart Growth on Earnings Throughout the Retail Sector in Urban and Rural Counties," *Institute of Industrial Relations Working Paper,* UC Berkeley, 10/05; Dube, Jacobs, and Wertheim, "Internal Wal-Mart Memo Validates Findings of UC Berkeley Study," 11/26/05; Jerry Hausman and Ephraim Leibtag, "Consumer Benefits from Increased Competition in Shopping Outlets: Measuring the Effect of Wal-Mart," 10/05; Hausman and Leibtag, "CPI Bias from Supercenters: Does the BLS Know that Wal-Mart Exists?" *NBER Working Paper No. 10712,* 8/04; David Neumark, Junfu Zhang, and Stephen Ciccarella, "The Effects of Wal-Mart on Local Labor Markets," *NBER Working Paper No. 11782,* 11/05; Erin Johansson, "Wal-Mart: Rolling Back Workers' Wages, Rights, and the American Dream," American Rights at Work, 11/05; Wal-Mart Watch, "Spin Cycle"; CBC News, "Wal-Mart to cut ties with Bangladesh factories using child labour," 11/30/05; National Labor Committee, "10 to 13-year-olds Sewing 'I Love My Wal-Mart' Shirts," 12/05; Global Insight, "The Economic Impact of Wal-Mart," 2005.

The Short Run: Newsflash: Wal-Mart Cuts Wages!
November/December 2006

Wal-Mart has announced plans to cap wages and shift more positions from full-time to part-time, the *New York Times* reported in October. Sources told the *Times* that Wal-Mart is aiming for a 40% target but admit that the part-time share of the company's work-force has risen from 20% in late 2005 to 25-30% now. For Wal-Mart's workers, getting shifted from full-time to part-time means not only less income, but the possible loss of benefits like health coverage.

The company claims the changes are aimed at serving its customers better, although how cutting its workers' wages and benefits will translate into better customer service is, well, unclear. A more likely scenario: Wal-Mart reported a monthly same-store sales decline for November, something that hasn't happened since 1996, and is now quickly trying to fix its next-quarter financial results.   —*Barbara Sternal*

Article 2.5

WHAT CAN WE DO TO RAISE WAGES?

BY ARTHUR MacEWAN
May/June 2009; updated, March 2011

Dear Dr. Dollar:

Since the big problem in our national economy seems to be low wages for so many, how can we, or why can't we, just raise wages?

—Ben Leet, San Leandro, Calif.

A large part of the low wage story is explained by political power—political actions that have weakened unions and social support programs. So political action—in the other direction!—is a large part of what we can do to raise wages.

The biggest decline in wages took place in the 1980s and early 1990s. In 1993, average hourly wages, adjusted for inflation, were 18% below their 1972 peak. The 1980s started off with Ronald Reagan's firing of the air traffic controllers when they went on strike in 1981. This act directly weakened unions and was a harbinger of things to come. The pro-business appointments by Reagan and Bush I to the National Labor Relations Board (NLRB) allowed firms to aggressively resist unions' organizing efforts.

A recent report from the Center for Economic and Policy Research shows that during the 1980s and on into the early 1990s, over 25% of union election campaigns were marred by illegal firings. While the rate of illegal firings then dropped off substantially in the late 1990s, it jumped up again to over 25% in the Bush II era. The report points out that in the conditions of the 1980s, early 1990s, and since 2000, "almost one-in-five union organizers or activists [could] expect to be fired as a result of their activities in a union election campaign." With the NLRB favoring the employers, workers had little recourse against these illegal firings.

Also in the 1980s, the minimum wage was continually eroded by inflation. It slid down (in terms of 2008 prices) from $7.93 in 1981 to $5.82 in 1989, as the nominal minimum wage remained unchanged at $3.35 in this period. More recently, with the nominal minimum wage of $5.15 unchanged between 1997 and 2006, these years saw a similar erosion of the real minimum wage. In the absence of upward pressure at the bottom, employers could more easily maintain lower wages over a wide range.

Good social support programs—childcare, health care, housing subsidies, and other such programs—tend to redistribute income directly, but they also create upward pressure on wages because they give the people at the bottom more options. Yet the same rightward political shift that weakened unions also undermined social support programs. A process that was well underway in the 1980s reached its apex in the late 1990s when Bill Clinton presided over the "ending of welfare as we know it."

With the bottom of the labor market kept down by the lack of social support programs and a declining minimum wage, the bargaining power of workers at every level has been weakened. In 2008 (before the impact of the current downturn), the average real hourly wage was still 10% below the 1972 peak, even after a slow rise since the early '90s.

Although the current crisis is dramatically raising the unemployment rate and thus weakening workers' bargaining power, these circumstances also create possibilities for new, progressive programs. The Obama administration seems open to at least some of these programs. The President has voiced support for the Employee Free Choice Act that would greatly facilitate union organizing, and Obama's appointments to the NLRB will probably be more sympathetic to unions. On social programs, at least the door is open (a crack) to some positive developments with health care. On all these fronts, however, we cannot expect good results without popular efforts.

There are, however, limits to what we can accomplish domestically. Unions have been weakened by political actions, but they have also been weakened by international competition. Of course the nature of our economic connections to the rest of the world are shaped by political power, but with virtually any set of international connections it is difficult to maintain the high wages of U.S. workers while workers elsewhere live in poverty. A long-run strategy for improving workers' wages has to take account of all workers, not just those in the United States. ❏

Update, March 2011: In early 2011, the political aspects of wage determination became especially apparent. In several states, Republican administrations attacked state workers and their unions as responsible for states' fiscal crises. What is perhaps most significant about this attack is the upsurge of opposition that it has inspired. Whatever else results from this renewed attack on working people, it makes clear the importance of political decisions in determining workers' wages and rights.

The Short Run: Minimum Wage vs. Maximum Profit
July/August 2006

In June the Republican-run Senate rejected yet another proposal to increase the federal minimum wage, currently $5.15 an hour. This was the Democrats' ninth attempt to raise the minimum wage since 1997. Republican legislators insisted that while a higher wage floor would give some workers a raise, many others would suffer because employers would respond by cutting low-skill jobs. The Republicans' argument might hold more water if (1) past minimum-wage increases had led to job losses—on the whole they haven't; and (2) the average U.S. CEO were not earning 262 times the wage of the average worker—he is.

Perhaps CEOs and other upper-level managers could be tapped to cover some of the $0.70-an-hour raise that proponents are trying to give the lowest paid workers.   —*Barbara Sternal*

Article 2.6

MEASURING THE FULL IMPACT OF MINIMUM-WAGE LAWS

Workers who were earning less than the new wage floor are not the only ones who benefit from a higher minimum wage.

BY JEANNETTE WICKS-LIM
May/June 2006

Minimum-wage and living-wage laws have always caused an uproar in the business community. Employers sound the alarm about the dire consequences of a higher minimum wage both for themselves and for the low-wage workers these laws are intended to benefit: Minimum-wage mandates, they claim, will cause small-business owners to close shop and lay off their low-wage workers. A spokesperson for the National Federation of Independent Business (NFIB), commenting on a proposal to raise Pennsylvania's minimum wage in an interview with the *Philadelphia Inquirer*, put it this way: "That employer may as well be handing out pink slips along with the pay raise."

What lies behind these bleak predictions? Mark Shaffer, owner of Shaffer's Park Supper Club in Crivitz, Wisc., provided one explanation to the *Wisconsin State Journal*: "… increasing the minimum wage would create a chain reaction. Every worker would want a raise to keep pace, forcing up prices and driving away customers." In other words, employers will not only be forced to raise the wages of those workers earning below the new minimum wage, but also the wages of their co-workers who earn somewhat more. The legally required wage raises are difficult enough for employers to absorb, they claim; these other raises—referred to as ripple effect raises—aggravate the situation. The result? "That ripple effect is going to lay off people."

Ripple effects represent a double-edged sword for minimum-wage and living-wage proponents. Their extent determines how much low-wage workers will benefit from such laws. If the ripple effects are small, then a higher minimum (or living) wage would benefit only a small class of workers, and boosting the minimum wage might be dismissed as an ineffective antipoverty strategy. If the ripple effects are large, then setting higher wage minimums may be seen as a potent policy tool to improve the lives of the working poor. But at the same time, evidence of large ripple effects provides ammunition to employers who claim they cannot afford the costs of a higher wage floor.

So what is the evidence on ripple effects? Do they bloat wage bills and overwhelm employers? Do they expand the number of workers who get raises a little or a lot? It's difficult to say because the research on ripple effects has been thin. But getting a clear picture of the full impact of minimum and living wage laws on workers' wages is critical to evaluating the impact of these laws. New research provides estimates of the scope and magnitude of the ripple effects of both minimum-wage and living-wage laws. This evidence is crucial for analyzing both the full impact of this increasingly visible policy tool and the political struggles surrounding it.

Why Do Employers Give Ripple-Effect Raises?

Marge Thomas, CEO of Goodwill Industries in Maryland, explains in an interview with *The Gazette* (Md.): "There will be a ripple effect [in response to Maryland's recent minimum-wage increase to $6.15], since it wouldn't be fair to pay people now making above the minimum wage at the same level as those making the new minimum wage." That is, without ripple effects, an increase in the wage floor will worsen the relative wage position of workers just above it. If there are no ripple effects, workers earning $6.15 before Maryland's increase would not only see their wages fall to the bottom of the wage scale, but also to the same level as workers who had previously earned inferior wages (i.e., workers who earned between $5.15 and $6.15).

Employers worry that these workers would view such a relative decline in their wages as unfair, damaging their morale—and their productivity. Without ripple effect raises, employers fear, their disgruntled staff will cut back on hard-to-measure aspects of their work such as responding to others cheerfully and taking initiative in assisting customers.

So employers feel compelled to preserve some consistency in their wage scales. Workers earning $6.15 before the minimum increase, for example, may receive a quarter raise, to $6.40, to keep their wages just above the new $6.15 minimum. That employers feel compelled to give non-mandated raises to some of their lowest-paid workers because it is the "fair" thing to do may appear to be a dubious claim. Perhaps so, but employers commonly express anxiety about the costs of minimum-wage and living-wage laws for this very reason.

The Politics of Ripple Effects

Inevitably, then, ripple effects come into play in the political battles around minimum-wage and living-wage laws—but in contradictory ways for both opponents and supporters. Opponents raise the specter of large ripple effects bankrupting small businesses. At the same time, though, they argue that minimum-wage laws are not effective in fighting poverty because they do not cover many workers—and worse, because those who are covered are largely teens or young-adult students just working for spending money. If ripple effects are small, this shores up opponents' assertions that minimum-wage laws have a limited impact on poverty. Evidence of larger ripple effects, on the other hand, would mean that the benefits of minimum-wage laws are larger than previously understood, and that these laws have an even greater potential to reduce poverty among the working poor.

The political implications are complicated further in the context of living-wage laws, which typically call for much higher wage floors than state and federal minimum-wage laws do. The living-wage movement calls for wage floors to be set at rates that provide a "livable income," such as the federal poverty level for a family of four, rather than at the arbitrary—and very low—level current minimum-wage laws set. The difference is dramatic: the living-wage ordinances that have been passed in a number of municipalities typically set a wage floor twice the level of federal and state minimum wages.

So the mandated raises under living-wage laws are already much higher than under even the highest state minimum-wage laws. If living-wage laws have significant ripple effects, opponents have all the more ammunition for their argument that the costs of these laws are unsustainable for employers.

How Big Are Ripple Effects?

My answer is a typical economists' response: it depends. In a nutshell, it depends on how high the wage minimum is set. The reason for this is simple. Evidence from the past 20 years of changes to state and federal minimum wages suggests that while there is a ripple effect, it doesn't extend very far beyond the new minimum. So, if the wage minimum is set high, then a large number of workers are legally due raises and, relatively speaking, the number of workers who get ripple-effect raises is small. Conversely, if the wage minimum is set low, then a small number of workers are legally due raises and, relatively speaking, the number of workers who get ripple-effect raises is large.

In the case of minimum-wage laws, the evidence suggests that ripple effects do dramatically expand their impact. Minimum wages are generally set low relative to the wage distribution. Because so many more workers earn wages just above the minimum wage compared to those earning the minimum, even a small ripple effect increases considerably the number of workers who benefit from a rise in the minimum wage. And even though the size of these raises quickly shrinks the higher the worker's wage rate, the much greater number of affected workers translates into a significantly larger increase in the wage bills of employers.

For example, my research shows that the impact of the most recent federal minimum-wage increase, from $4.75 to $5.15 in 1997, extended to workers earning wages around $5.75. Workers earning between the old and new minimums generally received raises to bring their wages in line with the new minimum—an 8% raise for those who started at the old minimum. Workers earning around $5.20 (right above the new minimum of $5.15) received raises of around 2%, bringing their wages up to about $5.30. Finally, those workers earning wages around $5.75 received raises on the order of 1%, bringing their wages up to about $5.80.

This narrow range of small raises translates into a big overall impact. Roughly 4 million workers (those earning between $4.75 and $5.15) received mandated raises in response to the 1997 federal minimum-wage increase. Taking into account the typical work schedules of these workers, these raises translated into a $741 million increase to employers' annual wage bills. Now add in ripple effects: Approximately 11 million workers received ripple-effect raises, adding another $1.3 billion to employers' wage bills. In other words, ripple-effect raises almost quadrupled the number of workers who benefited from the minimum-wage increase and almost tripled the overall costs associated with it.

Dramatic as these ripple effects are, the real impact on employers can only be gauged in relation to their capacity to absorb the higher wage costs. Here, there is evidence that businesses are not overwhelmed by the costs of a higher minimum wage, even including ripple effects. For example, in a study I co-authored with University of Massachusetts economists Robert Pollin and Mark Brenner on the Florida ballot measure to establish a $6.15 state minimum wage (which passed overwhelmingly in 2004), we accounted for ripple-effect costs of roughly this same magnitude. Despite almost tripling the number of affected workers (from almost 300,000 to over 850,000) and more than doubling the costs associated with the new minimum wage (from $155 million to $410 million), the ripple effects, combined with the mandated wage increases, imposed an average cost increase on employers amounting to less than one-half of 1% of their sales revenue. Even for employers in the hotel and restaurant industry, where low-wage workers tend to be concentrated, the average cost increase was less than 1% of their sales revenue. In other words, a 1% increase in prices for hotel rooms or restaurant meals could cover the increased costs associated with both legally mandated raises and ripple-effect raises.

The small fraction of revenue that these raises represent goes a long way toward explaining why economists generally agree that minimum-wage laws are not "job killers," as opponents claim. According to a 1998 survey of economists, a consensus seems to have been reached that there is minimal job loss, if any, associated with minimum-wage increases in the ranges that we've seen.

Just as important, this new research revises our understanding of who benefits from minimum-wage laws. Including ripple-effect raises expands the circle of minimum-wage beneficiaries to include more adult workers and fewer teenage or student workers. In fact, accounting for ripple effects decreases the prevalence of teenagers and traditional-age students (age 16 to 24) among workers likely to be affected by a federal minimum-wage increase from four out of ten to three out of ten. In other words, adult workers make up an even larger majority of likely minimum-wage beneficiaries when ripple effects are added to the picture.

The Case of Living-Wage Laws

With living-wage laws, the ripple effect story appears to be quite different, however—primarily because living wage laws set much higher wage minimums.

To understand why living-wage laws might generate far less of a ripple effect than minimum-wage hikes, it is instructive to look at the impact of raising the minimum wage on the retail trade industry. About 15% of retail trade workers earn wages at or very close to the minimum wage, compared to 5% of all workers. As a result, a large fraction of the retail trade industry workforce receives legally mandated raises when the minimum wage is raised, which is just what occurs across a broader group of industries and occupations when a living-wage ordinance is passed.

My research shows that the relative impact of the ripple effect that accompanies a minimum-wage hike is much smaller within retail trade than across all industries. Because a much larger share of workers in retail receive legally required raises when the minimum wage is raised, this reduces the relative number of workers receiving ripple effect raises, and, in turn, the relative size of the costs associated with ripple effects. This analysis suggests that the ripple effects of living wage laws will likewise be smaller than those found with minimum-wage laws.

To be sure, the ripple effect in the retail trade sector may underestimate the ripple effect of living-wage laws for a couple of reasons. First, unlike minimum-wage hikes, living-wage laws may have ripple effects that extend across firms as well as up the wage structure within firms. Employers who do not fall under a living-wage law's mandate but who are competing for workers within the same local labor market as those that do may be compelled to raise their own wages in order to retain their workers. Second, workers just above living-wage levels are typically higher on the job ladder and may have more bargaining power than workers with wages just above minimum-wage levels and, as a result, may be able to demand more significant raises when living-wage laws are enacted.

However, case studies of living-wage ordinances in Los Angeles and San Francisco do suggest that the ripple effect plays a smaller role in the case of living-wage laws than in the case of minimum-wage laws. These studies find that ripple effects add less than half again to the costs of mandated raises—dramatically less than the almost tripling of costs by ripple effects associated with the 1997 federal minimum-wage increase. In other words, the much higher wage floors set by living-wage laws appear to reverse the importance of legally required raises versus ripple-effect raises.

Do the costs associated with living-wage laws—with their higher wage floors—overwhelm employers, even if their ripple effects are small? To date, estimates suggest that within the range of existing living-wage laws, businesses are generally able to absorb the cost increases they face. For example, Pollin and Brenner studied a 2000 proposal to raise the wage floor from $5.75 to $10.75 in Santa Monica, Calif. They estimated that the cost increase faced by a typical business would be small, on the order of 2% of sales revenue, even accounting for both mandated and ripple-effect raises. Their estimates also showed that some hotel and restaurant businesses might face cost increases amounting to up to 10% of their sales revenue—not a negligible sum. However, after examining the local economy, Pollin and Brenner concluded that even these cost increases would not be likely to force these businesses to close their doors. Moreover, higher productivity and lower turnover rates among workers paid a living wage would also reduce the impact of these costs.

Ultimately, the impact of ripple-effect raises appears to depend crucially on the level of the new wage floor. The lower the wage floor, as in the case of minimum-wage laws, the more important the role of ripple-effect raises. The higher the wage floor, as in living-wage laws, the less important the role of ripple-effect raises.

Making the Case

The results of this new research are generally good news for proponents of living- and minimum-wage laws. Ripple effects do not portend dire consequences for employers from minimum and living wage laws; at the same time, ripple-effect raises heighten the effectiveness of these laws as antipoverty strategies.

In the case of minimum-wage laws, because the cost of legally mandated raises relative to employer revenues is small, even ripple effects large enough to triple the cost of a minimum-wage increase do not represent a large burden for employers. Moreover, ripple effects enhance the somewhat anemic minimum-wage laws to make them more effective as policy tools for improving the lot of the working poor. Accounting for ripple effects nearly quadruples the number of beneficiaries of a minimum-wage hike and expands the majority of those beneficiaries who are adults—in many instances, family breadwinners.

However, ripple effects do not appear to overwhelm employers in the case of the more ambitious living-wage laws. The strongest impact from living-wage laws appears to come from legally required raises rather than from ripple-effect raises. This reinforces advocates' claims that paying a living wage is a reasonable, as well as potent, way to fight poverty. ❑

Sources: D. Fairris, et al., *Examining the Evidence: The Impact of the Los Angeles Living Wage Ordinance on Workers Businesses,* Los Angeles Alliance for a New Economy, 2005; V. Fuchs, et al., "Economists' Views About Parameters, Values and Policies: Survey Results in Labor and Public Economics," *Journal of Economic Literature*, Sept. 1998; R. Pollin, M. Brenner, and J. Wicks-Lim, "Economic Analysis of the Florida Minimum Wage Proposal, " Center for American Progress, 2004; R. Pollin and M. Brenner, "Economic Analysis of the Santa Monica Living Wage Proposal," Political Economy Research Institute, 2000; M. Reich et al., *Living Wages and Economic Performance,* Institute of Industrial Relations, 2003; J. Wicks-Lim, "Mandated Wage Floors and the Wage Structure: Analyzing the Ripple Effects of Minimum and Prevailing Wage Laws," Ph.D. dissertation, University of Massachusetts-Amherst, 2005.

The Short Run: Minimal Wage Increase
May/June 2008

Here's some good news for California's low-wage workers: in January, more than one million workers received a pay raise of 50 cents, to $8 an hour, as the state completed a two-step process of increasing the minimum wage. But now the bad news: because of inflation, the beneficial effects of the pay increase will be wiped out in just two years, according to the online newsletter "California Progress Report."

In addition, workers on the lowest rung of the wage ladder will only earn $16,640 in 2008. This is still below the federal poverty line for a family of three; in other words, working full time at the new minimum wage still won't cover the basic expenses of a small household. And this benchmark does not take into account California's relatively high cost of living.

An alternative to the periodic, hard-fought battles to enact minimum wage hikes that still fail to keep bottom-rung wages level with the cost of living would be to index the minimum wage to inflation. Under such a policy, the minimum wage would automatically adjust each year in step with a basic price index, allowing the lowest-paid workers to at least maintain their (very modest) spending power.   —*Jason Son*

Article 2.7

ACCESS TO PAID SICK DAYS VASTLY UNEQUAL

BY ELISE GOULD
April 2011

More than one-third of all workers--38%--have no paid sick days. When these workers get sick, they are either forced to go to work, or stay home without pay and risk losing their job. Access to sick days is also vastly unequal: As shown in the figure, workers at the top of the scale are more than four times more likely to have sick days than workers at the bottom of the wage scale. Only 19% of low-wage workers have paid sick days, compared with 86% of high-wage workers. These low-income workers are the ones who can least afford to lose pay when they are sick.

A 2010 study found that the vast majority of nations (163 in total, almost all of them much poorer than the United States) guarantee paid sick days for workers. A law giving American workers that same benefit could increase pro-ductivity in the workforce through heightened worker loyalty, reduced turnover, and reduced workplace illness. ❑

Note: This article originally appeared as an Economic Snapshot at the website of the Economic Policy Institute (www.epi.org/economic_snapshots).

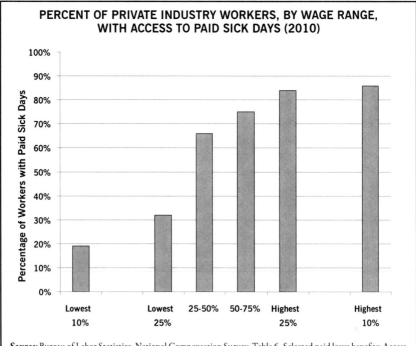

PERCENT OF PRIVATE INDUSTRY WORKERS, BY WAGE RANGE, WITH ACCESS TO PAID SICK DAYS (2010)

Source: Bureau of Labor Statistics, National Compensation Survey, Table 6, Selected paid leave benefits: Access, March 2010.

Article 2.8

IMPRISONED IN LOW WAGES
Limited access to education for people in prison leads to economic exclusion.

BY WILL GOLDBERG
July/August 2007

It's tough to get an education in prison. People in prison tend to start with lower educational levels than the general population, and spending time behind bars generally makes matters worse. Because schooling is a major factor in earnings potential, the incarcerated are being left farther and farther behind.

In New York State, 48.6% of people in prison do not have a high school diploma, as compared to 27.8% of the general population. From 1980 to 2000, the number of incarcerated black and white high school dropouts both tripled, and other disparities are immense. The rate of imprisonment among black men with college degrees has fallen, while a full 60% of black high school dropouts are now prisoners or ex-cons by the time they reach their mid-30s.

Lower levels of education already translate directly into lower earnings over a lifetime, as a 2002 Census Bureau study found (see figure).

This is compounded by the worsened prospects for employment and greater obstacles to job success that result from incarceration.

The economic penalties of incarceration begin with the stigma of a criminal record and snowball from there. A study conducted by sociologist Devah Pager found that applicants are much less likely to receive callbacks from potential employers if their resumes indicate that they have been incarcerated. Furthermore, each month someone cannot work because of incarceration, he or she loses ground in experience and personal connections; research indicates that the people serving the longest sentences suffer the largest loss in earnings. Sociologist Bruce Western has found that important survival skills for prison—"suspicion of strangers, aggressiveness, withdrawal from social interaction"—are detrimental to success at work. Western also found that Latino workers' average hourly wages dropped from $12.30 to $10.31 following incarceration; black workers' from $10.25 to $9.25.

GED programs have helped offset some of these effects. The Florida Department of Corrections found that recidivism, or repeat criminal offending, was 8.7% lower among graduates of GED programs; the benefits of education extended to groups at greatest risk for recidivism, including prior recidivists, black prisoners, and young males. Florida calculated that its GED program prevented the recidivism of approximately 100 people in prison annually, saving that state about $1.9 million a year.

Post-secondary education has been shown to be even more effective than the GED in reducing recidivism. James Gilligan, a director of mental health for the Massachusetts prison system and a prison psychiatrist for 25 years, found that a program through which hundreds of people in prison earned a college degree was 100% effective in preventing recidivism. The N.Y. Department of Correctional Services found that only 26.4% of people in prison who had earned a college degree re-offended, far lower than the recidivism rates of people in prison who had never enrolled in the program (47.4%) or those who had not completed it (44.6%).

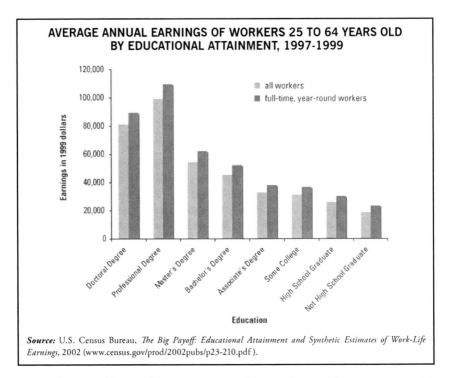

AVERAGE ANNUAL EARNINGS OF WORKERS 25 TO 64 YEARS OLD BY EDUCATIONAL ATTAINMENT, 1997-1999

Source: U.S. Census Bureau, *The Big Payoff: Educational Attainment and Synthetic Estimates of Work-Life Earnings*, 2002 (www.census.gov/prod/2002pubs/p23-210.pdf).

William Weld, Republican governor of Massachusetts from 1991 to 1997, previously unaware that college classes were available in prisons, responded to this news by declaring that Massachusetts should not grant the "privilege" of a college education to the incarcerated, or poor people would end up committing crimes in hopes of getting free higher education. This came at the same time as Jesse Helms and other "tough on crime" senators began to imply that awarding Pell grants to people in prison cut into federal funding set aside for unincarcerated students' education, though this was not the case. In 1994, Congress passed a crime bill that eliminated prisoner eligibility for the grants, a considerable setback for people in prison wishing to pursue a college education.

The alarmingly disproportionate levels of incarceration among black and Latino populations, in combination with all of these obstacles to future financial success upon release, result in troubling economic disadvantages. Giving people in prison, and released from prison, the tools they need to support themselves and to contribute meaningfully is both economically advantageous and morally necessary. Annette Johnson, member of the Board of Directors of the Prisoners' Reading Encouragement Project, testified in 2000 that education was an important part of criminal justice reform that would "make it more effective—indeed, more cost-effective—in preventing crime and restoring convicted persons to the community with a positive attitude and positive skills that will allow them to contribute to the economy and reclaim a wholesome place in family life."

Apart from the obvious advantage that education offers people who have been in prison in finding employment after release, quality educational programs help people in prison to have a better mindset both during and after incarceration. And prison education programs save money: the reductions in crime, incarceration, and social welfare costs, plus increased payroll and income tax revenues from employing people who would otherwise likely be re-imprisoned, more than compensate for their costs.

With the expansion of distance-learning technologies, it is easier and cheaper than ever to provide education to people in prison. The missing ingredient is the political will to view incarceration not just as punishment but also as an opportunity for recovery. ❏

Sources: Devah Pager, "The Mark of a Criminal Record," *American Journal of Sociology*, 108(5), 2003; Bruce Western, *Punishment and Inequality in America*, Russell Sage, 2006; Follow-Up Study of a Sample of Offenders Who Earned High School Equivalency Diplomas (GEDs) While Incarcerated in DOCS, www.prisonpolicy.org/scans/ny_ged.shtml; Annette Johnson, Testimony concerning the positive correlation between inmate education and reduction of recidivism, www.prisonreader.org/TestimonyEduc.html.

The Short Run: COBOL vs. Arnold
September/October 2010

Gov. Arnold Schwarzenegger's proposal to slash California state workers' wages until the legislature presents him with a budget he likes has been defeated by an unlikely hero: COBOL.

With California facing a $15.2 billion deficit and budget negotiations deadlocked, Schwarzenegger decided to cut the pay of over 200,000 state employees down to the federal minimum wage ($7.25/hour) until a budget agreement could be reached. But State Controller John Chiang is refusing to carry out the cuts, arguing that the task is too difficult since the payroll system is written in an outdated programming language known as COBOL.

Most legacy software is written in COBOL, but it is not used in new software and is rarely taught nowadays. Chiang estimates revising the system to alter wage rates on such a large scale would take six months.

This is not the first time COBOL has thwarted Schwarzenegger's attempts to hold state workers hostage in pursuit of an annual budget, but it may be the last. California is in the process of replacing its payroll system, a $283 million project to be completed in 2012.   —*Elizabeth Murphy*

Article 2.9

NIKE TO THE RESCUE?

Africa needs better jobs, not sweatshops.

BY JOHN MILLER

September/October 2006

"In Praise of the Maligned Sweatshop"

WINDHOEK, Namibia—Africa desperately needs Western help in the form of schools, clinics and sweatshops.

On a street here in the capital of Namibia, in the southwestern corner of Africa, I spoke to a group of young men who were trying to get hired as day laborers on construction sites.

"I come here every day," said Naftal Shaanika, a 20-year-old. "I actually find work only about once a week."

Mr. Shaanika and the other young men noted that the construction jobs were dangerous and arduous, and that they would vastly prefer steady jobs in, yes, sweatshops. Sure, sweatshop work is tedious, grueling and sometimes dangerous. But over all, sewing clothes is considerably less dangerous or arduous—or sweaty—than most alternatives in poor countries.

Well-meaning American university students regularly campaign against sweatshops. But instead, anyone who cares about fighting poverty should campaign in favor of sweatshops, demanding that companies set up factories in Africa.

The problem is that it's still costly to manufacture in Africa. The headaches across much of the continent include red tape, corruption, political instability, unreliable electricity and ports, and an inexperienced labor force that leads to low productivity and quality. The anti-sweatshop movement isn't a prime obstacle, but it's one more reason not to manufacture in Africa.

Imagine that a Nike vice president proposed manufacturing cheap T-shirts in Ethiopia. The boss would reply: "You're crazy! We'd be boycotted on every campus in the country."

Some of those who campaign against sweatshops respond to my arguments by noting that they aren't against factories in Africa, but only demand a "living wage" in them. After all, if labor costs amount to only $1 per shirt, then doubling wages would barely make a difference in the final cost.

One problem … is that it already isn't profitable to pay respectable salaries, and so any pressure to raise them becomes one more reason to avoid Africa altogether.

One of the best U.S. initiatives in Africa has been the African Growth and Opportunity Act, which allows duty-free imports from Africa—and thus has stimulated manufacturing there.

—Op-ed by Nicholas Kristof, *New York Times*, June 6, 2006

Nicholas Kristof has been beating the pro-sweatshop drum for quite a while. Shortly after the East Asian financial crisis of the late 1990s, Kristof, the Pulitzer Prize-winning journalist and now columnist for the *New York Times*, reported the story of an Indonesian recycler who, picking through the metal scraps of a garbage dump, dreamed that her son would grow up to be a sweatshop worker. Then, in 2000, Kristof and his wife, *Times* reporter Sheryl WuDunn, published "Two Cheers for Sweatshops" in the *Times Magazine*. In 2002, Kristof's column advised G-8 leaders to "start an international campaign to promote imports from sweatshops, perhaps with bold labels depicting an unrecognizable flag and the words 'Proudly Made in a Third World Sweatshop.'"

Now Kristof laments that too few poor, young African men have the opportunity to enter the satanic mill of sweatshop employment. Like his earlier efforts, Kristof's latest pro-sweatshop ditty synthesizes plenty of half-truths. Let's take a closer look and see why there is still no reason to give it up for sweatshops.

A Better Alternative?

It is hardly surprising that young men on the streets of Namibia's capital might find sweatshop jobs more appealing than irregular work as day laborers on construction sites.

The alternative jobs available to sweatshop workers are often worse and, as Kristof loves to point out, usually involve more sweating than those in world export factories. Most poor people in the developing world eke out their livelihoods from subsistence agriculture or by plying petty trades. Others on the edge of urban centers work as street-hawkers or hold other jobs in the informal sector. As economist Arthur MacEwan wrote a few years back in *Dollars & Sense*, in a poor country like Indonesia, where women working in manufacturing earn five times as much as those in agriculture, sweatshops have no trouble finding workers.

But let's be clear about a few things. First, export factory jobs, especially in labor-intensive industries, often are just "a ticket to slightly less impoverishment," as even economist and sweatshop defender Jagdish Bhagwati allows.

Beyond that, these jobs seldom go to those without work or to the poorest of the poor. One study by sociologist Kurt Ver Beek showed that 60% of first-time Honduran maquila workers were previously employed. Typically they were not destitute, and they were better educated than most Hondurans.

Sweatshops don't just fail to rescue people from poverty. Setting up export factories where workers have few job alternatives has actually been a recipe for serious worker abuse. In *Beyond Sweatshops*, a book arguing for the benefits of direct foreign investment in the developing world, Brookings Institution economist Theodore Moran recounts the disastrous decision of the Philippine government to build the Bataan Export Processing Zone in an isolated mountainous area to lure foreign investors with the prospect of cheap labor. With few alternatives, Filipinos took jobs in the garment factories that sprung up in the zone. The manufacturers typically paid less than the minimum wage and forced employees to work overtime in factories filled with dust and fumes. Fed up, the workers eventually mounted a series of crippling strikes. Many factories shut down and occupancy rates in the zone plummeted, as did the value of exports, which declined by more than half between 1980 and 1986.

Kristof's argument is no excuse for sweatshop abuse: that conditions are worse elsewhere does nothing to alleviate the suffering of workers in export factories. They are often denied the right to organize, subjected to unsafe working conditions and to verbal, physical, and sexual abuse, forced to work overtime, coerced into pregnancy tests and even abortions, and paid less than a living wage. It remains useful and important to combat these conditions even if alternative jobs are worse yet.

The fact that young men in Namibia find sweatshop jobs appealing testifies to how harsh conditions are for workers in Africa, not the desirability of export factory employment.

Oddly, Kristof's desire to introduce new sweatshops to sub-Saharan Africa finds no support in the African Growth and Opportunity Act (AGOA) that he praises. The act grants sub-Saharan apparel manufacturers preferential access to U.S. markets. But shortly after its passage, U.S. Trade Representative Robert Zoellick assured the press that the AGOA would not create sweatshops in Africa because it requires protective standards for workers consistent with those set by the International Labor Organization.

Anti-Sweatshop Activism and Jobs

Kristof is convinced that the anti-sweatshop movement hurts the very workers it intends to help. His position has a certain seductive logic to it. As anyone who has suffered through introductory economics will tell you, holding everything else the same, a labor standard that forces multinational corporations and their subcontractors to boost wages should result in their hiring fewer workers.

But in practice does it? The only evidence Kristof produces is an imaginary conversation in which a boss incredulously refuses a Nike vice president's proposal to open a factory in Ethiopia paying wages of 25 cents a hour: "You're crazy! We'd be boycotted on every campus in the country."

While Kristof has an active imagination, there are some things wrong with this conversation.

First off, the anti-sweatshop movement seldom initiates boycotts. An organizer with United Students Against Sweatshops (USAS) responded on Kristof's blog: "We never call for apparel boycotts unless we are explicitly asked to by workers at a particular factory. This is, of course, exceedingly rare, because, as you so persuasively argued, people generally want to be employed." The National Labor Committee, the largest anti-sweatshop organization in the United States, takes the same position.

Moreover, when economists Ann Harrison and Jason Scorse conducted a systematic study of the effects of the anti-sweatshop movement on factory employment, they found no negative employment effect. Harrison and Scorse looked at Indonesia, where Nike was one of the targets of an energetic campaign calling for better wages and working conditions among the country's subcontractors. Their statistical analysis found that the anti-sweatshop campaign was responsible for 20% of the increase in the real wages of unskilled workers in factories exporting textiles, footwear, and apparel from 1991 to 1996. Harrison and Scorse also found that "anti-sweatshop activism did not have significant adverse effects on employment" in these sectors.

Campaigns for higher wages are unlikely to destroy jobs because, for multinationals and their subcontractors, wages make up a small portion of their overall costs. Even Kristof accepts this point, well documented by economists opposed to sweatshop labor. In Mexico's apparel industry, for instance, economists Robert Pollin, James Heintz, and Justine Burns from the Political Economy Research Institute found that doubling the pay of nonsupervisory workers would add just $1.80 to the production cost of a $100 men's sports jacket. A recent survey by the National Bureau of Economic Research found that U.S. consumers would be willing to pay $115 for the same jacket if they knew that it had not been made under sweatshop conditions.

Globalization in Sub-Saharan Africa

Kristof is right that Africa, especially sub-Saharan Africa, has lost out in the globalization process. Sub-Saharan Africa suffers from slower growth, less direct foreign investment, lower education levels, and higher poverty rates than most every other part of the world. A stunning 37 of the region's 47 countries are classified as "low-income" by the World Bank, each with a gross national income less than $825 per person. Many countries in the region bear the burdens of high external debt and a crippling HIV crisis that Kristof has made heroic efforts to bring to the world's attention.

But have multinational corporations avoided investing in sub-Saharan Africa because labor costs are too high? While labor costs in South Africa and Mauritius are high, those in the other countries of the region are modest by international standards, and quite low in some cases. Take Lesotho, the largest exporter of apparel from sub-Saharan Africa to the United States. In the country's factories that subcontract with Wal-Mart, the predominantly female workforce earns an average of just $54 a month. That's below the United Nations poverty line of $2 per day, and it includes regular forced overtime. In Madagascar, the region's third largest exporter of clothes to the United States, wages in the apparel industry are just 33 cents per hour, lower than those in China and among the lowest in the world. And at Ramatex Textile, the large Malaysian-owned textile factory in Namibia, workers only earn about $100 per month according to the Labour Resource and Research Institute in Windhoek. Most workers share their limited incomes with extended families and children, and they walk long distances to work because they can't afford better transportation.

On the other hand, recent experience shows that sub-Saharan countries with decent labor standards *can* develop strong manufacturing export sectors. In the late 1990s, Francis Teal of Oxford's Centre for the Study of African Economies compared Mauritius's successful export industries with Ghana's unsuccessful ones. Teal found that workers in Mauritius earned ten times as much as those in Ghana—$384 a month in Mauritius as opposed to $36 in Ghana. Mauritius's textile and garment industry remained competitive because its workforce was better educated and far more productive than Ghana's. Despite paying poverty wages, the Ghanaian factories floundered.

Kristof knows full well the real reason garment factories in the region are shutting down: the expiration of the Multifiber Agreement last January. The agreement, which set national export quotas for clothing and textiles, protected the garment industries in smaller countries around the world from direct competition with China. Now China and, to a lesser degree, India, are increasingly displacing other garment producers. In this new context, lower wages alone are unlikely to sustain the sub-Saharan garment industry. Industry sources report that sub-Saharan Africa suffers from several other drawbacks as an apparel producer, including relatively high utility and transportation costs and long shipping times to the United States. The region also has lower productivity and less skilled labor than Asia, and it has fewer sources of cotton yarn and higher-priced fabrics than China and India.

If Kristof is hell-bent on expanding the sub-Saharan apparel industry, he would do better to call for sub-Saharan economies to gain unrestricted access to the Quad markets—the United States, Canada, Japan, and Europe. Economists Stephen N. Karingi, Romain Perez, and Hakim Ben Hammouda estimate that the welfare gains associated with unrestricted market access could amount to $1.2 billion in sub-Saharan Africa, favoring primarily unskilled workers.

But why insist on apparel production in the first place? Namibia has sources of wealth besides a cheap labor pool for Nike's sewing machines. The *Economist* reports that Namibia is a world-class producer of two mineral products: diamonds (the country ranks seventh by value) and uranium (it ranks fifth by volume). The mining industry is the heart of Namibia's export economy and accounts for about 20% of the country's GDP. But turning the mining sector into a vehicle for national economic development would mean confronting the foreign corporations that control the diamond industry, such as the South African De Beers Corporation. That is a tougher assignment than scapegoating anti-sweatshop activists.

More and Better African Jobs

So why have multinational corporations avoided investing in sub-Saharan Africa? The answer, according to international trade economist Dani Rodrik, is "entirely due to the slow growth" of the sub-Saharan economies. Rodrik estimates that the region participates in international trade as much as can be expected given its economies' income levels, country size, and geography.

Rodrik's analysis suggests that the best thing to do for poor workers in Africa would be to lift the debt burdens on their governments and support their efforts to build functional economies. That means investing in human resources and physical infrastructure, and implementing credible macroeconomic policies that put job creation first. But these investments, as Rodrik points out, take time.

In the meantime, international policies establishing a floor for wages and safeguards for workers across the globe would do more for the young men on Windhoek's street corners than subjecting them to sweatshop abuse, because grinding poverty leaves people willing to enter into any number of desperate exchanges. And if Namibia is closing its garment factories because Chinese imports are cheaper, isn't that an argument for trying to improve labor standards in China, not lower them in sub-Saharan Africa? Abusive labor practices are rife in China's export factories, as the National Labor Committee and *BusinessWeek* have documented. Workers put in 13- to 16-hour days, seven days a week. They enjoy little to no health and safety enforcement, and their take-home pay falls below the minimum wage after the fines and deductions their employers sometimes withhold.

Spreading these abuses in sub-Saharan Africa will not empower workers there. Instead it will take advantage of the fact that they are among the most marginalized workers in the world. Debt relief, international labor standards, and public investments in education and infrastructure are surely better ways to fight African poverty than Kristof's sweatshop proposal. ❑

Sources: Arthur MacEwan, "Ask Dr. Dollar," *Dollars & Sense*, Sept–Oct 1998; John Miller, "Why Economists Are Wrong About Sweatshops and the Antisweatshop Movement," *Challenge*, Jan–Feb 2003; R. Pollin, J. Burns, and J. Heintz, "Global Apparel Production and Sweatshop Labor: Can Raising Retail Prices Finance Living Wages?" Political Economy Research Institute, Working Paper 19, 2004; N. Kristof, "In Praise of the Maligned Sweatshop,"*New York Times*, June 6, 2006; N. Kristof, "Let Them Sweat," *New York Times*, June 25, 2002; N. Kristof, "Two Cheers for Sweatshops," *New York Times*, Sept 24, 2000; N. Kristof, "Asia's Crisis Upsets Rising Effort to Confront Blight of Sweatshops," *New York Times*, June 15, 1998; A. Harrison and J. Scorse, "Improving the Conditions of Workers? Minimum Wage Legislation and Anti-Sweatshop Activism," *Calif. Management Review*, Oct 2005; Herbert Jauch, "Africa's Clothing and Textile Industry: The Case of Ramatex in Namibia," in *The Future of the Textile and Clothing Industry in Sub-Saharan Africa*, ed. H. Jauch and R. Traub-Merz (Friedrich-Ebert-Stiftung, 2006); Kurt Alan Ver Beek, "Maquiladoras: Exploitation or Emancipation? An Overview of the Situation of Maquiladora Workers in Honduras," *World Development,* 29(9), 2001; Theodore Moran, *Beyond Sweatshops: Foreign Direct Investment and Globalization in Developing Countries* (Brookings Institution Press, 2002); "Comparative Assessment of the Competitiveness of the Textile and Apparel Sector in Selected Countries," in *Textiles and Apparel: Assessment of the Competitiveness of Certain Foreign Suppliers to the United States Market*, Vol. 1, U.S. International Trade Commission, Jan 2004; S. N. Karingi, R. Perez, and H. Ben Hammouda, "Could Extended Preferences Reward Sub-Saharan Africa's Participation in the Doha Round Negotiations?," *World Economy*, 2006; Francis Teal, "Why Can Mauritius Export Manufactures and Ghana Can Not?," *The World Economy*, 22 (7), 1999; Dani Rodrik, "Trade Policy and Economic Performance in Sub-Saharan Africa," Paper prepared for the Swedish Ministry for Foreign Affairs, Nov 1997.

Article 2.10

CHINESE WORKERS STAND UP
What is the real cause of rising wages in China?

BY JOHN MILLER
September/October 2010

"The Rise of Chinese Labor:
Wage Hikes Are Part of a Virtuous Cycle of Development"

The recent strikes at Honda factories in southern China represent another data point in an emerging trend: Cheap labor won't be the source of the Chinese economy's competitive advantage much longer.

The auto maker has caved and given workers a 24% pay increase to restart one assembly line. Foxconn, the electronics producer that has experienced a string of worker suicides, has also announced big raises. This is all part of the virtuous cycle of development: Productivity increases, which drive wages higher, forcing businesses to adjust, leading to more productivity growth.
—*Wall Street Journal* op-ed, June 9, 2010

Wages in China are in fact rising. But that hardly constitutes a "virtuous cycle of development" that is the inevitable result of market-led economic growth, as the *Wall Street Journal* editors contend.

Rather, higher wages in China are the hard-fought gains of militant workers who have used tightening labor markets as a lever to pry wage gains out of employers whose coffers have long been brimming with cash.

Labor unrest taking advantage of tightening labor markets is the story in China today—not abstract economic forces lifting wages, the tale the *Journal's* editors want to pass off as a paean to free-market economics.

A Changing Labor Outlook

In recent years rapid economic growth has indeed tightened the Chinese labor market, drying up the seemingly bottomless pool of jobseekers from the countryside. As of May 2010, job vacancies in China outnumbered the number of job applicants, according to the Chinese Labor Market Information Center.

And wages are rising for many. Pay for China's 150 million or so internal-migrant workers increased 16% in 2009 despite the global financial crisis, according to Cai Fang, head of the Institute of Population and Labor Economics at the Chinese Academy of Social Sciences.

Higher wages aren't about to break the corporate piggybank. In recent years the biggest increase in China's extraordinarily high national savings (which includes household and business savings) has come from retained earnings—the undistributed profits of Chinese corporations. Retained earnings did so much to boost the country's savings because low wages kept corporate profits high. For more than a decade, labor's share of national income has been on the decline in China as the corporate share has increased dramatically. On top of that, the strong productivity growth that the *Journal* editors laud has offset wage increases, keeping labor costs per unit of output in check. At the beginning of 2010 Chinese unit labor costs were no higher than in 2004.

Wage increases notwithstanding, working conditions in China remain oppressive, as even the *Journal* editors seem to recognize. In May 2010 a thirteenth worker attempted to commit suicide at a Foxconn factory in southern China. The world's largest maker of computer components, Foxconn supplies Apple, Dell, and Hewlett-Packard, among others. While working conditions at this Taiwanese-owned company are far from the worst in China, the hours are long, the assembly line moves too fast, and managers enforce military-style discipline.

Foxconn's string of suicides is just the tip of the iceberg. Early in 2008, the *New York Times* reported that worker abuse is still commonplace in many of the Chinese factories that supply Western companies. The *Times* quoted labor activists who reported unfair labor practices—child labor, enforced 16-hour days, and sub-minimum wages, among others—in factories supplying several U.S. firms including WalMart, Disney, and Dell. The activists also reported that factories routinely withhold health benefits, employ dangerous machinery, and expose workers to lead, mercury, and other hazardous chemicals. According to government statistics, an average of 187 Chinese workers die each day in industrial accidents; the equivalent U.S. figure is three.

The Real Virtuous Cycle

Rapid economic growth and rising productivity undoubtedly laid the groundwork for higher wages. But it is labor militancy that has exploited workers' improved bargaining position. The number of labor disputes in China doubled from 2006 to 2009. Workers have won wage increases in excess of 20% at several large export factories, including Foshan Fengfu Autoparts, the company that supplies exhaust pipes to Japanese automaker Honda, and Hon Hai Precision Industry Co., the Taiwan-based electronics manufacturer that supplies iPads and iPhones for Apple and a range of gadgets for Hewlett-Packard and Nintendo.

Predictably, the editors misrepresent how social improvement comes about with economic development. Not just in China but in the developed economies as well, improvements in working conditions have come about not due to market-led forces alone, but when economic growth was combined with social action and worker militancy.

The history of sweatshops in the United States makes that clear. The shirtwaist strike of 1909, the tragedy of the Triangle Shirtwaist fire two years later, and the hardships of the Great Depression inspired garment workers to unionize and led to the imposition of government regulations on the garment industry and other industries, beginning with the New York Factory Acts and extending to the Fair Labor Standards Act of 1938. The power of those reforms along with the postwar boom nearly eradicated sweatshops in the United States.

Since then, sweatshops have returned with a vengeance to the U.S. garment industry. Why? Declining economic opportunity is part of the answer. But severe cutbacks in the number of inspectors and a drop-off in union density paved the way as well. The U.S. experience confirms the take-away message from rising Chinese wages: Economic development by itself will not eliminate inhuman working conditions. Improvements in working conditions are neither inevitable nor irreversible.

Not only is labor organizing crucial for improving working conditions, but those organizing efforts need to be international if workers are to succeed in reaping durable gains from economic development.

China's case makes that clear. Rising wages in China have prompted footwear and apparel firms to shift their manufacturing elsewhere—to Indonesia, Bangladesh, and Vietnam, for example. Jim Sciabarrasi, head of sourcing and procurement at U.S.-based sneaker company New Balance, was clear about the reason for the firm's move. "Indonesia has a ready supply of workers and their wages are not going up as fast as in China," he told the *Boston Globe*.

Chinese workers attempting to organize and improve their situation always face the threat that their employer will simply pack up and depart for even lower-cost countries. This kind of threat, which helps employers resist demands for better wages and working conditions not just in China but elsewhere in the global South and in the developed economies as well, has been increasingly effective as globalization has weakened limits on the mobility of corporations. It throws into sharp relief the common interests of workers in all countries in improving conditions at the bottom, in robust full-employment programs that raise their incomes and enhance their bargaining power.

In that way, the rise of China's workers and the bold labor unrest there should benefit manufacturing workers across the globe, a virtuous cycle the *Wall Street Journal* editors would not only be loathe to recognize but have gone out of their way to obscure. ❑

Sources: David Barboza, "In Chinese Factories, Lost Fingers and Low Pay," *New York Times*, Jan. 5, 2008; William Foreman, "13th worker attempts suicide at Foxconn tech factory in southern China, report says," *Los Angeles Times*, May 27, 2010; Jenn Abelson, "Local sneaker firms are making it in Indonesia," *Boston Globe*, May 29, 2010; Norihiko Shirouzo, "Chinese Workers Challenge Beijing's Authority," *WSJ*, June 13, 2010; Elizabeth Holmes, "U.S. Apparel Retailers Turn Their Gaze beyond China," *WSJ*, June 15, 2010; "NW: Wage disputes in China put world on notice," NIKKEI, June 14, 2010; Aileen Wang and Simon Rabinovitch, "Why labor unrest is good for China and the world," Reuters, June 2, 2010; World Bank, China Quarterly Update, June 2010; James Areddy, "Accidents Plague China's Workplaces," *WSJ*, July 28, 2010.

Article 2.11

STATE WORKERS FACE A COMPENSATION PENALTY

BY ETHAN POLLACK
March/April 2011

The campaign against state and local workers is often justified with claims that they are privileged relative to their private-sector peers or have somehow been cushioned from the effects of the recent recession and slow recovery. Data from Wisconsin as well as Indiana, New Jersey, and Ohio prove that these claims are clearly false.

In Wisconsin, which has become a focal point in this debate, public servants already take a pretty hefty pay cut just for the opportunity to serve their communities, according to findings by Rutgers economist Jeffrey Keefe. The figure below shows that when comparing the total compensation (which includes non-wage benefits such as health care and pensions) of workers with similar education, public-sector workers consistently make less than their private-sector peers. Workers with a bachelor's degree or more—who make up nearly 60% of the state and local workforce in Wisconsin—are compensated between $20,000 a year less (if they just have a bachelor's degree) to over $82,000 less (if they have a professional degree).

True apples-to-apples comparisons require controlling for worker characteristics such as education in order to best measure a worker's potential earnings in a different sector or industry. Controlling for a larger range of earnings predictors—including not just education but also age, experience, gender, race, etc., Wisconsin public-sector workers face an annual compensation penalty of 11%. Adjusting for the slightly fewer hours worked per week on average, these workers still face a compensation penalty of 5% for choosing to work in the public sector.

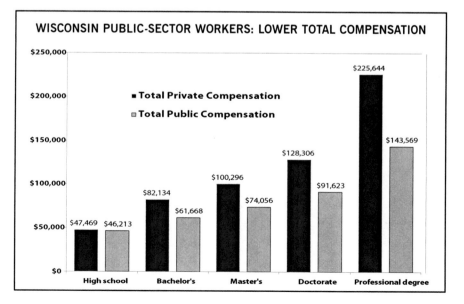

WISCONSIN PUBLIC-SECTOR WORKERS: LOWER TOTAL COMPENSATION

PUBLIC- AND PRIVATE-SECTOR WORKERS COMPARED

	Public-sector Penalty	Job experience		% w/ 4-yr degree	
		Public	Private	Public	Private
Indiana	7.5%	24.1 years	21.6	49%	24%
New Jersey	4.1%	24	22	57%	40%
Ohio	6%	23.2	21.7	49%	26%
Wisconsin	11%	22.5	21.3	59%	30%

The story is similar in Indiana, New Jersey, and Ohio. Public-sector workers in all of these states also face an annual compensation penalty—of 7.5%, 4.1%, and 6%, respectively. As in Wisconsin, a higher percentage of public-sector workers than private-sector workers in these states have a four-year college degree, as well as more job experience on average (see table).

The deficit that these states face is caused by the economic downturn and, in Wisconsin, a recent tax-cut package. It has nothing to do with the compensation of the people that educate our children, keep the streets safe and clean, keep dangerous chemicals out of our water, and keep insurance companies from taking advantage of us. These public servants are already paid less than those in the private sector, and nationally, this gap has actually been increasing over the past few decades, according to a report by University of Wisconsin-Milwaukee economists Keith Bender and John Heywood.

Instead of opportunistically using these hard times to target workers who—because of their public service—already take a substantial pay cut, state politicians should focus on creating jobs and boosting the incomes of all workers. ❏

A version of this article originally appeared as a "Snapshot" at the Economic Policy Institute website (epi.org).

Sources: Keith Bender and John Heywood, "Out of Balance: Comparing Public and Private Sector Compensation over 20 Years," National Institute on Retirement Security, Washington, D.C., April 2010, (sige.org); Jeffrey H. Keefe, "Are Wisconsin Public Employees Overcompensated?," Economic Policy Institute, Washington, D.C., February 10, 2011 (epi.org); Economic Policy Institute, Reports on public-sector worker undercompensation in Ohio, Indiana, and New Jersey, Washington, D.C., February 18, 2011 (epi.org).

Chapter 3

EMPLOYMENT AND UNEMPLOYMENT

Article 3.1

THE "NATURAL RATE" OF UNEMPLOYMENT
It's all about class conflict.

BY ROBERT POLLIN
September/October 1998

In 1997, the official U.S. unemployment rate fell to a 27-year low of 4.9%. Most orthodox economists had long predicted that a rate this low would lead to uncontrollable inflation. So they argued that maintaining a higher unemployment rate—perhaps as high as 6%—was crucial for keeping the economy stable. But there is a hitch: last year the inflation rate was 2.3%, the lowest figure in a decade and the second lowest in 32 years. What then are we to make of these economists' theories, much less their policy proposals?

Nobel prize-winning economist Milton Friedman gets credit for originating the argument that low rates of unemployment would lead to accelerating inflation. His 1968 theory of the so-called "natural rate of unemployment" was subsequently developed by many mainstream economists under the term "Non-Accelerating Inflation Rate of Unemployment," or NAIRU, a remarkably clumsy term for expressing the simple concept of a threshold unemployment rate below which inflation begins to rise.

According to both Friedman and expositors of NAIRU, inflation should accelerate at low rates of unemployment because low unemployment gives workers excessive bargaining power. This allows the workers to demand higher wages. Capitalists then try to pass along these increased wage costs by raising prices on the products they sell. An inflationary spiral thus ensues as long as unemployment remains below its "natural rate."

Based on this theory, Friedman and others have long argued that governments should never actively intervene in the economy to promote full employment or better jobs for workers, since it will be a futile exercise, whose end result will only be higher inflation and no improvement in job opportunities. Over the past generation, this conclusion has had far-reaching influence throughout the world. In the United

States and Western Europe, it has provided a stamp of scientific respectability to a whole range of policies through which governments abandoned even modest commitments to full employment and workers' rights.

This emerged most sharply through the Reaganite and Thatcherite programs in the United States and United Kingdom in the 1980s. But even into the 1990s, as the Democrats took power in the United States, the Labour Party won office in Britain, and Social Democrats won elections throughout Europe, governments remained committed to stringent fiscal and monetary policies, whose primary goal is to prevent inflation. In Western Europe this produced an average unemployment rate of over 10% from 1990-97. In the United States, unemployment rates have fallen sharply in the 1990s, but as an alternative symptom of stringent fiscal and monetary policies, real wages for U.S. workers also declined dramatically over the past generation. As of 1997, the average real wage for nonsupervisory workers in the United States was 14% below its peak in 1973, even though average worker productivity rose between 1973 and 1997 by 34%.

Why have governments in the United States and Europe remained committed to the idea of fiscal and monetary stringency, if the natural rate theory on which such policies are based is so obviously flawed? The explanation is that the natural rate theory is really not just about predicting a precise unemployment rate figure below which inflation must inexorably accelerate, even though many mainstream economists have presented the natural rate theory in this way. At a deeper level, the natural rate theory is bound up with the inherent conflicts between workers and capitalists over jobs, wages, and working conditions. As such, the natural rate theory actually contains a legitimate foundation in truth amid a welter of sloppy and even silly predictions.

The "Natural Rate" Theory Is about Class Conflict

In his 1967 American Economic Association presidential address in which he introduced the natural rate theory, Milton Friedman made clear that there was really nothing "natural" about the theory. Friedman rather emphasized that: "by using the term 'natural' rate of unemployment, I do not mean to suggest that it is immutable and unchangeable. On the contrary, many of the market characteristics that determine its level are man-made and policy-made. In the United States, for example, legal minimum wage rates ... and the strength of labor unions all make the natural rate of unemployment higher than it would otherwise be."

In other words, according to Friedman, what he terms the "natural rate" is really a social phenomenon measuring the class strength of working people, as indicated by their ability to organize effective unions and establish a livable minimum wage.

Friedman's perspective is supported in a widely-read 1997 paper by Robert Gordon of Northwestern University on what he terms the "time-varying NAIRU." What makes the NAIRU vary over time? Gordon explains that, since the early 1960s, "The two especially large changes in the NAIRU... are the increase between the early and late 1960s and the decrease in the 1990s. The late 1960s were a time of labor militancy, relatively strong unions, a relatively high minimum wage and a marked increase in labor's share in national income. The 1990s have been a time of labor peace, relatively weak unions, a relatively low minimum wage and a slight decline in labor's income share."

In short, class conflict is the spectre haunting the analysis of the natural rate and NAIRU: this is the consistent message stretching from Milton Friedman in the 1960s to Robert Gordon in the 1990s.

Stated in this way, the "Natural Rate" idea does, ironically, bear a close family resemblance to the ideas of two of the greatest economic thinkers of the left, Karl Marx and Michal Kalecki, on a parallel concept—the so-called "Reserve Army of Unemployed." In his justly famous Chapter 25 of Volume I of *Capital*, "The General Law of Capitalist Accumulation," Marx argued forcefully that unemployment serves an important function in capitalist economies. That is, when a capitalist economy is growing rapidly enough so that the reserve army of unemployed is depleted, workers will then utilize their increased bargaining power to raise wages. Profits are correspondingly squeezed as workers get a larger share of the country's total income. As a result, capitalists anticipate further declines in profitability and they therefore reduce their investment spending. This then leads to a fall in job creation, higher unemployment, and a replenishment of the reserve army. In other words, the reserve army of the unemployed is the instrument capitalists use to prevent significant wage increases and thereby maintain profitability.

Kalecki, a Polish economist of the Great Depression era, makes parallel though distinct arguments in his also justly famous essay, "The Political Aspects of Full Employment." Kalecki wrote in 1943, shortly after the 1930s Depression had ended and governments had begun planning a postwar world in which they would deploy aggressive policies to avoid another calamity of mass unemployment. Kalecki held, contrary to Marx, that full employment can be beneficial to the profitability of businesses. True, capitalists may get a smaller share of the total economic pie as workers gain bargaining power to win higher wages. But capitalists can still benefit because the size of the pie is growing far more rapidly, since more goods and services can be produced when everyone is working, as opposed to some significant share of workers being left idle.

But capitalists still won't support full employment, in Kalecki's view, because it will threaten their control over the workplace, the pace and direction of economic activity, and even political institutions. Kalecki thus concluded that full employment could be sustainable under capitalism, but only if these challenges to capitalists' social and political power could be contained. This is why he held that fascist social and political institutions, such as those that existed in Nazi Germany when he was writing, could well provide one "solution" to capitalism's unemployment problem, precisely because they were so brutal. Workers would have jobs, but they would never be permitted to exercise the political and economic power that would otherwise accrue to them in a full-employment economy.

Broadly speaking, Marx and Kalecki do then share a common conclusion with natural rate proponents, in that they would all agree that positive unemployment rates are the outgrowth of class conflict over the distribution of income and political power. Of course, Friedman and other mainstream economists reach this conclusion via analytic and political perspectives that are diametrically opposite to those of

Marx and Kalecki. To put it in a nutshell, in the Friedmanite view mass unemployment results when workers demand more than they deserve, while for Marx and Kalecki, capitalists use the weapon of unemployment to prevent workers from getting their just due.

From Natural Rate to Egalitarian Policy

Once the analysis of unemployment in capitalist economies is properly understood within the framework of class conflict, several important issues in our contemporary economic situation become much more clear. Let me raise just a few:

1. Mainstream economists have long studied how workers' wage demands cause inflation as unemployment falls. However, such wage demands never directly cause inflation, since inflation refers to a general rise in prices of goods and services sold in the market, not a rise in wages. Workers, by definition, do not have the power to raise prices. Capitalists raise prices on the products they sell. At low unemployment, inflation occurs when capitalists respond to workers' increasingly successful wage demands by raising prices so that they can maintain profitability. If workers were simply to receive a higher share of national income, then lower unemployment and higher wages need not cause inflation at all.

2. There is little mystery as to why, at present, the so-called "time-varying" NAIRU has diminished to a near vanishing point, with unemployment at a 25-year low while inflation remains dormant. The main explanation is the one stated by Robert Gordon—that workers' economic power has been eroding dramatically through the 1990s. Workers have been almost completely unable to win wage increases over the course of the economic expansion that by now is seven years old.

3. This experience over the past seven years, with unemployment falling but workers showing almost no income gains, demonstrates dramatically the crucial point that full employment can never stand alone as an adequate measure of workers' well-being. This was conveyed vividly to me when I was working in Bolivia in 1990 as part of an economic advising team led by Keith Griffin of the University of California-Riverside. Professor Griffin asked me to examine employment policies.

I began by paying a visit to the economists at the Ministry of Planning. When I requested that we discuss the country's employment problems, they explained, to my surprise, that the country *had no employment problems*. When I suggested we consider the situation of the people begging, shining shoes, or hawking batteries and Chiclets in the street just below the window where we stood, their response was that these people *were* employed. And of course they were, in that they were actively trying to scratch out a living. It was clear that I had to specify the problem at hand far more precisely. Similarly, in the United States today, we have to be much more specific as to what workers should be getting in a fair economy: jobs, of course, but also living wages, benefits, reasonable job security, and a healthy work environment.

4. In our current low-unemployment economy, should workers, at long last, succeed in winning higher wages and better benefits, some inflationary pressures

are likely to emerge. But if inflation does not accelerate after wage increases are won, this would mean that businesses are not able to pass along their higher wage costs to their customers. Profits would therefore be squeezed. In any case, in response to *either* inflationary pressures or a squeeze in profitability, we should expect that many, if not most, segments of the business community will welcome a Federal Reserve policy that would slow the economy and raise the unemployment rate.

Does this mean that, as long as we live in a capitalist society, the control by capitalists over the reserve army of labor must remain the dominant force establishing the limits of workers' strivings for jobs, security, and living wages? The challenge for the progressive movement in the United States today is to think through a set of policy ideas through which full employment at living wages can be achieved and sustained.

Especially given the dismal trajectory of real wage decline over the past generation, workers should of course continue to push for wage increases. But it will also be crucial to advance these demands within a broader framework of proposals. One important component of a broader package would be policies through which labor and capital bargain openly over growth of wages and profits after full employment is achieved. Without such an open bargaining environment, workers, with reason, will push for higher wages once full employment is achieved, but capitalists will then respond by either raising prices or favoring high unemployment. Such open bargaining policies were conducted with considerable success in Sweden and other Nordic countries from the 1950s to the 1980s, and as a result, wages there continued to rise at full employment, while both accelerating inflation and a return to high unemployment were prevented.

Such policies obviously represent a form of class compromise. This is intrinsically neither good nor bad. The question is the terms under which the compromise is achieved. Wages have fallen dramatically over the past generation, so workers deserve substantial raises as a matter of simple fairness. But workers should also be willing to link their wage increases to improvements in productivity growth, i.e., the rate at which workers produce new goods and services. After all, if the average wage had just risen at exactly the rate of productivity growth since 1973 and not a penny more, the average hourly wage today for nonsupervisory workers would be $19.07 rather than $12.24.

But linking wages to improvements in productivity then also raises the question of who controls the decisions that determine the rate of productivity growth. In fact, substantial productivity gains are attainable through operating a less hierarchical workplace and building strong democratic unions through which workers can defend their rights on the job. Less hierarchy and increased workplace democracy creates higher morale on the job, which in turn increases workers' effort and opportunities to be inventive, while decreasing turnover and absenteeism. The late David Gordon of the New School for Social Research was among the leading analysts demonstrating how economies could operate more productively through greater workplace democracy.

But improvements in productivity also result from both the public and private sector investing in new and better machines that workers put to use every day, with the additional benefit that it means more jobs for people who produce those machines. A pro-worker economic policy will therefore also have to be concerned with increasing investments to improve the stock of machines that workers have at their disposal on the job.

In proposing such a policy approach, have I forgotten the lesson that Marx and Kalecki taught us, that unemployment serves a purpose in capitalism? Given that this lesson has become part of the standard mode of thinking among mainstream economists ranging from Milton Friedman to Robert Gordon, I would hope that I haven't let it slip from view. My point nevertheless is that through changing power relationships at the workplace and the decision-making process through which investment decisions get made, labor and the left can then also achieve a more egalitarian economy, one in which capitalists' power to brandish the weapon of unemployment is greatly circumscribed. If the labor movement and the left neglect issues of control over investment and the workplace, we will continue to live amid a Bolivian solution to the unemployment problem, where full employment is the by-product of workers' vulnerability, not their strength. ❑

Sources: A longer version of this article appears as "The 'Reserve Army of Labor' and the 'Natural Rate of Unemployment': Can Marx, Kalecki, Friedman, and Wall Street All Be Wrong?," *Review of Radical Political Economics*, Fall 1998. Both articles derive from a paper originally presented as the David Gordon Memorial Lecture at the 1997 Summer Conference of the Union for Radical Political Economics. See also Robert Pollin and Stephanie Luce, *The Living Wage: Building a Fair Economy*, 1998; David Gordon, *Fat and Mean*, 1997; David Gordon, "Generating Affluence: Productivity Gains Require Worker Support," *Real World Macro*, 15th ed., 1998.

The Short Run: It's Finally Payday
March/April 2005

Albertsons, Ralphs Grocery, and Safeway's Vons Supermarkets will be cutting a large—and overdue—paycheck. The three grocery chains had used staffing agencies to hire more than 2,000 janitors, then failed to give these supposedly "temporary" workers employment benefits, paid some less than the minimum wage, and scheduled others to work 365 days a year, according to ABC News. Under a settlement reached in federal court in January, the janitors, who worked for the three chains between 1994 and 2001, will be sharing $22.4 million—$4,000 to $10,000 each. Meantime, the agency that hired out the janitors, Building One Service Solutions, has filed for bankruptcy protection.   — *Rolande Johndro*

Article 3.2

THE *REAL* UNEMPLOYMENT RATE HITS A 68-YEAR HIGH

BY JOHN MILLER
July/August 2009

Although you have to dig into the statistics to know it, unemployment in the United States is now worse than at any time since the end of the Great Depression.

From December 2007, when the recession began, to May of this year, 6.0 million U.S. workers lost their jobs. The big three U.S. automakers are closing plants and letting white-collar workers go too. Chrysler, the worst off of the three, will lay off one-quarter of its workforce. Heavy equipment manufacturer Caterpillar and giant banking conglomerate Citigroup have both laid off thousands of workers. Alcoa, the aluminum giant, has let workers go. Computer maker Dell and express shipper DHL have both canned many of their workers. Circuit City, the leading electronics retailer, went out of business, costing its 40,000 workers their jobs. Lawyers in large national firms are getting the ax. Even on Sesame Street, workers are losing their jobs.

The official unemployment rate hit 9.4% in May—already as high as the peak unemployment rates in all but the 1982 recession, the worst since World War II. And topping the 1982 recession's peak rate of 10.8% is now distinctly possible. The current downturn has pushed up unemployment rates by more than any previous postwar recession (see figure on p. 80).

Some groups of workers are already facing official unemployment rates in the double digits. As of May, unemployment rates for black, Hispanic, and teenage workers were already 14.9%, 12.7% and 22.7%, respectively. Workers without a high-school diploma confronted a 15.5% unemployment rate, while the unemployment rate for workers with just a high-school degree was 10.0%. Nearly one in five (19.2%) construction workers were unemployed. In Michigan, the hardest hit state, unemployment was at 12.9% in April. Unemployment rates in seven other states were at double-digit levels as well.

As bad as they are, these figures dramatically understate the true extent of unemployment. First, they exclude anyone without a job who is ready to work but has not actively looked for a job in the previous four weeks. The Bureau of Labor Statistics classifies such workers as

THE MAY 2009 UNEMPLOYMENT PICTURE (DATA IN THOUSANDS, NOT SEASONALLY ADJUSTED)	
Civilian Labor Force	154,336
Employed	140,363
Unemployed	13,973
Marginally Attached Workers	2,210
Discouraged workers	792
Reasons other than discouragement	1,418
Part-time for Economic Reasons	8,785
Slack work or business conditions	6,647
Could only find part-time work	1,898

Sources: Bureau of Labor Statistics, Tables A-1, A-5. A-12, A-13. Data are not seasonally adjusted because seasonally adjusted data for marginally attached workers are not available.

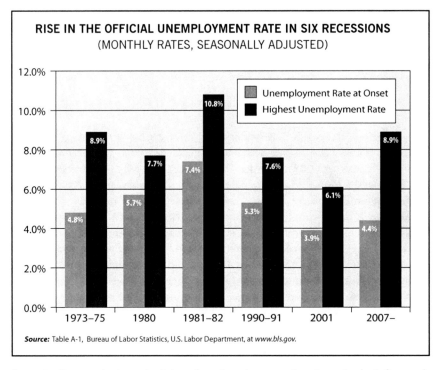

RISE IN THE OFFICIAL UNEMPLOYMENT RATE IN SIX RECESSIONS
(MONTHLY RATES, SEASONALLY ADJUSTED)

Source: Table A-1, Bureau of Labor Statistics, U.S. Labor Department, at *www.bls.gov*.

"marginally attached to the labor force" so long as they have looked for work within the last year. Marginally attached workers include so-called discouraged workers who have given up looking for job-related reasons, plus others who have given up for reasons such as school and family responsibilities, ill health, or transportation problems.

Second, the official unemployment rate leaves out part-time workers looking for full-time work: part-time workers are "employed" even if they work as little as one hour a week. The vast majority of people working part time involuntarily have had

Calculating the Real Unemployment Rate

The BLS calculates the official unemployment rate, U-3, as the number of unemployed as a percentage of the civilian labor force. The civilian labor force consists of employed workers plus the officially unemployed, those without jobs who are available to work and have looked for a job in the last 4 weeks. Applying the data found in the table yields an official unemployment rate of 9.1%, or a seasonally adjusted rate 9.4% for April 2009.

The comprehensive U-6 unemployment rate adjusts the official rate by adding marginally attached workers and workers forced to work part time for economic reasons to the officially unemployed. To find the U-6 rate the BLS takes that higher unemployment count and divides it by the official civilian labor force plus the number of marginally attached workers. (No adjustment is necessary for forced part-time workers since they are already counted in the official labor force as employed workers.)

Accounting for the large number of marginally attached workers and those working part-time for economic reasons raises the count of unemployed to 24.0 million workers for May 2009. Those numbers push up the U-6 unemployment rate to 15.9% or a seasonally adjusted rate of 16.4%.

their hours cut due to slack or unfavorable business conditions. The rest are working part time because they could only find part-time work.

To its credit, the BLS has developed alternative unemployment measures that go a long way toward correcting the shortcomings of the official rate. The broadest alternative measure, called "U-6," counts as unemployed "marginally attached workers" as well as those employed "part time for economic reasons."

When those adjustments are taken into account for May 2009, the unemployment rate soars to 16.4%. That is the highest rate since the BLS began calculating the U-6 rate in 1994. While not exactly comparable, it is also higher than the BLS's earlier and yet broader adjusted unemployment rate called the U-7. The BLS began calculating the U-7 rate in 1976 but discontinued it in 1994 in favor of the U-6 rate. In the 1982 recession, the U-7 reached 15.3%, its highest level. In fact, no bout of unemployment since the last year of the Great Depression in 1941 would have produced an adjusted unemployment rate as high as today's.

Why is the real unemployment rate so much higher than the official, or U-3, rate? First, forced part-time work has reached its highest level ever, going all the way back to 1956 and including the 1982 recession. In May 2009, 8.8 million workers were forced to work part time for economic reasons. Forced part-timers are concentrated in retail, food services, and construction; about a quarter of them are young workers between 16 and 24. The number of discouraged workers is high today as well. In May, the BLS counted 2.2 million "marginally attached" workers. That matches the highest number since 1994, when the agency introduced this measure.

With the economy in the throes of a catastrophic downturn, unemployment, no matter how it's measured, will rise dramatically and impose yet more devastating costs on society and on those without a job or unable to find full-time work. ❏

Sources: U.S. Dept. of Labor, "The Unemployment Rate and Beyond: Alternative Measures of Labor Underutilization," *Issues in Labor Statistics,* June 2008; John E. Bregger and Steven E. Haugen, "BLS Introduces New Range of Alternative Unemployment Measures," *Monthly Labor Review,* October 1995.

The Short Run: Canaries in the Coal Mine
September/October 2006

Left economic observers have long pointed out that Blacks in the United States are the first to feel the effects of an economic downturn. Recent unemployment data continue to make the point. "The unemployment rate, which usually moves in tenth-of-a-point increments, when it moves at all, jumped two-tenths in July, to 4.8 percent, the highest level in five months. *Nearly all of the increase was among African-Americans,*" the *New York Times* reported in August (emphasis added).

With all the talk about a possible recession, the unemployment statistics for Black people may turn out to be an early indicator of the impact of the Bush administration's economic policies on the rest of the U.S. population.

—Arthur Conquest

Article 3.3

HOW MIGHT BLACKS FARE IN A JOBLESS RECOVERY?

BY SYLVIA ALLEGRETTO AND STEVEN PITTS
November/December 2010

An economy officially in recovery that continues to shed jobs as if in recession, or experiences prolonged tepid job growth, is deemed a "jobless recovery." In a jobless recovery it takes an inordinate amount of time to recoup the jobs lost during the downturn. While the recession officially ended in June 2009, the employment picture remains quite dismal. At the lowest point for jobs, in December 2009, 8.4 million jobs were lost, which represented 6.1% of all jobs. To date job losses are still at 7.7 million, which represents 5.6% of all jobs. Since the onset of recovery, the monthly employment reports have been mixed, but the net employment level has fallen by an additional 439,000.

Figure 1 depicts the dynamics of recessionary job losses and jobless recoveries. Each line represents the trajectory of job growth from the onset of recession until jobs were finally recouped (when the line crosses the horizontal axis—which represents months since the onset of recession). The solid black line represents average job losses for recessions prior to 1990. (On average the pre-1990 recessions were about eleven months long and it took about 21 months to recoup pre-recessionary job level.)

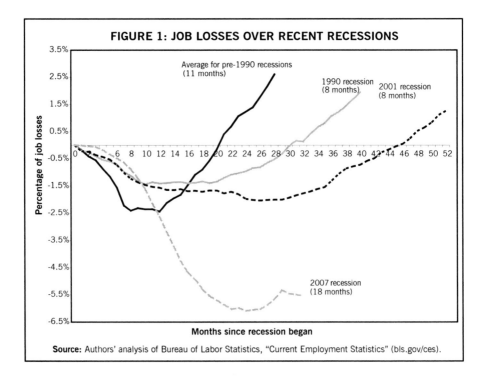

FIGURE 1: JOB LOSSES OVER RECENT RECESSIONS

Source: Authors' analysis of Bureau of Labor Statistics, "Current Employment Statistics" (bls.gov/ces).

Job losses due to the 1990 recession (the solid gray line) were just about 1.5%—quite shallow comparatively and the recession was officially just eight months long. But employment lingered at the trough for a long time and it took about 31 months to recoup those lost jobs. The downturn in 2001 (dotted black line) was also eight months long and about 2% of jobs were lost—again relatively mild—but it took 46 months to recoup those lost jobs.

It is clear from the chart that the recession that started in December 2007 (dotted gray line) led to a reduction in employment that far exceeded that of the previous recessions. This recession was 18 months long and ended in June 2009. Job losses were catastrophic. At its worst point jobs were down 8.4 million. Job growth turned positive in the spring of 2010—mostly due to the temporary hiring of Census workers. But shortly after Census workers were hired they were let go, and job growth once again turned negative. At this point it is clear that the labor market is in the realm of a jobless recovery—a prolonged period of negative or weak job growth. It will be a very long time before this economy recoups the enormous amount of jobs lost over this recession.

While it is difficult to predict exactly what might happen to black workers during this jobless recovery, it is instructive to examine what happened to black unemployment during the last jobless recovery, which followed the 2001 recession. Figure 2 provides key information.

The gray bars in the chart mark key dates of the last two recessions and recoveries.

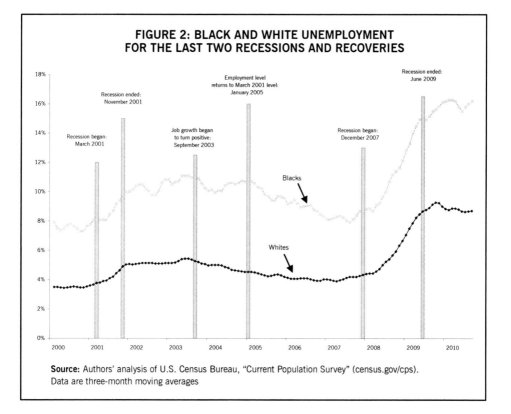

FIGURE 2: BLACK AND WHITE UNEMPLOYMENT FOR THE LAST TWO RECESSIONS AND RECOVERIES

Source: Authors' analysis of U.S. Census Bureau, "Current Population Survey" (census.gov/cps). Data are three-month moving averages

In examining the trend in black unemployment since the 2001 recession, there are six key dates:

- The beginning of the recession (March 2001)
- The official end of the recession (November 2001)
- When job creation turned positive (September 2003)
- When the employment levels returned to pre-recession level (January 2005)
- The beginning of recession (December 2007)
- The official end of the recession (June 2009)

As Figure 2 indicates, unemployment rates continued to rise after the official end of the recession in November 2001. Over the jobless recovery—from November 2001 to September 2003—unemployment increased from 9.8% to 11% for blacks and 4.9% to 5.4% for whites. Black unemployment rates did not begin to steadily fall until the total number of jobs had reached the pre-recession level (January 2005). The unemployment rates for whites started to fall just prior to September 2003—near the end of the jobless recovery.

Starting with the onset of the 2007 recession, again the black unemployment rate increased at a faster rate than did that of whites. Since the onset of recovery—in June 2009—the unemployment rate of blacks has increased by 1.4 percentage points, from 14.8% to 16.2%. The rate for whites at the start of recovery was 8.7%, and after an initial increase it is back to that same rate today.

If the 2001 pattern holds, it may well be that the current black unemployment rates will not begin to significantly abate until the employment level returns to its pre-recessionary level of December 2007. This will almost certainly take several years as the shortfall in jobs is currently at 7.7 million. In order to return the national unemployment rate to its December 2007 rate, the economy would need to create 290,000 jobs per month for five years; so far this year job creation has averaged 68,000 per month, even as the last four months have averaged -98,000 per month.

In other words, for many black workers and their families, the recovery will continue to feel like a deep recession for many years to come. ❑

Sources: Bureau of Labor Statistics, "Current Employment Statistics" (bls.gov/ces); National Bureau of Economic Research, "The NBER's Business Cycle Dating Committee" (nber.org/cycles/recessions.html and nber.org/cycles/sept2010.html).

Article 3.4

UNEMPLOYMENT INSURANCE: A BROKEN SYSTEM

BY MARIANNE HILL
September/October 2009

Millions of workers have lost their jobs in the current recession. Employment is down 12% in manufacturing, 7% in professional and business services, and more than 5% overall in the private sector compared to last year. Over 5.6 million people have lost their jobs since last June. The ranks of the unemployed are continuing to grow; the unemployment rate in June hit 9.5%. Good thing that unemployment insurance provides income to help tide these workers over this rough patch, right? Not so fast.

The share of unemployed workers receiving benefits has gradually shrunk since the 1970s. In 1975, over half of unemployed workers received regular benefits. But in 2008, only 37% of the unemployed did; in some states the figure was less than 25%. And so-called "discouraged workers," those who want but are not actively seeking employment, are not considered part of the labor force and so are not even included in these figures.

Unemployment insurance, in short, is not a benefit that everyone who loses a job can count on. Several groups are working to change this. The American Recovery and Reinvestment Act (ARRA), better know as the Obama stimulus package, provides temporary funding for states that expand their unemployment coverage, and so far this year 25 states have done so. Others, however, are resisting even a temporary expansion of coverage that would be fully federally funded.

Why Unemployment Compensation?

When unemployment insurance was established as a nationwide program in 1935, it was hailed as a means of enabling workers to protect their standard of living between jobs. With it, workers are better able to keep their homes and their health. It helps to stabilize family well-being and maintain the labor force in a region. By enabling workers to engage in longer job searches, unemployment compensation also improves workers' job choices. It even enhances employers' flexibility in hiring by making lay-offs less painful.

Unemployment insurance is also an important countercyclical tool: it bolsters consumer spending during economic downturns and then automatically drops off as the economy recovers and unemployment falls. Because it reduces the need for other forms of government intervention to raise demand in a downturn, the program has supporters across the ideological spectrum.

Coverage and benefits vary by state. The average weekly benefit in 2008 was $300—about 35% of the average weekly wage. Benefits are paid from state funds that are financed by a payroll tax on employers. This tax is levied on anywhere from the first $7,000 to the first $35,300 of each worker's annual earnings depending on the state; the national average is $11,482. The tax rate ranges from 0.83% to 5% of the taxable portion of wages, with a national average of 2.42%. (Who bears the cost of this tax is debated: economists have shown that whether or not a company is able to pass the cost of payroll taxes forward to customers or back to employees depends on conditions in its particular product and labor markets.)

Shifts in employment patterns and a tightening of eligibility requirements are behind the nationwide reduction in effective unemployment insurance coverage. Today almost 30% of the U.S. work force is employed in nonstandard work arrangements, including part-time, temporary, contract or on-call work, and self-employment. Most of these jobs are subject to the payroll tax that funds unemployment benefits—yet these workers often find they are ineligible. For instance, persons who are seeking only part-time employment do not qualify for unemployment benefits in many states. This affects women in particular, including heads of households, who often work part time due to dependent care responsibilities. People who work full time but only for part of the year may also find it difficult to qualify for unemployment benefits.

Many workers who are not eligible for benefits provide income that is critical to their families. In 2007, 41% of workers worked only part-time or part-year. Among heads of households, this figure, though lower, is still sizeable: in 2007, it was 32% overall and 42% for female family heads. Besides child care, elder care can also mean part-time or part-year work for many. Nearly one-third of working adults with older parents report missing some work to care for them.

Who Are the Unemployed?

Certain industries, regions, and workers are being hit harder than others this recession. In June, 15 states and the District of Columbia had unemployment rates of over 10%, but only one, North Dakota, had an unemployment rate below 5%. Michigan, Oregon, South Carolina and Rhode Island all had seasonally adjusted jobless rates of 12% or more.

Unemployment hits some population groups much harder than others—young people, people of color, and anyone with relatively few years of education. Among workers over 20 years of age, black men had the highest jobless rate in June at 16.4%. The rate for Hispanic women was 11.5%, for black women 11.3%, and for Hispanic men 10.7%. In contrast, the jobless rate was under 10% for both white men (9.2%) and white women (6.8%).

A combination of factors including occupational segregation, lower educational levels, and discrimination result in lower incomes for women and for black and Latino men, exacerbating the impact of higher unemployment. Data from 2005-2007 show that black women working year-round, full-time earned $15,900 a year less than white men; for Hispanic women the wage gap was $21,400. Lower-income families have fewer assets to see them through rough economic times, and their extended families are also hard-pressed as demands upon them increase. Nonprofits, another part of the social safety net, suffer from increased demand for services and decreased donations during recession. As a result, families of blacks, women and Hispanics suffer severe setbacks during a period of recession, and unemployment insurance can be especially critical to them.

Families in which one or more wage earners lose their jobs bear costs greater than just the lost wages. Savings are exhausted; rates of illness, both mental and physical, increase; debt levels often rise (inadequate medical insurance coverage is a major factor—in 2008, 60% of the unemployed lacked health insurance); and the pursuit of a college education or other training may be postponed. Studies have documented a rise in suicide rates, mental and physical illnesses, and domestic and other violence among the unemployed. These problems become widespread during recessions and become a burden on society, not just on individual families.

Promising Initiatives

Under the Obama stimulus package, states that elect to expand their programs in certain ways receive federal funds to finance these changes for at least two to three years. States can make unemployment benefits more available in a number of ways:

- Changing the base period used to determine whether a worker qualifies for benefits and if so, the amount he or she will receive.

- Making unemployment insurance available to certain individuals who are seeking only part-time work and/or to those who lost or left their jobs due to certain compelling family reasons (for example, domestic violence or a spouse relocating).

- Providing an additional 26 weeks of compensation to workers who have exhausted regular unemployment benefits and are enrolled in and making satisfactory progress in certain training programs.

- Paying an additional dependents' allowance of at least $15 per dependent per week to eligible beneficiaries.

Another potential reform relates to the extension of benefits beyond the regular 13- to 26-week period. States are required to offer extended benefits during periods of especially high unemployment (with half the cost covered by the federal government) only if certain trigger requirements are met—and that does not happen often. The ARRA offers states the option of adopting a new, less stringent trigger requirement. As of mid-July, 29 of the 30 states adopting the new trigger requirements have had extended benefits go into effect, compared with only six of the 20 states that have kept earlier triggers. Last year Congress authorized a separate program, Emergency Unemployment Compensation, to provide federally funded benefits after regular benefits are exhausted. The National Employment Law Project estimated that about 1.2 million workers would exhaust their benefits under *this* program before July 2009 and so become eligible for extended benefits.

A permanent expansion of coverage to a larger share of the unemployed, with or without an increase in benefit levels, would cost more than the average $23 per month in unemployment insurance taxes currently paid per worker. This could be achieved by expanding the portion of wages on which the tax is levied. To reduce

Article 3.5

MINING THE GOLDEN YEARS
The Return of Seniors to the Workforce

BY ROBERT LARSON
September/October 2009

With their retirement accounts seriously diminished, the surge of seniors back to work has recently become a focus of media attention. But the departure of older workers from the labor force first reversed itself in 1994. After falling for almost 50 years, seniors' labor force participation has been on the rise for over a decade, and as of the last business cycle peak 37% of seniors were employed, according to the Bureau of Labor Statistics. This striking development reflects changes in both public policy and corporate behavior, and has a variety of implications for labor strategizing.

Retirement timing is strongly influenced by changes in Social Security benefit requirements. The Republican "Contract with America" in 1994 mandated the removal of the Social Security earnings test, allowing workers 65 to 70 to work on the side without jeopardizing their benefits. Additionally, the retirement age for full Social Security benefits has been raised from 65 to 66 or 67 for workers born after 1937; this prolongs the time seniors stay on the clock.

Fundamental changes to corporate retirement plans also play an important role. Defined-benefit pensions put more burden and investment risk on the employer, whereas a defined-contribution plan, such as a 401(k), shifts the responsibility for building retirement assets onto the employee, who also bears the risk of outliving his or her savings. Twenty years ago, defined-benefit pensions and defined-contribution pensions each covered about one third of U.S. private-sector workers. Now defined-contribution plans cover twice as many workers as defined-benefit plans—42% to 21%.

The practical impact of this postponed retirement on younger workers is a subject of debate. The most prominent study of the subject, conducted in July 2008 by Jonathan Gruber and Kevin Milligan of the National Bureau of Economic Research, concluded that there was no strong evidence of older workers crowding out the young that was consistent across data sets, although they considered their conclusion to be "relatively weak." However, this was somewhat before the full gravity of the current recession was felt. Anecdotal evidence of intergenerational crowding has since grown rich, with the *Wall Street Journal* describing old and young workers competing in a "desperate scramble for work."

The rising labor market participation of workers over 55 has political implications as well. For one thing, it is red meat to advocates of raising the eligibility age for Social Security further and ultimately privatizing or abolishing it. Republican columnist William Saletan wrote in the *Washington Post* in 2006 that since people now live longer, Social Security should not pay out by age but by inability to work. This would mean working until you're physically incapable of an active retirement, a tough sell.

At the same time, the growth of older workers as a proportion of the workforce could represent a surprising opportunity for labor organizing. This is because unions are known to have a record of providing fringe benefits of special importance for older workers, including health insurance—a principle lure keeping seniors in the workforce—and pensions. For instance, unionized employees are 22.5% more likely to have a pension, and a far better one than their non-union counterparts, according to analyses by the Economic Policy Institute. Organizers working with mature adult workers could get a lot of mileage out of such advantages.

While people's visions of retirement vary from leisurely to productive, what's universal is the wish to be able to retire on your own terms. Punching in every day just to stretch health insurance coverage could force America's silver foxes and golden girls to make a winter of their autumn years. ❏

Sources: "Trends in Labor Force Participation in the United States," *Monthly Labor Review*, October 2006; Jonathan Gruber and Kevin Milligan, "Do Elderly Workers Substitute for Younger Workers in the U.S.?" National Bureau of Economic Research, July 2008; "Elderly Emerge as a New Class of Workers—and the Jobless," *Wall Street Journal*, Feb. 23, 2009; "Curse of the Young Old," *Washington Post*, March 19, 2006; *State of Working America 2008/2009*, Economic Policy Institute, 2009.

Article 3.6

WE NEED A (GREEN) JOBS PROGRAM

Clean-energy investment would promote job growth for a wide swath of the U.S. workforce.

BY JEANNETTE WICKS-LIM
September/October 2010

Fourteen months of an unemployment rate at or near 10% clearly calls for the federal government to take a lead role in job creation. The White House should push its clean-energy agenda as a jobs program but steer clear of all the hype about "green-collar" jobs. Green-collar jobs are widely perceived as job opportunities accessible only to an elite segment of the U.S. workforce—those with advanced degrees, such as environmental engineers, lab technicians, and research scientists. Such jobs are inaccessible to the 52% of unemployed workers with no college experience. The truth is, however, that clean-energy investments could serve as a powerful engine for job growth for a wide swath of the U.S. workforce.

My colleagues at the Political Economy Research Institute and I examined a clean-energy program that includes making buildings more energy efficient, expanding and improving mass transit, updating the national electric grid, and developing each of three types of renewable energy sources: wind, solar, and biomass fuels. Here's what we found.

First, clean-energy activities produce more jobs, dollar for dollar, than fossil fuel-related activities. This is because clean-energy activities tend to be more labor intensive (i.e., more investment dollars go to hiring workers than buying machines), have a higher domestic content (i.e., more dollars are spent on goods and services produced within the United States) and have lower average wages than fossil fuel-related activities. The figures in the table below show how a $1 million investment in clean-energy activities would create more than three times the number of jobs that would be created by investing the same amount in fossil fuels.

Second, many clean energy sector jobs would be accessible to workers with no college experience. The table also shows how the jobs created by a $1 million investment in clean energy would be spread across three levels of education: high school degree or less, some college, and B.A. or more. Nearly half of the clean energy jobs would be held by workers with a high school degree or less. These include jobs for construction laborers, carpenters, and bus drivers. Fewer than

---

JOB CREATION: CLEAN ENERGY VS. FOSSIL FUELS

Number of jobs created by investing $1 million in clean energy versus fossil-fuels activities, by education credentials

Education Credentials	Clean Energy	Fossil Fuels
Total	16.7 jobs (100%)	5.3 jobs (100%)
High school diploma or less	8.0 jobs (47.9%)	2.2 jobs (41.5%)
Some college, no B.A.	4.8 jobs (28.7%)	1.6 jobs (30.2%)
B.A. or more	3.9 jobs (23.3%)	1.5 jobs (28.3%)

one-quarter of clean-energy jobs would require a B.A. or more. The figures for the fossil fuels sector (second column) show that they are more heavily weighted toward jobs requiring college degrees.

Does this mean green investments will just create lots of low-paying jobs? No. The figures in the table below show that investing $1 million in green activities rather than fossil fuel-related activities would generate many more jobs for workers at *all three levels* of formal education credentials. Compared to the fossil fuels sector, the clean energy sector would produce nearly four times the number of jobs that require a high school degree or less, three times the number of jobs that require some college experience, and 2.5 times the number of jobs that require a B.A. or more. Green investments would produce more jobs at all education and wage levels, even while generating proportionately *more* jobs that are accessible to workers with a high school degree or less.

Workers are right to worry about whether these high school degree jobs would offer family-supporting wages. Construction laborers, for example, average at $29,000 annually—awfully close to the $22,000 official poverty line. In addition, women and workers of color have historically faced discrimination in the construction industry, which would be the source of a lot of the lower-credentialed jobs in the clean energy sector. Workers will need to do some serious organizing to put in place labor protections such as living-wage laws, strong collective bargaining rights, and affirmative action policies to insure that these jobs pay decent wages and are equally accessible to all qualified workers. ❏

Sources: Robert Pollin, Jeannette Wicks-Lim, and Heidi Garrett-Peltier, *Green Prosperity: How Clean-Energy Policies Can Fight Poverty and Raise Living Standards in the United States,* Political Economy Research Institute, 2009, www.peri.umass.edu/green_prosperity.

Article 3.7

WELFARE REFORM AND THE CAMPAIGN TO REGULATE AMERICAN WORKERS

BY FRANCES FOX PIVEN
Winter 2003—WorkingUSA

The Personal Responsibility and Work Opportunity Reconciliation Act of 1996 (PRWORA)—also known as "welfare reform"—was at least three decades in the making. The new welfare policy was enacted after a many-years-long campaign against existing welfare, or Aid to Families with Dependent Children (AFDC), by right-wing think tanks, politicians, and business organizations. The endlessly repeated arguments of the campaign asserted that Americans had been too generous, too kind. Generous AFDC benefits allowed women to opt out of wage labor, and encouraged them in loose sexual behavior and out-of-wedlock births. The result was that AFDC in fact increased poverty, or at least it increased the underlying poverty that would exist in the absence of the program. The solution, as Charles Murray famously recommended, was to eliminate welfare, and thus force people who had become "dependent," addicted to the handout, to confront the discipline of the labor market. At first, the Murray solution appeared too drastic, too radical for incremental American politics. But as the campaign persisted, something close to Murray's recommendation has in fact been implemented.

The main thrust of the new regime, sometimes known as "work first," has been to make wage work the only option for poor mothers, no matter how little they earn, no matter the lack of reliable child care, no matter the crisis-ridden character of their lives. The operating administrative principle of "work first" is that cash assistance should be hard to get, and hard to keep. Thus, federal law imposes a five-year lifetime limit on the receipt of assistance, and many states have imposed even more stringent limits. Federal law also requires the states to show that at least 50% of those on the rolls are working, and President Bush now proposes to raise that requirement to 70%. Even more importantly, although less obviously, the federal law gives the states—and the counties and private contractors to which the states devolve responsibility—wide latitude to sanction recipients with the loss of benefits if they transgress any of the myriad new rules of the system. And the states now also have the authority to rebuff, stall, or deny new applicants in a practice called "diversion."

Moreover, since federal grants to the states are not reduced when caseloads and expenditures fall, the states have a strong incentive to sanction, divert, and deny. The best-known consequence of the new regime, much heralded by politicians and the press, is that the rolls have fallen by more than half. We also know that, of those who have left the rolls, perhaps 50–60% are working fairly steadily, at wages of about $7 an hour. Even with full-time work, which many welfare-leavers do not have, this wage yields an income some $6 per hour short of what the Economic Policy Institute estimates is necessary for a bare-bones budget. Moreover, many leavers are not working, or are working only sporadically, and far less is known about their circumstances than about the welfare-leaver "successes" who are working. Even the successes now confront new trouble. As unemployment rose with the current recession, many employed ex-recipients found themselves jobless again. Because their work records were short and their earnings low, these workers were unlikely to be eligible for unemployment benefits. And welfare, at one time the real unemployment insurance program for low-wage women workers, was effectively walled off from many of them as well.

To understand why this harsh regime has become the policy of the nation, we need to look beyond welfare itself, and beyond welfare policy discussions, to a range of related changes that have occurred in domestic policy over the past three decades. Taken one-by-one, each policy change may seem credibly explained by particular policy discourses. But taken together, the changes suggest something larger at work, a multifaceted campaign oriented to intensifying labor market discipline, especially in the lower reaches of the workforce. To be sure, the political talk that justifies these policies is about other things, about restoring civil order, for example, or shoring up two-parent families, or giving workers a stake in the American dream. But so was the talk that justified the very similar campaign of the late nineteenth century about other things. Outdoor relief was eliminated or rolled back, people called "tramps" or "hobos" were rounded up, presumably to restore order, civility, and morality to American life. In both periods, the talk itself was politics, a politics to make a campaign to discipline working people palatable, even to working people themselves.

I now turn to the elements of the larger campaign that makes welfare reform comprehensible. It includes a three-decades-long assault on unions—in the workplace and in politics. Unions have many flaws, of course, but overall they raise wages and help workers secure some rights in the workplace. Since the early 1970s, big business has been determined to weaken unions for just those reasons.

This stance first became evident in the 1970s with the growing intransigence of management in contract negotiations where, for example, they began to insist on two-tier contracts with sharply lower wages and benefits for new employees, an arrangement that was insidious for its effects on union solidarity. The highlight of this stage of the anti-union war was the standoff between President Reagan and the air traffic controllers union, which resulted in mass layoffs of the striking workers. Since then, although less visibly, businesses have continued to lobby successfully for the rule changes and pro-business board appointments that have made the National Labor Relations Board, which oversees collective bargaining rights, virtually toothless. The result is that union density has plummeted, to pre-1930s levels.

Or consider contemporary new-style, top-down educational reform proposals. As usual, the rhetoric is about educational excellence. But the emphasis on standards and testing, on rote teaching methods, on phonics and classroom discipline suggests something more like the dumbing-down of public education. So does the cast of characters who are the main educational reformers, including the Business Roundtable and the testing companies. The push for privatization, another aspect of contemporary educational reform, has the added payoff of making public education a new field for profiteering, just as the privatization of the administration of welfare has made it a field for profiteering.

And then there is the growing trend of privatizing pensions. As with the privatization of schools, prisons, and welfare, the persistence with which backers of privatization of social security have pressed their cause reflects in part the profits that Wall Street will earn from these investments. But there is more to privatization than that. The rise of 401(k)s is illustrative. Employment-based social benefits, mainly in the form of pensions and health-care plans that depend on employers, have always been suspect for the simple reason that they are another way to tie workers who always face the risk of illness and the prospect of old age to the firm that employs them, no matter the other conditions of employment.

Labor historian Nelson Lichtenstein once said these programs should be understood as a form of serfdom. The increased reliance on 401(k)s underscores Lichtenstein's point. As a National Association of Manufacturers spokesman said in the aftermath of the Enron pension debacle: "When workers' savings are in company stock, they are more loyal, more committed to their work, more likely to raise product quality." Enron workers lost 1.3 billion of the 2 billion pension dollars they had invested in the company, and other workers' pensions also took big hits as a result of mutual fund investments in Enron's stock.

As private income-support programs have expanded, the public income-support programs initiated in the 1930s and enlarged in the 1960s have been rolled back. Cuts in cash assistance under welfare are an aspect of this, but these cuts are dwarfed by the changes that have occurred in social security, unemployment insurance, food stamps, and Medicaid. The great achievement of these programs taken together was that they made working people more secure in the face of the exigencies of old age, unemployment, illness, or disability. Unemployed people who knew they could get unemployment benefits were less terrified, less likely to take any job offered on any terms.

In the recession of the mid-1970s, more than two-thirds of the unemployed received these benefits. In the 1990s, only about one-third of the unemployed received unemployment insurance, largely because of arcane changes in the formulas determining eligibility. Or consider Old Age Survivors and Dependents Insurance, the program we call social security. When the program was inaugurated in 1935, the talk was about removing old people from a crowded labor market where they did not fare well, and where they undermined the bargaining power of younger workers.

Now, with little fanfare, the age of social security eligibility has been raised to age sixty-seven, albeit gently by one month a year so as not to provoke an outcry, and earnings by the old are treated more generously so as to encourage them to take the jobs that fast food restaurants, for example, offer. And not only has eligibility for food stamps been tightened, but because the administration of both the food stamp and Medicaid programs was always tied to welfare, welfare cutbacks have resulted in a marked decline in the percentage of eligible people who actually receive these other benefits.

And then there are the cutbacks in income support associated with welfare reform. Quite apart from the impact on family and community well-being, between 2.5 and 3 million women have been pushed into the labor market, some to get jobs, others to hunt for them. These numbers are significant. Millions of desperate women who otherwise would have been raising their children with welfare grants are scrambling for work. This is roughly equivalent to a two- to three-percentage-point increase in the unemployment rate in its impact on worker bargaining power, and, of course, it affects the bargaining power of lower-wage workers most directly. There are also cultural dimensions to welfare reform as a strategy for intensifying worker discipline, but before I turn to that, I want to say a little about the wider cultural campaign to celebrate markets and reinforce labor market discipline.

It hardly needs to be demonstrated that American politics has been overtaken by the celebration of markets associated with neoliberalism. One might view it as a renaissance of nineteenth-century laissez faire and its depiction of markets as operating according to something akin to natural law. This time, however, the deifying of markets gains credibility from the globalization of market exchange, which seems to make merely national governments helpless to intervene, except by putting domestic investment and trade at risk. This is not the occasion to scrutinize this view carefully, and I will have to be content with asserting that it is wildly exaggerated, especially when it is applied to the United States, since our domestic economy is huge, and our government has great economic and political power in setting the rules of the international economy. My point now is simply that this argument, pushed to extremes by ideological fanatics, undermines the democratic capacity of working people to press government for protective measures.

Moreover, neoliberalism or neo-laissez-faire has been shored up by a campaign to depict Wall Street as a game in which everyone can play, and everyone can win. This is part of the meaning of the expansion of 401(k)s. Hoodwinked workers whose pensions are invested in the stock market tie their hopes for a better life to the Dow Jones average. This investment and this illusion allays worker resentments about lagging wages and shrinking public benefits. It turns them away from the old struggles for better wages, better workplace conditions, and better public programs, as they watch the roulette wheel whirl in the vain hope that it will stop at their number.

Welfare reform is part of this cultural transformation. Consider the impact of the campaign against welfare on public opinion, as women on welfare were decried on all sides as dependent, meaning they were addicted to the dole, guilty of sexual excess and license, the contemporary progenitors of nineteenth-century-style moral iniquity. The new welfare regimen itself underlines this form of cultural teaching by stripping recipients of rights, and forcing them to perform very public and very demeaning tasks. If farmers who received federal crop subsidies were subject to the same invasive investigations as welfare recipients, the public understanding of the status of farmers and the meaning of the subsidies would also gradually shift.

In 1986, Mickey Kaus, a conservative critic of the old AFDC program, made explicit the purpose of a degrading welfare system when he said that the reason to put Betsy Smith to work sweeping streets and cleaning buildings was not only to deter Betsy Smith from having an illegitimate child but also so that the "sight of Betsy Smith sweeping streets after having her illegitimate child will discourage her younger sisters and neighbors from doing as she did." And, much as Kaus predicted, these new welfare rituals are having an impact on poor women. More importantly, they have an impact on all low-wage workers as welfare becomes more demeaning, and work, even low-wage and disrespected work, by contrast gains value.

So, who is doing this? And why? The campaign to intensify worker discipline dates from the early 1970s when corporate America was grappling with narrowing profit margins. The squeeze on profits resulted partly from intensifying competition from Japan and West Germany—only recall how the auto industry was thrown into disarray by the arrival of small and efficient cars on American markets—and partly from rising raw materials prices, especially rising oil prices.

The squeeze also resulted, however, from rising wages, and growing expenditures on income-support programs that undergirded wages. And business costs had also grown because of the expansion of workplace and environmental regulation. All these latter costs reflected the gains made by the protest movements of the 1960s, and the turbulence and electoral upsets they set in motion. No wonder the Great Society has become an epithet in the mouths of conservative critics.

The corporate response to these developments was to try to recover their competitive edge, to enlarge profits by lowering wages and social benefits, by pushing back regulation, and by slashing business taxes. To accomplish this, American business leaders who had grown fat and lazy during the 25 years after World War II, when America's economic preeminence was unchallenged, mobilized to do politics. They formed new peak business organizations, and revived old business organizations like the National Association of Manufacturers and the Chamber of Commerce, organizations that had virtually become dormant during the heady postwar years of business success. CEOs retooled themselves and became lobbyists, vice presidents for "public affairs" were created, and business became a major Washington presence, as a flourishing K Street demonstrates.

Lastly, business money flowed to politicians and their campaigns, to buy access and influence. In the area of social policy, however, business groups acted out their politics cautiously. In effect, they employed front men, the rightwing think tanks funded by business but presenting themselves as class-neutral intellectual arbiters of policy. The names are familiar: Heritage, Cato, the Hudson Institute, the American Enterprise Institute, the Manhattan Institute. The think tanks became the mouthpieces of a business class mobilized to do battle with the social policies inherited from the New Deal and the Great Society. They sponsored public intellectuals like George Gilder and Charles Murray, they wrote and published books, they deluged congressional offices with daily reports giving their take on policies, they promoted their spokespeople on TV talk shows, they flooded the newspapers with op-eds. And their agenda was the business agenda of dismantling the social protections painfully developed during the twentieth century. In significant measure, that agenda has succeeded.

What, then, can be done to restore the public policies that brought a measure of security to the lives of working and poor Americans?

Some hints at an answer are gained by sober scrutiny of periods of egalitarian reform in American history. The 1930s gave us federal protection of labor rights and the first national social welfare programs, including AFDC. The 1960s expanded those programs, and improved them too, bringing something like the rule of law to the administration of AFDC, for example. In both these periods, the poor and their advocates mobilized in protest, raised new demands, made trouble, enough trouble to penetrate electoral politics and threaten dominant electoral coalitions. If we look even further back into the nineteenth century, we can see a similar pattern in the success of the abolitionists. The abolitionists were despised and harassed for the issues they raised and the trouble they made, but their issues and their trouble broke up the intersectional national parties and created the conditions for civil war and emancipation.

What about now? Before September 11 there were clear signs that widening inequality in the United States, together with corporate abuse of democratic politics, was nourishing a new wave of protests. We could see it in the dramatic anti-corporate globalization demonstrations, in anti-sweatshop campaigns on campuses, in the resurgence of the labor movement, in living-wage campaigns in the cities. Those protests have been muffled by the war on terror, which, whatever else it is, has also become a mask, a charade to shield from view the public policies that made the rich richer and the poor poorer, within the United States and abroad. The vice president has said that the war on terror may take 50 years. But it is unlikely to succeed as a shield and diversion from the policies that encourage business greed and enforce labor discipline for 50 years. It may not even work for one year. People do regain their footing, and voices of dissent are important in helping to make that happen. ❑

Source: Mickey Kaus, "The Work Ethic State," *New Republic,* July 7, 1986.

Article 3.8

UNEMPLOYMENT: A JOBS DEFICIT OR A SKILLS DEFICIT?

BY JOHN MILLER AND JEANNETTE WICKS-LIM

January/February 2011

Millions of Americans remain unemployed nearly a year and a half after the official end-date of the Great Recession, and the nation's official unemployment rate continues at nearly 10%.

Why? We are being told that it is because—wait for it—workers are not qualified for the jobs that employers are offering.

Yes, it's true. In the aftermath of the deepest downturn since the Great Depression, some pundits and policymakers—and economists—have begun to pin persistently high unemployment on workers' inadequate skills.

The problem, in this view, is a mismatch between job openings and the skills of those looking for work. In economics jargon, this is termed a problem of "structural unemployment," in contrast to the "cyclical unemployment" caused by a downturn in the business cycle.

The skills-gap message is coming from many quarters. Policymaker-in-chief Obama told Congress in February 2009: "Right now, three-quarters of the fastest-growing occupations require more than a high school diploma. And yet, just over half of our citizens have that level of education." His message: workers need to go back to school if they want a place in tomorrow's job market.

The last Democrat in the White House has caught the bug too. Bill Clinton explained in a September 2010 interview, "The last unemployment report said that for the first time in my lifetime, and I'm not young … we are coming out of a recession but job openings are going up twice as fast as new hires. And yet we can all cite cases that we know about where somebody opened a job and 400 people showed up. How could this be? Because people don't have the job skills for the jobs that are open."

Economists and other "experts" are most likely the source of the skills-gap story. Last August, for instance, Narayana Kocherlakota, president of the Federal Reserve Bank of Minneapolis, wrote in a Fed newsletter: "How much of the current unemployment rate is really due to mismatch, as opposed to conditions that the Fed can readily ameliorate? The answer seems to be a lot." Kocherlakota's point was that the Fed's monetary policy tools may be able to spur economic growth, but that won't help if workers have few or the wrong skills. "The Fed does not have a means to transform construction workers into manufacturing workers," he explained.

The skills-mismatch explanation has a lot to recommend it if you're a federal or Fed policymaker: it puts the blame for the economic suffering experienced by the 17% of the U.S. workforce that is unemployed or underemployed on the workers themselves. Even if the Fed or the government did its darndest to boost overall spending, unemployment would be unlikely to subside unless workers upgraded their own skills.

The only problem is that this explanation is basically wrong. The weight of the evidence shows that it is not a mismatch of skills but a lack of demand that lies at the heart of today's severe unemployment problem.

High-Skill Jobs?

President Obama's claim that new jobs are requiring higher and higher skill levels would tend to support the skills-gap thesis. His interpretation of job-market trends, however, misses the mark. The figure that Obama cited comes from the U.S. Department of Labor's employment projections for 2006 to 2016. Specifically, the DOL reports that among the 30 fastest growing occupations, 22 of them (75%) will typically require more than a high school degree. These occupations include network systems and data communications analysts, computer software engineers, and financial advisors. What he fails to say, however, is that these 22 occupations are projected to represent less than 3% of all U.S. jobs.

What would seem more relevant to the 27 million unemployed and underemployed workers are the occupations with the *largest* growth. These are the occupations that will offer workers the greatest number of new job opportunities. Among the 30 occupations with the largest growth, 70%—21 out of 30—typically do not require more than a high school degree. To become fully qualified for these jobs, workers will only need on-the-job training. The DOL projects that one-quarter of all jobs in 2016 will be in these 21 occupations, which include retail salespeople, food-preparation and food-service workers, and personal and home care aides.

In fact, the DOL employment projections estimate that more than two-thirds (68%) of the jobs in 2016 will be accessible to workers with a high school degree or less. Couple this with the fact that today, nearly two-thirds (62%) of the adult labor force has at least some college experience, and an alleged skills gap fails to be convincing as a driving force behind persistent high unemployment.

LABOR MARKET MUSICAL CHAIRS

To understand the data discussed here, try picturing the U.S. labor market as a game of musical chairs, with a few twists. At any time, chairs (job openings) can be added to the circle and players can sit down (get hired). When the music stops at the end of the month, not all the chairs are filled. Still, many people—far more people than the number of empty chairs—are left standing.

Each month, the Bureau of Labor Statistics reports on what happened in that month's game of labor market musical chairs in its various measures of unemployment and in the Job Openings and Labor Turnover Survey (JOLTS). Here's how the BLS scorecard for labor market musical chairs works.

- **Job openings** is a snapshot of the number of jobs available on the last day of the month—the number of empty chairs when the music stops.

- **Hires** are all the new additions to payroll during the month—the number of people who found a chair to sit in while the music was playing. Because many chairs are added to the circle and filled within the same month, the number of hires over a month is typically greater than the number of openings available on the last day of that month.

- **Unemployed persons** are those who looked for a job that month but couldn't find one—the number of people who played the game but were left standing when the music stopped at the end of the month.

Low-Skill Workers?

If employers were having a hard time finding qualified workers to fill job openings, you'd think that any workers who are qualified would be snapped right up. But what the unemployment data show is that there remains a substantial backlog of experienced workers looking for jobs or for more hours in their existing part-time jobs in those major industries that have begun hiring—including education, healthcare, durable goods manufacturing, and mining.

Most telling are the *underemployed*—those with part-time jobs who want to work full-time. Today there are more underemployed workers in each of the major industries of the private economy than during the period from 2000 to 2007, as Arjun Jayadev and Mike Konczal document in a recent paper published by the Roosevelt Institute. Even in the major industries with the highest number of job openings—education and health services, professional and business services, transportation and utilities, leisure and hospitality, and manufacturing—underemployment in 2010 remains at levels twice as high or nearly twice as high as during the earlier period (measured as a percentage of employed workers).

Purveyors of the mismatch theory would have a hard time explaining how it is that underemployed workers who want full-time work do not possess the skills to do the jobs full time that they are already doing, say, 20 hours a week.

More broadly, workers with a diverse set of skills—not just construction workers—lost jobs during the Great Recession. Workers in manufacturing, professional and business services, leisure and hospitality, transportation and utilities, and a host of other industries were turned out of their jobs. And many of these experienced workers are still looking for work. In each of the 16 major industries of the economy unemployment rates in September 2010 were still far higher than they had been at the onset of the Great Recession in December 2007. In the industries with a large number of (cumulative) job openings during the recovery—education and health services, professional and business services, and manufacturing—experienced workers face unemployment rates twice what they were back in December 2007.

There are plenty of experienced workers still looking for work in the industries with job openings. To be faithful to the data, Kocherlakota and the other mismatch proponents would need to show that experienced workers no longer possess the skills to work in their industry, even though that industry employed them no more than three years ago. That seems implausible.

Statistical Errors

Still, the statistical oddity that Bill Clinton and many economists have pointed to does seem to complicate the picture. If the number of job openings is rising at a good clip yet the number of new hires is growing more slowly and the unemployment rate is stagnant, then maybe employers *are* having trouble finding qualified folks to hire.

Once you take a closer looks at the numbers, though, there is less here than meets the eye.

First, the *rate* at which job openings and new hires numbers change over time is not the right place to look. What we really need to know is how the number of unfilled job posts compares to the number of qualified workers employers hire over the same month. If employers in today's recovery are having a hard time finding workers, then the job openings left unfilled at the end of the month should be relatively high compared to the number of newly hired workers that month. In other words, if the number of positions left unfilled at the end of the month relative to the number of new hires rises *above* what we've seen during past recoveries, this would mean that employers are finding it harder to fill their positions with the right workers this time around.

But it turns out that the ratio of unfilled job openings to new hires is approximately the same during this recovery as in the recovery from the 2001 recession. In September 2010, fifteen months into the current economic recovery, the ratio of job posts left unoccupied at the end of the month to the number of monthly new hires stood at 69%—very close to its 67% level in February 2003, fifteen months into the last recovery. In other words, today's employers are filling their job openings with the same rate of success as yesterday's employers.

Comparisons that focus on the unemployment rate rather than on the number of new hires are even less meaningful. As hiring picks up at the beginning of an economic recovery, workers who had given up the job search start looking again. This brings them back into the official count of the unemployed, keeping the unemployment rate from dropping even as both job openings and new hires rise.

WHERE MISMATCHES MAY MATTER

The skills-mismatch theory does not go very far toward explaining stubbornly high U.S. unemployment. Still, there are unquestionably some unemployed and underemployed workers whose job prospects are limited by "structural" factors.

One kind of structural unemployment that does seem to fit the contours of the Great Recession to at least some degree is that caused by a mismatch of geography: the workers are in one part of the country while the jobs they could get are in another. The housing crisis surely has compromised the ability of unemployed workers to unload their single largest asset, a house, and move to another part of the country. Plus, job losses have been particularly heavy in regions where the housing crisis hit hardest.

But at the same time, lost jobs have been widespread across industries and there is little real evidence of geographic mismatch between job openings and unemployed workers. As labor economist Michael Reich reports, "economic decline and the growth of unemployment have been more widespread than ever before, making it unclear where the unemployed should migrate for greater job opportunities."

Even where there is a skills mismatch, that doesn't mean the government shouldn't get involved. On the contrary, government policies to boost economic demand can help significantly. When demand is high, labor markets become very tight and there are few available workers to hire. Workers previously viewed as "unemployable" get hired, get experience and on-the-job training, and see their overall career prospects brighten.

And, of course, government can fund expanded job-training programs. If the economy continues to slog along with low growth rates and persistent unemployment, the ranks of the long-term unemployed will rise. As they go longer and longer without work, their skills will atrophy or become obsolete and they will face a genuine skills-mismatch problem that will make job-training programs more and more necessary.

Not Enough Jobs

The reality of the situation—the widespread job losses and the long, fruitless job searches of experienced workers—make it clear that today's employment problem is a jobs deficit across the economy, not a skills deficit among those looking for work.

While it's true that any given month ends with some number of unfilled job openings, the total number of jobs added to the economy during this recovery has simply been inadequate to put the unemployed back to work. In fact, if every job that stood open at the end of September 2010 had been filled, 11.7 million officially unemployed workers would still have been jobless.

This recovery has seen far fewer job openings than even the so-called "jobless" recovery following the 2001 recession. Economists Lawrence Mishel, Heidi Shierholz, and Kathryn Edwards of the Economic Policy Institute report that cumulative job openings during the first year of this recovery were roughly 25% lower than during the first year of the recovery following the 2001 recession—that's 10 million fewer jobs. Even in the industries generating the most job openings in the current recovery—education and health services, professional and business services, leisure and hospitality, and manufacturing—the cumulative number of job openings has lagged well behind the figure for those industries during the first year of the recovery from the 2001 recession. (Only the mining and logging category, which accounted for just 0.5% of employment in 2007, has had more job openings during the first year of this recovery than during the first year of the 2001 recovery.)

Why has the pick-up in jobs following the Great Recession been worse than usual? The simple answer is that the recession was worse than usual. The sharp and extreme decline of output and employment in the Great Recession has severely dampened demand—that is, people have not had money to buy things. With the resulting lack of sales, businesses were not willing to either invest or hire; and this in turn has meant a continuing lack of demand.

If businesses have barely resumed hiring, it has not been for lack of profits. By the middle of 2010, corporate profits (adjusted for inflation) were about 60% above their low point at the end of 2008, well on their way back to the peak level of mid-2006. Also, in early 2010 non-financial firms were sitting on almost $2 trillion in cash. There was no lack of ability to invest and hire, but there was a lack of incentive to invest and hire, that is, a lack of an expectation that demand (sales) would rise. As is well known, small businesses have generally accounted for a disproportionately large share of job growth. Yet, since the onset of the Great Recession, small business owners have consistently identified poor sales as their single most important problem—and thus, presumably, what has prevented them from expanding employment.

The Role of Demand

Regardless of the lack of evidence to support it, the skills-mismatch story has seeped into media coverage of the economy. Take, for example, National Public Radio's recent Morning Edition series titled "Skills gap: holding back the labor market." In one segment, reporter Wendy Kaufman presents anecdotes about employers turning down record numbers of applicants and leaving job openings unfilled. Economist Peter Capelli then comes on and remarks, "You know, a generation ago you'd never expect that somebody could come into a reasonably skilled, sophisticated position in your organization and immediately make a contribution. That's a brand new demand." Now, that comment does not point to today's workers possessing fewer skills or qualifications. Rather, it suggests that employers have raised the bar: they are pickier than in the past.

That makes sense. We've seen that employers are successfully filling positions at about the same rate as in the recent past. What's different this time around is that employers have had up to six unemployed workers competing for every job opening left vacant at the close of the month. This is by far the highest ratio on record with data back to 2000. During the 2001 recession, that ratio rose to just over two unemployed workers for each opening. (In the first years of the "jobless recovery" following the 2001 recession, the ratio continued to rise, but it remained below three to one.) Clearly, these numbers favor the alternative explanation. Unfortunately, Kaufman doesn't even consider it.

That's too bad. Recognizing that a lack of demand for goods and services is to blame for the severe crisis of unemployment puts the focus squarely back on the federal government and on the Fed, which could help to remedy the problem —*if* they had the political will to do so. Millions of unemployed workers, organized and armed with an accurate diagnosis of the problem, could create that political will— unless they are distracted by a wrong-headed diagnosis that tries to blame them for the problem. ❑

Sources: Bureau of Labor Statistics Table A-14, Unemployed persons by industry and class of workers, not seasonally adjusted, historical data (bls.gov); Lawrence Mishel, Heidi Shierholz, and Kathryn Anne Edwards, "Reasons for Skepticism About Structural Unemployment," Economic Policy Institute, Briefing Paper #279, September 22, 2010 (epi.org); Arjun Jayadev and Mike Konczal, "The Stagnating Labor Market," The Roosevelt Institute, September 19, 2010 (rooseveltinstitute. org); Bureau of Labor Statistics, Job Openings and Labor Turnover (JOLTS) Highlights, September 2010 (bls.gov); Michael Reich, "High Unemployment after the Great Recession: Why? What Can We Do?," Policy Brief from the Center on Wage and Employment Dynamics, Institute for Research on Labor and Employment, University of California, Berkeley, June 2010 (irle.berkeley.edu/cwed); Narayana Kocherlakota, President Federal Reserve Bank of Minneapolis, "Inside the FOMC," Marquette, Michigan, August 17, 2010 (minneapolisfed.org); Lawrence Mishel and Katherine Anne Edwards, "Bill Clinton Gets It Wrong," Economic Policy Institute, Economic Snapshot, September 27, 2010 (epi.org); "Remarks of President Barack Obama—Address to Joint Session of Congress," February 24, 2009 (whitehouse.gov); "The Skills Gap: Holding Back the Labor Market," Morning Edition, National Public Radio, November 15, 2010 (npr.org).

Article 3.9

EMPLOYERS GO ON STRIKE—BECAUSE THEY CAN

The Journal editors support the bosses' strike demands.

BY JOHN MILLER
July/August 2010

> "EMPLOYERS GO ON STRIKE:
> CONGRESS KEEPS GIVING BUSINESS REASONS NOT TO HIRE"
>
> Yesterday [June 4th] Americans learned that the economy created a net total of 431,000 new jobs in May, including 411,000 temporary Census hires.
>
> The private economy—that is, the wealth creation part, not the wealth redistribution part—gained only 41,000 jobs, down sharply from the encouraging 218,000 in April, and 158,000 in March.
>
> Almost everything Congress has done in recent months has made private businesses less inclined to hire new workers. ObamaCare imposes new taxes and mandates on private employers. Even with record unemployment, Congress raised the minimum wage to $7.25, pricing more workers out of jobs.
>
> The "jobs" bill that the House passed last week expands jobless insurance to 99 weeks, while raising taxes by $80 billion on small employers and U.S-based corporations. On January 1, Congress is set to let taxes rise on capital gains, dividends and small businesses.
>
> —*Wall Street Journal*, "Review & Outlook," June 5, 2010

Employers surely have been on strike, but that's hardly news. Private sector hiring through the first four months of 2010 was no higher than in 2009. What there has been for job growth in the private sector is due to the decline in layoffs (and discharges) not an uptick in hiring. As of May nearly eight million fewer workers were on private payrolls than when the recession began in Dec. 2007.

Employers may be on strike, but they haven't missed a paycheck. The same, of course, can't be said for the 17.8 million workers the striking employers failed to hire. That number includes the 15 million officially counted as unemployed, and another 2.8 million workers who gave up looking for work or who could never get their first job during the recession. And honoring the demands issued by the *Wall Street Journal* editors would not help find them a job but rather would prolong the employers' strike.

Record Long-Term Unemployment

Unemployed workers have gone longer without a paycheck than any time in the last 62 years. In May the median or typical unemployment spell was 23.2 weeks (5.4 months). And 6.8 million workers, some 46% of the unemployed, had been unemployed over six months, the highest level of long-term unemployment on record (with data back to 1948). Even in the worst months of the early 1980s recession, when the jobless rate topped 10% for ten straight months, only one in four of the unemployed was out of work for more than six months.

Unemployed black workers, manufacturing workers, and workers in the transportation, utilities, financial, and information industries have all typically endured spells of unemployment 26 weeks or longer. In addition, the median unemployment spell increases unrelentingly with age, exceeding a half year for workers 35 or older and reaching 50 weeks, or nearly a year, for workers 65 and over.

The effects have been devastating. Just under one half of the unemployed have now gone without work longer than the traditional length of unemployment benefits (26 weeks). A third of the unemployed have gone a year or longer without a job. Congress has extended jobless benefits to a maximum of 99 weeks in states with high unemployment. Still the longer people are unemployed the more likely they are to eventually give up searching and drop out of the labor force.

There are few signs that unemployment will abate or its duration shorten, or that private sector hiring will spring back to life, anytime soon. In May 2010, there were still 5.5 officially unemployed workers for every job opening counted by the Bureau of Labor Statistics. With a backlog of 2.8 million workers wanting a job not accounted for in those figures, the official unemployment rate is likely to hover at near double-digits levels for the rest of 2010. In addition, with plenty of part-time employees who want full-time jobs, far more than during previous recoveries, employers will continue to add to those workers' hours before they hire additional workers.

Employers' Strike Demands

Employment readings admittedly vary month to month in any recovery, but the evidence is overwhelming: the private sector is not hiring.

Why not? The *Wall Street Journal* editors are only too happy to tell you: That pesky public sector keeps redistributing wealth, crushing whatever incentive employers might have had to hire workers. Health care mandates and taxes, a higher minimum wage, expanded jobless benefits, and, worst of all, the prospect of letting the Bush tax cuts expire.

The problems with the editors' list of strike demands are manifold. First, each and every one of these demands would redistribute wealth, the editors' supposed complaint about the public sector. But in this case that redistribution would favor employers, not workers. Not providing health care benefits, allowing the purchasing power of the minimum wage to deteriorate, skimping on social spending, cutting taxes on capital gains and dividends, and lowering the top income-tax bracket have all contributed to a massive redistribution of income to the wealthy over the last three decades, a trend the editors are dedicated to continuing.

Second, employers already have the financial wherewithal to hire new workers. Their costs are down, their profits are up, and they are rolling in dough. Corporate profits are back to pre-recession levels. The combination of rapid productivity gains and stagnant wages have slashed unit labor costs (compensation costs per unit of output) to lower levels than before the onset of the recession. And by the end of March 2010, non-financial corporations held 7% of all their assets in cash, the highest level since 1963.

Third, government spending is the source of much of what there has been in the way of new jobs. As the editors point out, almost all the jobs created in May 2010 were temporary Census hires. In addition, according to estimates from the Congressional Budget Office, the $895 billion government stimulus passed in early 2009 created jobs for between 1.2 million and 2.8 million workers during the first quarter of 2010. Even the lower estimate exceeds the 1.15 million hires in the private sector in the same time period, some of which should be directly attributed to the stimulus package.

No Restart Button

Finally and most importantly, the policies the editors attack are not what stand between us and massive hiring and sustained economic growth. Undoing those policies, as limited as they have been, and re-instituting the Bush tax cuts, would constitute little more than hitting the restart button. And what would be restarted is nothing other than the very forces that brought on the worst crisis since the Great Depression.

Consider this: The economy has grown only about half as quickly as typically follows a deep recession. Much of the reason has been sputtering consumer spending, held back by a lack of jobs, to be sure, and by the debt consumers racked up during the last two decades. The very polices advocated by the editors kept a lid on wages and concentrated income gains among those at the top, leaving most consumers to ring up more and more debt in an effort to keep up their standard of living. That debt burden, still a third higher than that in the mid 1990s relative to household income, continues to hamstring consumption. A recent Gallup Poll reveals that the modest increase in consumer spending over the last year came exclusively from well-to-do families. Consumers with an income over $90,000 a year increased their monthly expenditures by one-third from May 2009 to May 2010, while the monthly expenditures of consumers with incomes below $90,000 remained unchanged.

More government spending is needed to help jump-start the engine of economic growth. A good place to start is the Local Jobs for America Act of 2010, introduced by Rep. George Miller (D-Cal.). It would create or save approximately 1 million jobs by protecting or creating state and local government and nonprofit sector jobs. Those jobs are much needed since state and local governments have shed 231,000 jobs since August 2008.

But the engine of economic growth needs to be rebuilt as well. Employers are not the only ones on strike; lenders are as well. In 2009 total outstanding loans at FDIC insured banks dropped an epic 7.4%, the sharpest decline in lending since 1942. Without genuine reform that breaks the power of the mega-financial institutions, protects consumers and mortgage holders, and regulates financial transactions, lending will not resume. And what there is for economic growth will reward the employers the editors are so concerned about, while the jobs machine sputters and workers continue to endure long spells of unemployment. ❑

Sources: Sara Murray, "Lending Falls at Epic Pace," by Crittenden and Eckblad, *Wall Street Journal,* 2/24/10; "Chronic Joblessness Takes Toll," *Wall Street Journal,* June 2, 2010; Justin Lahart, "U.S. Firms Build Record Cash Piles," *Wall Street Journal,* June 10, 2010; Heather Boushey, "The Latest Employment Woes," Center For American Progress, June 4, 2010; "Estimated Impact of the American Recovery and Reinvestment Act on Employment and Economic Output from January 2010 Through March 2010," Congressional Budget Office; Dennis Jacobe, "Frugality Fatigue: Upper-Income Spending Surges 33%," gallup.com; Bureau of Labor Statistics, Household Data, Tables A-12, A-34, A-35, A-36, A-37, bls.gov.

Chapter 4

INTERNATIONAL LABOR MOVEMENTS

Article 4.1

LABOR INFLUENCE IN THE NEW SOUTH AFRICAN GOVERNMENT

BY PATRICK BOND
December 2009—WorkingUSA

Far more than in any other African country, a vibrant, explicitly socialist trade-union federation and a (nominally) communist party have formal representation in—and a hard-won informal influence over—the South African government, one re-elected in April with 66% of the vote (down from 70% in 2004). Such representation, however, tempts a well-rehearsed insult, namely that African National Congress (ANC) nationalism will permit the "Alliance" comrades to "talk left" now, in order to disguise the government's "walk right" later.

The discourse-reality gap is not solely South African. Nor is it merely a legacy of South Africa's long drawn-out, Soviet/Swedish-funded, occasionally workerist-influenced, and generally anti-imperialist liberation struggle, three decades of which included an erratic armed struggle, prior to the first democratic non-racial vote in April 1994. It can, more generally, be recognized from Frantz Fanon's "pitfalls of national consciousness" in most of newly post-colonial Africa. Recall how, in *The Wretched of the Earth*, Fanon condemned

> the transfer into native hands of those unfair advantages which are a legacy of the colonial period. Since the middle class has neither sufficient material nor intellectual resources (by intellectual resources we mean engineers and technicians) it limits its claims to the taking over of business offices and commercial houses formerly occupied by the settlers ... The national middle class discovers its historic mission: that of intermediary, ... the transmission line between the nation and a capitalism, rampant though camouflaged, which today puts on the mask of neocolonialism.

The South African Communist Party (SACP) and Congress of South African Trade Unions (Cosatu) leadership understand this power dynamic. Former President Thabo Mbeki completely marginalized the Alliance Left, leaving the SACP and Cosatu utterly powerless in Pretoria, merely begging for quite meager reforms and access during the post-apartheid era. But in turn, it was entirely because of this malign neglect that Mbeki and his closest allies were peacefully overthrown—first, vanquished in the ANC internal presidential elections in December 2007 and then booted from state power in September 2008. Two months later, several leading Mbekites left the ANC to form the Congress of the People (Cope) party on a good governance program, but the party only got 7.5% of the vote in the April 22 election. The other center-right party, the white-led Democratic Alliance, increased its margin from 4% from 2004 to 17% in 2008 and won the wealthiest province, the Western Cape, while several smaller parties—especially Zulu-nationalist Inkatha—declined precipitously, marking a stage where consolidations and more substantive centrist alliance-building would proceed.

Nevertheless, the war for hearts and minds in the ANC could not be won simply through rightward evacuations to Cope. Just prior to the April 22 general election, Cosatu general secretary Zwelinzima Vavi confessed the continuing adverse balance of forces, bluntly arguing, "We want to impose our working class hegemony. This is why others hate us like poison in the ANC." Added Cosatu president Sdumo Dlamini, "There is an anti-communist, anti-workers sentiment we are picking up. We can't accept that. This ANC was rescued by the workers. This is why I say it is a declaration of war."

Overall, Zuma's cabinet seems to offer the Alliance Left sufficient career concessions but, quite frankly, no real prospects for expanding a power base to achieve the "second stage" (from non-racial capitalism to socialism) of the "National Democratic Revolution." Nzimande's call to arms in the Umsebenzi Online edition two days before the inauguration reveals both hubris and a knowing cynicism about South Africa's notorious crony-capitalist party-patronage system:

> The electoral victory marks a significant rolling back of the huge ideological offensive waged by sections of the elites against the ANC and its allies. The electoral victory has thus significantly exposed both the bankruptcy and the distance between these elites from the concerns of ordinary workers and the poor of our country. In many ways these election results are an expression of the growing class cleavage in wider society between the haves (including now a small black group of tycoons as represented by Cope) and the have-nots . . .

> As the SACP we can proudly claim that we have achieved the main objectives of our main pillar in our 2009 Programme of Action, that of working for an ANC's overwhelming electoral victory. Indeed thousands of communists and all our structures were mobilized in this effort . . . However, we need to remind ourselves of the very clear directives given by our February Central Committee on communists deployed in government. This time around, the CC said, there must be a change in the manner in which communists relate and account to the SACP, much as they are deployed in the first instance as ANC cadres. In particular the

SACP will not allow itself to be used as a stepping stone to positions in the ANC and government only to be abandoned by some of those cadres once they occupy such positions . . .

We must refuse to be cowed down by neo-liberal ideological blackmail about what is to be done about this crisis. We believe that the only sustainable solutions that can effectively deal with the current capitalist crisis are leftist solutions, not more of the same liberal dogma whose failures are the direct cause of the current crisis. At no stage in the history of our democracy have we needed a developmental state, buttressed by popular power, than at this point in time.

Because such rhetoric pulls the reader leftwards with such confidence, the subsequent drift rightward will be all the more demoralizing. To be sure, incremental victories are not impossible, such as a potentially expensive National Health Insurance promise (which, Manuel and his neoliberal technical staff threaten, could be stalled for at least the next five years). Job losses, rising conflict over transport restructuring, and huge electricity price increases are certain flash points, as is a battle over Cosatu's demand to ban the outsourcing of workers through "labour brokers." Overall though, there is no reason yet to doubt Zuma when he repeatedly reassured financial institutions and Davos audiences, dating to late 2007, that "nothing will change" in terms of pro-business policies, no matter how vulnerable these have made South Africa. Although it may be too early to separate rhetoric from reality, neither the underlying social policy philosophy nor the economy that Zuma takes forward from the Mbeki era can be easily rejigged given the prevailing balance of forces, especially the weaknesses of the independent left. Assessing that weakness requires reviewing how the ANC attracted mass popular protests and then diverted and diffused them so effectively during the 2000s into a fight against Mbeki, not Mbekism.

Contours of a Class-Apartheid Transition

Perhaps no South African talked left and walked right with more confidence and eloquence than the mostly unlamented former president, Thabo Mbeki, who ruled not only from 1999–2008, but arguably also from 1994–99 as Nelson Mandela's deputy. He was a star pupil not only of Keynesianism at Sussex during the mid-1960s but subsequently of what South African political writer Raymond Suttner calls "Brezhnevite Marxism" at the Lenin Institute in Moscow. Mbeki served in the SACP politburo until 1990, when the new South African president, F.W. De Klerk, liberalized politics as the Berlin Wall fell. Mbeki was central in immediately drawing back the World Bank—whose last prior South African loan was in 1967—in part thanks to his old friend at Sussex, Geoff Lamb, a former SACP youth activist and then top Bank strategist credited with introducing the idea of homegrown structural adjustment to Africa during the 1980s.

The segue from racial to class apartheid could be read from more than a dozen World Bank "reconnaissance missions" from 1990–94 in all the main sectoral areas, in which the ANC shoe-horned the more radical Mass Democratic Movement allies into cooperation rather than conflict. Intermediary agencies like Anglo American

Corporation's Urban Foundation think tank and the Development Bank of Southern Africa (a World Bank junior partner) were crucial in shaping the transition in hotly contested fields like housing, water, energy, land, healthcare, and education. There was not a single aspect of social policy in which the "Knowledge Bank" pilot function of the World Bank and its local consultant corps were not a powerful factor.

Even before liberation, an October 1993 agreement to repay the apartheid debt—$25 billion in foreign loans from commercial banks, and somewhat more domestically—prevented the subsequent ANC government from meeting social spending goals. An interim constitution in November 1993 assured property rights and an "independent" (i.e. banker-biased, democracy-insulated) Reserve Bank. The International Monetary Fund had set the stage for other neoliberal economic policies—e.g. public sector wage and spending cuts—as a condition for a December 1993 $850 million loan, and the Fund's manager, Michel Camdessus, even compelled Mandela to reappoint the apartheid-era finance minister and central bank governor when the ANC took state power in May 1994. The General Agreement on Tariffs and Trade (soon to be the World Trade Organization) hit South Africa hard in mid-1994, as fast-declining manufacturing protection reversed the anticipated gains of liberation for workers.

By early 1995, the dissolution of the dual exchange control system (a "financial rand" used to deter international capital flight during the prior decade) and the encouragement of stock market investment by international finance meant first a huge inflow and then, on five separate occasions in the subsequent fifteen years, dramatic outflows and currency crashes of at least 25%. The first of these runs, in February 1996, followed a rumour (unfounded) that Mandela was ill, and it left the president and his team so psychologically shaken that they ditched their last left vestige, the Reconstruction and Development Programme ministry, and within four months imposed the hated "Growth, Employment, and Redistribution" agenda of neoliberalism.

Slowly deracializing class power had obvious macro manifestations of these types, but exactly the same dynamic was occurring in all the microdevelopmental arenas as well as in provinces and municipalities. Water, for example, was priced at "full cost recovery" by minister Kader Asmal, a populist social democrat, a policy that generated massive disconnections, a cholera epidemic, and a steady flow of protest riots and illegal reconnections. Housing policy was constructed by Joe Slovo—then SACP chair and housing minister—prior to his 1995 death, in a manner wholly consistent with the World Bank and Urban Foundation developer-driven, bank-centered philosophy.

The basis for a "government of national unity" which included DeKlerk's National Party and the Zulu-nationalist Inkatha party during the initial years of liberation was the reconciliation of several thousand elites in the liberation movement, white politics, and white business. Due in part to the political-economic cowardice of Archbishop Desmond Tutu—who remains extremely strong on symbolic political and ethical matters but weak on social justice—the Truth and Reconciliation Commission he chaired ensured that reconciliation would not touch, much less penalize, the vast majority of whites who were the main economic beneficiaries of apartheid. Successive Reserve Bank governors loosened exchange controls two dozen times from 1995 onwards, and finance minister Manuel let the capital flood out when in 1999 he gave permission for the relisting of financial headquarters for most of the largest companies on the London Stock Exchange. The firms that took the gap and permanently moved their historic apartheid loot offshore include Anglo American, DeBeers diamonds, Liberty Life insurance, Investec bank, Old Mutual insurance, Didata ICT, SAB Miller breweries (all to London), BHP Billiton metals (to Melbourne), and Mondi paper (to New York).

Although back in 1990 Mbeki had hurriedly quit the SACP to take advantage of the centering of mainstream South African politics, he never forgot how to deploy leftist rhetoric, as witnessed perhaps most publicly in his popularization of the phrase "global apartheid," first in mid-2000 when South Africa narrowly lost the hosting rights to the 2006 Soccer World Cup (to Germany thanks to a racist New Zealander's vote), and then again just prior to the 2002 United Nations World Summit on Sustainable Development in Johannesburg. That conference's main impact was the U.N.'s reification of "public-private partnerships" in areas as diverse as water, climate, and environmental management, and represented another example of a potentially transformative analysis denuded by local/global corporatism. However, under neoliberal conditions, none of the global strategies—especially the New Partnership for Africa's Development, dubbed "philosophically spot-on" by the U.S. State Department— could or can deliver the goods.

Degeneration set in within a year of Mbeki's ascent to the presidency, as witnessed in accusations that the Central Intelligence Agency and the industry known as "Big Pharma" controlled the Treatment Action Campaign (TAC). TAC is a grassroots movement ultimately successful not only in combating AIDS stigma, but in getting anti-retroviral drugs to 750,000 South Africans today. TAC's victory was an extraordinary accomplishment given that the price for a year's supply of medicines when it started the campaign exceeded $15,000. Other forms of delusion and schizophrenia characterized Mbeki's grip on power (e.g. a claim that three businessmen embarked on a 2001 conspiracy to unseat him). Mbeki's paranoid fear of leftists in and outside the Alliance reached a peak following the march of 30,000 social movement protesters against the U.N. environment summit on August 31, 2002: "They accuse our movement of having abandoned the working people, saying that we have adopted and are implementing neoliberal policies."

The Neoliberal Roll-Out

Just as he refused to acknowledge the link between HIV and AIDS or that (in 2008) Zimbabwe faced a "crisis," Mbeki and his ANC Political Education Unit would regularly deny critiques that his government served big businesses: "There are no facts that the anti-neoliberalism can produce to prove its accusations. Its statement characterizing the policies pursued by the ANC and our government since 1994 as the expressive of a neoliberal agenda are complete falsification of reality" (sic). Yet the evidence was so overwhelming that by 2006 it formed the core of the Alliance partners' critique of Mbekism, although the catalyst for the critique was by all accounts Mbeki's ham-fisted Machiavellian style:

• there was an immediate post-apartheid rise in income inequality, which was slightly tempered after 2001 by increased welfare payments, but which meant the Gini coefficient of inequality soared from below 0.6 in 1994 to 0.72 by 2006 (0.8 if welfare income is excluded);

• the official unemployment rate doubled (from 16% in 1994 to around 32% by the early 2000s, falling to 22% by the late 2000s—but by counting those who gave up looking for work, the realistic rate is closer to 40%) as a result of imported East Asian goods in relatively labour-intensive sectors (clothing, textiles, footwear, appliances and electronics) and capital-intensive production techniques elsewhere (especially mining and metals);

• the provision of housing to several million people has been marred by the facts that the units produced are far smaller than apartheid "matchboxes," are located further away from jobs and community amenities, are constructed with less durable building materials, come with lower-quality municipal services, and are saddled with higher-priced debt if and when credit is available;

• while free water and electricity are now provided to many low-income people, the overall price has risen dramatically since 1994, leading to millions of people facing disconnections each year when they cannot afford water consumption;

• the degeneration of the health system, combined with AIDS, has caused a dramatic decline in life expectancy, from 65 at the time of liberation to 52 a decade later;

• with respect to macroeconomic stability, the value of the Rand in fact crashed (against a basket of trading currencies) by more than a quarter in 1996, 1998, 2001, 2006 and 2008, the worst record of any major economy;

• South Africa's economy has become much more oriented to profit-taking from financial markets than production of real products, in part because of extremely high real interest rates (after a recent 3.5% spike during the mid-2000s, consumer and housing credit markets are badly strained by serious arrears and defaults);

• the two most successful major sectors from 1994-2004 were communications (12.2% growth per year) and finance (7.6%) while labour-intensive sectors such as textiles, footwear and gold mining shrank by 1-5% per year, and, overall, manufacturing as a percentage of GDP also declined;

• the government admits that overall employment growth was -0.2% per year from 1994-2004—but -0.2% is a vast underestimate of the problem;

• overall, the problem of "capital strike"—large-scale firms' failure to invest—continues, as gross fixed capital formation hovered between 15-17% from 1994-2004, hardly enough to cover wear-and-tear on equipment;

• where corporate profits were reinvested it sought returns from speculative real estate and the Johannesburg Stock Exchange: there was a 50% increase in share prices during the first half of the 2000s, and the property boom which began in 1999 had by 2007 sent house prices up by 400% (U.S. markets rose only by 60% prior to the banking collapse);

• businesses also invested their South African profits, but mainly not in South Africa: dating from the time of political and economic liberalization, most of the largest Johannesburg Stock Exchange firms shifted their funding flows and even their primary share listings to overseas stock markets;

• the outflow of profits and dividends due these firms is one of two crucial reasons South Africa's "current account deficit" has soared to amongst the highest in the world (in mid-2008 it was exceeded only by New Zealand) and is hence a major danger in the event of currency instability;

• the other cause of the current account deficit is the negative trade balance, which can be blamed upon a vast inflow of imports after trade liberalization, which export growth could not keep up with; and

• ecological problems have become far worse, according to the government's own commissioned research in the 2006 "Environmental Outlook" report, which according to the leading state official, "outlined a general decline in the state of the environment."

Countervailing claims of a "developmental state" under construction hinged upon a series of vast white-elephant projects:

• the Coega industrial complex aimed at attracting a persistently elusive aluminium smelter (by early 2008 electricity shortages made this unlikely as it would add 3.5% demand to the stressed grid while creating only 800 jobs);

• the Lesotho Highlands Water Project mega-dams which permit hedonistic water consumption in Johannesburg while unaffordably raising prices for Soweto township residents;

• several bloated soccer stadiums for the 2010 World Soccer Cup;

• the $5 billion arms deal;

• Pebble Bed Nuclear Reactors potentially costing tens of billions of dollars, alongside tens of billions more on coal-fired power plants notwithstanding South Africa's world-leading CO_2 emissions rate; and

• a $2.2 billion fast-rail network allowing wealthy travelers easy albeit expensive access between Johannesburg, Pretoria, and the O.R. Tambo airport.

To finance state infrastructure spending and steady tax cuts for corporations (tax rates are down from a rate of nearly 50% in 1994 to less than 30% today), Manuel engineered a parasitical growth process that looks impressive at surface level—a 5% GDP increase for much of the 2000s—but isn't when the downside is considered. The GDP growth fails to incorporate the depletion of non-renewable resources, and if the calculation is adjusted, South Africa would have a net negative per person rate of national wealth accumulation, according to even the World Bank.

Going into the Zuma era, South Africa has amongst the world's highest current account deficits and is the most economically vulnerable emerging market, according to *The Economist*. After the ANC's huge victory on April 22, South Africa is not politically "unstable" in the classical sense of potential government overthrow. But it is a society that is profoundly unstable because experience has shown that anti-neoliberal resistance can make a genuine difference. The police measured more than 30,000 "gatherings" (15 or more people in some form of protest, for which permission is typically applied for a week ahead of time) from 2004–07. Of these, 10% generated "unrest." But many tens of thousands more of spontaneous protests were not recorded, according to a recent survey by Johannesburg's two leading progressive research institutes.

Still, the late 2000s are probably going to be remembered as the good old days (like Zimbabwe's 1980s), in comparison to the economic devastation awaiting South Africa in coming months. Pincer pressures on Zuma will descend from above but also percolate up from below. The impending top-down austerity regime will not be surprising; it was projected in the International Monetary Fund's October 2008 Article IV Consultation and will strengthen the "1996 class project" (as the SACP call Mbekism, in honor of the year that homegrown structural adjustment was imposed as Mbeki declared, "Just call me a Thatcherite"). That project consists of ongoing technocratic neoliberalism and patronage-influenced resource flows associated with the state's numerous white elephant projects and Black Economic Empowerment. It is a project whose second wind appears imminent, notwithstanding the Alliance Left's current overconfidence. Manuel warned in the Financial Times late last year, "We need to disabuse people of the notion that we will have a mighty powerful developmental state capable of planning and creating all manner of employment." In April 2009, rejecting requests for bailouts in specific sectors, he announced to a Johannesburg business audience, "Expectations that government will socialize the costs of irrational exuberance cannot be entertained." But in reality, in spite of shifting from a small budget surplus to a substantial 3.8% deficit/GDP rate for 2009–10, that's precisely what Manuel has achieved since the mid-1990s by closely tracking South African economic policy onto the financial-speculative trajectory in the United States and Britain.

The IMF suggested that Manuel adopt five Washington Consensus austerity strategies last October, just three weeks before the institution's managing director, Dominique Strauss-Kahn, proclaimed that the IMF now supports a 2% budget stimulus "everywhere where it's possible. Everywhere where you have some room concerning debt sustainability. Everywhere where inflation is low enough not to risk having some kind of return of inflation, this effort has to be made." Pretoria should have qualified for such a Keynesian seal of approval, but no, according to IMF staff, Manuel should instead:

- run a budget surplus, i.e., "an increase in public saving so as to bring the structural public sector borrowing requirement to zero over the next few years," but bearing in mind that "cuts in the corporate income tax could boost growth";

- adopt privatization for "infrastructure and social needs," including electricity and transport by "relying more widely on public-private partnerships";

- maintain existing inflation-targeting (i.e. in the 3–6% target range, although inflation was more than 12% in 2008) and "raise interest rates further if supply shocks resume or domestic demand pressures do not dampen";

- "open the economy to greater international competition" by removing protections against international economic volatility, especially "further liberalization and simplification of the trade regime"; and

- remove worker rights in labour markets, including "backward-looking wage indexation" to protect against inflation.

To be sure, Manuel did not follow this advice immediately; the Alliance Left is powerful enough to prevent it if he tried any one of the five, especially right before a national election. But he is playing a complicated game to remain in genuine power in Pretoria while also apparently hankering for more than his present token role in multilateral financial maneuvers. The week before the April 2 G20 meeting in London, Manuel—as chair of the "Committee of Eminent Persons on IMF Governance Reform"— released a report aimed at putting the IMF at "the center of the world economy." This would entail a newly empowered ministerial-level Council (a politburo) with strategic decision-making capacity over "system stability, early warning and diagnosis, new lending facilities, and the selection of the Managing Director," who no longer necessarily will be a European citizen. Manuel, who chaired the IMF and World Bank board of governors in 2000 and the Development Committee after that, had long sought conditions for Bretton Woods Institution (BWI) relegitimization and recapitalization. In 2003, for example, he blithely confessed that BWI governance democratization was off the table: "I don't think that you can ripen this tomato by squeezing it." In 2005, when Paul Wolfowitz was named Bank president, Manuel pronounced him a "wonderful individual . . . perfectly capable." When Robert Zoellick and Strauss-Kahn were chosen as Bank and IMF leaders in 2007–08, Manuel grumbled to colleagues in South Africa but did not rock the Washington boat.

Conclusion: The Alliance-Left's Partial Radicalization

The recession—and potentially depression—will bring the contradictions of neoliberalism back to South Africa with a vengeance this year and next. In late May, government data showed a 6.4% quarterly GDP decline for early 2009, the worst since 1984. Even in late 2008 it was apparent that labour would suffer vast retrenchments, with a 67% reduction in average work hours per factory worker, the worst decline since 1970. The economy is likely to shed a half-million jobs in 2009, especially in manufacturing and mining. January 2009 alone witnessed a 36% crash in new car sales and 50% production cut, the worst ever recorded, according to the National Association of Auto Manufacturers. The anticipated rise in port activity has also reversed, with a 29% annualized fall in early 2009. The number of repossessed houses increased by 52% in early 2009 from a year earlier.

As if anticipating the crash of Manuel's project, and cognizant of the neoliberal era's inequality and rising social tension, the SACP had already in 2006 begun to talk much more radically than it had for many years. Their Bua Communisi! statement that year eloquently identified the neoliberal class project as resting upon three foundations: an uncritical "globalization made me do it" mentality (to borrow John Saul's phrase) that welcomed foreign trade and finance no matter the damage; an all-powerful presidency; and a modernizing centrist political party. The SACP saw this latter process as "a deliberate strategy to marginalize the SACP and Cosatu and perhaps (in the pre-2002 years) even to provoke a walk-out from the alliance." Contrary to hopes on the independent left, there was never a chance of a walk-out, and the extraordinarily hard work done by trade unionists and communists to revive Zuma paid off inside the ANC, setting back any talk of a Workers' Party by, probably, a decade.

However, while the independent left as an organized network force is in retreat today more so than at any other time since 1994, the local-level eruptions of protests have sometimes been far more effective, though to label these as manifestations of "left" activism would be an exaggeration. The high-profile "no-go zone" of Khutsong, not far from Johannesburg, was a telling example. The community there has struggled since the early 2000s, when an insensitive demarcation exercise placed Khutsong in the relatively poor Northwest Province, instead of a few kilometers away in Gauteng, the province housing Johannesburg and Pretoria. The extent to which extremely militant community activism—channeled impressively by SACP local leadership—generated dual power during the late 2000s surprised the country, and finally in 2008 the switch to Gauteng province was made. By the time of the 2009 election, the ANC was allowed back, welcomed by a mass rally. The working-class and poor of Khutsong, however, will face the problems of Orange Farm, Soweto, Alexandra, Tembisa, Vosloorus, Ivory Park, and so many other sites in Gauteng where protests have regularly shaken the municipalities.

Aside from the anti-retroviral medicines, a few major national social movement victories have been recorded since the early 2000s, such as a Clean Air Act pushed by environmentalists like groundWork, or the Free Basic Services (6000 liters of water, 50 kilowatt hours of electricity per family each month) promised by the state in 2000 though only grudgingly delivered. The latter was boosted in September 2009 when the Constitutional Court heard the case of several Sowetans who demanded a doubling of the free water allotment to 50 liters per person per day along with a prohibition of pre-payment meters (by which water is self-disconnected). They had won in the High Court in April 2008 but suffered a setback in the Supreme Court of Appeals in February. In local settings there are also occasional victories associated with insurgent protests from below, mainly in defending land invasions, or driving a mining company off indigenous-controlled territory (as happens periodically in titanium and platinum zones), or maintaining illegal water or electricity connections. However, these rare wins for independent-left forces pale in comparison to the social change that is conceivably possible if Alliance-left strategies prove successful.

The period immediately ahead will severely test the opportunities for genuine social democratic reforms, largely because the spike in the 2009 budget deficit—probably above 7% of national income (not the planned 3.8%) given how much worse the recession is than predicted—will set the stage for austere budgets in the future. This is an especially dangerous time given the vulnerabilities to a run on the currency, what with the prevailing current account deficit and shorter supply of foreign capital sloshing around the world. Power relations are fluid in this context. Late May was revealing, for in the same week as a bus drivers' strike that nearly shut down Johannesburg when solidarity strikes were threatened, plus a national one-day public-sector doctors' stay-away, 2000 metalworkers protested at the S.A. Reserve Bank to demand a 2% cut in interest rates (the Bank lowered by only 1%).

The latter was notable because it reflected not only the hunger and confidence of angry workers to move beyond the point of production to defend jobs, but also the arrogance of the central bank officials who refused to accept the metalworkers' memo of grievances. Union president Irvin Jim reacted: "Anyone who rejects peaceful demonstrations and refuses to accept petitions from the South African working class, who are experiencing extreme economic and social difficulties not of their own making, is inviting big trouble. You are warned." But the protest also attracted the first backlash by the ruling party—specifically, ANC general secretary Gwede Mantashe, formerly the mineworkers' leader—who argued the metalworkers were "counterproductive" and potentially damaging their own cause, because after all, the "door is open" to the Alliance partners. Replied Young Communist League president David Masondo, "Yes, the door is open but the opening is very small for the working class to make an impact. Business has its own way of putting pressure on government, including the threat of withdrawing investment. Workers must go public and strike."

Strike they did, again and again in the months after Zuma's election: clothing workers, doctors, municipal workers, miners, even the army (1500 of whose troops were nearly fired in the course of a battle over working conditions and rights to unionize), and many others. Nearly all got wage settlements above 10%. If Mantashe's Sophistic attempts at persuasion continue to fail, the next stage of the backlash would be intensified repression; Zuma was, after all, foremost an ANC military leader during most of his career in exile. In September 2009, Zuma appointed the notoriously brutal KwaZulu-Natal police minister Bheki Cele as the national police commissioner and gave a "shoot to kill" order (against criminals). The police have already wracked up a great deal of hits on left and community activists, including apparent involvement in an ethnically-tinged attack on the Durban shackdwellers' movement in September, and the shooting of a protester in a high-profile Mpumalanga township uprising a few months earlier.

The Alliance Left's radicalization might then finally follow the script that independent leftists always wrote: the contradictions of operating within a neoliberal nationalist political project would ultimately drive out the trade unions and serious communists, to start a new party that might contest seriously for state power in ten or fifteen years' time. In the meantime, the decommodification battles won in the initial stages of democracy by AIDS activists and community movements will probably be the kinds of experiences to build upon for both defensive and offensive purposes, as the economic crisis continues to take its toll. ❑

This paper was presented to the Gyeongsang University Institute for Social Studies (supported by the Korea Research Foundation's grant KRF 2007-411-J04602).

Sources: Frantz Fanon, *The Wretched of the Earth*, New York, 1967 [1961]; *Sunday Tribune*, "Cosatu warns if unions sidelined, it will be war," April 19, 2009; Mauma Letsoalo and Mmanaledi Mataboge, "Manuel caught in Cosatu's crosshairs," *Mail & Guardian*, 18 September 2009; Moletsane Malefane, "Battle for control of SA economy," *Sunday Times*, October 4, 2009; Mark Gevisser, *The Dream Deferred*, Johannesburg, 2008; William Gumede, *Thabo Mbeki and the Struggle for the Soul of the ANC*, Johannesburg, 2006; Deepak Gopinath, "Doubt of Africa," *Institutional Investor*, May 2003; Kerry Cullinan and Anso Thom, *The Virus, Vitamins and Vegetables*, Johannesburg, 2009; Thabo Mbeki, "Statement of the President of the African National Congress, Thabo Mbeki, at the ANC Policy Conference," Kempton Park, September 27, 2002; African National Congress Political Education Unit, "Contribution to the NEC/NWC Response to the 'Cronin Interviews' on the Issue of Neoliberalism," Johannesburg, September 2002, (archive.mg.co.za); Patrick Bond, "South Africa's 'Developmental State' Distraction," *Mediations: Journal of the Marxist Literary Group*, 24, 1, 2009 (mediationsjournal.org); *The Economist*, February 26, 2009; Freedom of Expression Institute and University of Johannesburg Centre for Sociological Research, "National Trends around Protest Action," February 2009, Johannesburg; Robert Lapper and Tom Burgis, "S Africans urged to beware left turn," *Financial Times*, October 27, 2008; Terence Creamer, "SA's fiscal response to crisis has been comparatively large, Manuel insists," *Creamer Media's Engineering News*, 6 April 2009; Dominique Strauss-Kahn, "Transcript of a Press Briefing by the IMF Managing Director," Washington, November 17, 2008 (imf.org); International Monetary Fund, "IMF Executive Board Concludes Article IV Consultation with South Africa," Public Information Notice (PIN) No. 08/137, October 22, 2008 (imf.org); Trevor Manuel, "Report of the Committee of Eminent Persons on IMF Governance Reform," letter to Dominique Strauss-Kahn, Pretoria, March 29, 2009; SACP, *Bua Komanisi!*, 5, 1, May 2006.

Article 4.2

ON STRIKE IN CHINA
A Chinese New Deal in the making?

BY CHRIS TILLY AND MARIE KENNEDY
September/October 2010

> *"[There will] never be a strike [at the Hyundai plant in Beijing]. Strikes in China would jeopardize the company's reputation."*
>   —Zhang Zhixiong, deputy chairman of the union at that plant, 2003

> *"About 1,000 workers at Hyundai's auto parts factory [in Beijing] staged a two-day strike and demanded wage increases. The action only ended when bosses offered an initial 15% pay rise followed by another 10% in July."*
>   —China Daily/Asia News Network, June 4, 2010

Workers in China are on the move. The media initially fixed on the downward trajectory of desperate workers jumping from the roofs of Foxconn, the enormous electronics manufacturer that assembles the iPhone and numerous other familiar gadgets, but soon shifted to the upward arc of strike activity concentrated in the supply chains of Honda and Toyota.

But the auto-sector strikes in China's industrialized Southeast, as well as in the northeastern city of Tianjin, are just the tip of the iceberg. June strikes also pulled out thousands of workers at Brother sewing machine factories and a Carlsberg brewery in the central part of the country; machinery, LCD, and rubber parts plants in the east-central Shanghai area; a shoe manufacturer further inland in Jiujiang; and apparel and electronics workers outside the auto sector in the Southeast and Tianjin. "There are fifteen factories launching strikes now," Qiao Jian of the Chinese Institute of Industrial Relations (CIIR) told us in mid-June. Since that time, still more strikes have been reported, and many others are likely going unreported by Chinese media, which despite their growing independence remain sensitive to government pressure. None of the strikes had approval by the All China Federation of Trade Unions (ACFTU), the only labor movement authorized by Chinese law.

This explosion of wildcat walkouts prompts several questions. Why did it happen? What do the strikes mean for China's low-wage, low-cost manufacturing model? Equally important, what do they imply for China's party- and state-dominated labor relations? China's labor relations scholars—an outspoken bunch—are animatedly discussing that last question in public and in private.

What Happened and Why

The spark for the recent strike wave was the May 17th walkout of hundreds of workers from a Honda transmission plant in Nanhai, near Guangzhou in the Southeast. According to research by Wang Kan of CIIR, the strike was an accident: two employees embroiled in a dispute with Honda consulted a lawyer who advised them to threaten a strike as a bluff and even drew up a set of demands for them. They apparently were as shocked as anyone when workers spontaneously walked out. Accident or not, the workers demanded a 67% raise. Two weeks later, they agreed to return to work with a 42% wage increase. By that time, copycat strikes had erupted at other Honda suppliers in the Southeast and at Hyundai; workers at Toyota suppliers soon followed suit, as did employees from other sectors and regions. Most of these actions won wage settlements in the 20% range.

Why did this strike wave happen now? The first thing to understand is that strikes in China did not begin in 2010. As Berkeley doctoral student Eli Friedman points out, "the number of strikes and officially mediated labor disputes in China [has] been increasing rapidly for at least fifteen years." So-called "mass incidents," of which experts estimate about a third to be strikes, numbered 87,000 in 2005, and were unofficially pegged at 120,000 in 2008. Mediated labor disputes, many of which only involve an individual, have grown even faster, rising in round figures from 19,000 in 1994 to 135,000 in 2000, 350,000 in 2007, and 700,000 in 2008. The huge increase in 2008 is due at least in part to new laws on labor contracts and labor mediation passed that year that bolster workers' ability to bring complaints.

Still, "the Honda strike marks a turning point," in the words of law professor Liu Cheng of Shanghai Normal University. "Previous strikes were mainly about enforcing labor law. This is the first successful strike about collective bargaining." Anita Chan, a labor researcher at the University of Technology in Sydney, agrees, saying the current strikers "are negotiating for their interests and not for their rights—it's a very different set of stakes." The Nanhai Honda action was also a breakthrough in that for the first time strikers demanded the right to elect their own union representatives—a demand to which the provincial union federation has agreed, though the election has not yet taken place. Many subsequent strikes reiterated this demand, although they have focused more on economic issues. Even the economic demands extend beyond wages: at Honda Lock, strikers demanded noise reduction measures to improve the work environment.

The long-term growth in strike activity owes much to demographic changes. Predominantly women, China's industrial workers hail overwhelmingly from the ranks of rural migrants, 140 million of whom live and work in the cities but lack long-term permission to stay there or receive social benefits there. When Deng Xiaoping's market liberalization first spurred rapid industrial growth in the 1980s, migrants were willing to "eat bitterness," enduring hardships and low wages to send remittances home to families who were worse off than they. This stoic attitude and decades of policies aimed at growth at almost any cost are reflected in the decline of labor's share of total national income from 57% in 1983 to 37% in 2005. Unpaid or underpaid overtime and only one or two days off a month—violations of Chinese law—became common in China's manufacturing sector.

But the new generation of migrants, reared in a time of relative prosperity and comparing themselves to their peers in the cities, expect more. "Our demands are higher because we have higher material and spiritual needs," a young Honda striker who identified himself only as Chen told Agence France-Presse. "Our strike demands are based on our need to maintain our living standards." With urban housing costs soaring, this has become a pressing issue. "I dream of one day buying a car or apartment," said Zhang, a 22-year-old man working at the same plant, "but with the salary I'm making now, I will never succeed."

Another long-run factor is the government's new willingness to tolerate strikes as long as they stay within bounds, in contrast to the harsh repression meted out in the 1980s and early 1990s.

Still the "Workshop of the World"?

The current wave of strikes owes its energy, too, to the lopsided policies China's government adopted in response to the global economic crunch. "With the global financial crisis, the income gap and social disparities worsened," commented Qiao of the CIIR. Panicking at the fall-off in demand for Chinese exports, authorities froze the minimum wage in 2009 even as the cost of living continued its upward march. They also put hundreds of billions of dollars into loans to help exporters and allowed employers to defer their tax payments and social insurance contributions.

Perhaps most important for workers' quality of life, provincial and local governments relaxed their enforcement of labor regulations—at a time when examples of hard-pressed businesses closing down and cheating workers out of months of back pay were becoming increasingly common. In Foshan, a government official declared in 2009 that employers violating the Labor Contract Law protecting basic worker rights would "not be fined, and will not have their operating licenses revoked." A year later, Honda workers in the city walked off the job.

But the business-friendly, worker-unfriendly government response to the crisis does not explain why *autoworkers* went out. "I don't know why the Honda workers went on strike, because their salaries and conditions are better than ours," Chen Jian, a 24-year-old worker at Yontai Plastics, not far from the Nanhai Honda plant, said to the *Guardian* newspaper. "We are not satisfied, but we will not go on strike. Some workers tried that last year and they were all fired. That is normal."

Despite Chen's puzzlement, his comments touch on the reason autoworkers led the way: power rooted in the specifics of the auto production process. Autoworkers wield a degree of skill that makes them more difficult to replace. Assembly line technology within the plant, and a division of labor that often locates fabrication of a particular part in a single plant, make it possible for a small number of strategically located workers to shut down the whole production process, a fact exploited by autoworkers around the world going back to the Flint sit-down strike in 1937. And Japanese-initiated just-in-time techniques have cut down inventories, speeding up the impact of strikes. Friedman reports that by the fourth day of the Nanhai strike, work at all four Honda assembly plants in China had ground to a halt due to lack of transmissions.

Pundits have speculated on whether the Chinese workforce's new demands will upend China's export machine. Andy Xie, a Hong Kong-based economist and business analyst formerly with Morgan Stanley, remarks, "To put it bluntly, the key competence of a successful [manufacturer] in China is to squeeze labor to the maximum extent possible." But in fact, Chinese manufacturing wages had already begun rising significantly in the years before the crisis—in part because of earlier strikes and protests. Some companies had already begun relocating work to Vietnam or

Bangladesh. Most observers, including Xie, expect incremental adjustment by businesses, not a stampede. Limited worker demands could even play into the Chinese government's goal of increasing productivity and shifting into higher value-added manufacturing, as well as expanding the buying power of Chinese consumers. But as James Pomfret and Kelvin Soh of Reuters write, China's Communist Party "has faced a policy tightrope. It must also ensure that strikes don't proliferate and scare investors or ignite broader confrontation that erodes Party rule."

"Taking the Same Boat Together to Protect Growth"

Where was the All China Federation of Trade Unions as the working class rose up? Friedman points out that though ACFTU leaders were concerned about defending worker interests in the crisis, they were equally concerned with defending employers' interests. The result was what the ACFTU called "mutually agreed upon actions," which combined promises to desist from job actions with what Friedman describes as "weakly worded requests for employers." "Taking the same boat together to protect growth," a joint March 2009 release by government, unions, and the employer association in Guangdong, was typical, imploring businesses to "work hard" to avoid layoffs and wage cuts—an appeal that seems to have had little real impact on employers.

This ACFTU stance grows directly out of the federation's longstanding focus on "harmonious enterprises," which is rooted in the unions' historic role in state enterprises. "Each trade union is under the control of the local Party branch," Lin Yanling of the CIIR told us. "So, Party, company, and union leadership are often the same." Indeed, the ACFTU typically invites companies to name their union officials; as a result, middle managers often hold those posts. Along the same lines, Shanghai Normal's Liu Cheng stated, "These company unions don't work. They have nothing to do but entertainment. In the summer, they buy watermelon for the workers to celebrate the festivals." Lin Yanling concluded, "Now is the time to change trade unions in China!"

Recommendations for change circulating within China vary widely. "Some local trade union leaders say to reform the trade union, you must sever the relation between the trade union and the local Party branch," said Lin. "If the local union would only listen to upper trade union officials, the problem could be solved." Local state and Party representatives are particularly closely tied to the local businesses, whereas the national officialdom has more often advocated for workers' interests, for example through the new 2008 labor laws. He Zengke, executive director of the Center for Comparative Politics and Economics, expressed support for shifting control to the national level: "Local government has historically supported business, but the [Party Secretary] Hu government is now asking them to pursue a balanced policy—also pro-people, pro-poor."

But Lin is skeptical of this limited fix, arguing that "if you want the unions to change, you need the workers to elect the trade union chairperson." Liu Cheng agrees, but also advocates for unions to have the right to litigate on behalf of workers. Liu argues it is premature to push for the right to strike, whereas Zheng Qiao of CIIR holds that this is a good opportunity to define that right. Qiao Jian of CIIR advocates democratizing unions within a revitalized tripartite (union federation/

employer association/government) system, but his colleague Lin insists, "That system will not function," because the unions don't yet have enough independence within the triad to adequately represent workers. The disagreements are passionate, if good-humored, since these scholars see the future of their country at stake.

Western observers, and some Hong Kong-based worker-rights groups, have gone farther to call for the right for workers to form their own independent unions— what the International Labor Organization calls "freedom of association." But labor relations experts within mainland China, and the strikers themselves, have so far steered clear of such radical proposals. Liu Cheng commented, "Without reform of the unions, I think freedom of association would result in disorder, and destroy the process of evolution. I don't like revolution—with most revolutions, there is no real progress, just a change of emperors." However, he did express the view that as the Chinese labor movement matures, it will reach a point when freedom of association will be possible and desirable.

"If People Are Oppressed, They Must Rebel"

But *will* the unions change—and will the Party and state let them? The question is complicated by the conflicting currents within the union federation itself and within China's official ideology. The same Party that promotes "harmonious enterprises" also enshrines Mao Zedong's dictum, "It's right to rebel." So perhaps it's not surprising that Li, a young striker at Honda's exhaust plant, told Agence France-Presse, "Safeguarding your own rights is always legitimate .... If people are oppressed they must rebel. This is only natural."

ACFTU responses to date, reported by Friedman and labor activist and blogger Paul Garver, reflect this mixed consciousness. At the Nanhai Honda strike that inaugurated the current wave, the local ACFTU leadership sent a group of 100 people with union hats and armbands to persuade the strikers to stand down. Whether by design or not, the conversation degenerated into a physical confrontation in which some strikers were injured, none severely. On the other hand, provincial-level union leaders then agreed to the strikers' demands to elect their own representatives. The top two Guangdong ACFTU officials, Deng Weilong and Kong Xianghong, subsequently spoke out in favor of the right to strike and pledged to replace current management-appointed officials with worker-elected ones.

When workers at the Denso (Nansha) car-parts factory in Guangzhou (also in Guangdong province) later went on strike, the local union response was different from that in Nanhai. The municipal union federation publicly supported the strikers, refusing to mediate between labor and management. There have even been signs of life from unions in other sectors: about a month after the Nanhai strike, the municipal union federation in Shenyang, in the far northeast of the country, hammered out the nation's first collective bargaining contract with KFC (whose fast-food restaurants blanket China), including a wage increase of nearly 30%.

On the government side, authorities in many provinces have responded to the strike wave with a wave of minimum-wage hikes. Premier Wen Jiabao declared in a June address to migrant workers, "Your work is a glorious thing, and it should be respected by society," and in August told the Japanese government that its companies operating in China should raise wages. Acknowledging that "a wide range of social conflicts have occurred recently," Zhou Yongkang, another top Party official, stated, "Improving people's livelihoods should be the starting and end point of all our work." In August, *BusinessWeek* reported that Guangdong's state legislature was discussing a law formalizing collective bargaining, empowering workers to elect local representatives, and even recognizing the right to strike—particularly noteworthy since Guangdong is China's industrial heartland. Still, pro-worker rhetoric is nothing new, the Guangdong provincial union federation is more progressive and powerful than most, and right around the time of Wen's June speech the Chinese government shut down a website calling for ACFTU democratization.

Amidst these cross-currents, China's labor relations scholars, aware that their own role is "marginal," as one of them put it, remain cautiously optimistic. "I think the situation will lead to union reform," said the CIIR's Zheng Qiao. When asked how activists in the United States can support the Chinese workers, her colleague Lin suggested, "Ask the big American brands to give a larger percentage back to the workers at their suppliers!" At Shanghai Normal, Liu Cheng reasoned through the prospects for change. "If the ACFTU does not do more, there will be more and more independent strikes, and in the end some kind of independent union. So the ACFTU will be scared, and the party will be angry with the ACFTU."

"So," Liu Cheng concluded, "the strike wave is a very good thing." ❏

Sources: Eli Friedman, "Getting through hard times together? Worker insurgency and Chinese unions' response to the economic crisis," paper presented at the International Sociological Association annual conference, Gothenburg, Sweden, July 2010; LabourStart page on China labor news, www.labourstart.org; James Pomfret and Kelvin Soh, "Special Report: China's new migrant workers pushing the line," Reuters, July 5, 2010; "The right to strike may be coming to China," *Bloomberg Businessweek*, August 5, 2010; ITUC/GUF Hong Kong Liaison Office, "A political economic analysis of the strike in Honda and the auto parts industry in China," July 2010.

Article 4.3

SOUTH KOREAN LABOR FACES REPRESSION

A "tiger economy" takes up battering rams against its unions.

BY DAN READ
May/June 2007

Last fall, South Korean riot police, along with hired "security" armed with claw hammers and battering rams, smashed their way into multiple offices of the Korean Government Employees Union (KGEU), dispersing or arresting the union staff and members inside and then sealing the offices shut. The crackdown against the KGEU—really, an all-out attempt to remove the union from the political landscape—is the latest flare-up in a long history of state and state-endorsed repression of independent trade unionism in the country.

By October 10th, despite stalwart resistance from union members, around 125 KGEU offices had been shut down, with many unionists arrested and some hospitalized.

The crackdown provoked a quick backlash from organized labor as a whole. On November 15, the Korean Confederation of Trade Unions (KCTU) declared that it would engage in a strike and subsequent actions if the state-sanctioned campaign of repression was not halted. When the government failed to respond, the KCTU followed up its threat with a nationwide four-hour warning strike involving around 138,000 workers.

The initial strike proved to be only the catalyst to a general strike a week later on November 22, with around 200,000 workers nationwide staying off the job and some 50,000 workers from varying industries taking to the streets in Seoul alone. Unions and labor rights supporters in at least 30 countries participated in coordinated solidarity actions that day as well. Demanding an end to government oppression against the labor movement and changes to new legislation on temporary and contingent employment—legislation that increases the already endemic vulnerability of certain sectors of the workforce—Korean workers stepped up the pressure with demonstrations in front of the National Assembly and further strikes.

This upsurge in union militancy is nothing new in a country whose workers have endured a long history of hostility from the state. The recent struggles highlight several ongoing problems afflicting Korean labor: continuing insecurity, an expanding share of the workforce confined to temporary labor contracts, and government and employer hostility toward trade union independence.

Prosperity at a Price

Despite its turbulent history, South Korea today—home to the eleventh largest economy in the world—is widely viewed as one of the most successful Asian nations. In contrast to its northern neighbor and to its own recent periods of undemocratic rule, the country has been held up by the Western media as a model of free market liberalism and prosperity. Dubbed one of Asia's "tiger" economies that grew spectacularly from the 1960s onwards—and in turn created a large working-class population—Korea has found a niche in the global economy producing and exporting agricultural produce and a range of competitively priced consumer goods.

Casual observers might believe that South Korea's embrace of "free-market" economic policies and its adoption of a Western parliamentary system have led to political liberty and economic abundance for all. Look beyond first impressions, though, and it's clear that the country's newfound prosperity is not widely shared among ordinary Koreans, many of whom face destitution, insecure employment conditions, and overwork. Out of a national workforce of just under 24 million, around eight million are "irregular" workers who endure shockingly long hours and poverty wages. What prosperity does exist is monopolized by a small propertied elite making up far less than 10% of the total population. The insecurity and inequality that characterize the country's economy have generated widespread dissent among workers—dissent which the South Korean republic in its varying forms has had a shameful record of dealing with via repression and intrigue.

Trade unionism, perhaps the most important form of this dissent, often faces attack on the grounds that independent trade unions, such as the currently persecuted KGEU, are illegal. This illegal status has its roots in the government's desire to rein in the labor force and ensure that labor market conditions remain favorable to employers. While this is arguably the case in any capitalist country, South Korea's dependence on foreign investment, on access to foreign markets, and on imports of raw materials—unlike the North, the South has little in the way of natural mineral resources—has led the state to impose a particularly severe set of policies aimed at controlling the country's workforce in the name of bolstering economic development.

In its efforts to cut labor costs and ensure a business-friendly economic climate, the government has employed all possible means to try to keep a lid on union organizing. In 2002, for instance, the government showed its displeasure at the founding of the KGEU by sending police to break up the union's inaugural conference; police arrested over 100 delegates, forcing the remaining membership to finish laying the groundwork for the union in secret.

In the face of the mounting uproar over the repression of the KGEU, the ruling Roh administration has often claimed it wishes to help public employee unions transform themselves from illegal organizations—or, more to the point, organizations refusing to comply with current policy—into legal ones. In reality, though, this would entail the independent unions being dissolved, then re-founded as entirely different groupings which would be straitjacketed into complying with what they see as unfair industrial laws. And, of course, the government's offer to "assist" unions like the KGEU has to be viewed in light of its willingness to use force to terrorize and subdue those who refuse.

Exploiting "Irregular Workers"

As the contingent sector of the workforce has grown, demands for labor law reform to improve conditions for temporary and other contingent workers have intensified. Last fall, key unions negotiated an agreement with the government to modify its proposed legislation so as to strengthen the protections afforded temporary workers. But then, on November 30, the government pushed a different bill through the National Assembly—one without any of the agreed-upon changes. The result: a controversial and unpopular piece of legislation, the "Irregular Workers Act," which now serves as a prime example of the kind of policy that the country's independent unions aim to combat.

In essence, the new law makes it *easier* for an employer to fire temporary workers. Like the "first employment contract" law proposed in 2006 in France, recalled in the face of mass protests in the streets of Paris, and like similar contracts forced on contingent workers elsewhere, the new law is designed to guarantee employers "flexibility" when it comes to hiring on contracts of less than two years. The French proposal would have permitted bosses to fire workers under age 26 without compensation or appeal if they had worked for the company for less than two years; likewise the Korean version, except that it affects the majority of the national workforce, young or otherwise.

A Future of Solidarity

Despite calls from labor organizations—both domestic and foreign—for the South Korean government to reverse its hostility to the labor movement, the environment of repression and persecution remains essentially the same. Still branding various unions as illegal, and still unwilling to repeal the hated law on irregular workers, the current administration remains steadfast in its desire to keep organized labor in a straitjacket.

What is clear is that the rapid growth of the "Asian tiger" economies, including South Korea, has a steep price. Emerging into a world of extreme competition and risk, newly developed countries find themselves in a frenzied struggle among nations for markets typically already dominated by established powers. Caught up in this process, the working class finds itself smothered and sidetracked, exploited to produce the cheapest goods for foreign consumption. In this environment, workers' struggles to stake a claim to the political terrain become all the more vital, as does the fight to ensure that their organs of defense, such as the unions, remain independent and committed to representing the interests of their members. And international solidarity can mean the difference between victory or defeat when it comes to defending workers' rights. The defense of the workers of South Korea will be no different. ❑

Article 4.4

THE ASSAULT ON LABOR IN CANANEA, MEXICO

BY ANNE FISCHEL AND LIN NELSON

September/October 2010

The actions taken in collusion between Grupo México and the Mexican government are an outrage. And if they can crush this very effective, independent union ... all independent unions in Mexico are at risk. And then other countries that are watching can say, "Well, if they can do it there, we can do it here too." And so I think that ... a union that is fighting for safe working conditions, fighting for decent treatment of the ... workers in those mines, if we can't stand behind that as a global labor movement, we're in trouble.

> —Leo Gerard, president, United Steelworkers Union

On the night of June 6, 2010, more than 3,000 federal and 500 state police descended on the city of Cananea, Mexico (population 32,000), 30 miles south of the Arizona-Mexico border, where Section 65 of the Union of Miners and Metallurgical Workers (the Mineros) has been on strike for three years. They drove workers out of the mine, pursued them to the union hall, and gassed all who took refuge inside, including women and children. Several people were injured in the melee and at least five miners were arrested.

The attack on the workers of Cananea was a bitter turn in the prolonged David-and-Goliath struggle between a proud union and a powerful transnational copper mining company, Grupo México, backed by a neoliberal Mexican government. The miners are striking to restore health and safety protections guaranteed by their union contract and to mitigate environmental damage to their region and community. More fundamentally, they are fighting for the survival of independent Mexican unions—for the power to organize, and protect workers and their communities from corporate abuse.

Fighting for the Right to Health and the Right to Strike

Grupo México doesn't respect the lives or the dignity of workers. It doesn't invest in safety or in reducing pollution. It is not interested in the hygiene of its worksites and it is not interested in rights or collective agreements.

> —Napoleón Gómez Urrutia, general secretary, Union of Miners
> and Metallurgical Workers

The Mineros union is at the forefront of an international movement defending workers and communities against neoliberal incursions. Although the U.S. media has largely ignored the Mineros' struggle, the strike has drawn global support from unions, including the United Steelworkers, the main union at Grupo México's U.S. plants. Steelworkers president, Leo Gerard, was quick to denounce the Mexican government's action, calling it "a reign of terror for the workers."

Grupo México became notorious in 2006 for its role in the Pasta de Conchos mining disaster in Coahuila, Mexico, in which 65 members of the Mineros union were killed. In the months leading up to the massive explosion in the mine, workers repeatedly warned of dangerous conditions, including a build-up of explosive methane gas. They were ignored by the company and by regulating agencies charged with overseeing mine safety in Mexico. On February 19, 2006, the mine blew up. Napoleón Gómez Urrutia, general secretary of the Mineros, accused Grupo México of "industrial homicide," and called for an investigation. Gómez was already well known for his opposition to neoliberal labor reforms and his focus on international labor solidarity. Under his leadership the Mineros forged alliances with the Steelworkers (United States and Canada) and with Grupo's key union at its Peruvian mines, the Federation of Metal Workers of Peru.

After Gómez Urrutia denounced the state's complicity in the Pasta de Conchos explosion, Calderón's government removed him from his leadership post. Gómez was charged with mishandling union funds and forced to flee to Canada, where he now lives as a guest of the Steelworkers. After an independent audit by a Swiss accounting firm exonerated Gómez and the union, Mexican courts threw out the charges and Gómez was officially reinstated as general secretary. Despite this, the government continued to seek his extradition, but Canada repeatedly refused. The Mineros refused to accept government control of their union and have re-elected Gómez Urrutia six times. In the United States, the AFL-CIO denounced Gómez' ouster as part of "the continuing suppression of the independent labor movement ... by the Mexican government."

In Cananea the Mineros have been on strike since July 2007, when 1,300 workers walked off their jobs citing dangerous health and safety conditions and contract violations that threaten the health and safety of the community. The violations were thoroughly documented by the Maquila Health and Safety Support Network (MHSSN), a bi-national group of occupational health experts who toured the mine in fall 2007. Among their findings: piles of silica dust, which can cause silicosis and lung cancer; dismantled dust collectors; and inadequate ventilation systems, respirators, and auditory equipment. MHSSN's report documents "a workplace being deliberately run into the ground" where workers are "exposed to high levels of toxic dusts and acid mists, operate malfunctioning and poorly maintained equipment, and work in ... dangerous surroundings."

Since then Grupo México and the union have waged a prolonged legal battle, as the company sought repeatedly to have the strike declared invalid. Under Mexican constitutional law, strikes must be honored unless invalidated by the courts; as long as union workers are striking, companies cannot hire replacement workers or resume production. In January 2008, the courts briefly sided with the company, and police ousted the workers from the mine. Helicopters bombed strikers with tear gas; police beat them with clubs; 20 miners were injured. The next day the court reversed its position and upheld the strike, forcing Grupo México to withdraw from the mine.

In February 2010, two and a half years into the struggle, the Supreme Court again declared the strike invalid, and terminated the union's contract. Mexico's Political Coordination Board, a governing body of the National Chamber of Deputies, urged the government to "avoid the use of public force against the strike movement" and instead consider revoking Grupo México's ownership of the Cananea mine concession "given their persistent refusal to resolve, by means of dialogue and negotiation, the strike that this mine's workers maintain." The Board called for a 30-day cooling-off period followed by negotiations. Looking broadly at the struggles against Grupo México at all its mining sites in Mexico, it called for a "legal, comprehensive and fair solution to the Cananea, Sonora, Sombrerete, Zacatecas, and Taxco, Guerrero miners' striking conflicts, within a frame of respect to the rights of unions' autonomy, strike, collective hiring, safety and hygiene and all other labor rights." Hoping that the Political Coordination Board's recommendations would win out, the workers continued to press their demands.

Imposing a Company Union on a Community

In May 2010, we traveled to Cananea with a delegation of labor educators and activists to meet union members and the Women's Front (the Frente) that works in solidarity with them. We stayed in the homes of mining families, met with union and Frente leaders, and were taken on a tour of the vast open pit mine. During the tour we saw for ourselves some of the conditions that impelled the miners to strike. We talked with Cananea's mayor about the state of the city's economy and with the head of the local hospital about Grupo México's problematic health and safety record. We returned to the United States prepared to support the growing movement of global solidarity that has coalesced around the Mineros. Two weeks later the government sent in the police, rupturing the constitutional protections that undergird Mexican labor law.

In a 2008 report the International Metalworkers Federation wrote, "The line between the Mexican government and Grupo México has remained blurry since Calderón took office ... and the two have worked in concert to plan and execute the assault on los Mineros." In fact, Mexico's ruling party, the Partido del Acción Nacional (PAN), has long pursued an openly neoliberal agenda. One of President Calderón's legislative priorities was to fundamentally restructure the relationships between labor, capital, and the state. Since winning the presidency for the first time in 2000, the PAN has championed the dismantling of contractual protections for workers. In Mexico, the process is known as "flexibilization," which allows companies to hire temporary and part-time workers without benefits or job security, and subcontract out jobs previously held by unionized workers. Grupo México has played a leading role in implementing flexibilization; as the Mineros explained to us, all of the union locals at Grupo's mines have been under assault, and several have been replaced by a *sindicato blanco*, a company union. In the days following the police incursion at Cananea, Grupo announced that all the strikers were welcome to return to work, as long as they agreed to join the *sindicato blanco*. With the mine secured, Grupo México, Minister of Labor Javier Lozano, and Sonora Governor Guillermo Padres quickly unveiled a new partnership: Grupo México will invest $120 million to rebuild and expand the mine, while the state will invest almost $440 million in new infrastructure and aid for economic development in Cananea.

Cananea's Place in Mexican History

The struggle for workers' rights is not new to Cananea. The city holds a special place in Mexican history. In June 1906, Mexican miners walked off the job, demanding equal pay with their U.S. co-workers. Their U.S. employer sent for Arizona vigilantes who fired into a crowd of striking miners, killing 23. The massacre in Cananea created outrage throughout Mexico and helped start the Revolution of 1910. The city is proud of its revolutionary and working-class history. Visitors are welcomed by a sign, "Cananea: the Proletarian City," and in one of the older neighborhoods, the "Neighborhood of the Martyrs of Cananea," streets are named for miners who died in the 1906 struggle. To millions of Mexicans, Cananea symbolizes their nation's long and incomplete struggle for political and economic independence, while the union is a standard-bearer in the battle for workers' rights.

The rights to organize and strike were written into the Constitution of 1917 and codified into labor law in 1931. The Mexican Constitution also charges the government with safeguarding resources essential to national development. Mining is high on the list, as are railroads and oil. In the 1960s, the government purchased the Cananea mine from its U.S. owner in accordance with Constitutional law. But in 1988, facing a debt crisis and a rapidly devaluing currency, then-President Salinas agreed to privatize state-owned industry. The concession to operate Cananea was auctioned off to a group of wealthy cronies, who created what is now Grupo México. While Grupo México is a relatively young company, its origins lie with one of the oldest U.S. miners, the American Smelting and Refining Company, or ASARCO (see box).

Undermining Health, Wasting the Environment

> Environment is the last thing that Grupo Mexico cares about. We see the destroyed mountains; we see the contamination; the acids in the atmosphere, the dust which is toxic to the people. [But] all GrupoMexico wants is the metal. To destroy, take the profits and leave the city in ruins, that is what they want.
> —Dr. Luis Calderón, medical director, El Ronquillo Hospital, Cananea

When Grupo acquired the Cananea mine in 1989, it immediately began to dismantle the historic social contract with the workers and the community. It closed the Workers Clinic, a well-equipped hospital run by the union and subsidized by the company, where miners and their families received treatment, including maternity and pediatric care. This left only the Ronquillo Hospital, a tiny, aging medical center owned and administered by the company. In 2008, in the midst of the strike, company officials summoned hospital personnel and announced the closure of the hospital. The company refused to pay for gasoline to transport dialysis patients to Hermosillo, four hours away; instead, hospital employees had to ask passersby for donations to buy gasoline. The community was left without access to health care. Dr. Calderón, the hospital's medical director, said, "They are stingy. They are exploiting a very rich mineral and there are positive things they could do to support the people. Instead Grupo Mexico has taken away all the benefits we used to receive in Cananea." The state of Sonora has since reopened the hospital, though at a very basic level of service.

Grupo México and ASARCO: A Case Study of a Corporate Shape-shifter

Grupo México began as ASARCO Mexicana. From its 1880s beginnings ASARCO operated mines in Mexico. ASARCO helped open Mexico to U.S. investment and economic control. ASARCO's mines produced fabulous wealth for its U.S. owners, while ASARCO's railroads trekked Mexico's ore across the border to ASARCO's smelters and refineries. At one time ASARCO had over 95 U.S. mines, smelters, and refineries, as well as holdings in Mexico, Chile, Peru, Australia, the Philippines, and the Congo.

In 1998, plagued by aging plants, contaminated sites, and the plunging price of copper, ASARCO put itself on the market and was purchased by its former Mexican affiliate. In 2002 ASARCO sold its lucrative Peruvian subsidiary, Southern Peru Copper, to its new owner, shifting its most potent assets across the border to Mexico. In 2005, ASARCO filed for Chapter 11 bankruptcy, citing lack of assets and environmental liabilities as the primary causes. The most prolonged and complex environmental bankruptcy in U.S. history was finally concluded in late 2009, when the company settled its claims and Grupo México regained control, over the strenuous objections of the Steelworkers. This closely watched bankruptcy left many communities struggling to complete remediation projects with modest funds; Texas State Senator Eliot Shapleigh called it an environmental test case for corporate polluters, while the Government Accounting Office warned of a precedent that could encourage corporations to use bankruptcy to evade the public trust.

After ASARCO was sold to Grupo México, workers at the Hayden, Arizona, plant complained about inadequate training for employees working with industrial chemicals and hazardous equipment. Workers reported that stocks of safety equipment were consistently low, and even gloves and toilet paper were often unavailable. In interviews conducted in summer 2006, workers told of accidents caused by inadequate training, fingers lost because of poor lockout procedures, broken limbs, and a co-worker who was electrocuted when the power was improperly shut down. The local union's president, Tony Mesa, told us, "You're like a number; you can be replaced. That's not part of the agreement when you hired on that I'm going to leave part of my fingers here or I'm going to leave my arm or my leg or my life."

Grupo México now proposes to consolidate ASARCO and Southern Copper Corporation into a single entity. This Mexican-U.S.-Peruvian conglomerate is well-engineered for today's global economic landscape, able to shift assets and investments across borders, dedicated to eliminating obstacles to profits, and relying on international financial instruments and compliant governments for backup. It is this corporate shape-shifter, and the threat it represents to workers and communities, that the Mineros are fighting in Cananea.

During our visit the Mineros warned of the dangers that mine wastes pose to Cananea's air and water supply and to the region's watershed. The town is bordered on the northwest by the ever-expanding mine and on the east by a valley filling up with mine waste. Cananea maps show the valley area as a leachate lake, or reservoir, into which chemicals used to separate copper from its impurities are drained. Mountains of mine wastes, known as "halis" or tailings, loom on the outskirts of the city. When the winds blow, the top layers of the tailings drift through town, often ending up as a fine powder inside residents' homes. We were told that on windy days the sky is grey and thick, and waste materials blow as far north as the Arizona border. Local historian Arturo Rodriquez Aguero says, "On a bad day, you can't see the mountains at all." Increasingly the town is being swallowed up as the mine and the leachate lake continue to expand.

When Grupo took over the mine it promised to provide electricity and water to the community as the government and previous corporate owners had done. Instead, the company refused to pay the town's electrical bills and demanded exclusive use of the majority of town wells. This left the city with an inadequate water supply and distribution system. The city is building new wells, but this will take time; for now, the majority of residents use the Sonora River, which is contaminated by mine wastes, for their household needs, including drinking water—or purchase purified water, if they can afford it.

There is growing concern about the movement of mine wastes through the San Pedro River watershed, which begins in Cananea and flows 140 miles north to its confluence at Winkleman, Arizona, site of an ASARCO smelter. The San Pedro has one of the most diverse bird populations in the United States, including 100 species of breeding birds and 300 species of migrating birds. Agustín Gómez-Álverez reports, "Acid mining drainage from mine tailings is currently reaching a tributary of the San Pedro River with heavy metals and sulfates in water and sediments." Cadmium, copper, iron, manganese, lead and zinc have become fluid parts of the regional ecosystem.

"With the Support of Our Friends"

The Minero's strike has been broken, at least temporarily, but the struggle continues. The attack in Cananea is only the first wave in the corporate/state onslaught against workers' rights and unions in Mexico. Eleven days after the government sent in the police, Gammon Gold, a Canadian company, fired 397 union workers at its Mexican mine, citing the "relentless distractions of union labor disruptions." According to the *Financial Post*, the company said the Labor Ministry's support of Grupo México has "emboldened other miners to take decisive action against the union."

As Grupo's profits mount ($337 million in the last quarter), the Mineros continue to fight. They rely on the support of a growing international movement. The Steelworkers union has a steady presence in Cananea and is working with the Mineros to create an international alliance to strengthen workers' rights. The International Federation of Chemical, Energy and Mine Workers has sent delegations to Cananea. The International Metal Workers Foundation has published two white paper reports about the Mineros' struggle; the IMF supports the findings of the independent International Tribunal on Trade Union Rights, which met for over a year to consider the growing crisis of labor in Mexico. In its May 2010 report, the Tribunal questioned "the illegal sentence that has terminated the employment relationship ... between workers and the company." The Tribunal condemned the "partiality" of the Mexican government which appeared "as if acting on behalf of employers," and expressed concern about "the continuing use of force to end labor disputes." It concluded, "Repeated use of force and abuse of the law could lead to social upheaval and social unrest, and to the closure of legal avenues to resolve labor problems."

On July 9, the Superior Court of Justice of the Federal District of Mexico dismissed the arrest warrant against Napoleon Gómez Urrutia, removing any legal base for a case against him. And amidst the frenzy of the World Cup in South Africa, the National Congress of Mineworkers and the Coalition of South African Trade Unions mobilized an international demonstration of support for the Cananea miners. These signals of support give hope to the Mineros in their ongoing struggle. Sergio Lozano, secretary of the Cananea local told us, "You help us overcome the barrier of the border. In the past this didn't happen so much. It makes a big difference."

Just as in 1906, the miners of Cananea are standing against the abuses of unregulated corporate power backed by a compliant state. As a recent email from a union member stated, "We have lost a battle, but our struggle continues. We remain hopeful that with the international support of our friends and allies, we can persist and win."

Postscript

On August 11th, two months after the federal police seized the mine, the Ninth District Judge in Sonora ruled that the Mineros' strike was still in existence and once again legally recognized. The judge found that the federal Attorney General and Secretary of Public Security had the authority to send police to inspect mine installations, but not to remove the strikers. The judge has granted a temporary injunction barring Grupo Mexico's replacement workers and the police from the mine until a permanent court ruling can be made. At least one replacement worker died in a mining accident and an estimated 25 have been injured on the job. As this article goes to press 800 miners and their supporters are waiting outside the gates to once again take control of the mine. ❏

Sources: Judy Ancel, "Mexican Government Threatens to Open Mine by Force," *The Cross Border Network*, June 2010; Barr, Heather et. al., "Workplace Health and Safety Survey and Medical Screening of Miners at Grupo México's Copper Mine, Cananea, Sonora, Mexico, *Maquiladora Health and Safety Support Network*, www.igc.org/mhssn, October 5–8, 2007; Garrett Brown, "Genuine Worker Participation—An Indispensable Key to Effective Global OHS," *New Solutions: A Journal of Occupational and Environmental Health*, 2009; Garrett Brown, "International OHS Through the Looking Glass of the Global Economy," *EHS Today*, January 2008; Gómez-Álvarez, Augustín, et al. "Estimation of potential pollution from mine tailings in the San Pedro River (1993-2005), Mexico-U.S. border," *Environmental Geology*, vol. 57, #7, 2009; "Hasta La Victoria: Napoleon Gómez Speaks," speech to ITUC, June 29, 2010, www.mua.org.au; International Metalworkers' Federation, "Report of IMF Fact Finding Mission to Mexico," July 2006, www.solidaritycenter.org; International Metalworkers' Federation, "An Injury to One: The Mexican Miners' Struggle for Union Independence." March 2008, www.imfmetal.org; International Metalworkers' Federation, "International Tribunal on Freedom of Association condemns Mexican government policies," www.imfmetal.org; Interview with Dr. Calderón, El Ronquillo Hospital, Cananea, Mexico, May 2010; Interview with Tony Mesa, Phoenix, Arizona, July 2006; Mara Kardas-Nelson, Lin Nelson, and Anne Fischel, "Bankruptcy as Corporate Makeover: ASARCO demonstrates how to evade environmental responsibility," *Dollars & Sense*, May/June 2010; Gerald Markowitz and David Rosner, "Deceit and Denial: The Deadly Politics of Industrial Pollution," UC Press, 2002; Ingrid Zubieta, "Cananea Copper Mine: Is it Safe for Workers?" NIEHS presentation, 2009; Ingrig Zubieta et al., "Cananea Copper Mine: An International Effort to Improve Working Conditions in Mexico," *International Journal of Occupational and Environmental Health*, 2009.

Article 4.5

COLOMBIA: BUILDING GLOBAL WORKER SOLIDARITY

BY AVIVA CHOMSKY

December 2007—WorkingUSA

For the past ten years, international solidarity organizations have been working with Afro-Colombian and indigenous communities displaced and affected by the giant Cerrejón coal mine in northern Colombia. Initiated by Exxon in the 1980s, the mine was sold to a consortium made up of three of the largest multinational mining companies in the world: BHP Billiton (Australian), Anglo-American (British-South African), and Glencore (now Xstrata, Swiss). Almost all of the coal is exported, primarily to the United States, Canada, and Europe.

The mine is located in Colombia's poorest province, La Guajira. The people who live there are Wayuu indigenous people—Colombia's largest indigenous group—who have maintained their language and culture over the 500 years of Spanish conquest, and Afro-Colombian and mestizo peasants, many of them descendants of communities of escaped slaves who settled there in the eighteenth century. La Guajira enjoyed little infrastructure or state presence. Most of the inhabitants farmed small plots, hunted, fished, and worked as day laborers on larger farms or ranches until the arrival of the mine began to inexorably devour their land and contaminate their air and water.

The open-pit coal mine employs mostly skilled workers who come from the immediate area. Not until 2006 did the union at the mine, Sintracarbón (the National Union of Workers in the Coal Industry), take note of the operation's effect on the communities. In August of that year, the union's president met with a Witness for Peace delegation that was investigating the impact of the mine on the local communities. He was shocked by the stories he heard from the international delegates and community members, and invited representatives of the solidarity organizations to return in November to help build relations between the union and the communities, and support the contract negotiations scheduled to begin that month.

It was a courageous step for Cerrejón's workers to reach out to the poor and marginalized communities that are in many ways victims of their employer's very existence. It was even more courageous—in some ways unprecedented—when workers voted to include a demand in their bargaining proposal that the company recognize the collective rights of the affected communities to negotiation, relocation, and compensation—three things the company has been adamantly denying.

International supporters organized to support what was a path-breaking and important commitment by the union to use the collective bargaining process to press the company on issues of human and community rights. We formed an International Commission in Support of Sintracarbón and the Communities Affected by Cerrejón (ICSSCAC). We requested—and received—a meeting with the mine's president during our November delegation, at which we delivered a fat folder of letters from unions, NGOs, and elected officials around the world demanding that the company negotiate in good faith with the union, and acknowledge the rights of the communities.

The union sent us daily updates on the negotiating process, which we distributed widely. We organized actions at the headquarters of the three companies that own the mine, and pressed some of the energy companies that purchase the coal in the U.S. and Canada to express their desire for a peaceful, fair, and negotiated solution.

What follows is a selection of correspondence between the union and the international support group leading up to, and during, the entire process. It reveals the union's growing commitment to the communities, and the importance of the international support and publicity we were able to provide during the negotiations. All of us felt that we were creating something new and exciting, and full of potential at a time when labor movements worldwide are struggling against extraordinarily unfavorable local and global environments.

José Arias is one of the new leaders of Sintracarbón. He is currently Interunion Secretary. In his union work he has focused on the social issues facing the Guajira people and he has struggled tirelessly for a more just and equitable treatment for the villages in the vicinity of the mine.

Jaime Delúquez Díaz is President of Sintracarbón and a member of the executive committee of the International Federation of Chemical, Energy, Mine and General Workers' Unions (ICEM). He has been an untiring leader in the struggle to create a new Colombia based on principles of social justice.

Freddy Lozano Villarreal is from Barranquilla, Colombia. He has been a union leader in Sintracarbón for twelve years, and is currently Secretary General of the Puerto Bolívar section. He is forty-eight years old, and has worked for El Cerrejón for twenty-one years.

Jairo Quiroz Delgado is a community social psychologist and is currently Secretary of Media and Publicity for Sintracarbón. He has been involved for many years in human rights struggles.

Field Communication

September 15, 2006
Dear Avi,

The National Union of the Coal Industry "SINTRACARBON" is preparing to present a negotiating proposal to the corporation Carbones del Cerrejón. Our proposal contains some basic points for discussion including the health, education, and welfare of the communities in the mining region, the workers' lack of economic resources, and other issues.

Avi, we know about your commitment, and that is why we are asking you to join with other supporters to accompany us in this conflict, so that we can carry out a field project together with the workers and the communities in the area of the mine that are affected by the coal operation.

Fraternally,
Jaime Delúquez
President, Sintracarbón

◆◆◆

NATIONAL AND INTERNATIONAL DECLARATION ON THE IMPACT OF THE CERREJON MINE EXPANSION ON THE COMMUNITIES IN THE MINING AREA

During the week of October 30 to November 3, 2006, a delegation of the National Union of Coal Workers (Sintracarbón) worked together with several international NGOs and the Wayuu indigenous rights organization Yanama to investigate the living conditions and health conditions in the communities in the area of the Cerrejón mine.

The delegation met with the communities of Patilla, Roche, Chancleta, Tamaquito, Albania, and Los Remedios, as well as the indigenous resguardo of Provincial and the displaced population of Tabaco. It carried out health clinics, conducted a public health survey, and listened to testimonies and life stories in all of these communities.

These communities are being systematically besieged by the Cerrejón company. The company begins by buying up the productive lands in the region surrounding the communities, encircling each community and destroying inhabitants' sources of work. . . The United Nations has established categories of "poverty" and "extreme poverty," but these communities have reduced to the conditions that we could call the "living dead." They do not have even the most minimal conditions necessary for survival. They are suffering from constant attacks and violations of their human rights by the Cerrejón company—a systematic process of annihilation to create despair so that they will negotiate from a position of weakness, desperation, and hopelessness, and agree individually to the company's terms.

Each of these communities has been reduced to a zone of misery. They have no schools, hospitals, or basic public services. Their water supply is unfit for human consumption. We also saw evidence of many cases of respiratory diseases, skin infections, mental health problems, and arthritis.

Upon finishing this stage of the investigation we conclude that the reality is far worse than we had imagined. The multinational companies that exploit and loot our natural resources in the Cerrejón mine are violating the human rights of these communities.

Sintracarbón has committed itself to the struggle of the communities affected by the mine's expansion. We invite all other unions and social organizations in Colombia and especially in the Guajira to join in the struggle of these communities for better conditions and quality of life and to take on the communities' problems as our own problems.

As a union committed to the struggle of these communities, we have established the short-term goal of working to help unify the affected communities, to participate in their meetings, to take a stand with the local and national authorities regarding the absence of public services in the communities, to begin a dialogue with the company about the reality we are now aware of, and to take a public stand locally, nationally, and internationally about the situation of the communities affected by the Cerrejón mine and its expansion.

SINTRACARBON STANDS WITH THE STRUGGLE FOR JUSTICE FOR THE COMMUNITIES AFFECTED AND DISPLACED BY THE CERREJON MINE! ¡¡¡¡SINTRACARBON PRESENTE!!!!

◆ ◆ ◆

Barranquilla, November 8, 2006
Compañera Avi Chomsky
Warm greetings:

All of us here in the Guajira would like to thank you and the members of your international delegation who we had the privilege of accompanying in the important task of bringing a voice of hope to the members of the communities surrounding the Cerrejón mining complex.

Beginning now we as a union are proposing that just as the company has a social responsibility for the way it runs its business, our union has a moral and political responsibility before the destruction that the Guajira communities are suffering at the hands of Cerrejón. The company generates huge profits through the misery, poverty, and uprooting of these populations. The communities have to pay a very high price for the company's profits.

—Jairo

◆ ◆ ◆

Excerpt from Sintracarbón bargaining proposal, presented to the Company on November 20.
CHAPTER XI

NEW ARTICLE 16. SUPPORT FOR SINTRACARBON'S PROGRAM IN SUPPORT OF THE COMMUNITY:
Upon the signing of this Contract, the Employer will support Sintracarbón's program in relation to the communities, aimed at bettering the quality of life in the Guajira Department.

FIRST PARAGRAPH:
Upon the signing of this Contract, the Employer will carry out improvements on the road from Cuestcitas to Riohacha according to the norms established by the Ministry of Transportation.

SECOND PARAGRAPH:
Upon the signing of this Contract, the CERREJON company, in accordance with international law and the Colombian constitution with respect to indigenous and Afro-Colombian communities, will implement and carry out a policy of RELOCATION and INDEMNIZATION for all of the communities affected by the coal complex.

CHAPTER XII
NEW ARTICLE 18. FORUM ON COAL POLICY:
Upon the signing of this Contract, the Employer will finance the organization and implementation of a forum about coal policy that will allow for the dissemination of information about the environmental, socio-economic, and health impacts of mining on the communities in the region.

◆◆◆

Communiqué 28
STATEMENT TO THE PUBLIC
Sintracarbón denounces the intransigent position that the Cerrejón company has been taking before our just bargaining proposal that we presented on November 20, 2006. During 31 days of negotiations the company has not presented serious responses, nor have they showed the will to negotiate.

We summarize below the most important points of our bargaining proposal:

* HEALTH: Among the company's workers there are approximately 700 who are currently suffering health problems. Their health coverage is being permanently altered with the complicity of Colombia's health plans (EPS Coomeva and ISS ARP), with the blessing of the Colombian state.

* EDUCATION: The high cost of education, the privatization of the education system, and the disappearance of the public universities, make it impossible for workers' sons and daughters to gain access to higher education without putting an enormous burden on their economic situation.

* WAGES: The most recent labor law reforms, Laws 50 and 789, along with the loss of purchasing power because of inflation, have reduced Colombian workers' salaries, and Cerrejón workers have not been immune to these problems. This situation has plunged many of our workers into insolvency.

* TEMPORARY WORKERS: We are asking that all workers in the Cerrejón coal complex be contracted on a permanent basis. Temporary workers are exploited; their fundamental rights are continually violated. Cerrejón has ignored this situation.

* COMMUNITIES: As a consequence of the expansion of the mining operation, neighboring communities like Patilla, Roche, Chancleta, Tamaquito 2, Provincial and Los Remedios have been turned into ghost towns. They have lost the capacity to survive through herding, farming and fishing. They have not had the opportunity to collectively negotiate reparations for the loss of their cultural patrimony, the loss of their ancestors, and everything else. The towns of Tabaco, Manantial, Caracolí, and others, have been abused and their human rights violated. These communities were displaced from their natural environment.

LONG LIVE OUR JUST BARGAINING PROPOSAL! DOWN WITH THE INTRANSIGENCE OF THE MULTINATIONAL BOSSES!
LONG LIVE THE STRUGGLE, ORGANIZATION AND UNITY!

◆◆◆

Communiqué 35
January 16, 2006; calling for a strike vote
In addition to labor demands, our petition includes social demands, such as those regarding subcontracted/temporary workers, and those regarding communities.
The communities near the mine, and the communities displaced by the mine's expansion, also have the right to collective negotiations. All of the communities should be relocated, preferably in conditions better than their current conditions. They should be paid compensation for the loss of their cultural patrimony, the loss of their ancestors. The current approach of individual negotiations should be halted.

◆◆◆

January 20, 2007, the union reported the results of the strike vote:
Strike vote results:
Out of 3,100 members, 2,421, or 76%, voted. 2,382, or 98% of those voting, voted in favor of a strike.

◆◆◆

Communiqué 44
STRIKE IMMINENT AT EL CERREJON

In spite of the Cerrejón mine's enormous profits in recent years, with the selling price of coal over $60 (USD) a ton, and with 28 million tons of coal in sales last year, the company has refused to come to a negotiated agreement with our union. During 45 days of negotiations the Sintracarbón negotiating committee has reiterated its desire to come to an agreement that would satisfy the workers' needs as expressed in our bargaining proposal. During the entire negotiating period Cerrejón has said nothing but NO to the needs that our union has expressed.

IF WE ARE FORCED TO STRIKE, WE WILL STRIKE! FOR OUR JUST BARGANING PROPOSAL! UNITY, ORGANIZATION, AND STRUGGLE!

◆◆◆

January 23, 2007
Message from Freddy to Avi
Avi, I just want to say a thousand thanks for the torrent of solidarity we have received, letters which in addition have gone to the company. Today we feel that we are no longer alone. I would like to ask you for one more thing, a message from the International Commission that I can read to the delegates in the meeting that we are holding in Riohacha on Thursday the 26th. It would be very important for the people at the meeting to hear a message of support from the international community. Again, thank you and we are not alone!

◆◆◆

January 24, 2007
Message from the International Commission
Many of us met Sintracarbón in August 2006, when the union's president, Jaime Delúquez, accepted our invitation to participate in an International Conference that we organized in Riohacha on the impact of mining in the Guajira.

The conference included international delegates, academics, members of NGOs, unionists, and representatives of communities affected by El Cerrejón.

We are an international coalition of people and organizations that feel involved, one way or another, in coal mining. Some of us are from the US and Canada, where we import large amounts of Colombian coal for our power stations. Others are from Australia, Switzerland, and England, the countries where the multinationals that own Cerrejón have their headquarters. Some of us are from regions affected by the same multinationals that have investments all over the world. Some are members of unions that are struggling for the same thing Sintracarbón is struggling for: the right to decent work, with decent pay and benefits.

But we are also aware that our struggles depend on others' struggles. We want decent work–but we also want to create a world in which everybody has the right to decent work and a decent life. We want to have electricity–but we don't want it to be produced at the cost of displaced communities and murdered unionists.

In our November delegation to accompany Sintracarbón, in which we visited the communities affected by the mine, we saw clearly that the Cerrejón workers shared our goals. Just as they committed themselves to finding a way to support the rights of the communities, we committed ourselves to supporting our collective struggle for a mining industry that respects the rights of everyone involved.

This is why we created our International Commission to support Sintracarbón in its negotiations, and this is why we today reiterate our strong commitment to maintain and strengthen our support for the union and for the communities affected by Cerrejón. Another world is possible, and we hope that together we can continue to create it.

◆ ◆ ◆

Communiqué 50
Today, Wednesday, January 31, the negotiating committees of Cerrejón Llc and Sintracarbón finished the revision and redaction of the new Collective Bargaining Agreement. At 3pm the two parties signed the Agreement, which will be in effect for the period 2007-2008.

We believe that the results show a positive outcome, according to our fundamental objectives in the negotiation, from the perspective of wages, educational benefits, social welfare and social security, subcontracted and temporary workers, and communities. In addition, Sintracarbón recovered its capacity for mobilization and its credibility in the local, national, and international spheres, as well as its capacity for struggle and mobilization of its members. ❑

Article 4.6

THE GLOBAL CRISIS AND THE WORLD LABOR MOVEMENT

BY DAN LA BOTZ

Summer 2009, New Politics

The world's working people face the greatest challenge in three generations. The economic crisis that began in the banking institutions of the United States last year has rapidly spread around the globe, creating a financial and industrial disaster. In one country after another, banks have failed, corporations have gone bankrupt, and millions around the world have lost their jobs. Governments from the United States to Europe to Asia and Latin America have responded by putting up trillions in one form or another to save the banks, to stabilize endangered corporations, and to stimulate their economies. Many nations have spent billions to create public works programs and have expanded unemployment benefits and new social programs, though no one believes that these begin to adequately deal with the problem. Working people around the world face all that goes with a crisis: joblessness, poverty, hunger, sickness, depression, drugs and alcohol, domestic abuse, and a rise in criminality, and worst of all, the fear for their future and their children's.

The Economic Crisis

The financial collapse triggered a more profound general economic recession, what is in its fundamental features a classic overproduction crisis. Underlying what seemed to be simply the collapse of a financial bubble is a more fundamental problem, the decline of the rate of profit in manufacturing. This is not simply a minor cyclical recession, but rather it is as Marxist economists such as Anwar Shaikh argues, a genuine economic depression that will be severe and long-lasting. The fall in the rate of profit in manufacturing led some investors to move into real estate and finance in search of higher profits, resulting in the bubble. With the burst of the bubble, the broader and deeper economic crisis in industry has been revealed. We now appear to be entering a classical depression, likely to be accompanied by deflation, that will last until enough capital has been destroyed through the elimination of outdated plants and equipment, to once again attract investors.

If this does prove to be a deep and long lasting depression that is feared by some, that will shape and condition the nature of working class response. During the Great Depression of 1929-1939, it took four years before workers in the United States began to organize and fight back, creating a new labor movement and reshaping American politics. The depth and length of that economic crisis led to a new social compact, but also to the reincorporation of labor into the Democratic Party. Whether this crisis will also produce a working class response, and whether this time America's working people will be able to create their own political party, will only become clear in the next few years.

The central preoccupation for the labor movement is unemployment, the seriousness of which has been recognized by various international organizations. The International

Monetary Fund's January 28 news release read: "World Growth Grinds to Virtual Halt, IMF Urges Decisive Global Policy Response." "The ILO message is realistic, not alarmist," said Juan Somavia, Director General of the ILO, "We are now facing a global jobs crisis." The Organization for Economic Cooperation and Development (OECD) said in Paris at the end of March 2008 that the economies of its 30 developed member nations would contract 4.3% overall that year while unemployment across its bloc will reach 10.1% by the end of 2010. The OECD also predicted unemployment in the Group of Seven (United States, United Kingdom, France, Germany, Italy, Canada, and Japan) would reach 36 million by the end of 2010. China alone, according to some experts, could lose 50 million jobs just among its internal migrant workers. Unemployment in March was 4.4% in Japan, 10% in Indonesia, 12% in Russia, and 20% in Spain.

Working People Unprepared

Working people are hardly prepared to face this crisis. The working class does not have independent organizations with which it can fight for itself and for society at large. The so-called parties of the working class—Democrats, Labour, Socialist, and Communist—long ago gave up their role as the champions of wage labor. Labor unions in most countries have long been subordinated to capital and government, and have become thoroughly bureaucratic and unresponsive to workers' needs. In some places company and gangster unions dominate the scene, while in other countries the so-called unions are really state institutions created to control workers.

Ideologically, the mass media, government institutions, and religious organizations have convinced many working people that capitalism has no alternative. In some countries the experience of bureaucratic communism or neoliberal social democracy has given socialism a bad name. And, in terms of their capacity and willingness to struggle, the working class in most counties with some very important exceptions—Latin America and China—has not gone into motion yet. The crisis spreads like a tsunami washing away the institutional gains of decades, destroying organizations, and threatening all in its path, yet in many places the workers do not even have an organization to help them retreat to higher ground in the face of the rising water.

Not Your Great-Grandparents' Capitalism

This is not your great-grandparents' capitalism. Capitalism in the twenty-first century is, more than ever, a world system. Since the 1930s the world capitalist system has changed in several ways, all of which affect both the nature of the current crisis and the response of the working class. Capitalism has expanded, and its penetration of peoples, states, and regions of the world has deepened. At the same time, almost everywhere the system has reduced government social welfare budgets and reorganized social welfare programs. In the course of these developments, capital also transformed its relationships to unions in the workplace and to labor parties in society.

How did all of these changes come about? With the end of World War II, the process of decolonization began in Africa and Asia as former colonies became independent nations, now open to new investment and trade relationships. The fall of communism in the Soviet Union and Eastern Europe by the early 1990s also opened up that region to private capitalist investment from the West. The collapse of communism in the Soviet Union, China's evolution to a capitalist economy, and the opening up of India's economy have brought about what Thomas L. Friedman called "the great doubling" of the world capitalist labor force, adding 1.3 billion workers.

Capital simultaneously reconfigured itself, organizing world production both through multinational corporations and through extramural buyer-supplier relations, with many industrial manufacturing jobs moving from developed countries to developing countries. Throughout the post-World War II period, then, capital flowed into these vast new regions, such as Asia, and Eastern Europe which had been thrown wide open to investment. Latin America also saw significant growth in foreign investment. Africa, except for South Africa, for the most part continued to have a post-colonial economy much like the old colonial one with investment in some agricultural export products, oil and mining.

The Expansion of Capital in Asia and Latin America

Most of the capitalist economic growth in the developing world occurred in Asia—countries like Japan, South Korea, Taiwan, Hong Kong, and Singapore—though after 1980 the Chinese communist government began to oversee a transformation to a capitalist economy through the use of state capital, off-shore Chinese capital, and investment from countries such as the United States. Within little more than a decade, China had been transformed into the fastest growing capitalist industrial economy on earth, its production largely driven by the U.S. market. India, too, entered upon the path of rapid capitalist industrial development by the 1990s. In Latin America, Brazil grew into one of the world's largest ten economies, with greater industrialization also taking place in Mexico.

During this same period, capitalism changed its methods from the Taylor-Ford model of industrial production, based on scientific management and assembly line production, to the post-Fordist, Japanese or lean production model, sometimes called "management by stress." Production managers in workplaces around the world introduced just-in-time warehousing and parts delivery systems, created workplace quality circles or teams, cut the workforce, and introduced more intense supervision. At the same time, corporations reduced the size of their core facilities and workforces through subcontracting or contracting-out, a strategy which also tended to reduce the role of labor unions and collective bargaining agreement. Japanese and Korean success in the auto industry, later imitated by European and American manufacturers, was largely based on these new production models.

One of the most important new developments in world capitalism, beginning around 1980, was the growth of the worldwide manufacturing model, that is, a manufacturing system based on production of parts taking place in various countries later to be assembled in another nation, and perhaps sold in yet another. The growth of satellites, fiber optic cable, and cell phones, the computerization of communications and of production controls, the development and spread of the inter-modal containerized cargo system adaptable to trucks, trains, ships, and planes, and the creation of a world finance system facilitated by information technology made such a world production model possible.

All three of these developments—the expansion of capitalism to the post-colonial and post-communist worlds, the development of lean production, and the world production model—were accelerated by the appearance beginning in 1980 of the neoliberal economic policy. Margaret Thatcher in the UK and Ronald Reagan in the United States first began to introduce the neoliberal model based on deregulation and privatization, open markets and free trade, tight money fiscal policies, cuts in government social welfare spending, and a concerted attack on labor unions. Later the international financial institutions—the International Monetary Fund (IMF), the World Bank, the World Trade Organization (WTO—formerly the GATT), would use structural adjustment policies to press these measures on developing countries.

The Post-War Arrangement

To understand the labor movement's response to the crisis today, we have to see it in the perspective of the post-war labor and political experience. There was a radical upsurge from below led by the resistance movements in France and Italy in the last years of the war. At the war's end, the Socialist and Communist Parties, however, succeeded in keeping the movement from taking a revolutionary turn. Still, the revulsion against Fascism and Nazism and the conservative political parties in Europe, led the populations to elect the social democratic parties in Western European governments.

While the situations and the timing varied from country to country, the tendency was toward the creation of social democratic welfare states in the post-war period; moreover these institutional reforms in labor relations and social welfare remained intact even when conservatives or Christian Democrats came to power. At the same time, in most Western European nations, the government and political system tended toward the integration of the labor unions into the political system as an electoral apparatus, just as the various forms of social democratic union participation or joint-management schemes integrated the unions into the economic system as junior partners.

The general post-war prosperity of the United States and the consistent improvements in the standard of living in Europe, combined with the welfare state measures, led to a period of relative social stability lasting from 1945 to about 1965 during which the labor unions and labor parties atrophied. In the United States the post-war New Frontier, Great Society, and War on Poverty measures of Democratic presidents John F. Kennedy and Lyndon B. Johnson established a similar though narrower and weaker welfare state in America. By and large, collective bargaining became ritualized as unions traded shop floor control for wage increases, cost-of-living clauses, and health and pension benefits. Automation of the plants in the 1950s and 60s led to a combination of intensified production and the gradual reduction of the size of the industrial workforce.

The Insurgency of the Late 1960s and Early 1970s

When a period of economic crisis and social conflict erupted in the late 1960s and 1970s, a New Left and a new worker insurgency in countries like Greece, Italy, France, Spain, and Portugal, and to a lesser extent in Germany, led the resistance. The French general strike of 1968, the Italian "hot autumn" of 1969-1970, and the nearly revolutionary upheavals of 1974-75 in Spain and Portugal raised the prospect of socialist revolution but proved incapable of breaking the grip of the reformist Socialist and Communist Parties and their labor federations over the largest and most strategic sections of the European working classes. Nevertheless, the tendency toward the absorption of the Socialist and Communists into the parliamentary system as moderate reformers, together with the institutionalization of labor relations, meant that the working class was too weak to stop imposition of the new capitalist order of post-Fordism, world production, and neoliberalism.

The labor insurgencies in the United States and Mexico in the same period found themselves thwarted in the first case by management and the labor bureaucracy and in the second case by the state party and its captive unions. In the United States, rebellions among miners, postal workers, teamsters, telephone workers, and African-American auto workers proved capable of overturning the old bureaucracy only in the case of the miners. In Mexico, the independent unions were created among university workers, established a small foothold in auto parts, and built a democratic current in the Mexican teachers' union. The Democratic Tendency led by the Mexican Electrical Workers, however, went down to defeat at the hands of the Army and the official union in 1975.

Neoliberalism and the Response

Throughout Europe, Japan, and the United States, with competition increasing and profits stagnating, it was the employers who in turn went on the offensive in the second half of the 1970s. The employers launched what shocked union officials called "class warfare," during a decade when every contract negotiation seemed to lead to conflict. When the economic offensive proved insufficient to recoup profits, the employers turned to political measures. The neoliberal period that began in 1980 saw the further political degeneration of left and nationalist political parties around the world. While the Labor, Social Democratic, and Communist parties of Europe had already begun in the pre-World War II or Popular Front period to play the role of reformist parties that would seek to administer the capitalist economy and its state rather than to transform or overthrow them, by the 1980s these parties had become in most cases little more than tepid center-left parties carrying out programs little different than their conservative and liberal counterparts.

The neoliberal offensive had more onerous impacts in other countries. In Mexico the Institutional Revolutionary Party stole the election of 1988 and installed Carlos Salinas de Gortari as president. It was he who privatized virtually all of the state industries except petroleum and power generation. In China in 1989, the Communist government smashed the democracy movement at the Tien An Mien square, a blow to both society at large and to the labor movement in particular.

By the 1990s, the Social Democrats of Europe and President Bill Clinton and the Democrats in the United States now converted to neoliberalism, enthusiastically privatized, deregulated, opened markets, cut the social welfare budget, and restrained labor unions. Consequently, as the working class saw its standard of living decline, its parties and unions lost their support. Throughout the neoliberal period of the 1980s and 1990s, in countries around the world, unions were driven from the halls of government, lost their weight in political party conclaves, and found themselves driven out in the cold. Unions, in fact, became the targets of a concerted attack by government and employers. In the neoliberal world, the union was at best a pathetic dependent and at worst a pariah.

Neoliberal policies affected unions in various ways: closing of older industrial plants often wiped out the strongest labor unions; direct government attacks on unions eliminated others; changes in labor legislation, particularly the promotion of "flexible" labor laws weakened union protections; contracting out (or outsourcing) replaced union workers with nonunion contract workers, while an employers' offensive debilitated unions and eroded contracts. Employers also hired immigrant workers at lower wages, often without benefits and frequently off the books.

While the government and employer attack on unions proceeded, it was often accompanied by a restructuring of production which resulted in a reconfiguration and a recomposition of the working class such that even in developing countries, industry and industrial workers tended to decline, while services and service workers grew, and casual employment multiplied. In developing nations there was a tendency for much of the workforce to become part of the underground economy. In some developing countries as much as quarter, a third, or even half of all workers labored in the informal economy without social security (health and pension), without labor unions, and without paying taxes. As the process advanced, workers often found job security imperiled, wages falling, and benefits diminishing. All of this was accompanied, of course, by a gradual and general decline in the standard of living of workers. Social inequality grew and poverty increased in developing countries.

During this period the ties between government and Communist, Social Democratic, Labor, nationalist, and populist parties and their respective labor federations were weakened. Whether in the former Soviet Union, Indonesia, or Mexico, the government-party-union connection—a connection often built on patronage and rife with corruption—was severed. In several countries—including the United States, Mexico, and Venezuela—under the pressure of events, the old political labor federations cracked up, rival labor federations multiplied, and in some cases the unions were virtually pulverized. Unions which once found strength through their ties to a leftist party that for long periods of time controlled one or another government, now found themselves cut loose from both government and party and set adrift in the choppy economic seas.

In most countries, during this period, unions suffered damaging attacks and sometimes crushing defeats. At the same time, in Bolivia or India for example, new social movements arose, sometimes calling themselves "unions," but representing not the industrial working class or government employees, or service workers, but rather groups such as the unemployed, the self-employed, the landless, the indigenous, and women. New unions for casual workers arose in Japan, Korea, and India. Combinations of the old unions, the new movements, the indigenous groups, dissident military factions, and old left political parties created new political forces, especially in Latin America, where massive struggles eventually brought some of them to power in one or another country.

Latin America: The Neoliberal Trend Resisted

The situation was different in Latin America from that in other parts of the world. The disappointments in democratization and the failures of the economy in the 1980s and 1990s led to the rise of social movements, political parties, and candidates that opposed neoliberalism and the Washington Consensus. Latin Americans resisted neoliberalism in various countries through a series of national general strikes, popular uprising, and attempted coups. By the late 1990s the struggle found expression in political campaigns. The continental shift to the left can be seen clearly in the series of elections over the last decade which brought to power in seven Latin American nations a series of presidents with politics described as ranging from populist, to social democratic, and, in some cases, some claim, revolutionary socialist.

In Venezuela, Hugo Chávez, a charismatic military officer and coup leader, was elected in 1999 and reelected in 2000 and 2006. He proclaimed a struggle for a Bolivarian socialism, what he calls "socialism for the twenty-first century." Chávez has won support from sections of organized labor, mobilized Venezuela's poor, and used the nation's oil wealth to finance campaigns—the Bolivarian Missions—to bring health, education, and welfare to the nation's needy. He has worked to build unity among Latin American nations to resist the United States. Chávez has in the past few years created the United Socialist Party of Venezuela (PSUV) and the National Union of Workers (UNT) as political instruments of his government's power. A charismatic populist whose methods involve a combination of direction from above and mobilization from below, Chávez's Bolivarian Revolution has been paused but not paralyzed by a reactionary bourgeois opposition, the power of the United States, and the vicissitudes of oil prices. More democratic forces with other visions of socialism tend to operate within the broad chavista movement rather than outside of it.

Ignacio "Lula" da Silva, a former steel worker, organizer of the Metalworkers Union, then of the Brazilian Labor Federation (CUT), and of the Workers Party (PT), has pursued more cautious and traditional economic programs. His government has been aligned with the banks and big construction companies, kept its support of the CUT and PT, and created a welfare program for the nation's poor. In the international arena, he has formed an alliance with China and India to block the United States in the World Trade Organization (WTO), and he too has worked for Latin American unity under the leadership of Brazil.

Evo Morales represents the explosion of the indigenous people onto the Latin American scene. An indigenous person himself, the head of a union of coca growers, a self-proclaimed socialist and leader of the Movement to Socialism (MAS), Morales has fought both to keep control of the country's national resources (gas and lithium) and for a national land distribution. His radical program has won broad support from the country's indigenous and poor people of the altiplano and fierce opposition from the European or mestizo people of the lowlands.

Within all of these countries, there exist mass labor and popular movements and revolutionary groupings, though nowhere does socialist revolution appear to be on the immediate agenda. While the most radical situations exist in Venezuela and Bolivia, to be successful there social movements would have to overcome both Chavez's personalistic model and the limits of the petroleum-based economy, while in the second it would have to surpass Morales' cautious pursuit of reform. Neither of those seems highly likely.

China in Crisis

At the new heart of contemporary world production in Guangdong Province, China, the sudden collapse of the American market and other world markets led to abrupt plant closings, layoffs, and in some cases worker protests and riots. China's growth rate fell to 6.8% in the last quarter of 2008, ending five years of growth at 10% or more. The IMF predicts China will grow by only 6.7% this year, though some think growth might only be 5%. Economists say that China needs an 8% growth rate to provide jobs to new entrants to its labor force.

Already by February there were 20 million Chinese without jobs heading home to their villages. "It's expected that 40 to 50 million or more migrant workers may lose their jobs in urban areas if the global economy keeps shrinking this year," wrote Tsinghua University's Professor Yu Qiao in a recent paper. And this does not include the permanent urban residents who will also lose jobs in this downturn. "Jobless migrant workers on this mass scale implies a severe political and social problem," said Yu. "Any minor mishandling may trigger a strong backlash and could even result in social turbulence." According to official Chinese government statistics of 2006 and 2007, the country's manufacturing industry then employed 44.5 million migrant workers and 33.5 million urban residents. The Chinese Academy of Social Sciences asserted in January that the real unemployment rate was 9.4%, and could be expected to rise.

The Chinese Ministry of Security reported that "mass incidents"—such as strikes and riots—numbered 10,000 in 1994, but by 2005, that had risen to 87,000. While the government stopped publishing the statistics, observers believe the numbers have risen even higher. "Without doubt, now we're entering a peak period for mass incidents ... In 2009, Chinese society may face even more conflicts and clashes that will test even more the governing abilities of the party and government at all levels," according to senior Xinhua agency reporter, Huang Huo.

While the state, party, and union ties broke in many countries, in China the Communist Party jealously guards its power and protects the All China Federation of Trade Unions (ACFTU).Yet even in China, the ACFTU has evolved in complex and varied ways and sometimes functions somewhat more independently and sometimes, even if rarely, in one or another situation in defense of workers. The local ACFTU union finds itself both assisted and challenged by independent workers' centers. Whether the state will be able to contain the rising tide will depend on whether or not workers can build labor and political organizations independent of the government, the Communist Party, and the ACFTU.

The Crisis, the Movement, the Left, and the Future

The left around the world finds itself in a difficult position, without in most places a strong socialist organization or a powerful labor movement. History suggests that from the onset of a depression to the beginning of a mass movement it may take years for the working class to absorb intellectually and emotionally what has happened to them and then finally assert their righteous indignation and begin to act. The key to the development of the labor and social movements and of a socialist movement in the United States and in Europe will be, as it was in the early 1930s, the development of militant minorities, ginger groups in the workplace and unions, in communities, and in the various social movements who take actions that challenge the status quo. Militant minorities, acting independently of the labor bureaucracy and of the liberal and Social Democratic parties have the capacity to set larger forces in motion. Once large numbers begin to go into motion, history suggests that that will lead suddenly to the development of new tactics and new strategies and of new political alternatives. We see perhaps the first signs of this in the appearance of the new Anti-Capitalist Party in France.

Even without forces, however, the incipient movement desires to put forward an alternative. The revolutionary left—tarred with the failures and atrocities of both social democracy and Stalinism and recognizing that programs are something to be constructed not proclaimed—hesitates to put forward a full-blown plan which it recognizes that it does not have the arguments to justify, the forces to fight for, or the power to impose. The development of a program will have to come with the development of new socialist left and, more important, of working class and popular movements.

We already begin to see such first attempts to project a program—not yet on a revolutionary basis—in the declarations of the Asia-Europe People's Forum in Beijing and the Social Forum in Belém. Their calls for socialization of finance and industry and for the administration of the economy democratically, raised by movements from below, point toward a possible future. Yet those programs and demands will be meaningless unless the labor and social movements can build the power to push them forward. During this period the revolutionary left, through militant minorities and the development of its programmatic ideas, may be able to lay the basis for revolutionary organizations, and even in some countries to construct a revolutionary party. ❑

Sources: Anwar Shaikh, panel, "What is the Nature of the Economic Crisis," at the Left Forum, New York City, April 19, 2009; Jon Garnaut, "Spectre of 50m job losses looms in China," *The Age*, January 19, 2009; Tania Branigan, "China fears riots will spread as boom goes sour," *The Observer*, January 25, 2009.

Article 4.7

THE STRUGGLE FOR WORKER RIGHTS IN EGYPT
Freedom of association and the right to organize and bargain collectively

BY JOEL BEININ
February 2010; updated March 2011

One of the less noticed events of the "January 25th Revolution," as Egyptians call the popular uprising that ousted President Hosni Mubarak in 2011, was the formation of the Egyptian Federation of Independent Trade Unions (EFITU). The new union federation was announced at a press conference on January 30, 2011 in Cairo's Tahrir Square, the epicenter of the popular movement. The EFITU emerged from a twelve-year upsurge in labor protest that witnessed over 3,500 strikes, sit-ins, and other collective actions involving over two million workers. This taught many Egyptians a crucial lesson: engaging in collective action could achieve something of value.

Workers electing strike committees and debating whether or not to accept strike settlement terms represented some of the most democratic public activities during the Mubarak era. During the September 2007 strike at Ghazl al-Mahalla, the largest textile mill in Egypt, strike committee member Muhammad al-'Attar told a crowd of workers, "Politics and workers' rights are inseparable. Work is politics by itself. What we are witnessing here right now, this is as democratic as it gets." (Liam Stack and Maram Mazen, "Striking Mahalla Workers Demand Govt. Fulfill Broken Promises," Daily Star Egypt, September 27, 2007.) Al-'Attar and others saw the workers' movement as an incubator for substantive—not merely formal—democracy from below.

It is still uncertain whether the January 25th Revolution will achieve this objective. As this article goes to press in March 2011, the generals ruling Egypt seem determined to prevent it. But the EFITU, whose ranks have swelled since Mubarak's ouster, has been among the more prominent forces pushing for more democracy and economic equity.

While it is too soon to say what will come next in Egypt, the article below provides background on the revolution, highlighting labor repression under Mubarak, the weakness of the state-allied Egyptian Trade Union Federation, and the growth of independent worker organization.

—Joel Beinin, March 26, 2011

In 1957 Egypt ratified ILO Convention No. 87 (1948) on Freedom of Association and Protection of the Right to Organize. In 1954 it ratified ILO Convention No. 98 (1949) on the Right to Organize and Collective Bargaining. However, compliance with these conventions was undermined by national legislation, close links between the Egyptian Trade Union Federation (ETUF) and the state apparatus, and intervention in trade union affairs by the security authorities (typically State Security Investigations, which is comparable to the United States' Federal Bureau of Investigation) in resolving strikes or other labor protests and in impeding independent labor organizations.

In 1957 the government permitted the establishment of the Egyptian Workers Federation, which subsequently became the ETUF, under the supervision of the Ministry of Labor (now called the Ministry of Manpower and Migration, or

MOMM) and the security forces. The government's acquiescence came only after it had repeatedly blocked the efforts of rank-and-file union members and democratically elected trade union leaders to form an independent federation. Many trade unionists accepted government supervision of the labor movement in 1957—either because they recognized that there was no other realistic option or because they sincerely believed that this was the best way to secure worker rights. Union leaders of that era and their successors were sometimes able to achieve gains for workers beyond those that the government was inclined to give or to resist policy initiatives that would have undermined workers' standards of living and fundamental rights.

Egypt's economic and political policies have changed substantially since the 1950s, and the ETUF's organizational structure has been modified several times. Although the ETUF is not formally part of the government, it has always been closely aligned with the state. Its leadership has always been firmly in the hands of the ruling party, whatever its ideology or name. Nonetheless, there have sometimes been policy differences and bureaucratic turf battles between the ETUF leadership and other factions of the ruling party. Under Presidents Sadat and Mubarak in the 1970s and 1980s, the ETUF leadership, along with many other trade unionists and citizens, resisted efforts to privatize the public sector. However, the ETUF leadership eventually went along with the Egyptian government in accepting the 1991 Economic Reform and Structural Adjustment Program (ERSAP) proposed by the IMF and World Bank. During the 1990s the ETUF leadership and many other Egyptians also opposed efforts to create what neoliberal economic theory calls a more "flexible" labor market—e.g., the enactment of laws and regulations cutting social benefits and making it easier to fire workers.

The ETUF executive committee or one of its 23 national general union affiliates sometimes stand up for worker rights; local union committees and individual members of local committees sometimes do so as well. But in the great majority of the struggles since the passage of the Unified Labor Law, the ETUF as an organization and its affiliates have effectively failed to defend worker rights.

Unified Labor Law of 2003: No Labor Rights for the Many

In 2003 the government enacted a "Unified Labor Law," which replaced all previous legislation dealing with employer-employee relations. ETUF resistance delayed the passage of the Unified Labor Law for nearly a decade, but it ultimately agreed to the legislation. The law preserved the ETUF's legal monopoly on trade union organization, its hierarchical structure, and the supervision of the ETUF by the MOMM.

One of the Unified Labor Law's most important new provisions permits workers to be hired on fixed-term (often called "temporary") contracts that may be renewed indefinitely. Previously, employers were required to grant workers permanent status after a probation period or dismiss them. Workers on fixed-term contracts are not eligible to join trade unions that may exist in their places of employment or vote in trade union elections. The government no longer routinely appoints workers to permanent positions in public-sector enterprises. In some public-sector enterprises the number of workers on fixed-term contracts is now larger than the number of workers on permanent contracts, even though many of these "temporary" workers have been employed full-time for years. Consequently, the local union committee may not legally represent a majority of the workers in some workplaces. This exclusion gives employers a legal tool to deny fundamental worker rights to a large and growing proportion of their workforce.

The Unified Labor Law has been criticized by many domestic and international rights advocates. According to the Egyptian Organization for Human Rights, it "contravenes both the Egyptian Constitution and international treaties ratified by Egypt. It constitutes a blatant attack on the working class, particularly with regard to contracts, dismissal, wages, workers' right to take strike action, and their representation on the Supreme [Higher] Council for Wages." A 2005 report of the International Confederation of Free Trade Unions (ICFTU) prepared for the World Trade Organization criticized the law in detail, noting its limits on collective bargaining, provisions granting administrative bodies the right to refuse to register a collective agreement, and limits on the right to strike. The ILO Committee of Experts on the Application of Conventions and Recommendations (CEACR) has criticized several aspects of the law, including its limits on freedom of association, collective bargaining, and the right to strike.

Case Study: Repression of Independent Trade Unionism at Ghazl al-Mahalla

The most egregious consequence of the Trade Union Law is that it requires all unions to be affiliated with the ETUF. In response to the efforts of Ghazl al-Mahalla textile workers to organize an independent trade union, Sa'id al-Gawhari, president of the General Union of Textile Workers (GUTW), an ETUF affiliate, reaffirmed that it is illegal to organize a union independently of the single trade union center recognized by the Egyptian state. The ILO CEACR has repeatedly stated that laws requiring all trade unions to belong to a single federation infringe on the freedom of association and violate Convention No. 87.

Strikes in December 2006 and September 2007 at Ghazl al-Mahalla (Misr Spinning and Weaving)—a public-sector firm and one of the largest industrial enterprises in Egypt with about 25,000 employees—were high points in the protest movement and inspired many other workers. As the ultimate employer, the government is directly responsible for repression of independent trade unionism there.

The local trade union committee did not support the December 2006 strike. Therefore, workers demanded that the ETUF executive committee impeach the committee. When the ETUF ignored this demand, some 14,000 workers signed a petition declaring "no confidence" in their trade union committee and demanding its impeachment. About 3,000 went further and sent formal letters announcing their resignations to ETUF headquarters. The ETUF bureaucracy ignored the workers' resignations and continued to deduct dues from their paychecks.

During the September 2007 strike, five members of the elected strike committee were arrested and pressured to reach a settlement behind the backs of their colleagues. They agreed only to submit the proposed agreement to a meeting of workers, who rejected it. After his release from jail, Muhammad al-'Attar told journalists, " We want a change in the structure and hierarchy of the union system in this country. . . . The way unions in this country are organized is completely wrong, from top to bottom. It is organized to make it look like our representatives have been elected, when really they are appointed by the government."

The Struggle for Independent Trade Unions

The 55,000 municipal real estate tax collectors are the only workers so far to have succeeded in establishing an independent union, the result of a protracted struggle that began over economic issues. Their wages were considerably lower than their counterparts employed directly by the Ministry of Finance. So they demanded wage parity and affiliation with the Ministry of Finance instead of the local municipalities.

During the fall of 2007 they organized escalating protests, including demonstrations and refusal to collect taxes. In December they went on strike. About 3,000 municipal real estate tax collectors and their family members sat for 11 days in front of the Ministry of Finance and other government offices in downtown Cairo. The strike ended when Minister of Finance Yusif Butros Ghali granted the municipal tax collectors a bonus equal to two months pay and raised their wages by approximately 325 percent, giving them wage parity with those employed by the General Tax Authority. The campaign of collective actions that led to this victory involved the largest number of workers in the entire wave of protests since 2004 and was the first coordinated mobilization of civil servants across Egypt.

The General Union of Bank, Insurance and Finance Employees (GUBIFE), an ETUF affiliate, did not support the struggle of the municipal tax collectors. Out of 11 local union committees of municipal tax collectors affiliated with the GUBIFE, only the Daqahliyya governorate (province) committee and half of the Giza governorate committee supported the protest. Therefore, the tax collectors elected representatives from each governorate to form a Higher Committee for the Real Estate Tax Collectors' Strike.

Higher Committee decided to remain in existence. Led by Kamal Abu 'Eita, its members resolved to build on their success and create an independent union. During 2008 the committee and its supporters gathered about 30,000 signatures of tax collectors who endorsed the creation of an independent union. Local union committees were elected in the governorates. On December 20, 2008, more than 1,000 municipal tax collectors from all over Egypt met in Cairo and declared the establishment of the Independent General Union of Real Estate Tax Authority Workers (IGURETA). Kamal Abu 'Eita and most of the members of the strike committee, including one elected from each governorate, became the IGURETA Constituent Council.

On April 21, 2009, the Constituent Council, supported by a demonstration of 300 union members, submitted an application to form a union to Minister of Manpower and Migration 'A'isha 'Abd al-Hadi. After intense negotiations, she accepted the application and did not act during the 30-day period during which she could have contested the legality of the new union. The creation of the first independent Egyptian trade union in over half a century was confirmed. The independent press and labor activists believe that 'Abd al-Hadi made this extraordinary decision as a result of her personal feud with ETUF President Hussein Megawer and that the rest of the government supported her in this because it was embarrassed over criticism of Egypt and the ETUF at the 2008 ILO conference and other international forums.

The tax collectors have several advantages over industrial workers like those of Ghazl al-Mahalla. They temporarily suspended collecting taxes and thereby directly threatened the government's revenues. Their independent unionization does not threaten the privatization of public-sector enterprises, and they are not employed by an institution with as much national political symbolism as Ghazl al-Mahalla.

Nonetheless, the ETUF has sought to impede the formation of their union at every step. After ETUF President Hussein Megawer failed to prevent the establishment of the new union, he proposed that the IGURETA affiliate with the ETUF. But the IGURETA leadership rejected this offer and insisted on maintaining their independence. In response, the ETUF pressured the Real Estate Tax Authority to suspend the activities of the IGURETA, and it filed legal complaints with the Public Prosecutor against IGURETA President Kamal Abu 'Eita and IGURETA leaders in the governorates of Qalyubiyya and Bani Suwayf. It accused them of calling for the establishment of the union (this charge is, of course, factually correct).

After the formation of the IGURETA, ETUF dues continued to be deducted automatically from members' paychecks, while collection of dues by IGURETA officials has been impeded. 'Abd al-Qadir Nada, deputy-treasurer of the IGURETA told a respected labor journalist, "Whenever we try fund raising [i.e., collecting dues] for the union, we get investigated for collected [sic] 'illegal funds.'" Moreover, Nada alleged that thugs working for the ETUF-affiliated GUBIFE insulted, slapped, pushed, and kicked Ahmad Abu'l Yazid, the head of IGURETA in Gharbiyya governorate, and IGURETA representative Ahmad 'Abd al-Sabur from Sharqiyya governorate.

On July 27, 2009, the Minister of Finance approved the establishment of a Social Fund for the IGURETA, similar to those of other unions. Its assets would be used to augment the government-established pensions of retirees. ETUF President Megawer opposed this decision and pressured the Minister of Finance to rescind it. Consequently, on August 5 the Minister of Finance effectively reversed his decision and assigned the fund to the ETUF-affiliated GUBIFE. In protest of this decision, on August 11 about 37,000 IGURETA workers throughout Egypt went on strike. The strike was suspended after one day when the Ministry of Finance promised to consider the IGURETA's demands. At the same time, the executive committee of the IGURETA decided to file a complaint against the ETUF with the ILO.

The IGURETA continues to consolidate itself as the representative of the great majority of the municipal tax collectors despite the persistent opposition of ETUF and GUBIFE leaders. Unexpectedly, in this case the Egyptian government has been more willing to tolerate independent unionism than the ETUF.

Another indication that government employees may be better positioned than others to establish independent unions given the current balance of forces in Egypt is the struggle of the 526,000 administrative workers in the Egyptian public school system. These administrators—who manage student affairs, order and distribute school books, organize examination materials, and work in accounting, human resources, and legal affairs departments—have been demanding wage parity with teachers. Like the tax collectors' refusal to collect taxes, a refusal to administer examinations would be a very powerful tool, which the education administrative workers have threatened to use.

Historically, the wages of teachers and administrators were the same (and very low). In 2007 the Egyptian parliament enacted a new teacher pay scale. Since the administrative workers are not classified as "educational staff," they did not receive similar pay increases. The ETUF-affiliated General Union of Educational Services Workers (GUESW) had not supported the education administrative workers. So, following the example of the IGURETA, the education administrative workers formed an independent committee to represent them. The committee organized local strikes in several schools and local education authorities in February and March 2009, a demonstration in front of parliament on March 9, and a national school strike on March 29.

In addition to wage demands, the committee advocates establishing an independent union. This was very likely why the GUESW supported two sit-in demonstrations in front of the ministries of Finance and Education on April 15, 2009. However, official support for the administrative workers was limited.

On August 15, 2009, several dozen members of their committee attempted to stage a sit-in protest in front of the government cabinet offices in downtown Cairo to demand that they receive their incentive pay. Security forces broke up the protest and detained the committee's coordinator, Fawzi 'Abd al-Fattah. He was subsequently banned from travelling to Cairo from his home in the Suez governorate, and the police seized funds he had been collecting to finance the protest movement. He ignored the travel ban and returned to Cairo to continue the protest. This struggle remains unresolved as of January 2010.

Even though they are relatively privileged compared to the education administrative workers, some teachers are also considering forming an independent trade union. They are receiving support and encouragement from an education-oriented NGO, the Egyptian Center for Education Rights.

Postal workers are also threatening to form an independent union. On May 18, 2009, postal workers in Kafr al-Shaykh governorate went on strike for six days after the manager of the Egyptian Post Authority refused to meet a delegation of postal workers from several governorates, even though he had set the time for the meeting. They demanded wage parity with the Egyptian Telecommunications Company (ETC) workers, who earn up to three times as much as the 52,000 postal workers. The postal workers are employed by the same ministry as the ETC workers, but their basic wage has not increased in five years. They also demanded that the 5,000 temporary workers employed by the Postal Authority receive permanent status and complained about a recently adopted performance appraisal system.

The following month, 200 postal workers attended a press conference in Cairo called to air their grievances. Ahmad Hamdi, head of the Fayyum trade union committee told the audience, "We have addressed the general union but unfortunately have had no response." Consequently, the postal workers' leaders at the press conference called for establishing an independent union. IGURETA President Kamal Abu 'Eita addressed the press conference and encouraged the postal workers to form a strike committee and move towards establishing an independent union.

Right to Strike

In April 1987 the government prosecuted railway drivers, who had gone on strike the previous year, in the Cairo State Security Emergency Criminal Court. The court exonerated all the defendants on the grounds that the International Covenant on Economic, Social and Cultural Rights, to which Egypt is a signatory, considers the right to strike a human right. Nonetheless, several strikes that occurred after this ruling—for example, at the Iron and Steel Company in Helwan (1989), and at Misr Spinning and Weaving Company in Kafr al-Dawwar (1994) were repressed with violent, even deadly, force. Although the 2003 Unified Labor Law explicitly legalizes strikes, it is not designed to protect workers' right to strike. The legislation permits a strike if two-thirds of the relevant general union executive committee approves it and the ETUF executive committee ratifies it. These bodies are in the hands of National Democratic Party (NDP) members loyal to the government.

According to the law, after a strike is approved, the union must give the employer a ten-day notice. It must also announce in advance the planned duration of the strike. Indefinite strikes to achieve demands are not legal. Strikes held while collective agreements are in force or during mediation or arbitration procedures are forbidden. These conditions are so restrictive that workers do not have an effective right to strike. Mufid Shihab, the Minister of Legal and Parliamentary Affairs, admitted, "The law in Egypt bans strikes. And this contradicts the international treaties we signed. But strikes must have regulations and guarantees so as not to affect vital state facilities. There are sectors where strikes should not be allowed."

In May 2009, under heavy pressure from workers and public opinion, the ETUF executive committee approved a strike at Tanta Flax and Oil Company. This is only the second strike the ETUF has ever approved as far as all the labor activists and journalists interviewed for this report can recall. The previous one was in 1993, when the General Union of Mining, Construction, and Carpentry supported a national strike of miners.

Case Study: ETUF Indecisively Supports a Strike at Tanta Flax and Oil Company (Kitan Tanta)

Tanta Flax and Oil Co. (Kitan Tanta) was established as a public-sector firm in 1954 and is the largest Egyptian enterprise producing linen, oil, and other flax products. At its peak it employed about 2,500 workers. In February 2005 the government sold the firm to a Saudi investor, 'Abd Allah al-Lilah al-Ka'ki. The current workforce is about 1,000.

Kitan Tanta workers struck (without ETUF authorization) in February 2007 to protest actions taken by the employer in violation of the law—an increase in working hours without additional pay, a reduction in incentive pay by about 50 percent, and introduction of a charge to workers for up to 30 percent of health care costs. As there was no resolution of these demands, there were further protests. Another strike on July 2, 2008 was supported by two (out of eleven) members of the trade union committee—Hisham 'Aql and Ra'fat Ramadan—though the ETUF did not authorize the action. On July 15, 'Aql, Ramadan and five other workers were fired for participating in the strike. The company has refused to implement court rulings finding that these dismissals were unjustified. The government has not compelled it to do so, even though an appeals court ruled on September 17, 2009, that all seven of the dismissed workers must be returned to their jobs.

The workers say that they did not receive their annual pay raise of 7 percent of their basic wage in July 2008 as required by Egyptian law. Moreover, despite the fact that the enterprise is profitable, workers have not received profit-sharing payments since it was privatized. Workers also say that their incentive pay is calculated on the basic wages they received in July 2004 rather than the current wage level; and the company did not increase their meal allowance to E£90 per month, as other firms in the textile industry have done since April 2007. In the spring of 2009 the Kitan Tanta workers resolved to resume their struggle against the much-hated Saudi owner. This time the GUTW and the ETUF executive committee approved a five-day strike beginning on May 31, 2009, in accordance with the Unified Labor Law, which requires that strikes be announced and their length specified in advance. However, the Kitan Tanta strike continued until mid- November and was suspended without a resolution of its major economic demands or the reinstatement of the fired workers.

Kamal 'Abbas, general coordinator of the Center for Trade Union and Workers Services, believes that the GUTW's strike authorization at Kitan Tanta "reflects an awareness on ETUF's part that its existence is under threat. . . . ETUF has really started to become aware of its own alienation, not only from labor leaders but in Egyptian society as a whole. This is a result of its complete submission to, and defense of, the government 's position."

Whatever the ETUF's reasons for supporting the Kitan Tanta workers' demands by authorizing a five-day strike, it ultimately abandoned them. On August 8, 2009, Zayn al-'Abidin Ahmad 'Ali, the ETUF deputy secretary general, attempted to con-vince the Kitan Tanta workers to call off their strike. 'Ali confirmed that ETUF President Hussein Megawer had ordered Sa'id al-Gawhari, President of the GUTW, to end the strike after his discussions with the Minister of Manpower and Migration and the company management. One of the fired strike leaders, Hisham 'Uql, main-tained that management made no firm commitments, only verbal promises. Al-'Uql said that the workers wanted management to negotiate directly with them.

In response to demands that they abandon the strike, Kitan Tanta workers planned a sit-in in front of the MOMM on August 9, 2009, but they had to abandon it because of pressure from the security authorities. However, they showed no sign of calling off the strike. On August 15, after the GUTW stopped providing workers with strike pay, they set up their own independent strike fund. The workers began the strike displaying banners proclaiming their support for ETUF President Hussein Megawer and GUTW President Sa'id al-Gawhari. By August, they had taken down those banners and were literally trampling them underfoot. They rejected an offer from Prime Minister Nazif of a month's pay in exchange for calling off the strike and continued to insist that their demands be addressed. On August 18, 2009, 850 workers proclaimed a hunger strike in Tanta while their colleagues demonstrated in front of the Prime Minister's office in Cairo.

Some workers did advocate returning the firm to the public sector at the start of the strike. Later, however, other leaders said that they did not want the firm to be returned to the public sector, but wanted to manage it themselves. The ETUF, as evidenced by al-Gawhari's statement, is not prepared to consider this position. ❏

Excerpted from "Justice for All: The Struggle for Worker Rights in Egypt," published by the Solidarity Center of the AFL-CIO.

Chapter 5

SEGMENTATION AND DISCRIMINATION
BY RACE, GENDER, AND IMMIGRATION STATUS

Article 5.1

HOW THE GREEN ECONOMY CAN PROMOTE EQUAL OPPORTUNITIES FOR WOMEN

BY JEANNETTE WICKS-LIM
July/August 2009

Create jobs. End the recession. Save the environment. What else can transforming our fossil fuel economy to a clean energy economy do? How about create unprecedented employment opportunities for women? Readers of Linda Hirshman's recent *New York Times* editorial may think this is a dubious claim. She sparked a debate over the gender bias in Obama's stimulus plan by asking, "Where are the new jobs for women?" She makes a good point. Transitioning to a clean-energy economy has the makings of a decent jobs program. Unfortunately, many of these jobs are in male-dominated industries such as construction.

Therefore, the next question we should ask is: "How do we get women into these new jobs?" Women would benefit significantly from gaining access to these male-dominated jobs that pay decent wages. Take for example the $18.72 average wage of carpenters, 99% of whom are men. This wage can cover the basic needs of a small family. Compare this to the $11.48 average wage of preschool teachers, 98% of whom are women. At this wage, a preschool teacher would have to work in excess of 25 hours more per week to support a similar living standard.

In fact, transforming our fossil-fuel economy to a clean-energy economy presents us with an unprecedented opportunity to make real headway in integrating male-dominated workplaces. This is precisely because so many federal dollars will be injected into the male-dominated construction industry.

First, the billions of dollars being injected into the construction industry through the American Recovery and Reinvestment Act (ARRA) can come with strings attached. Currently, construction contracts involving more than $10,000 in federal funds are covered by Executive Order 11246, which requires that contractors adopt affirmative-action goals to reduce the under-representation of women and minorities in their workforce. In other words, the ARRA dollars can be used to coax employers into adopting affirmative-action policies—the only policies that attack workplace segregation head-on.

Second, the federal government's deep pockets can support the very type of construction projects that are most successful at meeting affirmative action goals: large, long-term projects. Large construction projects have the capacity to absorb new workers while keeping adequate numbers of journey-level workers on a construction site. Long-term projects better accommodate the training needs of new workers who need time to develop their skills. An excellent example is the government's funding of high-speed rail corridors; over $8 billion have been committed to creating hundreds of miles of new rail service over the next several years.

Securing increased opportunities for women, however, requires more than just an increase in the reach of federal regulations into industries with a history of discrimination. We also need better enforcement of these regulations by the Office of Federal Contract Compliance Program. More adequate staffing would be a good place to start. We must also fund pre-apprenticeship and outreach programs, as well as wrap-around services (e.g., child care subsidies, mentoring) to increase the supply of qualified women.

It would, of course, be cheaper to simply re-hire currently unemployed male construction workers—not an insignificant fact in the midst of the worst recession since the Great Depression. However, programs such as the Apprenticeship Opportunities Project in Seattle have taught us that publicly funded construction projects can successfully raise the number of female apprentices in their workforce while remaining profitable. In other words, although buying into a tradition of discrimination may stretch our tax dollars further, it is not our only option.

We should not ignore other challenges that women face in the current recession, such as the severe cuts in funding to the female-dominated education industry. At the same time, the Obama administration's commitment to constructing a clean energy economy has put before us the best opportunity yet to integrate women into decent-paying male-dominated jobs. We must seize this opportunity. ❑

Article 5.2

COMPARABLE WORTH

BY AMY GLUCKMAN
September/October 2002

There must be something to an idea that the business press has recently labeled "crackpot," "more government humor," an attempt "to Sovietize U.S. wage scales," and one of ten "dumbest ideas of the century." The idea is comparable worth (or "pay equity"), a broad term for a range of policies aimed at reducing the pay gap between occupations traditionally filled by women and those traditionally filled by men.

Comparable worth proposals first appeared in the 1970s, when women's rights campaigners began to recognize that much of the pay gap between men and women occurred not because women were paid less for doing the exact same work, but because women workers were concentrated in occupations that paid less than male-dominated occupations.

Consider a nurse who earns less than a maintenance worker working for the same employer. (This is typical of the pay gaps researchers uncovered in studies of municipal pay scales in several U.S. cities in the 1970s.) The nurse is responsible for the well-being and even the lives of her patients, and the job typically requires at least two years of postsecondary education. The maintenance worker may have far less serious responsibilities and probably did not even need a high-school diploma to get the job. Why might he earn more? His job may be physically demanding and may entail unpleasant or risky working conditions (although so may hers!). But in many cases, any reasonable evaluation of the two jobs supports the nurse's claim that she should earn the higher salary.

Comparable worth advocates argue that this kind of pay gap is the result of gender bias. Historically, they claim, employers set wages in various occupations based on mistaken stereotypes about women—that women had little to contribute, that they were just working for "pin money." These wage differences have stuck over time, leaving the 60% of women who work in female-dominated occupations (as well as the small number of men who do) at a disadvantage. Studies show that even after other factors affecting wages are accounted for, the percentage of women in an occupation has a net downward effect on that occupation's average wage.

Mainstream economists take issue with this view. How do they explain the persisting wage gap between male-dominated and female-dominated occupations? The market, of course. Wages are not set by evaluating the requirements of each job, they claim, but rather by shifts in the supply of and demand for labor. In this view, the nurse-janitor pay gap represents the outcome of past employment discrimination against women. Discrimination in hiring kept women out of many occupations, resulting in an oversupply of women entering the traditionally-female jobs such as nursing. This oversupply kept wages in those fields low. Not to worry: as gender bias against women wanes and women are able to enter the full range of occupations, some economists argue, this situation will resolve itself and the pay gap between female- and male-dominated occupations will disappear.

As it turns out, the majority of women workers continue to labor within the confines of the "pink-collar" ghetto. Women have indeed entered certain professions in significant numbers over the past thirty years. Physicians were 10% female in 1972, but 27.9% female in 2000. Lawyers and judges were 3.8% female in 1972, but 29.7% female in 2000. But the extent of sex segregation in a wide range of occupations has barely budged during this time. Teachers (K-12) were 70% female in 1972; 75.4% female in 2000. Secretaries were 99.1% female in 1972; 98.9% female in 2000. Hairdressers were an identical 91.2% female in 1972 and in 2000! Retail sales clerks were 68.9% female in 1972; 63.5% female in 2000. On the other side, automobile mechanics were 0.5% female in 1972; 1.2% female in 2000. Plumbers were 0.3% female in 1972; 1.9% female in 2000. (Women moved into a few blue-collar jobs in greater—but still relatively low—numbers. For example, telephone installers were 0.5% female in 1972, but 13.1% female in 2000.) So either employers are still discriminating directly against women to a significant degree, or else the mainstream economists' predictions about the effects of waning job discrimination are wrong—or both.

Another analysis points to the lower wages women earn as the price they pay for choosing jobs that give them the flexibility to fulfill parenting responsibilities. For example, many women (and a few men) choose to become teachers so that they can be home with their children in the late afternoon and during school vacations. But leaving gender aside, do employees typically trade off lower wages for greater flexibility? Higher-paid jobs tend to have more flexibility, not less. If this argument has some relevance for women in female-dominated professions such as teaching, it ignores entirely the vast number of women in low-wage, female-dominated occupations: retail clerk, direct care worker, waitress, beautician. These jobs certainly don't offer their occupants flexibility in return for their low wages.

Conservative commentators also stress that the overall wage gap between men and women—women employed full time, year round earn about 74% as much as men—is reasonable because women on average have fewer years of work experience and less seniority. That's true, but accounts for only about 40% of the gap. That leaves about 15 to 16 cents on every dollar unaccounted for. (Ironically, it is deindustrialization and the resulting decline in men's wages—not growth in women's wages—that has been primarily responsible for the shrinking of the gender wage gap, down from 59% in 1970.)

So the work force continues to be segregated by sex, and women's wages continue to lag behind men's, if not as much as in the past. What can be done? Comparable worth advocates have used a variety of strategies: legislation, lawsuits, collective bargaining agreements. Typically, advocates call for employers to use job evaluation instruments that rate different jobs according to several criteria such as skill, responsibility, and working conditions. Job evaluation instruments like these are not new; many large corporations already use them in their ordinary personnel procedures.

Of course, a job rating scale does not automatically indicate how to weight different factors in determining compensation, and so does not in itself determine how much a job should pay. Usually, this piece of the puzzle comes from information about what employers actually do pay. In other words, these instruments don't exclude the market from consideration. Instead, they usually take market wages for various occupations as baseline data to determine how much value to assign to different job characteristics. Then, however, employees and employers can recognize jobs that fall off the curve—jobs that pay much more or much less than the broad average of jobs with the same rating. On this basis, workers can then push employers to raise the wages of "underpaid" jobs.

The comparable worth movement made a lot of headway in the 1970s and early 1980s, primarily in unionized, public-sector workplaces. However, comparable worth barely made a dent in the private sector. Even in the public sector, the movement's momentum slowed by the late 1980s. Today, Congress is again considering legislation authorizing workers to sue their employers in order to correct pay inequities between male- and female-dominated job titles and also between race-segregated job titles.

Comparable worth legislation, if enacted, could potentially give an enormous boost to low-wage women workers. One study estimates that "among those currently earning less than the federal poverty threshold for a family of three, nearly 50% of women of color and 40% of white women would be lifted out of poverty" by a national comparable worth policy that addressed both race-segregated and sex-segregated occupations.

However, comparable worth is not a cure-all. Since comparable worth typically addresses wage gaps within a single workplace, it does not help workers whose employers pay everyone the minimum wage. Without strong unions, comparable worth won't get very far even if new legislation were enacted; for one thing, it is unions that are most likely to be able to fund the expensive litigation necessary to force companies to revise their pay scales. At a deeper level, existing comparable worth policies largely accept how the U.S. economic system has typically rewarded different job factors. It is one thing to even out pay inequities between jobs that rate the same on existing job-evaluation instruments. It would be far more radical to rebuild our notions of fair compensation in a way that values the skills of caring, communication, and responsibility for people's emotional well-being that are critical to many female-dominated occupations. ❏

Sources: Deborah M. Figart and Heidi I. Hartmann, "Broadening the Concept of Pay Equity: Lessons for a Changing Economy" in Ron Baiman, Heather Boushey, Dawn Saunders, eds., *Political Economy and Contemporary Capitalism: Radical Perspectives on Economic Theory and Policy* (M. E. Sharpe, 2000); "In Pursuit of Pay Equity" in *Women at Work: Gender and Inequality in the '80s*, Economic Affairs Bureau, 1985; Paula England, "The case for comparable worth," *Quarterly Review of Economics and Finance* 39:3, Fall 1999; *Forbes*, December 27, 1999; *Statistical Abstract of the United States*.

Article 5.3

GULF COAST SHIPYARD WORKERS TAKE ON NORTHRUP GRUMMAN

An important strike on the Katrina-ravaged Mississippi coast lacks national labor support.

BY SALADIN MUHAMMAD
September/October 2007

On March 8 of this year, more than 7,000 asbestos workers, boilermakers, machinists, operating engineers, painters, plumbers and pipe fitters, sheet metal workers, carpenters, guards, laborers, and drivers at the Ingalls shipyard in Pascagoula, Miss., went on strike to demand a decent contract. The Ingalls workers are represented by fifteen unions; fourteen of them had voted down the first two contract offers from Northrop Grumman, the corporate owner of Ingalls and the U.S. military's third largest contractor.

Ironically, the Katrina disaster helped to create conditions that forced the Ingalls workers to see the necessity of struggle and solidarity, both for themselves and for ordinary people across the region. The workers "are fed up with what they see as abandonment and neglect of this region," said Ron Ault, president of the AFL-CIO Metal Trades. "Our members are the world's best shipbuilders, living in one of the nation's most devastated areas. Something has got to give."

After a nearly month-long strike—and facing mounting hardships—union members voted on April 4 to accept a contract that gave them only 28 cents more an hour than Grumman had offered in its first two proposals.

Simple reports of a "yes" vote on the contract, however, obscure many workers' deep dissatisfaction with the new contract, and with government complicity in Grumman's exploitation and disaster profiteering. The vote count was 1,370 in favor and 910 against, totaling only 2,300 of the nearly 5,000 members who had voted down the previous contract proposals and opted to strike. The nearly 3,000 union members who did *not* vote represent a silent majority who did not support the contract but who felt that they could not hold out on strike any longer.

The remarkable number of members who abstained from voting also reflects deep demoralization among the workers because of the broader trade union movement's lack of support for their strike. When a strike against a major corporation by workers on the disaster-ravaged Gulf Coast fails to garner national trade union support, that sends all of the region's workers a disheartening message: that the unions have not made the fight for a just post-Katrina reconstruction for working people a key part of their agenda. This lack of national solidarity limits the power of the working class in this region, with serious ramifications for workers throughout the region and for the development of a powerful movement for a just reconstruction.

Corporate Greed and Disaster Profiteering

The Ingalls strike was the first direct challenge to a major corporation on the Gulf Coast following the 2005 Katrina disaster. The workers demanded that Grumman share with them its corporate profits—swollen by the billions of dollars in disaster recovery funds it received from the federal government—to help them address the new economic realities they face in Katrina's aftermath.

Better wages and benefits, the strikers' key demands, are critical in the face of sharp post-Katrina increases in the price of everything from milk to gas to rent, which have brought many families to a financial breaking point. The workers made major sacrifices to restore operations at the shipyard within two weeks after Katrina, enabling Grumman to meet huge multibillion-dollar contract obligations. They felt that their efforts should be rewarded with a contract providing a decent raise as well as the vision and dental insurance coverage that their former contract lacked.

Grumman estimated the Katrina damages to its Gulf Coast operations at around $1 billion. However, the Navy gave Grumman $2.7 billion as an increase on existing contracts to cover recovery costs, and FEMA gave the company an additional $386 million. Out of all of this cash, Ingalls workers only got two weeks' pay. Plus, many had to replace their own tools and equipment even though these were lost or damaged in the flood and should have been paid for out of the recovery funds Grumman received.

The Politicians' Two Cents

By midday on the second day of the strike, the state's senior U.S. senator, Republican Trent Lott, had issued a statement calling for a quick resolution of the strike and saying that it was in the interest of "America's national security to make sure our military has the best tools to protect our nation." Federal mediators pressured the unions to settle. Aware of the pressure President Bush brought to bear on the striking West Coast longshore workers in the summer of 2002, some of the Ingalls workers feared he would likewise try to force them back to work by invoking the Taft-Hartley Act.

And despite the platform offered by their party's control of Congress, no leading Democratic politicians spoke out in support of the Ingalls workers' strike or against Grumman's hard line.

On March 13, close to 3,000 Ingalls workers conducted a six-mile march from the shipyard to downtown Pascagoula and back. The march was called by rank-and-file worker activists as an effort to draw national attention to the strike, and to show the connection between their struggle for a good contract and the struggle of the majority of the working people and communities throughout the Gulf Coast for a just reconstruction.

Silence of the Labor Federations

Throughout it all, the leadership of the AFL-CIO put out no call for national support for the Ingalls strike. Neither did Change to Win, the alternative federation formed in 2005 by the Service Employees International Union, the Teamsters, and several other unions. A number of active leaders of national and local unions, including several who themselves have been involved in major strikes requiring national support, have stated that their union locals were not notified by their national unions or federations about the strike, much less recruited to an organized labor-led campaign to support the Ingalls workers.

Perhaps this lack of support from the top of the union movement for the Ingalls strike should not have come as a surprise. In key respects the national union movement had been absent in August 2005 when hurricanes Katrina and Rita struck, failing to mobilize the power of the unions to demand that the U.S. government carry out an immediate rescue of the thousands of people who were suffering and dying in New Orleans and throughout the region.

AFL-CIO President John Sweeney's June 2006 announcement of the "AFL-CIO Gulf Coast Revitalization Program," a seven-year, $1 billion housing and economic development initiative for the region, while potentially a positive step toward building affordable housing and creating jobs for those most affected by Katrina, cannot shield Sweeney from criticism about the AFL-CIO's failure to build support for the Ingalls strike. Change to Win, which claims to be committed to reasserting labor's voice and rebuilding its capacity to fight back, must also take its share of the criticism.

Lessons Learned?

A year after Katrina struck, one magazine editorialized: "The Katrina catastrophe screams out for a serious alternative program for democratic reconstruction, with social justice." And likewise, the Ingalls strike, exemplifying as it did the struggles that workers throughout the Gulf Coast will continue to face, begs for the development of a major rank-and-file democratic workers' organization as one component of the ongoing reconstruction movement.

Along with substantial allocations of money, a just reconstruction of the Gulf Coast requires the protection of basic rights for workers, women, and historically oppressed communities in the region. Here, one strategy is illustrated by post-apartheid South Africa, where the trade unions conducted a massive "Workers Charter" campaign to fight for inclusion of basic worker democratic rights in the country's new constitution. Workers throughout the Gulf Coast region can mount a similar campaign for the inclusion of a workers' bill of rights within state and local government constitutions and charters.

A majority of the displaced Katrina survivors are Black, as are a disproportionate number of low-wage and blue-collar workers throughout the region—including 60% of the approximately 11,000 non-managerial workers at Ingalls. Black workers were a major force in voting down Grumman's initial contract proposals. Likewise, the leadership of Black workers will be critical to the task of building a powerful movement that brings together the struggle for the right of return for displaced survivors with the fight for a workers' bill of rights for all Gulf Coast workers.

Already some of the organizers and leaders of the March 13 march in Pascagoula are discussing the formation of a Gulf Coast Workers Alliance as a rank-and-file organizing framework, involving other unions, organizing dislocated workers throughout the Gulf Coast, and pushing local struggles out to the wider trade union movement.

But they cannot do it alone. Trade union leaders and labor activists throughout the country must voice criticisms within the labor movement about the national unions' lack of support for the Ingalls struggle and raise awareness about the need to build support for workers and others on the Gulf Coast. Trade union support is needed to help build a Gulf Coast workers' alliance and a labor solidarity network that builds national and international support for workers' struggles on the Gulf Coast. Those in the trade union movement who consider themselves part of labor's left or progressive wing have a special responsibility to help raise these criticisms and develop this support.

The Ingalls strike and the lessons it offers can serve as an important catalyst for building a united and more conscious labor movement and for strengthening the post-Katrina reconstruction movement throughout the region. ❑

The Short Run: Gender Pay Gap Hurts (Some) Men, Too!
November/December 2008

A new Department of Labor study, released in September, suggests that nice guys really do finish last. The study followed the salary histories of 12,000 workers since 1979. Among the results: men with traditional attitudes about gender roles made an average of about $12,000 more per year than men with egalitarian views (and $13,000 more per year than women with egalitarian views). In other words, the gender pay gap may not be just a matter of men versus women, but also of men with traditional ideas about gender roles versus everybody else.

The study's co-authors offer two likely explanations for the results: employers may discriminate against employees with egalitarian beliefs, and men with traditional worldviews may have corollary characteristics that make them more successful. Here's another possibility: traditional-minded men may tend to marry women with similar views who are less likely to have significant careers of their own. Having a homemaker for a spouse would allow these men to focus solely on advancing their careers. Men with egalitarian attitudes, on the other hand, may take on more responsibilities at home, which subtracts time from their professional pursuits.   —*Karina Wagnerman*

Article 5.4

INDIANA AND HONDA MOLD A WHITE WORKFORCE

Honda's new Indiana plant nets the company $141 million in subsidies—and a segregated workforce.

BY ROGER BYBEE
September/October 2008

"**H**onda gearing up for diversity." That was how Bloomberg News headlined its story last March on the opening of a new 2,000-worker Honda plant in the town of Greensburg, Ind., 50 miles southeast of Indianapolis.

The new plant comes with a hefty price tag of $141.5 million in taxpayer subsidies. Still, it will surely provide an economic boost for an idyllic place that National Public Radio noted "could be a movie set for an ideal American small town."

But a boost for workforce diversity? Hardly. Beneath the veneer of corporate doublespeak, Honda's entry into this corner of Indiana raises little-discussed issues of corporate location strategies and race, the role of government policy in reinforcing the exclusion of black workers from job opportunities, and the value of subsidizing corporations whose coffers are already overflowing.

Hiring Inside the Circle

Despite the prize the new plant represents for Indiana, some elected officials and union and civil rights leaders have blasted Honda's hiring policy there as discriminatory, saying it would exclude many black workers and laid-off union members. Why? Hiring at the new plant is limited to Marion County, which includes Indianapolis, along with 19 rural counties whose cumulative population is 96% white.

"This hiring radius is the worst form of discrimination," fumes state Rep. Dennis Tyler. Tyler represents the city of Muncie, which in recent years has hemorrhaged high-paying factory jobs, many held by black residents. "Our constituents pay state income and sales taxes, and therefore they directly helped bring Honda to Indiana through the targeted use of their tax dollars," Tyler and four other legislators wrote to the Indiana Economic Development Corporation, the state agency that pulled together the subsidy package for Honda.

Noting the large number of skilled and experienced autoworkers who are now jobless in central Indiana, the legislators declared, "For any Hoosier to be denied even the opportunity to apply for a position seems grossly unfair."

Honda contends that its hiring radius was established to ensure that workers were not commuting more than an hour, so bad weather would not mean absent workers and production tie-ups. Opponents say that newly hired workers who live far from the plant would likely move closer to Greensburg to avoid long commutes, especially in an era of $4-a-gallon gas.

But Gov. Mitch Daniels—a former Eli Lilly executive who later served as George W. Bush's budget director—and state Commerce Secretary Nathan Feltman were unwilling to challenge the hiring policy. Feltman, who heads up the economic development agency, told the *Indianapolis Star* that "the quasi-governmental agency isn't about to start dictating hiring policy in exchange for incentives."

However, as the *Wall Street Journal* noted, Honda and other carmakers have in fact become accustomed to accepting conditions on hiring and other matters in order to receive substantial incentive packages: "Honda's policy in Greensburg is a departure from the way it and other foreign auto makers have previously staffed plants in the U.S."

For instance, Alabama—long known for its reluctance to regulate corporate conduct—"required the company to consider workers from across the state," the *Journal* reported last October. "We wanted to spread opportunity across our state and wanted plants to be able to hire the best people in the state," explained the director of Talladega County's economic development authority. Hyundai Motor Co. also opened a plant in Alabama, in 2005, and agreed to take applications from anywhere in the state as a condition of the tax subsidy package it received.

George Washington University sociologist Gregory Squires argues that top Indiana officials failed to negotiate hiring terms that would have benefited all residents of the state. "They [Daniels and Feltman] are in a position to dictate over the use of public money," Squires said. "They at least ought to be negotiating the terms and conditions. When you're giving those kinds of subsidies, it's gross irresponsibility not to see that the public's needs are being met. And there ought to be clawback provisions" allowing the state to recover funds from the corporation if it moves the plant away or fails to meet job-creation goals.

Geography and Exclusion

The fight over Honda's hiring policy throws a spotlight on a quietly growing trend: large corporations siting new facilities in rural areas where they can select a workforce that is largely white, conservative, geographically dispersed and thus lacking social cohesion—and, for all those reasons, unlikely to unionize. "When corporations seek out greener pastures, they tend to seek out whiter ones as well, in part because of the presumption of a relatively greater attraction to unions on the part of blacks, in part to avoid equal opportunity requirements … and in part due to the perpetuation of traditional stereotypes and old-fashioned prejudice," Squires noted in his book *Capital and Communities in Black and White.*

"The data on unions is generally that blacks are more likely to join a union if they are able, and blacks, Latinos, and women are less anti-union than rural white workers," notes University of Indiana labor studies professor Ruth Needleman. "In general, when companies go to such rural locations, they do so to avoid people with union experience. At the same time, it is a way to avoid hiring blacks."

This pattern is pervasive, and is particularly evident in Indiana, says Needleman. "The fact is that African Americans do not live in rural Indiana, but the Klan does."

Indeed, the Ku Klux Klan has a long and deep history in Indiana. In the period around 1920, the Klan had a massive following in the state, holding events with crowds of 100,000 or more and claiming the governor and other top state elected officials as members. At that point, anti-Catholicism was the central appeal of the

Klan, but the group spread fierce hatred of blacks, Jews, and unionism as well.

Today, anti-black attitudes remain entrenched in much of rural Indiana. A remarkable 18 of the 20 counties within Honda's hiring radius have black populations of 2% or less. Postcard-perfect Greensburg has a particularly sordid history of racial exclusion. "In 1906, Greensburg's white residents pushed out most of its black population," according to sociologist James Loewen, author of *Sundown Towns: A Hidden Dimension of American Racism*. "By 1960, the entire county, which boasted 164 African American residents in 1890, was down to just three, all female. In the 2000 census, Greensburg still had only two black or interracial households among 10,260 residents." (In 2007, after Loewen wrote a newspaper column exposing Greensburg's past, a reception sponsored by the Indiana State Civil Rights Commission at which Loewen was to speak was cancelled, apparently at the behest of Gov. Daniels' office.)

Despite this history, last year former Mayor Frank Manus defended the town's reputation to the *Bloomington Times-Herald* in terms that reflected the local mindset: "I think there might have been something way back when, but, hell, we don't have anything like that now. We have several colored people who live in the city."

For its part, Honda has a record of siting plants in areas of low black population and imposing hiring requirements that effectively exclude large numbers of black job applicants. The Equal Employment Opportunity Commission under the Reagan administration, not regarded as an aggressive champion of civil rights, imposed a settlement in 1988 under which Honda had to pay $6 million in back wages to 370 black and/or female job applicants in Ohio. As in present-day Indiana, the core issue was a hiring radius that included rural, nearly all-white areas but excluded the city of Columbus with its significant black population. A 1988 study by professors Robert Cole and Donald Deskins found that "based on the population employment potential, one would expect 10.5% of Honda employees at Marysville [Ohio] to be black; in fact only 2.8% are." But in spite of this alarming precedent, Commerce Secretary Feltman said that the hiring radius issue came up only late in talks with Honda over the Greensburg plant.

Honda may have improved its minority hiring numbers following the Ohio case, but the company has made it hard to tell. In 2006, Honda was the target of an EEOC lawsuit initiated by a former diversity manager who claimed the company refused to provide her with data on the racial composition of its workforce. And today, despite Honda's claims to be seeking a diverse workforce for Greensburg, the actual figures on the percentage of black hires remain more closely guarded than Fort Knox. By now the first shift has been hired and trained and is almost ready to begin producing Honda Civics. But Honda declined to give any statistics on minority hiring, claiming only that "HMIN [Honda Manufacturing of Indiana] is extremely pleased that its associate population reflects the overall minority population and diversity of Indiana." Pressed on what this means, company spokesman Andrew Stoner responded, "I will not be able to elaborate further for you."

Commerce Secretary Feltman told *Dollars & Sense*, "We do not maintain hiring information for any companies. You will need to obtain this from Honda." Asked to explain why, given Honda's record in Ohio, the agency was not tracking minority hiring, Feltman responded, "No, you have this wrong—we do not collect data on information on minority hiring at the IEDC. We do have information on hiring as it relates to the job creation promises made to the state of Indiana, of course."

Efforts by state Rep. Tyler to obtain hiring data also proved fruitless, despite the fact that the Honda incentive package includes $50 million coming directly from the state. Tyler has also tried to win passage of a bill to block tax incentives for corporations that would restrict hiring to specific geographic areas. But the bill narrowly lost in the Democrat-controlled General Assembly. "There's a powerful fear factor at work about jobs now," he sighed. ❏

Sources: Wall Street Journal, March 24, 1988, April 12, 1988, and Oct. 10, 2008; *Indystar,* Oct. 1 and 18, 2007; *Greensburg Daily News,* July 22, 2006; *Indianapolis Star,* Oct. 18, 2007; Gregory D. Squires, *Capital and Communities in Black and White* (SUNY Press, 1994); James W. Loewen, *Sundown Towns: A Hidden Dimension of American Racism* (New Press, 2005); Greg LeRoy, *The Great American Jobs Scam* (Berrett-Koehler, 2005).

The Short Run: The Good News and the Bad News
January/February 2009

Employment at the tippy-top is looking good for Black people in the United States, as Barack Obama ascends to the presidency and Roland Burris (finally) settles into Obama's former U.S. Senate seat (net job increase: +1). The job picture for the rest of Black America? Not so good.

The Bureau of Labor Statistics reported a sharp decline in nonfarm payroll employment in December and an increase in the general unemployment rate from 6.8% to 7.2%. Meanwhile, the unemployment rate for Black men over the age of 20 rose from 12.1% to 13.4%. The official jobless rate for Black youth (ages 16 to 19) was even bleaker; it rose from 32.3% to 33.7% in the same period, while the unemployment rate for white youth increased from 18.4% to 18.7%. Find more grim news at bls.gov.   —*Chris Sturr*

Article 5.5

WAGES FOR HOUSEWORK
The Movement and the Numbers

BY LENA GRABER AND JOHN MILLER
July/August 2002

The International Wages for Housework Campaign (WFH), a network of women in Third World and industrialized countries, began organizing in the early 1970s. WFH's demands are ambitious—"for the unwaged work that women do to be recognized as work in official government statistics, and for this work to be paid."

Housewives paid wages? By the government? That may seem outlandish to some, but consider the staggering amount of unpaid work carried out by women. In 1990, the International Labor Organization (ILO) estimated that women do two-thirds of the world's work for 5% of the income. In 1995, the UN Development Programme's (UNDP) Human Development Report announced that women's unpaid and underpaid labor was worth $11 trillion worldwide, and $1.4 trillion in the United States alone. Paying women the wages they "are owed" for unwaged work, as WFN puts it, would go a long way toward undoing these inequities and reducing women's economic dependence on men.

Publicizing information like this, WFH—whose International Women Count Network now includes more than 2,000 non-governmental organizations (NGOs) from the North and South—and other groups have been remarkably successful in persuading governments to count unwaged work. In 1995, the UN Fourth World Conference on Women, held in Beijing, developed a Platform for Action that called on governments to calculate the value of women's unpaid work and include it in conventional measures of national output, such as Gross Domestic Product (GDP).

So far, only Trinidad & Tobago and Spain have passed legislation mandating the new accounting, but other countries—including numerous European countries, Australia, Canada, Japan, and New Zealand in the industrialized world, and Bangladesh, the Dominican Republic, India, Nepal, Tanzania, and Venezuela in the developing world—have undertaken extensive surveys to determine how much time is spent on unpaid household work.

The Value of Housework

Producing credible numbers for the value of women's work in the home is no easy task. Calculating how many hours women spend performing housework—from cleaning to childcare to cooking to shopping—is just the first step. The hours are considerable in both developing and industrialized economies. (See Table 1.)

What value to place on that work, and what would constitute fair remuneration—or wages for housework—is even more difficult to assess. Feminist economists dedicated to making the value of housework visible have taken different approaches to answering the question. One approach, favored by the UN's International Research and Training Institute for the Advancement of Women (INSTRAW), bases the market value of work done at home on the price of market goods and services that are similar to those produced in the home (such as meals served in restaurants or cleaning done by professional firms). These output-based evaluations estimate that counting unpaid household production would add 30-60% to the GDP of industrialized countries, and far more for developing countries. (See Table 2.)

A second approach evaluates the inputs of household production—principally the labor that goes into cooking, cleaning, childcare, and other services performed in the home, overwhelmingly by women. Advocates of this approach use one of three methods. Some base their calculations on what economists call opportunity cost—the wages women might have earned if they had worked a similar number of hours in the market economy. Others ask what it would cost to hire someone to do the work—either a general laborer such as a domestic servant (the generalist-replacement method) or a specialist such as a chef (the specialist-replacement method)—and then assign those wages to household labor. Ann Chadeau, a researcher with the Organization for Economic Cooperation and Development, has found the specialist-replacement method to be "the most plausible and at the same time feasible approach" for valuing unpaid household labor.

These techniques produce quite different results, all of which are substantial in relation to GDP. With that in mind, let's look at how some countries calculated the monetary value of unpaid work.

Unpaid Work in Canada, Great Britain, and Japan

In Canada, a government survey documented the time men and women spent on unpaid work in 1992. Canadian women performed 65% of all unpaid work, shouldering an especially large share of household labor devoted to preparing meals, maintaining clothing, and caring for children. (Men's unpaid hours exceeded women's only for outdoor cleaning.)

TABLE 1
**WOMEN'S TIME SPENT PER DAY PERFORMING HOUSEHOLD
LABOR, BY ACTIVITY, IN HOURS:MINUTES**

	Childcare Time	Cleaning Time	Food Prep Time	Shopping Time	Water/Fuel Collection	Total Country Time[a]
Australia (1997[b])	2:27	1:17	1:29	0:58	n.a.	3:39
Japan (1999)	0:24	2:37	n.a.	0:33	n.a.	3:34
Norway (2000)	0:42	1:16	0:49	0:26	0:01	3:56
U.K. (2000)	1:26	1:35	1:08	0:33	n.a.	4:55
Nepal (1996)	1:28	2:00	5:30	0:13	1:10	11:58

Note: Some activities, especially childcare, may overlap with other tasks
[a] Totals may include activities other than those listed.
[b] Only some percentage of the population recorded doing these activities. Averages are for that portion of the population. Generally, figures represent a greater number of women than men involved. *Sources:* Australia: <www.abs.gov.au/ausstats>; Japan: <www.unescap.org/stat>; Norway: <www.ssb.no/tidsbruk_en>; United Kingdom: <www.statistics.gov.uk/themes/social_finances/TimeUseSurvey>; Nepal: INSTRAW, *Valuation of Household Production and the Satellite Accounts* (Santo Domingo: 1996), 34-35; <www.cbs.nl/isi/iass>.

The value of unpaid labor varied substantially, depending on the method used to estimate its appropriate wage. (See Table 3.) The opportunity-cost method, which uses the average market wage (weighted for the greater proportion of unpaid work done by women), assigned the highest value to unpaid labor, 54.2% of Canadian GDP. The two replacement methods produced lower estimates, because the wages they assigned fell below those of other jobs. The specialist-replacement method, which paired unpaid activities with the average wages of corresponding occupations—such as cooking with junior chefs, and childcare with kindergarten teachers—put the value of Canadian unpaid labor at 43% of GDP. The generalist-replacement method, by assigning the wages of household servants to unpaid labor, produced the lowest estimate of the value of unpaid work: 34% of Canadian GDP. INSTRAW's output-based measure, which matched hours of unpaid labor to a household's average expenditures on the same activities, calculated the value of Canada's unpaid work as 47.4% of GDP.

In Great Britain, where unpaid labor hours are high for an industrialized country (see Table 1), the value of unpaid labor was far greater relative to GDP. The British Office for National Statistics found that, when valued using the opportunity cost method, unpaid work was 112% of Britain's GDP in 1995! With the specialist-replacement method, British unpaid labor was still 56% of GDP—greater than the output of the United Kingdom's entire manufacturing sector for the year.

In Japan—where unpaid labor hours are more limited (see Table 1), paid workers put in longer hours, and women perform over 80% of unpaid work—the value of unpaid labor is significantly smaller relative to GDP. The Japanese Economic

TABLE 2
VALUE OF UNPAID HOUSEHOLD LABOR
AS % OF GDP, USING OUTPUT-
BASED EVALUATION METHOD

Country	% of GDP
Canada (1992)	47.4%
Finland (1990)	49.1%
Nepal (1991)	170.7%

Source: INSTRAW, *Valuation of Household Production and the Satellite Accounts* (Santo Domingo, 1996), 62, 229.

TABLE 3
VALUE OF UNPAID HOUSEHOLD LABOR
IN CANADA AS % OF GDP, 1992

Evaluation Method	% of GDP
Opportunity Cost (before taxes)	54.2 %
Specialist-Replacement	43.0%
Generalist-Replacement	34.0%
Output-Based	47.4%

Source: INSTRAW, *Valuation of Household Production and the Satellite Accounts* (Santo Domingo: 1996), 229.

Planning Agency calculated that counting unpaid work in 1996 would add between 15.2% (generalist-replacement method) and 23% (opportunity-cost method) to GDP. Even at those levels, the value of unpaid labor still equaled at least half of Japanese women's market wages.

Housework Not Bombs

While estimates vary by country and evaluation method, all of these calculations make clear that recognizing the value of unpaid household labor profoundly alters our perception of economic activity and women's contributions to production. "Had household production been included in the system of macro-economic accounts," notes Ann Chadeau, "governments may well have implemented quite different economic and social policies."

For example, according to the UNDP, "The inescapable implication [of recognizing women's unpaid labor] is that the fruits of society's total labor should be shared more equally." For the UNDP, this would mean radically altering property and inheritance rights; access to credit; entitlement to social security benefits, tax incentives, and child care; and terms of divorce settlements.

For WFH advocates, the implications are inescapable as well: women's unpaid labor should be paid—and "the money," WFH insists, "must come first of all from military spending."

Here in the United States, an unneeded and dangerous military buildup begun [in 2002] has already pushed up military spending from 3% to 4% of GDP. Devoting just the additional 1% of GDP gobbled up by the military budget to wages for housework—far from being outlandish—would be an important first step toward fairly remunerating women who perform necessary and life-sustaining household work. ❑

Sources: Ann Chadeau, "What is Households' Non-Market Production Worth?" *OECD Economic Studies* No. 18 (Spring 1992); Economic Planning Unit, Department of National Accounts, Japan, "Monetary Valuation of Unpaid Work in 1996" <unstats.un.org/unsd/methods/timeuse/tusresource_papers/japanunpaid.htm>; INSTRAW, *Measurement and Valuation of Unpaid Contribution: Accounting Through Time and Output* (Santo Domingo: 1995); INSTRAW, *Valuation of Household Production and the Satellite Accounts* (Santo Domingo: 1996); Office of National Statistics, United Kingdom, "A Household Satellite Account for the UK," by Linda Murgatroyd and Henry Neuberger, *Economic Trends* (October 1997) <www.statistics.gov.uk/hhsa/hhsa/Index.html>; Hilkka Pietilä, "The Triangle of the Human Ecology: Household-Cultivation-Industrial Production," *Ecological Economics Journal* 20 (1997); UN Development Programme, Human Development Report (New York: Oxford University Press, 1995).

Article 5.6

MANAGED LABOR OR HUMAN RIGHTS
Conflicting Directions for Immigration Reform

BY DAVID BACON
December 2010—WorkingUSA

A political alliance is developing between countries with labor export policies and the corporations who use that labor in the global north. Many countries sending migrants to the developed world depend on remittances to finance social services and keep the lid on social discontent over poverty and joblessness, while continuing to make huge debt payments.

Corporations using that displaced labor share a growing interest with those countries' governments in regulating the system that supplies it. Increasingly, the mechanisms for regulating that flow of people are contract labor programs—called "guest worker" or "temporary worker" programs in the United States, or "managed migration" in the UK and much of the EU. With or without these programs, migration to the United States and other industrial countries is a fact of life. But does that mean that U.S. immigration policy should be used to increase corporate profits by supplying labor to industry at a price it wants to pay? Despite often using rhetoric that demonizes immigrants, the U.S. Congress is not debating the means for ending migration.

Nothing can end it—short of a radical reordering of the world's economy. Nor are waves of immigration raids and deportations intended to halt it. In an economy in which immigrant labor plays a critical part, the price of stopping migration would be economic crisis. Immigration policy is intended to manage the flow of people and determine their status in the United States, in the interest of those who put that labor to work.

Migrants are human beings first, however, and their desire for community is as strong as the need to labor. Or as the old shop floor saying goes, "We work to live; we don't live to work." The use of neoliberal reforms and economic treaties to displace communities, producing a global army of available and vulnerable workers, has a brutal impact on people. NAFTA and the existing and proposed free trade agreements between the United States and Central America, Peru, Colombia, Panama, South Korea, and Jordan not only do not stop the economic transformations that uproot families and throw them into the migrant stream—they push that whole process forward.

On a world scale, the migratory flow caused by displacement is still generally self-initiated. In other words, while people may be driven by forces beyond their control, they move at their own will and discretion, trying to find survival and economic opportunity, and to reunite their families and create new communities in the countries they now call home.

The idea of managing the flow of migration is growing. During the negotiations at the Hong Kong summit of the World Trade Organization (WTO) in 2005, a proposal was introduced for the first time to begin regulating the movement of people along with the movement of capital and goods. As the WTO further regulated the modes in which services are provided in the world economy, it began to propose regulating the movement of people themselves as the "providers of services" in what was called Mode 4. The Mode 4 program was originally proposed for skilled workers and executives, and included salespeople, corporate managers and specialists, foreign employees of corporate subsidiaries, and independent contractors like doctors and architects. Labor-exporting countries, however, have advocated expanding the range of jobs to include construction workers, domestic workers, and other less-skilled employment.

As in all guest worker programs, the visas of these workers would require them to remain employed, and they would be deported if they lost their jobs. Contractors would be allowed to recruit workers in one country and sell their labor in another. The visas would all be temporary, and the workers would not be able to become permanent residents. Countries contracting for these guest workers could regulate the number admitted and establish conditions under which they could be employed. The WTO opposes the regulation of any standards of employment, and says they should be regulated by the International Labor Organization (ILO) instead. Over many decades, however, the ILO has been unable to establish any mandatory standards or wages, or any enforcement mechanism to punish countries or corporations that violate its voluntary standards.

The economic reforms that displace communities, like privatization and the end of subsidies, are all mandated by the WTO and international trade agreements. Displacement therefore would continue under this scheme, while protection for workers and migrants would be voluntary and ineffective. Essentially, this would produce migrant labor on a huge scale, and give corporations and compliant governments the freedom to exploit it without regulation or limits.

A number of U.S. human rights and immigrant rights organizations issued a statement during the WTO negotiations opposing Mode 4, including the American Friends Service Committee, the National Network for Immigrant and Refugee Rights, the Committee in Solidarity with the People of El Salvador, Filipino Civil Rights Advocates, the Teamsters Union, United Food and Commercial Workers, Public Services International, and 55 others. They criticized the impact of the export of skilled workers on developing countries, and they predicted that the scheme would violate the rights of migrants themselves.

Migrant Rights International (MRI) also criticized the Mode 4 proposal. Genevieve Gencianos of MRI said global immigration policy should be based on the protection of migrants' rights rather than regulating their movement in the interest of employers. "Trade and investment liberalization," she said, "have eroded basic human rights. These include the right to quality public services (such as health and education), jobs at home, sustainable agriculture, indigenous knowledge, self-determination, and human security for all. These violations . . . have directly and indirectly driven people out of their home countries to become migrant workers abroad."

The stream of migrant labor is not all unskilled. Rajiv Dabhadkar, a former guest worker, engineer, and founder of the National Organization for Software and Technology Professionals (NOSTOP), describes "a significant new group of nations where the average citizen is poor, but the nation as a whole is technologically advanced and economically powerful, like China, India, Brazil, Russia and Thailand. Technical education in these countries is both cheap and advanced, thanks to the Internet and the easy movement of ethnic technocrats between the developed world and their countries of origin."

While sub-Saharan Africa needs 620,000 nurses to cope with the HIV/AIDS epidemic, Dabhadkar said, 23,000 health professionals leave the region every year for jobs in developed countries. Contract labor programs, especially those employing women, have mushroomed in East Asia, and now include 242,000 domestic workers in Hong Kong, 674,000 factory, construction, and domestic workers in South Korea, and 120,000 caregivers in Taiwan. "The migrant worker has been dehumanized and commodified." Gencianos said. "The WTO is effectively stripping the worker of his or her basic human rights." Because the impact is greatest on women, she predicted "irreversible negative social impacts to families left back home."

Protecting Migrants' Rights

While the current regime of migrant labor is a convenient arrangement for wealthy nations, it has severe disadvantages for poorer ones. The cost of maintaining and reproducing this international migrant labor force falls on countries least able to afford it. The remittances of migrant workers become the main source of income for the communities from which they come. Large corporations and industries of wealthy countries get the benefit of this labor force, and workers themselves pay the cost of maintaining it.

Developing countries do, however, have an alternative framework for protecting the rights and status of this migrant population. Both Gencianos and rights advocates urged that instead of regulating migration through the WTO, countries should ratify and implement the U.N. International Convention on the Protection of the Rights of All Migrant Workers and Members of Their Families. "Rather than reduce migrants to a factor of production, or a commodity to be exported and imported, migration policy must acknowledge migrants as human beings and address their dignity and human rights," the statement concluded.

The U.N. convention was adopted in 1990. It extends basic human rights to all migrant workers and their families, documented or undocumented. It supports family reunification, establishes the principle of equality of treatment with citizens of the host country in relation to employment and education, protects migrants against collective deportation, and makes both sending and receiving countries responsible for protecting these rights. All countries retain the right to determine who is admitted to their territories, and under what conditions people gain the right to work. The convention does not answer all questions posed by migration in a world economic system. But it takes two basic steps that still paralyze the U.S. debate: it recognizes the new global scale of migration and its permanence, and it starts by protecting the rights of people, especially those with the least power: migrants themselves.

In the U.S. immigration debate, proponents of restrictions usually argue they are only directed at undocumented immigrants. But maintaining this distinction between legal and illegal status has become a code for preserving inequality, a tiered system dividing people into those with rights and those without. Guest worker schemes set up similar tiers—in effect, another form of illegality or rightlessness. Once established, growing inequality eventually affects all immigrants, including legal or permanent residents. The 1996 debate over the Clinton immigration reform began by proposing increased enforcement against the undocumented, but ended by denying even legal immigrants Social Security and other benefits and rights they had previously enjoyed. The effects of inequality spread beyond immigrants to citizens as well, especially in a society that has historically defined unequal status by skin color and sex.

With twelve million undocumented people living in the United States, gaining legal status is obviously a central problem for immigrant communities. At the heart of many proposals by U.S. immigrant groups is relaxing restrictions on granting permanent residence visas. They would allow migrants to live and participate in community life in the United States and move to and from their countries of origin. The Coalition of Guatemalan Immigrants in the United States criticized Bush's comprehensive immigration reform proposal, for instance, because it failed to include "a process through which immigrants can obtain permanent residence, and eventual citizenship."

Political Rights

Citizenship is a complex issue in a world where transnational migrant communities span borders and exist in more than one place simultaneously. Residents of transnational communities do not see themselves simply as victims of an unfair system, but rather as actors capable of reproducing culture, of providing economic support to families in their towns of origin, and of seeking social justice in the country to which they have migrated. A sensible immigration policy would recognize and value the communities of migrants and see their support as desirable. It would reinforce indigenous culture and language, rather than treating them as a threat. At the same time, it would seek to integrate immigrants into the broader community around them and give them a voice in it, rather than promoting social exclusion, isolation, and segregation. It would protect the rights of immigrants as part of protecting the rights of all working people.

Transnational communities in Mexico are creating new ways of looking at citizenship and residence that correspond more closely to the reality of migration. In 2005 Jesus Martinez, a professor at California State University in Fresno, was elected by residents of the state of Michoacán in Mexico to their state legislature. His mandate was to represent the interests of the state's citizens living in the United States. "In Michoacán, we're trying to carry out reforms that can do justice to the role migrants play in our lives," Martinez said.

In 2006, Pepe Jacques Medina, director of the Comite Pro Uno in Los Angeles' San Fernando Valley, was elected to the Federal Chamber of Deputies on the Party of the Democratic Revolution (PRD) ticket with the same charge. Transnational migrants insist that they have important political and social rights, both in their communities of origin and in their communities abroad.

The Party of the Institutionalized Revolution and the National Action Party (PRI and PAN) control the Mexican national congress, and while they voted over a decade ago to enfranchise Mexicans in the United States, they only set up a system to implement that decision in April 2005. They imposed so many obstacles that in the 2006 presidential elections only 40,000 were able to vote, out of a potential electorate of millions. "It was limited," conceded Dominguez, "but it was the fruit of many years of fighting by organizations here in the U.S. It's not all we wanted, but it's a beginning. And most important, now that they've passed the law and started to create a process, there's no going back."

U.S. electoral politics could not remain forever immune from these expectations of representation, and they should not. After all, the slogan of the Boston Tea Party was "No taxation without representation." Those who make economic contributions have political rights. That principle requires recognition of the legitimate social status of everyone living in the United States. Legalization is not just important to migrants—it is a basic step in the preservation and extension of democratic rights for all people. With and without visas, 34 million migrants living in the United States cannot vote to choose the political representatives who decide basic questions about wages and conditions at work, the education of their children, their health care or lack of it, and even whether they can walk the streets without fear of arrest and deportation.

The migrants' disenfranchisement affects U.S. citizens, especially working people. If all the farm workers and their families in California's San Joaquin Valley were able to vote, a wave of living wage ordinances would undoubtedly sweep the state. California's legislature would pass a single-payer health plan to ensure that every resident receives free and adequate health care. If it failed to pass, San Joaquin Valley legislators, currently among the most conservative, would be swept from office.

By excluding from the electorate those who most need social change and economic justice, the range of possible reform is restricted, not only on issues of immigration, but on most economic issues that affect working people. Immigration policy and political and social rights for immigrants are integral parts of a broad agenda for change that includes better wages and housing, a national healthcare system, a national jobs program, and the right to organize without fear of firing. Without expanding the electorate, it will be politically difficult to achieve any of it. By the same token, it is not possible to win major changes in immigration policy apart from a struggle for these other goals. To end job competition, workers need the four million jobs promised by the Obama administration.

To gain organizing rights for immigrants, all workers need Congress to pass the Employee Free Choice Act. But jobs programs that exclude immigrants, especially the undocumented, not only reinforce inequality, but also undermine the very purpose of putting people to work and using their buying power to revitalize the economy. And if laws making it illegal for undocumented immigrants to hold a job and for employers to hire them are not eliminated, the reforms of the Employee Free Choice Act will not apply to 12 million immigrant workers with a long record of trying to organize to improve their wages and conditions.

Anti-immigrant hysteria has always preached that the interests of immigrants and the native born are in conflict and that one group can only gain at the expense of the other. In fact, the opposite is true. To raise wages, generally the low price of immigrant labor has to rise, which means that immigrant workers have to be able to organize effectively. Given half a chance, they will fight for better jobs and wages, schools, and health care, just like anyone else. When they gain political power, the working class communities around them benefit too.

Since it is easier for immigrants to organize if they have permanent legal status, a real legalization program would benefit a broad range of working people, far beyond immigrants themselves. On the other hand, when the government and employers use employer sanctions, enforcement, and raids to stop the push for better conditions—making organizing much more difficult—unions and workers in general suffer the consequences.

That vulnerability is only increased by the social exclusion and second-class status imposed by guest worker programs. De-linking immigration status and employment is a necessary step to achieving equal rights for migrant workers, who will never have significant power if they have to leave the country when they lose their jobs. Healthy immigrant communities need employed workers, but they also need students, old and young people, caregivers, artists, the disabled, and those who do not have traditional jobs.

Security and Solidarity

The global economy has turned insecurity into a virtue, praising it as necessary to increase flexibility and competitiveness. But working communities need a system that produces security, not insecurity. In evaluating proposals for immigration reform, security, equality, organization and community should be the watchwords used by human rights activists. Proposals to deny people rights or benefits because of immigration status move away from equality. Yet most people living in the United States believe in equal rights and status, even if there is often a gap between rhetoric and the concrete measures and laws necessary to achieve them. Ultimately, most migration in today's global economy is forced migration, a result of dislocation. Yet even in a more just world, migration will continue.

Today the huge global movement of people has connected families and communities over thousands of miles and many borders, creating links between people that will inevitably grow. Immigration policy should make that movement possible, instead of seeing everywhere the threat of terrorism. Freedom of movement is a human right. But selling workers to employers should not be the price for gaining it.

The Salvadoran American National Network points out that any long-term solution has to include "development and implementation of new economic and social policies in our home countries . . . thereby reducing migration flows to the United States." Changing corporate trade policy and stopping neoliberal reforms is as central to immigration reform as gaining legal status for undocumented immigrants. Minor modifications to trade agreements like NAFTA and the Central American Free Trade Agreement (CAFTA) will not alter their basic effect. Instead, working people need a common front to scrap those agreements, and to change the economic and political priorities they enforce.

Doing no harm is not enough, however. The United States, Europe, and Japan are wealthy societies, with the capacity and responsibility for repairing globalization's social damage. A fund to provide rural credit (without strings to big corporations) could allow indigenous Mixtec farmers to raise their productivity and stay on the land. It is not so far-fetched. The fair trade movement in wealthy countries already helps many rural producers form cooperatives to gain access to the markets of developed countries at a fair price.

Beyond equality is solidarity. U.S. workers have been forced into a global labor market. They have a direct interest in helping workers in other countries to organize and raise living standards, and in stopping U.S. military intervention in support of the free-trade system. Today, working people of all countries are asked to accept continuing globalization, in which capital is free to go wherever it wants. By that token, migrants must have rights and status equal to those of anyone else. People in Mexico, Guatemala, China, the United States, and every other country need the same things: secure jobs at a living wage; rights in their workplaces and communities; and the freedom to travel and seek a future for their families. The borders between countries should be common ground where they can come together, not lines to pull them apart. ❑

The Short Run: ICEcapades
July/August 2007

The Woodfin Hotel in Emeryville, Calif., is at the center of a political corruption scandal that has erupted in the middle of a long labor dispute. According to the Bay Area bilingual newspaper *El Reportero*, the hotel's president, a Republican Party donor, contacted Rep. Brian Bilbray (R-Calif.), chair of the House Immigration Reform Caucus. Bilbray then wrote to the head of Immigration and Customs Enforcement (ICE) to request that it investigate the status of the Woodfin employees fighting for a living wage. The hotel subsequently fired 21 of its most outspoken workers.

The workers were trying to get the hotel to comply with Measure C, the living wage law passed in 2005, as well as to recover $200,000 in back pay owed to them as a result of the conflict. The city of Emeryville has now ordered Woodfin to pay the back wages by July 31 of this year. One city councilor, John Fricke, describes the scandal as just one of a series of deceptions by hotel management. "I stand with the workers," he said at a recent rally, pointing out that the other three hotels in the city had complied with Measure C.

Woodfin's excuse for using ICE to intimidate its workers into accepting illegal working conditions, despite the fact that ICE policy discourages involvement in labor disputes? "We did so to be certain," claimed its manager, "[that] we were in compliance with all laws governing our business."

—*Sudeep Bhatia*

Article 5.7

"THEY WORK HERE, THEY LIVE HERE, THEY STAY HERE!"

French immigrants strike for the right to work—and win.

BY MARIE KENNEDY AND CHRIS TILLY
July/August 2007

France has an estimated half-million undocumented immigrants, including many from France's former colonies in Africa. The *sans-papiers* (literally, "without papers"), as the French call them, lead a shadowy existence, much like their U.S. counterparts. And as U.S. immigrants did in 2006 with rousing mass demonstrations, the French undocumented have recently taken a dramatic step out of the shadows. But the *sans-papiers* did it in a particularly French way: hundreds of them occupied their workplaces.

Snowballing Strikes

The snowflake that led to this snowball of sit-in strikes was a November immigration law, sponsored by the arch-conservative government of President Nicolas Sarkozy, that cracked down on family reunification and ramped up expulsions of unauthorized immigrants. The law also added a pro-business provision permitting migration, and even "regularization" of undocumented workers, in occupations facing labor shortages. The French government followed up with a January notice to businesses in labor-starved sectors, opening the door for employers to apply to local authorities for work permits for workers with false papers whom they had "in good faith" hired. However, for low-level jobs, this provision was limited to migrants from new European Union member countries. Africans could only qualify if they were working in highly skilled occupations such as science or engineering—but not surprisingly, most Africans in France are concentrated in low-wage service sector jobs.

At that point, African *sans-papiers* took matters into their own hands. On February 13, Fodie Konté of Mali and eight co-workers at the Grande Armée restaurant in Paris occupied their workplace to demand papers. All nine were members of the Confédération Générale du Travail (CGT), France's largest union federation, and the CGT backed them up. In less than a week, Parisian officials agreed to regularize seven of the nine, with Konté the first to get his papers.

The CGT and Droits Devant!! (Rights Ahead!!), an immigrant rights advocacy group, saw an opportunity and gave the snowball a push. They escorted Konté and his co-workers to meetings and rallies with other undocumented CGT workers, where they declared, "We've started it, it's up to you to follow." Small groups began to do just that. Then on April 15, fifteen new workplaces in Paris and the surrounding region sprouted red CGT flags as several hundred "irregular" workers held sit-ins. At France's Labor Day parade on May 1st, a contingent of several thousand undocumented, most from West African countries such as Mali, Senegal, and Ivory Coast, were the stars.

But local governments were slow to move on their demands, so with only 70 workers regularized one month into the sit-ins, another 200 *sans-papiers* upped the ante on May 20 by taking over twenty more job sites. Still others have joined the strike since. As of early July, 400 former strikers have received papers (typically one-year permits), and the CGT estimates that 600 are still sitting tight at 41 workplaces.

Restaurants, with their visible locations on main boulevards, are the highest profile strike sites. But strikers are also camping out at businesses in construction, cleaning, security, personal services, and landscaping. Though the movement reportedly includes North Africans, Eastern Europeans, and even Filipinos, its public presence has consisted almost entirely of sub-Saharan Africans, a stunning indication of the degree of racial segregation in immigrant jobs. Strikers are overwhelmingly men, though the female employees of a contract cleaning business, Ma Net, made a splash when they joined the strike on May 26, and groups representing domestics and other women workers began to demonstrate around the same time.

"To go around freely..."

The *sans-papiers* came to France by different means. Some overstayed student or tourist visas. Others paid as much as 7,500 euros ($12,000) to a trafficker to travel to the North African coast, clandestinely cross by boat to Spain, and then find their way to France. Strike leader Konté arrived in Paris, his target, two long years after leaving Mali. A set of false papers for 200 euros, and he was ready to look for work.

But opportunities for the undocumented are, for the most part, limited to jobs with the worst pay and working conditions. The French minimum wage is 8.71 euros an hour (almost $13), but strikers tell of working for 3 euros or even less. "With papers, I would get 1,000 euros a month," Issac, a Malian cleaner for the Quick restaurant chain who has been in France eleven years, told *Dollars & Sense*. "Without papers, I get 300." Even so, he and many others send half their pay home to families who depend on them. Through paycheck withholding, the *sans-papiers* pay taxes and contribute to the French health care and retirement funds. But "if I get sick, I don't have any right to reimbursement," said Camara, a dishwasher from Mali. He told *L'Humanité*, the French Communist Party newspaper, how much he wished "to go around freely." "In the evening I don't go out," he said. "When I leave home in the morning, I don't even know if I will get home that night. I avoid some subway stations" that are closely monitored by the police.

When asked how he would reply to the claim that the undocumented are taking jobs from French workers, Issac replied simply, "We are French workers—just without any rights. Yes, we're citizens, because France owned all of black Africa!"

Business Allies

The surprise allies in this guerrilla struggle for the right to work are many of the employers. When workers seized the Samsic contract cleaning agency in the Paris suburb of Massy, owner Mehdi Daïri first called the police. When they told him there was nothing they could do, he pragmatically decided to apply for permits for his 300-plus employees. "It's in everybody's best interest," he told *Le Monde*, the French daily newspaper. "Their action is legitimate. They've been here for years, working, contributing to the social security system, paying taxes, and we're satisfied with their work." He even has his office staff make coffee for the strikers every morning.

Though some businesses have taken a harder line against the strikers, the major business associations have called for massive regularization of their workforces. According to *L'Humanité*, André Dauguin, president of the hotel operators association, is demanding that 50,000 to 100,000 undocumented workers be given papers. Didier Chenet, president of another association of restaurant and hotel enterprises, declared that with 20,000 jobs going unfilled in these sectors, the *sans-papiers* "are not taking jobs away from other workers."

For the CGT, busy with defensive battles against labor "reforms" such as cutbacks in public employees' pensions, the strike wave represents a step in a new direction. The core of the CGT remains white, native-born French workers. As recently as the 1980s, the Communist Party, to which the CGT was then closely linked, took some controversial anti-immigrant stands. Raymond Chauveau, the general secretary of the CGT's Massy local, acknowledged to *Le Monde* that some union members still have trouble understanding why the organization has taken up this issue. But he added, "Today, these people are recognized for what they are: workers. They are developing class consciousness. Our role as a union is to show that these people are not outside the world of work." While some immigrant rights groups are critical of the CGT for suddenly stepping into the leadership of a fight other groups had been pursuing for years, it is hard to deny the importance of the labor organization's clout.

Half Empty or Half Full?

With only 400 of 1,400 applications for work permits granted four months into the struggle, the CGT is publicly voicing its impatience at the national government's insistence that local authorities make each decision on a case-by-case basis rather than offering broader guidelines. But Chauveau said he is proud that they have compelled the government to accept regularization of Africans in low-end jobs, broadening the opening beyond the intent of the 2007 law. And on its website, the CGT boasted that the *sans-papiers* "have compelled the government to take its first steps back, when that had seemed impossible since the [May 2007] election of Nicolas Sarkozy." Perhaps even more important for the long term is that class consciousness Chauveau mentioned. This is "a struggle that has changed my life," stated Mamadou Dembia Thiam of Senegal, a security guard who won his work authorization in June. "Before the struggle, I was really very timid. I've changed!" Changes like that seem likely to bring a new burst of energy to the struggling French labor movement. ❏

Resources: Confédération Générale du Travail, www.cgt.fr; Droits Devant!!, www.droitsdevant.org.

Article 5.8

MADE IN ARGENTINA
Bolivian Migrant Workers Fight Neoliberal Fashion

BY MARIE TRIGONA
January/February 2007

Dubbed "the Paris of the South," Buenos Aires is known for its European architecture, tango clubs, and *haute couture*. But few people are aware that Argentina's top fashion brands employ tens of thousands of undocumented Bolivian workers in slave-labor conditions. In residential neighborhoods across Buenos Aires, top clothing companies have turned small warehouses or gutted buildings into clandestine sweatshops. Locked in, workers are forced to live and work in cramped quarters with little ventilation and, often, limited access to water and gas. The *Unión de Trabajadores Costureros* (Union of Seamstress Workers—UTC), an assembly of undocumented textile workers, has reported more than 8,000 cases of labor abuses inside the city's nearly 400 clandestine shops in the past year. Around 100,000 undocumented immigrants work in these unsafe plants with an average wage—if they are paid at all—of $100 per month.

According to Olga Cruz, a 29-year-old textile worker, slave-labor conditions in textile factories are systematic. "During a normal workday in a shop you work from 7 a.m. until midnight or 1 a.m. Many times they don't pay the women and they owe them two or three years' pay. For not having our legal documents or not knowing what our rights are in Argentina, we've had to remain silent. You don't have rights to rent a room or to work legally."

Another Bolivian textile worker, Naomi Hernández, traveled to Argentina three years ago in hopes of a well-paying job. "I ended up working in a clandestine sweatshop without knowing the conditions I would have to endure. For two years I worked and slept in a three-square-meter room along with my two children and three sewing machines my boss provided. They would bring us two meals a day. For breakfast a cup of tea with a piece of bread and lunch consisting of a portion of rice, a potato, and an egg. We had to share our two meals with our children because according to my boss, my children didn't have the right to food rations because they aren't workers and don't yield production." She reported the subhuman conditions in her workplace and was subsequently fired.

Diseases like tuberculosis and lung complications are common due to the subhuman working conditions and constant exposure to dust and fibers. Many workers suffer from back injuries and tendonitis from sitting at a sewing machine 12 to 16 hours a day. And there are other hazards. A blaze that killed six people last year brought to light abusive working conditions inside a network of clandestine textile plants in Buenos Aires. The two women and four children who were killed had been locked inside the factory.

The situation of these workers shows that exploitation of migrant labor is not just a first-world/third-world phenomenon. The system of exploitative subcontracting of migrant workers that has arisen in U.S. cities as a result of neoliberal globalization also occurs in the countries of the global south—as does organized resistance to such exploitation.

Survival for Bolivian Workers

Buenos Aires is the number one destination for migrants from Bolivia, Paraguay, and Peru, whose numbers have grown in the past decade because of the declining economic conditions in those countries. More than one million Bolivians have migrated to Argentina since 1999; approximately one third are undocumented.

Even when Argentina's economy took a nosedive in the 1990s, Bolivians were still driven to migrate there given their homeland's far more bleak economic conditions. Over two-thirds of Bolivians live in poverty, and nearly half subsist on less than a dollar a day. For decades, migration of rural workers (44% of the population) to urban areas kept many families afloat. Now, facing limited employment opportunities and low salaries in Bolivia's cities, many workers have opted to migrate to Argentina or Brazil.

Buenos Aires' clandestine network of sweatshops emerged in the late 1990s, following the influx of inexpensive Asian textile imports. Most of the textile factory owners are Argentine, Korean, or Bolivian. The workers manufacture garments for high-end brands like Lacár, Kosiuko, Adidas, and Montage in what has become a $700 million a year industry.

In many cases workers are lured by radio or newspaper ads in Bolivia promising transportation to Buenos Aires and decent wages plus room and board once they arrive. Truck drivers working for the trafficking rings transport workers in the back of trucks to cross into Argentina illegally.

For undocumented immigrants in Argentina, survival itself is a vicious cycle. The undocumented are especially susceptible to threats of losing their jobs. Workers can't afford to rent a room; even if they could, many residential hotel managers are unwilling to rent rooms to immigrants, especially when they have children.

Finding legal work is almost impossible without a national identity card. For years, Bolivian citizens had reported that Alvaro Gonzalez Quint, the head of Bolivia's consulate in Buenos Aires, would charge immigrants up to $100—equivalent to a textile worker's average monthly pay—to complete paperwork necessary for their documentation. The Argentine League for Human Rights has also brought charges against Gonzalez Quint in federal court, alleging he is tied to the network of smugglers who profit from bringing immigrants into Argentina to work in the sweatshops.

A New Chapter in Argentina's Labor Struggles

Argentina has a notable tradition of labor organizing among immigrants. Since the 19th century, working-class immigrants have fought for basic rights, including Sundays off, eight-hour workdays, and a minimum wage. The eight-hour workday became law in 1933, but employers have not always complied. Beginning with the 1976-1983 military dictatorship, and continuing through the neoliberal 1990s, many labor laws have been altered to allow flexible labor standards. University of

Buenos Aires economist Eduardo Lucita, a member of UDI (Economists from the Left), says that although the law for an eight-hour workday stands, the average workday in Argentina is 10 to 12 hours. "Only half of workers have formal labor contracts; the rest are laboring as subcontracted workers in the unregulated, informal sector. For such workers there are no regulations for production rates and lengths of a workday—much less criteria for salaries." The average salary for Argentines is only around $200 a month, in contrast to the minimum of $600 required to meet the basic needs of a family of four.

Today, the extreme abuses in the new sweatshops have prompted a new generation of immigrant workers to organize.

"We have had to remain silent and accept abuse. I'm tired of taking the blows. We are starting to fight, *compañeros*; thank you for attending the assembly." These are the words of Ana Salazar at an assembly of textile workers that met in Buenos Aires on a Sunday evening last April. The UTC formed out of a neighborhood assembly in the working class neighborhood of Parque Avalleneda. Initially, the assembly was a weekly social event for families on Sundays, the only day textile workers can leave the shop. Families began to gather at the assembly location, situated at the corner of a park. Later, because Argentina's traditional unions refuse to accept undocumented affiliates, the workers expanded their informal assembly into a full-fledged union.

Since the factory fire that killed six on March 30, 2006, the UTC has stepped up actions against the brand-name clothing companies that subcontract with clandestine sweatshops. The group has held a number of *escraches*, or exposure protests, outside fashion makers' offices in Buenos Aires to push the city government to hold inspections inside the companies' textile workshops. Workers from the UTC also presented legal complaints against the top jean manufacturer Kosiuko.

At a recent surprise protest, young women held placards: "I kill myself for your jeans," signed, "a Bolivian textile worker." During the protest, outside Kosiuko's offices in the exclusive Barrio Norte neighborhood, UTC presented an in-depth research report into the brand's labor violations. "The Kosiuko company is concealing slave shops," said Gustavo Vera, member of the La Alemeda popular assembly. "They disclosed false addresses to inspectors and they have other workshops which they are not reporting to the city government." The UTC released a detailed list of the locations of alleged sweatshops. Most of the addresses that the Kosiuko company had provided turned out to be private residences or stores.

To further spotlight large brand names that exploit susceptible undocumented workers, the UTC held a unique fashion show in front of the Buenos Aires city legislature last September. "Welcome to the neoliberal fashion show—Spring Season 2006," announced the host, as spectators cheered—or jeered—the top brands that use slave labor. Models from a local theatre group paraded down a red carpet in brands like Kosiuko, Montagne, Porte Said, and Lacar, while the host shouted out the addresses of the brands' sweatshops and details of subhuman conditions inside shops.

"I repressed all of my rage about my working conditions and violations of my rights. Inside a clandestine workshop you don't have any rights. You don't have dignity," said Naomi Hernández, pedaling away at a sewing machine during the "fashion show."

After the show, Hernández stood up in front of the spectators and choked down tears while giving testimony of her experience as a slave laborer in a sweatshop: "I found out what it is to fight as a human being." She says her life has changed since joining the UTC.

Inspection-Free Garment Shops

To date, the union's campaign has had some successes. In April of 2006, the Buenos Aires city government initiated inspections of sweatshops employing Bolivians and Paraguayans; inspectors shut down at least 100. (Perhaps not surprisingly, Bolivian consul Gonzalez Quint has protested the city government's moves to regulate sweatshops, arguing that the measures discriminate against Bolivian employers who run some of the largest textile shops.) But since then, inspections have been suspended and many clothes manufacturers have simply moved their sweatshops to the suburban industrial belt or to new locations in the city. The UTC has reported that other manufacturers force workers to labor during the night to avoid daytime inspections.

Nestor Escudero, an Argentine who participates in the UTC, says that police, inspectors, and the courts are also responsible for the documented slave-labor conditions inside textile factories. "They bring in illegal immigrants to brutally exploit them. The textile worker is paid 75 cents for a garment that is later sold for $50. This profit is enough to pay bribes and keep this system going."

Since 2003, thousands of reports of slave-labor conditions have piled up in the courts without any resolution. In many cases when workers have presented reports to police of poor treatment, including threats, physical abuse, and forced labor, the police say they can't act because the victims do not have national identity cards.

Seeing their complaints go unheeded is sometimes the least of it. Escudero has confirmed that over a dozen textile workers have received death threats for reporting to media outlets on slave-labor conditions inside the textile plants. Shortly after the UTC went public last spring with hundreds of reports of abuses, over a dozen of the union's representatives were threatened. And in a particularly shocking episode, two men kidnapped the 9-year-old son of José Orellano and Monica Frías, textile workers who had reported slave-labor conditions in their shop. The attackers held the boy at knifepoint and told him to "tell your parents that they should stop messing around with the reports against the sweatshops." The UTC filed criminal charges of abandonment and abuse of power against Argentina's Interior Minister Aníbal Fernández in November for not providing the couple with witness protection.

The Road Ahead

Although the Buenos Aires city government has yet to make much headway in regulating the city's sweatshops, the UTC continues to press for an end to sweatshop slavery, along with mass legalization of immigrants and housing for immigrants living in poverty. Organizing efforts have not been in vain. In an important victory, the city government has opened a number of offices to process immigration documents free of charge for Bolivian and Paraguayan citizens, circumventing the Bolivian Consulate.

The UTC has also proposed that clandestine textile shops be shut down and handed over to the workers to manage them as co-ops and, ultimately, build a cooperative network that can bypass the middlemen and the entire piece-work system. Already, the Alameda assembly has joined with the UTC to form the Alameda Workers' Cooperative as an alternative to sweatshops. Nearly 30 former sweatshop workers work at the cooperative in the same space where the weekly assemblies are held.

Olga Cruz now works with the cooperative sewing garments. She says that although it's a struggle, she now has dignity that she didn't have when she worked in one of the piece-work shops. "We are working as a cooperative, we all make the same wage. In the clandestine shops you are paid per garment: they give you the fabric and you have to hand over the garment fully manufactured. Here we have a line system, which is more advanced and everyone works the same amount."

Fired for reporting on abusive conditions at her sweatshop, Naomi Hernández has also found work at the cooperative. "We are freeing ourselves, that's what I feel. Before I wasn't a free person and didn't have any rights," said Hernández to a crowd of spectators in front of the city legislature. She sent a special message and invitation: "Now we are fighting together with the Alameda cooperative and the UTC. I invite all workers who know their rights are being violated to join the movement against slave labor." ❑

Resources: To contact UTC activists at La Alameda assembly in Parque Avellaneda, email: asambleaparqueavellaneda@hotmail.com. To see videos of recent UTC actions, go to: www.revolutionvideo.org/agoratv/secciones/luchas_obreras/costureros_utc.html; www.revolutionvideo.org/agoratv/secciones/luchas_obreras/escrache_costureros.html.

Article 5.9

BUILDING A BETTER AUSTIN FROM BELOW

Immigrant workers confront the construction industry in Texas' state capital.

BY CARLOS PÉREZ DE ALEJO
September/October 2009

On June 11, 2009, three immigrant construction workers fell to their deaths when a scaffold gave way on the 11th floor of a high-rise apartment project near the University of Texas at Austin. The tragic deaths of Wilson Joel Irías Cerritos, Raudel Ramírez Camacho, and Jesús Ángel López Pérez sent chills through the Latino/a immigrant community in Austin. The loss of these three young workers from Mexico and Central America offered a bleak reminder of the dangers of working construction in the Lone Star State.

Texas is one of the fastest growing states in the country, boasting a massive population of over 24 million people and a booming construction industry to keep pace with its rapid development. Yet growth has come at a significant cost to those building the state's commercial buildings, resident housing, and infrastructure system.

A construction worker dies on the job every two-and-a-half days in Texas. According to the most recent statistics from the U.S. Department of Labor, 142 construction-related fatalities took place in 2007 alone, up from 131 the previous year. Statistics like these have made Texas the deadliest state for construction workers, with California at a distant second.

"The [construction] industry in Texas suffers from poor working conditions and a basic lack of health and safety protections," says Cristina Tzintzún of the Austin-based Workers Defense Project (WDP), a membership-based Latino/a immigrant workers' center. "Austin is a prime example of the problems that exist throughout the state."

For the past seven years, Workers Defense Project has mobilized thousands of Latino/a immigrant workers in Austin to combat rampant exploitation in the construction industry. WDP's increasingly strong base is a testament to their participatory organizing model, which prioritizes the leadership of those directly affected by social inequality. After years of grassroots organizing, alliance-building, and direct action, Workers Defense Project has begun the process of reigning in the worst abuses in the industry; and they're doing it from the ground up.

The Hidden Costs of Development

In mid-June 2009, WDP released a comprehensive report on the construction industry, *Building Austin, Building Injustice: Construction Working Conditions in Austin, Texas.* The study was done in conjunction with faculty from the University of Texas at Austin and from the University of Illinois in Chicago. Based on over a year of research into local, state and federal data, as well as 312 in-depth surveys onsite with construction workers and 20 interviews with local employers, *Building Austin* provides staggering data on the social and economic costs of the city's growth.

The city of Austin, known as the "Live Music Capital of the World," has been at the forefront of Texas' growth spurt. With its progressive character and vibrant music scene, Austin has attracted scores of new residents in recent years, becoming the second-fastest growing metropolitan area in the country. The physical evidence of the city's development is inescapable: cranes dominate the skyline in downtown, while the wooden skeletons of future homes can be found in neighborhoods across Austin. However, few Austinites look beyond the new buildings to consider the plight of the builders.

The workforce of Austin's construction industry, as in many cities in the United States, is largely composed of Latino immigrants. Over two decades of neoliberal reforms—defined by the drive to "liberate" the free market through extreme privatization and deregulation—have forced thousands of men and women from Mexico and Central America to leave their homes, and often their families, to find work in Austin and other cities of "El Norte." From 2000 to 2007, the Latino population in Austin expanded by 45%, while the proportion of Latino construction workers grew by 13%. These workers generally put in long hours for little and sometimes no pay, and their immigration status often leaves them at risk of being taken advantage of by unscrupulous employers.

"We're seeing more and more cases of wage theft every year," says Emily Timm, a Workplace Justice Coordinator who works on unpaid wage cases for WDP. "The level of abuse has been unsettling, particularly during the economic crisis."

Due to the number of unreported cases, it is impossible to determine the total amount of unpaid wages in the construction industry in Austin. However, WDP estimates that it handles close to $7 million worth of unpaid wage cases every year from construction workers. Because of their immigration status, undocumented workers suffer disproportionately from wage theft, along with other abuses in the industry.

WORKER PROTECTIONS IN FIVE STATES			
State	Workers' Compensation	Breaks	Ratio of Federal OSHA Investigations to Workers
Texas	Not required—employers can opt out of workers compensation	Workers in Texas are not entitled to rest breaks.	1 per 132,882
Tennessee	Required by state law.	30 min. break every 6 hrs. of work	1 per 66,954
North Carolina	Required by state law.	30 min. meal break after 5 hrs. of work for children under 16 yrs	1 per 35,025
New York	Required by state law.	30 min. meal break every 6 hrs. of work	1 per 71,882
Nevada	Required by state law.	10 min. break for every 3.5 hrs. worked. 30 min. meal break in 8 hr. shift	1 per 31,329

Sources: Rick Levy, AFL-CIO of Texas, General Counsel, 2008; "Can My Boss Do That?" www.canmybossdothat. com; AFL-CIO, *Death on the Job*, 18th ed., 2009.

In addition to wage theft, *Building Austin* uncovered rampant workplace violations. Fifty percent of surveyed construction workers reported not being paid overtime. Forty-five percent earned poverty level wages. One in five suffered a workplace injury requiring medical attention. Sixty-four percent lacked basic health and safety training, while many workers had to provide their own safety equipment.

An ill-equipped and largely toothless regulatory system has left dubious working conditions unchecked for years in the state's capital. The majority of workers surveyed had never even heard of the Occupational Health and Safety Administration (OSHA), much less other regulatory agencies. In fact, Texas has the fourth-lowest number of OSHA inspectors, despite its construction boom in recent years. According to *Building Austin*, not a single worker who experienced wage theft reported the crime to the Texas Workforce Commission, the Department of Labor, or the Austin Police Department, the agencies responsible for handling unpaid wages. Instead, many workers risked going to their employers directly to recover their due pay. Yet employers proved to be unreceptive. Upon confronting their boss, many workers were threatened with being fired or reported to immigration authorities. In some cases they were even threatened with physical violence.

Lax enforcement in the construction industry is the product of over two decades of severe deregulation, beginning with the administration of Ronald Reagan and continuing through the current economic crisis. During this period, reported the *Texas Observer*, "the emphasis shifted from enforcement to voluntary compliance." The Texas Workforce Commission, the state agency responsible for investigating wage and hour violations, has not performed a single field investigation since 1993, the year the State Legislature slashed its funding. Since then, investigations have been limited to telephone and email; satellite offices throughout the state have closed down; and only 24 labor law investigators are left to cover the entire state of Texas from a single office in downtown Austin.

In the absence of an effective regulatory system, Workers Defense Project has organized thousands of undocumented workers to build a more just and equitable construction industry from below.

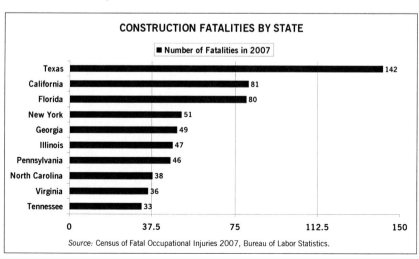

CONSTRUCTION FATALITIES BY STATE

■ Number of Fatalities in 2007

State	Fatalities
Texas	142
California	81
Florida	80
New York	51
Georgia	49
Illinois	47
Pennsylvania	46
North Carolina	38
Virginia	36
Tennessee	33

Source: Census of Fatal Occupational Injuries 2007, Bureau of Labor Statistics.

Building It from Below

Workers Defense Project emerged in response to the growing crisis of wage theft for immigrant workers in Austin. Founded in August 2002, WDP began as a largely white-male-led social-service organization, primarily focused on wage-claim issues. Yet after some staff changes, strategic planning, and careful capacity-building, WDP has developed into one of the most dynamic member-driven organizations in the city's labor movement.

"We've grown a lot over the years," says Tzintzún, who's been with WDP nearly since its inception. "We've become a democratically-run, base-building organization, with the belief that real power is derived from grassroots organizing by those most directly impacted by social and economic inequality."

Democratic participation by the membership of over 400 Latino/a immigrant workers is valued and encouraged at all levels of the organization. Members weigh in on key decisions through monthly general assembly meetings, weekly gatherings by the Construction Worker Committee, and through the board of directors—more than half of which is composed of immigrant workers. The increasing depth of participation, although not always a smooth process, has strengthened WDP as an organization, and the resolve of its members to step into the trenches of social change.

"As workers, it [WDP] gives us the sense that we have the power to change history," says Martín Ruiz, a member of WDP. "We're here because we're all members, all part of a family."

Ruiz came to the organization a year ago after an employer refused to pay him overtime. Since then he has been involved in several direct actions against employers, given a speech at the most recent May Day march, and played an active role in recruiting new members. He is now one of the main facilitators of WDP's leadership development course.

Rooted in the tradition of popular education, which emphasizes people's experience as the basis of education and action, WDP's leadership development course has expanded considerably over the years. What began as a class on worker's rights has grown to encompass complex issues such as globalization, race, immigration, gender equity, U.S. history, and public speaking. "The government will not deliver consciousness to the people," says Ruiz. "And the university will not focus on ones experience as a worker. Here they can learn from their own experience and the experience of others…it's a shared experience, and an experience of sharing."

The participatory education model of Workers Defense Project is designed to address the root causes of social inequality, providing a framework for workers to analyze their own experience. Yet it is more than an analytical tool. "Membership education is about recognizing and developing leaders," noted Bill Fletcher Jr. and Fernando Gapasin in *Solidarity Divided: The Crisis in Organized Labor and a New Path Toward Social Justice*. "It aims to provide a framework that members can use to…guide actions in their own interests."

Direct Action Gets the Goods

For many worker-members, WDP offers an introduction to direct action. Over the years, the worker center has recovered over $500,000 in unpaid wages. In some cases, employers are willing to concede what they owe through negotiation, while others require more convincing. When employers refuse to pay, WDP takes the fight to their doorstep, mobilizing dozens of worker-members and community allies to confront the problem head-on.

In late 2008, one of the nation's largest homebuilders, KB Home, gave in to over five months of public pressure from Workers Defense Project, paying nearly $7,000 in back wages to seven worker-members who built luxury homes for the housing giant. The campaign against KB came to a head in September when over 60 community supporters, union members, and faith community leaders joined WDP to occupy the home builders' main office in north Austin, demanding immediate payment for the seven workers. Bypassing the security guard, protesters flooded KB's main lobby, circling the reception desk to await a reply. The following day, KB contacted Workers Defense Project and agreed to pay.

In the process of struggling for immediate gains, direct action puts the strength of *collective* action on display, deepening a sense of solidarity among the workers and their allies in the community. "Instead of politicians giving us all the changes we need," notes Ruiz, "it [direct action] gives us the sense that we can change things, through uniting, through organizing ourselves." In a city with notoriously lax enforcement, WDP has taken labor law into its own hands, braiding workers and their allies into a common struggle for a more just workplace.

The release of *Building Austin, Building Injustice* has drawn much-needed attention to the dangers of Austin's construction industry. In response to the report, U.S. Labor Secretary Hilda Solis announced that OSHA inspectors from other states will descend on Texas to investigate abuses in the construction industry. For WDP, however, there is still work to be done. As Ruiz reminds us, the struggle is not only at the workplace, "it is also in our community, to get more people involved." ❑

Sources: "Dying to Build: Why Texas is the Deadliest State for Construction Workers," *Texas Observer*, June 12, 2009; Bill Fletcher Jr. and Fernando Gapasin, *Solidarity Divided: The Crisis in Organized Labor and a New Path Toward Social Justice*, UC Press, 2008. For more information, visit workersdefense.org and buildaustin.org.

Article 5.10

IMMIGRANT RIGHTS ARE LABOR RIGHTS
Postville and the lessons of the Hormel strike.

BY PETER RACHLEFF
September/October 2008

On May 12, 900 officers from the Immigration and Customs Enforcement (ICE) division of the Department of Homeland Security descended on the small northeast Iowa community of Postville (population 2,200), home to Agriprocessors, Inc., the largest kosher meatpacking plant in the United States. They raided the plant, arresting nearly 400 immigrant workers, men and women, most of them indigenous Guatemalans. Few spoke English; few even spoke Spanish. They were charged with felony "aggravated identity theft," placed in chains, and taken to a tent encampment in the fairgrounds of the nearby town of Waterloo. There, they were advised to plead guilty, processed rapidly by judges in yet other tents, sentenced to five months in prison, and carted away.

Many of the women were placed under house arrest and outfitted with electronic ankle bracelets. They became prisoners, unable to work but expected to care for their children, and dependent on the generous support proffered by local churches, neighbors, and labor and faith-based sympathizers from miles away. They were also told that, at the conclusion of the men's sentences, husbands and wives would switch positions (from prison to house arrest, and vice versa), and then all would be deported at the end of ten months. With felony convictions, they would forever be denied re-entry into the United States.

The ICE raid in Postville and similar raids across the country, and the horrendous working conditions at the plant that have since come to light, are among the most pressing challenges facing the labor movement today. But the seeds of the current situation for migrant workers in the United States were sown years ago, in the breaking of unions in the meatpacking industry and the neoliberal restructuring of the global economy.

Twenty-five years ago, U.S. labor activists like me thought we were enmeshed in a struggle against concessions, fueled by a process of deindustrialization and capital flight. In the Midwest, the epicenter of that formation was the Hormel strike of 1985–86. Hormel management wanted to reorganize everything about the work in their new flagship plant in Austin, Minn., from the calculation of wage payments to the sharpening of knives, with the aim of replicating these strategies company wide. They pushed veteran workers to retire, while insisting that remaining workers and new hires had no choice in a competitive industry but to accept management's terms. They made similar demands on Austin city officials—tax breaks, the construction of infrastructure at public expense, and subsidized access to electric power.

Hormel's behavior was typical of the meatpacking industry, which was being swept by tumultuous change in the early- to mid-1980s. Companies went out of business; new companies, often conglomerates, bought those facilities and rehired their workers at cut-rate wages. New plants were opened in small towns, away from urban centers, in search of isolated, even captive workforces.

Here and there, especially within the Hormel chain, local unions wanted to make a fight, but the international union, the United Food and Commercial Workers (UFCW), consistently undermined these efforts. The UFCW national strategy of "controlled retreat" turned into a thorough rout. By 1990, wages in the meatpacking industry had fallen 44% below their 1980 level. They have never recovered, while working conditions in this dangerous industry have deteriorated even further.

Meatpacking proved to be the canary in the coal mine for U.S. labor relations in the late 20th century. Steel, auto, electronics, newspaper publishing, corn processing, and farm implement manufacturing followed suit, with transportation, services, and public employment sliding downhill as well.

By the early 1990s it became apparent that what was happening was bigger than deindustrialization and corporate America's demands for concessions from its unionized workforce. A major paradigm shift was afoot in the global economy, with neoliberalism and its "race to the bottom" supplanting the Keynesian, demand-driven economics of the post-WWII era. Around the world, workers, peasants, and citizens were being sucked into a vortex of commodification and competition, with only shredded safety nets for protection. Some lost land, some lost jobs, and many lost their way of life. In response, many individuals and families moved. Immigration to the United States reached unprecedented levels.

Neoliberalism's grip on the world economy has created certain kinds of jobs, and has also created the workers who have little choice but to fill those jobs. The very forces that drove down wages and benefits and undermined working conditions in an industry like meatpacking have also driven workers and peasants in southern Mexico, Guatemala, El Salvador, Bosnia, India, Pakistan, and many, many other places to leave their home communities and find their way to jobs in meatpacking and poultry processing plants, or behind the wheels of taxi cabs, pushing gurneys in hospitals and mops in commercial skyscrapers, from the metropolises of New York City and Los Angeles to small Midwestern towns like Worthington and Willmar, Minn.—and Postville, Iowa.

Meanwhile, in the United States, some individuals and families sought to sell more labor, by taking two or three jobs or having more family members work for wages, but the markets paid less and less for their labor. By imperiling the economic security of native-born workers in industrialized countries, neoliberalism has also fanned the flames of nativism and xenophobia, providing fearful and angry workers with immigrant scapegoats as the objects of their furor. In the United States these dynamics seem scripted by a long history of racism and anti-immigrant nativism enforced by the state (the Chinese Exclusion Act of 1882, the immigrant quotas of 1923–24, the deportation of Mexicans and Filipinos in the 1930s, the internment of Japanese-Americans during WWII, etc.). It is little wonder that the regime that celebrates the dismantling of the Berlin Wall seeks to build a wall along the U.S./ Mexican border.

It is in these contexts that we must consider Postville, where Agriprocessors built a workforce willing to work hard and long for low wages. Responding to Agriprocessors' call for workers, hundreds of indigenous Guatemalans, driven from their rural communities by neoliberal economic policies, found their way to Postville and took those jobs. Add to these conditions an ineffective and out-of-favor federal administration, desperate in an election year to look tough on "illegal" immigration. Hence the ICE raid in May, the biggest immigration raid in U.S. history. As I write in late August, the *New York Times* has reported a similar raid on a factory in Laurel, Miss.

Such raids and legal railroading reflect ICE's redoubled efforts to criminalize immigrants in this worsening economic environment. In Minnesota, for instance, ICE arrests and prosecutions have increased 650% in the past five years. The state's Republican administration has rebuffed proposals to issue drivers' licenses to undocumented immigrants, to offer in-state tuition at public colleges to undocumented youth who have graduated from local high schools, and to order local police not to ask questions about immigration status when interviewing people in relation to other investigations.

All of this has fed representations of undocumented immigrants as "illegal" and "criminal," adding fuel to popular nativism and racism. Such forces have, not surprisingly, obscured and stifled the immigrant and labor rights movements that had roared into the public view in April and May 2005.

Agriprocessors is the largest kosher meatpacking plant in the United States, not only selling to Jewish communities across the country but also exporting their products to Israel. Only a few years ago the company was a poster child for "diversity" in the United States, hailed by "60 Minutes" and a best-selling book, *Postville: A Clash of Cultures in Heartland America* (Harvest Books, 2001). Both the highly praised author of the book and the award-winning TV news magazine show were so captivated by the presence of Orthodox Jews in small-town Iowa that they failed to ask many questions about who was actually working in the plant, how they were treated, and what they earned.

Now, in the wake of ICE's May 12 raid, which came in the midst of a UFCW union organizing campaign, Agriprocessors and Postville have become the poster children for the exploitation of labor in the United States within the neoliberal global economy. Commentators and consumers alike have had to give credence to the grim predictions of 1980s labor activists that management's attack on unions and workers would bring meatpacking "back to the jungle" of Upton Sinclair's heyday, the early 20th century. The brutality and horror of the May 12 raid and the ensuing judicial nightmare, detailed eloquently by interpreter Erik Camayd-Freixas in an impassioned public letter, grabbed widespread attention. Investigations by Conservative Jewish rabbis, the *Jewish Daily Forward*, the *New York Times*, the *Des Moines Register*, People for the Ethical Treatment of Animals, the House Judiciary Committee's Subcommittee on Immigration, and the Congressional Hispanic Caucus have unearthed far more than the employment of workers who lacked proper documentation.

"Jungle" stories abound: the employment of underage workers; work and safety violations; forced overtime; abuse of workers by foremen, including the physical beating of men and the sexual harassment of women; pressure to buy cars from certain dealers in order to keep jobs; and the distinctly non-kosher abuse of animals.

Alarms have also been sounded by an International Indian Treaty Council meeting in Guatemala that addressed the pressures on indigenous peoples to migrate in search of work; Jewish organizations that have asked how the treatment of workers in this plant and elsewhere should be included in the setting of kosher standards; the United Food and Commercial Workers' Union, which questioned whether the timing of the raid bore a relationship to a growing organizing drive in the plant; and advocates for immigrants' rights from around the world.

Hormel's Austin plant was not only the icon of the corporate attack on workers in the mid-1980s but also the epicenter of an impassioned solidarity movement to resist that attack. Today, Postville is the locus of a revived immigrant and labor rights movement which had sputtered after the great immigrant rights marches of the spring of 2005. On Sunday, July 27, led by Jewish organizations such as Twin Cities Jewish Community Action and the Chicago-based Jewish Council on Urban Affairs, with the support of the New York City-based Hebrew Immigrant Aid Society, buses converged on Postville from the Twin Cities, Milwaukee, Chicago, and LaCrosse, Wisc., while others drove in smaller groups from Madison, Iowa City, Des Moines, and elsewhere. Nearly 2,000 people rallied on behalf of immigrant and labor rights, calling for lost wages and accrued vacation pay for the detained immigrants, the establishment of a $100,000 hardship fund by Agriprocessors, management neutrality in the face of workers' efforts to unionize, and the passage in Iowa of a "Meatpackers' Bill of Rights" like one Minnesota passed in 2007. The coalition also called for humane immigration reform, better federal oversight of working conditions, and a national environment that respects worker justice.

Jewish leadership of the protest reflected two years of work on the notion of *hekhsher tzedek*, the expansion of kosher guidelines to include worker treatment; several months of organizing in both the Twin Cities and Chicago; and the determination to tell the owners of Agriprocessors that their exploitation of workers cannot be done in the name of Jews. While in Postville, labor, social justice, and immigrant rights activists mixed with Jewish activists, sharing experiences and stories as well as phone numbers and e-mail addresses. Following an interfaith service at St. Bridget's Catholic Church, which has been the center of assistance to the immigrant families, protestors marched a mile to the Agriprocessors plant (where there was a large sign reading "Now Hiring"). At a children's park, a group of Postville children, who had experienced the raids as pulling their friends out of school, read a poem together titled "I Am Latino," modeled after a poem, "I Am A Jew," that they'd learned while studying the Holocaust in school.

In the weeks since the march, grassroots organizations have met and begun to lay out a plan of action, including internal education about worker and immigrant rights through churches, synagogues, and community organizations; expanding a base for *hekhsher tzedek* in Jewish and non-Jewish organizations and families; raising material aid for immigrant families still victimized by the ICE raid; organizing a rapid response network in anticipation of future raids; lobbying Congress for humane, migrant-friendly immigration reform; and expanding the network of people and organizations in our communities who are committed to justice for immigrants, workers, and immigrant workers.

While there has been significant participation and support in the Twin Cities from UFCW Local 789 and some support from UNITE-HERE, SEIU, and the Workers' Interfaith Network, there is much work yet to be done to bring the formal labor movement on board this project. If we are to learn from the failures of the mid-1980s, when major labor organizations stood apart from—and even undermined—local union struggles, with disastrous consequences, activists from inside and outside unions must insist that the labor movement at all its levels bring its solidarity and resources to the new historic campaign, one that recognizes that labor rights and immigrant rights are tightly woven together.

Indeed, Agriprocessors is now actively seeking to drive a wedge between labor rights and immigrant rights. In late August the company petitioned the U.S. Supreme Court to overturn a 2005 NLRB representation election held by their Brooklyn, N.Y., distribution center workers, on the grounds that the workers were undocumented and, therefore, do not have the right to vote on union representation. Immigrant workers, citizens or not, documented or not, have exercised this right for nearly three-quarters of a century, and it was most recently affirmed by the Supreme Court in a 1984 decision. But now this rogue employer is asking the Supreme Court to overturn those precedents on the grounds that the workers (whom they hired!) should never have been allowed to work and, therefore, should not have been able to vote in a union representation election. It is time for the entire labor movement to respond with one voice: "Immigrant rights are labor rights." ❏

Chapter 6

UNIONS AND ORGANIZING STRATEGY

Article 6.1

THE *REAL* AUDACITY OF HOPE
Republic Windows Workers Stand Their Ground

BY KARI LYDERSEN and JAMES TRACY
January/February 2009

The 2008 holiday season is one of high hopes and high anxiety. Barack Obama's November victory raised expectations of meaningful change, while the Department of Labor estimates over a half million jobs were lost in November alone.

Workers at Chicago's Republic Windows and Doors weren't waiting for the White House when they learned that they were losing their jobs due to a plant closing. They occupied their workplace, insisted on receiving their full vacation and sick days pay—and won. Whether it be the shape of things to come or just a fleeting moment remains to be seen. Their action forced the mainstream media to show the faces behind the statistics—ones filled with pride and defiance, not pity and powerlessness.

Last fall, workers at Republic noticed that important pieces of equipment had disappeared from their Goose Island warehouse. Alarmed, they notified their union, United Electrical Radio and Machine Workers of America, Local 1110 (otherwise known as UE), an independent union with a tradition of direct action. Republic's management assured the union that no plant closure was afoot; and that the equipment would be replaced with modernized pieces.

Not willing to take the company's word for it, the union covertly monitored the plant, and watched as trucks removed the very machinery needed to produce windows and doors. Meanwhile as the foreclosure crisis unfolded, Republic lost most of its contracts for new home construction.

Then on Tuesday, December 2, employees were told what they feared had been coming for a long-time. Friday, the plant would be shuttered. They were to come pick up their checks and file for unemployment. Company officials blamed the closing on the economic crisis, and on Bank of America, who they said clamped down on their credit despite a federal bailout package of $25 billion in taxpayer money.

"When we arrived to pick up our checks, we were told that we would not be getting paid for our accrued sick days," said Melvin Maclin, Local 1110's Vice President and Republic employee of seven years. Their health insurance was also cut off on Friday, December 5, despite an earlier promise it would extend until December 15. "At that point we had been told so many lies, we didn't know what to believe."

At look at Republic shows the faces of both organized labor past and present. A warehouse that produces actual products, instead of simply distributing them, is a rarity in de-industrialized America. The workers—largely Latino, many black, and a few white—reflect the shifts in Chicago's population and the composition of the blue-collar sections of the working-class. Plant closures are a common part of the Midwest experience. What makes this saga uncommon is what the workers decided to do about it.

They voted to occupy the factory in order to force the company to pay their accrued vacation time as well as comply with the federal WARN Act of 1988, which mandates that companies give 60 days notice when plants are closed or mass layoffs are planned, or pay each employee 60 days severance. Illinois law had actually extended the required notice time to 75 days.

The workers took turns sitting on the shop floor, rotating roughly in the shifts they would have normally worked. Members of local labor and community organizations continuously visited, offering words of support and freshly cooked food. Victor Emeric, a driver with Teamsters Local 705, delivered several boxes of food and underscored what he felt as the importance of the Republic action.

"Support is very important; so is solidarity. We're hoping that the outcome of this is positive for the workers," he said. "I hope that elected officials do the right thing, I try to remain optimistic, but past experience teaches me to know better than that."

The union and company officials had reached an agreement that the workers would not be forcefully removed from the plant as long as they kept it safe and secure and only workers and union staff were allowed on the shop floor. (Supporters congregated in the small lobby and outside on the sidewalk, even in freezing rain and snow.)

Nonetheless, during the first few days of the sit-in rumors flew via text message and email that police would be ordered to evict workers from the plant. But officers keeping watch at the site seemed sympathetic to workers, perhaps another sign of how the economic crisis has affected such a wide swath of Americans and created alliances and empathy among those who wouldn't have felt it before.

One police officer, dispatched to observe the occupation from across the Republic parking lot, refused to speak on the record about his feelings, or the position of the Chicago Police Department. But from his patrol car, he then eloquently explained how the economy was destroying the futures of everyday people "just trying to survive," as plants close and pension plans disappear.

On day four of the occupation, the union began negotiations with company and Bank of America officials, as workers and supporters waited eagerly for word of the outcome. Monday evening crowds waving picket signs and chanting "Si se puede" crowded around a bonfire in a trash can and formed a line to deliver donated food hand to hand into the factory.

Donte Watson, 30, said he was furious at company officials because he was proud of all the effort he had put into this job for eight years and had assumed he would work there for decades more and then retire. He was also angry that the company would close with orders still to fill because he didn't want customers to be let down. "People put their blood, sweat, and tears into this company; it was our company too, not just the owners," he said. "They knew this was coming and they didn't say a word to us. They owed us more respect than that. We don't want anything extra, we just want what we are owed." The negotiations were continued to Tuesday, and then to Wednesday. Meanwhile during the day on Wednesday JPMorgan Chase bank offered a $400,000 line of credit to help pay the workers. Finally, on late Wednesday evening workers voted to accept a proposal from Bank of America creating $1.75 million in credit to pay health benefits for two months, severance and accrued vacation time.

It was a huge victory, a group of 260-some determined workers and their supporters convincing a major financial institution to reverse its position. But the bank didn't agree to the union's larger demand, that it finance the company to allow it to remain open. This was a tough question to tackle from political, legal, and ethical standpoints: if a company is failing financially, to what extent if any is a bank—a private institution—required to subsidize them? And how does the equation change when that private institution has just received an infusion of $25 billion in public money?

The Republic Windows and Doors situation is complicated by insinuations that the owners were trying to move the plant to Iowa, perhaps to avoid having union workers. The owner had incorporated a similar business in Iowa, according to a trade journal cited in the *New York Times*, and that might explain the moving of equipment.

As this went to press, the workers were thrilled with their victory and the results of their direct action. But they also weren't satisfied with taking the money—enough to survive for several months—and still having to find new jobs in this cut-throat economy. Yet they clearly demonstrated that in a shifting economic and political context, collective action can bring real results. Protests in support of Republic workers at Bank of America branches in Philadelphia, San Francisco, and Reno resulted in arrests of activists and added to the national attention of the occupation.

The tactic of a takeover evoked memories of the Flint Sit-Down Strike of 1936 that established the United Auto Workers' presence in the auto industry. Chicago has a long history of labor militancy and events there have often set the tone and tempo of the labor movement as a whole. In 1886, the Haymarket demonstrations, and subsequent massacres and trials of anarchist activists became a hallmark of the battle for the eight-hour day. Turn of the century strikes of clothing workers against Hart, Shaffner and Marx in Chicago led by Sidney Hillman later led to the founding of the Amalgamated Clothing Workers.

"With this economic crisis and unemployment, there are no other jobs," said Dagoberto Cervantes, 41, as his five-year-old son danced around with a picket sign on Monday evening.

This example has boosted the spirits of other workers facing what might be the dawn of the next depression. Across town, at the Congress Plaza Hotel, workers have been on strike for five years. Augustina Bahena, a Congress worker remarked, "Republic workers have given us all a lot of hope, and maybe some new ideas. The bailout needs to help workers. A corporation can't receive millions of dollars just to finance layoffs."

Back at Republic, the workers are talking about starting a co-op to run the factory, reminiscent of labor movements of the past and the factory takeovers by Argentine workers following the financial meltdown of the late 1990s.

Such a move would be a challenging undertaking, especially in this desperate financial climate. But the economic crisis has given people the sense they can no longer simply survive by laying low and not making waves. The status quo is no longer safe. As the workers realized when faced with the plant's closing and denial of their wages, people have no choice but to take matters into their own hands. ❏

The Short Run: Whose Internet?
January/February 2008

The Internet can be a powerful tool for democracy, but apparently not in the workplace.

The National Labor Relations Board ruled in December that employers can prohibit their workers from using company e-mail for union organizing. By a vote of 3-2, the NLRB found that a company may prohibit its employees from using its e-mail system for "non-job related solicitations," and messages about a union rally and other workplace-organizing activities are not "job-related."

In a statement responding to the decision, AFL-CIO Organizing Director Stewart Acuff said the ruling is "clearly counter to the long-established practice of workers being able to talk to one another at the job about unions and their rights."

On the other side of the computer screen, the UK *Independent* relayed a story in early January suggesting that employers are ramping up their surveillance efforts in order to prevent unionization.

"Starbucks managers monitored Internet chat rooms and eavesdropped on party conversations in a covert campaign to identify employees agitating for union representation," the *Independent* reported. —*Larry Peterson*

Article 6.2

THE IWW AND SOLIDARITY UNIONISM AT STARBUCKS

BY STAUGHTON LYND AND DANIEL GROSS

September 2007—WorkingUSA

No new organizing strategy has lifted very far off the ground in the real world. In none of them can one find any strategy for combating the flight of capital to low-wage economies.

All are constrained by the assumptions of a Social Democratic mindset: first one finds a "progressive" national union leader, then that leader calls for the creation of a labor party, then that labor party peacefully ushers in a new day. It is as if history had stopped in 1913, before the betrayal of socialism by most of the world's Social Democratic parties in August 1914 demonstrated the inadequacy of that perspective once and for all.

In the meantime, a group of organizers for the Industrial Workers of the World (IWW, aka the "Wobblies") have pursued what at first glance may seem a more conventional strategy: to pursue direct action and to file Unfair Labor Practices (ULPs) charges with the National Labor Relations Board pursuant to Sections 7 and 8 of the Labor Management Relations Act (LMRA), while wholly avoiding the provisions for elections set out in Section 9 of the Act.

First, this commentary offers a rationale for such a bifurcated organizing strategy. In the remainder of what follows, Daniel Gross of the IWW tells the story of using this approach at the Starbucks Coffee Co.

From the very beginning, the Wagner Act, or National Labor Relations Act (later, as amended, the LMRA), had two contradictory objectives. The first goal of the Wagner Act was to protect workers when they acted together, whether to picket, to strike, or to form a union. Before 1935, workers pursued this objective by seeking to prevent courts from issuing injunctions in labor disputes: that is, by getting the government off their backs. Between enactment of the Norris–LaGuardia Act in 1932 and passage of the Wagner Act three years later, workers got very little assistance from either the government or national unions, but they also were freer to engage in self-activity than at any time before or since. Not coincidentally, these were the years of successful general strikes in Minneapolis, Toledo, and San Francisco, and of a very-nearly successful national textile strike.

The Wagner Act represented a different approach. When workers engaged in direct action and organizing, the federal government stepped forward to protect them. A worker or group of workers, who believed their right to engage in "concerted activities for the purpose of . . . mutual aid or protection" had been infringed, could file a ULP charge. The government would investigate, and if it agreed, thenceforth represent the complaining worker or workers before an administrative law judge.

However, this proffered aid came with a price. The draftspersons of the bill (and, one presumes, the large Congressional majority that voted for it) had a second objective, namely, labor peace. The Wagner Act's preamble says more about achieving the uninterrupted flow of commerce than about creating a workplace equivalent of the

First Amendment. The essential idea, often repeated by Senator Wagner himself, was: Let workers organize unions; let unions then act for their members in collective bargaining and, if need be, in restraining anarchic direct action by individual workers; and, paradoxically, by thus creating freedom, the undesirable exercise of freedom will be restrained. It was a statutory embodiment of Herbert Marcuse's idea of repressive tolerance.

The cruel corollaries of this two-headed approach soon became apparent. Despite language to the contrary in the law itself, workers who went on strike could be "replaced," that is, fired. Once a collective bargaining agreement was ratified that prohibited strikes during the life of the contract—as almost all CIO contracts did from the very beginning—workers could no longer wildcat at will. Direct actions in opposition to decisions at the "core of entrepreneurial control," like closing a factory and taking away your job, were presumptively disfavored. Even minority workers who asked consumers to boycott their boss because of the employer's discrimination were subject to discipline for engaging in concerted activity on their own, rather than filing a grievance. "Workplace contractualism," that is, negotiation of collective bargaining agreements by unions empowered by law to act as the exclusive representative of all workers in an appropriate bargaining unit, shouldered aside the solidarity and collective direct action on which workers had always depended.

The means for thus disempowering the rank and file was, of course, Section 9. This is the part of the Act that provides for union elections. In the minds of most union organizers and administrators of the Act, the pieces fit together this way: Section 7 (especially the words that guarantee the right to form a union) is what workers do before a union is recognized; Section 9 is how unions put themselves in position to act on behalf of their membership after a Labor Board election.

It is, simply, an unholy bargain. In unionized workplaces, the right to strike exists only in a predictable and hence easily controlled manner at the end of the union-negotiated contract. On account of the dues check off, unions are accountable to their members only in instances of extreme misconduct. The "labor movement," feisty and irreverent, has become the "union movement," whose functionaries have essentially the same lifestyle as the bosses they ostensibly combat. And not incidentally, a domesticated, tabby cat union movement has altogether failed to find the means or the will to combat the downsizing and closing of manufacturing plants in the United States as capital has moved, first to the South, and then to other countries.

The best potential answer to these intractable and often unacknowledged problems may be a small network of organizers who are trying to revive the IWW.

Let us begin by acknowledging the grave problems faced by this effort.

1. The majority of IWW members in New York City are in food warehousing and distribution. Significant organizing is taking place at the ports in New Jersey and Los Angeles. Still, a great deal of IWW organizing continues in small service establishments such as bookstores, restaurants, health food stores, and the like. These enterprises are not what Lenin had in mind by a capitalist economy's "commanding heights."

2. Wobblies, like so many other radicals in the 1920s and 1930s, believed that industrial unionism would, of necessity, be more class-conscious, and more politically radical, than the craft unionism of the old American Federation of Labor (AFL). That has not proved to be the case.

3. IWW theory has not progressed beyond the 1905 Preamble. Solitary comrades like the late Marty Glaberman and Stan Weir have had to try to do the theoretical work that the IWW should have done.

4. In the absence of a coherent theoretical framework evolving in response to new conditions, present-day Wobblies have, in practice, done that which their founding brothers and sisters would have abhorred: they have turned to the instrumentalities of the state to establish revolutionary unions. That is, Wobblies have engaged in elections sponsored by the NLRB (pursuant to Section 9 of the LMRA) as well as filing ULP charges with the NLRB (pursuant to Section 7).

Given the dismal state of affairs for workers in the United States, why look to the work of IWW organizers for a path through the minefield of Social Democracy?

The second part of this article suggests the beginning of an answer. The limitations of Wobbly organizing also contain latent strengths. For example, small enterprises that offer a service are vulnerable to consumer picketing, perhaps the easiest and most protected form of direct action available to workers and their supporters. Also, in warehouses in Brooklyn and among truck drivers in Los Angeles, the IWW has begun to reach out to enterprises that directly impact industrial manufacturing.

The IWW's orientation to worldwide class solidarity makes it possible to organize in ways that traditional unions eschew. Even rank-and-file formations within traditional trade unions often support efforts to keep foreign workers out of the U.S. labor market. Such opposition to immigrant workers recapitulates Samuel Gompers' support for Chinese exclusion. In contrast, independent truckers in Los Angeles, working with the IWW, succeeded in shutting down the port of Los Angeles on May 1, 2007, in support of nationwide immigrant rights protests. Ernesto Navarez, spokesperson for the drivers, explained that the Port Authority knew the truckers were going to strike, and by calling it a legal holiday, avoided liability for the shutdown. "We forced them to recognize May Day."

This article considers organizing at Starbucks in New York City as a case study in a strategy we call "solidarity unionism." Workers for Starbucks are not able to seek NLRB-sponsored elections, even if they wish to do so. This is because Starbucks maintains that the appropriate bargaining unit for workers/employees would be a prohibitively large multistore unit. (The IWW campaign at Starbucks did test the waters with an election petition in 2004. When the NLRB in Washington, D.C. accepted the unit question for appellate review, baristas withdrew their petition because a lengthy delay was guaranteed and a nullification of the election was probable given the Republican majority on the Board.)

Perforce, therefore, Starbucks workers have not used the statutory mechanism designed to produce exclusive bargaining representatives with the power to bargain away their members' rights to concerted direct action. However, Starbucks workers have made persistent and creative use of Section 7. As a result, the narrative in the succeeding discussions tells the important story of how one might use Section 7 to build a new workers' movement while maintaining a healthy distance from NLRB-sponsored elections under Section 9.

The State of Affairs in Retail

Retail workers receive wages far below what is needed to live with dignity. In 2003, a cashier earned an average of $8.40 per hour. Food counter workers earned $6.99 per hour. In contrast, Starbucks made a profit of over $560 million in 2006 in revenues of $7.8 billion and Starbucks Chairman Howard Schultz received $102 million in compensation.

It is often supposed that retail workers are kids looking for beer and video game money. In New York City, 47% of retail workers are at least 35 years old and 69% are over 25. And, 48% of retail workers have children under the age of 18.

In retail, full-time employment is on the way out in favor of "flexibility." Starbucks employs 150,000 people, 80% of whom are part-time. Starbucks Chairman Schultz downgraded every retail hourly position in the company to part-time, with no guaranteed number of work hours per week. A Starbucks worker can get fifteen hours of work for one week, thirty hours the next week, and ten hours the week after that.

Health benefits provided by the company are a far-off dream for most retail workers. Starbucks has claimed that it provides health care to all its employee "partners." But first of all, Starbucks employees without a guaranteed workweek must work 240 hours per quarter to qualify for coverage. Second, even workers who qualify must pay premiums, co-pays, and deductibles that they often cannot afford. After repeated public challenges from the IWW Starbucks Workers Union (SWU), the company conceded that only 42% of Starbucks employees (including management personnel whose higher pay makes health care more affordable) were covered by company health care. The percentage of employees covered dropped over 2006 to just 40.9%. Seventy-five thousand Starbucks employees in the United States are without health care from the company and are either uninsured or rely on other sources, including Medicaid, for coverage.

According to government statistics, in 2001 over 80,000 retail workers suffered from muscular-skeletal disorders such as carpal tunnel syndrome. Repetitive stress injuries are common at Starbucks. Management deliberately understaffs and endlessly insists on "speed of service." Moreover, Starbucks fails to implement the most elementary ergonomic standards. Every drink served requires an unnecessarily long reach to place the cup on Starbucks' trademark half-moon counter, depositing $20 bills requires workers at many Starbucks shops to bend almost to the floor and workers are often not permitted to shift from one task to another.

Starbucks' Misconduct Against Workers

Laura de Anda, 21 years old, in her hat and green apron, has just started her shift at Starbucks and after two years on the job, it is hard to manage a smile. Born and raised in Chicago's Mexican immigrant neighborhood, Pilsen, Ms. de Anda moved to New York to pursue her dream of getting an education in the arts.

The line for Starbucks' specialty coffees like the latte and Frappuccino, a cold drink blending coffee, ice, and special flavoring or whipped cream, is almost out the door. Staffing is short as usual, so Ms. de Anda is moving extra quickly at the espresso bar, running to ring customers up at the registers while espresso shots are shooting and milk is steaming at the bar. When she has a few free seconds, she spins to the back counter to prepare the Frappuccino mix before it runs out. The din of the steaming milk, blenders, and workers sprinting back and forth would be overwhelming to the uninitiated, yet Ms. de Anda holds her own.

It seems that every time she turns around an assistant manager or the store manager is right on her back, nagging or nit-picking. "The lemon loaf is on the wrong side of the banana loaf. . . . Your shirt is too wrinkled. . . . There's a fingerprint on the front door. . . . You took too long waiting in line to go to the bathroom." Ms. de Anda has heard it all. The managers' bonuses are tied to selling more and more things to customers who do not need them, and getting fewer "baristas" to do more work so as to hold down labor costs. Thousands of dollars in revenue later, night has fallen and Ms. de Anda has meticulously cleaned the espresso bar, inside and out. There is supposed to be a third worker but the manager "forgot" to put someone else on the schedule.

Before leaving, the two workers present must scrub the bathroom, do the dishes, sweep and mop the floor, vacuum the pastry case, haul the milk into the bar refrigerator, take out the trash, Windex all the glass, restock the cups, and fill the condiment bar. The store closes at 12:30 a.m. on Saturday and they have forty-five minutes to complete these assigned tasks. They will be disciplined if at the end of that time anything is not sparkling.

Starbucks management expects workers to stay after their shifts when it is busy no matter what after-work commitments they may have. Working the closing and then the opening shifts—dubbed the "clopener" according to some Starbucks workers—is a common source of frustration. And heaven forbid if you have to leave work a little early to get to a doctor's appointment.

The grandmother of one Starbucks barista died a few hours before a shift was to begin. The worker called the manager to explain that she was responsible for her grandmother's funeral and burial arrangements, and could not make it to work that day. The manager first expressed disbelief in the worker's explanation and then ordered her, on threat of termination, to call other baristas so as to cover her shift.

Ms. de Anda finishes on time and walks to the subway station for her thirty-five-minute ride to Brooklyn. Exhausted, she closes her fierce brown eyes and immediately falls asleep.

There is not much to smile about. Promised wage increases have never materialized. Ms. de Anda is not getting enough hours of work each week to deal with her bills. While Starbucks pays freight costs for coffee or paper cups, labor "inputs" must deliver themselves to the boss and a thirty-day pass on the subway costs $76. In short, Ms. de Anda is mired in retail worker poverty.

Discrimination, sexual harassment, infantilization, verbal abuse, camera surveillance, and arbitrary write-ups are the order of the day in retail. For Starbucks barista

Suley Ayala, psychological torment took the form of religious discrimination. Ms. Ayala, a mother of four from Ecuador, is a practicing Wiccan. For almost four years at Starbucks, she proudly wore an important Wiccan symbol that she almost never takes off, a modest pentagram necklace. After Ms. Ayala began to organize with her coworkers, management claimed that the necklace was a distraction to customers and demanded that she remove it. Ms. Ayala refused. Management sent her home without pay. A few weeks later, they ousted her from work again. On both occasions, Ms. Ayala was understandably distraught and angry, leaving work on the verge of tears. Not only was she forced to leave work in a very humiliating fashion, the unpaid wages undermined her ability to support her family.

But then something happened. After Ms. Ayala was told to leave, a coworker and fellow member of the SWU put on Suley's pentagram and was sent home too. Coming on top of public protest, a legal filing, and media pressure, this direct action broke the company's will on the issue as management correctly anticipated that store operations would be disrupted every time they sent Ms. Ayala home. Suley has not been sent home since and Starbucks has reimbursed her for lost pay.

An injury to one is an injury to all.

Labor Unions Selling Workers Short

According to the Bureau of Labor Statistics, only 5% of retail workers are union members. What is worse is that union membership means so little. Walk around a unionized New York City grocery store and ask members about their union. Many will not know if they are members or not. Few will know the name of their union. Even fewer see any value in membership.

There are many reasons for the absence of traditional unions in the retail sector. The multinational retailers are extremely powerful and fiercely anti-union. Traditional unions do not like the ratio between the funds they would have to expend to organize and the dues income they could expect if successful. Furthermore, the yearly turnover of the workforce in retail establishments is extremely high. When workers bounce around continuously from one employer to another, as they do in retail establishments, the NLRB election process takes too long. Government certification of an appropriate bargaining unit often involves employer appeals that require two or three years to resolve. All this is what leaders of traditional unions have in mind when they say (privately) that retail workers are "unorganizable."

Solidarity Unionism

Members of the SWU are the first union members in any of the more than 6,000 company-owned Starbucks stores in the United States. The union was begun by Starbucks workers in New York City fed up with living in poverty and being mistreated. The SWU now has a public presence at ten Starbucks stores in four states and dues-paying IWW members are quietly organizing at several other establishments.

In addition to absolutely central changes with respect to dignity and respect, there have been tangible gains. For example, Starbucks baristas in New York City have won three wage increases, increasing their pay by almost 25% in a period when retail wages in the city have been essentially stagnant. When the campaign started in 2004, baristas in New York City began at only $7.75 an hour and they were among the highest-paid workers in the chain. Currently, New York City baristas begin at $8.75 an hour, and when periodic "merit" raises and tips are included, many workers now earn about $10 an hour. In addition, many Starbucks workers around the country have received unexpected wage increases that they attribute to the organizing drive.

The SWU has made serious inroads on Starbucks' refusal to guarantee a minimum workweek. Starbucks asked every barista in New York City how many work hours per week they desired, assuring workers that "within reason" the company would seek to comply with their requests. IWW baristas now generally work the number of hours they demand each week. After continual pressure from the union, Starbucks has finally stopped denying the existence of repetitive strain dangers. The company dedicated its September 2004 Safety and Security Bulletin to repetitive stress injuries, admitting that the espresso bar was a particular problem. Information about repetitive stress, including exercises designed to reduce this kind of injury, was made part of a new employee manual, and Starbucks' employee orientation now includes how to perform these exercises. The union still demands a comprehensive ergonomic evaluation by an expert of whom the SWU approves, and scheduling of appropriate numbers of workers on the shop floor.

The solidarity unionism process is straightforward. Workers, rather than outside organizers, reach out to potential new members, worker by worker. Baristas organize around issues of common concern regardless of whether a majority of workers in a given workplace, or group of workplaces, are union members. SWU members have engaged in a plethora of creative and provocative direct actions to win concessions from Starbucks. When a critical mass of Starbucks workers has formed a shop floor committee, workers (together with members from other stores and supporters) will march into the store at peak hours to give the boss a list of demands. Typically, the demands include a living wage, guaranteed work hours, appropriate staffing, respect, and an ergonomically sound environment. There may be militant picketing and managers known to harass workers who are a minute late to work may find their pictures together with a list of their misdeeds on leaflets handed to customers. A favorite tactic (borrowed from the late Saul Alinsky) is for a group of unionists to enter the store at peak hours, buy drinks, and pay for them one penny at a time.

There is more. Disgusted at having to work around rodent or insect infestation at many New York City Starbucks stores, baristas called a press conference in front of one store that featured a giant thirty-foot inflatable rat. SWU member Sarah Bender was reinstated after supporters formed "Billionaires for Bush and Starbucks Chairman Howard Schultz," entered Sarah's store in full aristocratic regalia, and presented a framed union-buster of the year award to the manager who fired her. The Billionaires called for the abolition of the labor movement and praised the inequitable distribution of wealth under capitalism.

They said that Starbucks was their kind of company.

Solidarity has poured in from around the world. IWW baristas took part in the historic immigrant protests on May 1, 2006, that reclaimed May Day for the entire U.S. working class. A "Justice from Bean to Cup!" initiative seeks to link SWU to the farmers who grow the coffee that baristas sell. A delegation of SWU activists has just returned from Ethiopia where they sought to connect with coffee farmers who grow beans for Starbucks. A protest coalition in Scotland served free Zapatista-grown Fair Trade coffee outside one store and handed out information about union-busting and exploitative land practices in Mexico.

In this context—but only in this context—the activities of SWU members in the legal arena make an important contribution. The first ULP charges filed by Starbucks baristas in New York City resulted in a settlement requiring the company to reinstate two discharged workers and to rescind company-wide policies that forbade employees to share written union information and to wear union pins.

In the immediate aftermath of this settlement, Starbucks again began breaking the law. Six IWW baristas are out of work at the moment because of illegal terminations. Wobbly baristas and their supporters are fighting these terminations in the streets and at the Labor Board. In March 2007, the Labor Board issued yet another complaint against Starbucks for massive union busting including retaliatory terminations. The legal victories have been an important platform from which the SWU has articulated its message through the corporate media. This last complaint generated coverage in the *New York Times*, the *Washington Post*, and National Public Radio, among other outlets.

It is a testament to the courage of coworkers and the breadth of support around the world that in the face of such retaliation, the SWU still enjoys consistent growth.

Solidarity Union Power and Challenges Ahead

Solidarity unionism, like any other form of unionism, faces great difficulties. Any union drive in the United States, regardless of form, can expect determined employer opposition. Just two days after the first union of Starbucks baristas announced its existence, Starbucks Chairman Schultz issued an anti-union voicemail distributed in stores throughout North America.

Solidarity unionism also faces challenges that are to some extent unique. The great "pro" of the model is a "con" as well: solidarity unionism requires continuous participation by its members. The benefits accruing to an energized, mobilized working class are clear. However, being mobilized without respite can be draining and, for some, is unsustainable. The costs of perpetual struggle must be considered and counteracted. A critique of conventional collective bargaining should not stand in the way of agreements with the boss about particular issues, reduced to writing and made known throughout the workplace.

When a company decides to "do business" with a traditional union, the employer can look to the trade union bureaucracy to contain and suppress the spontaneous militancy of union members. A solidarity union cannot and would not wish to provide the same assurances. Therefore, a solidarity union must be prepared to do more than a bureaucratic union to compel profit-maximizing corporations to concede on issues of concern.

The bottom line is that there are no shortcuts in solidarity unionism. The state of rest provided by the dues check-off is not available. Because the union is the workers, because every member is an organizer, because in solidarity unionism we have no leaders; the union lives and dies with the initiative and activity of its members. ❑

Article 6.3

SEIU CIVIL WAR PUTS LABOR-MANAGEMENT "PARTNERSHIP" IN A NEW LIGHT

BY STEVE EARLY
September/October 2009

During his campaign for AFL-CIO president this fall, ex-coal miner Rich Trumka extended the olive branch to corporate America—despite the latter's demonstrated lack of enthusiasm for reinstating organized labor as its junior partner. "Here's the deal," he told a Reuters reporter. "For employers who want to work with us and want to work with workers, we'll be the best friend they ever had." In another interview, Trumka touted "a new compact" in which "collective bargaining is part of the solution" to the nation's economic woes and union members' contributions to society are more highly valued. Amid unrelenting business opposition to the Employee Free Choice Act, however, any plan to renew the social compact model that governed labor relations in the post-World War II era has had few takers on the management side.

One notable exception is Kaiser Permanente (KP), the giant California-based hospital chain and health maintenance organization. Kaiser was founded as a pioneering pre-paid medical plan. It was embraced by California unions to such a degree that it became known as "the HMO that labor built." By 2007, Kaiser's nationwide workforce was 130,000 strong, and its 96,000 union members made it one of most heavily unionized non-profit health care providers. After a series of disruptive (but not always successful) strikes from the late 1970s to the early 1990s, 27 different Kaiser unions formed a coordinating council with help from the AFL-CIO in 1995.

As described in *Healing Together*, their goal was to "exchange information about particular local struggles" and begin "developing a joint strategy and structure" for more effective bargaining and strike activity. At the time KP was losing $250 million a year and facing pressure "to better match the cost structures of competing HMOs." So labor and management ended up trying to create a less adversarial relationship that would, as a by-product, expand worker influence in running Kaiser and improve its delivery of care.

The resulting "Labor-Management Partnership"—which according to the authors has produced more than "a decade of labor peace"—was not "the product of an ideological conversion to labor-management cooperation." Rather, it evolved "out of a pragmatic judgment" that the parties "would have more to lose separately and jointly by going further down the road of escalating conflict." Partnership proponents point to subsequent gains for workers in job security, pension coverage, and standardized wage rates plus opportunities to participate in decision-making beyond the scope of normal contract bargaining—gains that required strong union involvement.

The four labor relations experts who produced *Healing Together* were hired in 2001 as paid consultants to the Kaiser-financed trust fund set up to administer the partnership. Several are well-known advocates of greater labor-management cooperation. So, notwithstanding their claim to "independence as outside researchers," they would appear to have an interest in proclaiming the partnership to be a great success. The authors believe it "has implications for two of the greatest challenges facing the nation today: how to improve, if not fix, a broken health care system" and how to revive a system of collective bargaining "that has collapsed."

The AFL-CIO likewise remains quite bullish about this experiment. At a July forum in Washington, D.C., outgoing AFL-CIO president John Sweeney credited Kaiser and the partnership for "improvements in patient outcomes, reductions in medical errors, better preventative care, cost savings, and a better, more satisfying work environment for everyone involved." In particular, Sweeney cited the "significant work" of one element of the partnership, "unit-based teams," in "bringing doctors, nurses, technicians, pharmacists, and other caregivers together on behalf of patients."

Unfortunately, neither Sweeney's upbeat report nor *Healing Together*—because of the timing of its publication—address the latest developments at Kaiser: a bitter shop-floor struggle in which management has sided with the Service Employees International Union (SEIU) against the latter's own rebellious members at Kaiser. That conflict began last winter when the partnership's largest local union participant, the 150,000-member United Healthcare Workers-West (UHW), was put under trusteeship by SEIU President Andy Stern following a major challenge to Stern's leadership by UHW members and officers.

Although supportive of the Kaiser partnership and a key player in building it, in 2007 and 2008 UHW had resisted pressure from Stern to make continuing contract concessions to California nursing home operators. These deals were supposed to expand union organizing opportunities but, as documented by UHW, they deprived workers of important job rights, prevented them from functioning as patient advocates, and failed to produce significant gains in either wages or dues-paying membership. Stern responded to this dissent by trying to dismember UHW and transfer all 65,000 of its long-term care workers to a new, more management-friendly statewide local with leaders appointed by him. When the affected UHW workers balked at this plan, Stern removed all of UHW's democratically elected officers and replaced them with his own appointees, triggering a rank-and-file revolt.

Soon after UHW's offices and treasury were seized, a majority of the 48,000 Kaiser employees represented by UHW petitioned to leave SEIU and join the National Union of Healthcare Workers (NUHW), a rival union created by former UHW president Sal Rosselli and other ousted activists. Unfortunately, the National Labor Relations Board is not a great protector of "employee free choice" for unionized workers seeking to change unions. The board upheld SEIU's legal claim that no vote should be held at Kaiser until next summer, when the current five-year contract expires. To force a vote then, NUHW must survive on voluntary membership contributions during the months ahead, plus re-sign all of its supporters on new election petitions.

Meanwhile, more than 700 UHW stewards have quit in disgust or been removed by SEIU after they refused to sign the loyalty oath required by Stern's trustees. Kaiser has eagerly exploited the resulting dismantling of the shop floor organization

UHW had built up for the purposes of strong contract enforcement and defending workers' rights, both on the job and inside the union. At Kaiser today, rank-and-file confidence in the value of partnering and management's commitment to that process is, by most reports, very low. Kaiser's "unit-based teams"—the basic building blocks of worker participation much lauded by the authors—are in complete disarray, SEIU-represented workers report.

"I've never seen this many terminations without just cause," says Lisa Tomasian, who works at Kaiser's Santa Clara Medical Center. "Many of us are facing discipline on trumped-up charges by managers who we used to hold accountable as shop stewards."

According to Tomasian, the open bargaining championed by UHW has been replaced by secret meetings between management and SEIU trustees. The latter "agreed to huge cuts in our pension," Tomasian charges. "SEIU brought four stewards to meet with Kaiser after the deal was made. They were told to just listen and ask no questions. SEIU appointees claimed that, by including these four people, democracy was served. Meanwhile, our lump-sum payout will get smaller and smaller until it's gone as an option altogether in 2012."

"Kaiser is truly in bed with SEIU," agrees former UHW leader Ralph Cornejo, now an organizer for NUHW. "Relationships that our stewards had built with the administration ended from one day to the next when the trusteeship was imposed. Kaiser is feeling like they can do just about anything now, and get away with it. Many members feel the union is irrelevant. The other unions know the partnership is doomed if this continues."

In *Healing Together*, Kaiser is nevertheless lauded for its partnership-related organizing rights agreement—a privately negotiated deal similar to what labor may need elsewhere if the Employee Free Choice Act is defeated or its card-check provision is dropped. Kaiser's pledge of non-interference in new organizing drives has led to a union success rate of 80% in 29 campaigns involving 7,400 workers. Overall, between 1997 and 2006, unions in the Kaiser coalition grew from about 55,000 to 86,000 members in all, via card-check recognition, bargaining unit accretion, and additional hiring.

Yet, when workers opted to organize with a union outside the partnership, Kaiser managers reacted like any other anti-union bosses. For example, in 2004, a group of Kaiser call center reps in Alameda, Calif., chose to organize with backing from the Communications Workers of America. Kaiser refused to recognize their "card majority," thereby buying more time for "Vote No" campaigning in a hotly contested NLRB election that was a case study in why workers need labor-law reform. Even after losing, Kaiser management continued to spend heavily on "union avoidance," engaging in bad-faith bargaining for more than a year. Without the benefit of first contract arbitration (one of the provisions of the Employee Free Choice Act bill) and not strong enough to strike, the frustrated and demoralized Alameda workers eventually voted by a narrow margin to decertify the Communications Workers union.

This outrageous management interference—which no partnership union protested at the time—was a taste of things to come. In Kaiser facilities today, management has weighed in clearly and repeatedly on the side of SEIU's occupying army of appointed staffers. As 17-year Kaiser worker Richard Schofield from West Covina, Calif., said in a recent letter of protest to SEIU, after he was removed as an elected shop floor leader:

"Requiring stewards to 'bow down' and sign a pledge of allegiance to SEIU-UHW is in direct conflict with all that we accomplished through partnership activities. Where is the collaborative spirit that the LMP was founded on? Does anyone really think that directing stewards to sign such a document will not contaminate the more democratic environment that has been created?"

For Schofield and many other longtime union activists at Kaiser, next year's representation contest between NUHW and SEIU-UHW can't come soon enough.

"You don't need a weather man to see which way the wind is blowing," he says. "SEIU is on the wrong side of this storm" because "without trust and honesty, there will never be a relationship between leadership and rank-and-file. The eventual outcome is always with the majority no matter how long and hard the fight." ❏

Source: Tom Kochan, Robert McKersie, Adrienne Eaton, and Paul Adler, *Healing Together: The Labor-Management Partnership at Kaiser Permanente*, Cornell ILR Press, 2009.

The Short Run: Unionize for Safety
May/June 2009

Amid all the jingoistic hoopla about the rescue of the merchant marine container ship *Maersk Alabama* from Somali pirates, an important fact about the crew was almost lost: They might not have survived without their labor unions.

In an interview on NBC's "Today" show after the rescue, Third Engineer John Cronan explained how they kept control of their ship: "We're American seamen. We're union members. We stuck together and did our jobs." The vessel's eight officers and engineers are members of either Masters, Mates & Pilots or Marine Engineers' Beneficial Association; the 12 unlicensed crew members are represented by the Seafarers International Union. The presidents of the three unions issued a joint statement on April 16:

"The training provided to American merchant marine officers and crew at the institutions jointly operated by America's labor unions and our contracted United States-flag shipping companies, including Maersk, are among the finest in the world. The quality of the training, the experience and expertise of the instructors, and the modern, state-of-the-art facilities and curricula ensure that American mariners will have the best possible information and training available so that when a situation such as this arises, they can respond efficiently and effectively."

—*Linda Pinkow*

Article 6.4

AUSTIN, MINNESOTA AND THE LEGACY OF THE IWW

BY PETER RACHLEFF

September 2005—WorkingUSA

Austin, Minnesota, some one hundred miles south of the Twin Cities and home to the George A. Hormel and Company meat-packing firm since the early 1920s, has been the site of not just one, but two significant chapters in U.S. labor history. In the mid-1930s, Hormel workers organized the Independent Union of All Workers (IUAW), extended it from the packinghouse to most of the city's workers, and then reached more than a dozen other communities in the Upper Midwest. Half a century later, during 1985–1986, Hormel workers, organized in United Food and Commercial Workers' (UFCW) Union Local P-9, launched a strike that set the tone nationally for the labor movement's struggle against concessions, plant closings, and deunionization. Both of these struggles, I suggest, were infused with the visions, ideas, and strategies of the Industrial Workers of the World (IWW).

I want to begin with two personal anecdotes as illustrations of how legacies are sustained and transmitted. These anecdotes also confirm the wisdom of my mentor, David Montgomery, who advised his students that serious labor historians must become familiar not only with archives and libraries but also union halls and picket lines. David's advice continues to bear fruit, not just for me, but for the entire cohort of labor historians he trained and inspired, who are now scattered around the country.

In the winter of 1986, in my capacity as chairperson of the Twin Cities Local P-9 Support Committee, I opened an envelope postmarked "Santa Rosa, California." Inside I found a check for $5 and a handwritten note. "This is all I can spare from my monthly social security check," it read, "and I'd like you to take it and buy groceries for those striking Hormel workers and their families." It was signed "Marian Nilson." My curiosity was piqued. Who was this woman and why was she sacrificing from her own meager income to support these strikers? So I wrote back to her, thanking her for her contribution, but also asking my questions.

When Mrs. Nilson responded, I learned that, in the mid-1930s, she and her husband Carl had left the Twin Cities for Austin, where he had secured a job with the newly created state Bureau of Workers' Education. Under its auspices and with the newly organized IUAW providing many of his students, Carl taught classes in labor history, labor law, parliamentary procedure, and even music. He also assumed the editorship of the IUAW's mimeographed newspaper, *The Unionist*, which was distributed free to every home in Austin. Marian wrote a book review column for *The Unionist* and helped organize the IUAW's Ladies Auxiliary. She also maintained a library in the union hall that featured works by John Reed, Upton Sinclair, and Edward Bellamy. This was her personal connection to the Hormel strikers, or at least their parents' and/or grandparents' generation.

Additional correspondence taught me more about Marian Nilson, about the IUAW, and about the dynamics of legacies within the labor movement. Her father, she explained to me, had been an organizer for the Knights of Labor in St. Paul in the 1880s, and, while he liked their vision of solidarity (expressed in their slogan, "An Injury to One is the Concern of All"), he had tired of their attention to ritual. When the IWW was created in 1905, he leapt at the opportunity to become a "Wobbly." Were he still with us in 1986, she assured me, he would have wanted to support the Hormel strikers.

My second anecdote suggests other historical threads that wove experiences from the early 20th century together with those from the 1980s. In the fall of 1984, I was part of a group of Twin Cities labor activists who attended a solidarity rally in the Austin Labor Center. When I walked into the hall, a wall display of old union buttons caught my eye. At first glance, they appeared to be from the IWW, bearing the familiar globe with its latitude and longitude lines. Upon closer examination, however, I discovered that they read "IUAW" rather than "IWW." They were dues buttons, each a different color, denoting a different month from the summer of 1933 through the spring of 1937.

Radicals and Activists

By talking to old-timers and active union members and by conducting some preliminary research, I learned that between those years in the Great Depression, the IUAW organized locals in more than a dozen cities in Minnesota, Iowa, Wisconsin, and North and South Dakota and influenced the emerging labor movement from Oklahoma to the Canadian border. The IUAW sought not only to organize packinghouse workers but also to organize "wall-to-wall," from manufacturing and transportation to retail and service workers. Their efforts—expressed in organizing drives, strikes, strike support, local politics, and cultural activities—threatened entrenched power throughout the region.

While an impressive cast of radicals and activists, both itinerant and local, helped create and spread the IUAW, no one had a greater influence than Frank Ellis. The feisty ex-Wobbly not only shaped the union's transformative vision, its all-encompassing structure, its commitment to democracy and solidarity, and its use of direct action tactics, but he also imprinted his combative personality into the union's character. In his late forties, Ellis had a labor record that dated from the 1904 St. Joseph, Missouri, meat-packing strike; free speech fights from Omaha to Seattle before World War I; the IWW's historic struggles in Centralia, Illinois, and Everett, Washington; a lengthy list of arrests, including an indictment for criminal syndicalism in Omaha; and a seat on the IWW's national executive board in the early 1920s. He was widely known as an effective stump speaker who put forward a "one big union philosophy." During his travels, Ellis had not only mastered butchering skills, but he had also learned a new sausage casing fermentation process. In 1928, Hormel hired him as a foreman to run its new casing department.

Keeping a low profile at first, Ellis helped other experienced labor activists get jobs. He later told an interviewer:

> I'd send out and get rebels that I knew from other towns to come in and go to
> work, and I'd work them during the rush season, see. Then, when it came to layoff

time, instead of laying them off, I'd go to some other boss and say, "Here, I've got a good man. And I hate like hell to lay him off. Can you use him? And I'll take him back as soon as business starts up." And I'd place him in the plant and scatter him out. Well, he was an old union man. He knew what to do. I didn't have to tell him. He knew the idea was to get in there with the gang and to get them emotionally moved so that they'd be ready to organize when the time came.

Ellis and his cadre of activists built a strong shop-floor organization, beginning in the spring of 1933. They used direct action to challenge managerial authority. That summer they stopped production in the hog kill to force foremen to tear up Community Chest pledge cards and that fall, they walked off the job to join members of the Farm Holiday Association in picketing roads into Austin as part of their campaign for higher hog prices. Rank-and-file workers were inspired and attracted to the IUAW by these actions, and they joined by the hundreds. They were ready for the confrontation that would bring them their first contract and increased wages.

In the country's first officially recorded sit-down strike, Hormel workers took over their plant on November 10, 1933, and held it—and millions of dollars' worth of equipment and semiprocessed meat—for the next three days. IUAW leaders insisted that company management come into the plant for negotiations, where, according to local folklore, they felt a rise in temperature every time they turned down a union demand at the bargaining table. Governor Floyd Olson, elected in 1930 on the Farmer Labor ticket, refused Jay Hormel's request that he call in the National Guard and instead rushed to Austin to mediate a settlement. Between Olson's apparent pro-union sympathies and managerial concerns that the meat might spoil, an agreement was reached. Shop-floor militancy and extensive solidarity characterized the IUAW, reflecting the legacy of the IWW. They relied on direct action to resolve grievances on the spot. One union veteran told an oral historian: "Frank Ellis would sit down at the union hall. They would call him up and say: 'Come on over, the department is sitting down . . .' Frank would go over to one of the departments, and here the people were madder than hell, sitting against the wall, refusing to work. . . . They'd get the grievance settled right on the job." Ellis himself told an interviewer: "Most of our strikes were sit down, sit down right on the job and not do a damn bit of work until we got it settled."

The IUAW spread by offering a militant role model and active solidarity to other workers, from barbers and beauticians to truckers and warehouse workers. They sent "teams" of rank-and-file "volunteer organizers" into other communities, organized mass meetings featuring the kind of stump speaking that had been practiced on soap boxes by the IWW, and then offered practical support on picket lines and in food pantries. The IUAW put forward a vision that echoed the Wobblies'. In the summer of 1937, one activist looked back over the past four years:

> Above all, Austin's unionization is not a shallow thing, but a master organization that penetrates far into the very lives of workers . . . It is not merely a matter of wages and more money to spend. Within this program of unionization lies the basis of things that are far reaching and more important. With unionization comes a new freedom—a freedom of the individual that will grow in importance

as the organizational experience grows older. A new freedom of thought, of action and knowledge, are products of workers' lives protected through organizations of their own choosing.

Working Class Militancy and Labor Repression

Although the IUAW could not maintain its organizational independence and integrity as the U.S. collective bargaining system took hold in the later 1930s and World War II years, and the labor movement reached legitimacy and a level of incorporation, the Hormel union (United Packinghouse Workers of America–Congress of Industrial Organizations (CIO), Local 9, then United Packinghouse Workers and Butcher Workmen, American Federation of Labor (AFL)–CIO, Local 9, then United Food and Commercial Workers' Union, Local P-9) maintained practices of shop-floor militancy and extensive solidarity. From the late 1970s to the early 1980s, when Hormel built a new plant and insisted on a complete reorganization of the production process and payment systems, workers enjoyed impressive control over their work, wages, and benefits that kept up with the best in the industry, a local union renowned for its internal democracy and rank-and-file participation, and a dignified status within their community, their industry, and their union.

Global, national, and local forces combined to set the stage for the new regime of the late 1970s to the early 1980s. Economic stagflation, corporate reorganization, capital flight and plant closings, technological change and the reorganization of production, and a ferocious shakeout in the meatpacking industry led Hormel management to drop its paternalistic practices and turn up the screws on workers. At the same time, the Vietnam War generation of workers came of age, in the plant and in the union hall. They did not merely react to this changed environment and these new pressures. They drew on the legacy of the IUAW and its creative adaptation of the legacy of the IWW.

This new generation of activists had been schooled by the 1930s generation. They had spent countless hours at the appropriately named "Lefty's Bar and Grill," listening to Frank Ellis himself expound his "one big union philosophy" and discuss union strategy. Pete Winkels, who would be elected business agent, was the son and nephew of two key activists from the thirties, Oscar and John Winkels, who had regaled him and his friends with stories of their shop-floor tactics. They also pored over back issues of *The Unionist*, meeting minutes, photos, and other memorabilia in the Austin Labor Center. As they found the business unionism of the 1970s ineffective in the face of the company's demands for concessions and pressures to speed up production, their interest in the IWW's legacy of direct action and solidarity grew.

Most of them had been hired into the beef side of the operations and put to work on night shift. There, they began to experiment with slowdowns and other tactics that responded directly to the pace of production. By the late 1970s, led by shop steward Jim Guyette, a third-generation Hormel worker, they had made the loin cooler a center of opposition to the proposed concessionary agreement that the company insisted upon as a condition for building a new plant in Austin rather than elsewhere. They focused on the no-strike clause in the "new plant agreement," and, although they fell short of defeating it, they garnered 502 negative votes, which gave them their new name—the "502 club." From their base in the nightshift loin cooler and the beef operations more generally, the "502 club" promoted an increasingly confrontational agenda.

They used an effective slowdown to win equal pay for all members of given departments regardless of seniority. They resisted organizational changes being promoted by the UFCW international. In 1981, Guyette was elected to the local's executive board, which also gave him a seat on the Hormel chain's bargaining committee, representing workers in eight plants, and he became the leading opponent to granting any further concessions to the company. Not content to be a lone voice, he began to publish a bulletin that informed members what was being discussed at the bargaining table. When Hormel and the union agreed to a wage freeze and cost of living adjustment cuts, Guyette and his cohort used the bulletin to rally opposition to the changes, leading to a "no" vote.

The new plant opened, even without contractual commitments to concessions, in the summer of 1982. Hormel workers found themselves in nightmarish working conditions. Technological innovations were introduced with little concern for safety. Chain speed was so fast that workers often stumbled into one another as they fell behind. Some were seriously cut. Carpal tunnel syndrome became epidemic. Grievances mounted. Meanwhile, turmoil was mounting in the meatpacking industry across the country. Big companies went out of business or declared bankruptcy and their plants were reopened with wages slashed by 50% or more. Hormel announced that they wanted to reopen their chain agreement for the purpose of negotiating big wage and benefit cuts.

In December 1983, Jim Guyette was elected president of Local P-9, and he began a campaign to change the union from the shop floor to the Hormel chain. He chose to sit in on grievance hearings and to use the in-plant union bulletin to inform the members about their outcomes. At chain contract negotiations, he urged unity in the face of demands for concessions. As in the 1930s and 1940s, direct action and solidarity were becoming the lifeblood of the union.

The Struggle for Rank-and-File Unionism

This time around, however, the legacy of the IWW was confronted not only by a determined, powerful corporate employer, but also by a bureaucratic union deeply enmeshed in a labor relations system that gave it legal advantages. Outside of Austin, Hormel workers were incorporated within geographically based local unions in which retail clerks dominated numerically and petty bureaucracies beholden to the national union ran day-to-day affairs. Although Guyette and the growing cohort of P-9 activists took their concerns directly to rank-and-file Hormel workers in Ottumwa, Iowa; Fremont, Nebraska; Dallas, Texas; and Atlanta, Georgia, their locals' representatives on the chain bargaining committee refused to join in Guyette's opposition to concessions. The company got its way in 1984.

But in the late summer of 1985, the Austin contract was coming due. Local P-9's activists worked the shop floor urging resistance to concessions, and they organized motorcycle brigades to the other Hormel plants, where they pitched tents, sat down over campfires with local workers, and solicited solidarity. At the least, they asked Hormel workers to refuse to do work in case the Austin workers walked out of the company's flagship plant. At the most, they asked the workers to consider honoring picket lines if they were put up. Meanwhile, Local P-9's leadership turned to maverick labor strategist Ray Rogers, asking him to devise a campaign that might pressure Hormel. While Rogers' financial strategy did not find the company's Achilles heel, it did provide a framework within which rank-and-file participation, family involvement, and an extensive solidarity network were built. And in August 1984, the union's membership voted by 92% versus 8% to reject the company's demands for wage, benefit, and work rule concessions and launch their historic strike. Over the next six or so months, Local P-9 built on its IWW/IUAW legacy and Rogers' vision of a participatory membership to construct a movement culture unlike anything created by a labor organization at least since the 1950s.

Union activity, dare I say class struggle, became a way of life for hundreds of families. This newfound social-political network became a source of education and personal/collective change for them. Rank-and-file packinghouse workers and their families studied political economy and labor history, became public speakers, painted murals and wrote songs, and reached beyond the community they had known all their lives to travel to New York City, California, and England, to explain their struggle to others, to solicit support, and to preach a vision of labor/class unity.

The audiences they reached, from rallies and marches in Austin to union halls across the country and into other parts of the world, were captivated by the stories they heard, the example they saw, and the possibility that was awakened for them. The union created an "Adopt-a-Family" program to link individual local unions to individual strikers and their families. More than two dozens of "P-9 Support Committees" sprang up and more than 3,000 local unions sent monetary aid to the strikers. Support also came from nineteen different countries beyond the borders of the United States. Tens of thousands of supporters visited Austin personally, marching, rallying, joining picket lines, delivering food or money, and making intimate connections with the strikers and their families. While most of the support and sense of connection came from other workers and other trade unionists, P-9's model of IWW-style unionism caught the imaginations of embattled farmers, veteran peace activists, idealist college students, folksingers and visual artists, and more. It had indeed become the center of a new movement culture.

The IWW's Legacy

While this strike failed—many of the strikers lost their jobs, the company was able to impose the concessions it sought—I would not hasten to term the struggle itself a failure, any more than other IWW struggles, or the struggles of the IUAW in the 1930s, which fell short of materializing the vision put forward by the likes of Frank Ellis and his comrades. The greatest gift of this legacy—beyond even its brilliant strategies and tactics, its models for effective organization, its vision of social justice, all of which remain valid and valuable today—is the example that each of these struggles provides that workers can take charge of their own struggles, that they can generate a movement culture, and that they can create the conditions through which they themselves can grow and change into human beings far bigger, far better than this capitalist system ever intended for them to be. This is the richest vein of the IWW's legacy that emerged twice in Austin, Minnesota, so that we, later, could say: "See, it *is* possible." ❑

Sources: E. Arnesen, J. Greene, and B. Laurie, eds. 1998. *Labor histories: Class, politics, and the working class experience*; *Austin Herald*, November 9, 10, and 11, 1933; *Austin American*, January 25, 1935; F. Blum, *Toward a democratic work process*, 1953; H. DeBoer, Interview with Randy Furst, Dave Riehle, Sal Salerno, and Peter Rachleff. Minnesota Historical Society, 1986; F. Ellis, Oral history interviews with Martin Duffy, Minnesota Historical Society, 1997; S. Godfredson, R. Helstein, and J. Winkels, Oral history interviews with Roger Horowitz and Rick Halpern. State Historical Society of Wisconsin, 1986; R. Halpern, *Down on the killing floor: Black and white workers in Chicago's packinghouses,*1997; R. Helstein, Oral history interview with Mark Smith. State Historical Society of Iowa, 1975; R. Horowitz, *"Negro and white, unite and fight": A social history of industrial unionism in meatpacking,* 1997; G. Lipsitz, *A rainbow at midnight: Labor and culture in the 1940s*, 1994; J. Metzgar, *Striking steel*, 2000; P. Rachleff, *Hard-pressed in the heartland: The Hormel strike and the future of the labor movement*, 1993; P. Rachleff, "Organizing 'wall-to-wall': The independent union of all workers 1933–1937" in *"We are all leaders": The alternative unionism of the early 1930s*, ed. S. Lynd, 51–71, 1993; Records of the Twin Cities Local P-9 Support Committee. Minnesota Historical Society; F. Schultz, "History of our union," *Unionist*, May 7:1971; *Unionist*, November 8 and 15, 1935, and August 7, 1937; W.J. Warren, *Struggling with Iowa's pride: Labor relations, unionism, and politics in the rural midwest since 1877*, 2000; S. Weir, *Singlejack solidarity*, 2004.

Article 6.5

LABOR'S CAPITAL
Putting Pension Wealth to Work for Workers

BY ADRIA SCHARF
September/October 2005

Pension fund assets are the largest single source of investment capital in the country. Of the roughly $15.5 trillion in stock equity in the U.S. economy, $3.1 trillion, or 20.1%, is directly held by employee pension plans. Pensions own $8.5 trillion in total assets. These vast sums were generated by—and belong to—workers; they're really workers' deferred wages.

Workers' retirement dollars course through Wall Street, but most of the capital owned *by* working people is invested with no regard *for* working people or their communities. Pension dollars finance sweatshops overseas, hold shares of public companies that conduct mass layoffs, and underwrite myriad anti-union low-road corporate practices. In one emblematic example, the Florida public pension system bought out the Edison Corporation, the for-profit school operator, in November 2003, with the deferred wages of Florida government employees—including public school teachers. (With just three appointed trustees, one of whom is Governor Jeb Bush, Florida is one of the few states with no worker representation on the board of its state-employee retirement fund.)

The custodians of workers' pensions—plan trustees and investment managers—argue that they are bound by their "fiduciary responsibility" to consider only narrow financial factors when making investment decisions. These professionals maintain they have a singular obligation to maximize financial returns and minimize financial risk for beneficiaries—with no regard for broader concerns. But from the perspective of the teachers whose dollars funded an enterprise that aims to privatize their jobs, investing in Edison, however promising the expected return (and given Edison's track record, it wasn't very promising!), makes no sense.

A legal concept enshrined in the 1974 Employee Retirement Income Security Act (ERISA) and other statutes, "fiduciary responsibility" does constrain the decision-making of those charged with taking care of other people's money. It obligates fiduciaries (e.g., trustees and fund managers) to invest retirement assets for the exclusive benefit of the pension beneficiaries. According to ERISA, fiduciaries must act with the care, skill, prudence, and diligence that a "prudent man" would use. Exactly what that means, though, is contested.

The law does *not* say that plan trustees must maximize short-term return. It does, in fact, give fiduciaries some leeway to direct pension assets to worker- and community-friendly projects. In 1994, the U.S. Department of Labor issued rule clarifications that expressly permit fiduciaries to make "economically targeted investments" (ETIs), or investments that take into account collateral benefits like good jobs, housing, improved social service facilities, alternative energy, strengthened infrastructure, and economic development. Trustees and fund managers are free to consider a double bottom line, prioritizing investments that have a social pay-off so long as their expected risk-adjusted financial returns are equal to other, similar, investments. Despite a backlash against ETIs from Newt Gingrich conservatives in the 1990s, Clinton's Labor Department rules still hold.

Nevertheless, the dominant mentality among the asset management professionals who make a living off what United Steelworkers president Leo Gerard calls "the deferred-wage food table" staunchly resists considering any factors apart from financial risk and return.

This is beginning to change in some corners of the pension fund world, principally (no surprise) where workers and beneficiaries have some control over their pension capital. In jointly managed union defined-benefit (known as "Taft-Hartley") plans and public-employee pension plans, the ETI movement is gaining ground. These types of pension funds provide for direct or indirect employee influence over investment decisions. Taft-Hartley plans are overseen by union trustees, and state pensions typically include employees on their oversight boards. By contrast, non-union corporate pension plans and defined contribution plans like 401(k)s provide for no employee voice in decision-making.

"Taft-Hartley pension trustees have grown more comfortable with economically targeted investments as a result of a variety of influences, one being the Labor Department itself," says Robert Pleasure of the Center for Working Capital, an independent capital stewardship-educational institute started by the AFL-CIO. Concurrently, more public pension fund trustees have begun adopting ETIs that promote housing and economic development within state borders. Most union and public pension trustees now understand that, as long as they follow a careful process and protect returns, ETIs do not breach their fiduciary duty, and may in certain cases actually be sounder investments than over-inflated Wall Street stocks.

Saving Jobs: Heartland Labor Capital Network

During the run-up of Wall Street share prices in the 1990s, investment funds virtually redlined basic industries, preferring to direct dollars into hot public technology stocks and emerging foreign markets, which despite the rhetoric of fiduciary responsibility were often speculative, unsound investments. Even most collectively bargained funds put their assets exclusively in Wall Street stocks, in part because some pension trustees feared that if they didn't, they could be held liable. (During an earlier period, the Labor Department aggressively pursued union pension trustees for breaches of fiduciary duty. In rare cases where trustees were found liable, their personal finances and possessions were at risk.) But in the past five years, more union pension funds and labor-friendly fund managers have begun directing assets into investments that bolster the "heartland" economy: worker-friendly private equity, and, wherever possible, unionized industries and companies that offer "card-check" and "neutrality." ("Card-check" requires automatic union recognition if a majority of employees present signed authorization cards; "neutrality" means employers agree to remain neutral during organizing campaigns.)

The Heartland Labor Capital Network is at the center of this movement. The network's Tom Croft says he and his allies want to "make sure there's an economy still around in the future to which working people will be able to contribute." Croft estimates that about $3 to $4 billion in new dollars have been directed to worker-friendly private equity since 1999—including venture capital, buyout funds, and "special situations" funds that invest in financially distressed companies, saving jobs and preventing closures. Several work closely with unions to direct capital into labor-friendly investments.

One such fund, New York-based KPS Special Situations, has saved over 10,000 unionized manufacturing jobs, according to a company representative. In 2003, St. Louis-based Wire Rope Corporation, the nation's leading producer of high carbon wire and wire rope products, was in bankruptcy with nearly 1,000 unionized steelworker jobs in jeopardy. KPS bought the company and restructured it in collaboration with the United Steelworkers International. Approximately 20% of KPS's committed capital is from Taft-Hartley pension dollars; as a result, the Wire Rope transaction included some union pension assets.

The Heartland Labor Capital Network and its union partners want to expand this sort of strategic deployment of capital by building a national capital pool of "Heartland Funds" financed by union pension assets and other sources. These funds have already begun to make direct investments in smaller worker-friendly manufacturing and related enterprises; labor representatives participate alongside investment experts on their advisory boards.

"It's simple. Workers' assets should be invested in enterprises and construction projects that will help to build their cities, rebuild their schools, and rebuild America's infrastructure," says Croft.

"Capital Stewardship": The AFL-CIO

For the AFL-CIO, ETIs are nothing new. Its Housing Investment Trust (HIT), formed in 1964, is the largest labor-sponsored investment vehicle in the country that produces collateral benefits for workers and their neighborhoods. Hundreds of union pension funds invest in the $2 billion trust, which leverages public financing to build housing, including low-income and affordable units, using union labor. HIT, together with its sister fund the Building Investment Trust (BIT), recently announced a new investment program that is expected to generate up to $1 billion in investment in apartment development and rehabilitation in targeted cities including New York, Chicago, and Philadelphia. The initiative will finance thousands of units of housing and millions of hours of union construction work. HIT and BIT require owners of many of the projects they help finance to agree to card-check recognition and neutrality for their employees.

HIT and BIT are two examples of union-owned investment vehicles. There are many others—including the LongView ULTRA Construction Loan Fund, which finances projects that use 100% union labor; the Boilermakers' Co-Generation and Infrastructure Fund; and the United Food and Commercial Workers' Shopping Center Mortgage Loan Program.

Since 1997, the AFL-CIO and its member unions have redoubled their efforts to increase labor's control over its capital through a variety of new programs. The AFL-CIO's Capital Stewardship Program promotes corporate governance reform, investment manager accountability, pro-worker investment strategies, international pension fund cooperation, and trustee education. It also evaluates worker-friendly pension funds on how well they actually advance workers' rights, among other criteria. The Center for Working Capital provides education and training to hundreds of union and public pension fund trustees each year, organizes conferences, and sponsors research on capital stewardship issues including ETIs.

Public Pension Plans Join In

At least 29 states have ETI policies directing a portion of their pension funds, usually less than 5%, to economic development within state borders. The combined public pension assets in ETI programs amount to about $55 billion, according to a recent report commissioned by the Vermont state treasurer. The vast majority of these ETIs are in residential housing and other real estate.

The California Public Employees' Retirement System (CalPERS) is an ETI pioneer among state pension funds. The single largest pension fund in the country, it has $153.8 billion in assets and provides retirement benefits to over 1.4 million members. In the mid-1990s, when financing for housing construction dried up in California, CalPERS invested hundreds of millions of dollars to finance about 4% of the state's single-family housing market. Its ETI policy is expansive. While it requires that economically targeted investments earn maximum returns for their level of risk and fall within geographic and asset-diversification guidelines, CalPERS also considers the investments' benefits to its members and to state residents, their job creation potential, and the economic and social needs of different groups in the state's population. CalPERS directs about 2% of its assets to investments that provide collateral social benefits. It also requires construction and maintenance contractors to provide decent wages and benefits.

Other state pension funds have followed CalPERS' lead. In 2003, the Massachusetts treasury expanded its ETI program, which is funded by the state's $32 billion pension. "It doesn't hurt our bottom line, and it helps locally," state treasurer Timothy Cahill told the *Boston Business Journal*. His immediate priority will be job creation. Washington, Wisconsin, and New York also have strong ETI programs.

In their current form and at their current scale, economically targeted investments in the United States are not a panacea. Pension law does impose constraints. Many consultants and lawyers admonish trustees to limit ETIs to a small portion of an overall pension investment portfolio. And union trustees must pursue ETIs carefully, following a checklist of "prudence" procedures, to protect themselves from liability. The most significant constraint is simply that these investments must generate risk-adjusted returns equal to alternative investments—this means that many deserving not-for-profit efforts and experiments in economic democracy are automatically ruled out. Still, there's more wiggle room in the law than has been broadly recognized. And when deployed strategically to bolster the labor movement, support employee buyouts, generate good jobs, or build affordable housing, economically targeted investments are a form of worker direction over capital whose potential has only begun to be realized. And (until the day that capital is abolished altogether) that represents an important foothold.

In 1978, activists Randy Barber and Jeremy Rifkin first urged the U.S. labor movement to wield greater control over its pension wealth in *The North Will Rise Again*. Today, workers' pension funds own vastly more capital. Pensions prop up the U.S. economy. They're a point of leverage like no other. Union and public pension funds remain the most promising means for working people to shape the deployment of capital on a large scale, while directing assets to investments with collateral benefits. If workers and the trustees of their pension wealth recognize the power they hold, they could alter the contours of capitalism. ❏

Sources: Michael Calabrese, "Building on Success: Labor-Friendly Investment Vehicles and the Power of Private Equity," *Working Captial: The Power of Labor's Pensions*, 2001. California Public Employees' Retirement System <www.calpers.ca.gov>. EBRI Pension Investment Report, First Quarter 2005 (2005). Teresa Ghilarducci, "Small Benefits, Big Pension Funds, and How Governance Reforms Can Close the Gap," *Working Capital: The Power of Labor's Pensions*, 2001. Doug Hoffer, "A Survey of Economically Targeted Investments: Opportunities For Public Pension Funds: A Report for the Vermont State Treasurer and the State Retirement Boards," 2004. Edward Mason, "Cahill to Boost Pension Fund Investments," *Boston Business Journal*, 2004.

The Short Run: Scrooge Says No to Unions
January/February 2009

The International Labor Rights Forum, a Washington, D.C.-based advocacy organization, announced its list of the "worst companies for the right to associate" in December. The five corporations named by the group: Nestle, Dole, Del Monte, Russell (owned by Fruit of the Loom), and Wal-Mart. Together, the five multinationals managed to violate workers' rights to form and join unions in nearly every continent—in Cambodia, Canada, Colombia, Costa Rica, Guatemala, Honduras, Pakistan, Peru, the Philippines, Russia, the United States, and Uzbekistan.

The group's report (titled "Work for Scrooge") outlines violations ranging from harassment to murder against workers attempting to organize. And in a post-9/11 twist, union membership is now being equated with terrorism. In the Philippines, the report alleges, "Dole and the Armed Forces of the Philippines have collaborated on anti-union propaganda programs," including mandatory "'symposiums' during work where every member was accused of being part of the New People's Army, targeted as a terrorist organization by the Filipino government."   —*Amy Gluckman*

Article 6.6

UNIONIZATION OF NURSES IN THE UNITED STATES
Worker Power, Autonomy, and Labor Democracy

BY HERMAN BENSON
May 2010—WorkingUSA

It was a moment of high hopes and great expectations in Phoenix on December 7, 2009. Three major unions of registered nurses were merging forces into a new national organization, National Nurses United (NNU). To thunderous applause from some 150 delegates, one of the three newly elected co-presidents proclaimed that this creation of the "largest union of direct care nurses is about a century overdue." And it is truly the largest and most promising union of registered nurses ever created in the United States: the three founding affiliates—the California Nurses Association (CNA), the Massachusetts Nurses Association (MNA), and the United American Nurses (UAN)—report a combined membership of 150,000.

An inspiring campaign of ambitious organizing and political action by the new union was proposed by one of its incoming leaders: to unite all working registered nurses in a single union to deploy maximum power in health care, to advance the interests of nurses in solidarity with nurses around the world, to battle for quality health care for all, to achieve effective collective bargaining representation, and to campaign for patient rights and for safe patient-to-nurse ratios in hospitals. Its new executive director declared that immediately after the convention, NNU would become an "organizing machine" that would set out to unionize all unorganized nurses in the country.

Supporters of the merger hail its formation as a long overdue step toward establishing a powerful and united force to represent the interests of the nation's 2.5 million nurses, in politics and on the job. Marilyn Albert, a registered nurse and experienced unionist, sees the formation of the new NNU as a part of the movement to "reverse the decline of labor" that will "amplify the voice of nurses to a national level." Her reaction is not the product of a momentary flash of enthusiasm; it is based on decades of experience. For thirty years, she served as a shop steward and organizer for 1199/ Service Employees International Union (SEIU) then left to join the California Nurses, where she is now an organizer. Her enthusiasm, even exhilaration, was shared by the delighted convention delegates and is widespread, but not unanimous because the evolution of nurse unionism in the United States has never been simple.

A quick look at the founding components of the new NNU reminds us that the course can be complicated and even confusing.

United American Nurses. Three top UAN leaders opposed merging into the NNU: President Ann Converso, Vice President Jan Croft, and Director Kathleen Gettys. With the support of UAN delegates from a majority of the smaller locals, together a reported one-fifth of the total UAN membership, they boycotted the union's conference that had been called to decide on the merger and blocked it from assembling a constitutional quorum to conduct business. But delegates from four locals, representing 80% of the members, remained in the hall to replace Converso as chair and vote for the merger.

The two sides battled it out in court: In one suit, a federal court rejected the application of Converso supporters for an injunction to block the merger. In an opposing federal suit, merger advocates sought a federal court order barring interference with their plans. As the UAN now enters the new union, it lists some 40,000 members among its various state affiliates, but it is not clear how many will stay for the long haul. At best, the UAN comes in as a shadow of its earlier self. Not long ago, with over 100,000 members, the UAN was by far the largest nurses' union in the nation. But in 2007, UAN affiliates with some 60,000 members, including state nurses associations in New York, Ohio, Washington, and Oregon, seceded from the UAN, reducing it to its current level of 40,000.

National Federation of Nurses. In 2007, when the UAN was beginning to function more and more like a traditional union, four state affiliates split. They seemed nervous over the prospect of subordination to a higher authority. They demanded that the UAN break off any cooperative ties to the SEIU, obviously fearing domination or infiltration by it. After seceding from the UAN, these four nurses' associations, together with other former UAN affiliates, set up their own new national nurses group, the National Federation of Nurses, in January 2009. The prime mover in this new national union is the 30,000-member New York State Nurses Association. The National Federation of Nurses claims a total of 70,000 members in all its state affiliates. They had hoped to join the American Federation of Labor–Congress of Industrial Organizations (AFL–CIO) but were rebuffed by President John Sweeney. The National Federation of Nurses (NFN), then, is a loose confederation of labor organizations, each of which wants all the advantages of combination with none of the commitments. The defining element of its constitution is the guarantee of complete autonomy for all affiliates.

Massachusetts Nurses Association. The MNA joins the NNU with 23,000 members. The union has a robust democratic tradition, reflected in its website, but it is not yet clear how enthusiastically the membership welcomes the merger. On December 9, just one day after the NNU founding convention, dissenting MNA members, skeptical of the merger, formed a caucus independent of the leadership. Its supporters had begun by opposing the merger; now they are convinced that they must organize for the future to resist what they fear could be an erosion of the MNA's autonomous rights in the larger national body and a disquieting drift away from its traditional democracy.

They cite the MNA merger referendum as one basis for their misgivings: on the eve of the merger, the MNA leadership had arranged for a membership referendum. Votes would be cast in person at a statewide membership meeting that was set for a weekday when most members were scheduled to work, and on Cape Cod, in the remote eastern edge of the state. Only a few hundred attended. At the meeting, one member of the MNA Board of Directors tried to motion for a statewide referendum by mail; he was simply ruled out of order. The leadership announced that that the merger had been approved "overwhelmingly." But few of the union's 23,000 had voted; the actual count was 390 to 124.

California Nurses Association. Spearheading the new union is the CNA, whose leadership and membership seem, unlike its two partners, wholeheartedly committed to the new venture. According to reports of the merger agreement, the CNA will dominate the new union: Rose Ann DeMoro, CNA executive director, becomes its executive director, and the CNA gets a majority on the new national executive board.

The CNA left the American Nurses Association (ANA) in 1993 after an insurgent group took over the California state affiliate, broke with ANA professionalism, and transformed the CNA into an explicitly labor organization. As such, it affiliated with the AFL–CIO in 2006. By establishing its own National Nurses Organizing Committee, it reached out beyond California to become a national nurses' union that now brings 86,000 members into the new union.

In the years that followed its departure from the ANA, the CNA earned a reputation as an active, militant, progressive, proselytizing organization. In setting out to organize around the country, it engaged in jurisdictional battles with other unions, including the SEIU.

Reports from nurses to the Association for Union Democracy have been mixed. Marilyn Albert, who speaks from experience, says that the CNA represents "real social movement unionism" and that its leaders transformed a conservative nurses association, under the control of nurses in management, into a real union that undertook to organize the unorganized. On the other hand, nurses in Florida have complained that the CNA had agreed with one hospital chain to abandon organizing efforts at one or more sites in return for the company's neutrality toward organizing at other sites, apparently making an arrangement similar to one that touched off a bitter battle in the California SEIU. (The CNA did not reply to a request for comment.) In Nevada, in contrast, nurse Sally Johnson, an informed and enthusiastic unionist and former SEIU member, reports that a vigorous CNA campaign in Reno has just achieved a contract superior to any others.

In any event, there are miles to go before registered nurses can be united into a single predominant union. A majority of those registered nurses who are already organized remain dispersed among other unions, independent of the new organization. Of these, the National Federation of Nurses claims 70,000; American Federation of Teachers, 40,000. Thousands of other nurses are organized in unions like the Operating Engineers, American Federation of Government Employees, American Federation of State, County and Municipal Employees, Teamsters, and independents like the New York Professional Nurses Association. A major player is the SEIU, which is the principal union in health care and claims to have enrolled 85,000 registered nurses.

Service Employees International Union. For a time, the SEIU was embroiled in an intense rivalry with the CNA, so bitter that in 2008 it actually led to a push and shove confrontation that fell just short of a brawl. That year, the CNA had sent representatives into Ohio, where it urged nurses to reject the SEIU in a collective bargaining election; it succeeded in forcing the SEIU to withdraw from the election and abandon efforts to organize health-care workers at local Catholic hospitals. In retaliation, the SEIU sent a mass of pickets into Detroit in an effort to disrupt sessions of a *Labor Notes* conference where CNA executive director Rose Ann DeMoro was scheduled to speak. Conference participants blocked pickets from breaking into the hall, but DeMoro felt forced to withdraw from the conference. The CNA charged that the SEIU made sweetheart deals with management; the SEIU accused the CNA of scabbing and union busting.

But early in 2009, the war came abruptly to an end with a surprise peace pact. The SEIU and the CNA ended hostilities, agreed to cooperate, and peaceably parceled out nurses where the two had been competing before. Since reaching the nonaggression pact with the CNA, the SEIU seems to have deemphasized its own effort to organize nurses, but it is hard to believe that SEIU president Andy Stern will abandon the field. Earlier in 2008 he told the SEIU convention, "One fundamental test of any agreement [with employers] should be that it speeds up the day when all workers in health care, public sector, and private services can be united in our union." For the moment, however, he is overwhelmed by other things, devoting enormous resources to digest the 150,000 California locals he put into trusteeship and trying to ward off the challenge from the new National Union of Healthcare Workers in California. As the new CNA-UAN-MNA union—NNU—takes off, Stern is still there in the wings.

Earlier Attempts at Unifying Nurses

The formation of the new NNU is not the first attempt to bring nurses into one national union. In 2002, with the California nurses in the lead, five unions agreed to form the American Association of Registered Nurses, which would combine the CNA, the Massachusetts Nurses, the Maine State Nurses Association, the Pennsylvania Association of Staff Nurses, and the United Health Care Workers of Missouri into one national union with some 70,000 members. But according to one participant, the deal fell through, mainly because some partners insisted upon a loose structure that would guarantee strict autonomy to the affiliates and concentrate upon mutual aid and lobbying for common aims; but the CNA, according to the report, wanted a more centralized traditional union-international structure and went its own way. The desire for autonomous rights undermined the desire for unity.

Around 2006, the UAN, by far the largest nurses' union with its 108,000 members, seemed a likely candidate to lead the charge. But its potential leadership role vanished when those four affiliates walked away with 60,000 members. The UAN failure to fulfill the role of unifier points to a continuing dilemma. What brought those 108,000 nurses under the UAN banner was the call for autonomous rights inside the ANA. The disaffected affiliates were impelled to depart, it now seems clear, because they feared that their rights would be threatened in a strong, vigorous national union— a misgiving that was reinforced when the UAN began cooperating with the SEIU. The very impulse for autonomy that created the UAN in the end undermined it.

Earlier, the most promising contender for the role of unifier had been the SEIU. After the affiliation of most of health and hospital Local 1199, it developed into an 1.8-million-member union through assorted mergers with smaller unions. It earned a reputation as a militant, progressive union that organized exploited racial minorities and substantially raised their standard of living. It became the dominant union, by far, in health care, especially among the non-professional ancillary personnel. When it reached out to registered nurses, however, its appeal had limited effect. It claims to have enrolled 85,000 nurses, not in their own separate SEIU-linked union but distributed among the various SEIU health-care locals around the country.

At this point, in line with a grandiose reorganization plan, the SEIU program aims to recruit an additional million members to revive the dwindling power of the labor movement, rebuild the American economy, change Washington, neutralize big capital, and create ties with worker organizations the world over. To accomplish these ambitious goals, the union centralizes extensive powers in the hands of the international president who proposes to turn the whole cadre of appointed staff and elected officers, local and international, into a kind of quasi-military operation speaking with one voice not only to the outside world but also to the SEIU membership. Whatever its virtue, the plan has at least this one flaw: it comes into head-on collision with nurses' insistence on autonomous rights. And so the SEIU, domineering over its membership in the lofty goal of leading the nation, has squandered its opportunity of leading registered nurses.

What set the stage for all these events is the long convoluted story of nurses' unionism.

From "Professionalism" to Unionism

The historical trend among registered nurses has been a shift away from narrow "professionalism" toward unionism, that is, a realization by at-the-bed staff nurses that, like all other employees, their working conditions must be protected and their rights nailed down by unions in collective bargaining. For decades, the principal voice for nurses had been the ANA. Founded in 1911 as a professional society for developing ethical standards, lobbying, public relations, and education, it rejected collective bargaining and was hostile to unionism. But in the mid-1940s, when staff nurses sought representation on the job, the ANA established a separate bargaining division. It was necessarily a complicated set-up because the ANA continued to be management-controlled while federal law required that labor organizations be free of management domination.

The structure provided a limited degree of self-government for employed staff nurses. Each ANA state affiliate set up its own separate quasi-autonomous collective bargaining unit, but financing and final administrative control remained in the hands of nonunion boards of directors. In time, staff nurses demanded a greater degree of autonomy.

These quasi-union state groups joined together in the UAN, still controlled by the ANA and dependent on it for financing. In 2001, representing those 108,000 nurses, the UAN joined the AFL–CIO. Registered nurses were now identified as part of the organized labor movement. In 2003, the UAN became a fully autonomous organization financed by per capita payments from its own affiliates. For a time it remained loosely affiliated with the ANA but is now effectively independent.

Throughout all these permutations and combinations, registered nurses have drifted toward unionism. Union enthusiasts, however, want a more deliberate, activist, organizing unionism. Dispersed now among all the organizations that compete for nurses, these enthusiasts look for a unifying force that can organize the drive to bring together most of the nation's 2.5 million registered nurses. But can it succeed where the American Association of Registered Nurses, the UAN, and the SEIU have failed? The experience of at least seventy years indicates that one stubborn barrier to the formation of a single strong union is the conflict between centralization and autonomy. The challenge is to find a way to combine the nurses' quest for union power with their persisting aspiration for autonomous rights.

Autonomy, Democracy, and Union Power

In moving from professionalism to unionism, nurses retain pride in their profession and a realization of their central role in health care. They are won over to unionism as a curb on the authority of imperious management. In unions, this desire for rights and recognition is translated into an insistence that registered nurses should control nurses' unionism, all of which explains why the demand for autonomy is so popular a rallying cry. They identify with the labor movement and affiliate with the AFL–CIO because they realize that they need the power of the labor movement in health-care battles in the larger society. They insist upon autonomy to protect the power of nurses within that labor movement.

However, the growing trend within the labor movement today is in the opposite direction, away from rights down below toward the imposition of authoritarian control from above and the obliteration of local autonomy. To organize the unorganized, to reverse labor's decline, to meet the centralized power of management—it is argued—unions must centralize power in the top leadership, reduce the role of elected stewards, and limit dissent by requiring elected officers and appointed staff to speak with one voice inside the union to the membership and outside to the public. This trend is graphically evident in the SEIU and in the building trades, especially in the formation of various regional and district councils whose structure turns locals into administrative shells and enables the officials to deny many of the rights that federal law, the Labor-Management Reporting and Disclosure Act of 1959, intended to protect. (Ironically, those union leaders who insist upon unbridled, super-centralized power as a necessary means of confronting hostile management are precisely those who, in real life, propose to increase union membership in agreement with cooperating employers.)

And so, at this point in the evolution of the American labor movement, the demand of nurses for union autonomy is a welcome and necessary counterweight to an encroaching authoritarianism and to the pressure for conformity. But autonomy has its own limitations. It does not assemble the resources and create the structure needed to fight labor's tough battles. For that you do need a measure of centralizing authority. In that respect its critics do have a point. Autonomy can limit arbitrary authority, but it is no substitute for a strong centralizing force.

With self-governing rights, a local union or an affiliate of a larger international can stimulate local initiative, negotiate contracts to suit their special needs, elect shop stewards to enforce contracts, pay attention to members' grievances, set local dues levels, retain their own attorneys, elect leaders, and pay officers free from international political dictate, even organize and intervene in politics in their own jurisdictional area. It can do everything essential to stimulate initiative and convince members that the union is theirs. But it cannot meet the needs of the larger labor movement to organize nationally, to coordinate dealing with corporations nationally and globally, to act as a force in national politics, and to organize the millions of unorganized. For that, a union needs the authority to tax subsidiaries, a certain measure of discipline in national affairs, and a national strike fund for mutual support.

If power centralized in the hands of officers at the international level has the potential for abuse, so does autonomy at the local level because autonomy is not necessarily synonymous with honest or democratic unionism. In some of our major unions, as in the Teamsters and construction trades, local officers have utilized the autonomous right to create regimes that are self-serving, repressive, and sometimes corrupt. None of the nurses' unions, not the nationals, not the locals, have ever been the subjects of such corruption scandals, and in this respect these unions are many notches above most others. Nevertheless, some leaders who jealously guard their own local autonomous rights against interference from any larger national body turn out to be leery of dissenters who assert the same kind of rights in their union.

In the big—and very autonomous—New York State Nurses Association, the leaders took the union out of the UAN even though, in an "opinion" referendum, two-thirds of the voters rejected the move. Disciplinary charges were filed against 23 nurses who had campaigned against disaffiliation. (The union backtracked and dismissed the charges only after three of the intended victims had filed suit in federal court.)

And so it is not a matter of idealizing or demonizing either autonomy or centralized union power as opposing principles. The practical question is how to deal with the persisting clash between the manifest need for union power and the insistent aspiration for autonomy. The question continues to bedevil those who want to build a strong union for nurses.

One "solution" is to suppress autonomy as heresy, eliminate its partisans, and construct a centralized system in which the leading cadre moves in lockstep. Some union leaders brandish the need for strong national unions as a club to enforce conformity, curb autonomous local rights, and centralize power in the hands of an authoritarian officialdom. That approach may have some success in restoring union power in the United States. Or it may prove to be self-defeating. Whatever the future holds, the authoritarian spirit among leaders has failed to unify the scattered forces of nurse unionism.

There is another way: it calls for integrating the requirements of union power with the deep-seated aspiration for autonomous rights so that each strengthens the other. That need, the need to temper centralized power with individual rights, was confronted in the formative days of the American republic.

After the Articles of Confederation turned the United States into a loose combination of sovereign states with an ineffectual central government, the new U.S. Constitution proposed to create a national government armed with enough power to sustain a strong nation capable of acting on the world scene. To allay the fears of those who argued that centralized power posed the danger of tyranny, a Bill of Rights, in ten amendments, was added. The disturbing trend of established labor leadership today is toward concentrated power and watered-down rights—all power but no bill of rights, or only lip service to it.

As an empty abstraction, the idea of reconciliation already receives a token bow of respect; some of our major unions feel impelled to write what they call a Bill of Rights into their own constitutions. In most cases, these provisions prescribe nothing more, or even less, than what is already required by federal law and lack effective enforcement procedures, or are violated in actual practice. None of this has had much effect on life in unions, but it does remind us that hypocrisy is the homage that vice pays to virtue. After the SEIU 2008 international convention wrote a feeble bill of rights into its constitution, the international president, backed by a compliant international executive board, promptly clamped a repressive trusteeship over United Healthcare Workers-West, the 140,000-member California local whose leadership had been critical of SEIU president Stern.

The spirit that motivates the desire for autonomous rights can be a force that enhances union power when it is linked to respect for individual rights. It is precisely that spirit, that resentment against domination from above, that leads workers who resent arbitrary rule by employers to unionism. It is the quality that a healthy labor movement should cultivate in its own interests. It is that quality that domineering officialdom represses.

When unions respect workers' rights on the job and in the union hall and assure them that the movement truly belongs to them, union members can serve as an army of proselytizers, defending the labor movement and advancing its program in the broad population. With that kind of respect for members' rights, the labor movement recruits millions of representatives to speak on its behalf in churches, clubs, societies, lunchrooms, and diners.

The challenge for progressives is to find a way to combine the quest for union power with the insistence on autonomous rights. True in the labor movement generally, this precept is especially true among nurses, where a strong nurses' union can satisfy the quest for autonomy by offering union democracy—not the simulacrum of democracy, not deferential holiday bows to democracy, not democracy confined to printed constitutions—but actual democracy in the life of the union.

Democracy?

Social philosophers may find it difficult to define; derogators may find it easy to obfuscate; but we know what it is when we do not see it. In unions, there are practical tests for preserving or introducing democracy.

Full Transparency. Abolish restrictive rules imposed on the pretext of a false or exaggerated need for "confidentiality." Keep members fully informed on finances, actions of executive boards, salaries of staff and officers. Comply with the provisions of federal law that require unions to keep members informed of their legal right to fair elections, free speech, due process in trials, and the right to appeal to courts and government agencies for recourse against abuse.

Provide Genuine Due Process. Establish an appeals board outside of the union power structure, modeled upon the UAW Public Review Board but with greater guarantees that the process for the selection of its members will assure their independence and impartiality. As in the UAW, the appeals board should have the right to review and even reverse decisions of the union's president or international executive board on issues such as disciplinary charges and trials, imposition of trusteeships over locals, election disputes, and accusations of corruption and malicious and arbitrary treatment of members—in general, on any matter that involves democratic rights.

It is also essential to enforce rules for fair job referrals in union hiring halls, encourage the use of the Internet as a tool for democratic discussion, especially during union elections and referendums, and refrain from restrictions on independent websites run by rank-and-file members. The unions must recognize the right of members to discuss social and union issues with the media and in public and with elected public officials without being subjected to retaliatory discipline. In addition, unions must encourage the election rather than appointment of job stewards and business agents, and submit proposed collective bargaining agreements to the affected membership for ratification vote.

It is essential that unions abolish meeting attendance rules that invariably have the effect of disqualifying an overwhelming majority of members from running for office. End the requirement of years of continuous good standing that bar dedicated long-time unionists from candidacy because they may have inadvertently fallen a few days in arrears or who are disqualified when dues records are inefficiently recorded or maliciously manipulated. To promote debate, unions must provide discussion pages in union publications, especially during elections and referendums.

Where it is advisable to establish huge mega-locals, they must provide for the election of officers of subunits or chapters and payment of their salaries. Where so-called intermediate organizations like district and regional councils effectively take over functions traditionally performed by local unions, they should require the direct election of council officers by the membership of affiliated locals and membership referendums on due structure. In the distribution of dues income, they must give locals enough money to pay salaries to their elected officers and retain attorneys when needed.

Conclusion

This compilation, this laundry list of specific measures, is intended to bring the subject of democracy in unions down from the outer space of intellectual speculation to the realm of practical life in unions. This or that single proposal may be discounted as trivial or inapplicable. (As lawmakers are careful to note, if any portion is ruled inappropriate, it shall not invalidate the rest.) The spirit behind it is what counts, the spirit that is missing in the broader labor movement. Hopefully, now that nurses are firmly linked to that movement, they will help imbue it with that spirit.

The model of unabashed authoritarian unionism has not succeeded in uniting nurses, or even coming close. And yet the need and the desire for a unifying force remains. In merging three separate unions into one NNU, the new union appeals to that desire for a united, effective, progressive union. But can the new NNU succeed where others have failed? As nurses move away from narrow professionalism, union advocates are still divided between those who see the need for coordinated power and those who insist upon the rights of autonomy. If anything can bring them together, it is the magnetic force of union democracy. ❏

Article 6.7

MINEWORKERS' DIRECT ACTION
Occupations and Sit-Ins in South Africa

BY SHAWN HATTINGH
September 2010—WorkingUSA

Even today, racist attitudes permeate mining institutions in South Africa. The fact that South African mines continue to have some of the worst working conditions and safety records in the world is telling. Each year, hundreds of workers die in accidents underground, while thousands more die of work-related diseases such as silicosis. Obviously, the mining bosses in South Africa do not particularly care about this because after all, for them, it is only insignificant "others" dying underground.

The mining sector in South Africa, however, merely reflects the attitudes and practices of the broader society. The elite in the country, as a whole, treat the majority of people with utter disdain, or at best with condescending paternalism. For bosses and politicians, workers and the poor in South Africa are simply human fodder for the country's mines, factories, and electoral machine. Naturally, being subjected to such a dehumanizing system has led to a seething anger among workers and the poor, and rightfully so. It is also this anger that often bursts into struggle and direct action—whether in the form of community protests or wildcat strikes.

Since mid-2009, the anger that people have been feeling toward the system and the exploiting elite has once again erupted: this time, in the form of a series of mine occupations. Considering the history of extreme exploitation and racism in the mining industry, it is perhaps no coincidence that workers decided to take the fight to their bosses in this arena through embarking on sit-ins and occupations. Indeed, the main grievances of the workers involved in these occupations centered on issues that have deep historical roots: the racist attitudes of managers, unsafe working environments, precarious working conditions, unpaid wages, and bad wages.

Crocodile River Mineworkers Start the Mine Occupations

The first of a string of six mine occupations which occurred over the last few months in South Africa took place in July 2009 at the Crocodile River Mine. In order to avoid adhering to aspects of South Africa's labor legislation and to lower the costs of employment, the management of Crocodile River Mine was hiring contract workers through another company, JIC, which was operating as a labor broker. In fact, a large percentage of the workforce at Crocodile River Mine was employed as contract workers, which also meant that legally, the mine did not have to implement any proper health and safety workplace standards. For the workers, this meant that they could be fired more easily than permanent workers, they could be paid less, they could be denied benefits that permanent workers were entitled to, and they could be denied the right to work in a safe environment.

For these reasons, the contract workers at Crocodile River Mine embarked on various actions such as picketing to try to persuade the bosses to hire them on a permanent basis. Initially, they were supported by the second largest union in the country, the National Union of Mineworkers (NUM). The protest actions by the workers appeared to have initially brought some success as the management made a promise that all contract workers would indeed be hired on a permanent basis and that their grievances would be addressed. Nonetheless, months passed and these concerns failed to be addressed. Frustrated, 560 contract workers eventually decided to occupy the mine on Thursday, July 9, 2009, in a bid to get management to meet their demands. In doing so, they shut down the mine's operations and blockaded themselves underground. Not only were the bosses of the mine caught off guard, but union officials from the NUM were also caught unaware, and from the start, it was clear that the workers were undertaking the occupation through self-initiative. On hearing that workers were occupying the mine, the NUM did send officials down to the mine and they tried to persuade the workers to end their sit-in. This, however, initially failed and soon after, the mine management called in the police and acquired a court interdict against the workers.

Throughout the two days of the mine occupation, negotiations between the union and the bosses continued until eventually an agreement was reached. The agreement stated that a new round of negotiations would take place between management and the union to look at the possibility of hiring all contract workers on a permanent basis. Upon hearing this, the workers occupying the mine decided to surface. Yet, as soon as they had exited the mine, the management once again reneged on its promises and fired all of the 560 workers that were involved in the occupation. To add insult to injury, the police also laid charges of trespassing and kidnapping against the workers. It was clear from these draconian actions that the state and the company involved were trying to intimidate the workers and prevent the idea of mine occupations from spreading.

The Platinum Mining Strike and the Kroondal Mine Occupation

The state and bosses' strategy of trying to terrorize workers into abandoning any idea of occupying mines has turned out to be a dismal failure. In the weeks that followed the Crocodile River Mine occupation, a second mine occupation occurred—this time at the Aquarius Platinum Kroondal Mine in Rustenburg.

The occupation of the Kroondal Mine had its roots in a strike that occurred in the platinum mining sector in August 2009. Workers across Rustenburg—whether at the Kroondal Mine or the mines owned by another company, Impala Platinum—went out on strike for higher wages. Most of the workers were members of the NUM and were demanding at least a 14% increase. From the start, the strike was marked by a high degree of militancy. Several days into the strike, however, the negotiators from the NUM announced that they had reached an agreement with the bosses and that as a result, workers could expect a 10% increase. Workers at both Impala Platinum and the Kroondal were angered by this and felt that the union bureaucracy and negotiating team had sold them out. For this reason, most of the workers remained out on strike.

Officials from the NUM then rushed to Rustenburg and tried to intervene to bring the strike to a halt. At Impala Platinum's Rustenburg mine, they received a hostile reception from the workers. When the NUM deputy president insisted that the workers accept the corporation's offer and return to work, some of the workers responded by throwing stones and physically attacking him. Meanwhile, at the Kroondal mine, the workers there too remained out on strike and refused to budge. With the NUM having accepted the bosses' offer, the continued strike action lost its legal status and essentially became a wildcat strike. The Kroondal Mine management used this as a pretext to fire the 3,900 workers who had elected to continue the strike.

Protests were then organized by the workers to demand their reinstatement. During these protests, the police and mine security harassed the workers, opened fire on them on numerous occasions, and set trained dogs on them. The outcome was that three strikers were killed. Under intense pressure, the Kroondal Mine managers were eventually forced to reinstate the workers. Nevertheless, as soon as the workers returned to work, they discovered that the bosses had erased their employment histories and had terminated some of their benefits. This then led to a second wildcat strike. Once again, management fired the workers involved and refused to even issue them their Unemployment Insurance Fund (UIF) certificates. With this, 32 of the workers decided to embark on an occupation of the mine.

The 32 workers managed to get through the mines' security systems and gained access to the underground section of the mine. Immediately, they also tried to barricade themselves in. They also stated that they would not resurface until they had been issued their UIF certificates so that they could claim the unemployment benefits that were due to them. The management of the mine reacted callously and, without delay, summoned the police. On arrival, police task force members descended into the mine and proceeded to attack the workers to force them to resurface. In the process, some sort of altercation ensued and both the miners and a couple of police force members were injured. The police allege that this involved workers setting off explosive booby traps to prevent being arrested. Whether or not this was the case, and considering the police's brutal role in the preceding wildcat strikes, it seems quite likely that the altercation involved workers merely trying to defend themselves against further violence at the hands of the state's representatives.

In the end, however, all 32 of the workers participating in the action were arrested and charged with attempted murder, malicious damage to property, trespassing, and assault. In addition, the families of the workers who were hospitalized as a result of the clash with the police were denied visiting rights. Sadly, far from supporting them or even offering them any form of solidarity, NUM officials turned their backs on their own members. In the aftermath of the occupation, the NUM released a cold statement saying: "We therefore call on the law enforcement agencies to ensure that those who are involved in all these irregular activities are arrested and that no one disguises criminal activity as labor matters." It was this type of attitude that eventually led the 32 workers to join a rival union, the Metal and Electrical Workers Union of South Africa (MEWUSA). Despite its problems, which include a high level of centralization and bureaucratization, MEWUSA at least offered the workers some assistance and managed to secure them legal representation, bail, and visiting rights for the families of the workers who had been hospitalized.

The Two Rivers and Bokoni Mine Occupations

While the ruthless crushing of the Kroondal Mine occupation was occurring, another mine occupation erupted in Mpumulanga at the Two Rivers Mine. On

October 19, 2009, over 100 workers staged a sit-in to demand that a racist manager be fired and four of the workers he had recently dismissed be reinstated. Within hours, hundreds of workers had joined in the sit-in and had completely shut down production. The bosses were clearly under pressure due to the workers' actions and agreed to investigate the conduct of the manager in question and to reinstate the four workers. By early November, however, the four workers had still not been rehired. As a consequence, 1,400 workers decided to once again occupy Two Rivers. They remained underground for over 40 hours until management finally gave in and took concrete steps to reemploy their four colleagues.

With this victory, the occupation was called off. Yet, despite the promises of the Two River Mine bosses, no investigation into the manager in question was ever conducted, and anger among the workers continued to boil just beneath the surface. Matters were compounded when the management at the mine failed to pay workers their end-of-year bonuses and overtime. As a result of this, on January 20, 2010, about 50 workers decided to once again embark on a wildcat strike and occupy the mine.

In a coordinated effort, over 100 workers at the Bokoni Mine several hundred kilometers away from Two Rivers also decided to occupy their workplace and refused to leave their shifts. Their demands and reasons for embarking on their occupation were also similar to those at Two Rivers Mine: they wanted the appalling safety standards at the mine addressed, they wanted the bonus system reexamined, and they wanted a racist manager to be fired.

Similar to the previous occupations in the preceding months, the workers involved in these two occupations had undertaken them independently of their unions. As such, the workers' actions were based on self-initiative and self-organization. When the bureaucrats from the workers' unions—in the form of the NUM and the Association of Mineworkers Union—learned of the occupations, instead of supporting them, they condemned them. In fact, both unions called for the occupations to end immediately, and the NUM bureaucracy even went as far as accusing the workers involved in the Two Rivers Mine occupation of kidnapping their members. They also called for the police to intervene and end both of these occupations. As it turned out, the NUM members that were supposedly kidnapped at Two Rivers were in fact willingly involved in the occupation.

The owners of the two mines—African Rainbow Minerals and Impala Platinum—immediately embarked on an intimidation campaign to try and get the workers to surface. Traditional leaders were called in by the companies to instruct the workers to end the occupations. When this failed, the two companies obtained court orders to evict the workers. The workers at first simply ignored the court orders and continued with the occupations.

Nonetheless, on January 22, 2010, a large police contingent was sent down the Bokoni Mine with the intention of forcing the workers out. Under the threat of violence, the workers eventually elected to end the occupation. Likewise, when police presented an interdict to the Two Rivers mine workers, on the same day, they also decided to resurface. While the NUM said that they would engage with the workers and management to tackle the reasons why the workers embarked on the occupations, an NUM spokesman also said the union was pleased that the occupations were over and that production would soon be back to normal.

As has also happened with all of the previous occupations, the management at the Bokoni Mine elected to go on the attack in the aftermath and it fired the 100 workers involved in the occupation.

Discussion

Despite the defeats that have accompanied most of the occupations of South African mines over the last several months, the actions of the workers have been inspiring and promising—most notably, the direct action, self-initiative, and self-organization that accompanied all of the occupations. What was not inspiring were the actions of the union bureaucrats, who not only abandoned their members, but often actively worked against them. Thus, the series of occupations once again revealed that workers in South Africa not only face the bosses and politicians as an enemy but they also often face an enemy in the form of union bureaucrats. As such, if workers are going to emancipate themselves, they are not only going to have to struggle against bosses and politicians, but also against union bureaucracy.

Indeed, what is perhaps really needed in South Africa is for workers to reclaim their unions from a bureaucratic class and to transform them into self-managed, radically democratic, non-hierarchical, and decentralized unions. In other words, unions that are controlled from the bottom-up by the members themselves and not the bureaucrats. It is in this struggle that anarchists can make a huge contribution with our knowledge of anarcho-syndicalist unionism and ideas of self-management, self-organization, and opposition to hierarchies. Of course, the challenges in trying to transform the existing unions into participatory organizations are immense.

It has not been unknown for the unions to send officials from their head offices to intervene in, and in some cases, even block, meetings that discuss the need for bottom-up participatory unions. Linked to this, some union bureaucrats have resorted to sidelining and even expelling members who raise difficult questions about the growing centralization within unions. Despite this, the struggle to bring about self-managed, non-hierarchical, revolutionary, and radically democratic unions or organs is vital—whether through transforming existing unions or beginning to organize new ones, and/or bypassing unions via workers themselves establishing links with one another by creating joint councils and/or committees. The reason for this is that without such unions or committees, it is going to be difficult for any workplace occupation to succeed or for workers to move toward a truly free society in a process of self-emancipation.

Another challenge that the occupations have faced besides brutal repression by the bosses and the state is that they have gotten relatively little support from the surrounding community or community-based movements—who, to some extent, have been unaware that these actions have been taking place. If the occupations are going to begin to succeed, then this needs to change and widespread support needs to foster. In countries where occupations have been successful, sometimes to the point of even transforming factories into worker self-managed institutions as in Argentina, community support and solidarity played a vital role.

The potential is certainly there for this to happen in South Africa as radical community-based organizations and workers have at times linked up to take on mining companies around environmental issues. There are, however, serious obstacles preventing this from becoming a widespread phenomenon at the moment. These, to a large degree, have revolved around the fact that the largest union federation, the Congress of South African Trade Unions (COSATU), is in an alliance with the ruling party and has often actively prevented members from trying to create links with community activists—who are critical of the state. Again, this perhaps points toward the need for workers to act independently of their unions through creating independent structures such as worker committees, which could welcome the participation of everyone regardless of union or movement affiliation.

Perhaps one of the biggest challenges in South Africa is also how to begin to transform the occupations we have seen, which have been largely defensive struggles, into a real challenge to the elite through fighting for worker self-management. Of course, the best process for such a transformation to take place is in struggle itself and through the self-education that accompanies it. Indeed, already, some workers in South Africa—although in a very small minority—have begun to think about the possibility of worker self-management and how to get there. It is also in this context that anarchists can offer solidarity and support to these workers. This could involve sharing our vision and ideas—without trying to dominate or impose—around a free, non-hierarchical, and self-managed society: in other words, a society that is the antithesis of the oppressive one we are currently forced to live in. Linked to this, anarchists could also play a role in sharing ideas about how we could possibly get to such a society and how the means and the ends should be compatible as far as possible. In fact, the ideas associated with anarchism could make a massive contribution to the mine occupations that have been emerging in South Africa as these ideas themselves were also born in struggle. ❑

Sources: Luli Callinicos, *A People's History of South Africa: Gold and Workers 1886–1924* , Johannesburg: Ravan Press, 1980; NGO Pulse, "Mining Industry Must Act on Silicosis," November 17, 2009 (ngopulse.org); Kea' Modimoeng, "Minister is determined to give labour broking short shrift," *Times Live*, August 16, 2009 (timeslive.co.za); Chanel de Bruyn, "Aquarius' Kroondal mine reopened after protest action," *Mining Weekly*, November 23, 2009 (miningweekly. com); James Macharia, "Striking Implats miners attack union leaders," *Mail&Guardian*, September 4, 2009 (mg.co.za); Mamethlwe Sebei and Weizmann Hamilton, "Rustenburg miners' strike," December 9, 2009 (socialistsouthafrica.co.za); Chanel de Bruyn, "Illegal sit-in halts production at SA Platinum Mine," *Mining Weekly*, October 19, 2009 (miningweekly.com); Kea' Modimoeng, "Protests go underground," *Times Live*, November 8, 2009 (timeslive.co.za); "Cops end Limpopo mine sit-in," News 24, January 21, 2010 (news24.com); South African Press Association, "Lydenburg Mines Refuse to Surface," January 21, 2010; "Sit-ins end at two S. Africa platinum mines," Reuters, January 22, 2010; Shawn Hattingh, "Mine occupations in South Africa," February 4, 2010 (anarkismo.net); José Antonio Gutiérrez, "Workers without bosses: workers' self-management in Argentina," May 31, 2005 (anarkismo.net); Victor Munnik, "Solidarity for environmental justice in Southern Africa," a report for groundWork, November 2007 (groundwork.org.za).

Article 6.8

THE REVIVAL OF THE STRIKE IN U.K. EMPLOYMENT RELATIONS

BY ALAN TUCKMAN
September 2010—WorkingUSA

In recent years, workers at British Airways have gone on strike multiple times, responding to privatization, deregulation, and the degradation of labor standards throughout the airline industry. Alan Tuckman analyzes these and other recent strikes by British workers, including some conducted without the formal support of unions. In this excerpt from a longer article, he asks whether these industrial actions might be part of a new upsurge in strike activity, which has been declining in Britain since the early 1980s. During that period, the Conservative government of Margaret Thatcher instituted new laws making strikes more difficult: for instance, before calling a strike, unions had to conduct a postal ballot of all workers who might be involved. For Thatcher's government, restrictions on the right to strike were part of a broader attack on labor. According to Tuckman, the Conservative government "eradicated compulsory union membership, regulated internal union government, dismantled statutory support for collective bargaining, removed statutory floors to wages, and curtailed individual employment rights." The New Labor government that came to power under Tony Blair in 1997 did not repeal the Conservative restrictions on workers' right to strike.

Today, in the wake of the 2008 economic crisis, Britain is one of many countries demanding concessions from public-sector workers, including layoffs, wage and pension cuts, and poorer working conditions. Across Europe, governments have promoted these policies on the argument that they are necessary to reduce budget deficits and maintain their countries' access to international credit. Yet in Ireland, Greece, and Spain, workers have responded with strikes and public protests. Tuckman asks whether British workers, drawing on their own recent experience striking under difficult legal and economic circumstances, might do the same. —*Eds.*

When Unite, the union representing British Airways (BA) cabin staff, voted to take industrial action in late 2009, it became increasingly apparent that there was something at stake deeper than the immediate issues in dispute: the cuts in staffing on long-haul flights. The very scale of the vote in favor of strike action, 92% supporting strike action, in the context of a historically divided workforce, was symptomatic of a deeper malaise.

The transition of BA from national "flag carrier" to private sector airline has been turbulent. Along with privatization, and the loss of the security of being underwritten by the U.K. exchequer, the company was also integral to the deregulation of airline routes. This increasingly opened the routes they dominated around the main London airports of Heathrow and Gatwick to competition, especially from the burgeoning low-cost carriers principally entering the market for short-haul flights.

BA sought to maintain dominance in the lucrative long-haul Atlantic flights, especially for business passengers, through alliance with American Airlines, although this has had long-term problems with regulatory authority. It is also currently in the process of a merger with Iberia, the Spanish national airline. Its strategy toward short-haul, increasingly dominated by the economy airlines, has fluctuated. The economy airlines have not only managed to reduce services to passengers, but they have also squeezed labor costs, with pay and conditions far lower than those traditionally found in the long-established "heritage" airlines. Recent studies distinguish between "high-road" strategy, which entails high-commitment workforce with employer partnership with trade unions, and "low-road" strategy, which seeks tight control over labor and trade union avoidance.

In BA, we can see dramatic shifts between these strategies. In the run-up to privatization and the years immediately following, they stressed customer care and invested in training and commitment in staff, while later, increasingly undermined the "high-road" strategy, forcing insecurity of staff, marginalizing the trade unions, and undermining established conditions of service. Arguments for privatization and around deregulation of airlines also stressed that the discipline of the market would somehow alleviate the propensity for militant action by workers.

Management after privatization tried, similarly to other airlines in the period, to cultivate "emotional labor" and a service culture adopting "putting people first" training in the attempt to move from the "militaristic and bureaucratic." However, whatever the managerial intention, and there are many accounts of "how BA turned its culture around," the introduction of a service culture did not bring with it servility. The strategy into the 1990s had been to establish the airline as focusing on, and perhaps pruned to, the long-haul business traveler, a strategy that had made BA the world's most profitable airline. However, with a new chief executive, the strategy shifted to challenge the burgeoning economy airlines on the short-haul routes.

This strategy, to establish a "virtual airline," prompted the mobilization of resistance from various sectors of the workforce. However, there may have been some hesitancy as, although there was a call for three-day strike action from cabin crew, many called in sick instead and created even greater chaos to schedules by longer absence.

BA workers are highly unionized, a heritage of state enterprise roots but unchanged since privatization. However, the very pattern of this unionization has reflected internal strife between airline staff as well as some ironic quirks of recent trade union history in the U.K.. While different unions have represented the range of staff employed by the airline, the majority have traditionally been organized by the Transport and General Workers Union (TGWU) with the cabin crew in a semi-autonomous branch of the British Airways Stewards and Stewardesses Association (BASSA). However, in opposition to the supposed militancy of BASSA, some cabin crew broke away to form Cabin Crew '89, which itself merged with the Engineering and Electrical Union, which then became a section within Amicus. In a final twist, in 2007, the TGWU and the union Amicus themselves merged to become Unite, bringing the cabin crew back into the same union. Given this history of antagonism, the equanimity of cabin crew from both BASSA and Cabin Crew '89 in the current dispute is indicative of the depths of the conflict with BA management.

Changes to BA staff's terms and conditions have been introduced piecemeal over two decades, usually through management "divide and rule" strategy. Not only are different groups set against each other—as currently pilots are against cabin crew, and the main London Heathrow-based staff are against the more peripheral and predominantly short-haul Gatwick—but there are now increasing discrepancies between staff appointed since the 1997 disputes. Settlements have also tended to include downgrading of conditions for new recruits so that a declining proportion of BA staff hold onto what are seen as prime pay and conditions, not just in industry terms compared with those offered by economy airlines but also against other BA staff in similar jobs. The squeezing of pay to new recruits now means that crew employed by BA at Gatwick now earn less than half that of crew based at Heathrow where the dispute is most solid.

In 2003, check-in staff staged a wildcat strike opposing the introduction of a "virtual airline" with the suspicion that most of the work would be contracted out and the workers that remained would be squeezed. This very same issue was to reappear two years later in the catering operation Gate Gourmet, which had been sold off by BA but was now squeezing labor costs. As part of the cost reduction opposed by staff in 1997, BA had sold off its catering operation to Swissair, which was then sold on to Gate Gourmet when Swissair went bankrupt. While action in 2005 had been an illegal wildcat, the strike action proposed to start in December 2009 followed procedure for official action. A ballot was held, with 80% of cabin crew voting, which gave a vote of around 92% in favor. However, before the planned strikes, the action was declared illegal by the courts in an action brought by BA.

Cabin crew staged seven days of strike action in March 2010 with some controversy concerning how many had reported for work and how many flights managed to remain scheduled. BA instituted contingencies, which involved leasing aircraft and crew from another airline as well as use as many of its own and could have crewed with flight deck staff trained to cover for cabin crew. An organization, the Professional Cabin Crew Council, also appeared to claim to represent staff opposed to the strike action. It fielded silhouetted spokespeople for some discussions about the dispute and while claiming not to be a trade union on its website (www.mypccc.co.uk), it seeks membership with an aspiration to represent cabin crew in negotiations concerning pay and conditions. In the negotiations with Unite, there was agreement to reinstate 184 of 500 cabin crew whose withdrawal from long-haul flights had been one of the initial issues in the dispute. With no real resolution, and perhaps trying to break the deadlock, Unite called a further 20 days of strike action for May based on their existing ballot.

According to the union, there were still unresolved issues: the removal of free and concessionary travel and disciplinary action being taken against fifty crew accused of breaking company rules in relation to the strike. This includes four dismissed for "promoting the strike," including branch officers of BASSA. Finally, there were still issues around the pay cuts and changes to working conditions unresolved. BA wanted to recruit new staff on long-haul flights on lower pay, reduce allowances for time having to stay away from home, and cut bonuses. They also wanted to impose a two-year pay freeze.

Initial injunction delayed the official union action in December, with another ballot having to be called in February and action then in March. However, when this action led to escalation, with management withdrawing travel concessions to striking cabin crew and disciplining fifty strikers, this ballot itself was challenged when further strike action was called.

While the union reporting of the result appears thorough, and if anything beyond the normal practice of just posting such results on union notice boards, the missing of the eleven spoiled papers from some of the union communications meant that the strike could be delayed by an interim injunction, which was subsequently overturned.

What emerges is a pattern of bullying and attempts to undermine union organization at the airline, occasionally interrupted by conciliatory overture in attempts to cheapen labor. BA, while announcing losses through the strike and the effect of volcano ash, also had a cash reserve of U.K.£2 billion to hold it through.

The negotiations that had been taking place periodically through the last twenty days of strike in May and June were obviously deadlocked on what the union considered the "no cost" issue of travel concessions. One session of negotiations was broken up when protesters— members of the Socialist Worker Party, not members of Cabin Crew—broke into the Acas building where the talks were being held. A dispute also broke out about one of the union negotiators "tweeting" a commentary from the meeting. The tweets generally told a story of frustration at the stalemate.

The fight was over the cost of labor and the reduction in subsistence for cabin crew. In the resolution of the previous disputes, BA had been able to install a bridgehead of cheaper labor cost. There was also periodic suggestion that BA would create an economy airline, with staff on inferior conditions to those at BA itself, to challenge rivals and recapture short-haul connection flights. Now, the pay and conditions of staff at the core of BA business, those on the long haul, was under challenge. They were also staff on whom BA was ultimately dependent for the "competitive advantage" of quality service to hold the business customers.

With service industries, as against manufacturing , there is often an issue of proximity of the "reserve army" of cheap labor used to challenge unionized workers. Typically, this is represented by the move of manufacturing to the periphery, from the U.S. or Western European economies to Latin America, Eastern Europe, or Asia, but may also operate the other way as peripheral workers are drawn to migration. However, in some services, perhaps epitomized by the airline industry, battle lines are closely placed with passengers' immediate travel requirement to move from one place to another, meaning direct confrontation with the transparency of different working conditions. Labor costs are forced down and recourse to "subsistence" becomes a conflict over immediate work expenses and living conditions considered acceptable when away from home. Many of the disputes concerning cabin crew, while the company has claimed no loss of pay, revolve around loss of this element of subsistence.

Breaking Out of the Legal Straightjacket?

A commentator in the *Guardian* has recently argued that "the impact of the series of successful injunctions risks undermining the relationship between unions and their members. Fearful of being taken to court, some unions may prefer not to risk a strike ballot but, where members have a genuine grievance, the result is a spontaneous walk-out." Such a walkout occurred at BA over the dispute at Gate Gourmet in 2005.

Without the right to strike in the U.K., unions become liable for damages for any losses through breach of contract while strikers lose any protection against dismissal. This has not always been a deterrent from strike action, the most widespread wave occurring in the chemical construction sector around the seemingly unprovoking *Posted Worker Directive* (96/71/EC) of the European Union. This directive allowed companies within the EU taking up a contract in another member state to move home-based workers to work on the contract and the terms and conditions under which they are to be employed, creating major disparities in wages between countries in the EU.

In early 2009, a strike broke out at the Lindsey Oil Refinery on the south bank of the River Humber in the north east of England and owned by the French company Total. Engineering construction workers opposed the employment of Italian workers, under the Posted Worker arrangements, for subcontract work on plant construction. Unusual for the U.K., the engineering construction workers were still covered by a national agreement, the "blue book," where these have tended to disappear elsewhere in the private sector. Construction workers, especially in specialist areas, need to be highly mobile moving from one contract to another even when employed by the same company. There is certainly job insecurity at the end of work on one contract and the search for the next.

Such circumstances establish informal networks taking shape among essentially migrant workers as work sites continually reestablish and reconfigure useful intelligence in the anticipation of the future need for work. Such networks, the use of text messages and the Internet, began to mobilize industrial action across different large engineering sites––chemical plants, other refineries, and electricity generation plants––around the northeast where there was a concentration of such sites and across other parts of the U.K.. While there where attempts to present the strikes as xenophobic, the unions stressed that they were not against the posted workers but a challenge to "the lack of wage transparency" under which they were working.

The strikes where essentially spontaneous and unofficial, carried out without a ballot. Given the insecurity of employment, there is no clear indication whether any retaliation occurred against strikers, and at least in the Lindsey strike, the unions were not required to repudiate the action "because the employers preferred to negotiate with unions rather than ad hoc striking workers," according to a London School of Economics working paper. Essentially, trade unions may be forced into a withdrawal. These strikes ignored the procedures and relied on informal networks. An influential critique of union "partnership" in the U.K. argues "mobilization" as an alternative.

Clear gender differences in income were obvious with male wage tending to be substantially higher. While some local authorities sought means to mask these differentials in the new pay scales through bonus enhancements or other plus payments, others leveled down men's wage to those of women. Notably, there appears to be no evidence of any authority raising the pay levels of predominantly "female jobs" to those of the "male jobs."

The Resurgence of the Strike?

At the time of writing, there are a number of uncertainties that may have an impact on the predicted resurgence of strike action in the U.K. First, the actual details of cuts in public spending—the main spark for such action—are yet to be finalized. On the possibility of privatization, there were suggestions that some remaining public sector activity may be transformed to worker cooperatives devolving budget responsibility onto the workforce. All so far that has been promised is that the changes inherent in the cuts will represent a historic reversal in the pattern of public spending.

While the initial spark for a resurgence of strike action may be the public sector, one of the justifications has been presented as a sharing of the misery, applying to the public sector the rationalization and intensification, as well as changes in conditions such as pension scheme, which have become usual in the private sector. The strikes we have explored here indicate that this is not unproblematic and discontent and "injustice" is being mobilized in the private sector as well as in the public; it is only perhaps the insecurity of employment that has stifled this. What the strikes at BA also indicate is the very perseverance of trade unions and collective action in privatized industries, characteristics that were supposed to be made extinct by the realities of the free market.

Rather than any reform of the U.K. laws on industrial action, given the "right to strike," escalation may begin debate in government and the press, advocating for tightening the restriction, and as was suggested in 1997, removing all rights to withdraw labor from sections or even all public sector workers. Rights not currently extended to the armed forces and police and being periodically proposed for prison officers may be proposed for refuse collection and other essential service providers.

The cases of BA and Lindsey Oil indicate that the "wildcat" strike has also not disappeared, and as in the case of the chemical construction workers, can be mobilized and spread rapidly through informal network. What is clear, if there is no repeal of industrial action legislation, is that if workers in the U.K. were to move toward a general strike against the government budget cuts, it would not be under any trade union control even if particular union leaders may have sympathy for such action. Rules as they are would make any such action illegal as not in furtherance of a trade dispute. ❏

Sources: Sarah Arnott, "BA's most bitter dispute heads into a tailspin," *The Independent*, May 12, 2010; BA-v-Unite, 2010, *British Airways -v- unite in the royal court of justice*, Folio No HQ10X01825, May 17 2010, London: The Strand; H. Beynon, "False hopes and real dilemmas: The politics of the collapse in British manufacturing," *Critique* (16):1–22, 1983; John Bowers, Michael Duggan, and David Reade, *The Law of Industrial Action and Trade Union Recognition*, Oxford and New York: Oxford University Press, 2004; Colin Burgon, "A rubbish pay dispute," *The Guardian*, November 24, 2009; Pilita Clark, "Walsh throws down gauntlet to strikers," *Financial Times*, June 7, 2010; Linda Dickens and Mark Hall, "The changing legal framework of employment relations," in *Industrial Relations: Theory & Practice*, ed. T. Colling and M. Terry, 298–322, Chichester: Wiley, 2010; Gill Dix, John Forth, and Keith Sisson, *Conflict at work: The pattern of disputes in Britain since 1980*. London: Acas, 2008; "Care for a downgrade?" *The Economist* 344(8024):63–4, 1997; Irena Grugulis, and Adrian Wilkinson, "Managing culture at British Airways: Hype, hope and reality," *Long Range Planning* 35(2):179–94. 2002; John Hendy and Gregor Gall, "British trade union rights today and the Trade Union Freedom Bill," in *The right to strike: From the Trade Disputes Act 1906 to a Trade Union Freedom Bill 2006*, ed. K. Ewing, 247–75, Liverpool: Institute of Employment Rights, 2006; Arlie Russell Hochschild, *The managed heart*, Berkeley: University of California Press, 1983; H. Hopfl, "Culture and commitment: British

Airways," in *Case studies in organizational behaviour*, eds. D.K. Gowler, Legge, and C. Clegg, London: Paul Chapman Publishing, 1993; B. Kersley, C. Alpin, J. Forth, A. Bryson, H. Bewley, G. Dix, and S. Oxenbridge, *Inside the workplace: Findings of the 2004 Workplace Employment Relations Survey*, London and New York: Routledge, 2006; C. Kilpatrick, "British jobs for British workers? U.K. industrial action and free movement of services in EU law," LSE Working Paper 16/2009; I. Lang, "Forward" to *Industrial Action and Trade Unions*, London: Department of Trade and Industry, HMSO 1996; J. McIlroy, "Unfinished business-the reform of strike legislation in Britain," *Employee Relations* 21(6):521–39, 1999; N. Millward, A. Bryson, and J. Forth, *All change at work? British employment relations 1980–1998, as portrayed by the Workplace Industrial Relations Survey*, London & New York: Routledge 2000; A. Perkins, "British Airways ruling: When judges came to the aid of the workers," *The Guardian*, May 21, 2010; M. Upchurch, *Creating a sustainable work environment in British Airways: Implications of the 2010 cabin crew dispute*, London: Global Work and Employment Project, Middlesex University, 2010; J. Walters, "New BA boss to force redundancies," *The Observer*, May 7, 2000; M. Weaver and A. Gabbatt, "BA strike third day—How it happened," *Guardian* blog (guardian.co.uk/news/blog/), accessed July 7, 2010.

Chapter 7

MANAGEMENT MODELS:
OLD AND NEW, GOOD AND BAD

Article 7.1

SCRIPTED TALK
From "Welcome to McDonald's" to "Paper or plastic?" employers control the speech of service workers.

BY ADRIA SCHARF
September/October 2003

> Now one of the very first requirements for a man who is fit to handle pig iron as a regular occupation is that he shall be so stupid and so phlegmatic that he more nearly resembles in his mental make-up the ox than any other type... He is so stupid that the word "percentage" has no meaning to him, and he must consequently be trained by a man more intelligent than himself into the habit of working in accordance with the laws of this science before he can be successful.
> —Frederick Winslow Taylor, The Principles of Scientific Management (1911)

"**G**ood evening and welcome to Cineplex Theater. Can I get you the super-combo popcorn-soft-drink special this evening?"

"Just a small drink," you say, your "hi, how are you" preempted by the question.

The worker at the snack counter takes your money, hands you a cup, and sends you off with a flat "thank you and enjoy the show."

The exchange may feel unnatural, even awkward. But scripted talk is more than just an annoying quirk of the modern service economy. It represents a deep form of managerial control—a regimentation of the labor process so total that it extends even to speech. Scripts are a fact of life for retail and service workers whose employers make use of a time-worn early-20th century managerial strategy: Taylorism.

In the 1910s and 1920s, a harsh new management system swept the nation's stockyards and factories. It called for managers to break jobs down into easily replicable, often mind-numbing, steps. The originator and foremost proponent of the system, Frederick W. Taylor, called his approach "scientific management," as it purported to apply scientific principles to the production process.

Taylor advocated strict separation between "thinking" and "doing." Managers and engineers in the central planning department were to do the "thinking"; workers, the "doing." He emptied labor of discretion and skill by reducing jobs to series of regimented tasks, eliminating all unnecessary body movements. A foreman with a stopwatch monitored and timed performance.

In the manufacturing sector, Taylorism was met with resistance from workers who saw their jobs deskilled and their control over the shop floor eroded. Over time, management developed more participatory practices like quality circles and suggestion systems that aim to elicit worker effort through overtures of collaboration. (And many manufacturing operations continue to rely primarily on Taylorist methods).

But in large swaths of the economy—especially in the service, retail, and clerical occupations that employ up to 42% of the U.S. workforce—old-fashioned Taylorism is expanding. And in service jobs that require workers to interact with customers, Taylorist control extends to the words workers utter. From "Welcome to McDonalds" to "Paper or plastic?" scripted talk is the rule for much "interactive service work." It's found in operations where volume sales drive profit, industry competition is intense, and where management takes a uniform, cookie-cutter approach to delivering a service—for example, in chain fast-food joints, coffee houses, and restaurants, and in call centers and mass-retail stores.

Corporate scripting of speech expands the deskilling of workers to personal and social terrain. Not only are workers' bodily movements broken down into standardized subtasks, monitored intensively, and clocked, but their ability to converse with consumers and sometimes with each other is also subject to company control. The surveillance once performed by a foreman takes stealthy and invasive new forms in the service economy. Retail and restaurant companies use undercover "secret shoppers" to monitor workers' adherence to company scripts, while call centers—which employ 3% of the U.S. workforce—use sophisticated new technologies to record workers' every interaction with customers.

Managers argue that Taylorism is efficient. And to many time-harried consumers, it offers predictable service and reduces kinks and slowdowns produced by disorganization. But the human toll of this mode of control is steep. And it turns out that the benefits may not be as great as managers—or Taylor himself—have claimed. Indeed, the expansion of Taylorism into the service sector has replicated all the problems that it caused in mass production—profound worker alienation, physical exhaustion, and stress—which contribute to astronomical quit rates in Taylorized jobs. Moreover, research suggests that other more humane ways of organizing work can be equally effective.

Regimented Talk

At Taylorized service companies, work is organized much like in mass production assembly plants. "At McDonald's, almost every decision about how to do crew people's tasks has been made in advance by the corporation," says sociologist Robin Leidner in her book *Fast Food, Fast Talk*. Counter workers at McDonald's follow the Six Steps of Window Service: greet the customer, take the order, assemble the order, present the order, receive payment, thank the customer and ask for repeat business.

The specific way they speak to customers may even be subject to rules. Leidner says McDonald's workers were instructed to say "May I help you, ma'am," rather than "Can I help someone?"

At Starbucks coffee shops, workers are supposed to greet the customer within 30 seconds from the time he or she enters the store; chat with the customer before taking the order; "call out" the coffee drink to the barista according to company specs (listing the temperature, the size, the modifiers, then the name of drink, in that order); then make eye contact and say "Have a nice day."

Clocked Talk

Telephone operators now typically handle 1,000 calls a day, and their job-cycle time (for example, the length of time it takes to answer a directory assistance request) averages just 20 seconds, according to Cornell University economist Rosemary Batt.

In interactive service work, whether at the drive-through window of a fast-food restaurant or a call-center computer station, speed is paramount. Employers time each step of the work procedure and drive workers to complete transactions at top speed so as to maximize volume and minimize labor costs. Scripting of speech is essential to this end.

Fast-food drive-through window workers must greet customers almost instantly—often within three seconds from the time the car reaches the menu board. Digital timers—visible to the worker, manager, and sometimes the customer—are wired to sensors buried underneath the drive-through lane. They measure how long it takes the worker to issue the greeting, take the order, and process the payment. When a worker falls behind the "targeted time goal" for a particular subtask, timers spur her on with chimes, sirens, or recorded messages. Sales of timers have doubled each year since 1994, according to the *Wall Street Journal*.

Former McDonald's CEO Jack Greenberg claimed that unit sales increase 1% for every six seconds saved at the drive-through. Because restaurant profits lie in shaving seconds off of "window time," store managers strive for drive-through times of 90 seconds (the industry average is 204 seconds).

Slick Talk

Many consumers have come to expect national fast-food corporations to require their workers to follow standardized scripts. A new generation of corporate scripts, though, has taken more insidious forms.

Chains like Starbucks write employee scripts to sound not merely polite, but chatty and sincere. "We're effectively required to make small talk," says James Boone*, who works the register at a Starbucks in southern Louisiana. "The company provides a list of questions it suggests we use to start the small talk, like 'How's that weather?' 'How's the family?' We're not supposed to talk about politics. And we have to close with 'Have a nice day.'" Should the customer actually be an undercover

---

Workers' names have been changed.

secret shopper sent by management to evaluate workers, Boone knows he'll get points docked for not saying "Have a nice day."

Mass retail stores, restaurants, and call centers also require their workers to participate in subtle or overt sales work. Besides simply ringing up purchases, taking a menu order, or answering consumer questions, workers are directed to hawk products, services, gimmicks, or expensive menu items in every service encounter. Because many workers find this task manipulative, awkward and alienating, employers enforce their compliance through covert surveillance.

Secret Shoppers and Digital Recording Technology

Fekkak Mamdouh, Director of the Restaurant Opportunities Center of New York (ROC-NY), a worker center, has a term for secret or mystery shoppers. "We call them 'busters.' Few of them will tell the boss that everything is perfect." Mamdouh knows of workers who were fired based on mystery shoppers' allegations.

Companies like Starbucks, the Olive Garden, and Marriott Hotels contract with mystery shopper companies to dispatch "service quality auditors"—secret shoppers—who, disguised as regular customers, monitor worker performance. Most national restaurant chains and hotels, and many mass retailers, now contract with mystery shopper companies. Virtually all of Taco Bell's 5,300 restaurants receive at least one visit from a clandestine auditor each month.

Rochelle Thomas* has worked for five years at the Seattle franchise of a national Italian restaurant chain. Headquarters makes sure that Thomas' store is "secret shopped" every two weeks. "When we take the dinner order, we have to suggestively sell five things: a drink, a side dish, a dessert, specials, and a special offer. You have to mention all five." Suggestive selling means naming specific high-price menu items. "We can't say, 'Would you like something to drink?' We have to say, 'Can I start you off with a glass of chianti?' If they have kids, we suggest sparkling water." At any one of her tables, an undercover monitor may be checking to make sure she complies with the suggestive selling requirements. "If you get a 'bad shopper' [meaning a bad report], the restaurant gives you terrible shifts for a week as punishment, and fewer tables. And they say if you get a couple of bad ones, they'll fire you."

The uncertainty makes secret shoppers an economical way for companies to control workers. Because workers don't know when they are actually being secret shopped, they modify their behavior as if they were always being watched.

At call centers, workers simultaneously talk on the telephone and navigate through computer screens. As in restaurants and chain stores, adherence to scripts is monitored and enforced. A 2002 survey of 735 North American call centers shows that 93% monitor customer-service agent calls, an increase over the past two years, according to the book *Call Center Operation: Design, Operation, and Maintenance*. Forty percent monitor both workers' voices and their computer screens. And modern monitoring techniques go beyond supervisors' occasionally listening in for "quality assurance purposes." Sophisticated new digital tapping technologies ensure that every transaction is either heard or recorded. Furthermore, supervisors may convert a voice transaction to text, do word searches, and even e-mail the interaction transcript to higher-ups in the company for disciplinary action or "training opportunities." And they can alternate among multiple workers' screens to monitor an entire group. Secret monitoring modes enable supervisors to observe workers undetected. Finally, some "quality monitoring systems" claim to measure customer service representatives' stress levels and other emotional indices. Sales of call-recording software reached $323 million last year, up $45 million since 2001, and the market-analysis firm Datamonitor predicts sales will hit $538 million a year by 2007, according to the *New York Times*.

Call-center workers are required to sell corporate products, services, and special offers—not just in "outbound" centers like telemarketing firms, but in "inbound" centers that answer toll-free calls as well. "There's an attempt to convert any service call into a sales call," says Batt. And workers know that if they deviate from the script, they may face disciplinary action.

The covert monitoring exacerbates stress and physical exhaustion. Rochelle Thomas explains, "We have to greet the table within 30 seconds of sit-down—to at least welcome the customer and say 'I'll be right with you.' We take their drink order within three minutes. After food hits the table, within three minutes we check back to make sure everything is OK. If I'm working a whole section, I have to push myself all night because the 30-second rule doesn't change, even if I'm juggling 10 tables. There's just no slack." It's not surprising that chain restaurants have a median worker-turnover rate of 125% per year. In the call-center industry, turnover rates are typically 35% to 50% per year, and far higher in some companies.

In the capitalist employment relationship, employers by definition have the right to direct the work of employees. But Taylorism takes the logic of managerial authority to an extreme. It applies intensive managerial control to the bodily movements and behavior of working people. In requiring workers to perform scripted talk, it produces alienation from one's own words and from one another. As sociologist Robin Leidner puts it, the "standardization of human interactions does encroach on social space not previously dominated by economic rationality. It shifts the meanings of such fundamental values as individuality and authenticity, raising troubling issues of identity for workers and customers."

Another Way is Possible

There are other, better, ways to organize service work. The Communication Workers of America has developed contract language on working procedures in call centers. The language prevents managers from using monitoring to discipline workers. Recordings are to be used for training purposes only. The union is also developing new formulas for sales quotas and call handling time.

Economist Rosemary Batt found that call center jobs organized as self-managed teams were far more productive in terms of sales volume and customer service than Taylorized call center jobs within the same company. The self-managed teams could decide how to conduct their work and interact with customers, and they set group goals and regulated themselves.

Finally, in the United States there are an estimated 1,000 to 5,000 worker cooperatives, or businesses owned by worker-members, and many more collectives—nonhierarchical organizations that are not cooperatives but do make decisions democratically. In worker cooperatives and collectives, authority resides in the workforce as a whole. For instance, at the Seward Café, a collectively owned and managed restaurant in Minneapolis, there is no manager. A set of job descriptions defines the basic work procedures but allows flexibility within those descriptions. Speech is not scripted. "As a consensus organization, we value a whole variety of different ways of communicating and interpreting what's happening. We value the fact that workers aren't censored," says Tom Pierson, a counter worker at the café. He says that speed is not compromised. But even if it were, the tradeoff would certainly be worth it. ❑

Resources: Rosemary Batt, "Work Organization, Technology, and Performance in Customer Service and Sales," *Industrial and Labor Relations Review*, July 1999; Harry Braverman, *Labor and Monopoly Capital*, Monthly Review Press,1974; Robin Leidner, *Fast Food, Fast Talk*, California University Press, 1993; George Ritzer, *The McDonaldization of Society*, Pine Forge Press, 1996; Duane Sharp, *Call Center Operation: Design, Operation, and Maintenance*, Digital Press, 2003.

The Short Run: Wal-Mart Pulls the Plug on Another Union
March/April 2005

The only unionized Wal-Mart store in the western hemisphere will be closing its doors this spring. The mega-retailer had been in negotiations with union officials since last fall, when over 200 workers at its Jonquiere, Quebec, site joined the United Food and Commercial Workers (UFCW) Local 503. When the company and the union failed to reach agreement, the union asked the Quebec Ministry of Labor to impose binding arbitration.

Wal-Mart has cited the store's "fragile" economic condition as the official reason for its impending closure, but the announcement fits a larger pattern of shut-downs in response to union drives. In 2000, Wal-Mart closed the deli section of its Jacksonville, Texas, store when 11 meat cutters decided to join the UFCW.

Undeterred, the UFCW has unionization applications in progress in a dozen locations elsewhere in Canada, including nearby Sainte-Hyacinthe, Quebec.　　　　　　　　　　　　　 *—Tyler Hauck*

Article 7.2

HOPE AND EXHAUSTION AT THE HOTEL BAUEN

Seven years in, workers trudge on and forge ahead at Argentina's recuperated businesses.

BY ELISSA DENNIS

September/October 2010

From the front window of an 11th-floor room in Buenos Aires' BAUEN Hotel, one can see festive crowds in blue and white parading along Avenida Corrientes. Hundreds of thousands of *porteños* are celebrating the bicentennial of the city's first government independent of Spain on May 25, 1810.

Inside the hotel, some workers sport red t-shirts with a large number seven on the back, celebrating another sort of independence: seven years of worker self-management. Since 2003, the hotel's housekeepers, doormen, seamstresses, and front desk clerks have operated the 200-room hotel, not taking orders from any boss, occupying the property with no legal rights of ownership. As one of about 200 "recuperated businesses" resurrected by workers after abandonment by their owners, the BAUEN is a leader in a tiny yet startlingly creative alternative economy that emerged out of the chaos of Argentina's 2001 economic crash.

Seven years in, BAUEN workers express a mix of pride, hope, fear, confidence, and exhaustion. They are tired of running a hotel where only two of the three elevators function and they can't afford to open the pool; earning ridiculously low salaries; operating under constant threat of eviction; making decisions by consensus at wearisome assembly meetings. Yet they cherish their role as grandparents of the recuperated business phenomenon, providing expertise, encouragement, and meeting venues for workers gathering the courage to take their workplaces into their own hands.

A new wave of recuperations is bringing energy to the movement, as workers build on their predecessors' experience, acting quickly to form cooperatives and resume production. The recuperated business model could get another boost if Argentina's legislature adopts bankruptcy law modifications supported by President Cristina Kirchner giving worker cooperatives more legal legitimacy.

The BAUEN's Rise and Fall

Squinting just a little at the scene outside, it is not hard to picture a similarly gleeful crowd in the streets 32 years ago, when soccer-crazed Argentina hosted and won the 1978 World Cup. Construction of the BAUEN (Buenos Aires Una Empresa Nacional) was part of the World Cup frenzy. The military dictatorship ruling Argentina wanted to boost nationalism and redirect popular attention away from the atrocities of its "Dirty War," when 30,000 Argentineans were kidnapped, tortured, and killed. The international soccer tournament provided impetus for revitalizing the capital city, including construction of luxury hotels for wealthy World Cup fans and business elites. Politically connected businessman Marcelo Iurcovich borrowed millions of dollars from Argentina's national bank to finance the BAUEN's construction.

Conjuring 1978 is not difficult from the BAUEN's rooms: there is the lime green headboard with attached swivel lights by the bed; matching green chairs, suitcase stands, and table with pop-up mirror; and wall speakers that used to play piped-in music. During the 1980s, the BAUEN was the place to be in Buenos Aires, says front desk clerk Luís Gonzalez, 49, who was a doorman and messenger at the hotel from 1984 to 1995. "There were two five-star hotels in the city: the Sheraton and the BAUEN," Gonzalez says, gazing towards the nondescript restaurant in one corner of the lobby and remembering an elegant piano bar and elevator entrance to the flashy second floor disco.

By the late 1980s, staff noticed a decline, as Iurcovich turned his attention to constructing the more lucrative BAUEN Suites around the corner. The hotels were connected through tunnels allowing guests to access the pool, bars, and performance venues in the two buildings. Those tunnels would later allow the owner to secretly empty the BAUEN of its furnishings, and the workers to secretly prepare the hotel for re-occupancy.

Argentina's dictatorship ended in 1983, but the nation's economic woes were just beginning, as President Raul Alfonsín's reliance on foreign debt and failure to control inflation led to a vicious cycle of more debt and IMF-imposed austerity measures. His successor Carlos Menem privatized the electric, railway, and phone companies in the 1990s, creating devastating unemployment. When he pegged the peso to the U.S. dollar, a flood of cheap imports destroyed domestic industrial production, bankrupting factories and throwing more people out of jobs.

With unemployment at 30% and 5.2 million people living below the poverty line, the unfamiliar sight of homeless people on city streets startled Argentineans. While the well-to-do hustled their money out of the country in the late 1990s, the unemployed organized street blockades, and a few locked-out worker groups pioneered the recuperation model. Crisis and revolt came to a head when President Fernando de la Rua froze bank accounts to prevent further capital flight, shocking the middle class into action. Raucous pot-banging demonstrations in the capital on December 20-21, 2001, led to de la Rua's resignation and the spectacle of four presidents over several weeks.

Amid this political chaos, Iurcovich sold the BAUEN in 1997 to Chilean investor Felix Solari, who apparently only made one $4 million payment toward the contracted purchase price of four to five times that amount, then tried unsuccessfully to renegotiate the deal as the economy slid into recession. He let the hotel decline, firing the last 60 workers and chaining the building shut on December 28, 2001.

Rebirth

BAUEN veterans light up with excitement describing their return 15 months later. "We started with zero," says Arminda Palacios, 73, who had stitched the hotel's curtains and pillowcases for 20 years, and who snuck into the boarded-up building from the adjacent hotel with 20 co-workers to find the BAUEN emptied of valuables, with piles of rubble in the lobby.

First they cleaned the hotel's event spaces and secured city permission to hold performances. They secretly repaired the guest rooms, working without pay for a year before they could rent rooms. Gonzalez describes how they cut a small door in the wood boarding up the front entrance to let people into events. In lieu of paying for tickets, attendees helped with the surreptitious renovations.

"There were just a few of us, but everyone worked willingly, and we put all our strength into proving we can run this hotel without a boss," says front desk clerk Elisa Vera, 56. Workers took turns living in the hotel, protecting their work from eviction and looters.

BAUEN workers acted out of self-preservation in an economy where there were no jobs available, particularly for older workers. "There was no other option," says Marcelo Ruarte, 70, who started at the hotel in 1980 as a doorman, and now handles the BAUEN media office. Yet, like the 400 Zanon Ceramics workers who refused to accept being locked out of their Patagonia factory, and the 52 Brukman seamstresses who stood up to police trying to evict them from the Buenos Aires textile factory where they had labored for decades, the BAUEN workers unwittingly found themselves leaders of a new social movement.

In dozens of closed businesses nationwide in the early 2000s, workers' efforts to reclaim their livelihoods caught the attention of students as well as church and community members, who brought food and supplies, and rallied by the thousands to defend workers' rights to resume production. The recuperations struck a nerve, Ruarte explains, because "it is dignifying a human being, the recuperation of an individual as part of society."

During Buenos Aires' bicentennial week, the BAUEN lobby is bustling with hotel guests, including the attendees of an international women's museum conference and a University of Georgia student orchestra. Locals come for evening performances: a play about Sacco and Vanzetti, a working class film festival, and a performance by Zanon workers about their recuperation. The new towels are fluffy, the rooms have wi-fi, the location can't be beat, and workers are proud of the service they provide and the 142 jobs they have created.

"I came for the wonderful courage of the workers," says Graciela Ulloque, 41, who started as a housekeeper in 2005 and now apprentices to seamstress Palacios, from whom she learns the workers' story as they sip their daily *mate*, an infused tea that is wildly popular in Argentina. Housekeeper Florencia Gonzalez, 45, says opportunities for training and advancement far exceed those at her previous job as a domestic worker, though at a salary of 1,200 pesos (approximately $300) per month, it is difficult to support her three daughters. Workers earn the same base salary, veterans and department supervisors earn 100 pesos per month more, and there are small bonuses for punctuality and performance.

New hires say a key part of the BAUEN experience is learning to argue at the assemblies, where after six months each member has a vote. "We quarrel like a family," Palacios explains, "but at the end we have consensus."

Signs of Strain

The assembly quarrels contribute to what veterans describe as strains on the cooperative's cohesiveness. As Luís Gonzalez observes the lobby scene, he thinks the hotel should provide a couple of computers for guests, and the restaurant could lure lunchtime patrons with a salad bar. But he shrugs that such suggestions get lost in the tedium of assemblies.

The camaraderie of the early days has dissipated, leaving a general malaise, Vera notes, and she worries that the cooperative model is not sustainable. "Now there are more of us, and we do less," she says. Some jobs aren't done well, and there is a sense of "let someone else do it." With no one in control, workers have more freedom, creating more confusion.

"There's not much discipline," Gonzalez agrees. They stopped their earlier practice of hiring workers' family members, which had led to allegiances detrimental to worker unity. Still Gonzalez laments that not everyone pulls their weight, and worries that for the hotel to succeed, "People need to have more consciousness of what they have."

At a 50% occupancy rate, the hotel's revenues cover ongoing expenses, but the cooperative constantly juggles priorities for improvements, Ruarte says, noting they have invested more than $1 million of revenues back into the hotel.

Lack of investment capital is the recuperated businesses' biggest challenge. Not owning their buildings or equipment, the cooperatives have no collateral with which to access credit, making it difficult to grow.

The legal limbo provides additional uncertainty. There are 206 recuperated businesses nationwide, representing approximately 9,300 workers, according to a recent study by the Open College Program in the College of Philosophy and Letters at the University of Buenos Aires. The majority of these recuperated businesses have secured an "expropriation" from their provincial government, giving the worker cooperative the legal right to use the business' equipment to continue production. Andrés Ruggeri, director of the Program, explains that the expropriation "freezes the judicial process of bankruptcy, but doesn't annul it," preventing the equipment from being sold while the workers are using it.

Most expropriations are for two years, subject to renewal or conversion to permanent status at the discretion of future politicians, Ruggeri explains. The expropriation mandates an "indemnification" payment to the business' creditors, to be paid in the temporary expropriations by the government, or in the permanent expropriations by the cooperative over a 20-year term, based on a government appraisal of the value of the business' equipment after two years of cooperative ownership. But Ruggeri says no appraisals have been completed for the permanent expropriations, nor have the provincial governments made indemnification payments for the temporary cases.

The BAUEN cooperative had a temporary expropriation. But despite Solari's ownership claim, the Iurcovich family sold the property again in 2005 to a firm called Mercoteles. Although apparently an entity controlled by Iurcovich, that "new" owner secured forgiveness of the multimillion dollar debt to the state bank, and in August 2007, a court declared Mercoteles the owner and ordered the workers' eviction. With 3,000 people protesting, the workers fought off eviction, but are again occupying the premises illegally as the case heads for the Supreme Court. Although veterans shrug off the threat of eviction, workers are constantly on alert. "We hear rumors, and we start to mobilize," Ulloque says.

New Generations of Recuperations

BAUEN workers stay motivated by their mentor role. "We were the children of circumstance," Ruarte says. "Now we're the parents of the solution."

"We got an attorney and we met with the BAUEN workers," explains Carlos Visuara, 46, one of 17 longtime employees who reclaimed the Arrufat chocolate factory in January 2009. The 77-year-old business, famous nationwide for its chocolate Easter eggs, fired most of its 300 workers as sales declined in recent years, shutting the doors in December 2008.

Workers acted quickly to re-enter their workplace and resume chocolate production just two weeks later. Occupying a building with no light or water, they took turns spending nights in the factory and secured community support to prevent removal of the equipment. Arrufat workers won their temporary expropriation in January 2010, and the energized 20 men and eight women of the cooperative produced 220,000 pounds of Easter eggs this spring.

Immediately restarting production is the most critical lesson new worker groups have learned from the earlier generation, asserts Esteban Magnani, author of a 2005 book about recuperated businesses, *The Silent Change*. Earlier groups occupied their building, formed a cooperative, secured community support to prevent eviction, sought legal standing, and only then began to produce. But the lengthy legal and political process drained workers' energy, clients were lost, and owners had a chance to loot the property. Starting production before getting approvals shifts the balance of power to the workers, Magnani explains.

Legal Legitimacy

Declaring "Argentina is a great recuperated factory," President Cristina Kirchner in March sent to Parliament proposed modifications to the country's bankruptcy law, following up on a 2007 campaign promise to legitimize recuperations. The modifications would require the bankruptcy court to: 1) prioritize continuation of the bankrupt company's production; and 2) give equal weight to debts owed to the company's workers as to other creditors. Currently, workers' unpaid wages and benefits, often comprising years of back pay, are not considered in a bankruptcy proceeding. If at least two-thirds of the company's workers organize a cooperative and present a viable management plan, the bankruptcy judge would have to consider ordering continuation of the business under worker management. Currently, such an order is an exception rather than an alternative the judge must consider.

The reforms would allow workers to deal directly with the bankruptcy court instead of being locked into the protracted process of expropriations, Magnani explains. And workers could use their back pay towards the cooperative's purchase of the company.

Ruggeri notes that while the modifications provide critical technical changes to the law, the reforms will only be valuable if accompanied by a concomitant public policy initiative to sustain the cooperatives, including access to credit and favorable financing mechanisms, and the creation of advisory and training bodies. "Otherwise, the law will facilitate the formation of a lot of cooperatives, but they will be very vulnerable," he says. He believes some version of the reforms will pass, though notes that there is a delicate balance of power between Kirchner allies and opposition legislators, and that even Kirchner allies, motivated by their own or their supporters' business interests, have rejected similar measures before.

BAUEN Dreams

With the BAUEN's legal complexities, it is not clear if these reforms would help the hotel cooperative. But workers make time for legislative lobbying, keeping an eye on their Supreme Court case, and on a new expropriation case working through Buenos Aires' provincial government. Meanwhile, they wash sheets, carry luggage, clean bathrooms, check in guests, and argue in assemblies about projects to prioritize for next year. Ruarte wants to see the old disco converted to a gym, and to hire a chef to bake the morning *medialunas*. Ulloque would like a sewing machine that could put the BAUEN logo on sheets and towels. For Palacios, "I love this hotel like a child. My great dream is that some day before I die the workers can own the hotel. They deserve it, they have sacrificed so much. They are the real owners." ❑

Resources: *Pagina 12*, www.pagina12.com.ar; University of Buenos Aires Open College Program, www.recuperadasdoc.com.ar.

The Short Run: Striking Results
March/April 2006

For the first time in six years, the Vietnamese government has raised the country's minimum wage in foreign-owned factories by nearly 40%, effective April 1, Labor Notes reported in February. Workers in Vietnam's two biggest cities will now earn $55 in monthly wages, $50 and $45 elsewhere in the country. The hike came after two months of heavy protests, including wildcat strikes by more than 40,000 workers in numerous Asian-owned export factories.

Alain Cany, chairman of the European Chamber of Commerce in Vietnam, viewed the strikes with trepidation. One of Vietnam's attractions for foreign investors, Cany wrote, "has been the fact that the work force is not prone to industrial action." Cany further warned, "Should such incidents occur again, this could have a detrimental effect on the economic climate in Vietnam in general, leading to a downturn in the economy and to foreign-invested business." Many Vietnamese workers are evidently not getting the message: strikes have continued in the weeks since the minimum-wage hike was announced.   *—Liv Gold*

Article 7.3

VENEZUELA'S COOPERATIVE REVOLUTION
An economic experiment is the hidden story behind Chávez's 'Bolivarian Revolution.'

BY BETSY BOWMAN AND BOB STONE
July/August 2006

Zaida Rosas, a woman in her fifties with 15 grandchildren, works in the newly constructed textile co-op Venezuela Avanza in Caracas. The co-op's 209 workers are mostly formerly jobless neighborhood women. Their homes on the surrounding steep hillsides in west Caracas were almost all self-built.

Zaida works seven hours a day, five days a week, and is paid $117 a month, the uniform income all employees voted for themselves. This is much less than the minimum salary, officially set at $188 a month. This was "so we can pay back our [government start-up] loan," she explained. Venezuela Avanza *cooperativistas* have a monthly general assembly to decide policy. As in most producer co-ops, they are not paid a salary, but an advance on profits. Workers paying themselves less than the minimum wage in order to make payments to the state was, Zaida acknowledged, a bad situation. "We hope our working conditions will improve with time," she said.

To prepare the co-op's workers to collectively run a business, the new Ministry of Popular Economy (MINEP) had given them small scholarships to train in cooperativism, production, and accounting. "My family is a lot happier—I've learned to write and have my 3rd grade certificate," she said.

Zaida is now also part of a larger local web of cooperatives: her factory is one of two producer co-ops, both built by a local bricklayers' cooperative, that, along with a clinic, a supermarket co-op, a school, and a community center, make up a so-called "nucleus of endogenous development." These *nucleos* are at the core of the country's plan for fostering egalitarian economic development.

U.S. media coverage of Venezuela tends to center around the country's oil and the—not unrelated—war of words between President Hugo Chávez and the White House. Chávez, for example, likes to refer to George W. Bush as "Mr. Danger," a reference to a brutish foreigner in a classic Venezuelan novel. Somewhat more clumsily, Defense Secretary Donald Rumsfeld recently compared Chávez to Hitler. While this makes for entertaining copy, reporters have missed a major story in Venezuela—the unprecedented growth of cooperatives that has reshaped the economic lives of hundreds of thousands of Venezuelans like Zaida Rosas. On a recent visit to Caracas, we spoke with co-op members and others invested in this novel experiment to open Venezuela's economy from the bottom up.

Explosion of Cooperatives

Our first encounter with Venezuela's co-op movement was with Luis Guacarán, a taxi co-op member who drove us to the outskirts of Caracas. Settled into the rainy trip, we asked Luis what changes wrought by the Chávez government had meant for him personally. Luis replied that he now felt that as a citizen he had a right to share in the nation's oil wealth, which had always gone to an "oligarchy." The people needed health, education, and meaningful work; that was reason enough for Chávez to divert oil revenues in order to provide these things. Two of Luis's five sons are in the military, a daughter is studying petroleum engineering, another has a beauty shop. All were in vocational or professional studies.

Almost everyone we met during our visit was involved in a cooperative. The 1999 constitution requires the state to "promote and protect" co-ops. However, it was only after the passage of the Special Law on Cooperative Associations in 2001 that the totals began to skyrocket. When Chávez took office in 1998 there were 762 legally registered cooperatives with about 20,000 members. In 2001 there were almost 1,000 cooperatives. The number grew to 2,000 in 2002 and to 8,000 by 2003. In mid-2006, the National Superintendence of Cooperatives (SUNACOOP) reported that it had registered over 108,000 co-ops representing over 1.5 million members. Since mid-2003, MINEP has provided free business and self-management training, helped workers turn troubled conventional enterprises into cooperatives, and extended credit for start-ups and buy-outs. The resulting movement has increasingly come to define the "Bolivarian Revolution," the name Chávez has given to his efforts to reshape Venezuela's economic and political structures.

Now MINEP is trying to keep up with the explosion it set off. While pre-Chávez co-ops were mostly credit unions, the "Bolivarian" ones are much more diverse: half are in the service sector, a third in production, with the rest divided among savings, housing, consumer, and other areas. Cooperativists work in four major sectors: 31% in commerce, restaurants, and hotels; 29% in transport, storage and communications; 18% in agriculture, hunting, and fishing; and 8.3% in industrial manufacture. Cooperativism is on the march in Venezuela on a scale and at a speed never before seen anywhere.

Most cooperatives are small. Since January 2005, however, when the government announced a policy of expropriation of closed industrial plants, MINEP has stood ready to help workers take control of some large factories facing bankruptcy.

DEMOCRACY: ECONOMIC AND POLITICAL

Alongside the co-op movement, Venezuelans are engaged in building a new form of local political democracy through so-called Communal Councils. Modeled on Brazil's innovative participatory budgeting process, these councils grew out of the Land Committees Chávez created to grant land titles to the many squatters in Caracas's barrios. If a community of 100 to 200 families organizes itself and submits a local development plan, the government grants land titles. Result: individuals get homes, and the community gets a grassroots assembly.

The councils have budgets and make decisions on a range of local matters. They delegate spokespersons to the barrio and the municipality. Today, a few thousand Communal Councils exist, but within five years the government plans to bring all Venezuelans into local counsels. In conjunction with cooperativization in the economy, the Community Council movement may portend the creation of a new decentralized, democratic polity.

If the unused plant is deemed of "public utility," the initiation of expropriation proceedings often leads to negotiation with the owners over compensation. In one instance, owners of a shuttered Heinz tomato processing plant in Monagas state offered to sell it to the government for $600,000. After factoring in back wages, taxes, and an outstanding mortgage, the two sides reached an amicable agreement to sell the plant to the workers for $260,000, with preferential loans provided by the government. In a more typically confrontational example, displaced workers first occupied a sugar refinery in Cumanacoa and restarted it on their own. The federal government then expropriated the property and turned it over to cooperatives of the plant's workers. The owners' property rights were respected inasmuch as the government loaned the workers the money for the purchase, though the price was well below what the owners had claimed. Such expropriated factories are then often run by elected representatives of workers alongside government appointees.

There are strings attached. "We haven't expropriated Cumanacoa and Sideroca for the workers just to help them become rich people the day after tomorrow," said Chávez. "This has not been done just for them—it is to help make everyone wealthy." Take the case of Cacao Sucre, another sugar mill closed for eight years by its private owners, leaving 120 workers unemployed in a neighborhood of grinding poverty. The state's governor put out a call for the workers to form a co-op. After receiving training in self-management, the mill co-op integrated with the 3,665-strong cane growers' co-op. In July 2005, this large cooperative became the first "Social Production Enterprise." The new designation means that the co-op is required to set aside a portion of its profits to fund health, education, and housing for the local population, and to open its food hall to the community as well.

With only 700 plants on the government's list of closed or bankrupt candidates for expropriation, cooperativization of existing large-scale facilities is limited, and so far a bit slow. Unions are identifying more underproducing enterprises. But there is a long way to go.

Cooperatives are at the center of Venezuela's new economic model. They have the potential to fulfill a number of the aims of the Bolivarian revolution, including combating unemployment, promoting durable economic development, competing peacefully with conventional capitalist firms, and advancing Chávez's still-being-defined socialism.

Not Your Grandfather's WPA

Capitalism generates unemployment. Neoliberalism aggravated this tendency in Venezuela, producing a large, stable group of over-looked people who were excluded from meaningful work and consumption. If not forgotten altogether, they were blamed for their plight and made to feel superfluous. But the Bolivarian revolution is about demanding recognition. In March of 2004 Chávez called Venezuelans to a new "mission," when MINEP inaugurated the *Misión Vuelvan Caras* program— Mission About-Face. Acting "from within themselves and by their own powers" to form cooperatives, the people were to "combat unemployment and exclusion" by actually "chang[ing] the relations of production."

In Venezuela, *"vuelvan caras"* evokes an insurgent general's command to his troops upon being surrounded by Spaniards in the war of independence. In effect: stop playing the role of the pursued; turn and attack the enemy frontally. The new enemy is unemployment, and the goal of full employment is to be achieved by groups—especially of the unemployed—throwing in their lot with each other and setting to work together. *Vuelvan caras* teaches management, accounting, and co-op values to hundreds of thousands of scholarship students. Graduates are free to seek regular jobs or form micro-enterprises, for which credit is offered; however, co-ops get priority for technical assistance, credits, and contracts. But the original spark—the collective entrepreneurship needed for cooperativization—is to come from the people. Over 70% of the graduates of the class of 2005 formed 7,592 new co-ops.

Vuelvan Caras seems to be paying off. Unemployment reached a high of 18% in 2003 but fell to 14.5% in 2004, and 11.5% in 2005. MINEP is planning a *"Vuelvan Caras II,"* aiming to draw in 700,000 more of the jobless. But with a population of 26 million, Venezuela's battle against structural causes of unemployment has only begun.

Economic Development from Within

Cooperatives also advance the Chávez administration's broader goal of "endogenous development." Foreign direct investment continues in Venezuela, but the government aims to avoid relying on inflows from abroad, which open a country to capitalism's usual blackmail. Endogenous development means "to be capable of producing the seed that we sow, the food that we eat, the clothes that we wear, the goods and services that we need, breaking the economic, cultural and technological dependence that has halted our development, starting with ourselves." To these ends, co-ops are ideal tools. Co-ops anchor development in Venezuela: under the control of local worker-owners, they don't pose a threat of capital flight as capitalist firms do.

The need for endogenous development came home to Venezuelans during the 2002 oil strike carried out by Chávez's political opponents. Major distributors of the country's mostly imported food also supported the strike, halting food deliveries and exposing a gaping vulnerability. In response, the government started its own parallel supermarket chain. In just three years, Mercal had 14,000 points of sale, almost all in poor neighborhoods, selling staples at discounts of 20% to 50%. It is now the nation's largest supermarket chain and its second largest enterprise overall. The Mercal stores attract shoppers of all political stripes thanks to their low prices and high-quality merchandise. To promote "food sovereignty," Mercal has increased its proportion of domestic suppliers to over 40%, giving priority to co-ops when possible. Venezuela still imports 64% of the food it consumes, but that's down from 72% in 1998. By cutting import dependence, transport costs, and middlemen while tapping local suppliers, Mercal aims to wean itself from its $24 million-a-month subsidy.

Displacing Capitalism and Building Socialism

Another reason the architects of the so-called "Bolivarian revolution" are vigorously pushing the co-op model is their belief that co-ops can meet needs better than conventional capitalist firms. Freed of the burdens of supporting costly managers and profit-hungry absentee investors, co-ops have a financial buoyancy that drives labor-saving technological innovation to save labor time. "Cooperatives are the businesses of the future," says former Planning and Development Minister Felipe Pérez-Martí. Not only are they non-exploitative, they outproduce capitalist firms, since, Pérez-Martí holds, worker-owners must seek their firm's efficiency and success. Such a claim raises eyebrows in the United States, but a growing body of research suggests that co-ops can indeed be more productive and profitable than conventional firms.

To test whether co-ops can beat capitalist firms on their own terms, a viable co-op or solidarity sector must be set up parallel to the securely dominant capitalist one. Today Venezuela is preparing this "experiment." More than 5% of the labor force now works in cooperatives, according to MINEP. While this is a much larger percentage of *cooperativistas* than in most countries, it is still small relative to the size of a co-op sector that would have a shot at out-competing Venezuela's capitalist sector. Chávez's supporters hope that once such a sector is launched, cooperativization will expand in a "virtuous circle" as conventional workforces, observing co-ops, demand similar control of their work. Elias Jaua, the initial Minister of Popular Economy, says, "The private sector can understand the process and incorporate itself into the new dynamic of society, or it will be simply displaced by the new productive forces which have a better quality production, a vision based much more on solidarity than consumption." One could claim that MINEP's credits, trainings, and contracts prejudice the outcome in favor of co-ops. But *Vuelvan Caras* graduates are free to take jobs in the capitalist sector. And MINEP's policy of favoring employee-owned firms is not that different from U.S. laws, subsidies, and tax benefits that favor investor-owned ones.

Finally, by placing the means of production in workers' hands, the co-op movement directly builds socialism. Cooperativization, especially of idle factories occupied by their workforces, promotes "what has always been our goal: that the workers run production and that the governments are also run by the workers," according to Labor Minister María Cristina Iglesias. Co-ops, then, are not just means to what Chávez calls "socialism for the 21st century": they actually constitute partial realizations of it.

Managing the Experiment's Risks

Cooperativization is key to achieving the aims of the Bolivarian revolution. But the revolution's leaders acknowledge that a long struggle lies ahead. Traditional capitalist enterprises still dominate Venezuela's economy. And even if all of the country's current cooperativization programs succeed, will that struggle—and it will be a struggle—result in socialism? Michael Albert of *Z Magazine* grants that co-ops may be more productive, and he strongly supports Venezuela's experiment. But in the absence of plans for de-marketization, he has doubts that it will reach socialism. For the effect on cooperatives themselves of "trying to out-compete old firms in market-defined contests may [be to] entrench in them a managerial bureaucracy and a competitive rather than a social orientation," leading to a market socialist system "that still has a ruling managerial or coordinator class." Albert's concern is well founded: the history of co-ops from the Amana colonies of Iowa to the Mondragón Cooperative Corporation in the Basque country shows that even when they start out with a community-service mandate, individual co-ops, or even networks of co-ops, tend to defensively re-internalize capitalist self-seeking and become indistinguishable from their competitors when made to compete alone against an array of capitalist firms in a capitalist economy.

Disarmingly, members of Chávez's administration acknowledge these risks. Juan Carlos Loyo, deputy minister of the popular economy, noting that community service has been part of the cooperative creed since its beginning, asks for patience: "We know that we are coming from a capitalist lifestyle that is profoundly individualistic and self-centered." Marcela Maspero, a national coordinator of the new, Chavista UNT labor federation, acknowledges "the risk of converting our comrades into neo-liberal capitalists." In Venezuela's unique case, however, construction of a viable co-op sector is the goal of a government with considerable financial resources, and its aim of thereby building socialism is also a popular national project. In Venezuela, success is therefore a plausible hope. A loose analogy would hold with May 1968 if both the de Gaulle government and the French Communist Party had been in favor of student-worker demands for *auto-gestion* or self-management.

There are problems, of course. Groups may register as "phantom co-ops" to get start-up grants, then simply walk away with the money. And since co-ops are favored in awarding government contracts, there is a significant amount of fraud. "There are cooperatives that are registered as such on paper," Jaua, the former head of MINEP, reports, "but which have a boss who is paid more, salaried workers, and unequal distribution of work and income." SUNACOOP admits that its enforcement is spotty. Many of the new cooperatives have also suffered as a result of inadequate self-management training. Government authorities are attempting to address these problems by increasing visits to local co-ops, augmenting training and support services, and decentralizing oversight to local councils.

Despite the obstacles, the new co-ops, with government support, are building a decentralized national movement with its own momentum and institutions. This May, the National Executive Cooperative Council (CENCOOP) was launched. The council is made up of five co-op members from each of Venezuela's 25 states, elected by their State Cooperative Councils, which are in turn elected by Municipal Councils composed of local cooperativists. CENCOOP will represent Venezuela at the International Cooperative Alliance—the global body embracing 700 million individual members in hundreds of thousands of cooperatives in 95 countries.

The pre-Bolivarian co-op movement at first felt left out, and criticized hasty cooperativization. But its advice was sought at each stage of the planning for CENCOOP, and it finally joined the council, sharing its valuable experience with the new movement. The new state and municipal co-op councils are part of a plan to decentralize MINEP's functions. Having helped organize CENCOOP, MINEP Superintendent Carlos Molina says his office will adopt a hands-off approach to assure the cooperative movement's increasing autonomy. Today, however, many of the new co-ops remain dependent on MINEP's support.

A Movement's Opponents

Whatever success cooperativization achieves carries its own risks, both internal and external. So far, the Chávez government has compensated capitalists for expropriations and has targeted for co-op conversion only firms that are in some sense in trouble. But at a certain point, workers in healthy firms, seeing their cooperativist neighbors enjoying newfound power in the workplace and a more equal distribution of income, may want to cooperativize their firms too. And having for years had profit extracted as a major portion of the value their labor has created—in many cases enough to cover their firm's market value many times over—won't they have grounds to demand transfer without compensation? In short, to further expand and strengthen revolutionary solidarity before new counter-revolutionary efforts take root, won't the revolution have to start a real redistribution of productive wealth—to cooperativize firms directly at the expense of Venezuela's capitalists? Sooner or later, Venezuela's cooperative experiment will have to address this question.

After joining in the World Social Forum in Caracas in last January, we caught some glimpses of the "Bolivarian revolution" moving at full speed, and we've followed it since then. We are convinced that for those around the world who believe "another world is possible," the stakes of this experiment are enormous. Predictably, then, it faces genuine external threats. The short-lived coup in April of 2002 and the destructive strike by oil-industry managers that December were the works of a displaced and angry elite encouraged by the United States at every step. And the campaign continues: State Department-linked groups have been pumping $5 million a year into opposition groups that backed the coup. Yet the democratizing of workplaces proceeds relentlessly, bringing ever more Venezuelans into the revolutionary process. This inclusion is itself a defense since it expands, unites, and strengthens the resistance with which Venezuelans would greet any new effort to halt or divert their revolution. ❑

Sources: Many valuable articles have been collected at www.Venezuelanalysis.com, including: C. Harnecker, "The New Cooperative Movement in Venezuela's Bolivarian Process" (from *Monthly Review Zine*) 5/05; S. Wagner, "*Vuelvan Caras*: Venezuela's Mission for Building Socialism of the 21st Century," 7/05; "Poverty and Unemployment Down Significantly in 2005," 10/05; F. Pérez-Martí, "The Venezuelan Model of Development: The Path of Solidarity," 6/04; "Venezuela: Expropriations, cooperatives and co-management," *Green Left Weekly*, 10/05; M. Albert, "Venezuela's Path," Z-Net, 11/05; O. Sunkel, *Development from Within: Toward a Neostructuralist Approach for Latin America* (L. Rienner Publ., 1993); H. Thomas, "Performance of the Mondragón Cooperatives in Spain," in *Participatory and Self-Managed Firms*, eds. D. C. Jones and J. Svejnar (Lexington Books, 1982); D. Levine and L. D'A. Tyson, "Participation, Productivity and the Firm's Environment," in *Paying for Productivity: A Look at the Evidence*, ed. A. Blinder (Brookings Inst., 1990); D. Schweickart, *After Capitalism* (Rowman & Littlefield, 2002); M. Lebowitz, "Constructing Co-management in Venezuela: Contradictions along the Path," *Monthly Review Zine* 10/05; Z. Centeno, "Cooperativas: una vision para impulsar el Desarrollo Endogeno," at www.mci.gob.ve.

Article 7.4

POST-APARTHEID VINEYARDS
Land redistribution begins to transform South Africa's wine country

BY WILLIAM G. MOSELEY
January/February 2006

As I walked through the rows of grape vines with a representative of one of South Africa's few worker co-owned vineyards, I could tell that he was proud of what his group had accomplished. Nearly all of the 60 members of the Bouwland partnership trust are coloured or black farm workers. They own a controlling share of the Bouwland vineyard and wine label, producing 17,000 bottles of wine per year, with exports to Europe and Canada. By all accounts, this is an amazing achievement for an effort that is only three years old. But the group is also nervous. They are still heavily dependent on the expertise and equipment of their white partners, and they must repay a substantial commercial bank loan. This project and others like it represent a small but growing number of worker-owned vineyards in post-Apartheid South Africa. These efforts embody the hopes, dreams, and challenges of those who aspire to make the new South Africa a reality for the working poor.

In 1994, the African National Congress (ANC) took power in South Africa under the leadership of Nelson Mandela, formally ending decades of state-sponsored discrimination. Among a wide range of exclusionary policies during the Apartheid era were restrictions on the ownership of farmland by non-whites outside of the homelands or Bantustans—a policy that left only 13% of the country's land for the entire majority black population. This led to complete white domination of commercial agriculture, particularly in the Western Cape Province, an area often thought of as the historical hearth of white farming. Of all of South Africa's provinces, agriculture in the Western Cape is the most commercialized and export-oriented. Wine exports in particular have skyrocketed since Apartheid ended and the international community lifted sanctions. While South African wines were once unheard-of in North American and European supermarkets, they now compete with wines from their southern hemisphere counterparts, mainly Chile and Australia, for a share of the "good value" wine market (i.e., reasonable-quality wines of low to moderate price). In fact, South Africa's wine production nearly quadrupled between 1994 and 2004, and the country is now the eighth or ninth largest wine producer in the world. But what has this growth meant for South Africa's historically disadvantaged groups, particularly the farm workers who comprise one of the poorest segments of the country's population? What is the ANC government doing, if anything, to ensure that the wealth from growing wine exports trickles down to the poorest workers?

While many North Americans are familiar with the struggle against Apartheid and the subsequent political opening in the 1990s, fewer may be aware of efforts to transform South Africa's economy. The ANC has promised to redress the legacy of discriminatory land ownership policies in the farming sector through a land reform program that facilitates the transfer of land from whites to blacks (a generic term in

South Africa that encompasses people of African, mixed race and Indian origin). In fact, the government has pledged to redistribute 30% of the country's agricultural land by 2014. Land reform is part of a broader transformation strategy for South Africa's agricultural sector aimed at increasing black participation in decision-making. The wine industry in the Western Cape is one instance where the effects of that strategy are visible, and this is significant given its economic importance to the province, its growing export potential, and the history of white dominance.

The Coloured Farm Worker Population and the South African Wine Industry

Wine production in South Africa's Western Cape Province dates back to the 17th century, when the Dutch established an outpost at Cape Town to provision ships sailing from Europe to the Far East. Because the area's local Khoisan population was sparse and unaccustomed to agricultural labor, the Dutch brought slaves from East Africa, Madagascar, and the East Indies to work their farms. The farm laborer population evolved into a mixed race or mulatto group, locally referred to as coloureds, who now comprise 60% of the Western Cape's population.

Even though slavery was abolished in 1834, conditions on farms remained difficult and wages were low. The historic relationship between white farmers and farm workers has often been described in terms of paternalism and dependency. Permanent farm workers (as opposed to seasonal laborers) lived on the farms, often for multiple generations. In addition to meager wages, permanent workers typically received housing, food, and wine. Many farm workers bought goods on credit at the company stores their bosses owned and fell into the classic debt-bondage cycle. The provision of cheap wine to workers as a component of compensation, known as the "tot or dop" system, was used to attract and retain workers in a low-wage industry (and the poorest white farmers were often the greatest abusers of this practice). While this practice has been illegal since the 1960s, and more strictly monitored in the post-Apartheid era, alcoholism continues to be a major problem among farm workers.

Raising grapes required a tremendous amount of labor, so those farms with larger areas in grape production often employed 30 to 60 permanent workers who lived on the farm with their families. Spouses and children would then join the workforce at key moments in the agricultural season. Until the end of Apartheid, wine production remained limited because international sanctions blocked exports. Furthermore, other than the dreg wine reserved for the coloured farm workers in the Western Cape, wine consumption was reserved largely for whites—blacks in other parts of the country were encouraged to drink beer.

Post-Apartheid Agriculture

Since the end of Apartheid, shifts in the international political economy, as well as a number of policies and programs at the national level, have had a profound impact on commercial agriculture and on the wine industry in particular. At the international level, the biggest change was the end of sanctions on products that were clearly South African. This change had little impact on exports whose origin was ambiguous, such as table fruit, whose sale continued unabated in Europe during the Apartheid era. But as origin and label are extremely important for all but the cheapest wines, the end of sanctions represented a huge opening of markets for the South African wine industry. As a result, South African wine production went from 38.9 million liters in 1994 to 153.4 million liters in 2004. Today, there are some 4,400 farming units that produce wine grapes in South Africa. Almost all are in the Western Cape because the Mediterranean climate in this region favors their production. The livelihoods of over 108,000 South Africans depend on the wine industry.

Once Apartheid ended, international financial institutions such as the World Bank and the IMF pressed South Africa to adopt neoliberal economic policies that encouraged export orientation and free trade. Key donors, including the United States, pushed the ANC government to focus narrowly on establishing a procedural democracy, rather than pursuing a broader vision of democracy involving economic justice. The ANC would also come under pressure from the World Bank to adopt a policy of negotiated land reform based on the principle of willing seller/willing buyer, rather than a more radical alternative.

Within this international context, the formerly Marxist ANC government developed five sets of policies that would affect wine farming: 1) liberalizing agricultural trade and deregulating the marketing of agricultural products; 2) abolishing certain tax concessions and reducing direct subsidies to farmers; 3) introducing a minimum wage and other protections for farm workers; 4) implementing land reform policies and programs; and 5) setting broad goals for black empowerment and transformation in the agricultural sector.

In order to ensure food self-sufficiency at the national level, and to cater to an important constituency of the conservative National Party, Apartheid-era governments provided white commercial farms with a range of subsidies and tariff protections. The ANC government subsequently moved toward a dramatic liberalization of South African agricultural policy. This shift was motivated not only by external pressures, but also by the need to redirect resources away from agricultural subsidy programs to other areas, and by little sympathy in the new government for the situation of white commercial farmers. The increasingly competitive commercial agriculture sector has led to the loss of smaller and more marginal farms. With farms going out of business—and with commercial farmers seeking to avoid offering newly required legal protections to workers—the number of permanent farm laborer positions has dropped.

Land Redistribution and Transformation in the Agricultural Sector

Since the late 1990s, land redistribution programs have provided government grants to help blacks and coloureds acquire land when they are not in a position to benefit from land restitution. This program provides approximately $3,080 per eligible individual for the purchase of farmland (or more if the beneficiary contributes additional capital). In the Western Cape, the majority of land redistribution beneficiaries are current or former farm workers. Because farmland is relatively expensive in the province (especially vineyard appropriate land), large groups of beneficiaries, often

50 to 100 people, must pool their grants in order to buy a farm. In some instances, farms are purchased outright at market prices from willing sellers and then run independently by the land redistribution beneficiaries. In other instances, people use their grants to buy a portion of an existing farm, going into partnership with a white farmer. This second approach, known as a share equity scheme, is the only approach used to date with vineyards.

The reasons why vineyards have not been purchased outright number at least two: the purchase price of most vineyards is so high that it would take a vast number of grantees to purchase one; and there are certain advantages to going into partnership with an established wine grape farmer who presumably already has the know-how and contacts needed to run a successful vineyard. As of early 2005, there were 101 government land redistribution projects in the Western Cape, and of these nine were share equity schemes producing wine grapes. To put this in perspective, there are 7,185 commercial farms in the Western Cape, of which roughly 2,372 produce 100 tons or more of grapes annually. As such, land redistribution projects only constitute 1.4% of all farms in the Western Cape, and projects focused on the production of wine grapes make up less than half of one percent of all farms in this category. However, in addition to the nine government supported share equity schemes, there are also a number of worker co-owned vineyards that have been privately financed by progressive commercial farmers, international donors, foundations, and local wine industry groups.

South Africa's land redistribution program has been criticized from both right and left. Many conservative white South Africans believe that black or coloured farmers are incapable of effectively managing commercial farms. They see land redistribution as a waste of the government's money at best and, at worst, a program that could lead to collapse of the agricultural sector. Current problems with neighboring Zimbabwe's land reform process, including a series of disputed farm occupations by black war veterans, have only further fueled these fears.

Critics of the program from the political left, and even center, have focused on several issues. First, the pace at which the program is redistributing land has been exceptionally slow. By mid-2005, a little less than 3% of the formerly white-owned land had been redistributed to black or coloured South Africans, a long way from the 30% targeted for redistribution by 2014. Second, critics are questioning the "willing seller/willing buyer" principle that relies on the voluntary sale of commercial farms at market value, as the government does not have anything close to the level of resources needed to purchase 30% of white-owned farmland at market prices by 2014. Third, whether the large-scale, commercial orientation of the land redistribution program is appropriate has come into question at a time when so many commercial farms are going under. Finally, there are some specific concerns about share equity schemes because this mechanism may be manipulated by white farmers to obtain capital without actually relinquishing control. Furthermore, some have questioned how realistic it is to go into partnership with someone who may previously have been the autocratic "boss."

In addition to land redistribution, the South African government has a broader plan for transformation in the agricultural sector. This includes setting targets to increase the representation of blacks in management positions, to increase black ownership of agro-enterprises, and to increase the supply of produce to supermarkets by black-owned farms. Increasing black participation in the management of farms is key because farm workers have been excluded for years from the business and management side of farming. While farm workers are highly skilled in certain tasks, such as the pruning of grape vines, under Apartheid few blacks and coloureds were able to develop the managerial and business skills needed to run commercial farms. Moving farm workers into management positions will develop a cadre of black people who could go on to run successful commercial farms of their own.

While encouraging ownership of wineries and wine labels by black business interests is important for economic equality in South Africa, this is not the same as ownership by farm workers. Farm ownership by the emerging black upper class of business entrepreneurs does not automatically help the poor; worker-owned wineries and vineyards have a better chance of doing so.

Three Worker Co-Owned Vineyards

The Bouwland partnership trust, the Nelson's Creek New Beginnings project and the Nuutbegin trust represent three different models of worker co-owned vineyards. The Bouwland partnership trust came into being in 2003, when 60 land redistribution beneficiaries (of whom 55 are farm workers from the nearby Beyerskloof and Kanonkop vineyards) bought a 76% share of the 56-hectare Bouwland vineyard from Beyerskloof outside of Stellenbosch (of which 40 hectares is planted in Pinotage, Cabernet Sauvignon, and Merlot grapes). The trust's membership is roughly half male and half female (see photo), a split that is not only required by the government to receive grants, but that reflects the significant presence of women as farm workers in the South African wine industry. The group went into partnership with the winemaker for Beyerskloof and Kanonkop and with the owner of a London-based wine distribution firm. Using land redistribution grants from the government, and a commercial bank loan, they purchased both a majority share of the vineyard and a stake in the established Bouwland wine label.

The Bouwland trust operates with a somewhat complicated labor arrangement. Rather than working on their land during off hours, the trust shares the cost of a team of workers with Beyerskloof (which includes many trust members) that spends 40% of its time on the Bouwland land. The Bouwland property has no infrastructure, but rather relies on Beyerskloof for the use of its equipment and tasting room. With the exception of one full time employee who is involved in marketing and management, nearly of all of the group's shareholders have kept their day jobs as farm laborers on the nearby Beyerskloof and Kanonkop vineyards. The group currently produces and sells 17,000 cases of wine annually but is just breaking even, largely because they are paying off a loan. Their wine is sold in local supermarkets and exported to the UK, the Netherlands, Belgium, Denmark, Germany, and Canada. They currently are working with their Canadian distributor to expand exports to the United States. This is a solid project with a bright future, but the group is wrestling with the fact that it has yet to turn a profit, as well as some concerns about its dependence on Beyerskloof.

The Nelson's Creek New Beginnings Project is the oldest and most celebrated worker-owned vineyard in South Africa. This project began in 1997 when the owner of Nelson's Creek winery and vineyard gave 9.5 hectares of land to 18 of his workers as an expression of thanks for their efforts on his farm. The vineyard has subsequently grown to 13.5 hectares (the additional land was purchased from Nelson's Creek), producing Chardonnay, Cabernet Sauvignon and Merlot grapes. The group has its own wine label, New Beginnings, and sells wines to local supermarkets, along with exports to Germany and the Netherlands. Export opportunities to the United States are being explored. The group is reliant on Nelson's Creek for equipment, management, and winemaking expertise. The New Beginnings project is turning a profit and its members are using the money to buy food and consumer goods and pay their children's school fees.

The Nuutbegin trust began in 2000 when 99 farm workers from the Waterskloof and Fransmanskloof vineyards obtained land redistribution grants to purchase a 50% share of a long-term lease from the municipality for 25 hectares of prime vineyard land. The other two partners, the owners of the Waterskloof and Fransmanskloof vineyards, each have a 25% stake in the project. The group produces Merlot, Shiraz, and Cabernet Sauvignon grapes which are sold to the Thandi winery, in which the Nuutbegin trust has a 7% stake. Thandi produces a variety of wines, sourcing its grapes from four different worker co-owned vineyards in the area. Significantly, this is the first wine label to be fair-trade accredited in the world. While this accreditation should allow Thandi to fetch a small premium on the global market, Nuutbegin's 7% share in the label means that its returns from this end of the business are more limited. All of the shareholders have maintained their day jobs as farm workers, and they coordinate with the owners of Waterskloof and Fransmanskloof to schedule time to work the vines at Nuutbegin. Like Bouwland, this group has yet to turn a profit, and they are somewhat concerned about their continuing dependence on their white partners.

The Way Forward

As these case studies make clear, land redistribution and black empowerment in the wine industry are extremely challenging. High land prices and capital costs, not to mention the need for sophisticated business and wine-making expertise, mean that worker co-owned vineyards and wine labels are few in number, slow to start, and often dependent on the good graces of white employers and partners. It is important to note that the real money to be made in viticulture is in the selling of wine, not in the production of grapes. So vineyards with their own labels, such as the Bouwland and New Beginnings projects, have an advantage. Furthermore, because land, investment, and capital costs are so high, new projects must take on significant debt obligations that severely limit profits in the early years. Unlike Bouwland and Nuutbegin, New Beginnings did not incur significant debt; thus it can generate dividends for its membership more quickly and so benefit from a higher level of worker interest in the project.

The role of government land redistribution initiatives in the viticulture sector may always be minimal because the costs are so high. Interestingly, there has been more private support for black empowerment in viticulture than any other agricultural subsector, probably because the opportunity for new markets and profits is so high. This presents both an opportunity and a danger. On the positive side, private money means additional support for projects such as New Beginnings. But there is also a danger that private backers may see black empowerment and fair trade solely as means to earning greater profits rather than as paths toward economic justice. The key to lasting change will be having policy makers, academics, and consumers who are attuned to the difference between vineyards and wine labels that are truly co-owned by workers and those that are co-owned by black business interests with no or nominal participation of the workers.

Alas, what should North American and European wine consumers with a conscience do? I say seek out, and demand that your local wine market order, those South African labels that are co-owned and produced by farm workers. Yes, the South African land redistribution program is not perfect, but a growing market for worker-friendly wines will make existing ventures more profitable and encourage more white wine-makers to go into partnership with their workers. This is more than just fair trade—it is about creating a marketplace that rewards those working for change and economic justice, a world where workers really benefit from the fruits of their labor. ❑

Sources: C. Mather, "The Changing Face of Land Reform in Post-Apartheid South Africa," *Geography*, 87(4), 2002; P. Scully, "Liquor and Labor in the Western Cape, 1870-1900," in Crush, J. and C. Ambler (eds), *Liquor and Labor in Southern Africa*, Ohio University Press, 1992; G. Williams, G., "Black Economic Empowerment in the South African Wine Industry," *Journal of Agrarian Change*, 5(4), 2005; F.J. Zimmerman, "Barriers to Participation of the Poor in South Africa's Land Redistribution" *World Development* 28(8), 2000.

The Short Run: There They Go Again
July/August 2005

Hard as we try, we just can't keep up with Wal-Mart's crimes against workers. The company's Cross Lanes, W.V., store recently implemented a new policy that requires employees "to work almost any shift, any day of the week, whenever management asks," reports *Labor Notes* this month. Workers must agree to be available for work between 7:00 a.m. and 11:00 p.m., seven days a week, or lose their jobs. It sounds like a good way to get rid of employees with seniority and family obligations—we suppose that's the point.

—*Amy Gluckman*

Article 7.5

QUALITY IN, WORKERS OUT?
Companies Adopt Six Sigma

BY AMY GLUCKMAN
September/October 2003

"**M**y friend's company laid off every single salesperson in all of their stores around the country, in one morning. Then they immediately rehired them, but only the ones who had been averaging less than $16 an hour in commissions. All the best salespeople were laid off permanently. They got rid of commissions; now it's strictly hourly. Then they hired in a bunch of new people at around $7.00 an hour. And there's all kinds of other crazy stuff going on. He thinks it has something to do with Six Sigma, whatever that is."

This story, from a friend, was my introduction to Six Sigma, one of today's hottest management tools. The company was Circuit City. As it turns out, Circuit City's decision last February to lay off 3,900 high-performing salespeople and eliminate commissions may have had nothing to do with Six Sigma. *Wall Street Journal* reporter Carlos Tejada, who covered the story, doesn't think it did. Circuit City spokesperson Steve Mullin said the company does not disclose the nature or results of its Six Sigma program, and would not say whether last February's events were an outgrowth of it. But unions around the country are worried that Six Sigma is just one more cover story for companies implementing this kind of downsizing, along with speed-ups and other workplace changes that have been hitting U.S. workers hard since the 1980s.

Six Sigma Basics

Six Sigma is not new; it grew out of a quality-improvement effort at Motorola in the 1980s. When Motorola management publicized the billions of dollars in cost savings it claimed Six Sigma had achieved, other companies began to adopt the program, among them General Electric (GE). Former CEO Jack Welch—"Neutron Jack" to the one-fourth of GE's U.S. workforce whose jobs the company eliminated or exported in the 1980s—adopted Six Sigma as practically a company religion. GE claimed $750 million in Six Sigma-based gains in the first three years. Since the late 1990s, Six Sigma has spread beyond the manufacturing sector. Today, a growing list of service and retail businesses are adopting the program, including Citibank, Federal Express, Capital One, and Macy's. New York City is tapping Jack Welch to train school principals in the approach, and according to *USA Today*, federal homeland security officials are bringing in Six Sigma consultants to beef up the war on terror. Six Sigma has spawned a proliferating industry of consultants, seminars, software, and books that commend the program in glowing terms.

So what's behind all the hype? Six Sigma is a statistics-heavy approach to corporate planning and quality improvement. It's the newest in a long series of corporate quality schemes: Quality Circles, Total Quality Management (TQM), the Team Concept, ISO 9000, and so on. Some boosters call it "TQM on steroids." The sigma in Six Sigma is a statistics term for a measure of variation from an expected outcome. A sigma of six represents a near-perfect rate of only 3.4 defects per million opportunities. (An "opportunity" is any measurable outcome, from the strength of welds in a jet engine to the hold times at a call center.) The basic Six Sigma formula is summed up as DMAIC: define the requirements of a process or product to meet customer wishes, measure performance, analyze what's causing defects, improve the process to reduce them, and control the process to maintain improvements.

Despite its name, what seems to differentiate Six Sigma from earlier programs like TQM are not the statistical tools, which have been in use for decades, but rather the way companies implement the program. Certain individuals receive intensive training and become "green belts" or "black belts," certified to lead three- to five-month Six Sigma projects that are geared at overcoming a particular defect in a product or process. Apart from the small number of people who serve on the project teams, most non-supervisory employees typically don't participate in the program, other than to provide information to project teams—and, of course, to adopt whatever changes in work processes management decides on based on the team's results. Employees at Circuit City and Air Canada, for example, indicated that they only learned about their companies' adoption of Six Sigma by accident or through the grapevine. GE was an exception: virtually all workers received a brief "Six Sigma lite" training. But even at GE, management has not enlisted workers in Six Sigma nearly as much as it did under earlier quality programs, according to Ric Casilli, business agent at a GE local in Lynn, Massachusetts, and a member of his union's national bargaining committee.

This is in contrast to TQM, which often involved universal participation in trainings and teams. Six Sigma advocates tout the fact that improvement projects are carefully chosen by top management and limited to those with a clear bottom-line impact. This, they say, is an advantage over TQM, where each of the many quality teams might decide to work on a project of its own choosing.

Occasionally, Six Sigma teams uncover innocuous, common-sense improvements. A team at a Milwaukee hospital discovered that some patient specimens were getting lost because there was a hole in the pneumatic tube that carried specimen jars down to the lab. At Starwood Hotels, a Six Sigma team found a software package that enabled them to e-mail rather than fax information to conference planners looking for hotel space. But in many cases, the "improvements" are ones that enhance the bottom line at workers' expense.

Good for Workers?

After years of experience with quality and teamwork programs, unions are wary of Six Sigma. Perhaps their foremost concern is that the program is just Taylorism in a new guise. Six Sigma teams gather data to uncover workers' expertise, then turn that expertise into a knowledge base that can be transferred away: to other, less skilled workers; to cheaper workers overseas; to computers or robots. The fact that GE is perhaps the most well-known example of a Six Sigma company only reinforces this concern, given that it was Welch who was well known for saying that he'd like to put all GE factories on barges so they could be moved around the world in search of the cheapest labor.

It's one thing to collect data on how well a machine tool is working. But as more and more companies outside the manufacturing sector adopt Six Sigma, the program's focus on data collection can become a justification for intensified surveillance of employees. A company called Witness Systems sells software that can record voice, data, e-mails, web searches, and online chats. The company boasts that Starwood Hotels "has leveraged eQuality [the software] as part of its Six Sigma process." Its website quotes a Starwood manager who says he "can use eQuality to isolate particular challenges by recording 100 percent of calls ... by an associate's login ID." In other words, in the name of collecting data to make process improvements, the company can zero in on any one customer service employee's every word and keystroke.

Because the whole point of Six Sigma is to reduce variation in a process or product, the program can end up introducing infuriating rigidities into workers' jobs. At Circuit City, for example, department managers are told exactly how many hours of staffing they must employ in their departments each week. One week a department might be slotted for 140 hours of staffing, the next week for 170. Even if business is brisk, managers are not permitted to give anyone more hours. (Of course, this kind of ever-variable scheduling is impossible with a staff of full-time employees, so the policy institutionalizes the replacement of full-time staff with part-timers who, just coincidentally, receive no benefits.) One department manager said, "With Six Sigma, we're not supposed to look at the people any more, just meet the numbers. The pressure for the numbers is incredible."

At Loews Hotels, any employee who interacts with hotel guests has to worry about a different set of numbers: in this case, "10, 5, First and Last." Hotel workers are required to make eye contact when any guest is 10 feet away, greet the guest at five feet, and be the first and last to speak in the conversation. Six Sigma expert Peter Pande sees this kind of performance standard as a plus because it's "a way to make 'attentiveness' measurable"—and under Six Sigma, everything has to be measurable. This fact alone, applied to complex human interactions, shapes job requirements that are increasingly mind-numbing.

Companies don't usually come out and say that their Six Sigma projects have led to layoffs. Just the opposite: they're more likely to claim, as consultant Jim Bandrowski puts it, that if the company can use Six Sigma methods to cut costs or meet customers' needs better, the business will grow and jobs will be created. But many analysts predict that Six Sigma will fit right into the downsizing trend that many workers know well after years of corporate restructuring. Pamela Sachs, head of the flight attendants union at Air Canada, says that the airline has carried out a downsize-speedup cycle: first cutting the number of flight attendants on the plane with a commensurate reduction in the amount of service provided to passengers, but then restoring the former service level with fewer flight attendants on board. Since the airline adopted Six Sigma, she says, it reinstituted a detailed five-page checklist for supervisors to use when they observe crew members on a flight. She views the checklist as a way management can collect precise information on how flight attendants do their work, information that facilitates the reassignment of more work to fewer people. Even if Six Sigma projects are not the direct impetus for layoffs, companies can use its tools to figure out how to function with fewer workers afterwards. When Six Sigma does achieve cost savings, notes Stephen Tormey, international representative with the UE, "They're not about to share it with us."

Crisis/Opportunity

Six Sigma is just a small piece of the increasingly raw deal U.S. workers have been getting over the past thirty years. Nonetheless, pro-labor analysts believe it's important for workers and unions to respond in a proactive and nuanced way when companies adopt the program. Charley Richardson of the Labor Extension Program at the University of Massachusetts-Lowell advocates "continuous bargaining." In other words, he says, unions should neither accept nor reject Six Sigma and related corporate initiatives outright. Rather, they should evaluate each instance—each process change, each invitation to join a team—according to consistent criteria and bargain accordingly. Will jobs be created or destroyed? What will the company give in return for worker participation in this instance?

With this kind of careful response, Six Sigma may present workers with opportunities as well as challenges. Like earlier quality-control programs, Six Sigma is sold to workers as a way to give workers a say, solve workplace problems, and make everyone better off. If these benefits fail to materialize, the discrepancy can be a means of raising workers' consciousness about their situation, according to Steven Vallas, professor of history, technology, and society at Georgia Institute of Technology. In a study of four manufacturing plants, he found that "by drawing attention to the limited authority that workers were actually allowed," these programs "tended to heighten worker suspicion and distrust and to foster patterns of solidarity that were difficult for managers to control." Activists and researchers have long criticized quality-control programs as a way to co-opt workers and unions by pretending to give them a voice on the job. By design, Six Sigma offers more limited channels for worker involvement than earlier programs, so perhaps co-optation is less of a risk. But in any case, Vallas' research suggests that Six Sigma could—ironically—open up new and unexpected opportunities for true worker empowerment. ❏

Article 7.6

WORKER-OWNERS AND UNIONS: WHY CAN'T WE JUST GET ALONG?

BY DAN BELL
September/October 2006

You have probably heard the story of the scorpion that convinces a frog to carry it across a river. Halfway across, the scorpion stings the frog, which means both will drown. The frog does not understand; the scorpion explains, "I couldn't help myself. It's my nature."

In the abstract, worker-owned enterprises and labor unions would appear to have much in common. Both share the goal of improving pay and working conditions. Both aim to give workers a say in the workplace. And both belong on any progressive's short list of strategies for building a more just economic system.

But when unions and worker-owned businesses actually interact, they sometimes act more like the fabled arachnid.

The Ohio Employee Ownership Center at Kent State, where I work, provides preliminary technical assistance on worker buyouts. I once met with a group of employees exploring a worker buyout of a failing paper mill in southwest Ohio. When I asked them why they thought they would do any better, they gave me an example. Pointing to a large machine, they explained that it broke down regularly, resulting in lost production. Any repairs they could make were only temporary, until permanent replacement parts could be installed. They went on to explain that the mill had been bought and sold three times over the past two years. Two owners ago the parts had been purchased, but they were still sitting in a storeroom. When these employees became the owners, they were going to install the parts.

But would the workers really cooperate with management as employee owners, and would management really cooperate with them and empower them to make decisions and act independently? Or, as with the scorpion, were the decades of confrontational labor-management relations so engrained in the nature of both groups that they would sink their own company? In that instance we'll never know, because the buyout effort did not go forward.

Competing Models?

Worker-owned businesses can take a variety of forms, from full-fledged worker cooperatives to companies whose structure and management practices are indistinguishable from ordinary capitalist firms except for the fact that their employees own some or all of the company's shares (see "The Many Forms of Worker Ownership"). Because most of the manufacturing companies where worker buyouts have been used to avert plant closures were unionized, unions have had to grapple with reshaping their role in this new context.

While unions and worker-owners share many aims, there are also profound differences. True cooperatives address working conditions through direct democracy at the company level. Members have the right to participate in making decisions on matters such as compensation and business planning. Co-op members do not like being restricted in their decision-making by factors external to the cooperative—even factors like industry-wide collective bargaining agreements. When co-ops interact with other co-ops, they typically form secondary cooperatives controlled by the member co-ops, which run them to serve their common needs. One might say that co-ops tend toward decentralization.

In contrast, unions depend on numbers to build their strength. They need to maintain a degree of discipline among their locals, insisting on relative uniformity around key issues. Unions' most effective strategy for bringing about changes in the workplace is the collective refusal to work. If the central leadership cannot count on each local to follow its direction, the threat of a strike loses credibility. Thus, unions depend on centralization in order to create enough power to offset that of the owners.

Why Worker-Owners Need Unions

Moreover, union representation might seem to be superfluous for worker-owners, who after all are supposed to have decision-making authority by virtue of being owners. Most ESOPs are not structured so as to give workers significant decision-making authority. But even in the most democratic ESOP, a union can have an important role to play. One way to look at the role of unions is to observe the balance of power that exists between the three branches of government in the United

---

THE MANY FORMS OF WORKER OWNERSHIP

The term "worker ownership" can describe a variety of business structures. At one end of the spectrum, the worker-owned cooperative model rejects the very notion that capital should control the business and enjoy an unlimited return. To the contrary, as political economist David Ellerman describes it, in the cooperative model labor hires capital, governance is based on membership in the firm, and the return to capital is limited. As a result, investors are not easily attracted. Workers themselves typically have little capital to invest. So co-ops are rarely found in capital-intensive industries; most of the 400 for-profit co-ops in the United States are in labor-intensive service industries, which do not require expensive tools.

Another model involves direct worker ownership of voting stock. Unlike the cooperative, this model accepts the capitalist system but rejects the capitalist. Here, the workers accept the assumption that control and profits should be allocated according to the number of shares one owns, but reject absentee ownership of shares by those who do not work at the firm. Only a handful of worker-owned companies are structured this way because workers typically lack capital to invest and are averse to risking the little they may have.

By far the most common structure of worker ownership is the Employee Stock Ownership Plan, or ESOP, which has been used in over 11,000 U.S. companies since first being written into legislation in 1974. About 9,225 ESOPs are active today, according to the National Center for Employee Ownership. ESOP participants often share ownership of

States. The legislative branch makes the laws, as the board of directors in a company sets policy by which management must manage. The executive branch implements or executes the laws on a daily basis, as management runs the day-to-day operations. Even in those ESOPs where the worker-owners have the right to participate in electing the board of directors, that right does not protect any individual employee from the power that management enjoys to hire and fire, for example. Just as the judicial branch protects individual citizens from the misuse of power by an executive, the union protects individual workers from the arbitrary use of power by management.

Collective bargaining is another role that unions play. A union can help worker-owners to assess their situation in the context of industry-wide working conditions and compensation practices. And via the union, information flows both ways. In a cooperative or an ESOP practicing so-called open book management, the employees have full access to the company's financial information. With such transparency, the union negotiating team does not have to guess about what the company can afford; it has the information required to calculate what is available for compensation. Using this as a frame of reference, the union is also in a better position to bargain for strong agreements throughout the industry.

Access to group rates on benefits like health insurance or multi-employer pensions can be another advantage that unions bring, especially in the case of cooperatives, which tend to be much smaller than ESOP companies.

Unions also bring a ready-made communication structure, which can be helpful in building an ownership culture among workers who are accustomed to having little say in the business.

---

the company with large investors. Moreover, in most companies with ESOPs the worker-owners not only accept that capital, not labor, has the right to govern the business, but also allow someone else to vote their shares of that capital.

The ESOP itself is a trust that receives tax-deductible retirement contributions from the company. Two characteristics set ESOPs apart from other retirement plans, such as 401(k)s. First, ESOPs are not only allowed, but required, to invest a majority of their assets in the employer company's own stock. Second, an ESOP can borrow money to acquire stock, releasing shares to individual participants as future contributions are made. While employees may not possess credit, cash, or collateral, the ESOP provides a vehicle for the sponsoring employer to fill this gap with the credit, cash, and collateral of the company itself. In other words, ESOPs provide workers with a tax-advantaged structure for financing the acquisition of their company.

The legal owner of the capital is the ESOP trust, overseen by a trustee appointed by the board of directors. In managing the ESOP's assets, under current law the trustee is allowed to consider only the workers' interest in increasing the value of their retirement holdings—not their interests as employees with concerns such as job security.

While worker buyouts to avoid shutdowns account for only about 3% of all ESOPs, a majority of these are companies with union representation prior to the buyout. Without the leadership, structure, and protection afforded by a union, employees generally cannot build common cause quickly enough to present themselves as viable buyers, before machinery has been moved out and customers turned away.

Some of the positive synergies between union representation and worker owner-ship were at play in a Toledo textile firm. In 1991, GenCorp was planning to close down an unprofitable division, but instead agreed to sell it to the 200-plus employees as Textileather. The Amalgamated Clothing and Textile Workers Union (ACTWU) supported the buyout and joined with management in building successful employee participation. Training in participatory practices was implemented from the begin-ning, and an effective jointly led employee involvement structure resulted in a 28% increase in productivity, a 40% drop in scrap, and greatly reduced machine down-time in the first year. The company was immediately profitable. Ultimately, though, Textileather's worker-owners decided that their primary goal was job security, not ownership. In 1996, when the acquisition debt was paid off, management and workers agreed to sell the company. The buyer not only paid 160% of the valuation price, but also agreed to increase wages, bring in additional work creating more jobs, and give the employees the first right of refusal if it decided to sell the plant in the future.

At another worker-owned firm, an initially strong union-ESOP relation-ship failed to prevent a breakdown of the worker-ownership structure. Republic Engineered Steels' 4,500 employees, spread among eight plants in four states and primarily organized by the United Steelworkers (USWA), chose to buy their divi-sion from steel giant LTV in 1989 to avoid a shutdown. The new contract defined a structure for employee participation: Work groups would meet regularly to iden-tify opportunities for change. They could implement actions that affected only their area; other proposals would be kicked up to the department level, the plant level, and in some cases to a corporation-wide joint labor-management committee. To get this structure to work, 100 managers and their corresponding 100 union represen-tatives trained jointly for a week to become co-facilitators. Union and management also formed a joint committee to direct the ownership training program.

With a solid foundation of worker-owner participation, the company suc-cessfully cut $80 million out of its annual $800 million expenses in only 18 months—not by cutting compensation, but by implementing employees' ideas for improving operations.

Two events changed the picture. First, to provide equity for the buyout, employ-ees had agreed to roll over $20 million from their LTV retirement plan in exchange for preferred stock that paid annual dividends at 16%. In order to retire this expensive debt, management convinced the employees to let the company go public. But man-agement miscalculated the price the shares would obtain, disappointing the workers and shaking their confidence in company leadership. Furthermore, in an attempt to enhance the company's reputation with its new outside shareholders and raise its share price, management became less sensitive to the priorities of its worker-owners.

Then, in the late 1990s the price of steel took a deep plunge. Instead of respond-ing to the crisis by taking advantage of the participatory structures that had so methodically been created, management fell back on its traditional MO, imple-menting changes with no worker input. When management made plans to open a new plant where it could get the most concessions from the local government—a decision that would have put many of its Massillon, Ohio, worker-owners on the street—the union became so frustrated that it sought out an investor to buy the company, giving up ownership in order to dislodge an entrenched management.

Unions have other ways of getting management's attention, short of selling the company. Some choose the traditional union weapon: the strike. In 1998, the worker-owners at the 100% employee-owned Republic Storage Systems, represented by the Steelworkers, chose to go on strike, ostensibly over a few pennies. In fact, this was their way of expressing a vote of no confidence in the CEO. Soon after, the CEO did resign, and the employees found a new leader they were prepared to follow. In fact, in 2003, when the entire plant was severely damaged by a flood, employees came in on their own time to clean it up.

Communication and Transparency

Union members are conditioned to be suspicious of management. Worker buy-outs are far more likely to be successful if workers and management build trust; the experience of a number of companies shows that the best way for managers to build that trust is to operate with transparency and open up workers' access to information.

The union bargaining committee at Dimco-Gray, a 100% employee-owned company with about 110 worker-owners, was refusing to budge on management's proposed profit sharing formula. Management wanted to reserve an amount equivalent to 5% of the company's assets before paying out 50% of the remainder as profit-shares to the employees. The bargaining committee members decided the trigger for profit sharing should be no more than 3% of assets.

The impasse was broken after an Ohio Employee Ownership Center trainer met with the committee. After reviewing the basics of the profit and loss statement and the balance sheet, employees asked, "Where does the company's share go?" The trainer explained that it went to build up the company's equity, in the same way that the principal portion of monthly mortgage payments increases a homeowner's equity. The union team realized that the issue was not how much do *we* get and how much do *they* get. As a 100% employee owned company, the employees get it all. The question is, rather, how much do *we* take out for current consumption, and how much do *we* re-invest for a stronger retirement. Agreement on the contract was reached the very next day.

At Republic Engineered Steels, a group of 50 employee-owners, half blue collar and half white collar, attended an offsite peer-training workshop. Believing the program to be a sham, some of the union members had signed up to be trainers so they could expose it. I recall overhearing some union participants discussing how the company had brought them there to be brainwashed. But when they realized they were getting real information, they became much more supportive of the changes and became the company's best trainers. Their reversal in attitude got the attention of others, who had known them to be outspoken skeptics.

Reasonable Doubt

Although workers and companies can clearly benefit from maintaining union representation following a worker buyout, unions have historically been skeptical about worker ownership. For one thing, they have had to contend with a string of companies that have engaged in deceptive practices in connection with creating ESOPs or selling plants to workers.

For instance, the International Brotherhood of Teamsters has good reason to be suspicious of employee ownership. In the 1980s, when deregulation was exposing trucking companies to lower-cost competition, the Teamsters refused to negotiate any changes to the master contract. At the same time, the union did not object if individual locals chose to exchange specific items in the contract for an equivalent amount of company stock held in an ESOP.

With this hands-off position, neither opposing nor encouraging employee ownership, the union left its locals at the mercy of the companies. Some trucking company owners were able to get away with matching their workers' concessions with stock in assetless "front" companies that leased their trucks from the owner's separate asset-holding company. When the front companies failed, the workers had neither revenue nor assets to give their stock any value.

One of the Ohio Employee Ownership Center's first employee buyout efforts was with Atlantic Foundry in Akron, Ohio. The owners had announced a shutdown because the foundry was unable to turn a profit. A quick analysis showed that the revenues did cover the direct costs, generating a gross profit, and that with sufficient sales volume, the buyout would be able to cover its indirect and debt service costs.

Despite this good news, the Steelworkers showed little initial support for the buyout effort and eventually took a clear position opposing it. Why was the union not willing to help these workers save their jobs?

The reason the foundry was losing money was its pension obligations to past workers; the plant simply did not generate sufficient income to cover this additional non-operating expense. Deeper analysis revealed that the owners had withdrawn a significant amount of non-operating assets and placed them in a separate company, whose balance sheet did not show the obligations to the retirees. The owners had offered to sell the company "for a song" as long as the workers took the retiree obligation with them. The union believed that the new company would fail if saddled with this obligation, and that the retirees would then have a more difficult time going after the original owners.

In the case of a deceptive sale, as with Atlantic Foundry, the union did exactly the right thing. Had the Steelworkers not drawn attention to the deceptive offer, the workers would have taken on more debt—the obligation to the retirees—than the operation could service. This would have left them bankrupt and unemployed—and left the retirees with a more difficult legal battle in any attempt to salvage their pensions. In essence, the active employees and the seller were negotiating a sale based on the risk capital of an absent voice: the retirees. The union brought that voice to the table. With this transparency, a more feasible transaction might have been possible. For example, negotiators could have placed a fair value on the retiree obligation; a trust could have been funded with a note from the new worker-owned company, equal to the fair market value of the operating business, and with cash from the seller to cover the balance. Of course, this was exactly the outcome that the unethical sellers were attempting to avoid. Not surprisingly, the foundry still sits idle today, two decades later.

Unions also have legitimate concerns about worker buyouts leading to decertification of the union. For the most part, if a company does not have a union before becoming worker-owned, it probably will not form a union afterward. Employees reason, "If we didn't need a union when we were owned by someone else, why would we need one now that we own the place?" Similarly, companies that have a union before the buyout often continue with the union under worker ownership. However, in some instances sellers have forced workers to disband their union as a condition of the buyout deal. In the case of Plymouth Locomotive, the owners refused to sell to a union workforce. The UAW agreed to decertification in order to let the buyout move forward. In the case of the Brainard Rivet Division of Textron, the employees did not decertify; the union local simply ceased to exist when the plant was closed. When Fastener Industries, a successful 100% employee-owned company, offered the Brainard workers the opportunity to reopen as a subsidiary, the workers agreed not to re-establish the union.

On the other hand, organizing drives sometimes do succeed at employee-owned companies where workers view the union as a mechanism for reshaping the ESOP along more democratic lines. At Voto Sales and Manufacturing in Steubenville, Ohio, for example, the management controlled the initial board of directors following the buyout, allowing them to put a hand-picked trustee in charge of the ESOP. In other words, while owning only a minority of the company stock, management had positioned itself as the controlling shareholder group. The workers brought in a union as a way to establish a balance of power. After establishing a Steelworkers local, the employees were able to get the ESOP modified to pass through voting rights directly to the participants, in effect, bringing management under the control of the owners again.

Finally, unions have a duty to workers across an industry as well as to those in a particular workplace. Recently a worker co-op member contacted me looking for guidance on resolving a difficult conflict between his co-op and the union that organizes a few of its employees. Most of the workers at this site had supported the worker buyout and joined the co-op. A few of the workers, who are represented by a union, chose not to become members. In order to generate the surplus necessary to pay off the acquisition debt, the members agreed to reduce their wages and benefits. However, the union insisted that the terms of the collective bargaining agreement not be altered. The co-op members believed that to stick to the contract would be unfair to the members who were not in the union, because they were making sacrifices to help the co-op survive. And if all of the members were compensated as the union members expected to be, the business would fail. Since one of the principles of a co-op is autonomy from outside organizations, it seemed inappropriate for the union to be insisting on sticking to the contract, when even the members affected were willing to adapt.

But the co-op members had to recognize that the union was not dealing with their company in a vacuum. A union has to bargain with the entire industry and try to get the best possible deal for all of its members. Any time a local agrees to a lower-cost contract with one employer, that undercuts the union's bargaining position with all other employers. Each employer will expect to get the same contract as the competition, so the result is that wages fall. Industry-wide worker solidarity is just as important to union members as autonomy is to co-op members.

As it turns out, in this instance both the need to respect an industry-wide collective bargaining agreement *and* the co-op members' right to compensate everyone fairly and according to cooperative values can probably be satisfied. For the co-op members, their compensation is not wages per se, but rather an advance on their profit share. If the union-member employees are to receive higher pay in accord with their contract, that can be offset by giving them a smaller share of the surplus as owners. The nonunion co-op members, who get a smaller "advance" now, will receive a larger profit-share down the road.

The Road Ahead

Can worker-owners and unions get along? Notwithstanding the profound differences between worker ownership and union representation as strategies for improving working conditions and giving workers a voice, and in spite of unions' sometimes valid skepticism, the simple answer is: They must! Globalization has exposed both the labor movement and worker-owned cooperatives to intense competition within a framework of laws and policies that relentlessly favor corporations over workers. To respond effectively, workers need a varied toolkit; they cannot afford to abandon solidarity merely because different groups pursue different strategies.

The collaboration between the Hotel Employees and Restaurant Employees union (HERE) and Cooperative Home Care Associates, a large, Bronx, N.Y.-based co-op, provides a good case study. When HERE sought to organize CHCA's employees, the workers, who already had significantly better pay and working conditions than most home health aides, initially showed little interest. CHCA's management, on the other hand, saw an opportunity: a successful industry-wide organizing campaign would raise the payroll of the competition closer to the co-op's costs.

CMCA's managers believed a union organizing drive would benefit their co-op. Likewise, creating co-ops may benefit a union's organizing work, according to Lisabeth Ryder, an American Federation of State, County, and Municipal Employees (AFSCME) administrator. Ryder believes that when public-sector jobs are contracted out to large corporations, unions such as AFSCME, instead of repeating traditional organizing drives that face growing obstacles and often fail, could help the privatized workers to turn their units into worker-owned cooperatives that could then bid against the corporation for the government contract.

Today, the worker-ownership and labor movements are engaged in an expanding dialogue. In June [2006], several union leaders participated in a symposium in Halifax, Nova Scotia, on cooperatives and their workers. In September, the Canadian Worker Co-op Federation hosted over a dozen regional labor leaders at a two-day workshop in Saskatoon to explore the development of a joint strategy for worker-driven interventions to avert plant closures. Retired Steelworkers President Lynn Williams set the tone for the meeting with a brief review of his union's development of a proactive position on employee buyouts. Participants ended the meeting by forming the Prairie Labour-Worker Cooperative Council; with the Ohio Employee Ownership Center as a model, the council aims to create a regional program and infrastructure to support worker buyouts and foster collaboration between the worker-ownership and labor movements.

The U.S. Federation of Worker Cooperatives hopes that its effort to engage labor leadership at its biannual conference this October in New York will prove just as successful as that of its Canadian counterpart.

As unions and co-ops engage in further discussion and collaboration, they may discover unexpected synergies between the two strategies. Ideally, such collaborations will turn out to strengthen and invigorate both the union staff and members and the worker-owners who are willing to cross over and work together toward a common goal of empowering workers. ❑

This article was adapted with permission from a paper presented at a symposium held by the Master of Management—Co-operatives and Credit Unions Program, St. Mary's University, Halifax, Nova Scotia in June 2006.

The Short Run: Invisible Hand Caught in the Cookie Jar
September/October 2007

Hershey, the largest candy producer in the United States, announced in February that it would eliminate 1,500 jobs in Pennsylvania and transfer some of its operations to Mexico. But the plan has backfired, according to Bloomberg News. Hershey's second-quarter profits fell 96%, with net earnings falling to $3.55 million, from $97.9 million a year earlier. Bloomberg also reported that, partly as a result of its plan to offshore jobs, Hershey has lost market share to its main rival, Mars Inc. "We understand the missteps over the past few quarters," said Hershey CEO Richard Lenny, "and we are aggressively addressing them."

Shipping U.S. jobs overseas to cut labor costs isn't the worst business practice the candy industry has seen, by a long shot. A UNICEF report in the late 1990s helped to publicize the use of child slaves—mostly 12- to 16-year-old boys trafficked form neighboring Mali—to harvest cocoa beans in Cote D'Ivoire, the world's leading cocoa producer and exporter. In 2001, the chocolate and cocoa industries reached an agreement aimed at reducing the use of child labor in cocoa production. But the group Anti-Slavery International has stated that "[b]ecause of the way the chocolate industry buys its cocoa, it is not possible to ensure that slaves or other forms of illegal exploitation have not been used in its production." —*Sudeep Bhatia*

Article 7.7

THE JOBS CRISIS AND THE ART OF FLEXIBLE LABOR

BY DAN DIMAGGIO
January/February 2011

On Sunday, October 3 [2010], an ad in the Minneapolis *Star Tribune* from the temp agency ProStaff advertised 300 immediate call-center positions. By Wednesday the agency had upped this number, hiring 550 unemployed and under-employed Twin Cities residents like me to fill these jobs. The majority were people of color, including hundreds of African Americans—no surprise given that as of 2009 African-American unemployment in the Twin Cities stood at three times that of whites (20.4% vs. 6.6%). We were promised work through October 22, with the caveat that we must be "flexible."

After interviewing for the job on Monday we were told to show up early Tuesday morning for eight hours of training. So we arranged babysitters, reshuffled schedules at our other jobs, and canceled meetings and classes. Then on Monday evening we were called and told training had been moved to 1 p.m. on Tuesday. We rescheduled everything again, dutifully displaying our flexibility.

We weren't supposed to be done with training until 8, or 9, or 10 p.m., depend-ing on which member of the ProStaff team you'd talked to the night before, but when we arrived Tuesday at 1 p.m., the company trainer smiled and told us, "Don't worry, we'll have you out of here by 5!" As if anyone without a job wants to make less money—especially when they've already paid for a babysitter. This "flexible" approach to time is entirely one-sided; ProStaff's time sheets are calculated down to the second.

At some point during the training, we also learned that most of the shifts we'd signed up for had been changed. And that we were going to be working weekends, despite explicitly being told during our interviews that this was a Monday through Friday job. Then we found out that the actual job wouldn't start until Thursday, though we were repeatedly told that we had to be available immediately. That's the thing about temp work—you have to always be available, able to "flexibly" adjust to all your employers' whims. In return, they have to guarantee you … nothing.

The supervisor in charge of training laughed whenever she repeated her favorite sentence: "You must be FLEXIBLE, FLEXIBLE, FLEXIBLE." Eventually she realized she might be offending some of us, and apologized by saying, "We're sorry, this is just the nature of this work"—the phrase that excuses any and all behavior by businesses that hire temps.

Finally, in the middle of the night Thursday, after four hours of training and one day of work, we all received a dreaded phone call: our jobs were gone. No one had been calling the call center with regard to the class-action settlement we were hired to take questions about. Just like that, over 500 people were returned to the ranks of the jobless.

We woke up Friday morning to headlines announcing the loss of an addi-tional 95,000 jobs nationally, with the unemployment rate steady at 9.6% and the underemployment rate rising to 17.1%. Saturday's *Star Tribune* seemed to mock us with its headline "For Jobless, No Relief."

Unfortunately, working through temp agencies like ProStaff has become the only option for many without jobs. Among the 64,000 private-sector jobs added nationwide in September, the Bureau of Labor Statistics reported that "temporary help services accounted for most of" the 28,000 jobs added in professional and business services.

The "flexibility" mantra of these jobs means desperation, disposability, accommodation, quiescence. It means acting as much as possible like a commodity rather than a human being. Commodities don't complain. They don't have families or lives. They don't write articles denouncing temp agencies.

You have to wonder how far American workers will continue to bend before they either break or snap back. If we get ourselves organized, maybe the next time 500 of us receive a call in the middle of the night informing us that we've been laid off, we can produce a better response than just rolling over and going back to sleep. It's long past time to wake up from this nightmare. Temps of the world unite! We have nothing to lose but our flexibility! ❑

Sources: Algernon Austin, "Uneven Pain: Unemployment by Metropolitan Area and Race," Economic Policy Institute, epi.org, August 2010; Bureau of Labor Statistics, October 2010; "Temporary downturn? Temporary staffing in the recession and the jobless recovery," *Focus*, Spring 2005; Alazraki Melly, "Paid Off for Layoffs: CEOs Who Cut More Jobs Got Paid 42% More Money in 2009," *Daily Finance*, September 2010.

Chapter 8

LABOR, GLOBALIZATION, AND TRADE

Article 8.1

CONTEMPORARY WORKERS' STRUGGLES AGAINST NEOLIBERALISM

BY PETER RACHLEFF
December 2006—WorkingUSA

What do flight attendants, auto workers, college professors, clerical workers, and public employees have in common? We—and most of our counterparts in the United States, Latin America, Europe, Asia, Africa, indeed, all over the world—are under the gun, the gun of "neoliberalism."

More than 150 years ago, Karl Marx and Frederick Engels ended their *Communist Manifesto* with the call: "Workers of the World, Unite! You have nothing to lose but your chains." However, for the next century and a half, rather than unite on a global basis, workers competed with each other for privileges, advantages, and jobs, falling prey to nationalism and racism, even to the point of fighting wars to the death against each other.

Now, perhaps for the first time in the history of the capitalist system, capital is attacking labor all over the world, in all industries, with the same techniques, demands, and pressures. As grim as the recent past, present, and immediate future might appear, with wage and benefit cuts, economic insecurity, draconian reorganizations of work rules and job descriptions, declining rates of unionization, and declining effectiveness of conventional strikes, the prospects for the emergence of a global labor movement have never been better.

Capitalism emerged from the Great Depression and World War II with a reorganized political economy. Keynesianism—the promotion of macroeconomic growth through the manipulation of aggregate demand—became the dominant government, business, and labor policy framework, and it became the dominant school of thought in academic economics throughout the world.

Governments "fine-tuned" inflation and unemployment through regulating interest rates and increasing or decreasing demand, relying on deficit spending or budget surpluses. Employers and unions collectively bargained contracts, which began with the premise that increases in productivity would be rewarded with increases in wages, enabling large numbers of workers to become meaningful consumers.

A critical political-economic context for this system was the particular world order in which the United States and U.S.-based businesses dominated the European and Asian economies that had been devastated by World War II. This world order was legitimated by military as well as economic power at the height of the Cold War. Much of the rest of the world, only recently freed from European colonialism, became available for U.S. exploitation of national resources, labor, and markets. For an entire generation, most Americans, including workers, experienced a rising standard of living and economic security—all the more impressive by comparison to the Depression that many of them had experienced in their own lifetimes.

This system began to fray in the mid-1960s and was spinning apart by the mid-1970s. The uses of deficit spending to cover the costs of both the "War on Poverty" and the Vietnam War—what my first economics teacher called "trying to have guns and butter at the same time"—drove the relationship between inflation and unemployment beyond their assumed parameters. The more both of these wars appeared to be progressing in the wrong direction, the more money had to be borrowed or printed, and then thrown at the problems.

Inflationary policies that had once spurred growth now seemed to block it. A new economic term was coined: "stagflation." In early 1972, economists reported that the "Phillips curve" (which described that relationship) had "shifted" from 4% to -4% to 7% to -7%—almost as if they were astronomers announcing the discovery of a new moon around Saturn. Mortgage rates shot up to 20% and beyond. Keynesianism had entered a deep, potentially fatal, crisis.

Meanwhile, the global context was changing. Japan and West Germany were recovering from their war setbacks and becoming sources of competition for U.S. businesses. Middle Eastern countries were finding their own voices, overcoming their tendencies towards competition with each other, and forming OPEC (the Organization of Petroleum Exporting Countries), raising the price of fuel and petroleum-based products rapidly. President Richard Nixon was forced to take the United States off the gold standard, not only feeding domestic inflation but also weakening the strength of the upper hand the United States had enjoyed as the world's banker. The ability of the U.S. government and U.S.-based capital to shift the burden of their problems onto others, while remaining within the structures and practices of Keynesianism, was fading.

To make matters even worse, corporate employers faced an increasingly militant working class at home. Rather than being assuaged by a generation of wage and benefit increases, unionized workers demanded more compensation, less work, and more time off. African-American workers, whose boat had not yet been lifted by the rising tide of Keynesian growth, demanded not only political and civil rights, but sought to use their increased political power to gain jobs, higher wages, and access to better housing, education, and health care. Public employees—from hundreds of thousands of postal workers across the country, to teachers and municipal and state employees—organized and demanded collective bargaining rights, seeking to raise their compensation and solidify their employment futures. In the first half of the 1970s, U.S. workers averaged close to 400 "large strikes" (more than 1,000 participants) per year.

With the rise of working-class militancy, the growing appeal of black power and feminist ideologies (some of which quite openly questioned capitalism), the antiwar movement and the failure of the Vietnam War, the crisis of the presidency (Nixon and Agnew both leaving office in disgrace), an energy crisis in which city upon city urged its residents to turn down their thermostats and put on more sweaters, the rise of mortgage rates to a level that crippled the housing industry, the fiscal crisis of New York City, seemingly out-of-control inflation, alienated and militant workers, ghetto revolts, and more, there seemed to be a political and ideological crisis of legitimacy just as deep as the economic crisis of Keynesianism and global capitalism. It is little surprise that this conjuncture generated deep structural, organizational, and ideological shifts among leading global capitalists, particularly those based in the United States.

Fundamental shifts in the nature and function of capitalism do not lead to a new full-blown vision and practice overnight. Rather, a series of projects, conversations, campaigns, experiments, and ideas—some of which succeeded, some of which failed, some implemented by individual capitalists, some implemented by individual governments—gradually became the practice of the bourgeois class and the key economic and political institutions they controlled: "supply-side economics," deindustrialization, capital flight, the formation and strengthening of transnational economic institutions like the International Monetary Fund (IMF), the World Bank, and the World Trade Organization (WTO), the use of "permanent replacements" to undercut strikes and bust unions, demands for "concessions" in wages and benefits, the introduction of "lean" production and decentralization (so-called post-Fordism). In addition, pressures on state and local governments to underwrite corporate investments combined and were spun with a burgeoning antigovernment ideology, promoting tax cuts, on the one hand, and slashing social expenditures on education, health care, and services, on the other.

In the place of the government-provided "safety net," this ideology hailed individual responsibility, self-discipline and, increasingly, Christian fundamentalism. The cohesive class strategy to be known as "neoliberalism" was taking shape.

Why is it called "neoliberalism"? This name harkens back to the philosophical and economic "liberalism" that accompanied the emergence of free market capitalism out of the government-controlled eras of feudalism, mercantilism, and colonialism. This initial "liberalism," championed by the likes of Adam Smith, John Stuart Mill, and John Locke, celebrated the market, unencumbered by government interference, as a "rational" and "efficient" institution in which providers of inputs would be rewarded in proportion to the value of their contributions. As capitalists—bankers and corporate execs, their lawyers, political agents, and media flaks—responded to what they saw in the 1970s as the crisis of Keynesianism, particularly its government-provided social benefits, its willingness to constrain corporate behavior, and its implicit "social contract" between employers and their unionized workers, they sought to restore a "market" environment, on a global as well as a national basis, in which they would have a free hand to invest where they wanted, employ whom they wanted for whatever wages and benefits they wanted to pay, and buy and sell wherever they wanted. This is their "neoliberalism."

Twenty to twenty-five years of experience give us the hindsight to see the key elements of "neoliberalism" as well as to make a preliminary accounting of its consequences. These elements include:

• *Free Trade.* This includes more than the absence of tariffs, taxes, and customs duties. It means the right to export and invest capital, buy materials, manufacture parts, sell products, and transport materials and products without concern for government regulations. Notice that labor may not move freely unless demanded as guest workers.

• *Financialization.* Through speculation, credit, and stock manipulations, finance capital siphons wealth not only from the working class, but also from manufacturing, retail, and other industries. The total daily turnover of financial transactions in international markets rose from $2.3 billion in 1983 to $130 billion in 2001. With each transaction, the representatives of financial capital took a commission, transferring capital from one sector to another. Within some sectors, such as airlines, banks and other lenders gained ownership of planes, collecting fat monthly leases even as one airline after another lost money.

• *Deregulation.* Beginning with the Staggers Act of 1978, which substantially deregulated transportation, government oversight and control over corporate economic behavior has diminished. Interestingly, notice that labor is typically still subject to controls, for example, over the right to strike.

• *Commodification.* Services and goods, which were once available on the basis of citizenship or community membership, have become commodities with price tags. Water, telecommunications, electricity, culture, and even clean air become available only to those who can afford to pay for them. Popular rights of access and use become scarce goods, the property of the elite.

• *Privatization.* Around the world, governments, sometimes under pressure from the IMF and the World Bank, have sold off public enterprises. Even in the most economically advanced economies, outsourcing and contracting out encouraged private sector competition for public sector provision of essential services (education, the postal service, transportation, and infrastructure).

• *Accumulation by dispossession.* The combination of commodification and privatization forms the basis for a return of what Marx called "primitive accumulation." New capital is created by actively stripping small owners and producers—individually or collectively, as the basis for the state—of their use rights or ownership of goods (land in many countries) and services. These commodities and the industries that produce them become private property, sources of profit and wealth for the bourgeois class who purchases them.

• *Cut labor costs.* By shrinking the unionized sector of the workforce and reducing the power of unions, employers cut wages and benefits while increasing productivity. More and more workers are positioned as casual, temporary, adjunct, and contingent. They replace higher-paid, veteran workers with newly hired workers, immigrants, or workers employed outside the United States altogether via international outsourcing. During the era of neoliberalism in the United States, for instance, workers have lost 20% of their net pay while adding 160 hours—a whole month—to their average work year. Workers who cannot keep up their consumption by selling more individual and family labor or taking on more credit are forced to consume some of the assets they might have accumulated. Thus, in 2005, American families spent down $600 *billion* of their savings embodied in their home equity.

• *Cut the social wage.* By reducing government-provided social services in education, health care, and the like, workers are forced to purchase goods and services (commodification), sell more labor or work more hours to purchase what they need, or just plain go without. For example, the number of Americans without health insurance has increased from approximately 37 million to 47 million since Bill and Hilary Clinton announced that there was a health case "crisis" that they were going to "fix."

• *Increase inequality.* Under such practices, it should be little surprise that inequality has skyrocketed throughout the world, particularly in the United States itself. Forty-five percent of American workers earn less than $13.25, which amounts to $27,600 a year. This is more than seven of the top 10 categories in job growth projected for the next 10 years. Between 1972 and 2001, earnings for the top 10% of income earners rose 34%, only about 1% per year. They rose 87% for the top 1%, those earning over $402,000 per year. For the top one-tenth of one percent, those earning more than $1.7 million per year, income rose 181%, and the top one-hundredth of one percent, those earning more than $6 million per year, income rose 497%.

These elements have added up to what commentators have called a "one-sided class war" or a "race to the bottom," all over the world. Workers from Chile to Canada, from India to South Africa, from France to China have faced pressures to boost their productivity and lengthen their work weeks, with wage cuts, diminished social and economic security, and reduced public services, along with a silencing of their political voices. While these practices have been wrapped within ideologies of individual freedom and promises of macroeconomic growth, they have been experienced as "Work harder and get less to show for it" by most workers.

Insecurity has become the order of the day. In the United States, not only do 47 million men, women, and children not have health insurance, but one-third of companies employing 200 or more workers provide no health benefits to retirees, and only one worker in four has even been promised a pension.

Neoliberalism and Emboldened Capitalist Despotism

David Harvey, in his book, *A Brief History of Neoliberalism*, makes a compelling argument that neoliberalism has failed to regenerate macroeconomic growth. GNP and GDP figures for the 1990s and first decade of the 21st century lag well behind comparable measures for the 1960s and 1970s. Drawing on the research of French economists Gerard Dumenil and Dominque Levy, Harvey confirms the evidence of capital's extraordinary transformation to maintain and expand power through the superexploitation of the working class.

Neoliberalism should be understood as a strategy to restore the class power of the national and global elites which came under fire in the 1960s and 1970s. Indeed, it has been successful in promoting increased economic inequality within and between countries and increased concentrations of wealth and political power. "Structural adjustment" programs in poor countries, on the one hand, and tax cuts and reduced social spending in highly developed countries, on the other, have put proportionately more money in rich people's pockets and less in poor people's.

Despite its theoretical disdain for the state, neoliberalism in practice has embraced interventionist state practices, from the breaking of strikes to the waging of war. The more securely the state has been taken in hand by the elite, the more confidently its powers are wielded to protect and further their interests. As for the nation-state itself, far from withering away under globalization, it has become all the more armored and armed.

Despite its lionization of individual freedom, neoliberalism in practice has promoted fundamentalist restrictions on human behavior, on the one hand, and the commodification of social relations, on the other. It has also undermined the social rights (to education, pensions, social security, health care, recreation, and more) that generations of men and women struggled and sacrificed to gain and which became the material floor upon which we could pursue our quests for individual freedom.

Like every other political, cultural, and ideological structure to emerge out of capitalism at a particular stage of its development, neoliberalism is both reality (wage and benefit cuts, etc., are all too real) *and* smokescreen. It has rapidly become the dominant discourse in elections, school board meetings, collective bargaining negotiations, classrooms, and popular media. It appears as if "there is no alternative."

Neoliberalism and Global Resistance

But, of course, as throughout history, there are alternatives, and they are emerging at the levels of ideas and movements. In just the last decade, we have seen the emergence of the Zapatistas in Chiapas, the Hugo Chávez administration in Venezuela, the factory occupations in Argentina, the shack dwellers' movement in South Africa, the young workers' movement in France, the anti-dam movement in India, a nascent labor movement in China, and more. The World Social Forum movement has sought to find ways to knit these and other movements together, albeit with fits and starts, breakthroughs and setbacks.

Despite the limited progress so far, the idea that "another world is possible" is spreading. Here in the United States, the spread and deepening of neoliberalism has had widespread consequences. Barbara Bowen, president of the Professional Staff Congress, the 20,000-member faculty union at the City University of New York, presented a paper to the "How Class Works" conference at the State University of New York at Stony Brook in June 2006, pointing out that 70% of the new college-level teaching jobs created throughout the United States are for casual, temporary, part-time, adjunct labor.

When 10,000 mechanics responded to management demands for a 50% reduction in jobs and a 26% reduction in wages and benefits by striking, Northwest Airlines implemented a strategy that combined outsourcing to nonunion facilities in the United States and outside the United States, the employment of permanent replacements through inside contracting, the filing of bankruptcy to gain leverage over not only the mechanics but all of the unions at the airline, and the threat of walking away from their already underfunded pensions. From Northwest to Delta, from Delphi to GM, so-called "legacy" employers (that is, those with retirees to whom they have financial obligations) have announced that they can no longer "compete" if they are forced to live up to those obligations. When the state of Minnesota announced that it was running a budget deficit, the Republican governor unilaterally decided to drop 30,000 adults from "MinnesotaCare," the state-subsidized health care program. And so it goes.

The story is much the same across the globe. In South Africa, the post-apartheid government's adoption of neoliberalism has placed not only decent paying jobs beyond the reach of millions of its citizens, but also housing, electricity, health care, and water. In Brazil, the Workers' Party has failed to stop or even slow the displacement of indigenous people from rainforests, allowing the clear-cutting of trees for massive soybean farms and other corporate enterprises.

In India, Coca-Cola redirects the water of underground aquifers to enable it to manufacture its sugary soft drinks while family and village wells go dry. In Chile, social security has been privatized and wage-earners and their families are forced to tie their futures to the stock market. In China, millions of peasants and small-village residents migrate to rapidly growing, polluted cities with inadequate infrastructure and social services in order to find jobs, which have relocated in search of lower and lower wages.

Everywhere we look, working people's lives are more intolerable. Workers throughout the world face the same enemy. It is not a particular corporation or a particular state; it is not even a transnational institution like the World Bank, the WTO, or the IMF. No, it is the very organization of the world economic system, neoliberalism. Even though individual struggles—of particular groups of workers, in particular countries—have been notably unsuccessful in the past two decades, there has been an impressive and important growth in the structures, practices, and relationships of international communication, organization, and solidarity. Protests against the WTO, the IMF, and the World Bank, on the one hand, and conventions of the World Social Forum and its regional branches, on the other, have laid some foundations for global workers' movements. Little by little, Internet communications, the solicitation of solidarity funds or even solidarity actions, are adding substance to these relationships.

For lack of space, this commentary only briefly elucidates some new forms of resistance to neoliberal capitalism, but it is my hope that they identify and clarify the wretched global conditions and the challenges that are emerging in the capitalist system today. I conclude with four fundamental requirements crucial to identifying and challenging neoliberal capitalism:

• First, we must recognize the beast that is ravaging the lives of working people the world over.

• Historians and social scientists must convey to the working class and poor how and why neoliberalism has arisen with such force and the characteristics of its operation.

• By providing knowledge and awareness of the perniciousness of neoliberalism, the basis for class-consciousness and global solidarity and the construction of a global resistance movement are possible.

• Armed with recognition of the destructiveness of neoliberal capitalism, it is my hope that activists will place individual struggles for justice within their universal context and seek ways and means to build transnational solidarities, not in some utopian future, but in the here-and-now.

While neoliberal capitalism seeks to portray itself as invincible to struggles for justice by workers and peasants through control over the media and education, activists must grasp the quandary and communicate accurately that resistance from below is possible, and that specific struggles may expand into a mass global movement to create a revolution of its own. ❑

Sources: G. Dumenil and D. Levy, *Capital Resurgent: Roots of the Neoliberal Revolution*, trans. D. Jeffers, Harvard University Press, 2004; David Harvey, *A Brief History of Neoliberalism*, Oxford University Press, 2006; Karl Marx and Friedrich Engels, *Communist Manifesto*, Penguin Group, 2002 (1848).

Article 8.2

THE GLOBALIZATION CLOCK
Why corporations are winning and workers are losing.

BY THOMAS PALLEY
May/June 2006

Political economy has historically been constructed around the divide between capital and labor, with firms and workers at odds over the division of the economic pie. Within this construct, labor is usually represented as a monolithic interest, yet the reality is that labor has always suffered from internal divisions—by race, by occupational status, and along many other fault lines. Neoliberal globalization has in many ways sharpened these divisions, which helps to explain why corporations have been winning and workers losing.

One of these fault lines divides workers from themselves: since workers are also consumers, they face a divide between the desire for higher wages and the desire for lower prices. Historically, this identity split has been exploited to divide union from nonunion workers, with anti-labor advocates accusing union workers of causing higher prices. Today, globalization is amplifying the divide between people's interests as workers and their interests as consumers through its promise of ever-lower prices.

Consider the debate over Wal-Mart's low-road labor policies. While Wal-Mart's low wages and skimpy benefits have recently faced scrutiny, even some liberal commentators argue that Wal-Mart is actually good for low-wage workers because they gain more as consumers from its "low, low prices" than they lose as workers from its low wages. But this static, snapshot analysis fails to capture the full impact of globalization, past and future.

Globalization affects the economy unevenly, hitting some sectors first and others later. The process can be understood in terms of the hands of a clock. At one o'clock is the apparel sector; at two o'clock the textile sector; at three the steel sector; at six the auto sector. Workers in the apparel sector are the first to have their jobs shifted to lower-wage venues; at the same time, though, all other workers get price reductions. Next, the process picks off textile sector workers at two o'clock. Meanwhile, workers from three o'clock onward get price cuts, as do the apparel workers at one o'clock. Each time the hands of the clock move, the workers taking the hit are isolated. In this fashion globalization moves around the clock, with labor perennially divided.

Manufacturing was first to experience this process, but technological innovations associated with the Internet are putting service and knowledge workers in the firing line as well. Online business models are making even retail workers vulnerable—consider Amazon.com, for example, which has opened a customer support center and two technology development centers in India. Public sector wages are also in play, at least indirectly, since falling wages mean falling tax revenues. The problem is that each time the hands on the globalization clock move forward, workers are divided: the majority is made slightly better off while the few are made much worse off.

Globalization also alters the historical divisions within capital, creating a new split between bigger internationalized firms and smaller firms that remain nationally centered. This division has been brought into sharp focus with the debate over the trade deficit and the overvalued dollar. In previous decades, manufacturing as a whole opposed running trade deficits and maintaining an overvalued dollar because of the adverse impact of increased imports. The one major business sector with a different view was retailing, which benefited from cheap imports.

However, the spread of multinational production and outsourcing has divided manufacturing in wealthy countries into two camps. In one camp are larger multinational corporations that have gone global and benefit from cheap imports; in the other are smaller businesses that remain nationally centered in terms of sales, production and input sourcing. Multinational corporations tend to support an overvalued dollar since this makes imports produced in their foreign factories cheaper. Conversely, domestic manufacturers are hurt by an overvalued dollar, which advantages import competition.

This division opens the possibility of a new alliance between labor and those manufacturers and businesses that remain nationally based—potentially a potent one, since there are approximately 7 million enterprises with sales of less than $10 million in the United States, versus only 200,000 with sales greater than $10 million. However, such an alliance will always be unstable as the inherent labor-capital conflict over income distribution can always reassert itself. Indeed, this pattern is already evident in the internal politics of the National Association of Manufacturers, whose members have been significantly divided regarding the overvalued dollar. As one way to address this division, the group is promoting a domestic "comp etitiveness" agenda aimed at weakening regulation, reducing corporate legal liability, and lowering employee benefit costs—an agenda designed to appeal to both camps, but at the expense of workers.

Solidarity has always been key to political and economic advance by working families, and it is key to mastering the politics of globalization. Developing a coherent story about the economics of neoliberal globalization around which working families can coalesce is a key ingredient for solidarity. So too is understanding how globalization divides labor. These narratives and analyses can help counter deep cultural proclivities to individualism, as well as other historic divides such as racism. However, as if this were not difficult enough, globalization creates additional challenges. National political solutions that worked in the past are not adequate to the task of controlling international competition. That means the solidarity bar is further raised, calling for international solidarity that supports new forms of international economic regulation. ❑

Article 8.3

FIELDS OF FREE TRADE
Mexico's Small Farmers in a Global Economy

BY TIMOTHY A. WISE
November/December 2003

In Cancún, Mexico, on the stifling afternoon of September 10, Korean farm leader Lee Kyung Hae scaled the police barricades, which were keeping 10,000 protesting farmers from storming the World Trade Organization (WTO) talks, and thrust a knife into his own heart. His self-sacrifice proved to be a catalyst for the disparate protesters and a solemn reminder of the toll trade liberalization has taken on the world's poorest farmers. When the talks collapsed four days later, it became clear that the ship of free trade had foundered badly on the shoals of its captains' hypocrisy on farm policy.

Mexican farmers provided the protests' largest contingent, and not just because the meeting took place on their own embattled soil. Based on their experiences under the North American Free Trade Agreement (NAFTA) and the free-trade model that it embodies, they had a lot to say. Farmers of maize and other grains, who produce for subsistence and for local and regional markets, have been hardest hit by liberalization, with imports from the United States driving prices down to unsustainable levels. But much of the export sector has suffered as well, with gains in industrial tomato farming more than offset by sharp declines in coffee, Mexico's most important export crop in both employment and output.

Mexico's small-scale farmers came together last winter to demand that their government renegotiate NAFTA's agricultural provisions and establish new policies for the countryside. While they have thus far failed to win a commitment from the pro-free trade administration of Vicente Fox to renegotiate NAFTA, last spring they secured new funds for rural development and a promise to assess the agreement's impact on small farmers and to take measures to defend and promote the sector. Whether the movement can hold Fox to those promises remains to be seen, but the farmers' rejection of the neoliberal model is here to stay.

A closer look at the experiences of Mexican farmers of corn and coffee—the country's largest domestic and export crops which directly support some 20 million of the country's 100 million people—illustrates the perils of agricultural trade liberalization. Farmers' responses to the crisis and their policy proposals present a useful starting point for an alternative approach to rural development, one that recognizes the limits of trade, the importance of domestic food sources, and the value of peasant production.

Unrealized Promises

Although some policy-makers still point to Mexico as a success story, there is a growing consensus that the free trade experiment—which began well before NAFTA's inception in 1994—has not lived up to expectations. Its failures are all the more striking given Mexico's indisputable success in transforming one of the world's most protected economies into one of the most open and in attracting the foreign investment needed to capitalize such a transformation. Since 1985, when Mexico began its rapid liberalization process, exports have doubled and foreign direct investment has nearly tripled. According to the promises of free-trade proponents, with inflation in check, Mexico should have reaped the rewards of liberalization. It hasn't. Growth has been slow, job creation has been sluggish, wages have declined, poverty has increased, and the environment has taken a beating.

In many ways, Mexico got what NAFTA promised: trade and investment. Unfortunately, these have not translated into benefits for the Mexican population as a whole or into improvements in the country's fragile environment. And there is little question that rural Mexico has suffered the greatest decline.

NAFTA versus Maize

When NAFTA was negotiated, Mexico's leaders promised the agreement would help modernize the countryside, converting low-yield peasant plots into highly productive commercial farms growing fruits, vegetables, and other export crops for the U.S. market. Farmers who could not modernize or export would be absorbed as workers into the rising export industrial sector and the expanding service sector. Sensitive to the important role of corn in Mexico's culture and economy—over 3 million farmers grow corn, triple the employment in the maquiladora export assembly sector—NAFTA included a 15-year phase-out period for corn tariffs along with strict import quotas. Such a phased "tariff-rate quota" system was designed to ensure a gradual transition to competition with more developed and highly subsidized U.S. producers.

Farmers were confronted with a far different reality. After negotiating these protections for its corn farmers, the Mexican government proceeded to throw them overboard. Citing supply shortages for basic grains, the government unilaterally approved imports over NAFTA's quotas and then declined to collect tariffs. The decision reflected the growing power of agribusiness interests within Mexico, which coveted access to cheaper and lower-quality U.S. corn. The livestock industry wanted cheap feed, the beverage industry sought inexpensive corn sweetener, and a growing processed-food industry wanted to reduce its input costs for flour.

The result was free-trade shock treatment for corn farmers. Instead of a difficult long-term adjustment to competition with U.S. farmers, they faced the near-impossible challenge of fully liberalized trade just three years into NAFTA. Imports doubled and the price of corn fell nearly 50%. At the same time, the Mexican government was phasing out its price-support system, the final step in bringing Mexico into compliance with the Uruguay Round Agreement on Agriculture (URAA). Though CONASUPO, the main government agency managing supplies and prices, did not fold until 1998, price supports for most crops were eliminated in 1989. Corn and beans saw support into the mid-1990s, though at reduced levels. Facing fiscal pressures after the peso crisis and bailout of the banking sector, the government also reduced other rural support and modernization programs.

Corn farmers and other grain growers responded with an aggressive effort to stay on the land. Their organization, the National Association of Commercial

Enterprises (ANEC), brings together over 180,000 producers, mostly small- and medium-scale landowners working 25 acres or less and selling the majority of their produce in local and regional markets. ANEC has bought abandoned state storage facilities, developed its own marketing infrastructure, promoted regional trade, and fostered sustainable agriculture practices. It is estimated that members earn prices 10% to 12% higher than the free market can provide.

"We do not and will not accept that we are mere surplus, that we are not productive, not competitive, that we are a burden for the country," said an ANEC leader at the group's 2000 General Assembly. "We are productive now ... we can be more productive in the future ... but only if the role of the small and medium peasant producers is revalued." Despite ANEC's success in revaluing the contributions of small farmers, the import flood still threatens to drown many growers, with producer prices below the cost of production.

Disinterest and Disinvestment

The farm crisis is not simply a problem of imports, or even of the structural imbalances between the United States' industrial agriculture and Mexico's more traditional farming. In corn fields, those differences are stark, with the United States farming nearly four times the acreage at over three times the yield, resulting in eleven times Mexico's output. That glut of American corn, which is subsidized at a per-acre level at least triple that of Mexico, sells at less than half the price of Mexico's traditional maize. Such disparities prompted farmers' initial demand to exclude corn from NAFTA, a position the government later watered down to the 15-year tariff-rate quota and a vague U.S. promise to consider reducing its farm subsidies.

At the heart of the crisis, though, is a long-term structural decline in international prices for agricultural and other non-oil commodities. According to the World Bank, real prices for non-oil commodities have fallen by an average of 50% since 1980 to their lowest levels in a century. Global overproduction has been fed by rising productivity in industrial agriculture and the neoliberal mantra to export, export, export. For many developing countries, World Bank and International Monetary Fund policies have mandated a deepening dependency on a few commodities and a turn away from the diversification that characterized Latin American development strategies in the 1960s and 1970s. This dependency, in turn, makes countries particularly vulnerable when commodity prices fall sharply.

Small farmers are even more vulnerable when their government abandons them. True to its neoliberal ideals and its URAA commitments, the Mexican government dismantled most of the agencies that had bought and sold farm produce, provided credit and technical assistance, and administered price supports and subsidies. The percentage of the government budget devoted to agriculture fell by half, to just 4.6% of outlays. Farm subsidies dropped 58% in real terms. The promised modernization of Mexican agriculture through public investment withered on the free-trade vine. New irrigation, an explicit government goal prior to NAFTA, never materialized, with the amount of new irrigated land falling from 100,000 acres in 1991 to a post-NAFTA average of just 17,000 acres per year. Lending by both government and private-sector rural credit programs declined 75% after 1994, when NAFTA took effect, while rural bankruptcies increased sixfold.

Nor did foreign investment, the free-trade elixir for all development ills, step in to slow the bleeding. A paltry 0.2% of the $128 billion in foreign direct investment that flowed into Mexico from 1994 to 2002 went to agriculture. Just three activities—hog farming, horticulture (fruits and vegetables), and flowers—claimed 94% of that total, and almost 90% ended up in the two Mexican states that already had the most modern agriculture.

According to one government-commissioned study, overall investment levels as a percentage of agricultural GDP declined from a healthy 11% in 1980 to 6% in 1985, then dropped to 3% just prior to NAFTA's signing. They have remained under 2% since NAFTA took effect. If its goal was to modernize Mexican agriculture, the liberalization project has been a dismal failure.

Winning Through Exports?

In a free-trade world it is almost a given that if you're not part of the trading, you're part of the problem. NAFTA's apologists could claim that Mexico's inefficient grain farmers were just not competitive in a market freed of distortions. As the cold logic of comparative advantage separated the high-value wheat (or, in this case, corn) from the uncompetitive chaff, they needed to find more productive uses for their labor or their land. With few prospects for efficiency gains on poor lands suffering disinvestment and a rural credit vacuum, farmers who wanted to stay in agriculture would have to switch crops and export.

For small farmers in Mexico's rugged highlands, coffee might have seemed a likely solution. It was already the country's largest export crop, and the second largest commodity export after oil. Before NAFTA, Mexico was the world's fourth largest coffee producer, and its shade-grown arabica beans were highly valued on the international market. Better still, there would be no competition with U.S. producers.

Free Trade's Unkept Promises

NAFTA took effect in 1994, but the "neoliberal" experiment began in the mid-1980s following Mexico's 1982 debt crisis. Ten years into NAFTA and nearly twenty years into neoliberalism, the track record, drawn from official World Bank and Mexican government figures, is poor:

•Economic growth has been slow. Since 1985, Mexico has seen average annual per capita real growth of just 1%, compared to 3.4% from 1960 to 1980.

•Job growth has been sluggish. There has been little job creation, falling far short of the demand from young people entering the labor force. Manufacturing, one of the few sectors to show significant economic growth, has registered only marginal net job creation since NAFTA took effect.

•The new jobs are not good jobs. Nearly half of all new formal-sector jobs created under NAFTA do not include any of the benefits mandated by Mexican law (social security, vacations, holidays, etc.). One-third of the economically active population works in the informal sector.

•Wages have declined. The real minimum wage is down 60% since 1982, 23% since NAFTA's inception. Wages in all sectors have followed suit.

•Poverty has increased. According to Mexico's most respected poverty researchers, the number of households living in poverty has grown 80% since 1984, with nearly 80% of Mexico's people now below the poverty line, up from 59% in 1984. Income distribution has become more lopsided, making Mexico one of the hemisphere's most unequal societies.

•The rural sector is in crisis. Four-fifths of rural Mexicans live in poverty, over half in extreme poverty. Migration levels remain high despite unprecedented risks due to increased U.S. border patrols.

•Imports surpass exports. The export boom has been outpaced by an import boom, in part due to intrafirm trade within multinationals.

•The environment has deteriorated. The Mexican government estimates that from 1985 to 1999, the economic costs of environmental degradation amounted to 10% of annual GDP, or $36 billion per year. These costs dwarf economic growth, which amounted to only $9.4 billion annually.

So much for economic theory. Mexico's coffee farmers have been living their own free-trade nightmare, and it has little to do with NAFTA. In 1989, the U.S. and Mexican governments pulled out of the International Coffee Agreement (ICA), a supply-management arrangement between major producing and consuming countries that had kept supplies and prices at relatively stable and sustainable levels. The target price had been $1.20 to $1.40 per pound. Such "market-distorting" schemes are proscribed by the Organization for Economic Cooperation and Development and the Agreement on Agriculture of the GATT (General Agreement on Tariffs and Trade), the precursor to the WTO.

The result was as predictable as it was devastating to small coffee farmers. Prices plummeted to below the costs of production (about $0.60 a pound in Mexico) as stored coffee flooded the market and free competition among producing countries bid down prices. Five years of low prices (1989-94) ended temporarily when destructive frosts in Brazil in 1994 and 1997 killed off coffee trees in the world's largest producing nation. But when Brazil's new, high-yield coffee plantations came back on the market, prices fell even lower.

The market was further glutted by the entry of Vietnam, which grew from a virtual nonproducer in 1990 into the second largest coffee producer in the world by 2000. The World Bank and other development agencies had heavily promoted coffee as a viable export crop for small farmers in Vietnam and elsewhere, offering loans and other inducements. It worked, but by 2000, depressed prices had even low-cost producers in Vietnam scrambling to survive. By 2002, even the lowest-cost producers were unable to recoup their production costs.

Mexico's coffee farmers were especially hard hit by the price drop. They grow some of the world's best coffee, but at costs higher than many of their competitors. The sector is dominated by small farmers on shady hillside plots, with yields lower than Brazil's ecologically damaging but high-yield plantations. And the Mexican government added neoliberal insult to free-trade injury by eliminating INMECAFE, the Mexican coffee institute that had marketed and promoted Mexican coffee from its 285,000 producers.

In one of Mexico's poorest coffee-growing states, the Coffee Producers of Oaxaca (CEPCO), a grassroots organization of nearly 30,000 small-scale producers from nine indigenous groups, responded to the crisis with an impressive array of independent initiatives designed to "appropriate the production process for the producers." The members created their own credit union, mobilized women farmers, and promoted direct sales from their collective to marketers and consumers in the fair-trade movement. CEPCO campaigns encouraged farmers to produce certified organic coffee, bringing substantially higher prices for some 8,000 member families.

International market prices now hover around $0.50 a pound (and producers usually get far less than that). Organic fair-trade coffee pays producers $1.41 a pound, a dramatic price premium. But while the fair-trade and organic markets are growing quickly, they still account for a very small percentage of the market—currently about 3%. As even the most ardent fair-trade advocates acknowledge, niche markets can't solve a worldwide overproduction problem that affects far more producers than fair-trade consumers could ever sustain.

CEPCO's organic producers aside, most Mexican coffee farmers are in dire straits. Even high-quality arabica beans now receive low prices from international buyers. The national coffee farmer association in Mexico reports a 40% decline in coffee production in the past three years, a 55% decline in coffee exports, and a 70% decline in income from coffee sales. Many producers are letting the beans rot on the trees, since it makes little economic sense to harvest them. Clearly, if there is going to be a solution to coffee farmers' free-trade woes, it will come from a reversal of free-trade policies. An international coalition of coffee farmer organizations has called for a return to supply management and international assistance in keeping the lowest quality coffee off the market.

Mobilizing for Change

CEPCO's and ANEC's efforts have not been enough to reverse the overwhelming impacts of unregulated globalization and the Mexican government's abandonment of small-scale farmers. That is why coffee and corn growers have joined other farmers' groups in demanding policies and trade agreements that recognize and value the social, economic, and environmental contributions of small producers. Their demands are hardly radical, but their implications are entirely subversive to the neoliberal model. The farmers' movement has demanded:

1. A moratorium on the agricultural provisions of NAFTA, if not their renegotiation;

2. Emergency and long-term agricultural development programs;

3. Viable rural credit institutions providing adequate and affordable credit;

4. Government investment in rural infrastructure and communities;

5. Food safety and quality for Mexican consumers (a response to the importation of genetically modified corn from the United States);

6. Recognition of the rights of indigenous communities.

The April 2003 agreement with the Fox administration represented one important battle in a longer war. In the long run, the farmers' movement is demanding a return to an inclusive government development strategy in which trade and foreign investment are but two of many economic means to an end. They are not the ends in themselves.

If the WTO meetings in Cancún are any indication, farmers will continue to be a thorn in the side of the liberalization juggernaut. Via Campesina, an international farmer alliance that claims over 100 million members, put the issue front and center in Cancún. Arguing that agricultural products are more than just commodities and rural communities are more than just laborers, the group demanded that agriculture be removed from the WTO. They advanced the new concept of "food sovereignty"—the right of every country to decide how it will meet the food needs of its people, free of the strictures of WTO rules.

With negotiations on the proposed Free Trade Area of the Americas slated for November, we can look forward to further conflict. Current drafts include significant agricultural liberalization, following through on the U.S. promise that the Free Trade Area of the Americas will be a "NAFTA for the hemisphere." Before signing any deal, the peoples of Latin America and the Caribbean would do well to talk to Mexico's farmers. ❏

Sources: Timothy A. Wise, Hilda Salazar, and Laura Carlsen, *Confronting Globalization: Economic Integration and Popular Resistance in Mexico* (Kumarian Press 2003); Timothy A. Wise, "NAFTA's Untold Stories: Mexico's Grassroots Responses to Economic Integration," (Interhemispheric Resource Center, June 10, 2003); Charis Gresser and Sophia Tickell, "Mugged: Poverty in Your Coffee Cup," (Oxfam International, 2002); Alejandro Nadal, "The Environmental and Social Impacts of Economic Liberalization on Corn Production in Mexico," (Oxfam GB and WWF International, September 2000).

Article 8.4

INTERNATIONAL LABOR STANDARDS

BY ARTHUR MacEWAN
September/October 2008

Dear Dr. Dollar:

U.S. activists have pushed to get foreign trade agreements to include higher labor standards. But then you hear that developing countries don't want that because cheaper labor without a lot of rules and regulations is what's helping them to bring industries in and build their economies. Is there a way to reconcile these views? Or are the activists just blind to the real needs of the countries they supposedly want to help?

—Philip Bereaud, Swampscott, Mass.

In 1971, General Emilio Medici, the then-military dictator of Brazil, commented on economic conditions in his country with the infamous line: "The economy is doing fine, but the people aren't."

Like General Medici, the government officials of many low-income countries today see the well-being of their economies in terms of overall output and the profits of firms—those profits that keep bringing in new investment, new industries that "build their economies." It is these officials who typically get to speak for their countries. When someone says that these countries "want" this or that—or "don't want" this or that—it is usually because the countries' officials have expressed this position.

Do we know what the people in these countries want? The people who work in the new, rapidly growing industries, in the mines and fields, and in the small shops and market stalls of low-income countries? Certainly they want better conditions—more to eat, better housing, security for their children, improved health and safety. The officials claim that to obtain these better conditions, they must "build their economies." But just because "the economy is doing fine" does not mean that the people are doing fine.

In fact, in many low-income countries, economic expansion comes along with severe inequality. The people who do the work are not getting a reasonable share of the rising national income (and are sometimes worse off even in absolute terms). Brazil in the early 1970s was a prime example and, in spite of major political change, remains a highly unequal country. Today, in both India and China, as in several other countries, economic growth is coming with increasingly severe inequality.

Workers in these countries struggle to improve their positions. They form—or try to form—independent unions. They demand higher wages and better working conditions. They struggle for political rights. It seems obvious that we should support those struggles, just as we support parallel struggles of workers in our own country. The first principle in supporting workers' struggles, here or anywhere else, is supporting their right to struggle—the right, in particular, to form independent unions without fear of reprisal. Indeed, in the ongoing controversy over the U.S.-Colombia Free Trade Agreement, the assassination of trade union leaders has rightly been a major issue.

Just how we offer our support—in particular, how we incorporate that support into trade agreements—is a complicated question. Pressure from abroad can help, but applying it is a complex process. A ban on goods produced with child labor, for example, could harm the most impoverished families that depend on children's earnings, or could force some children into worse forms of work (e.g., prostitution). On the other hand, using trade agreements to pressure governments to allow unhindered union organizing efforts by workers seems perfectly legitimate. When workers are denied the right to organize, their work is just one step up from slavery. Trade agreements can also be used to support a set of basic health and safety rights for workers. (Indeed, it might be useful if a few countries refused to enter into trade agreements with the United States until we improve workers' basic organizing rights and health and safety conditions in our own country!)

There is no doubt that the pressures that come through trade sanctions (restricting or banning commerce with another country) or simply from denying free access to the U.S. market can do immediate harm to workers and the general populace of low-income countries. Any struggle for change can generate short-run costs, but the long-run gains—even the hope of those gains—can make those costs acceptable. Consider, for example, the Apartheid-era trade sanctions against South Africa. To the extent that those sanctions were effective, some South African workers were deprived of employment. Nonetheless, the sanctions were widely supported by mass organizations in South Africa. Or note that when workers in this country strike or advocate a boycott of their company in an effort to obtain better conditions, they both lose income and run the risk that their employer will close up shop.

Efforts by people in this country to use trade agreements to raise labor standards in other countries should, whenever possible, take their lead from workers in those countries. It is up to them to decide what costs are acceptable. There are times, however, when popular forces are denied even basic rights to struggle. The best thing we can do, then, is to push for those rights—particularly the right to organize independent unions—that help create the opportunity for workers in poor countries to choose what to fight for. ❑

Article 8.5

OUTSIZED OFFSHORE OUTSOURCING

The scope of offshore outsourcing gives some economists and the business press the heebie-jeebies.

BY JOHN MILLER
September/October 2007

At a press conference introducing the 2004 *Economic Report of the President*, N. Gregory Mankiw, then head of President Bush's Council of Economic Advisors, assured the press that "Outsourcing is probably a plus for the economy in the long run [and] just a new way of doing international trade."

Mankiw's comments were nothing other than mainstream economics, as even Democratic Party-linked economists confirmed. For instance Janet Yellen, President Clinton's chief economist, told the *Wall Street Journal*, "In the long run, outsourcing is another form of trade that benefits the U.S. economy by giving us cheaper ways to do things." Nonetheless, Mankiw's assurances were met with derision from those uninitiated in the economics profession's free-market ideology. Sen. John Edwards (D-N.C.) asked, "What planet do they live on?" Even conservative House Speaker Dennis Hastert (R-Ill.) said that Mankiw's theory "fails a basic test of real economics."

Mankiw now jokes that "if the American Economic Association were to give an award for the Most Politically Inept Paraphrasing of Adam Smith, I would be a leading candidate." But he quickly adds, "the recent furor about outsourcing, and my injudiciously worded comments about the benefits of international trade, should not eclipse the basic lessons that economists have understood for more than two centuries."

In fact Adam Smith never said any such thing about international trade. In response to the way Mankiw and other economists distort Smith's writings, economist Michael Meeropol took a close look at what Smith actually said; he found that Smith used his invisible hand argument to favor domestic investment over far-flung, hard-to-supervise foreign investments. Here are Smith's words in his 1776 masterpiece, *The Wealth of Nations*:

> By preferring the support of domestic to that of foreign industry, he [the investor] intends only his own security; and by directing that industry in such a manner as its produce may be of the greatest value, he intends only his own gain, and he is in this, as in many other cases, led by an invisible hand to promote an end, which was no part of his intention.

Outsized offshore outsourcing, the shipping of jobs overseas to take advantage of low wages, has forced some mainstream economists and some elements of the business press to have second thoughts about "free trade." Many are convinced that the painful transition costs that hit before outsourcing produces any ultimate benefits may be the biggest political issue in economics for a generation. And some recognize, as Smith did, that there is no guarantee unfettered international trade will leave the participants better off even in the long run.

Keynes's Revenge

Writing during the Great Depression of the 1930s, John Maynard Keynes, the pre-eminent economist of the twentieth century, prescribed government spending as a means of compensating for the instability of private investment. The notion of a mixed private/government economy, Keynes's prosthesis for the invisible hand of the market, guided U.S. economic policy from the 1940s through the 1970s.

It is only fitting that Paul Samuelson, the first Nobel Laureate in economics, and whose textbook introduced U.S. readers to Keynes, would be among the first mainstream economist to question whether unfettered international trade, in the context of massive outsourcing, would necessarily leave a developed economy such as that of the United States better off—even in the long run. In an influential 2004 article, Samuelson characterized the common economics wisdom about outsourcing and international trade this way:

Yes, good jobs may be lost here in the short run. But …the gains of the winners from free trade, properly measured, work out to exceed the losses of the losers. … Never forget to tally the real gains of consumers alongside admitted possible losses of some producers. … The gains of the American winners are big enough to more than compensate the losers.

Samuelson took on this view, arguing that this common wisdom is "dead wrong about [the] *necessary* surplus of winning over losing" [emphasis in the original]. In a rather technical paper, he demonstrated that free trade globalization can sometimes give rise to a situation in which "a productivity gain in one country can benefit that country alone, while permanently hurting the other country by reducing the gains from trade that are possible between the two countries."

Many in the economics profession do admit that it is hard to gauge whether intensified offshoring of U.S. jobs in the context of free-trade globalization will give more in winnings to the winners than it takes in losses from the losers. "Nobody has a clue about what the numbers are," as Robert C. Feenstra, a prominent trade economist, told *BusinessWeek* at the time.

OFFSHORED? OUTSOURCED? CONFUSED?

The terms "offshoring" and "outsourcing" are often used interchangeably, but they refer to distinct processes:

Outsourcing – When a company hires another company to carry out a business function that it no longer wants to carry on in-house. The company that is hired may be in the same city or across the globe; it may be a historically independent firm or a spinoff of the first company created specifically to outsource a particular function.

Offshoring or *Offshore Outsourcing* – When a company shifts a portion of its business operation abroad. An offshore operation may be carried out by the same company or, more typically, outsourced to a different one.

ATTRIBUTES OF JOBS OUTSOURCED

- No Face-to-Face Customer Servicing Requirement
- High Information Content
- Work Process is Telecommutable and Internet Enabled
- High Wage Differential with Similar Occupation in Destination Country
- Low Setup Barriers
- Low Social Networking Requirement

The empirical issues that will determine whether offshore outsourcing ultimately delivers, on balance, more benefits than costs, and to whom those benefits and costs will accrue, are myriad. First, how wide a swath of white-collar workers will see their wages reduced by competition from the cheap, highly skilled workers who are now becoming available around the world? Second, by how much will their wages drop? Third, will the U.S. workers thrown into the global labor pool end up losing more in lower wages than they gain in lower consumer prices? In that case, the benefits of increased trade would go overwhelmingly to employers. But even employers might lose out depending on the answer to a fourth question: Will cheap labor from abroad allow foreign employers to out-compete U.S. employers, driving down the prices of their products and lowering U.S. export earnings? In that case, not only workers, but the corporations that employ them as well, could end up worse off.

Bigger Than A Box

Another mainstream Keynesian economist, Alan Blinder, former Clinton economic advisor and vice-chair of the Federal Reserve Board, doubts that outsourcing will be "immiserating" in the long run and still calls himself "a free-trader down to his toes." But Blinder is convinced that the transition costs will be large, lengthy, and painful before the United States experiences a net gain from outsourcing. Here is why.

First, rapid improvements in information and communications technology have rendered obsolete the traditional notion that manufactured goods, which can generally be boxed and shipped, are tradable, while services, which cannot be boxed, are not. And the workers who perform the services that computers and satellites have now rendered tradable will increasingly be found offshore, especially when they are skilled and will work for lower wages.

Second, another 1.5 billion or so workers—many in China, India, and the former Soviet bloc—are now part of the world economy. While most are low-skilled workers, some are not; and as Blinder says, a small percentage of 1.5 billion is nonetheless "a lot of willing and able people available to do the jobs that technology will move offshore." And as China and India educate more workers, offshoring of high-skill work will accelerate.

Third, the transition will be particularly painful in the United States because the U.S. unemployment insurance program is stingy, at least by first-world standards, and because U.S. workers who lose their jobs often lose their health insurance and pension rights as well.

How large will the transition cost be? "Thirty million to 40 million U.S. jobs are potentially offshorable," according to Blinder's latest estimates. "These include scientists, mathematicians and editors on the high end and telephone operators, clerks and typists on the low end."

Blinder arrived at these figures by creating an index that identifies how easy or hard it will be for a job to be physically or electronically "offshored." He then used the index to assess the Bureau of Labor Statistics' 817 U.S. occupational categories. Not surprisingly, Blinder classifies almost all of the 14.3 million U.S. manufacturing jobs as offshorable. But he also classifies more than twice that many U.S. service sector jobs as offshorable, including most computer industry jobs as well as many others, for instance, the 12,470 U.S. economists and the 23,790 U.S. multimedia artists and animators.

In total, Blinder's analysis suggests that 22% to 29% of the jobs held by U.S. workers in 2004 will be potentially offshorable within a decade or two, with nearly 8.2 million jobs in 59 occupations "highly offshorable." Table 1 provides a list of the broad occupational categories with 300,000 or more workers that Blinder considers potentially offshorable.

Mankiw dismissed Blinder's estimates of the number of jobs at risk to offshoring as "out of the mainstream." Indeed, Blinder's estimates are considerably larger than earlier ones. But these earlier studies either aim to measure the number of U.S. jobs that will be outsourced (as opposed to the number at risk of being outsourced), look at a shorter period of time, or have shortcomings that suggest they underestimate the number of U.S. jobs threatened by outsourcing. (See "Studying the Studies," below.)

Global Arbitrage

Low wages are the reason U.S. corporations outsource labor. Table 2 shows just how large the international wage differentials were for computer programmers in 2002. Programmers in the United States make wages nearly *ten times* those of their counterparts in India and the Philippines, for example.

Today, more and more white-collar workers in the United States are finding themselves in direct competition with the low-cost, well-trained, highly educated workers in Bangalore, Shanghai, and Eastern and Central Europe. These workers often use the same capital and technology and are no less productive than the U.S. workers they replace. They just get paid less.

This global labor arbitrage, as Morgan Stanley's chief economist Stephen Roach calls it, has narrowed international wage disparities in manufacturing, and now in services too, by unrelentingly pushing U.S. wages down toward international norms. ("Arbitrage" refers to transactions that yield a profit by taking advantage of a price differential for the same asset in different locations. Here, of course, the "asset" is wage labor of a certain skill level.) A sign of that pressure: about 70% of laid-off workers in the United States earn less three years later than they did at the time of the layoff; on average, those reemployed earn 10% less than they did before.

And it's not only laid-off workers who are hurt. A study conducted by Harvard labor economists Lawrence F. Katz, Richard B. Freeman, and George J. Borjas finds that every other worker with skills similar to those who were displaced also loses out. Every 1% drop in employment due to imports or factories gone abroad shaves 0.5% off the wages of the remaining workers in that occupation, they conclude.

Global labor arbitrage also goes a long way toward explaining the poor quality and low pay of the jobs the U.S. economy has created this decade, according to Roach. By dampening wage increases for an ever wider swath of the U.S. workforce, he argues, outsourcing has helped to drive a wedge between productivity gains and wage gains and to widen inequality in the United States. In the first four years of

TABLE 1: MAJOR OCCUPATIONS RANKED BY OFFSHORABILITY

Occupation	Category	Index Number	Number of Workers
Computer programmers	I	100	389,090
Telemarketers	I	95	400,860
Computer systems analysts	I	93	492,120
Billing and posting clerks and machine operators	I	90	513,020
Bookkeeping, accounting, and auditing clerks	I	84	1,815,340
Computer support specialists	I and II	92/68	499,860
Computer software engineers: Applications	II	74	455,980
Computer software engineers: Systems software	II	74	320,720
Accountants	II	72	591,311
Welders, cutters, solderers, and brazers	II	70	358,050
Helpers—production workers	II	70	528,610
First-line supervisors/managers of production and operating workers	II	68	679,930
Packaging and filling machine operators and tenders	II	68	396,270
Team assemblers	II	65	1,242,370
Bill and account collectors	II	65	431,280
Machinists	II	61	368,380
Inspectors, testers, sorters, samplers, and weighers	II	60	506,160
General and operations managers	III	55	1,663,810
Stock clerks and order fillers	III	34	1,625,430
Shipping, receiving, and traffic clerks	III	29	759,910
Sales managers	III	26	317,970
Business operations specialists, all other	IV	25	916,290

Source: Alan S. Blinder, "How Many U.S. Jobs Might Be Offshorable?" *CEPS Working Paper* #142, March 2007, figures from Bureau of Labor Statistics and author's judgments.

this decade, nonfarm productivity in the United States has recorded a cumulative increase of 13.3%—more than double the 5.9% rise in real compensation per hour over the same period. ("Compensation" includes wages, which have been stagnant for the average worker, plus employer spending on fringe benefits such as health insurance, which has risen even as, in many instances, the actual benefits have been cut back.) Roach reports that the disconnect between pay and productivity growth during the current economic expansion has been much greater in services than in manufacturing, as that sector weathers the powerful forces of global labor arbitrage for the first time.

Doubts in the Business Press?!

Even in the business press, doubts that offshore outsourcing willy-nilly leads to economic improvement have become more acute. Earlier this summer, a *BusinessWeek* cover story, "The Real Cost of Offshoring," reported that government statistics have underestimated the damage to the U.S. economy from offshore outsourcing. The problem is that since offshoring took off, *import* growth, adjusted for inflation, has been faster than the official numbers show. That means improvements in living standards, as well as corporate profits, depend more on cheap imports, and less on improving domestic productivity, than analysts thought.

TABLE 2: AVERAGE SALARIES OF PROGRAMMERS

Country	Salary Range
Poland and Hungary	$4,800 to $8,000
India	$5,880 to $11,000
Philippines	$6,564
Malaysia	$7,200
Russian Federation	$5,000 to $7,500
China	$8,952
Canada	$28,174
Ireland	$23,000 to $34,000
Israel	$15,000 to $38,000
USA	$60,000 to $80,000

Source: CIO magazine, November 2002, from Merrill Lynch *Smart Access Survey.*

Growing angst about outsourcing's costs has also prompted the business press to report favorably on remedies for the dislocation brought on by offshoring that deviate substantially from the non-interventionist, free-market playbook. Even the most unfazed pro-globalization types want to beef up trade adjustment assistance for displaced workers and strengthen the U.S. educational system. But both proposals are inadequate.

More education, the usual U.S. prescription for any economic problem, is off the mark here. Cheaper labor is available abroad up and down the job-skill ladder, so even the most rigorous education is no inoculation against the threat of offshore outsourcing. As Blinder emphasizes, it is the need for face-to-face contact that stops jobs from being shipped overseas, not the level of education necessary to perform them. Twenty years from now, home health aide positions will no doubt be plentiful in the United States; jobs for highly trained IT professionals may be scarce.

STUDYING THE STUDIES

When economist Alan Blinder raised alarm bells in 2006 about the potentially large-scale offshoring of U.S. jobs, his results were inevitably compared to earlier research on offshore outsourcing. Three studies have been especially influential. The 2002 study (revised in 2004) by Forrester Research, a private, for-profit market research firm, which estimated that 3.3 million U.S. service sector jobs would move offshore by 2015, caused perhaps the biggest media stir. It was picked up by *BusinessWeek* and the *Wall Street Journal*, and hyped by Lou Dobbs, the CNN business-news anchor and outspoken critic of offshoring.

Forrester researcher John McCarthy developed his estimate by poring over newspaper clippings and Labor Department statistics on 505 white-collar occupations and then making an educated guess about how many jobs would be shipped offshore by 2015.

The Forrester study projects actual offshoring, not the number of jobs at risk of offshoring, so its estimate is rightfully lower than Blinder's. But the ample possibilities for technological change between now and 2015 convince Blinder that the Forrester estimate is nonetheless too low.

A 2003 study by University of California economists Ashok Bardhan and Cynthia Kroll estimated that about 11% of all U.S. jobs in 2001 were vulnerable to offshoring. Bradhan and Kroll applied the "outsourceability attributes" listed in Figure 1 to occupations where at least some outsourcing either has already taken place or is being planned.

Blinder considers the Bardhan and Kroll estimate for 2001 to be comparable to his estimate that 20% to 30% of the employed labor force will be at risk of offshore outsourcing within the next ten to twenty years, especially considering that Bardhan and Kroll do not allow for outsourcing to spread beyond the occupations it is currently affecting. This is like "looking only slightly beyond the currently-visible tip of the iceberg," according to Blinder.

The McKinsey Global Institute (MGI), a research group known for its unabashedly favorable view of globalization, has done its best to put a positive spin on offshore outsourcing. Its 2003 study, which relied on the Forrester offshoring estimates, concluded that offshoring is already benefiting the U.S. economy. For instance, MGI calculates that

Trade adjustment assistance has until now been narrowly targeted at workers hurt by imports. Most new proposals would replace traditional trade adjustment assistance and unemployment insurance with a program for displaced workers that offers wage insurance to ease the pain of taking a lower-paying job and provides for portable health insurance and retraining. The pro-globalization research group McKinsey Global Institute (MGI), for example, claims that for as little as 4% to 5% of the amount they've saved in lower wages, companies could cover the wage losses of all laid-off workers once they are reemployed, paying them 70% of the wage differential between their old and new jobs (in addition to health care subsidies) for up to two years.

While MGI confidently concludes that this proposal will "go a long way toward relieving the current anxieties," other globalization advocates are not so sure. They recognize that economic anxiety is pervasive and that millions of white-collar workers now fear losing their jobs. Moreover, even if fears of actual job loss are overblown,

for every dollar spent on a business process outsourced to India, the U.S. economy gains at least $1.12. The largest chunk—58 cents—goes back to the original employer in the form of cost savings, almost exclusively in the form of lower wages. In addition, 30% of Indian offshoring is actually performed by U.S. companies, so the wage savings translate into higher earnings for those companies. The study also argues that offshore outsourcing frees up U.S. workers to do other tasks.

A second MGI study, in 2005, surveyed dozens of companies in eight sectors, from pharmaceutical companies to insurers. The study predicted that multinational companies in the entire developed world will have located only 4.1 million service jobs in low-wage countries by 2008—a figure equal to only 1% of the total number of service jobs in developed countries.

But the MGI outsourcing studies have serious limitations. For instance, Blinder points out that MGI's analysis looks at a very short time frame, and that the potential for outsourcing in English-speaking countries such as the United States is higher than elsewhere, a fact lost in the MGI studies' global averages.

In their 2005 book *Outsourcing America*, published by the American Management Association, public policy professors Ron Hira and Anil Hira argue that MGI's 2003 report "should be viewed as a self-interested lobbying document that presents an unrealistically optimistic estimate of the impact of offshore outsourcing." For instance, most of the data for the report came from case studies conducted by MGI that are unavailable to the public and unsupported by any model. Moreover, the MGI analysis assumes that the U.S. economy will follow its long-term trend and create 3.5 million jobs a year, enough to quickly reemploy U.S. workers displaced by offshoring. But current U.S. job creation falls far short of that trend. A recent White House fact sheet brags that the U.S. economy has created 8.3 million jobs since August 2003. Still, that is less than 2.1 million jobs a year, and only 1.8 million jobs over the last 12 months.

MGI's Farrell is right about one thing. "If the economy were stronger," she says, "there wouldn't be such a negative feeling" about work getting offshored. But merely assuming high job growth doesn't make it so.

wage insurance schemes do little to compensate for the downward pressure offshoring is putting on the wages of workers who have not been laid off.

Other mainstream economists and business writers go even further, calling for not only wage insurance but also taxes on the winners from globalization. And globalization has produced big winners: on Wall Street, in the corporate boardroom, and among those workers in high demand in the global economy.

Economist Matthew Slaughter, who recently left President Bush's Council of Economic Advisers, told the *Wall Street Journal*, "Expanding the political support for open borders [for trade] requres making a radical change in fiscal policy." He proposes eliminating the Social Security-Medicare payroll tax on the bottom half of workers—roughly, those earning less than $33,000 a year—and making up the lost revenue by raising the payroll tax on higher earners.

The goal of these economists is to thwart a crippling political backlash against trade. As they see it, "using the tax code to slice the apple more evenly is far more palatable than trying to hold back globalization with policies that risk shrinking the economic apple."

Some even call for extending global labor arbitrage to CEOs. In a June 2006 *New York Times* op-ed, equity analyst Lawrence Orlowski and NYU assistant research director Florian Lengyel argued that offshoring the jobs of U.S. chief executives would reduce costs and release value to shareholders by bringing the compensation of U.S. CEOs (on average 170 times greater than the compensation of average U.S. workers in 2004) in line with CEO compensation in Britain (22 times greater) and in Japan (11 times greater).

Yet others focus on the stunning lack of labor mobility that distinguishes the current era of globalization from earlier ones. Labor markets are becoming increasingly free and flexible under globalization, but labor enjoys no similar freedom of movement. In a completely free market, the foreign workers would come here to do the work that is currently being outsourced. Why aren't more of those workers coming to the United States? Traditional economists Gary Becker and Richard Posner argue the answer is clear: an excessively restrictive immigration policy.

Onshore and Offshore Solidarity

Offshoring is one of the last steps in capitalism's conversion of the "physician, the lawyer, the priest, the poet, the man of science, into its paid wage laborers," as Marx and Engels put it in the *Communist Manifesto* 160 years ago. It has already done much to increase economic insecurity in the workaday world and has become, Blinder suggests, the number one economic issue of our generation.

Offshoring has also underlined the interdependence of workers across the globe. To the extent that corporations now organize their business operations on a global scale, shifting work around the world in search of low wages, labor organizing must also be global in scope if it is to have any hope of building workers' negotiating strength.

Yet today's global labor arbitrage pits workers from different countries against each other as competitors, not allies. Writing about how to improve labor standards, economists Ajit Singh and Ann Zammit of the South Centre, an Indian nongovernmental organization, ask the question, "On what could workers of the world unite" today? Their answer is that faster economic growth could indeed be a positive-sum game from which both the global North and the global South could gain. A pick-up in the long-term rate of growth of the world economy would generate higher employment, increasing wages and otherwise improving labor standards in both regions. It should also make offshoring less profitable and less painful.

The concerns of workers across the globe would also be served by curtailing the ability of multinational corporations to move their investment anywhere, which weakens the bargaining power of labor both in advanced countries and in the global South. Workers globally would also benefit if their own ability to move between countries was enhanced. The combination of a new set of rules to limit international capital movements and to expand labor mobility across borders, together with measures to ratchet up economic growth and thus increase worldwide demand for labor, would alter the current process of globalization and harness it to the needs of working people worldwide. ❏

Sources: Alan S. Blinder, "Fear of Offshoring," CEPS Working Paper #119, Dec. 2005; Alan S. Blinder, "How Many U.S. Jobs Might Be Offshorable?" CEPS Working Paper #142, March 2007; N. Gregory Mankiw and P. Swagel, "The Politics and Economics of Offshore Outsourcing," Am. Enterprise Inst. Working Paper #122, 12/7/05; "Offshoring: Is It a Win-Win Game?" McKinsey Global Institute, August 2003; Diane Farrell et al., "The Emerging Global Labor Market, Part 1: The Demand for Talent in Services," McKinsey Global Institute, June 2005; Ashok Bardhan and Cynthia Kroll, "The New Wave of Outsourcing," Research Report #113, Fisher Center for Real Estate and Urban Economics, Univ. of Calif., Berkeley, Fall 2003; Paul A. Samuelson, "Where Ricardo and Mill Rebut and Confirm Arguments of Mainstream Economists Supporting Globalization," *Journal of Economic Perspectives* 18:3, Summer 2004; Alan S. Blinder, "Free Trade's Great, but Offshoring Rattles Me," *Wash. Post,* 5/6/07; Michael Mandel, "The Real Cost of Offshoring," *Business Week,* 6/18/07; Aaron Bernstein, "Shaking Up Trade Theory," *Business Week,* 12/6/04; David Wessel, "The Case for Taxing Globalization's Big Winners," *WSJ,* 6/14/07; Bob Davis, "Some Democratic Economists Echo Mankiw on Outsourcing," *WSJ;* N. Gregory Mankiw, "Outsourcing Redux," gregmankiw.blogspot.com/2006/05/outsourcing-redux; David Wessel and Bob Davis, "Pain From Free Trade Spurs Second Thoughts," *WSJ,* 3/30/07; Ajit Singh and Ann Zammit, "On What Could Workers of the World Unite? Economic Growth and a New Global Economic Order," from *The Global Labour Standards Controversy: Critical Issues For Developing Countries,* South Centre, 2000; Michael Meeropol, "Distorting Adam Smith on Trade," *Challenge,* July/Aug 2004.

Article 8.6

WOMEN OF NAFTA

BY MARTHA OJEDA, FELICITAS CONTRERAS, AND YOLANDA TREVIÑO
September/October 2007

The outstanding collection *NAFTA From Below: Maquiladora Workers, Farmers, and Indigenous Communities Speak Out on the Impact of Free Trade in Mexico*, combines worker testimony with analytical and historical essays to provide a devastating picture of the effects of neoliberal international trade policies—culminating in the North American Free Trade Agreement (NAFTA)—on workers throughout Mexico. The book, available in both English and Spanish, also offers inspiring accounts of resistance to those policies.

The book's early chapters focus on *maquiladora* workers in the north of the country, addressing key labor issues such as health and safety, environmental concerns, and freedom of association. Later chapters take up organizing by agricultural workers in the south, especially in the state of Chiapas, in response to neoliberal "reforms." That the Zapatista uprising in Chiapas began on January 1, 1994, the very day that NAFTA went into effect, was no accident.

One of the book's achievements is to show how the struggles of industrial workers in the north of Mexico are related to those of agricultural workers in the south. Knitting these struggles together is one of the central aims of the Coalition for Justice in the Maquiladoras, which produced *NAFTA From Below*. The coalition has helped bring *maquila* workers and organizers from the north together with members of grassroots *campesino* and indigenous groups in the south to help strengthen cooperative projects in both regions and to share information about the history of organized struggle in the workplace. Women's strong leadership roles in workplace struggles in the north have been of particular interest to organizers in the south, especially as former agricultural workers from the south migrate to work in *maquiladoras* near the northern border.

Women played a central role in the struggle of workers at a Sony plant in Nuevo Laredo for a democratic union, described in the selections that follow. The events at Sony vividly illustrate the frequent conflicts between Mexico's corrupt official unions and rival independent unions that Chris Tilly and Marie Kennedy describe (pp. 26-30). The Sony workers' struggle was also a key early test of NAFTA's labor side-agreement, the North American Agreement on Labor Cooperation, and the bodies it established, known as National Administrative Offices (NAOs), to investigate violations.

These excerpts include testimony from Martha Ojeda (co-editor of *NAFTA From Below*, with Rosemary Hennessy), a *maquila* worker from 1973 to 1994 who is now executive director of the Coalition for Justice in the Maquiladoras; from Felicitas (Fela) Contreras, an activist with CETRAC (Center for Workers and Communities) in Nuevo Laredo who worked at the Sony plant from 1985 through 1998; and from Yolanda Treviño, a former Sony worker who testified before the NAO as part of the Sony workers' NAFTA complaint.

MARTHA A. OJEDA: Official history is always written so that the reality people were living is hidden. If everyone told the part they lived or knew, the truth would be in their collective word.

In 1979 Sony arrived in my town [Nuevo Laredo].... Sony manually assembled audiocassettes and Beta videocassettes. In 1982, after the first devaluation of the peso, there were more than 1,000 workers working three shifts in five plants, and by then the workers were also producing the VHS videocassette and the 3.5 inch diskette.

They began to bring machines for semiautomatic and automatic assembly of the cassettes. The plastic molding injection plant was providing the plastic cases and the components for the audio and video plants. It was the boom of assembly line production.

In this era children with birth defects began to be born, but the company doctor said that this happened because the parents were alcoholics or because they had genetic problems. By 1993 there were 2,000 employees in seven plants in three shifts. There was a lot of overtime, but still it wasn't enough to meet production quotas.

The molding ingestion plants never stopped working; they were going three shifts seven days a week. For the first time the company proposed 12 hour shifts for four and three days a week. This implied that Sony got their production, because the machines were running around the clock, but they avoided paying overtime. This twelve-hour shift was unknown to workers because it didn't exist in the Federal Labor Law.

It was in this labor and political context that in October 1993 we visited Fidel Velázquez, the CTM national leader, in Mexico City and solicited union elections within the framework of the CTM. All of the *maquilas* were affiliated with this union because it was the only one; if you didn't belong to them there was no other alternative for workers anywhere. But the leaders negotiated the contract with the company even before it was established in the locality.

Fidel told us that he agreed with the elections (but he never said when they would be). We trusted his word and began the process that the Federal Labor Law sets down for forming the union sections.

On January 1, 1994, we were informed of the Zapatista uprising, but equally surprising to us was to find out in the newspaper on January 4 that Chema Morales had declared that on the order of Fidel Velázquez he would be the new Secretary General of the *maquilas*—without sectionals—and, worst of all, he was already named to the Labor Board at the state level because of his position as Secretary General, not only of the Maquila Union but also of the Workers Federation of Nuevo Laredo.

Shocked, we tried to communicate with Fidel Velázquez, but our efforts were in vain. Then we learned that he was coming to Ciudad Victoria, the capital of Tamaulipas, on January 12. We traveled all night. But when we arrived it was obvious that they would not let us enter. We guessed that Fidel would come in by the side door and we waited there until he arrived with the media.

I demanded publicly that he retract his authorization of Chema Morales as Secretary General. Then I asked for a public debate with him and with Chema. I don't know if I was the only woman from the provinces who had publicly challenged him, but what I do know is that so much corruption repulsed me and gave me the courage to make sure that the two of them, both Chema and Fidel, would be exposed even to the President of the Labor Board of the state who was present. He had authorized naming Chema to be Secretary General even though he had never worked in the *maquilas*, and according to the union by-laws that was one of the requirements.

In the face of the media and all of the evidence, Fidel looked ridiculous and he had no alternative but to accept that there would be union elections. So he declared that he would send a national representative to hold them. When I went to say good-bye to him at the podium he told me, "You are going to eat fire." And I told him, "I'm ready." But I never imagined what he was referring to.

FELICITAS ("FELA") CONTRERAS: In 1993 they began to change the delegates in all of the *maquiladoras* who were not agreed with the CTM. I heard that there were going to be elections in all the *maquilas*, not only in Sony, and we were asking when Sony's turn would be. But before the elections they were changing the delegates. They fired the ones we wanted and after work we had meetings to change the delegates so that they would really be for us. We met in one house and another with Martha because we wanted to change the delegates who were imposed by the CTM. I would get home at 4:00 or 5:00 in the morning. We always were hiding here and there, and that is how we put together a slate, even though they fired our candidates.

Those union delegates who were with Chema Morales (of the CTM) developed their slates with the old delegates from Sony… They preferred Chema instead of our democratic union. In April of 1994 the day arrived for the elections, and Chema's representative from the union and a representative of Fidel Velázquez were set up in the parking lot of Plant #7. We had our slate, but they didn't give us a chance to let our other co-workers know that the voting was taking place.

Representatives of Fidel Velázquez and of the company were there. They told the people to go to the parking lot and they arranged to meet the other shift and take them out to vote. They said on this side go all those in favor of the blue slate, on the other side those in favor of the CTM slate. Our slate won because everyone came to our side. But Fidel's representative said that the other delegates from the CTM won. And so we said, "How is that possible if we are all here, voting for our slate? We were the majority. What are we going to do?" We were really mad! Those who were working came out and we took to the streets to protest that they were doing this fraudulent election, and we made signs that said, "We want democratic elections!!"

YOLANDA TREVIÑO: On Saturday April 16, which was my day off, I went to plant #3 to see what resolution Mayor Horacio Garza had been able to make as to when we would have new elections. The *compañeras* who had spoken with him told us that he wasn't going to help us. That's when we started to hold our protest on the sidewalk in front of the plants, showing our frustration, but in a peaceful manner. We didn't stop anyone who wanted to from going into work and we didn't commit any act of violence.

We continued protesting in this way until Horacio Garza and Maricela López arrived. We had a meeting there with Horacio and he told us to stop the protest and that afterwards he would help us. We answered that the only thing we wanted was

Señor Avila's word that they would hold new elections. But he said no. So Horacio Garza left and soon afterward the police and the firemen arrived. The girls were afraid when they saw the police and some of them asked if the were going to take us away, but we told them if we didn't act violently then they shouldn't either.

But that wasn't the case. Francisco Xavier Rios [Vice President of Human Resources at Sony] signaled to the police with a motion of his hand to enter through a side door, and they positioned themselves on the inside lot of the company. Then without any warning the police began to push us with their Plexiglas shields and their billy clubs. They beat us badly; they knocked a *compañera* unconscious, a woman named Alicia Soto, and they pushed the rest of us down with their shields, insulting us all the while, calling us names like "goddamn bitches."

I have been told that the company claims that the police didn't commit any acts of violence and that they only person who acted violently was Alicia who attacked the police with a magazine. I ask you: how is it possible that a 24 year old woman can harm a group of 35 well-armed police agents carrying Plexiglas shields and billy clubs? How is it possible to say they didn't commit acts of violence when my friend Alicia was knocked out by a blow to the head and has had problems ever since? I have here the newspaper *El Mañana*, dated 17 April, which shows very clearly a picture of Alicia unconscious. If they don't want to read the newspapers they should just look at their own videos because they were filming the entire attack.

FELICITAS ("FELA") CONTRERAS: They had pressed charges against us—Martha Ojeda and various others—because Sony had lost millions with the work stoppage. They issued a summons for us to appear at the police department and told us that our lives were not even worth enough to pay for the company's losses.

They wanted us to say that Martha was responsible, and they pitted us against each other. They told Lupe that I had confessed that Martha was doing it all, and they told me that Lupe confessed that Martha told us to stop working. But of the 40 they called to testify all of us said, "We are all responsible, and so you will have to arrest all of us not just Martha." All of our *compañeras* were outside the police department yelling that they would have to arrest everyone. But since there were more than a thousand and we didn't all fit in the cells, after hours of interrogations and threats they let us go.

On the fifth day, in the early morning, around 5:00 am the governor –Manuel Cavazos Lerma- ordered that they state police from Reynosa, Matamoros and Cd. Victoria be brought in. The police arrived and the soldiers with machine guns and rifles. And they said to you, "Get out of here or I'll kill you." According to them they came to restore order, and with blows and kicks. They awakened us and ran after those who were sleeping on the sidewalk. You were waking up with a gun pointing in your face and they were yelling, "Get out or we will kill you."

We withdrew, and we were like this for five days and nights. In those days the trucks tried to mow us down because they wanted to take out the production, but we were all sleeping in the main gate so they couldn't cross and take it out.

Unfortunately, we didn't get it. We didn't get our union, and they fired a lot of people without giving them any severance payment because they said that they were leaders of the movement. We stayed there because we wanted an independent union.

In 1994 NAFTA was signed, and they said that the rights of workers would not be violated. But they beat us up and violated our rights. With the help of CJM and the lawyers from ANAD a demand was presented to the NAO. In 1995 we had a hearing and we all went to San Antonio to testify. Sony brought lawyers from New York and they said that our testimony was a lie, but we took the newspapers and the evidence, the videos. We won this trial, but we didn't really win anything because they didn't punish or fine Sony and we never had the elections or anything. They just put in these offices [the NAO] just to prop us NAFTA.

For me NAFTA was no good. The workers are still just as poor. The only difference is that now there are many settlements, *colonias*, many squatters, a lot of insecurity and a contaminated river. Before I used to drink water from the river and now you cant, and you cant go into it either. Our air is contaminated. There is a lot of sickness. There is a lot of illiteracy. The only one NAFTA helped were the businessmen because they are the ones that have gotten rich. And now they say, "I am going to China; I screwed the Mexicans so now I'm going to screw the Chinese." That is what says with me about NAFTA. We are poor and screwed.

MARTHA A. OJEDA: Each one of my *compañeras* risked her life, her children, and her family. They kidnapped Yolanda and threatened her. They persecuted the others, calling them on the phone and intimidating them. Wherever any of them are, because there were many and I will never forget one, to each of them I render homage and a special tribute to their *"coraje"*—their courage and bravery—for trying to reclaim workers' right to freedom of association. For resisting and never giving up.

That is what NAFTA left me after 20 years in the *maquilas*: it gave me the opportunity to denounce at a global level the failure of this agreement and of the side agreements and to share the rebellion and resistance of my *compañeras*. It taught me that there is a world of solidarity. It clarified the horizon we are looking for, and above all the hope to reach it with a team like this team of women, united until the end. ❑

To order NAFTA From Below *or for more information, visit www.coalitionforjustice.net write to The Coalition for Justice in the Maquiladoras, 4207 Willowbrook Dr., San Antonio, TX 78228, or call 210-732-8324.*

Article 8.7

IS CHINA'S CURRENCY MANIPULATION HURTING THE U.S.?

BY ARTHUR MacEWAN
November/December 2010

Dear Dr. Dollar:

Is it true that China has been harming the U.S. economy by keeping its currency "undervalued"? Shouldn't the U.S. government do something about this situation?
—Jenny Boyd, Edmond, W.Va.

The Chinese government, operating through the Chinese central bank, does keep its currency unit—the yuan—cheap relative to the dollar. This means that goods imported *from* China cost less (in terms of dollars) than they would otherwise, while U.S. exports *to* China cost more (in terms of yuan). So we in the United States buy a lot of Chinese-made goods and the Chinese don't buy much from us. In the 2007 to 2009 period, the United States purchased $253 billion more in goods annually from China than it sold to China.

This looks bad for U.S workers. For example, when money gets spent in the United States, much of it is spent on Chinese-made goods, and fewer jobs are then created in the United States. So the Chinese government's currency policy is at least partly to blame for our employment woes. Reacting to this situation, many people are calling for the U.S. government to do something to get the Chinese government to change its policy.

But things are not so simple.

First of all, there is an additional reason for the low cost of Chinese goods— low Chinese wages. The Chinese government's policy of repressing labor probably accounts for the low cost of Chinese goods at least as much as does its currency policy. Moreover, there is a lot more going on in the global economy. Both currency problems and job losses involve much more than Chinese government actions— though China provides a convenient target for ire.

And the currency story itself is complex. In order to keep the value of its currency low relative to the dollar, the Chinese government increases the supply of yuan, uses these yuan to buy dollars, then uses the dollars to buy U.S. securities, largely government bonds but also private securities. In early 2009, China held $764 billion in U.S. Treasury securities, making it the largest foreign holder of U.S. government debt. By buying U.S. government bonds, the Chinese have been financing the federal deficit. More generally, by supplying funds to the United States, the Chinese government has been keeping interest rates low in this country.

If the Chinese were to act differently, allowing the value of their currency to rise relative to the dollar, both the cost of capital and the prices of the many goods imported from China would rise. The rising cost of capital would probably not be a serious problem, as the Federal Reserve could take counteraction to keep interest rates low. So, an increase in the value of the yuan would net the United States some jobs, but also raise some prices for U.S. consumers.

It is pretty clear that right now what the United States needs is jobs. Moreover, low-cost Chinese goods have contributed to the declining role of manufacturing in the United States, a phenomenon that both weakens important segments of organized labor and threatens to inhibit technological progress, which has often been centered in manufacturing or based on applications in manufacturing (e.g., robotics).

So why doesn't the U.S. government place more pressure on China to raise the value of the yuan? Part of the reason may lie in concern about losing Chinese financing of the U.S. federal deficit. For several years the two governments have been co-dependent: The U.S. government gets financing for its deficits, and the Chinese government gains by maintaining an undervalued currency. Not an easy relationship to change.

Probably more important, however, many large and politically powerful U.S.-based firms depend directly on the low-cost goods imported from China. Wal-mart and Target, as any shopper knows, are filled with Chinese-made goods. Then there are the less visible products from China, including a power device that goes into the Microsoft Xbox, computer keyboards for Dell, and many other goods for many other U.S. corporations. If the yuan's value rose and these firms had to pay more dollars to buy these items, they could probably not pass all the increase on to consumers and their profits would suffer.

Still, in spite of the interests of these firms, the U.S. government may take some action, either by pressing harder for China to let the value of the yuan rise relative to the dollar or by placing some restrictions on imports from China. But don't expect too big a change. ❑

The Short Run: The Smelly American
September/October 2007

Are the inexorable laws of global capitalism causing corporations to export their manufacturing and service operations to low-wage countries, or is it just that U.S. workers are boorish, lazy slobs? Secretary of Labor Elaine Chao says it's the latter. A recent article in *Parade* magazine entitled "How safe is your job?" quotes Chao as expressing her concern for the competitiveness of the U.S. workforce. "American employees must be punctual, dress appropriately, and have good personal hygiene," Chao said. "They need anger-management and conflict-resolution skills, and they have to be able to accept direction. Too many young people bristle when a supervisor asks them to do something."

Chao has since claimed that her comments were taken out of context, Labor Notes reports. Evidently, she thinks that in addition to all their other flaws, U.S. workers are too stupid to recognize an insult when they hear one.

—*Allison MacDonald*

Article 8.8

WHY THE LOSS OF MANUFACTURING JOBS?

BY ARTHUR MacEWAN
September/October 2010

Dear Dr. Dollar,

Many times I have read (in writings by former Secretary of Labor Robert Reich, for example) or heard it said (by President Obama, for example) that technology is eliminating more manufacturing jobs in the United States than rising imports. Is that true?

—Kevin Rath, Oakland, Calif.

The former labor secretary and the president are right—at least if by "technology" we mean all sources of increases in output per worker, whether by greater use of machinery, work reorganization, or plain old speed-up.

Consider the years from 1990 to 2007. In this period, the supply of manufactured goods in the United States (production plus imports) roughly doubled (in inflation-adjusted, or "real," terms). Had the share of imports stayed the same and had productivity (output per worker) stayed the same, employment too would have roughly doubled (assuming workers worked just as many hours, an issue I will come back to below). But that's not what happened. In 2007, manufacturing employed about 76% as many people as in 1990, 13.431 million as compared to 17.695 million.

In fact, both productivity and the share of imports in total supply increased substantially between 1990 and 2007. Output per worker in manufacturing rose dramatically, by roughly 88% in real terms. Imports rose from 27% of the total supply of manufactured goods in the United States in 1990 to 48% in 2007. So the amount of domestic output, instead of doubling along with the doubling of supply, increased by only 43% (in real terms).

To figure out which of these factors—productivity or the share of imports in total supply—had the larger quantitative impact on employment, let's look at two fictitious cases that allow us to examine each factor separately:

Case 1: *Productivity increases by 88%, but the share of imports stays the same.* If supply doubles, domestic output will also double. Employment will rise, but only by approximately 6% because with an 88% increase in productivity, each worker is yielding a larger output. Only 6% more workers are necessary to produce twice as much output.

Case 2: *The import share increases from 27% to 48%, but productivity stays the same.* If supply doubles, domestic output will rise by 43% (as it actually did). And if productivity stays the same, employment would therefore also increase by 43%.

It is clear that the increase in productivity had a quantitatively larger impact in limiting employment growth than did the increase in the share of imports.

Job-loss in manufacturing presents serious problems. Some people lose their jobs and most are unlikely to get jobs that pay equivalent wages, even if overall employment picks up. These people suffer, and so do their families and communities. More broadly, the strong unions that developed in manufacturing are weakened, undercutting the economic and political strength of all working people.

But these negative impacts don't have to take place. There is no good reason why we have to accept the choices of cutting foreign trade or cutting jobs, of reducing technological change or reducing jobs, or, for that matter, of destroying the environment (e.g., off-shore drilling and clear cutting of forests) or destroying jobs. Instead we can find ways to prevent the costs of economic changes from falling on workers, their families, and their communities.

One positive step would be to assure that productivity gains yield shorter work-weeks with no cut in pay—that is, no loss in the number of jobs. After all, this has happened before. Also, we need to establish the conditions for rebuilding strong unions in all segments of the economy—for example, by passing the Employee Free Choice Act and assuring that the National Labor Relations Board does its job. In addition, we need an array of good social programs such as, "Medicare for all" so people don't lose their health care benefits when they lose their jobs. Likewise, better support for education and training programs for all workers—not just those affected by imports—are essential to facilitate their adjustment to change.

There may be good reasons to place some restrictions on technological changes or foreign trade—for example, when they generate environmental destruction, when they place workers in danger, or in conditions of virtual slavery (in the exporting countries). When we are forced to choose between the gains from trade or technology versus the well-being of workers directly affected, most often we should choose the well-being of the workers. The real solution to these problems, however, is to find ways to change the choices.

Whatever steps we take, we need to recognize that foreign trade is not the only cause—not even the quantitatively most important cause—of the decline in manufacturing employment. ❑

Chapter 9

LABOR AND ECONOMIC CRISIS

Article 9.1

INEQUALITY, POWER, AND IDEOLOGY
Getting It Right About the Causes of the Current Economic Crisis

BY ARTHUR MacEWAN
March/April 2009

It is hard to solve a problem without an understanding of what caused it. For example, in medicine, until we gained an understanding of the way bacteria and viruses cause various infectious diseases, it was virtually impossible to develop effective cures. Of course, dealing with many diseases is complicated by the fact that germs, genes, diet and the environment establish a nexus of causes.

The same is true in economics. Without an understanding of the causes of the current crisis, we are unlikely to develop a solution; certainly we are not going to get a solution that has a lasting impact. And determining the causes is complicated because several intertwined factors have been involved.

The current economic crisis was brought about by a nexus of factors that involved: a growing concentration of political and social power in the hands of the wealthy; the ascendance of a perverse leave-it-to-the-market ideology which was an instrument of that power; and rising income inequality, which both resulted from and enhanced that power. These various factors formed a vicious circle, reinforcing one another and together shaping the economic conditions that led us to the present situation. Several other factors were also involved—the growing role of credit, the puffing up of the housing bubble, and the increasing deregulation of financial markets have been very important. However, these are best understood as transmitters of our economic problems, arising from the nexus that formed the vicious circle.

What does this tell us about a solution? Economic stimulus, repair of the housing market, and new regulation are all well and good, but they do not deal with the underlying causes of the crisis. Instead, progressive groups need to work to shift each of the factors I have noted—power, ideology, and income distribution—in the other direction. In doing so, we can create a *virtuous* circle, with each change reinforcing the other changes. If successful, we not only establish a more stable economy, but we lay the foundation for a more democratic, equitable, and sustainable economic order.

A crisis by its very nature creates opportunities for change. One good place to begin change and intervene in this "circle"—and transform it from vicious to virtuous—is through pushing for the expansion and reform of social programs, programs that directly serve social needs of the great majority of the population (for example: single-payer health care, education programs, and environmental protection and repair). By establishing changes in social programs, we will have impacts on income distribution and ideology, and, perhaps most important, we set in motion *a power shift* that improves our position for preserving the changes. While I emphasize social programs as a means to initiate social and economic change, there are other ways to intervene in the circle. Efforts to re-strengthen unions would be especially important; and there are other options as well.

Causes of the Crisis: A Long Time Coming

Sometime around the early 1970s, there were some dramatic changes in the U.S. economy. The twenty-five years following World War II had been an era of relatively stable economic growth; the benefits of growth had been widely shared, with wages rising along with productivity gains, and income distribution became slightly less unequal (a good deal less unequal as compared to the pre-Great Depression era). There were severe economic problems in the United States, not the least of which were the continued exclusion of African Americans, large gender inequalities, and the woeful inadequacy of social welfare programs. Nonetheless, relatively stable growth, rising wages, and then the advent of the civil rights movement and the War on Poverty gave some important, positive social and economic character to the era—especially in hindsight!

In part, this comparatively favorable experience for the United States had depended on the very dominant position that U.S. firms held in the world economy, a position in which they were relatively unchallenged by international competition. The firms and their owners were not the only beneficiaries of this situation. With less competitive pressure on them from foreign companies, many U.S. firms accepted unionization and did not find it worthwhile to focus on keeping wages down and obstructing the implementation of social supports for the low-income population. Also, having had the recent experience of the Great Depression, many wealthy people and business executives were probably not so averse to a substantial role for government in regulating the economy.

A Power Grab

By about 1970, the situation was changing. Firms in Europe and Japan had long recovered from World War II, OPEC was taking shape, and weaknesses were emerging in the U.S. economy. The weaknesses were in part a consequence of heavy spending for the Vietnam War combined with the government's reluctance to tax for the war because of its unpopularity. The pressures on U.S. firms arising from these changes had two sets of consequences: slower growth and greater instability; and concerted efforts—a power grab, if you will—by firms and the wealthy to shift the costs of economic deterioration onto U.S. workers and the low-income population.

These "concerted efforts" took many forms: greater resistance to unions and unionization, battles to reduce taxes, stronger opposition to social welfare programs, and, above all, a push to reduce or eliminate government regulation of economic activity through a powerful political campaign to gain control of the various branches and levels of government. The 1980s, with Reagan and Bush One in the White House, were the years in which all these efforts were solidified. Unions were greatly weakened, a phenomenon both demonstrated and exacerbated by Reagan's firing of the air traffic controllers in response to their strike in 1981. The tax cuts of the period were also important markers of the change. But the change had begun earlier; the 1978 passage of the tax-cutting Proposition 13 in California was perhaps the first major success of the movement. And the changes continued well after the 1980s, with welfare reform and deregulation of finance during the Clinton era, to say nothing of the tax cuts and other actions during Bush Two.

Ideology Shift

The changes that began in the 1970s, however, were not simply these sorts of concrete alterations in the structure of power affecting the economy and, especially, government's role in the economy. There was a major shift in ideology, the dominant set of ideas that organize an understanding of our social relations and both guide and rationalize policy decisions.

Alan Greenspan, Symbol of an Era

One significant symbol of the full rise of the conservative ideology that became so dominant in the latter part of the 20th century was Alan Greenspan, who served from 1974 through 1976 as chairman of the President's Council of Economic Advisers under Gerald Ford and in 1987 became chairman of the Federal Reserve Board, a position he held until 2006. While his predecessors had hardly been critics of U.S. capitalism, Greenspan was a close associate of the philosopher Ayn Rand and an adherent of her extreme ideas supporting individualism and *laissez-faire* (keep-the-government-out) capitalism.

When chairman of the Fed, Greenspan was widely credited with maintaining an era of stable economic growth. As things fell apart in 2008, however, Greenspan was seen as having a large share of responsibility for the non-regulation and excessively easy credit (see article) that led into the crisis.

Called before Congress in October of 2008, Greenspan was chastised by Rep. Henry Waxman (D-Calif.), who asked him: "Do you feel that your ideology pushed you to make decisions that you wish you had not made?" To which Greenspan replied: "Yes, I've found a flaw. I don't know how significant or permanent it is. But I've been very distressed by that fact."

And Greenspan told Congress: "Those of us who have looked to the self-interest of lending institutions to protect shareholders' equity, myself included, are in a state of shocked disbelief."

Greenspan's "shock" was reminiscent of the scene in the film "Casablanca," where Captain Renault (Claude Rains) declares: "I'm shocked, shocked to find that gambling is going on in here!" At which point, a croupier hands Renault a pile of money and says, "Your winnings, sir." Renault replies, *sotto voce*, "Thank you very much."

Following the Great Depression and World War II, there was a wide acceptance of the idea that government had a major role to play in economic life. Less than in many other countries but nonetheless to a substantial degree, at all levels of society, it was generally believed that there should be a substantial government safety net and that government should both regulate the economy in various ways and, through fiscal as well as monetary policy, should maintain aggregate demand. This large economic role for government came to be called Keynesianism, after the British economist John Maynard Keynes, who had set out the arguments for an active fiscal policy in time of economic weakness. In the early 1970s, as economic troubles developed, even Richard Nixon declared: "We are all Keynesians now."

The election of Ronald Reagan, however, marked a sharp change in ideology, at least at the top. Actions of the government were blamed for all economic ills: government spending, Keynesianism, was alleged to be the cause of the inflation of the 1970s; government regulation was supposedly crippling industry; high taxes were, it was argued, undermining incentives for workers to work and for businesses to invest; social welfare spending was blamed for making people dependent on the government and was charged with fraud and corruption (the "welfare queens"); and so on and so on.

On economic matters, Reagan championed supply-side economics, the principal idea of which was that tax cuts yield an increase in government revenue because the cuts lead to more rapid economic growth through encouraging more work and more investment. Thus, so the argument went, tax cuts would reduce the government deficit. Reagan, with the cooperation of Democrats, got the tax cuts—and, as the loss of revenue combined with a large increase in military spending, the federal budget deficit grew by leaps and bounds, almost doubling as a share of GDP over the course of the 1980s. It was all summed up in the idea of keeping the government out of the economy; let the free market work its magic.

Growing Inequality

The shifts of power and ideology were very much bound up with a major redistribution upwards of income and wealth. The weakening of unions, the increasing access of firms to low-wage foreign (and immigrant) labor, the refusal of government to maintain the buying power of the minimum wage, favorable tax treatment of the wealthy and their corporations, deregulation in a wide range of industries and lack of enforcement of existing regulation (e.g., the authorities turning a blind eye to offshore tax shelters) all contributed to these shifts.

Many economists, however, explain the rising income inequality as a result of technological change that favored more highly skilled workers; and changing technology has probably been a factor. Yet the most dramatic aspect of the rising inequality has been the rapidly rising share of income obtained by those at the very top (see figures below), who get their incomes from the ownership and control of business, not from their skilled labor. For these people the role of new technologies was most important through its impact on providing more options (e.g., international options) for the managers of firms, more thorough means to control labor, and more effective ways—in the absence of regulation—to manipulate finance. All of these gains that might be associated with new technology were also gains brought by the way the government handled, or didn't handle (failed to regulate), economic affairs.

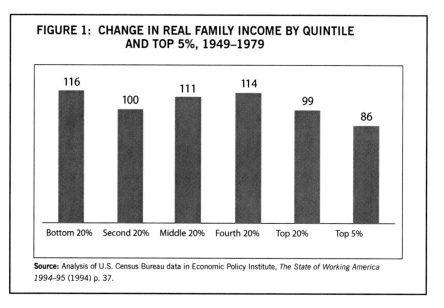

FIGURE 1: CHANGE IN REAL FAMILY INCOME BY QUINTILE AND TOP 5%, 1949–1979

Source: Analysis of U.S. Census Bureau data in Economic Policy Institute, *The State of Working America 1994–95* (1994) p. 37.

Several sets of data demonstrate the sharp changes in the distribution of income that have taken place in the last several decades. Most striking is the changing position of the very highest income segment of the population. In the mid-1920s, the share of all pre-tax income going to the top 1% of households peaked at 23.9%. This elite group's share of income fell dramatically during the Great Depression and World War II to about 12% at the end of the war and then slowly fell further during the next thirty years, reaching a low of 8.9% in the mid-1970s. Since then, the top 1% has regained its exalted position of the earlier era, with 21.8% of income in 2005. Since 1993, more than one-half of all income gains have accrued to this highest 1% of the population.

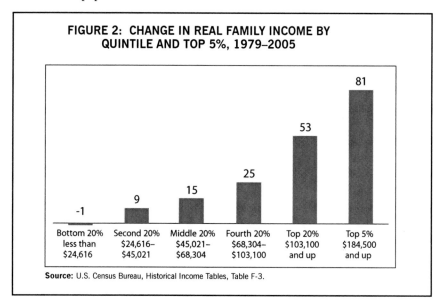

FIGURE 2: CHANGE IN REAL FAMILY INCOME BY QUINTILE AND TOP 5%, 1979–2005

Source: U.S. Census Bureau, Historical Income Tables, Table F-3.

Figures 1 and 2 show the gains (or losses) of various groups in the 1947 to 1979 period and in the 1979 to 2005 period. The difference is dramatic. For example, in the earlier era, the bottom 20% saw its income in real (inflation-adjusted) terms rise by 116%, and real income of the top 5% grew by only 86%. But in the latter era, the bottom 20% saw a 1% decline in its income, while the top 5% obtained an 81% increase.

The Emergence of Crisis

These changes, especially the dramatic shifts in the distribution of income, set the stage for the increasingly large reliance on credit, especially consumer and mortgage credit, that played a major role in the emergence of the current economic crisis. Other factors were involved, but rising inequality was especially important in effecting the increase in both the demand and supply of credit.

Credit Expansion

On the demand side, rising inequality translated into a growing gap between the incomes of most members of society and their needs. For the 2000 to 2007 period, average weekly earnings in the private sector were 12% below their average for the 1970s (in inflation-adjusted terms). From 1980 to 2005 the share of income going to the bottom 60% of families fell from 35% to 29%. Under these circumstances, more and more people relied more and more heavily on credit to meet their needs—everything from food to fuel, from education to entertainment, and especially housing.

While the increasing reliance of consumers on credit has been going on for a long time, it has been especially marked in recent decades. Consumer debt as a share of after-tax personal income averaged 20% in the 1990s, and then jumped up to an average of 25% in the first seven years of the new millennium. But the debt expansion was most marked in housing, where mortgage debt as a percent of after-tax personal income rose from 89% to 94% over the 1990s, and then ballooned to 140% by 2006 as housing prices skyrocketed.

On the supply side, especially in the last few years, the government seems to have relied on making credit readily available as a means to bolster aggregate demand and maintain at least a modicum of economic growth. During the 1990s, the federal funds interest rate averaged 5.1%, but fell to an average of 3.4% in the 2000 to 2007 period—and averaged only 1.4% in 2002 to 2004 period. (The federal funds interest rate is the rate that banks charge one another for overnight loans and is a rate directly affected by the Federal Reserve.) Corresponding to the low interest rates, the money supply grew twice as fast in the new millennium as it had in the 1990s. (And see the sidebar on the connection of the Fed's actions to the Iraq War.)

The increasing reliance of U.S. consumers on credit has often been presented as a moral weakness, as an infatuation with consumerism, and as a failure to look beyond the present. Whatever moral judgments one may make, however, the expansion of the credit economy has been a response to real economic forces—inequality and government policies, in particular.

The Failure to Regulate

The credit expansion by itself, however, did not precipitate the current crisis. Deregulation—or, more generally, the failure to regulate—is also an important part of the story. The government's role in regulation of financial markets has been a central feature in the development of this crisis, but the situation in financial markets has been part of a more general process—affecting airlines and trucking, telecommunications, food processing, broadcasting, and of course international trade and investment. The process has been driven by a combination of power (of large firms and wealthy individuals) and ideology (leave it to the market, get the government out).

The failure to regulate financial markets that transformed the credit expansion into a financial crisis shows up well in three examples:

The 1999 repeal of the Glass-Steagall Act. Glass-Steagall had been enacted in the midst of the Great Depression, as a response to the financial implosion following the

---

Joseph Stiglitz on the War and the Economy

On October 2, 2008, on the Pacifica radio program Democracy Now!, Amy Goodman and Juan Gonzalez interviewed Joseph Stiglitz about the economic situation. Stiglitz was the 2001 winner of the Nobel Prize in Economics, former chief economist at the World Bank, and former chair of President Clinton's Council of Economic Advisers. He is a professor at Columbia University. Following is an excerpt from that interview:

AMY GOODMAN: Joseph Stiglitz, you're co-author of *The Three Trillion Dollar War: The True Cost of the Iraq Conflict.* How does the bailout [of the financial sector] connect to war?

JOSEPH STIGLITZ: Very much. Let me first explain a little bit how the current crisis connects with the war. One of the reasons that we have this crisis is that the Fed flooded the economy with liquidity and had lax regulations. Part of that was this ideology of "regulations are bad," but part of the reason was that the economy was weak. And one of the reasons the economy was weak was oil prices were soaring, and part of the reason oil prices were soaring is the Iraq war. When we went to war in 2003, before we went, prices were $23 a barrel. Futures markets thought they would remain at that level. They anticipated the increase in demand, but they thought there would be a concomitant increase in supply from the low-cost providers, mainly in the Middle East. The war changed that equation, and we know what happened to the oil prices.

Well, why is that important? Well, we were spending—Americans were spending hundreds of millions—billions of dollars to buy—more, to buy imported oil. Normally, that would have had a very negative effect on our economy; we would have had a slowdown. Some people have said, you know, it's a mystery why we aren't having that slowdown; we repealed the laws of economics. Whenever anybody says that, you ought to be suspect.

It was actually very simple. The Fed engineered a bubble, a housing bubble to replace the tech bubble that it had engineered in the '90s. The housing bubble facilitated people taking money out of their . . . houses; in one year, there were more than $900 billion of mortgage equity withdrawals. And so, we had a consumption boom that was so strong that even though we were spending so much money abroad, we could keep the economy going. But it was so shortsighted. And it was so clear that we were living on borrowed money and borrowed time. And it was just a matter of time before, you know, the whole thing would start to unravel.

stock market crash of 1929. Among other things, it required that different kinds of financial firms—commercial banks, investment banks, insurance companies—be separate. This separation both limited the spread of financial problems and reduced conflicts of interest that could arise were the different functions of these firms combined into a single firm. As perhaps the most important legislation regulating the financial sector, the repeal of Glass-Steagall was not only a substantive change but was an important symbol of the whole process of deregulation.

The failure to regulate mortgage lending. Existing laws and regulations require lending institutions to follow prudent practices in making loans, assuring that borrowers have the capacity to be able to pay back the loans. And of course fraud—lying about the provisions of loans—is prohibited. Yet in an atmosphere where regulation was "out," regulators were simply not doing their jobs. The consequences are illustrated in a December 28, 2008, *New York Times* story on the failed Washington Mutual Bank. The article describes a supervisor at a mortgage processing center as having been "accustomed to seeing babysitters claiming salaries worthy of college presidents, and schoolteachers with incomes rivaling stockbrokers'. He rarely questioned them. A real estate frenzy was under way and WaMu, as his bank was known, was all about saying yes."

One may wonder why banks—or other lending institutions, mortgage firms, in particular—would make loans to people who were unlikely to be able to pay them back. The reason is that the lending institutions quickly combined such loans into packages (i.e., a security made up of several borrowers' obligations to pay) and sold them to other investors in a practice called "securitization."

Credit-default swaps. Perhaps the most egregious failure to regulate in recent years has been the emergence of credit-default swaps, which are connected to securitization. Because they were made up of obligations by a diverse set of borrowers, the packages of loans were supposedly low-risk investments. Yet those who purchased them still sought insurance against default. Insurance sellers, however, are regulated—required, for example, to keep a certain amount of capital on hand to cover possible claims. So the sellers of these insurance policies on packages of loans called the policies "credit-default swaps" and thus were allowed to avoid regulation. Further, these credit-default swaps, these insurance policies, themselves were bought and sold again and again in unregulated markets in a continuing process of speculation.

The credit-default swaps are a form of derivative, a financial asset the value of which is derived from some other asset—in this case the value of packages of mortgages for which they were the insurance policies. When the housing bubble began to collapse and people started to default on their mortgages, the value of credit-default swaps plummeted and their future value was impossible to determine. No one would buy them, and several banks that had speculated in these derivatives were left holding huge amounts of these "toxic assets."

Bubble and Bust

The combination of easy credit and the failure to regulate together fueled the housing bubble. People could buy expensive houses but make relatively low monthly payments. Without effective regulation of mortgage lending, they could get the loans even when they were unlikely to be able to make payments over the long run. Moreover, as these pressures pushed up housing prices, many people bought houses simply to resell them quickly at a higher price, in a process called "flipping." And such speculation pushed the prices up further. Between 2000 and 2006, housing prices rose by 90% (as consumer prices generally rose by only 17%).

While the housing boom was in full swing, both successful housing speculators and lots of people involved in the shenanigans of credit markets made a lot of money. However, as the housing bubble burst—as all bubbles do—things fell apart. The packages of loans lost value, and the insurance policies on them, the credit-default swaps, lost value. These then became "toxic" assets for those who held them, assets not only with reduced value but with unknown value. Not only did large financial firms—for example, Lehman Brothers and AIG—have billions of dollars in losses, but no one knew the worth of their remaining assets. The assets were called "toxic" because they poisoned the operations of the financial system. Under these circumstances, financial institutions stopped lending to one another—that is, the credit markets "froze up." The financial crisis was here.

The financial crisis, not surprisingly, very quickly shifted to a general economic crisis. Firms in the "real" economy rely heavily on a well-functioning financial system to supply them with the funds they need for their regular operations—loans to car buyers, loans to finance inventory, loans for construction of new facilities, loans for new equipment, and, of course, mortgage loans. Without those loans (or with the loans much more difficult to obtain), there has been a general cut-back in economic activity, what is becoming a serious and probably prolonged recession.

What Is to Be Done?

So here we are. The shifts in power, ideology, and income distribution have placed us in a rather nasty situation. There are some steps that will be taken that have a reasonable probability of yielding short-run improvement. In particular, a large increase in government spending—deficit spending—will probably reduce the depth and shorten the length of the recession. And the actions of the Federal Reserve and Treasury to inject funds into the financial system are likely, along with the deficit spending, to "un-freeze" credit markets (the mismanagement and, it seems, outright corruption of the bailout notwithstanding). Also, there is likely to be some re-regulation of the financial industry. These steps, however, at best will restore things to where they were before the crisis. They do not treat the underlying causes of the crisis—the vicious circle of power, ideology, and inequality.

Opportunity for Change

Fortunately, the crisis itself has weakened some aspects of this circle. The cry of "leave it to the market" is still heard, but is now more a basis for derision than a guide to policy. The ideology and, to a degree, the power behind the ideology, have been severely weakened as the role of "keeping the government out" has shown to be a major cause of the financial mess and our current hardships. There is now widespread support among the general populace and some support in Washington for greater regulation of the financial industry.

Whether or not the coming period will see this support translated into effective policy is of course an open question. Also an open question is how much the turn away from "leaving it to the market" can be extended to other sectors of the economy. With regard to the environment, there is already general acceptance of the principle that the government (indeed, many governments) must take an active role in regulating economic activity. Similar principles need to be recognized with regard to health care, education, housing, child care, and other support programs for low-income families.

The discrediting of "keep the government out" ideology provides an opening to develop new programs in these areas and to expand old programs. Furthermore, as the federal government revs up its "stimulus" program in the coming months, opportunities will exist for expanding support for these sorts of programs. This support is important, first of all, because these programs serve real, pressing needs—needs that have long existed and are becoming acute and more extensive in the current crisis.

Breaking the Circle

Support for these social programs, however, may also serve to break into the vicious power-ideology-inequality circle and begin transforming it into a virtuous circle. Social programs are inherently equalizing in two ways: they provide their benefits to low-income people and they provide some options for those people in their efforts to demand better work and higher pay. Also, the further these programs develop, the more they establish the legitimacy of a larger role for public control of—government involvement in—the economy; they tend to bring about an ideological shift. By affecting a positive distributional shift and by shifting ideology, the emergence of stronger social programs can have a wider impact on power. In other words, efforts to promote social programs are one place to start, an entry point to shift the vicious circle to a virtuous circle.

There are other entry points. Perhaps the most obvious ones are actions to strengthen the role of unions. The Employee Free Choice Act may be a useful first step, and it will be helpful to establish a more union-friendly Department of Labor and National Labor Relations Board. Raising the minimum wage—ideally indexing it to inflation—would also be highly desirable. While conditions have changed since the heyday of unions in the middle of the 20th century, and we cannot expect to restore the conditions of that era, a greater role for unions would seem essential in righting the structural conditions at the foundation of the current crisis.

Shifting Class Power

None of this is assured, of course. Simply starting social programs will not necessarily mean that they have the wider impacts that I am suggesting are possible. No one should think that by setting up some new programs and strengthening some existing ones we will be on a smooth road to economic and social change. Likewise, rebuilding the strength of unions will involve extensive struggle and will not be accomplished by a few legislative or executive actions.

Also, all efforts to involve the government in economic activity—whether in finance or environmental affairs, in health care or education, in work support or job training programs—will be met with the worn-out claims that government involvement generates bureaucracy, stifles initiative, and places an excessive burden on private firms and individuals. We are already hearing warnings that in dealing with the financial crisis the government must avoid "over-regulation." Likewise, efforts to strengthen unions will suffer the traditional attacks, as unions are portrayed as corrupt and their members privileged. The unfolding situation with regard to the auto firms' troubles has demonstrated the attack, as conservatives have blamed the United Auto Workers for the industry's woes and have demanded extensive concessions by the union.

Certainly not all regulation is good regulation. Aside from excessive bureaucratic controls, there is the phenomenon by which regulating agencies are often captives of the industries that they are supposed to regulate. And there are corrupt unions. These are real issues, but they should not be allowed to derail change.

The current economic crisis emerged in large part as a shift in the balance of class power in the United States, a shift that began in the early 1970s and continued into the new millennium. Perhaps the present moment offers an opportunity to shift things back in the other direction. Recognition of the complex nexus of causes of the current economic crisis provides some guidance where people might start. Rebuilding and extending social programs, strengthening unions, and other actions that contribute to a more egalitarian power shift will not solve all the problems of U.S. capitalism. They can, however, begin to move us in the right direction. ❑

The Short Run: Failure to Communicate
November/December 2008

The pink slip has gone digital. In October, electric car manufacturer Tesla Motors decided to close its Detroit-area facility and lay off most of the 100 workers there. Tesla posted a blog announcing the layoffs on the company website—two days before notifying the workers themselves, according to the online auto industry newsletter Jalopnik.com. After disclosing the shut-down of the Detroit-area office, the blog post went on to say that "good communication" is "of paramount importance as Tesla grows." Yup.

Tesla terminated about 90% of its Detroit employees; the rest were told to report to company headquarter in San Jose. However, they will have to relocate to southern California with no pay increase, moving assistance, or help in selling their homes. —*Jason Son*

Article 9.2

SHOULD WE BE TALKING ABOUT LIVING WAGES *NOW*?

BY JEANNETTE WICKS-LIM

March/April 2009

The Department of Labor announced in January that the U.S. economy shed 2.8 million jobs in 2008, bringing the national unemployment rate to 7.2%—its highest level in 16 years. In today's economic climate, the worst since the Great Depression, are the raises demanded by living-wage campaigns a luxury? Should living-wage campaigns take a back seat to pulling the economy out of recession?

For many, the answer is no. Campaigns across the country continue to build on the widespread success of a movement that has put into place more than 140 living-wage laws since the mid-1990s. Take the Hartford Living Wage Task Force in Connecticut, which is trying to expand the number of workers guaranteed a living wage under its original 1997 law. Or Santa Fe's Living Wage Network, which fought for, and won, a cost-of-living increase to its living wage rate for 2009. Or the Nashville Movement in Tennessee, a group laying the groundwork for a campaign to establish a brand new ordinance.

They are right. Today's economic turmoil challenges us to create practical policies to meet the *heightened* imperative of living wages, not to abandon them.

Why do we need living-wage campaigns? Let's consider first the current legal wage floor. At $7.25 per hour, the federal minimum wage as of July 2009, a full-time year-round worker will bring home $15,080—less than the official poverty threshold of $17,330 for a family of three.

Moreover, poverty experts roundly criticize that official poverty line as too severe. According to the National Survey of American Families, nearly two-thirds of people in households with incomes above the poverty line but below twice that level reported serious economic hardships—failing to pay their rent, having their phone disconnected, worrying about running out of food, or relying on the emergency room for routine medical care.

Consider a more realistic poverty line: the "basic budget" thresholds developed by the Economic Policy Institute as a measure of the income required for "a safe and decent standard of living." These range between two and three times the official poverty line depending on local living costs such as housing. For a family of three, a full-time year-round worker would need to earn between $16 and $24 an hour to reach these basic budget thresholds. Two workers would each need to earn between $8 and $12 per hour. The living-wage ordinances enacted in recent years have typically required rates in this range—on average $10.80, or about 50% above the federal minimum wage.

These basic budgets, however, leave out not only extras such as restaurant meals, but also essential, if not immediate, items such as savings for education, retirement, or even emergencies. Any cut in hours or spell of unemployment can immediately compromise these families' ability to meet their basic needs. Unfortunately, these will be all-too-common occurrences in today's economic climate, which will expose the lowest-paid workers to increasingly severe hardships. This is because businesses tend to let the wages of the lowest-paid workers stagnate or fall unless prodded by a minimum-wage hike or a near-full-employment economy. In the 1980s, for instance, the federal minimum wage remained the same for ten years. Over this period, the lowest-paid workers saw their real (i.e., inflation-adjusted) wages *fall* by 15%.

In other words, to put living-wage campaigns on hold would not simply mean that conditions for low-wage workers and their families would not improve. Instead, these families would face worsening economic hardships.

But perhaps that's inevitable during a recession. Today, with economic indicators falling by the day, can businesses afford to pay a living wage without slashing jobs?

We can learn from the experience of New Jersey's state minimum-wage hikes in the early 1990s: from $3.35 to $3.80 in 1990, then to $4.25 in 1991, and finally to $5.05 in 1992. These three raises, about 10% to 20% each, amounted to a 40% overall rise in the wage floor once adjusted for inflation. The first hike took place in April 1990 when the economy was nearing a business cycle peak. The second and third hikes, however, took place on the heels of the 1990 recession. Economists studied their effects extensively among the businesses likely to be hit hardest—fast-food restaurants—and found no significant negative impact on employment.

One reason businesses can absorb these costs is that for most, minimum-wage hikes require only modest adjustments. For example, in 2003 Santa Fe passed an $8.50 citywide minimum wage. The average low-wage worker, who earned $6.91, received about a 23% raise. The resulting cost increases for restaurants—the most heavily affected businesses—equaled 3% of their sales revenue. In other words, a typical restaurant could offset the entire expense of the minimum-wage hike with a 3% price increase, say, 60¢ on a $20 meal. Unsurprisingly, the city's new wage floor appears to have had no negative impact on jobs.

Even in today's sharp downturn, businesses can likely absorb similar minimum-wage hikes. To see this, consider that U.S. restaurant sales rose by 2.8% between November 2007 and November 2008, almost two percentage points faster than inflation. This is despite a 5% rise in restaurant prices over the same period. In other words, overall sales in this sector grew, albeit sluggishly, even as restaurants raised their prices *and* the recession deepened.

Based on the Santa Fe experience, and using extremely pessimistic assumptions about future sales trends, I estimate that a 20% minimum-wage hike would require, as before, just a 3% price increase to cover these businesses' higher costs.

What can living-wage campaigns draw from these experiences, given that transforming a minimum wage into a living wage requires more dramatic raises on the order of 50%? An obvious possibility is to structure a living-wage ordinance as a series of raises, 10% to 20% each, which gradually achieve an adequate living-wage rate. An added precaution may be in order since we simply do not have extensive data on the impact of minimum-wage hikes during similar economic conditions: each raise could be followed by a year of evaluation, used in turn to adjust future raises up or down. This, by the way, is another lesson Santa Fe's experience offers: the city required exactly such an evaluation before raising its initial $8.50 minimum to $9.50 in 2006.

To turn the economy around we need a significant boost in economic activity—an increase in the demand for businesses' goods and services, not minor adjustments to business costs. This is the logic behind President Obama's stimulus package.

Widespread public support for raising minimum-wage rates (in 2006, more than 60% of voters in six states passed state minimum-wage hikes) suggests, however, that we want not only decent schools, decent medical care, decent roads, and a decent environment, but also decent-paying jobs. To create such jobs, living-wage requirements must be tied to the stimulus plan's funding. Without such mandates, private sector businesses that are the main focus for job creation are unlikely to pass some of that stimulus money along in the form of raises for their lowest-paid workers. Current living-wage laws provide a model: these laws impose living-wage requirements on businesses that contract with, or receive subsidies from, local governments.

Today's economic crisis highlights the vulnerability of the lowest-paid workers and virtually ensures that their living standards will worsen. These facts compel us to pursue living-wage policies with even greater force. Two policy prescriptions are especially important. First, the economic recovery plan, with its extensive government subsidies, provides a tool to impose living-wage requirements. Second, a broader, longer term living-wage policy of multi-step raises guided by interim economic impact studies will allow us to sensibly wean our economy off of poverty wages. Past experience tells us that our economy, even today, can adjust to such a policy. ❏

The Short Run: Herald Scoops Globe
July/August 2008

It seems everyone who has even the slightest eye on print journalism knows about the rampant cost-cutting in today's newsrooms—that is, everyone except the editorial staff of the *Boston Globe*. *Globe* reporters heard about management's proposed 10% salary cut only when a *Globe* mailroom employee questioned the plan at a paper-wide "town meeting."

According to the *Boston Phoenix* (a weekly), the Boston Newspaper Guild (BNG), which represents the *Globe*'s editorial staff, had received the wage-cut proposal a week prior to the meeting at the *Globe*, but BNG president Dan Totten neglected to inform union members of the measure. As a result, staffers first heard about the proposal at the meeting—or read about it in an article in the *Globe*'s archrival, the *Boston Herald*, two days later. But the *Herald* has no reason to be smug, as it will be laying off upward of 160 union members this summer. —*Carrie Battan*

Article 9.3

CORPORATE AMERICA'S COUNTER-STIMULUS STRATEGY

Firms decide to shut profitable plants while spurning buyers.

BY ROGER BYBEE
May/June 2009

"Is it too late? I hope not," said an exasperated Anthony Fortunato, president of the 260-worker United Steelworkers (USW) Local 2604 at an ArcelorMittal steel mill in Lackawanna, N.Y., as he and his members watched the mill being systematically taken apart.

An eager buyer has been pressing the company—the world's largest steel firm—for at least two months to sell the mill and thus keep the profitable operation open and the jobs alive. Fortunato is hoping the buyer will remain interested despite ArcelorMittal's aggressive drive to gut the mill. ArcelorMittal is rushing to dismantle complex, custom-built ovens and other equipment that will take months to replace.

Day by day, the dismantling continues relentlessly, with each step reducing the value of the mill. "Our members are getting sick watching this happen," said Fortunato.

Arcelor's plans to close the Lackawanna mill are occurring against the backdrop of a widely supported effort by President Barack Obama to stimulate the nation's flat-lining economy with the $787 billion American Recovery and Reinvestment Act. But even as Obama is moving to counter the nation's economic free-fall, major corporations are moving in the opposite direction when it comes to maintaining employment and consumer demand. A recent survey showed 71% of CEOs expecting more layoffs in the coming six months.

Not only are they accelerating the pace of outsourcing to low-wage nations like China, but there have been several recent instances of corporations closing profitable plants in the United States and then refusing to sell them to other companies interested in keeping the plants open and retaining the current workforce.

"These jobs aren't coming back"

The Lackawanna mill isn't ArcelorMittal's only closure. ArcelorMittal is also shutting down its Hennepin, Ill., steel mill, even though other firms have expressed strong interest in buying that mill, reports USW Local 7367 president David York.

At a moment when unemployment around Hennepin—about 100 miles west of Chicago—has hit 10%, ArcelorMittal is preparing to discard the 285 USW members who have performed the hard work of steel production.

The plant has been consistently profitable, earning $48.4 million even in a recessionary year like 2008. Yet ArcelorMittal is intent on shipping one product line to low-wage Brazil and another to France. Moreover, ArcelorMittal has rebuffed a proposal by another major steel company to buy the Hennepin mill and keep it running.

The Hennepin workers have little prospect of finding jobs paying anywhere close to the $70,000 their old jobs averaged, including overtime and productivity bonuses, says York. Few family-supporting jobs are available nearby.

And ArcelorMittal's strategy is not unique. Last fall, the Cerberus private equity group, through its NewPage subsidiary, shut down a highly profitable, technologically advanced paper mill in Kimberly, Wisc. Cerberus is headed by John Snow, former Treasury secretary under George W. Bush; Dan Quayle, former vice president under George H.W. Bush; and Richard Feinberg, who personally raked in $330 million in compensation from Cerberus in 2007. USW Local 2-9 President Andy Nirschl speculates that Cerberus (the name is derived from the mythological dogs who guard the gates of Hades) essentially wanted to raise paper prices by reducing capacity, regardless of the human cost to 600 workers and their families.

"This wasn't like the usual scenario we've seen again and again," says Nirschl, "where a corporation moves jobs to Mexico or China to increase their profits by paying less than a dollar an hour. This was a case of a corporation taking a productive, profitable plant and closing it, refusing to sell it to anyone." The paper mill turned a profit of $66 million in 2007, says Nirschl. Four firms showed interest in buying the plant, but Cerberus and NewPage remained uninterested, frankly admitting that it had no plan at all to market the plant to another buyer.

Meanwhile, many major firms are adopting what can best be described as a "counter-stimulus" economic program, precisely following what Nirschl called "the usual scenario." The *New York Times* reported on a massive wave of job offshoring and wholesale divesting of product lines.

"These jobs aren't coming back," John E. Silvia, chief economist at Wachovia in Charlotte, N.C., told the *Times*. "A lot of production either isn't going to happen at all, or it's going to happen somewhere other than the United States. There are going to be fewer stores, fewer factories, and fewer financial services operations. Firms are making strategic decisions that they don't want to be in their businesses."

"The decimation of employment in legacy American brands such as General Motors is a trend that's likely to continue," said Robert E. Hall, an economist at Stanford University's Hoover Institution.

Productive Base Goes Out the Window

Mark Meinster, a representative of the United Electrical Workers (UE) international, said that this latest round of job destruction is simply an intensification of trends visible in recent decades, but made all the more galling because of the wanton closing of profitable plants at a time when good jobs are increasingly scarce. "We see this every day," said Meinster. For the past 20 years, you have everything from out-and-out trickery to private equity firms transferring debt from a money-losing operation to a profitable plant, and then shutting down the plant and stripping its assets. "Meanwhile, our productive capacity completely goes out the window."

Meinster helped to coordinate the December sit-down strike at Chicago's Republic Windows and Doors. Workers there faced both an employer secretly moving equipment to a new non-union plant in Iowa and the Bank of America—which received $20 billion in grants and $118 billion in loan guarantees from the bank bailout—cutting off the firm's line of credit, which, in turn, deprived workers of vacation and severance pay.

With the plant already closed, the workers decided to take over the plant, thereby taking control of Republic's valuable inventory and holding it hostage. The result: Bank of America re-opened the financial spigot, the workers were paid, an environmentally oriented firm bought the plant and will be rehiring the workers, and the sit-down achieved worldwide fame.

The Republic sit-down also inspired non-union workers, faced with a plant closing at the Colibri Group jewelry factory in East Providence, R.I., to stage a sit-in. The action resulted in 15 arrests while intensifying pressure on the firm's owner, the Founders' Group private-equity firm.

UE Western Regional President Carl Rosen, who played a leading role in backing the sit-down strike, noted that the action—both illegal and highly unusual in the United States—ignited enormous support, including from President Obama. "We made our message everybody's message," explained Rosen. "This economy is failing because workers cannot buy back what they are making. Corporations are being bailed out and workers are being sold out."

"We're willing to sell"

As a Luxembourg-based firm owned by an Indian-born billionaire living in London, ArcelorMittal is clearly following the "take the money and run" model of Anglo-American capitalism. This system is far harsher than the Western European model in which employers' incentives have been more influenced by social-democratic traditions and the ongoing strength of the labor movement.

In Lackawanna, ArcelorMittal's foot-dragging on a potential sale could soon mean the loss of 260 jobs. "Until yesterday [March 26], the company was not admitting that they even had heard of any interested buyers," said USW Local 2604 president Fortunato. But the forceful intervention of Sen. Chuck Schumer (D-NY) finally produced a meeting between ArcelorMittal's U.S. CEO James Ripley and one interested buyer.

"At this point, we don't know the results of the negotiations," Fortunato told *Dollars & Sense*, the frustration and anxiety evident in his voice. The outcome of the negotiations may depend on whether ArcelorMittal's decision to aggressively dismantle the steel operation has made purchasing the existing, hollowed-out plant and re-starting production far more difficult and costly than simply beginning production from scratch.

The involvement of members of the U.S. Congress at Lackawanna—as at Hennepin and Kimberly—has forced the corporations to claim that they were willing to sell the plants and retain jobs. But once the meetings were concluded, corporate interest in selling and saving the jobs of local workers rapidly melted away. For example, a Cerberus/NewPage official was asked recently whether the company had any plans in place to market the Kimberly plant. The response: "No."

Cooperation: A One-Way Street

Particularly frustrating for Local 2604 is the fact that the union made such extensive efforts to assist the corporation. It lobbied successfully for a two-thirds reduction in their electricity costs, lined up training grants, and supported reductions in sales- and property-tax rates for the corporation. "We as a union have done a lot to help the company. They've tried to tell us we're not competitive as a plant. If that's the case, why not sell us?"

Rather than being grateful for the union's efforts to lower its costs, ArcelorMittal instead changed its internal accounting procedures so that the Lackawanna plant actually booked a loss, by charging that plant more for shipping and supplies from other ArcelorMittal plants around the United States. In that way, ArcelorMittal aimed to evade New York's higher corporate taxes, Fortunato suspects. Until ArcelorMittal made that shift in accounting, the plant had been consistently showing a profit of about $6 million a month.

With annual wages typically running in the $40,000-to-$50,000 range, his members will have a hard time finding comparable-paying work. Fortunato believes the real unemployment rate in Lackawanna, near the similarly hard-hit industrial city of Buffalo, is about 25% to 30%. "Our guys will have to work two or three jobs to make what they earn here," he said.

The process of watching the Lackawanna mill being slowly dismantled, with custom-made parts being wrecked by being disassembled or simply scrapped, is difficult for the workers who invested their lives in the plant, says Fortunato. "Our guys are getting sick at what they're scrapping."

The steelworkers in Illinois also complain of the corporation's indifference to commitments by the public to subsidize ArcelorMittal. ArcelorMittal's decision to locate its U.S. headquarters in Chicago unleashed a flow of incentives, including $2 million in assistance for furnishing corporate offices.

At the Hennepin plant, the union's current contract commits ArcelorMittal to keeping the plant open through the agreement and maintaining its viability through adequate investment. The union has taken the case to arbitration.

What Benefits? What Retraining?

As major corporations continue to undermine the impact of Obama's stimulus efforts by slashing jobs, the conventional wisdom among leading economists and elected officials in both parties is that worker retraining is the best public-policy response. As the *New York Times* put it recently, "For decades, the government has reacted to downturns by handing out temporary unemployment insurance checks, relying upon the resumption of economic growth to restore the jobs lost. This time, the government needs to place a greater emphasis on retraining workers for other careers."

But this approach, while conveniently allowing elected officials to sidestep an uncomfortable confrontation with corporations' unilateral control over the fate of workers and communities, has little empirical support as a successful strategy for "adapting" to deindustrialization and the offshoring of jobs. As the supply of family-supporting jobs is reduced, workers are essentially losing at a game of musical chairs in which good jobs are disappearing and not being replaced. When displaced workers successfully complete retraining programs, they are generally unable to find jobs comparable in pay and benefits to the ones they lost.

"Out of a hundred laid-off workers," says *New York Times* economics writer Louis Uchitelle in his book *The Disposable American: Layoffs and Their Consequences*, "27 are making their old salary again, or more, and 73 are making less, or not working at all." But even if retraining were an effective strategy, the very politicians who tout it as a solution have been unwilling to fund training in a serious way. Funding for training has plummeted from $20 billion in 1979 to just $6 billion last year (in constant dollars), according to one expert cited by the *Times*. These cutbacks in funding would seem to indicate that leading politicians, especially in the Bush era, were never quite sincere in their willingness to match their proclaimed faith in the power of retraining with an equivalent level of funding.

Further, the traditional unemployment-compensation safety net has been shredded over the past four decades, reaching a much smaller percentage of workers than in past, less severe recessions. During the 1975 recession, unemployment compensation reached 75% of the jobless and thus was a significant factor in restoring consumer demand. But thanks to radical cuts in unemployment compensation eligibility rammed through by the Reagan administration, only 45% of the unemployed received any benefits during the much more severe recession of 1982-83. The National Association of Manufacturers was delighted with the cutbacks in eligibility, crowing that under the old rules, "there was no incentive to go back to work under that program."

By 2003, the number of unemployed workers eligible for benefits had fallen further from the 1982 level of 45% down to just 41%, according to the Ohio-based

---

Corporate Royalty Ignores Workers' Years of Loyalty

Corporations are often accused of having an imperious, Marie Antoinette-style attitude toward their workers, unaware and uncaring about their daily struggles to provide for their families.

Marie Antoinette, wife of Louis XVI, was informed that the poor of Paris were too poor to afford bread. Her infamous response: "Let them eat cake." She was later beheaded in 1793 during the French Revolution.

But in the case of ArcelorMittal, which is preparing to shut down steel mills in Hennepin, Ill. and Lackawanna, N.Y., the comparison to Marie Antoinette may not be much of an exaggeration. The workers and local communities have been bewildered by the corporation's commitment to closing the profitable mills despite offers from other firms that wanted to keep them open.

Meanwhile, corporate CEO Lakshmi Mittal lives in near-royal grandeur in London in a $125 million home right next to the posh Kensington Palace. Mittal's home was constructed by combining the former Russian and Egyptian embassies. The swimming pool is inlaid with jewels, and the estate includes a 20-car garage. Lakshmi Mittal has a personal fortune estimated at $25 billion.

For the wedding of his daughter Vanisha, who is also a member of the corporation's board of directors, Mittal shelled out $55 million. If you're wondering how even the super-rich could manage to spend such a sum on a wedding, it might help to know that the five-day celebration was capped by a party—at Versailles.

That's right—Versailles, the magnificent and legendary palace that King Louis XVI gave to his 19-year-old bride, Marie Antoinette, as a wedding present. *Plus ça change...*

group Public Policy Matters. While Obama's American Recovery and Reinvestment Act may begin to reverse some cutbacks in eligibility, it remains to be seen how widely these changes will positively affect the fates of the jobless.

Needless Job Losses

The toll of unemployment extends far beyond a drop in family income, access to health care, and a loss of self-esteem for the displaced worker. Peter Dreier, a political scientist at Occidental College, recently released a study showing that each 1% increase in the national U.S. unemployment rate produces an additional 47,000 deaths, with 26,000 of the fatalities cardiac-related, 1,200 due to suicides, and 831 due to homicides.

Given these grim realities about passively accepting the consequences of deindustrialization, coupled with growing resentment about the greed and malfeasance of Wall Street, the egregious damage to workers and communities imposed by firms like Cerberus and ArcelorMittal may raise corporate investment decisions to a high-profile political issue. Corporations are closing profitable, productive plants in the midst of a severe economic crisis, and then capriciously refusing to seriously consider selling the plants to keep them open.

This would be unthinkable in a number of Western European democracies like Germany and Sweden that have long required that corporations provide a compelling rationale for shutdowns to regional government labor-market bodies. Most other Western European nations offer workers and communities some degree of protection from the effects of shutdowns, although not as extensively as in Germany or Sweden, nor with the same degree of worker and community participation in decisions about the company's plans.

In the United States, the increasingly destructive impact of arbitrary corporate decisions to close plants amidst a severe economic crisis may finally unleash public demands to place corporations' conduct under democratic constraints. ❏

Sources: Roger Bybee, "Pulp Friction: A private equity firm's decision to shut down a profitable paper mill devastates a Wisconsin community," *In These Times*, Jan. 2009; Peter S. Goodman and Jack Healy, "Job Losses Hint at Vast Remaking of Economy," *New York Times*, Mar. 7, 2009; Matt Glynn, "ArcelorMittal says it's willing to sell Lackawanna plant," *Buffalo News*, Mar. 26, 2009; Stanley Reed, "Mittal & Son: An inside look at the dynasty that dominates steel," *BusinessWeek*, Apr. 16, 2007; New release, Northwestern University Medill News Service, Oct. 7, 2005; Making Steel.com, Feb. 21, 2007; Peter Dreier: "This Economy is a Real Killer," Huffington Post, Mar. 10, 2009, Barry Bluestone and Bennett Harrison, *The Deindustrialization of America: Plant Closings, Community Abandonment, and the Dismantling of Basic Industry* (NY: Basic Books, 1982); Lawrence Rothstein, *The Fight Against Plant Closings* (Auburn Books: Dover Mass. and London, 1986); Mark Richtel, "A Sea of Unwanted Imports, *New York Times*, Nov. 18, 2008; William K. Tabb, "Financialization Appropriation," *Z Magazine*, June 2008; William K. Tabb, "Four Crises of the Contemporary World Capitalist System," *Monthly Review*, October 2008; Vinaya Saksena, "15 arrested at EP rally," *Pawtucket Times*, Mar. 20, 2009.

Article 9.4

CREATING DECENT JOBS: THE ROLE OF UNIONS

BY JEANNETTE WICKS-LIM
January/February 2010

The turmoil of the current recession is deflecting attention from a longer-term challenge facing the U.S. economy: how to create decent jobs. Even before the recession, nearly two-thirds of U.S. jobs failed the "decent job" test—they paid too little to cover a small family's basic needs. Between now and 2016, the strongest job growth will be largely in low-pay occupations, according to Department of Labor projections. So barring any structural changes, the U.S. economy will be no better at producing jobs that can support a worker and his or her family at a very basic living standard in 2016 than it was in 2006.

Collective bargaining through labor unions could brighten this forecast, raising the quality of future jobs even if the economy continues to produce the same types of jobs. Bringing the unionized share of the U.S. workforce back up to around its level in the 1970s—admittedly no easy task—would lift an estimated 2.5 million additional jobs over the decent-job threshold in 2016.

A reasonable definition of a decent job is one with the minimum pay and benefits necessary to provide a healthy and safe standard of living for a small family. This benchmark is substantially above the U.S. Census Bureau's official poverty threshold, widely viewed as far too low. Based on very basic family budgets the Economic Policy Institute has developed, a decent job has to pay at least $17 an hour with health and retirement benefits, or $22 an hour without.

A recent Labor Department report examines trends through 2006 to predict the jobs picture in 2016. Here are the ten occupations slated to add the most jobs: orderlies and nursing/home-health aides; registered nurses; retail salespersons; customer service representatives; food preparation and serving workers; general office clerks; personal/home-care aides; postsecondary teachers; janitors; and accounting clerks. In only two—RNs and postsecondary teachers—do the majority of existing jobs meet the decent job standard. The other eight fall short.

It's no surprise, then, that an analysis of the complete 2016 jobs projection shows little change in the overall proportion of decent jobs. By my estimates, in 2016 some 35.2% of all jobs will meet this standard, barely changed from the 2006 figure of 34.8%. These projections pre-date the current recession, and so reveal a long-term problem likely to persist well after the economy revives.

If we cannot count on a raft of novel, more lucrative occupations in the next several years, then expanding the number of decent jobs will require improving the compensation of jobs in existing occupations. Unions enable workers to do exactly that. Suppose union representation rose by a meaningful amount, say ten percentage points to about 24%, by 2016. The proportion of decent jobs in 2016 would rise by an estimated 1.5 percentage points to 36.7%, representing an additional 2.5 million decent jobs. This is four times the projected increase if union representation levels remain the same.

But what about globalization? Forget about more decent jobs—how can U.S. workers stop decent jobs from disappearing in an increasingly integrated world economy with a large supply of labor that is cheaper than any in the United States, whether unionized or not?

One answer is to focus on jobs that are not off-shore-able and on sectors in which U.S.-based firms have a competitive edge. Clean energy initiatives fit the bill: they involve activities that can only be done locally such as retrofitting buildings. Plus, renewable energy is an area where U.S.-based firms' technological edge counts.

This strategy has another potential benefit for workers: greater international solidarity. By reducing the pressure they face from the global "race to the bottom," robust clean-energy job growth would better position U.S. workers to focus on cross-border organizing that can raise the floor of the global labor market.

What would it take to bring an additional 10% of U.S. workers into unions? That is the subject of another article. But the fact that the Employee Free Choice Act, which would make it easier for workers to join unions, is under serious consideration in Congress gives reason for hope. Any policies that expand opportunities for workers to join unions would help ensure that employment growth in the coming years produces decent jobs. ❏

Sources: *Creating Decent Jobs in the United States: The Role of Labor Unions and Collective Bargaining*, peri.umass.edu; Constance F. Citro and Robert T. Michael, eds., *Measuring Poverty: A New Approach*, National Academy Press, 1995; Arlene Dohm and Lyn Shniper, "Employment outlook 2006-2016: Occupational employment projections to 2016," *Monthly Labor Review*, Nov. 2007; David Howell, Dean Baker, Andrew Glyn, and John Schmitt, "Are Protective Labor Market Institutions at the Root of Unemployment? A Critical Review of the Evidence," *Capitalism and Society* 2(1), 2007; James Heckman, "Comments on 'Are Protective Labor Market Institutions at the Root of Unemployment? A Critical Review of the Evidence'," *Capitalism and Society* (2)1, 2007; James Lin and Jared Bernstein, What We Need To Get By, Economic Policy Institute, 2008.

Article 9.5

HARASSMENT: THE RECESSION'S HIDDEN BYPRODUCT

BY JANE SLAUGHTER
August 2009—Labor Notes

The recession numbers focus on the out of work, the nearly 10% of the workforce who are unemployed. Not counted in the stats of workplace misery are those still "lucky to have a job."

A *Labor Notes* survey this month found harassment in the workplace at unprecedented levels, with a sharp uptick since the recession began. It may be that a measurable chunk of the unemployed have been harassed out of their jobs, fired rather than laid off.

Union members report increases in verbal abuse, discipline including discharge, crackdowns on attendance, surveillance, hassling to work faster, forced overtime, and a concerted effort to get rid of older workers. "It's at a level that I have not seen equaled in my 20 years with the company," said Seattle UPS driver Dan Scott.

As a rule, recessions are a time for management to bear down in all sorts of ways, as the order to do more with less comes down the supervisory food chain.

Now, unions may be less prepared than ever to resist the harassment. In previous rounds of concessions, many surrendered work rules that had given workers flexibility or some say over their workday. Some took two-tier contracts that diluted solidarity on the job. And many older workers who knew—and defended—a less onerous workplace are gone.

Mark Bass, president of a Longshoremen's local in Mobile, Alabama, said foremen are rushing dockworkers and blackballing those who don't speed up.

"It has not always been this way," Bass added. "We had a large group of longshoremen retire who knew the longshoreman industry and had the union at heart. Now with the newcomers that don't know the history and the story that goes from one to the other, we are faced with the challenge of educating our people."

A recession is a hard time to do that. "At least I've got a job," many say. And union leaders feel pressed to save jobs, not job standards. Still, some locals are hearing members' desire for day-to-day respect.

Brown Dog Bites

UPS made its plans for the recession clear with a video shown to workers late last year. CEO Scott Davis warned that companies come out of a recession three ways: weakened, not at all, or leaner and stronger. UPS bosses—long expert at micromanagement—intend to take the third path.

Scott, the Seattle driver, said managers are putting on the brown uniform and riding along with drivers in record numbers. From an average of three or four rides per month, he says, they've increased to that many per week. They choose perfectly sorted trucks, open doors for drivers, walk really fast—everything to speed up on measurement day.

"You have to fight the urge to walk as fast as they're walking. If I had a nickel for every time he said, 'let's go, let's move it,'" Scott said. "It's perpetual chatter the whole day."

If the numbers at the end of a ride day are higher than on a regular day, that's proof the worker has been "stealing time."

UPS made $400 million in the first quarter of this year, despite recession blues. Telecommunications giant AT&T is even better off, pulling down $12.9 billion in 2008. But once the AT&T contract expired April 4, 2009, says Dan Coffin, a business agent with Communications Workers Local 1298 in Connecticut, suspensions skyrocketed.

Because AT&T has a two-tier contract, management is intent on getting rid of first-tier workers. Walt Cole is a case in point. He and other Local 1298 installers were transferred temporarily to U-Verse, which installs TV and Internet lines. They brought their higher pay and contract rights with them.

"Management hated paying us $30 an hour," said Cole. "We had things to say about work rules being violated, we filed grievances, we were a thorn in their side."

When Cole exercised his contractual right not to work on his day off—a right not shared by the U-Verse second-tier workers—he was suspended. When he ducked into a restaurant for carry-out and forgot to lock his truck, he was put on final warning for a year—despite a 10-year record of no discipline. Now he's fired. "When the contract expired," Cole said, "you could almost see them rubbing their hands and saying, 'This is the time to get rid of people.'"

Sick and Tired

Hospital workers, too, report that penalties are ratcheting up, with suspensions substituting for progressive discipline. A punitive approach to medication or practice errors has employees fearing for their jobs—and could pressure workers to cover up mistakes rather than report them.

Judy Sheridan-Gonzalez, a nurse at Montefiore Medical Center in New York, says nurses are harassed to punch out and finish their paperwork off the clock or to work through their meal breaks to finish on time.

At the University of Chicago Medical Center, the endowment took a hit from the stock market crash, and the president decided on 9% cuts to come through the recession leaner. Layoffs mean blue-collar and clerical workers are working short-handed and lunches are denied, according to Teamsters Local 743 rep J Burger.

Workers are bumping into new jobs where they're pressured to be up to speed within 30 days. Burger said many find the environment "so nasty and hostile they said they were leaving." The local managed to negotiate severance pay.

At the same time management created a new non-union position, "advanced pharmacy tech," that does bargaining unit work. "They're using them to snitch on people," said Burger. "We've gone from one or two grievances every two months to 15 outstanding."

Get the Old Guy

At the L'Oreal hair dye factory in New Jersey, chemical compounder Tom Walsh says management is targeting older workers to discipline and then fire. As a part-time business agent for RWDSU-UFCW Local 262, Walsh sees a similar crack-down across the wide variety of workplaces he represents.

"They write them up for every little thing, it doesn't matter how minor, and then it progresses to the next step till they've got their foot out the door," Walsh said.

Scott, the UPS steward, said each of the four drivers he represented in manage-ment reviews in two months' time has had more than 20 years.

At other UFCW-represented companies, workers on sick leave for more than thirteen weeks are fired. Walsh notes that lower managers are not immune: "They got rid of pretty much anybody over the age of 40 and brought in a bunch of young kids right out of college."

No Rolling Over

Some CWA locals at AT&T are using the fact that their contract is expired to take action against harassment. In Northern California, when two members of Local 9404 were disciplined for refusing overtime, the local called a grievance strike.

Overtime work isn't required, after a 2001 agreement stripped it from the con-tract. "We had to defend that," said President Carol Whichard, who remembers hating year after year of forced overtime as a technician in the field.

Whichard called the strike at 8:30 a.m., and by 10 a.m., 600 workers had driven their vehicles back to the garages and were holding picket signs. By 5 p.m. the disci-pline was removed. Workers were paid a half day.

In Southern California AT&T is cracking down on bathroom breaks for inside workers. Managers say "lost time" should equal no more than two hours a month—about five minutes a day. Local 9503 steward Wynter Hawk says managers keep track, letting workers know how much they've used. They call it "a courtesy."

"I say, 'Your courtesy is kind of like harassment,'" she said. "Do they think when they get to the end of the month people will just hold it?"

Stewards are considering a mass pee-in, in which all workers would clock out at the same time.

At UPS, Dan Scott, a member of Teamsters for a Democratic Union, counsels fellow drivers to fight speedup by following UPS's thick rulebook to a tee. "They encourage us to hydrate throughout the day, stretch after each break and at the beginning of the day, take all breaks and lunches in full," he said.

Scott believes the union's untapped resource is the customers.

"People relate to their driver, how hard they work," he said. "They are the face of the company. How much trouble would it be for a local or the international to run an ad saying, 'UPS is harassing your driver. Ask your driver what it's like.' Start that chatter." ❏

Article 9.6

SAME OUTPUT + FEWER HOURS = ECONOMIC CRISIS?

Today's economic crisis is less about the quantity of output than the distribution of income and leisure.

BY ALEJANDRO REUSS
September/October 2010

During the current crisis, real (inflation-adjusted) GDP per capita for the U.S. economy declined for six consecutive quarters. It has since increased for four consecutive quarters, though the figure for the second quarter of this year remains well below the pre-crisis peak. This might seem like an indication that real GDP per capita is a good measure of economic well-being. We're in a severe crisis, everyone thinks things are bad, and GDP is down. Even though GDP has been growing again recently, we're still not back to the level of prosperity before the crisis.

Consider, however, that real GDP per capita for the second quarter of 2010 was higher than it was in the second quarter of 2005—and in fact for every previous quarter in U.S. history. Now, hardly anyone thinks that things are better in the United States today, economically, than they were in 2005—or that, excepting about three years between 2005 and 2008, things are better economically now than they have ever been before. It can't be that our only problem is having fewer goods and services (as measured by real GDP per capita), since similar levels back in 2005 were not considered a disaster.

One alternative explanation is that the level of GDP does not matter as much as the change in GDP. Maybe we've gotten used to higher levels of affluence, and now miss the extra goods and services. At first blush, that doesn't seem like the issue

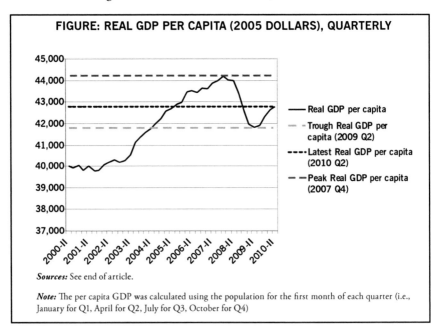

FIGURE: REAL GDP PER CAPITA (2005 DOLLARS), QUARTERLY

— Real GDP per capita
--- Trough Real GDP per capita (2009 Q2)
----Latest Real GDP per capita (2010 Q2)
— —Peak Real GDP per capita (2007 Q4)

Sources: See end of article.

Note: The per capita GDP was calculated using the population for the first month of each quarter (i.e., January for Q1, April for Q2, July for Q3, October for Q4)

either. The difference between the pre-crisis peak in real per capita GDP and even the trough of the recession is surprisingly small, less than 6%. Many people, counting on their incomes not only to remain at the higher (pre-crisis) level but to keep increasing, however, undoubtedly made spending decisions that are now difficult to reverse—like buying a house of a certain size and location or sending one's children to a certain college. Even if the decline in incomes were spread evenly across the population, for those living close to the limits of their means, it might be difficult to "scale back."

Of course, the impact of the recession has not fallen equally on everyone, and that is much closer to the crux of the problem. The unemployed have borne the brunt of the recession. The official number of unemployed people in the U.S. labor force dipped below 6.5 million just before the recession, in the first half of 2007. Today, it stands at nearly 15 million. For the unemployed themselves, this means not only a loss of income but also of an important source of personal identity and self-esteem, of a major part of their social lives, and of future career prospects. For millions of others, mass unemployment means increased insecurity and anxiety about their own futures.

Real U.S. GDP in 2009 was nearly the same as in 2006—just under $13 trillion. (The Bureau of Economic Analysis reports figures of $12.8806 trillion (in 2005 dollars) for 2009 and $12.9762 trillion for 2006). While these measures of total output produced are nearly identical, the figures for the number of workers employed and the number of work hours required to produce that output are strikingly different. In 2006, about 138.7 million workers (16 years and older) were employed, compared to only about 134.4 million in 2009. The total time spent at work, by all workers 16 and over, was 18 billion hours less in 2009 than in 2006.

Producing the same quantity of output in fewer hours means that labor productivity has increased. There are several possible causes: increased intensity or pace of work (or "speed up"), increased worker skill, improved production methods, or greater quantity or quality of tools used. During the current crisis, multiple factors may have been involved. High unemployment itself reduces workers' bargaining power. Employers know that there are plenty of unemployed workers who are desperate for a job. Meanwhile, workers who do have jobs are desperate to keep them. This makes it relatively easy for employers to push down wages or demand a faster pace of work. It may also be that workers' average skill level has increased, if for no other reason than that less-skilled workers are disproportionately represented among those laid off. There may also have been innovation in production methods and technology that explain part of this productivity increase.

Increased productivity is not intrinsically a bad thing. It can mean being able to produce more goods—and a higher "standard of living"—without additional work hours. Increases in productivity have been a major source of economic growth in capitalist economies. As long as demand for goods and services keeps pace with rising productive capacity, productivity increases generally fuel rising real output. In principle, increased productivity can also mean being able to produce the same amount of goods in fewer work hours. Fewer work hours can mean more leisure time and a higher quality of life.

The increase in productivity over the last few years, however, has not been matched by an increase in demand for goods. Overall demand now stands around the same level as a few years ago and at a significantly lower level than at the peak of the last boom, even as overall productive capacity has increased. The managers of capitalist enterprises do not set workers to produce goods just because they can, but because they (the managers) believe that this output can be sold at a profit. The decline in demand, then, means that some productive resources go unused—in the form of shuttered factories and idle machinery, and a dramatic decrease in employment and work hours.

This decline in work hours has not been distributed sensibly or equitably among all members of the population—in the form of a shorter regular working week, more vacation time, or an earlier retirement. Therefore, we have the strange paradox that today the U.S. economy produces about as much output (real goods and services) as it did in 2006, and requires billions fewer work hours to do so, which sounds like a good thing. And yet, as a result, we find ourselves in a disastrous crisis—millions have lost their jobs and main sources of income, while uncounted millions live in fear of a similar fate.

Karl Marx and Friedrich Engels wrote, over 150 years ago, that capitalist economies, in which goods are produced only if they can be sold, and will not be produced at all if they cannot be sold for a profit, had created a new kind of economic crisis: "an epidemic that, in all earlier epochs, would have seemed an absurdity—the epidemic of overproduction." Economic crises in previous societies, Marx and Engels understood, had been caused by an inadequate supply of goods, the results of drought, flood, war, and the like. In capitalist societies, for the first time in human history, there appeared crises as a result not of too little productive capacity, but of too much—"too much civilization, too much means of subsistence, too much industry, too much commerce."

Marx and Engels spoke of "too much means of subsistence, too much industry" with a sort of grim irony. They did not mean that there was really too much productive power compared to peoples' needs or wants, but compared to their buying power (what later economists termed "effective demand"). It is certainly questionable whether endlessly producing more goods and services is really the key to making us better off—as opposed to enjoying greater leisure time, a more pleasant environment, greater economic security, less economic inequality, greater autonomy at work, etc. However, there's no reason that the development of greater productive power must exact the enormous toll of human suffering that it can—and, very often, does—in a capitalist economy. ❑

Sources: Bureau of Labor Statistics, Labor Force Statistics (CPS), Table A-1, "Employment status of the civilian population by sex and age," www.bls.gov/webapps/legacy/cpsatab1.htm; Bureau of Labor Statistics, "Persons at work in agriculture and related and in nonagricultural industries by hours of work," 2006, ftp.bls.gov/pub/special.requests/lf/aa2006/aat19.txt; Bureau of Labor Statistics, "Persons at work in agriculture and related and in nonagricultural industries by hours of work," 2009, ftp.bls.gov/pub/special.requests/lf/aat19.txt; Bureau of Economic Analysis, Table 1.1.6. Real Gross Domestic Product, Chained Dollars (A) (Q), bea.gov/national/nipaweb/SelectTable.asp; Census Bureau, Table 1. "Monthly Population Estimates for the United States, April 1, 2000, to July 1, 2010," www.census.gov/popest/national/NA-EST2009-01.html; Karl Marx and Friedrich Engels, *The Communist Manifesto.*

Article 9.7

GREECE AS A DEMONSTRATION PROJECT

Will the Black Sheep Bite Back? Will the PIIGS? What about US?

BY MIKE-FRANK EPITROPOULOS
May/June 2010

There has been an avalanche of coverage on Greece's economic situation in the past few months. Most of the coverage rightly attempts to diagnose the underlying problems of Greece's government deficit and national debt, and how they might affect the value of the euro and the integrity of the eurozone. But, as anyone who has followed this story knows, Greece is not alone in this precarious situation. It is lumped into a group of EU countries that have been labeled the "PIIGS"—Portugal, Ireland, Italy, Greece, and Spain. Additionally, it is known that some of the other countries in this group have worse problems and are larger than Greece, which could have an even greater negative impact on the EU and the value of the euro. So, why the focus on Greece?

The Greek situation is both complicated and simple.

Greece has long had a bloated public sector that has employed disproportionate numbers of the population. This system has not operated on market or even traditional public sector principles, but rather on *rousféti*, or patronage. This means that there have typically been more civil servants employed than necessary, with shorter working hours and more lax conditions of service. All of these things have become targets for neoliberal reform around the world, as we are seeing harsh, IMF-style austerity measures once again being pushed as conditions on countries that find themselves in a bind.

Next, the Greek state has long been known as a bastion of corruption. In the financial press, Greece is often described as a leader in black-market economic activity. In 2006, under the conservative New Democracy (ND) government (recently voted out of office), Finance Minister Giorgos Alogoskoufis "redefined" the always-problematic measure of social and economic well-being, Gross Domestic Product (GDP), by essentially adding an estimate of Greece's well-known "black market" activities. In doing so, the government proudly announced that Greece and Greeks were 25% wealthier overnight! More importantly, the Greek government got on board with the global neoliberal program, catering to both domestic and foreign capital, and Washington.

Beyond this, Greece is at the top of the list in military spending as a percentage of GDP in the EU. At the same time, Greek teachers are next to last in salaries in the EU. In the past few years, riot police have beaten and tear-gassed teachers and students more frequently than any other groups. Both the ND and their competitors in Greece's two-party stranglehold, the Pan-Hellenic Socialist Movement (PASOK), have consistently been more in line with the neoliberal economic agenda and tougher in the social arena than their reputation in the West as the "black sheep" of Europe would suggest.

In December 2008, a police officer shot and killed 15-year-old Alexis Grigoropoulos in Athens. Since the shooting occurred in the Exarchia neighborhood of the capital, many identified the incident with the anarchists, for whom Exarchia is a traditional center of activity. The police's claims that the youth had attacked them, however, did not jibe with eyewitness accounts of the event. Greek society was outraged by the incident, and protests ensued across the country, lasting for weeks. The murder of Alexis was the spark that triggered the demonstrations and riots, but the causes were many and had been simmering under the surface of Greek daily life for a long time. Among those were the neoliberal policies of the ND government, such as the privatization of public services and cuts in social spending, in addition to police brutality, overt corruption and scandals, and poor job prospects and working conditions for youth, to name just a few.

While youth and students from universities down through the elementary schools took the lead in organizing and conducting the demonstrations—many of which caused significant property damage, leading to a backlash against the protesters in some circles—a broad spectrum of Athenian society, including left political parties, unions, parents, and immigrant groups also joined in. It was this broad-based anti-government and anti-brutality outpouring that acted as a check against abuse and misrepresentation of events by the mainstream media in Greece. When the media portrayals of events didn't correlate with what the people in the streets and their families directly experienced, the media's credibility suffered. Mainstream news organizations were forced to modify or retract earlier reports of events. The legitimacy of both the media and the government suffered as parents listened to their kids, and as people from all walks of life and classes condemned the killing of Alexis, the government crackdown on dissent, and the sensationalized and inaccurate media depictions of the protests.

In the past few years, Europe has faced serious riots not just in Greece, but also in France, England, and Italy. Government elites in both Europe and the United States have expressed overt concern about these uprisings, especially with the backdrop of the greatest economic downturn since the Great Depression. In France, President Nicolas Sarkozy backed down on education reforms, saying that, "We don't want a European May '68 in the middle of Christmas." Alluding to the increasing number of Greek youth who are relegated to low-wage, part-time, no-benefit jobs, he added, "...The slogan of the Greek students about 'the 600 euro generation' could easily catch on here."

For U.S. intelligence and security officials, Greece has long been a focus of attention, going back to the U.S. government's *de facto* support for Greece's military junta (1967-1974). Today, the United States views Greece as a centerpiece of "counterinsurgency" doctrine, especially with regard to suppressing leftist and anarchist forces. Among the more familiar tactics employed in such counterinsurgency efforts is infiltrating opposition groups with provocateurs. In the context of the December 2008 riots in Greece, Paul J. Watson of Prison Planet reported that

> police masquerading as anarchists were committing acts of wanton violence to inflame tensions and provide a pretext for a brutal crackdown on legitimate demonstrators protesting against police brutality and the mishandling of the economic crisis.

These are the kinds of tactics that lie at the heart of many counterinsurgency strategies, and can be expected as government responses to anti-authoritarian dissent, especially during a period of economic crisis. Recently, José Trabanco, an independent writer based in Mexico, reported in an article on the website of the Centre for Research on Globalization on official concerns about potential civil unrest in the United States, as elites begin to grasp the magnitude of the economic crisis. This may not square with recent positive economic news, but we should be just as wary of numbers and projections from the White House as we are from credit-rating agencies.

And this is the crux of why Greece is in the spotlight now.

Greeks, like other Europeans, have a history of bold protest, direct action, and civil disobedience. They have shown willingness to fight for their own class interests, time and again. And this current crisis is no different. It is fine that Greek Prime Minister George Papandreou, German Chancellor Angela Merkel, and even President Barack Obama pay lip service to cracking down on financial speculators and the big banks. But none of them has moved seriously to regulate, restrict, or punish them. In the United States, we bailed the banks out with taxpayer money. In Greece, the government is introducing punitive austerity measures on the working and middle classes to pay for the "accounting magic" that Wall Street consultants, like Goldman Sachs and JP Morgan, provided to the previous government.

Americans should arguably be *more* angry about the bailout of Wall Street than they already are. U.S. taxpayers are funding not only TARP and other corporate bailouts, but even the largesse of the Greek business and political elite. How? It was Goldman Sachs and J.P. Morgan that were hired to hide the magnitude of the Greek debt. Meanwhile, the executives on Wall Street continue to get paid spectacularly generous bonuses and serious financial regulatory reform is not currently on the radar in Washington. So it should also be clear is that these global bankers' actions have global consequences.

Why *shouldn't* we Americans feel slighted? Barack Obama won the presidency on the slogans of "Hope" and "Change," but the system continues to work for elites at the expense of ordinary people, here and abroad. On recent TV panel discussions in Greece, the mainstream political parties present the austerity measures as "necessary" and "responsible" solutions to a national problem. The government has even characterized the austerity drive as a "war effort," arguing that Greeks should rally together to help pay for the crisis and return to traditional, hard-working Greek ways. Some are even resorting to invoking Barack Obama's slogan of "Hope"!

Yet the government is trying to impose the costs of the crisis squarely on the worse-off. The Bank of Greece recently admitted that the lion's share of public revenues is collected from working- and middle-class households, while the rich and super-rich evade taxes. Meanwhile, it is precisely the working and middle classes that are targeted by the austerity measures. Besides that, austerity measures are arguably the *opposite* of what is needed during recessions and looming depressions.

The real issue, then, is *resistance*. The Greek unions and public have been striking and demonstrating against the austerity measures by stating in clear class terms that, "We are not sacrificing to pay interest to the leaders!" The mainstream and business media analyses of the crisis in Greece and the PIIGS have focused on the potential impact on the euro. Given the choice, however, between the currency (and the perpetrators that created the crisis) bearing the adjustment costs and pain, or the Greek people paying for those costs in prolonged unemployment and poverty, who can reasonably argue for the latter? There are indications that mainstream union leadership will compromise with the government on austerity measures that cut wages and benefits. The question is whether the traditionally protest-oriented and militant Greek people will meekly accept what they see as an unjust solution to this difficult problem.

The global banks, corrupt politicians, and financial speculators are engaging in real economic warfare by betting against Greece and the euro. As one PASOK parliamentarian, Mimis Androulakis, pointed out, "...the often-used casino analogy is faulty because a problem gambler at a casino is betting *his own* money, while these guys are using *other people's* money!"

Mainstream apologists argue that "there is no alternative" but for the working and middle classes to pay for the damage the banks and politicians have left. Greeks, however, are giving a class-conscious response. It's not that they don't want to deal with the crisis, but that many insist on taking it out of the hides of the perpetrators.

So why has the focus been on Greece? To see if public-relations media blitzes, calls to national unity and patriotism, along with fear and repression, can squelch a traditionally militant and class-conscious working class. The Greek workers have historically been willing to take to the streets to defend their own material interests— their pay, their education, their healthcare, and their pensions. They know that saying "Hope!" is not enough, especially when the perpetrators of the current global economic catastrophe continue to operate unencumbered and unscathed.

If the Greeks do not quietly accept the austerity measures, as the American public seems to be doing once again, there may have to be a more forceful *demonstration effect* in the form of violent confrontation between the people and the state. Whose state is it after all? And whose "mess" is this? The working people of Greece—or anywhere in the world, for that matter—should not have to pay and/ or suffer for the crimes and risks of global financial speculators.

Big business does not desire and will not stand for insubordination at this juncture. The non-productive paper economy that has taken control of the global economy is not sustainable for people or governments. There is frustration across the ideological spectrum around the world. The selfish interests that global financial capital is pursuing are naked. We must demand that these people be reined in. It is time for the "black sheep" to bite back. But then there are the PIIGS of Europe and us, here, in the United States. Let us recall the late Howard Zinn and ask: Which is worse at this moment in history—civil disobedience or civil *obedience*? ❑

Sources: Peter Boone and Simon Johnson, "Greece Saved For Now—Is Portugal Next?" Huffington Post, April 11, 2010, co-posted on BaselineScenario.com; Peter Boone and Simon Johnson, "Standing at Thermopylae: Greek Economic Situation Worsening Fast," Huffington Post, April 8, 2010; Peter Boone and Simon Johnson, "Greece And The Fatal Flaw In An IMF Rescue," Huffington Post, April 8, 2010; Kevin Gallagher, "The Tyranny of Bond Markets: Credit rating agencies helped cause the financial crisis—and as they rear their heads again, it's time for Obama to get tough." *The Guardian*, April 9, 2010; Diana Johnstone, "The Fall of Greece: Yes, It Really is a Capitalist Plot," CounterPunch, March 10, 2010; Paul Krugman, "Learning from Greece," *New York Times*, April 10, 2010; Landon Thomas, Jr., "As Greek Bond Rates Soar, Bankruptcy Looms," *New York Times*, April 6, 2010; Paul J. Watson, "CIA Preparing To Install Military Government In Greece?" PrisonPlanet.org; Robert Wielaard, "Europe Offers Greece 30 Billion Euros in Loans to Deal With Debt Crisis" Associated Press, April 11, 2010.

Article 9.8

FULL EMPLOYMENT AS THE ANSWER FOR EUROPE

BY ROBERT POLLIN
March/April 2011

The economic crisis in Western Europe today—including, most seriously, Greece, along with the other PIIGS economies, Portugal, Ireland, Italy, and Spain—is fundamentally a crisis of neoliberalism. Neoliberalism is the package of economic measures whose guiding principles include deregulation of financial markets and the displacement of full employment, in favor of inflation control, as the central concern of macroeconomic policy.

Financial market titans have always been the biggest cheerleaders for neoliberalism. Of course, they never appreciated having government regulators tell them how to run their businesses. Big-time financiers also know that inflation will almost always lower the value of the financial assets they own and manage for their clients. Even moderate inflation therefore cuts into their profits.

Neoliberal policies have been ascendant throughout the world since the mid-1970s, and especially since Margaret Thatcher took office in the United Kingdom in 1979 and Ronald Reagan became the U.S. president in 1980. Over this 35-year span, neoliberalism has produced persistent financial crises, along with greater unemployment and sharply rising inequality throughout the world. But there has also always been a solution to crises readily at hand within the neoliberal recipe book: to impose austerity on the majority of middle- and working-class families and the poor—squeezing their incomes and social services to find the funds to clean up the mess created by ruling elites.

The European crisis should be properly seen as marking yet another failure of neoliberalism. But this failure has not created a demand for a return to an economic policy framework centered around full employment. This is despite the fact that creating an economy with an abundance of decent employment opportunities—a "full-employment" economy, as we are using the term—is a matter of basic ethics. Without full employment, the fundamental notion of equal rights for everyone—the core idea emanating from the Enlightenment and elaborated upon in both the liberal and socialist traditions—faces insurmountable obstacles in practical implementation.

Rather, to date, the crisis has only elicited ever more severe variants on the standard neoliberal austerity policies, even with political parties in power that are socialist in name, as in Greece, Portugal, and Spain. The main justification for such measures is that—in the spirit of Margaret Thatcher's famous dictum of the late 1970s—"there is no alternative."

In fact, as the Greek experience is demonstrating every day, austerity policies are self-defeating. By imposing severe cuts in incomes for ordinary people, they reduce the ability of these people to spend money, which in turn means fewer sales for businesses. Without seeing strong market opportunities ahead of them, businesses then become less willing to invest in expanding their operations and, in particular, hiring new workers.

It is true that constructing a viable full-employment agenda is always a challenge, but most especially so out of the wreckage created by neoliberalism. To begin with, full employment is not simply a matter of everyone spending their days trying to scratch out a living. If that were our definition of full employment, austerity would work perfectly, by forcing people to become "employed"—doing anything to stave off destitution. A meaningful definition of full employment entails an abundance of decent jobs.

What kind of full-employment policy could work in Europe in the current globalized age? Such a policy should strive for an officially measured unemployment rate below 4%. To achieve this would entail channeling more public and private investments to those industries that both generate high levels of social benefit and also produce an abundance of jobs anchored to the domestic economy.

Two clear areas of interest here are energy and education. Building a clean-energy economy—i.e., an economy powered by solar power, wind, and other renewable energy sources and that achieves high levels of energy efficiency—is highly effective for generating jobs per euro of spending. And by a significant margin, education is the *most* effective source of domestic job-creation per euro of spending.

There are two reasons for this. The first is labor intensity, i.e. how much of the total increase in new spending is devoted to hiring workers as opposed to spending on buildings, machines, land, and energy itself. The second factor is relative domestic content per euro of overall spending—that is, how much of total spending remains within the Greek, Spanish, or other EU economies as opposed to leaking out of the domestic economy through imports and outsourcing. With education, by far the largest share of total spending is for people working directly in local communities.

With renewable energy and energy efficiency, the employment boost is not as high as with education, but it is far higher than spending the same amount of money on oil imports. Consider, for example, an economy-wide project to increase the energy efficiency of the country's existing stock of buildings. This would create major energy savings throughout each of the oil-importing EU economies, and each euro saved would be one that is not spent on imported oil.

Of course, investments in education and clean energy also deliver major social and environmental benefits. Spending on education is the foundation for building a productive economy over the long term. Investments in energy efficiency will both lower greenhouse gas emissions and save money for both businesses and consumers over time. These investments, along with those to build a renewable energy infrastructure, will also diminish the country's dependence on foreign oil.

Of course, one has to figure out how to pay for the full-employment economy. Technically speaking, the problem is actually simpler to solve than it appears. In the short term, the European Central Bank only has to emulate what Ben Bernanke has already undertaken at the Federal Reserve. Under the banner of "quantitative easing," the Fed is now buying up long-term U.S. Treasury bonds, as a way to lower long-term interest rates and stimulate private borrowing. If the ECB would undertake basically the same operation now on a scale similar to the Fed, the result would be a two-fold benefit. It would contribute toward lowering interest rates on long-term European government bonds. It would also remove a significant share of the toxic sovereign debt from the balance sheets of the private European banks.

This would allow the private banks to refocus on making loans for productive investments and job creation rather than obsessing over crisis management. But the banks would then also have to be prepared to make loans to support job creation, rather than hyper-speculation. This means that, along with full employment, Europe needs to establish a new, viable system of financial regulations, committed to supporting the productive economy and job creation. In short, the real solution to the crisis in Europe today is to abandon the failed policies of austerity and neoliberalism, and begin the long transition toward establishing full employment and financial stability as the centerpieces of economic renewal. ❑

The Short Run: No Union with That Latte
July/August 2008

Erik Forman, a Starbucks barista at the Mall of America in Minnesota, was illegally fired in July for "discussing a written warning with his peer." He recently got his job back after the National Labor Relations Board charged Starbucks with anti-union malfeasance, according to StarbucksUnion.org, the website of an IWW effort to unionize the coffee chain.

Starbucks is notorious for its anti-union stance: since 2004, the NLRB has charged the company with illegal union busting in three states. Starbucks claims to be a "socially responsible" company, but many of its employees may disagree. The average wage of a Starbucks barista is a meager $7.60 an hour, and only 40.9% of its workforce has the company health insurance. That makes Wal-Mart, which covers 47% of its employees, look good—not an easy feat.   —*Karina Wagnerman*

Article 9.9

THE BETRAYAL OF PUBLIC WORKERS

It's not only bad politics for states to use their budget crises to bust unions—it's bad economics.

BY ROBERT POLLIN AND JEFFREY THOMPSON
March 2011; The Nation

The Great Recession and its aftermath are entering a new phase in the United States, which could bring even more severe assaults on the living standards and basic rights of ordinary people than we have experienced thus far. This is because a wide swath of the country's policy- and opinion-making elite have singled out public sector workers—including schoolteachers, healthcare workers, police officers and firefighters—as well as their unions and even their pensions as deadweight burdens sapping the economy's vitality.

The Great Recession did blow a massive hole in state and municipal government finances, with tax receipts—including income, sales and property taxes—dropping sharply along with household incomes, spending and real estate values. Meanwhile, demand for public services, such as Medicaid and heating oil assistance, has risen as people's circumstances have worsened. But let's remember that the recession was caused by Wall Street hyper-speculation, not the pay scales of elementary school teachers or public hospital nurses.

Nonetheless, a rising chorus of commentators charge that public sector workers are overpaid relative to employees in comparable positions in the private sector. The fact that this claim is demonstrably false appears not to matter. Instead, the attacks are escalating. The most recent proposal gaining traction is to write new laws that would allow states to declare bankruptcy. This would let them rip up contracts with current public sector employees and walk away from their pension fund obligations. Only by declaring bankruptcy, Republican luminaries Jeb Bush and Newt Gingrich argued in the *Los Angeles Times*, will states be able to "reform their bloated, broken and underfunded pension systems for current and future workers."

But this charge is emanating not only from the Republican right; in a front-page story on January 20, the *New York Times* reported on a more general trend spreading across the country in which "policymakers are working behind the scenes to come up with a way to let states declare bankruptcy and get out from under crushing debts, including the pensions they have promised to retired public workers."

Considered together, state and local governments are the single largest employer in the US economy. They are also the country's most important providers of education, healthcare, public safety and other vital forms of social support. Meanwhile, the official unemployment rate is stuck at 9%—a more accurate figure is 16.1%—a full eighteen months after the recession was declared over. How have we reached the point where the dominant mantra is to dismantle rather than shore up state and local governments in their moment of crisis?

Why States Need Support During Recessions

The Wall Street–induced recession clobbered state and local government budgets. By 2009, state tax revenues had fallen by fully 13% relative to where they were in 2007, and they remained at that low level through most of last year. By comparison, revenues never fell by more than 6% in the 2001 recession. Even during the 1981–82 recession, the last time unemployment reached 9%, the decline in state tax revenues never exceeded 2%. These revenue losses, starting in 2008, when taken together with the increased demand for state services, produced an average annual budget gap in 2009–11 of $140 billion, or 21% of all state spending commitments.

Unlike the federal government, almost all state and local governments are legally prohibited from borrowing money to finance shortfalls in their day-to-day operating budgets. The state and local governments do borrow to finance their long-term investments in school buildings, roads, bridges, sewers, mass transit and other infrastructure projects. They have established a long record of reliability in repaying these debt obligations, even during the recession. Nevertheless, these governments invariably experience a squeeze in their operating budgets during recessions, no matter how well they have managed their finances during more favorable economic times.

If, in a recession, states and municipalities are forced to reduce their spending in line with their loss in tax revenues, this produces layoffs for government employees and loss of sales for government vendors. These cutbacks, in turn, will worsen conditions in the private market, discouraging private businesses from making new investments and hiring new employees. The net impact is to create a vicious cycle that deepens the recession.

As such, strictly as a means of countering the recession—on behalf of business interests as well as everyone else in the community—the logic of having the federal government providing stimulus funds to support state and local government spending levels is impeccable. The February 2009 Obama stimulus—the American Recovery and Reinvestment Act (ARRA)—along with supplemental funds for Medicaid, has provided significant support, covering about one-third of the total budget gap generated by the recession. But that leaves two-thirds to be filled by other means. ARRA funds have now run out, and the Republican-controlled House of Representatives will almost certainly block further funding.

In 2010 roughly another 15% of the budget gap was covered by twenty-nine states that raised taxes and fees-for-services. In general, raising taxes during a recession is not good policy. But if it must be done to help fill deepening budgetary holes, the sensible way to proceed is to focus these increases on wealthier households. Their ability to absorb such increases is obviously strongest, which means that, unlike other households, they are not likely to cut back on spending in response to the tax hikes. In fact, ten states—New York, Illinois, Connecticut, North Carolina, Wisconsin, Oregon, Hawaii, Vermont, Rhode Island and Delaware—have raised taxes progressively in some fashion.

Of course, the wealthy do not want to pay higher taxes. But during the economic expansion and Wall Street bubble years of 2002–07, the average incomes of the richest 1% of households rose by about 10% per year, more than three times that for all households. The richest 1% received fully 65% of all household income growth between 2002–07.

One charge against raising state taxes in a progressive way is that it will encourage the wealthy to pick up and leave the state. But research on this question shows that this has not happened. We can see why by considering, as a hypothetical example, the consequences of a 2% income tax increase on the wealthiest 5% of households in Massachusetts. This would mean that these households would now have $359,000 at their disposal after taxes rather than $370,000—hardly enough to affect spending patterns significantly for these households, much less induce them to relocate out of the state. At the same time, a tax increase such as this by itself will generate about $1.6 billion for the state to spend on education, healthcare and public safety.

But even with the ARRA stimulus funds and tax increases, states and municipalities have had to make sharp cuts in spending. More severe cuts will be coming this year, with the ARRA funds now gone. These include cuts that will reduce low-income children's or families' eligibility for health insurance; further cuts in medical, homecare and other services for low-income households, as well as in K–12 education and higher education; and layoffs and furloughs for employees. The proposed 2012 budgets include still deeper cuts in core areas of healthcare and education. In Arizona, the governor's budget would cut healthcare for 280,000 poor people and reduce state support for public universities by nearly 20%. In California, Governor Brown is proposing to bring spending on the University of California down to 1999 levels, when the system had 31% fewer students than it does today.

State and Local Government Workers Are Not Overpaid

Even if state and local government employees are not responsible for the budgetary problems that emerged out of the recession, are they nevertheless receiving bloated wage and benefits packages that are holding back the recovery? Since the recession began, there has been a steady stream of media stories making such claims. One widely cited 2009 Forbes cover article reported, "State and local government workers get paid an average of $25.30 an hour, which is 33% higher than the private sector's $19.... Throw in pensions and other benefits and the gap widens to 42%."

What figures such as these fail to reflect is that state and local government workers are older and substantially better educated than private-sector workers. Forbes is therefore comparing apples and oranges. As John Schmitt of the Center for Economic Policy Research recently showed, when state and local government employees are matched against private sector workers of the same age and educational levels, the public workers earn, on average, about 4% less than their private counterparts. Moreover, the results of Schmitt's apples-to-apples comparison are fully consistent with numerous studies examining this same question over the past twenty years. One has to suspect that the pundits who have overlooked these basic findings have chosen not to look.

State Pension Funds Are Not Collapsing

Not surprisingly, state and local government pension funds absorbed heavy losses in the 2008–09 Wall Street crisis, because roughly 60% of these pension fund assets were invested in corporate stocks. Between mid-2007 and mid-2009, the total value of these pension funds fell by nearly $900 billion.

This collapse in the pension funds' asset values has increased their unfunded liabilities—that is, the total amount of benefit payments owed over the next thirty years relative to the ability of the pension funds' portfolio to cover them. By how much? In reality, estimating the total level of unfunded liabilities entails considerable guesswork. One simply cannot know with certainty how many people will be receiving benefits over the next thirty years, nor—more to the point—how much money the pension funds' investments will be earning over this long time span. The severe instability of financial markets in the recent past further clouds the picture.

Thus, these estimates vary by huge amounts, depending on the presumed rate of return for the funds. The irony is that right-wing doomsayers in this debate, such as Grover Norquist, operate with an assumption that the fund managers will be able to earn returns only equal to the interest rates on riskless US Treasury securities. Under this assumption, the level of unfunded liabilities balloons to the widely reported figure of $3 trillion. To reach this conclusion, the doomsayers are effectively arguing that the collective performance of all the Wall Street fund managers—those paragons of free-market wizardry—will be so anemic over the next thirty years that the pension funds may as well just fire them and permanently park all their money in risk-free government bonds. It follows that the profits of private corporations over the next thirty years will also be either anemic or extremely unstable.

But it isn't necessary to delve seriously into this debate in order to assess the long-term viability of the public pension funds. A more basic consideration is that before the recession, states and municipalities consistently maintained outstanding records of managing their funds. In the 1990s the funds steadily accumulated reserves, such that by 2000, on average, they were carrying no unfunded liabilities at all. Even after the losses to the funds following the previous Wall Street crash of 2001, the unfunded share of total pension obligations was no more than around 10%. By comparison, the Government Accountability Office holds that to be fiscally sound, the unfunded share can be as high as 20% of the pension funds' total long-term obligations.

A few states are facing more serious problems, including New Jersey, Illinois and California. New Jersey is in the worst shape. But this is not because the state has been handing out profligate pensions to its retired employees. The average state pension in New Jersey pays out $39,500 per year. The problem is that over the past decade, the state has regularly paid into the system less than the amount agreed upon by the legislature and governor and stipulated in the annual budgets. For 2010 the state skipped its scheduled $3.1 billion payment altogether. However, even taking New Jersey's worst-case scenario, the state could still eliminate its unfunded pension fund liabilities—that is, begin running a 100% fully funded pension fund—if it increased the current allocation by about 4% of the total budget, leaving 96% of the state budget allocation unchanged.

In dollar terms, this worst-case scenario for New Jersey would require the state to come up with roughly $4 billion per year to cover its pension commitments in an overall budget in the range of $92 billion. Extracting this amount of money from other programs in the budget would certainly cause pain, especially when New

Jersey, like all other states, faces tight finances. But compare this worst-case scenario with the bankruptcy agenda being discussed throughout the country.

To begin with, seriously discussing a bankruptcy agenda will undermine the confidence of private investors in all state and municipal bonds—confidence that has been earned by state and municipal governments. When the markets begin to fear that states and municipalities are contemplating bankruptcy, this will drive up the interest rates that governments will have to pay to finance school buildings, infrastructure improvements and investments in the green economy.

Then, of course, there is the impact on the pensioners and their families. For the states and municipalities to walk away from their pension fund commitments would leave millions of public sector retirees facing major cuts in their living standards and their sense of security. Something few Americans understand is that roughly one-third of the 19 million state and local employees—i.e., those in fifteen states, including California, Texas and Massachusetts—are not eligible for Social Security and will depend exclusively on their pensions and personal savings in retirement. In addition, public sector pensions are not safeguarded by the federal Pension Benefit Guaranty Corporation. Unlike Wall Street banks, state pensioners will receive no bailout checks if the states choose to abrogate their pension fund agreements.

Getting Serious About Reforming State Finances

Of course, there are significant ways the public pension systems, as well as state and local finances more generally, can be improved. The simplest solution, frequently cited, involves "pension spiking"—that is, practices such as allowing workers to add hundreds of hours of overtime at the end of their careers to balloon their final year's pay and their pensions. This has produced serious additional costs to pension obligations in some states and municipalities, but it is still by no means a major factor in explaining states' current fiscal problems.

But states and municipalities also have to follow through on the steps they have taken to raise taxes on the wealthy households that are most able to pay. They should also broaden their sources of tax revenue by taxing services such as payments to lawyers, as well as by taxing items purchased over the Internet. And they have to stop giving out large tax breaks to corporations as inducements to locate in their state or municipality instead of neighboring locations. This kind of race to the bottom generates no net benefit to states and municipalities.

Finally, state and local governments are in the same boat as the federal government and private businesses in facing persistently rising healthcare costs. As was frequently noted during the healthcare debates over the past two years, the United States spends about twice as much per person on healthcare as other highly developed countries do, even though these other countries have universal coverage, longer life expectancies and generally healthier populations. These costs weigh heavily on the budgets of state and local governments, which finance a large share of Medicaid and health benefits for state employees. The problem is that we spend far more than other countries on medications, expensive procedures and especially insurance and administration. We also devote less attention to prevention. It remains to be seen how much the Obama healthcare reform law—the 2010 Patient Protection and Affordable Care Act—will remedy this situation. It is certainly the case that more must be done, especially in establishing effective controls on the drug and insurance industries.

These are some of the long-run measures that must be taken to bolster the financing of education, healthcare, public safety and other vital social services, as well as to support investments in infrastructure and the green economy. If states declare bankruptcy they will break their obligations to employees, vendors, pensioners and even bondholders, which will undermine the basic foundations of our economy. As we emerge, if only tentatively, from the wreckage of the Great Recession, this is precisely the moment we need to strengthen, not weaken, the standards of fairness governing our society. ❑

Chapter 10

LABOR
AND MILITARISM

Article 10.1

U.S. IMPERIALISM, MILITARISM, AND THE LABOR UNIONS

BY BILL FLETCHER, JR.
March 2005—WorkingUSA

Organized labor in the United States has had difficulty interacting with the global justice movement. Not only are they different labor-market sectors with different traditions, but more importantly they have no strategic agreement on the nature of the enemy. While there are many critical remarks one can make about the global justice movement, this article focuses on the challenges facing organized labor in addressing not simply the global justice movement, but also the issue of global justice as such by building international working-class solidarity.

To its credit, organized labor in the United States, beginning with the demonstrations against the World Trade Organization (WTO) in Seattle in 1999, paid greater attention to what can broadly be defined as global justice than it had in the past. The specific focus, however, was on trade-related issues and their impact on the United States The growing interest in the global justice movement—here defined as those forces united in their opposition to neoliberal globalization—stumbled when the American Federation of Labor-Congress of Industrial Organizations (AFL-CIO) chose to mount a campaign against China's inclusion in the World Trade Organization.

This campaign was a mistake in many ways, not the least of which is that the focus of the campaign was, by definition, on China as the problem. By any objective measure, China is not the principal problem in terms of global economic development. The problem is the WTO, the trade regime of which it is a part, and the manner in which global capitalism is restructuring itself. The current conditions of restructuring are actually the essence of what activists, scholars, and progressive labor leaders call "globalization," and are precisely the issue which U.S. organized labor had difficulty grasping. In fact, in the days leading up to the Seattle demonstrations, the notion of challenging the existence and *raison d'être* of the WTO was ridiculed by some in the AFL-CIO who held that because the international community needs a mechanism for regulating trade, the WTO is what is on the table, driving the global agenda, and therefore, we must reform it to serve the interests of working people.

That the WTO was a Clinton-supported project presented apparent difficulties for many union leaders, fearing that open opposition to the WTO would mean undercutting labor's alleged friend in the White House. Few people wanted to acknowledge that the WTO was as rotten in its essence as raw meat sitting in the hot sun. At the same time and in a more progressive direction, in 2000 the AFL-CIO and some of its affiliates became increasingly interested in educating their members to some of the issues of global justice.

Educating the American Working Class

Elements of what had been called the "Common Sense Economics Education Program" (originated in 1997) were utilized to create a union member-oriented "global fairness" education effort. There were two problems that emerged. First, as with Common Sense Economics, there was and remains a faltering commitment both within the AFL-CIO and most of its affiliates to developing a truly comprehensive educational program. This is something that haunts the U.S. trade union movement. The trade union movement often confuses *education* with *information provision* and does not realize what is necessary if we truly wish to interact with our members on the questions of ideas and analyses. Education is about critical reasoning skills, dialogue *plus* the addition of new information. It fundamentally concerns providing a frame of analysis in order for the "student" to look at an issue—or the world for that matter—and understand it in its complexities. An uneducated membership is a membership that cannot lead. It is a passive membership that will continue to view the union as a third-party institution, rather than its own organization.

The second problem with the program was that the conceptualization of global justice and global fairness by the trade union movement was somewhat restricted to concerning itself with the activities of multinational corporations and trade agreements. While this is certainly part of neoliberal globalization, it is not the whole story. This became much clearer in the aftermath of the Sept. 11, 2001 terrorist attacks and the response of most of U.S. organized labor to them. The Sept. 2001 terrorist attacks were in part a right-wing response, by Muslim clerical fascists, to U.S.-led globalization. In a sweeping analysis of America's quest for dominance in the post-World War II period, Noam Chomsky argues that the U.S. "imperial grand strategy" is an effort to gain global hegemony as the world's only superpower. However, Chomsky notes, the American pursuit of global dominance at any cost leads to the decline of U.S. legitimacy throughout the world, while it threatens the future of human survival.

The U.S. trade union movement had carried out no work to discuss with its members the broader features of globalization, including the military aspect of it. There was limited internal discussion regarding the nature of the various forms of opposition to neoliberal globalization. While rank-and-file members might hear or learn something about organized labor protesting neoliberal governments, there was little discussion of more reactionary responses to neoliberal globalization both within the United States—for example, the Oklahoma City bombing and the right-wing militia movements at home—and clerical fascism and anti-immigrant xenophobia overseas.

War and the Erosion of Worker Rights

In the wake of Sept. 11, the U.S. trade union movement tended to revert to a "World War II paradigm"—to the policy of assuming that national unity could be built in response to the crisis. The World War II paradigm suggests that organized labor in the United States decided during World War II that the fight against fascism trumped virtually everything else, including worker rights in the United States. Thus, during World War II, leaders of organized labor generally accepted the no-strike pledge and wage and price controls.

There was national unity against fascism. Organized labor expected that at war's end, capital would depart from its regular assortment of attacks on the working class, including strike-breaking and union-busting. The extent to which capital retreated from its aggressive stance against labor is another question, but that image was driven very intensely into the minds and memories of leaders of organized labor, including those who were not even active at that time.

Following the Sept. 11 attacks, there seemed to be the expectation on the part of many union leaders that Bush would change his spots, recognize the importance of workers and unions, and refrain from his vehemently anti-worker/anti-union approach toward domestic issues. Things did not work out that way. Instead, the Bush administration chose to wage a war on two fronts: against Iraq and against the American working class. As JoAnn Wypijewski asserted in 2003: "For workers, there is always a war at home and a war abroad, and it is not enough—it will never be enough—to oppose one without the other."

The deeper problem, however, is that the U.S. trade union movement is and has been caught in a ferocious bind. This labor movement, over the last 120 years, has developed within the context of a capitalist country with imperial ambitions that have now translated into foreign policy adventures. The U.S. government has justified the rise in foreign interventions in the name of patriotism and the defense of American lives and property. With certain exceptions, the official trade union movement, as opposed to, for example, the Industrial Workers of the World (IWW) that emerged a century ago, tended to support U.S. foreign policy almost without question. Labor's historic support for U.S. war policy is an expression of what it believes to be its patriotic duty. Organized labor's unconditional support for U.S. intervention has proved ineffective in building a strong labor movement because this approach fails to recognize the connection between U.S. foreign policy and the actions and plans of U.S. corporations.

During the Cold War, support for U.S. foreign policy was again seen as a patriotic step within much of organized labor. Yet, with the various actions of the AFL-CIO in particular, but most of organized labor generally, the credibility of U.S. organized labor came to be questioned internationally. First the AFL, and then later the AFL-CIO either created pro-Cold War institutions to support the struggle against "communism" and the Left, or it collaborated with institutions set up or supported by the U.S. government that had the same purpose. Among the most infamous of such institutions was the American Institute for Free Labor Development (AIFLD), which oversaw AFL-CIO-backed trade unionism in Latin America. Similar institutions were also established that worked in Europe, Africa, and Asia.

The work of the AFL-CIO's foreign labor operations usually targeted left-led worker organizations, including through the establishment of rival worker organizations (including unions) that were well resourced. This work also went beyond traditional trade union activity. To the extent to which the AFL-CIO—and I am using this to refer to the officialdom of U.S. organized labor, as most unions supported the policies of the institution known as the AFL-CIO—supported or assisted in coups and disruptions. The AFL-CIO's mischief includes disruption in British Guiana in 1964, Vietnam in the 1960s and 1970s, Chile in 1973, and South Africa during the 1980s. The AFL-CIO's actions were seen around the world, not as an expression of the interests of the U.S. working class, but rather as an arm of the U.S. state, thus the notion of the AFL–*CIA*—a reference often heard in the global South when speaking of the "old days."

To summarize at least part of the problem: organized labor in the United States has refused to acknowledge, or in the worst cases has supported, the imperial ambitions of the U.S. government. Labor's foreign policy legacy has left an inability to identify a broad front against neoliberal globalization within its ranks and the working class as a whole. The residue of labor's past has dampened progressive sentiment and encouraged right-wing populism. Organized labor's inconsistent response to neoliberal globalization has produced a strategic paralysis within the labor movement to respond to the specifics of U.S. foreign policy that undermines workers.

Corporate Neoliberalism and Global Justice

Organized labor has been unable to speak with rank-and-file members about how to understand the connections between U.S. foreign policy and the growth of the multinational corporations. Labor's inconsistency has produced a faint response to the North American Free Trade Agreement (NAFTA), the WTO, and other neoliberal policies of both the Clinton and Bush administrations. Moreover, organized labor has not resolutely responded to U.S. war policies. Ultimately, U.S. foreign military intervention has cleared the ground—as if with a political daisy cutter—of all opposition to neoliberal globalization.

In order for the union movement to understand the question of global justice, organized labor must understand the problem of *empire*, or if one prefers, *imperial ambitions*. There is simply no way to avoid it, particularly in today's world. The reason? One, the American working class resides in a world where corporate/government connections are strengthening, and with them increased repression of progressive and democratic forces in the face of unfolding globalization.

The linkage between corporations and government, at first glance, seems to contradict neoliberal ideology, but that is largely because neoliberal ideology exists to obscure the reality. As evident during the Reagan administration—a time when the world came to understand the growth of neoliberalism—the government more openly served the interests of the corporations. This was through various mechanisms, including but not limited to privatization schemes, tax policies, the choice of personnel for elected government positions and administrative positions, and expansion of the scope of international trade agreements.

In the aftermath of the Cold War, American imperial ambitions have become more blatant as the United States attempts to lead or direct the reorganization of global capitalism. That reorganization is linked not only to trade deals, but also to changes in the production process, wealth polarization on a global scale, and, as noted, repression to enforce neoliberal globalization. Understood more broadly, globalization comes to be seen as the reorganization of capitalism, accomplished through trade agreements *as well as* military operations. U.S. foreign policy, then, is not a side note to globalization, but the instrument for spreading, strengthening, and enforcing neoliberal globalization. If organized labor continues to ignore neoliberal globalization in its entirety, including U.S. foreign policy, the result will continue to produce ineffective, if not outright bad strategy that harms working people in the United States and throughout the world.

The period after World War II has been characterized—in the North, Midwest, and West Coast—as having relatively stable union/business relations. To be sure, there were periods of militant strikes and other upsurges, but the record demonstrates that unions were largely accepted as part of the scene. Labor activist and critic Stan Weir demonstrates that workers have constantly engaged in rank-and-file action, in most cases against the practices of employers and business unions. Unions in the U.S. South and Southwest, of course, were never accepted, and contrast with this picture of labor/capital compromise that is now undermined. Nevertheless, labor unions played a major role in the Democratic Party at both the national and local level, although in general they functioned more like interest-group trade associations than representatives of a workers' movement. In the international realm, particularly during the height of the Cold War, organized labor in the United States was useful to the American government, and to U.S. capital as well, in opposing left-wing labor movements around the world. After all, the AFL-CIO had labor credentials.

Social peace on the basis of some level of a *modus vivendi* between capital and organized labor was needed not only in the United States, but also around the world. This largely reflected the demands of the post–World War II period and the Cold War. The immediate need for reconstruction in the aftermath of the war, and the prospect of competition with the then-Soviet Union, as well as the rise of domestic left-wing forces in various countries, have driven capital and its allies in government toward two simultaneous approaches. One, crush domestic dissent—including in the United States (such as the creation of "Red Clauses" that had to be inserted into union constitutions prohibiting "communists" from attaining or retaining union office, as well as the expulsion of unions representing more than one million workers from the Congress of Industrial Organizations)—via the mechanism of "anticommunism." Thus, opposition forces that seemed to push the limits on capitalist democracy were challenged as being allegedly subversive, and therefore subject to repression.

The second approach was one of accommodation with the official trade union movement, and to some extent, their cooptation into some sections of the state apparatus. This approach of semi-accommodation was not directed at the official trade union movement alone, but toward most of the working class. The aim was to win it away from any appeal of working-class radicalism. The drive toward some semblance of social peace was also advanced by sections of capital that recognized that trade unions were useful in terms of keeping other sections of capital "honest," so to speak, that is, keeping wages out of capitalist competition. That day is gone. We should have no illusions. The capital–working class compromise is in tatters. The union movement is as useless to capital and the U.S. state as a bicycle is to a fish, to borrow from an old feminist expression.

Here, however, is the challenge: when one has built a labor movement on the basis of an incorrect assessment of reality, and based on the provision of incomplete and often inaccurate information to its members and supporters, it is problematic to shift gears. How does one correct the inaccuracies? How does one explain ways to build new alliances, such as with the so-called "Teamsters and Turtles"? How does one explain that those once condemned overseas a decade or more ago must now be embraced, whereas those once supported have often turned out to be our staunchest opponents? How does one explain U.S. capital's unpatriotic stance in abandoning the American worker, and policies of naked aggression and implied genocide that this same U.S. capital encourages in U.S. foreign policy?

How does one respond to questions continuously raised during the delivery of the AFL-CIO's *Common Sense Economics* education program of the 1990s? Participants would respond very favorably to the trainings and to the workshops themselves, but they would inevitably ask the following: *"Can we get more for this?"* That is a great question, and one that an educator always wants to hear. They would also ask: *"Why did we not know this before?"* The answer to that latter question goes to the heart of the history and culture of organized labor in the United States.

U.S. Military Intervention and Working-Class Patriotism

What is needed within U.S. organized labor is an understanding of how other trade union movements outside of the United States (and other social movements more generally) understand the operations of U.S. foreign policy and its implications for workers on a global scale. This is a very difficult discussion because it runs up against the assumptions upon which the U.S. trade union movement has been built. It is an uncomfortable discussion because it also challenges the way organized labor thinks of itself and how labor thinks it is viewed overseas. Nevertheless, a discussion of labor's troubled relationship with U.S. foreign policy is a discussion that must take place, without which there will be no international solidarity.

The second point is that the union movement must fuse the discussion of global justice—with a critique of multinational corporations, the U.S. imperial state, and a critical examination of American foreign policy. Such a discussion is especially difficult because it forces an examination of the manner in which the conception of patriotism has been manipulated by both capital and political leaders to advance their unsavory business. Such a discussion also compels a reexamination of how labor has been so often seduced by appeals to patriotism.

Let us look, for instance, at the U.S. intervention in Iraq. The American people were sold a bill of goods. The allegations of weapons of mass destruction and imminent threats were fabrications, pure and simple, by the U.S. government's own admission. The desire to invade Iraq dates back at least to 1991 when differences emerged in the context of the Gulf War over whether the United States should take the war to Baghdad and overthrow Saddam Hussein. Those differences simmered, and some conservatives began shortly thereafter to envision the resolution of the Saddam Hussein question, so to speak. Iraq became a virtual obsession among conservative hawks that made their way to leadership positions in the George W. Bush White House.

Supporters of U.S. invasion of Iraq included individuals who went on to help form the Project for a New American Century, a conservative think-tank which advanced a proposal for a more aggressive U.S. foreign policy. The George W. Bush administration adopted this obsession with Iraq, and it has subsequently been revealed in testimony by Richard A. Clarke that immediately following Sept. 11, 2001, the search was on for an alleged Iraqi connection, even though intelligence sources demonstrated no evidence.

The U.S. Labor Movement and the Iraq War

Although the AFL-CIO raised questions about the war somewhat late in the game, once the war started the federation felt compelled to issue a statement supporting the troops, and by implication, supporting the war. The AFL-CIO statement implied that supporting the troops was identified with workers' patriotic duty. In a cover letter on March 20, 2003, John Sweeney, the AFL-CIO's president, said: "When our nation is at war I strongly believe that we need to come together in support of our troops on the front lines." In all fairness, it should be stated that Sweeney did criticize "President Bush's insistence on military action rather than further diplomatic efforts" and there were, in effect, two statements (see below). One was a cover letter, while the other was the official statement. The different tone reflects the struggle over the message, particularly given the politics of the Bush era. The contradictory tone of the AFL-CIO is reflected in the statement on March 20, 2003:

> History will judge whether the actions taken by the United States will be seen as just and necessary. And Americans will judge if the foreign policy of the Bush administration is one that keeps the United States more secure in a dangerous world. While our fellow citizens are in harms' way, we are united in support of them and their families.

Yet on the very same day, John Sweeney noted in his cover letter "On the War with Iraq" that:

> The AFL-CIO stands firmly behind our troops. These brave men and women are America's best. The Iraqi regime is a brutal dictatorship that is a threat to its neighbors and its own citizens. We support fully the goal of ridding Iraq of weapons of mass destruction. . . . Now that a decision has been made, we are unequivocal in our support of our country and America's men and women on the front lines as well as their families here at home.

For the Bush administration to suggest—and for the U.S. trade union movement to implicitly accept—that Americans in opposition to the war do not support the troops is the height of insult. The notion that opponents of the war should be silent because the troops have already been deployed is ludicrous.

Opponents of the U.S. military intervention in Iraq have supported the troops by stating that they should be brought home. The U.S.-led invasion of Iraq violated international law by launching an assault on a sovereign nation that demonstrated no evidence of presenting a threat to its neighbors, let alone to the United States. International law and precedent only recognizes the notion of preemptive strike when there is a provable, imminent military threat, which was not the case in Iraq. Instead, a sham case for aggression was established. To borrow from the terminology used by former Marine Corps general and two-time Medal of Honor winner, Smedley Butler, "the U.S. military thus is used as a gang by the powers-that-be." Yet the trade union movement has been all-too-cautious about calling things as they are. Can we look forward to the day when our movement will even entertain a discussion in which today's version of General Butler's warning is heard? Consider General Butler's own words from over 60 years ago:

> War is just a racket. A racket is best described, I believe, as something that is not what it seems to the majority of people. Only a small inside group knows what it is about. It is conducted for the benefit of the very few at the expense of the masses. . . . I helped make Mexico, especially Tampico, safe for American oil interests in 1914. I helped make Haiti and Cuba a decent place for the National City Bank boys to collect revenues in. I helped in the raping of half a dozen Central American republics for the benefits of Wall Street. The record of racketeering is long. I helped purify Nicaragua for the international banking house of Brown Brothers in 1909–1912 (where have I heard that name before?). I brought light to the Dominican Republic for American sugar interests in 1916. In China I helped to see to it that Standard Oil went its way unmolested.

Organized labor in the United States has been held in check by its interpretation of patriotism and by its failure to critically evaluate U.S. foreign policy. Thus, we have on the one hand the surprise and support that greeted AFL-CIO President John Sweeney at the 2000 International Confederation of Free Trade Unions (ICFTU) World Congress in Durban, South Africa with his strong denunciation of neoliberal globalization, contrasted with the general inability or unwillingness of organized labor in the United States to speak with union members about the nature of U.S. foreign policy, not to mention the difference between patriotism versus culpability in a crime.

Solidarity and Shared Objectives

Is there any hope? The answer is "yes," but it depends entirely on the willingness and ability of the U.S. trade union movement to cross a line into what has hitherto been a forbidden zone for U.S. trade unionism. This forbidden zone is a political space where the U.S. trade union movement begins to look at the interconnections among multinational corporations, U.S. capital, and U.S. foreign policy. It is a space where labor begins to question the motives and actions of the U.S. government, particularly the role of the U.S. government in crushing progressive social movements around the world. It is a space where labor dares to ask whether there is a role the U.S. trade union movement can play, not simply in a partnership with unions in other countries. The U.S. trade union movement must seek to be a champion of *consistent democracy*, both at home and abroad. Consistent democracy, *the demand for obliteration of privilege*, is the real core of a genuine global justice movement. And that global justice movement desperately needs organized labor advancing a program of international *solidarity* against neoliberal globalization.

It is worth concluding this essay with a note on the concept of solidarity. Some unions no longer use the word solidarity—whether with respect to domestic or international working-class struggles. Union leaders apparently believe that it is antiquated and unrecognized by their memberships, and therefore should be dropped from trade union lexicon in favor of the word *unity*. Although there is certainly no problem with the word unity, expunging the word solidarity is a major mistake.

Solidarity is something akin to unity but by no means conveys the equivalent. Unity often assumes a similar context or environment. The beauty of the word and concept of solidarity is that it suggests the active bridging of the gap between the *known* and the *unfamiliar*. In that sense, solidarity is a clear step toward a higher level of unity. Some may think of solidarity as a rhetorical exercise. The late leader of Mozambique, Samora Machel, put it best: "Solidarity is not an act of charity, but mutual support in pursuit of shared objectives."

Solidarity is the process of bridging that gap with the unfamiliar—whether on the basis of geography, industry, race, ethnicity, or gender, to name a few. Solidarity is a process of building a linkage where one does not exist; a linkage tied to a common project or opposition to a common enemy. Cross-border solidarity develops when there is mutual respect and no sense of one domination, privilege, or elitism by the outsiders. Solidarity means a coming together of partners—voluntarily—but with shared objectives, as suggested by President Machel.

Thus, global unionism does not or should not be seen as resulting from the expansion of U.S.-based so-called "international unions," but rather by creating a new international partnership of workers. The initial developments of U.S.-based international unions nearly always contained a bias in favor of the American perspective. A genuine, global unionism, and its corresponding institutions, cannot afford to have such a bias. International working-class solidarity may result in a reformation of existing international bodies, and/or it may result in the creation of new bodies. In either case, this solidarity must represent a voluntary coming together, rather than the imposition of *unity* on someone by someone else who thinks they know better. That is not solidarity, but rather imperial arrogance. Thus, when thinking about renewed trade unionism and global justice, the concept of genuine solidarity must be at the core. ❏

Sources: AFL-CIO, *Common Sense Economics*, www.aflcio.org/issuespolitics/education/, 2004; Smedley Butler, "On Interventionism," excerpt from a speech delivered in 1933 by Major General Smedley Butler, USMC, www.fas.org/man/smedley.htm; Daniel J.Cantor and Juliet B. Schor,

Tunnel Vision: Labor, the World Economy and Central America, South End Press, 1987; Noam Chomsky, *Hegemony or Survival: America's Quest for Global Dominance*, Henry Holt and Company 2003; Richard A. Clarke, *Against All Enemies: Inside America's War on Terror*, Free Press, 2004; Nelson Lichtenstein, *Labor's War at Home: The CIO in World War II*. Temple University Press, 2003; Samora Machel, *Samora Machel: An African Revolutionary, Selected Speeches and Writings*, St. Martin's Press, 1985; Beth Sims, *Workers of the World Undermined: American Labor's Role in U.S. Foreign Policy*, South End Press, 1991; John Sweeney, "AFL-CIO statement on the war in Iraq to National and International Unions, State Federations and Central Labor Councils, Trade and Industrial Departments, and Allied Organizations," aflcio.org, March 20, 2003; John Sweeney 2003, "On the war with Iraq," aflcio.org, March 20, 2003; Gore Vidal, *Perpetual War for Perpetual Peace: How We Got to Be So Hated*, Thunder's Mouth Press, 2002; Stan Weir, *Singlejack Solidarity*, ed. George Lipsitz. University of Minnesota Press, 2004; JoAnn Wypijewski, "History is Not Frozen in the Past: Labor in the Dawn of Empire," *Counterpunch*, May 10, 2003; Michael D. Yates, *Naming the System: Inequality and Work in the Global Economy*, Monthly Review Press, 2003.

The Short Run: Don't Work for Halliburton
July/August 2005

CorpWatch released its alternative annual report on Halliburton in time for the corporation's shareholder meeting in Houston this May. Halliburton, including its subsidiary Kellogg Brown & Root (KBR), is, of course, one of the big winners in the contest for prized Iraq reconstruction contracts, and CEO David Lesar is no doubt touting the company's 2004 revenues of over $20 billion. But as CorpWatch points out, Halliburton currently faces federal investigations by the F.B.I., the Securities and Exchange Commission, and the Department of Justice; a class action suit by former employees alleging systematic accounting fraud; and two suits brought by families of Halliburton employees killed in Iraq, alleging the company misrepresented the risks of the jobs and intentionally endangered employees. And the company "still hasn't repaid the $212.3 million dollars the Defense Contract Audit Agency says Halliburton overcharged for fuel transportation in Iraq."

[Continued on p. 386...]

Article 10.2

YOUTH OF COLOR RESIST MILITARY RECRUITING

BY ANISHA DESAI AND MARYAM ROBERTS
July/August 2009

In 2006, high school senior Stephanie Hoang started working with Better Alternatives for Youth—Peace (BAYPeace), educating her peers about the potential risks of joining the military and helping to build alternative education and employment opportunities. For Hoang, her truth-in-recruitment work is more than just an internship. "It's my peers being affected. [Recruiters] are looking at me and thinking that I'm the person they want in the military."

More than just looking at Hoang and her peers, military recruiters today have unprecedented access to students and youth, particularly in poor neighborhoods. "There are generally more army recruiters on campus than college counselors," explains Elmer Roldan, fundraising director at Community Coalition in South Central Los Angeles, "and a more aggressive strategy to militarize them than to prepare them for college." He notes that recruiters target the best and brightest students, particularly young women.

In spite of this access, the number of recruits rose only slightly between 2005 and 2007, and the share of Black and Latino recruits fell. Community organizations including BAY-Peace and Community Coalition contributed to this drop-off through their truth-in-recruitment work. As Ann Lennon of the Carolina American Friends Service Committee (AFSC) explains, "The military sometimes makes promises that it can't keep; it's important to know which ones they can." AFSC put together a series of questions potential recruits can ask to help them separate myth from fact in areas such as job training, funds for education, and post-traumatic stress disorder and other potential consequences of combat.

But in 2008, as the economic crisis took a firm hold, recruitment numbers began to rise. "Jobs with stability are rarities," Lennon explains. "Options are narrowing and we have people that may have been in the work force that are now thinking about going into the military." In 2008, 185,000 men and women signed up for military service —the highest number since 2003. Many of the new recruits come from the groups hardest hit by the crisis. The National Priorities Project (NPP) report on FY2008 Army recruiting reveals that with unemployment climbing to 7.6% last year—and to 12.6% in the Black community—the steepest climb in recruiting came from lower-middle-class neighborhoods with median incomes in the $40,000 range. Black recruits account for over 95% of the increase over 2007 in overall Army recruitment numbers. Black and Native American women were recruited at high rates: around a quarter of recruits from these groups were women, compared to only about 14% of white recruits.

Amid ongoing economic instability, community and peace groups are working to build alternative opportunities. The Carolina AFSC, in alliance with green-economy groups, is developing sustainable training and employment opportunities.

"People need to know what all of their options are," says Lennon. "We have examples of people that have created their own jobs and economies."

Community Coalition works with students in the New World Foundation's Civic Opportunities Initiative Network (COIN) pilot program. Through COIN, youth leaders will be mentored and paid to do social justice organizing. This grant will keep talented students in their communities, working to create new opportunities for their peers.

Suzanne Smith, former research director at NPP, notes that carrying on two wars is "draining resources from other areas." The solution she proposes "is to shrink our global [military] footprint." The economic crisis provides the perfect moment to start redirecting funds away from unsustainable military solutions and into the areas that community-based organizations have identified as priorities: education, health support for veterans, community-based solutions to violence and militarism, and economic development to create economic opportunities outside the military. ❏

Sources: National Priorities Project, "Army Recruitment in FY 2008: A Look at Age, Race, Income, and Education of New Soldiers," nationalpriorities. org; Better Alternatives for Youth-Peace, baypeace.org; Community Coalition, cocosouthla.org; American Friends Service Committee, afsc.org; North Carolina Choices for Youth, ncchoicesforyouth.org.

[...continued from p. 384.]

The Short Run: Don't Work for Halliburton
July/August 2005

Halliburton's business activities may be fraudulent, but its treatment of injured employees is downright criminal. While on a lunch break last December at a base near Mosul, Iraq, construction worker Mark Baltazar fell victim to one of the most deadly bombing attacks to date. After being deemed healthy enough to continue work in Iraq by KBR medics, Baltazar was forced to quit to seek appropriate treatment back home. According to journalist David Phinney reporting on CommonDreams.org, "Because he worked for Halliburton's KBR, which uses Cayman Island subsidiaries to employ 70% of its workers, Baltazar is not eligible for state unemployment insurance." He's struggling to get by on the $368 disability check he receives every two weeks and has been denied the $1,000 a week he is owed under the Defense Base Act for his injuries. Meanwhile, he suffers from blurred vision and post-traumatic stress disorder and is unable to work. Other KBR employees injured in Iraq have reported similar treatment by the company.   —*Michael Rebne*

Article 10.3

IRAQ'S WORKERS STRIKE TO KEEP THEIR OIL

BY DAVID BACON
September/October 2007

The Bush administration has no love for unions anywhere, but in Iraq it has a special reason for hating them. They are the main opposition to the occupation's economic agenda, and the biggest obstacle to that agenda's centerpiece—the privatization of Iraq's oil. At the same time, unions have become the only force in Iraq trying to maintain at least a survival living standard for the millions of Iraqis who still have to earn a living somehow in the middle of the now four-year-old war.

This summer [2007], Iraqi popular anger over starvation incomes and oil rip-offs boiled over. On Monday, June 4, the largest and strongest of Iraq's unions, the Iraqi Federation of Oil Unions (IFOU), launched a strike to underline its call for keeping oil in public hands, and to force the government to live up to its economic promises. Workers on the pipelines that carry oil from the rigs in the south to Baghdad's big refinery stopped work.

This was a very limited job action which still allowed the Iraqi economy to function. Nonetheless, Iraqi Prime Minister Nouri al-Maliki responded by calling out the army and surrounding the strikers at Sheiba, near Basra. Then he issued arrest warrants for the union's leaders. On June 6, the union decided to postpone the strike plans for five more days. Facing the possibility that a renewed strike could escalate into shutdowns on the rigs themselves, or even the cutoff of oil exports, the source of the income stream that keeps his regime in power, Maliki blinked. He agreed to the union's principal demand—that implementation of the oil law be delayed until October, while the union gets a chance to pose objections and propose alternatives.

This will undoubtedly get Maliki in trouble in Washington, where his government will be accused of weakness, incompetence, and a failure to move on the oil law, one of the key political benchmarks it is under pressure to achieve. In Iraq, however, Maliki faces a fact that U.S. policymakers refuse to recognize—the oil industry is a symbol of Iraqi sovereignty and nationalism. Handing control to foreign companies is an extremely unpopular idea.

Some of the oil workers' demands reflect the desperate situation of workers under the occupation. They want their employer—the government's oil ministry—to pay for wage increases and promised vacations, and give permanent status to thousands of temporary employees. In a country where housing has been destroyed on a massive scale and workers often live under primitive conditions in dilapidated structures, the union wants the government to turn over land for building homes. Since 2003, the Oil Institute, a national technical training college for the industry's workers and technicians, has miraculously continued holding classes and training technicians. Yet the ministry won't give work to graduates, despite the war-torn industry's desperate need for skilled labor. The union demands jobs and a future for these young people.

Fighting for these demands makes the union popular, and enhances its nationalist credentials. Iraqis see it defending the interests of the millions of workers who have to make a living and keep food on the table for their families. On the other hand, the U.S. authorities, which imposed a series of low-wage laws at the beginning of the occupation, look to ordinary Iraqis like an enemy bent on enforcing poverty.

But one demand overshadows even these basic needs—renegotiation of the oil law that would turn the industry itself over to foreign corporations. And it is this demand that has brought out even the U.S. fighter jets, which have circled and buzzed over the strikers' demonstrations. In Iraq, the hostile maneuvering of military aircraft is not an idle threat to the people below. This standoff reflects a long history of actions in Iraq, by both the Iraqi government and the U.S. occupation administration, to suppress union activity.

Iraq has a long labor history. Union activists, banned and jailed under the British and its puppet monarchy, organized a labor movement that was the admiration of the Arab world when Iraq became independent after 1958. Iraq's oil industry was nationalized in the 1960s, like that of every other country in the Middle East. The Iraqi oil union became, and still is, the industry's most zealous guardian. Saddam Hussein later drove its leaders underground, killing and jailing the ones he could catch.

When Saddam fell, Iraqi unionists came out of prison, up from underground, and back from exile, determined to rebuild their labor movement. Miraculously, in the midst of war and bombings, they did. The oil workers union in the south is now one of the largest organizations in Iraq, with thousands of members on the rigs, pipelines, and refineries. The electrical workers union is the first national labor organization headed by a woman, Hashmeya Muhsin Hussein.

Together with other unions in railroads, hotels, ports, schools, and factories, they've gone on strike, held elections, won wage increases, and made democracy a living reality. Yet the Bush administration, and the Baghdad government it controls, has continued to enforce a Saddam-era law that outlawed collective bargaining, has impounded union funds, and has turned its back (or worse) on a wave of assassinations of Iraqi union leaders. Following the June strike, Iraq's oil minister ordered officials of the state oil industry to refuse to recognize or bargain with the IFOU.

President Bush says he wants democracy, yet he will not accept the one political demand that unites Iraqis above all others. They want the country's oil (and its electrical power stations, ports, and other key facilities) to remain in public hands.

The fact that Iraqi unions are the strongest voice demanding this makes them anathema. Selling the oil off to large corporations is far more important to the Bush administration than a paper commitment to the democratic process. And the oil workers' union has now emerged as one of the strongest voices of Iraqi nationalism, protecting an important symbol of Iraq's national identity, and, more important, the only source of income capable of financing the country's post-occupation reconstruction.

The administration and those U.S. legislators trying to impose the oil law might take note that they are requiring the Maliki government to betray one of the few reasons Iraqis have for supporting it—its ability to keep the oil revenue in public hands.

With a no-bid, sweetheart contract with occupation authorities in hand, Halliburton Corporation came into Iraq in the wake of the troops in 2003. The company tried to seize control of the wells and rigs, withholding reconstruction aid to force workers to submit. The oil union struck for three days that August, stopping exports and cutting off government revenue. Halliburton left the oil districts, and the Oil Ministry regained control.

The oil and port unions then forced foreign corporations, including Seattle-based Stevedoring Services of America and the Danish shipping giant Maersk, to give up similar sweetheart agreements in Iraq's deepwater shipping facilities. Muhsin's electrical union is still battling to stop subcontracting in the power stations—a prelude to corporate control. The occupation has always had an economic agenda. In 2003 and 2004 occupation czar Paul Bremer published lists in Baghdad newspapers of the public enterprises he intended to auction off. Arab labor leader Hacene Djemam bitterly observed, "War makes privatization easy: first you destroy society; then you let the corporations rebuild it."

The Bush administration won't leave Iraq in part because that economic agenda is still insecure. Under Washington's guidance, the Iraqi government wrote a new oil law in secret. The Iraq study commission, headed by oilman James Baker, called it the key to ending the occupation. That law is touted in the U.S. press as ensuring an equitable division of oil wealth. Iraqis see it differently. They look at the means it sets up for welcoming foreign oil companies into the oil fields, and the control it would give them over setting royalties, deciding on production levels, and even determining whether Iraqis themselves get to work in their own industry. Iraqi unions charge it will ensure that foreign corporations control future exploration and development, in one of the world's largest reserves, through so-called production sharing contracts that favor multinational oil corporations. Such contracts have been rejected by most oil-producing countries, including those of the Middle East.

In May, Hassan Juma'a Awad, president of the IFOU, which had been banned from the secret negotiations, wrote a letter to the U.S. Congress. "Everyone knows the oil law doesn't serve the Iraqi people," he warned. The draft law "serves Bush, his supporters and foreign companies at the expense of the Iraqi people." The union has threatened to strike if the law is implemented.

After Muhsin and IFOU general secretary Faleh Abood Umara toured the United States in June, Leo Gerard, president of the United Steel Workers of America, which represents U.S. oil workers, backed up the Iraqis' demand. In a July 31 letter to key Congress members, Gerard warned that "the oil privatization law now under consideration by Iraq's government is designed to benefit the multinational oil companies; not the Iraqi people. ... Iraq's oil is a national resource that should not be privatized [or] used as any kind of 'benchmark' of the Iraqi government's success or failure."

Like all Iraqi unionists, Juma'a says the occupation should end without demanding Iraq's oil as a price. "The USA claimed that it came here as a liberator, not to control our resources," he reminded Congress.

Congressional opponents of the war can only win Iraqis' respect if they disavow the oil law. Gerard told those representatives that "the views of this labor movement should be heard much more clearly in Washington than they have been to date," and noted that "they believe strongly that sectarian strife will ease, and that unions will be able to act with substantially more freedom when the U.S. military presence has ended." The steel workers, he said, wanted Congress to "oppose the privatization of Iraq's oil resources, correct the inequities present in Iraqi labor policy, and continue to support an end to the U.S. military presence in Iraq." ❑

Article 10.4

IN HARM'S WAY

The Working Class on the War Front and the Home Front

BY RODNEY WARD
May/June 2003

> "Old man Bush wasn't half the president his son is. When the father was president, I only took a 15% pay cut. Now that his idiot son is president, I get to take a 40% pay cut. Way to go, George!"
> —a US Airways Fleet Services union activist

> "I've had enough of being fired at from all directions. I just want to go home."
> —a U.S. Marine, speaking to BBC News

First, the obvious: In Iraq, a U.S. and allied military made up of working-class soldiers has fought against a working-class Iraqi military. But the war tears at the lives of working people in the United States as well. As Martin Luther King observed about an earlier war, the bombs raining down on the "enemy" also jeopardize the futures and livelihoods of people in poor and working-class communities in the United States.

On any number of dimensions, the war in Iraq is hurting working people back home. The U.S. soldiers who return will find their benefits slashed by Congress and their prospects limited by continuing economic stagnation. The massive cost of the war and occupation robs resources from those who can least afford it and exacerbates federal and state budget crises. In turn, the social safety net is unraveling further, just as wartime anxiety pushes the economy back toward recession.

The Bush administration is using wartime insecurity as a pretext to strip union rights from many federal workers and to intensify the criminalization of immigrant communities. In the private sector, entire industries—most notably, the airlines—are using the moment as an opportunity to bludgeon unions and savagely restructure their workplaces. As the invasion of Iraq winds down, an unwelcome occupation begins that will drain more resources away from meeting urgent human needs; just as important, it will prolong an atmosphere of crisis that gives cover for those whose agenda is to weaken the union movement and workers' rights.

Working Warriors

The modern U.S. military is vaunted as an all-volunteer force, but the truth is more complex. Conscription was ended in 1973 as a result of antiwar protest at home and, more important, among soldiers. Since then, the Department of Defense has built a voluntary military, primarily on a system of economic incentives. The military targets communities that have been devastated by disinvestment for recruitment, and military service has become a primary economic opportunity structure for working-class communities, disproportionately so for people of color.

Oskar Castro of the Youth and Militarism Project of the American Friends Service Committee (AFSC) points out that "most people didn't sign up because they were gung-ho warriors. Most people signed up for the college money and wonderful career opportunities, leadership skills and respect" that military recruiters offer—attractive promises to a young person whose alternatives are a dead-end job or unemployment. Researchers at the Rand Corporation found that low personal or family income and unemployment (particularly long term) increase the chances that someone will enlist. Not surprisingly, the military "seems to resemble the makeup of a two-year commuter or trade school outside Birmingham or Biloxi," *New York Times* reporters David Halbfinger and Steven Holmes note. As a result, close observers of military enlistment like the Central Committee for Conscientious Objectors refer to today's recruitment strategy as a "poverty draft."

Half of the 3.2 million soldiers in the U.S. military are reservists. In addition to the emotional trauma soldiers and their loved ones experience during a wartime mobilization, reservists also endure significant economic hardships. As they are activated from civilian jobs, many face dramatic pay cuts and disruption of health benefits. Tod Ensign of Citizen Soldier, an advocacy group for soldiers, explains, "Take an EMT making $42K driving an ambulance, enough to support a wife and two or three kids in a working-class suburb of New York City. They will earn $18K-22K once activated. Setting aside the risk of war, these people are taking heavy hits, often 30% to 50% cuts in pay!" Though some unionized workers have contractual pay protections in the event of reserve call-up, most reservists are out of luck. Civilian bills at best stay the same; with one parent absent, child care costs may go up. One New York City reservist explained that activation would mean his family would lose their home.

And when the war is over, the GIs will return home to find that politicians—many of whom used privilege to avoid military service themselves—are mouthing support while actually pulling the rug out from under soldiers' futures. On March 20, the Congress overwhelmingly passed a resolution to "express the gratitude of the Nation to all members of the United States Armed Forces." Then, early the next morning, the House of Representatives voted to cut funding for veterans' health care and benefit programs by nearly $25 billion over the next ten years. The cuts are designed to accommodate the massive tax cuts the Bush administration has been pursuing—while the war diverts the public's attention. The government track record on ignoring postwar problems like Agent Orange, post-traumatic stress disorder, and Gulf War Syndrome does not bode well for the soldiers fighting the current war. Says the AFSC's Castro, "Even the military doesn't support the troops. Families are not supported. When it comes to dollars and cents, the military doesn't put its money where its mouth is."

Speaking of money, Defense Secretary Donald Rumsfeld's strategy for the Iraq war was based on the cost-cutting, lean, just-in-time production model favored by corporate restructuring consultants. Rumsfeld apparently quashed the logistics plans of experienced officers, pressuring them to stage far fewer personnel and much less hardware in the Gulf than they considered adequate. Observers of the impact of lean restructuring in the corporate world report that increased workplace injuries are a major result. One wonders what impact importing this model into the battlefield will have on soldiers and civilians.

Union Busting as Homeland Security

Meanwhile, on the home front, both public- and private-sector workers are suffering a savage assault. The fiscal crisis brought about by war spending, recession, and tax cuts for the wealthy is squeezing public workers at all levels, resulting in wage freezes and elimination of entire departments. Thousands of public-sector workers are losing their jobs. Treasury Department worker Renee Toback reports that her department was told their budget would be "taxed" to pay for the war in Iraq.

At the same time, thousands of federal workers in the hastily cobbled-together Department of Homeland Security have been stripped of their union rights in the name of national security. The Department of Defense is developing plans to do the same. Are fearful employees with no voice on the job in the best position to protect national security? No. But it's no surprise that the administration's agenda prioritizes union busting over public safety. AFL-CIO Organizing Director Stewart Acuff says, "The most outrageous thing they [the Bush administration] said was that they had to remove union rights from the Department of Homeland Security when all of the people who answered the call on September 11, all of the firefighters and cops who died trying to save people, were union members! And 90% of the people who cleaned up in the aftermath were union members as well." Against this backdrop, the administration has also called for the privatization of as many as 800,000 non-postal federal jobs. If Bush succeeds, this move would replace large numbers of union jobs with non-union ones at lower pay and with less accountability; it would strike a huge blow at the strength of public-sector unions. (Naturally, Bush also plans to privatize Iraqi health care and education.)

Diane Witiak, an American Federation of Government Employees (AFGE) spokeswoman, describes the current atmosphere: "If you dare to oppose the administration, you're almost considered a traitor. We resent that the administration considers unionization and patriotism incompatible. In fact, [unionization is] essential. [The administration] will go back to the old cronyism and favoritism that the Civil Service Act corrected. It's only a matter of time before Bush starts with the private sector!"

Much as Witiak predicted, the administration is using the national-security pretext to erode the rights of some private-sector workers as well. Last year, Homeland Security Director Tom Ridge called the president of the west coast longshore union. He claimed a strike would harm national security and threatened dockworkers with replacement by military personnel. Ultimately, it was management that locked out the dockworkers, but Bush invoked the Taft-Hartley Act and threatened to prosecute International Longshore and Warehouse Union members who engaged in any kind of work slowdown or other industrial action.

More broadly, efforts are under way in Congress to ban strikes by airline workers and to pass a number of other anti-worker measures. Among these are expansion of the restrictive Railway Labor Act's jurisdiction to include certain industries now under the umbrella of the National Labor Relations Act, making it harder for workers in these sectors to win union recognition and severely limiting their right to strike. Another legislative initiative would eliminate "card-check," the system of conducting a union recognition election once a certain number of representation petition cards have been signed by workers at a particular facility. In recent years, card-check has been the chief mechanism of successful union organizing drives. The AFL-CIO's Acuff points out that "the direction the government is moving in will indeed have a chilling effect on mobilizations, collective activity, demonstrations and direct action, all necessary parts of contract and bargaining campaigns and union strength. This administration, by law and by culture, is trying to stigmatize or make illegal the kinds of activity that are necessary to build union workplace strength."

What Does a Terrorist Look Like?

Wartime is always dangerous for immigrant communities. When the towers collapsed on September 11, they crushed the movement to give undocumented immigrants amnesty. Since then, immigrants have been subject to a dramatically stepped-up campaign by the federal government to find and deport them. Rachael Kamel, AFSC education director, points to "growing attempts to criminalize immigrant workers—all now justified in the name of security." As the next episode in the now-permanent war on terror, the war in Iraq only serves to extend the period in which such policies appear legitimate.

For example, the Social Security Administration (SSA) sends so-called no-match letters to employers when it finds that a worker's Social Security number does not match SSA records. These letters serve to intimidate workers, since employers can threaten to turn them in to the Immigration and Naturalization Service (INS). The number of no-match letters has increased 800% since 9/11. Similarly, special registration of immigrants from a select list of countries, mostly in the Middle East and Southern Asia, has snared thousands of people with minor visa infractions, many of whom face deportation. (Of bizarre note is the case of Iraqi exile Katrin Michael. She met with President Bush on March 14 to recount the gas attack she survived, and then found herself on the INS deportation list the next week, according to a *Washington Post* story.)

All of this has a powerful impact on worker organization because, for the past decade, immigrant workers have been the bedrock of aggressive labor organizing campaigns in economically strategic states like California, Texas and New York. Last year in Los Angeles, 60 workers active in organizing the Koreatown Assi Supermarket were placed on indefinite suspension after their names appeared on no-match letters. And the same Homeland Security rules that stripped newly-federalized airport screeners of union rights also banned immigrant workers in those positions. As a result, 7,000 immigrant airport security screeners—some of whom had just succeeded in winning union representation—have been fired.

Shock and Awe for Airline Workers?

Amid official and unofficial repression against public sector workers and immigrant communities, the economy appears stalled and is likely heading for a double-dip recession. The World Bank is already estimating that the Iraq war will reduce worldwide economic growth by one-half of a percentage point during the first six months of this year.

When the economy is weak, the industries most affected make cuts wherever they can, and workers bear the brunt of industry restructuring. The airline industry continues to be the crucible of this restructuring; as such, it provides an instructive case study. Before the war, the industry's Air Transport Association predicted 70,000 layoffs (100,000 if a terrorist attack accompanied the war) in addition to the thousands already cut since September 11, as well as $4 billion in additional losses. Editorials intoned about "Airline Apocalypse."

True to their word, airlines began shedding employees by the thousands as soon as the bombs started to fall on Baghdad. Continental laid off 1,200, with more to come, Northwest, 4,900, while United and American plan to get rid of thousands more. Jeff Matthews, the Aircraft Mechanics Fraternal Association's national contract coordinator at Northwest, told Reuters: "Northwest is using the Iraq conflict as an excuse to justify mass layoffs planned before the conflict started. The number of planned layoffs is far larger than would be justified based on the number of planes Northwest is removing from service." One United employee and Marines veteran describes wartime layoffs as United's own campaign of "shock and awe."

All of these airlines have succeeded in, or are in the process of, extracting concessions on levels unheard of in the history of the industry. Of particular importance has been US Airways' use of the war as leverage to terminate the defined-benefit pension plan for its pilots. At a time when defined-benefit plans are underfunded by about $300 billion in the United States, this is alarming. U.S. Rep. Bernie Sanders (I-Vt.) warned in the *Wall Street Journal* that "this could set a horrible precedent by making it easier for companies to renege on the retirement promises they made to their workers." Nomi Prins, author of the book *Money for Nothing*, points out, "The poor stock market is offering a convenient excuse for companies that already desired to reduce future plan benefits."

The airlines cite the war as a major reason for the concessions they demand. United mechanic Jennifer Salazar-Biddle remarked, "The crisis is real, but the graft is unbelievable." In fact, executive compensation in the midst of the industry's crisis has shocked and awed even Republicans. Responding to reports of the doubling of Delta CEO Leo Mullin's compensation package, Sen. John McCain (who champions eliminating airline workers' right to strike) exclaimed, "You ought to be ashamed of yourself." Nonetheless, a new bailout is in the works for the airline industry. The bailout bill does include a cap on executive compensation, but at 2002 levels—a good example of closing the barn doors after the escape. It also requires the airline companies to reduce operating costs, a provision that will primarily bleed workers. The only bone the bill offers airline workers is a meager extension of their unemployment benefits.

Chain of Change

Wars have always had a deep impact on working people. In addition to the slaughter of war, wars have often undermined the strength of working class organization. Government repression tied to World War I all but destroyed the Industrial Workers of the World and the Socialist Party. Workplace regimentation in World War II played an important role in the long-term bureaucratization of unions, replacing militant shop floor activity with safer routinized grievance and arbitration procedures.

On the other hand, soldiers returning from war have also played an important role in reviving struggles at home. At the end of World War II and during the Vietnam War, opposition to the war surfaced among GIs, along with discussions of soldiers' rights to free speech and even to unions. Soldiers returning from Vietnam played an important role in the antiwar movement as well as rebellions within a variety of unions, most notably the wave of auto-worker wildcat strikes from 1969 to 1972. African-American soldiers returning from both of these wars parlayed their wartime experiences into civil-rights activism.

There are some hopeful signs that workers will fight back against the current wave of assaults on their rights. Transportation Security Administration (TSA) employees are continuing to organize themselves with AFGE in spite of TSA director James Loy's directives to the contrary. AFGE succeeded in securing a one-year moratorium on the de-unionization of the Department of Homeland Security. Federal workers in Seattle and dozens of other localities have begun a campaign of public rallies to protest privatization.

Time will tell how working people in the military will respond to what they are enduring today. One thing is clear, though: The immediate impact of the war has been to strengthen the hands of corporations and weaken unions and other worker organizations while placing thousands of working people in harm's way. In the long term, whether grassroots activists can turn this tide will depend on how they understand and address the class dimensions of this and future wars. ❑

Resources: Soldiers & Veterans: Citizen Soldier, citizen-soldier.org; Military Families Speak Out, mfso.org; Veterans for Common Sense, veteransforcommonsense.org; National Gulf War Resource Center, ngwrc.org; Immigrant Rights: National Network for Immigrant and Refugee Rights, nnirr.org; Labor: US Labor Against War, uslaboragainstwar.org; Dept. of Homeland Security Workers, dshworkers.org; Association of Flight Attendants, afanet.org; Airline Mechanics Fraternal Association, amfanatl.org; See also: David Cortright, *Soldiers in Revolt: The American Military Today,* Anchor Press/Doubleday, 1976; Kim Moody, *An Injury To All*, Routledge, 1997.

Article 10.5

CONSCRIPTED BY POVERTY

BY ANNA SUSSMAN
November/December 2007

Providing economic alternatives has been key to the successful demobilization of nearly 30,000 child soldiers in eastern Congo.

Ronaldo is covered with a thin layer of sawdust. As the sun sets over a hilltop woodshop in eastern Congo, the 16-year-old takes a moment to rest, wiping his brow with a cloth. He's been sawing all day, cutting wood for chairs, tables and shelves. The work is hard and physically demanding, but it's better than his last job: child soldier.

Two years ago, at the age of 14, Ronaldo, whose name has been changed to protect his identity, joined a local armed rebel group.

"I thought it would give me a better life," he said.

He says he joined voluntarily. But advocates here say that Ronaldo's recruitment was not exactly voluntary: while he was not forced with a gun or knife, Ronaldo, like thousands of other child soldiers in the Congo, was compelled to join an armed group by extreme poverty. "My family didn't have enough food or money," he says. "That's why I decided to join."

In the Democratic Republic of the Congo, more than 33,000 young people have been associated with armed groups in recent years, mostly in the troubled eastern Congo region. UNICEF officials and international aid agencies operating here say the child soldier epidemic in eastern Congo can be traced largely to economics. Across the globe there are many reasons children join armed groups—some are forcibly abducted, for example, while others are looking for revenge or prestige. But advocates here are finding that poverty is the driving force: many children enlist for the minimal food and shelter it will provide them.

"In such a poor country as the Democratic Republic of the Congo, there are economic factors that drive children towards joining armed groups or forces," says Pernile Ironside, a protection specialist with UNICEF in eastern Congo. "Families tend to be very large, so there is a certain allure for children to join up with a military group, where they are able to get enough food to eat," she said. "Occasionally parents, as well, drive children to join [an armed group], recognizing that they can't meet the needs of their child and that the child may be better off in their view by leaving the family and joining up with a group."

That's why UNICEF, along with other international agencies, is focusing its demobilization efforts on economic solutions.

"Fundamentally the reason is economic," says Murhabazi Namegabe, who directs a child soldier demobilization center in Bukavu. "Ninety-nine percent of these children come from poor families. The main problem we are dealing with is how to provide assistance for their families."

In Congo, where civil war has raged since President Mobutu Sese Seko was overthrown in 1997, young people have grown up in a climate of brutal warfare in which families are regularly slaughtered, homes burned, and villages destroyed.

Although the war is officially over and the country held democratic elections last year, the fighting continues today as ethnic, political, and government factions battle along Congo's mineral-rich border with Rwanda.

The eastern Congo region is controlled by more than a dozen armed groups, many battling over the valuable mineral resources abundant in this region of the country: gold, diamonds, and coltan (short for columbite-tantalite), a mineral widely used in the manufacture of electronic gadgets like mobile phones, computer chips, and VCRs. But the billions of dollars extracted from the ground here are enjoyed by an elite few, while hundreds of warlords and soldiers on the ground vie for control over civilian territories with brutal force.

Many children, including Ronaldo, have joined local "Mai-Mai" militias, decentralized armed groups operating across the region who claim they are engaging in self-defense against the government and ethnic rebel groups. Others are conscripted by the national army, says Ironside.

But amid the fighting, UNICEF is successfully negotiating for the removal of children from armed groups. Today, nearly 6,000 former child soldiers are learning income-generating activities like sewing, woodworking, and bicycle repair. This way, children like Ronaldo will be able to survive without the patronage of an armed group, says Ironside.

Restricting Re-recruitment

The "skill-building" demobilization programs championed by UNICEF and others, like Save the Children, began several years ago and have been hugely successful. In all, 29,000 child soldiers have been demobilized in the Congo since 2002. But at the same time the financial security promised by armed groups continues to draw in poor children.

"Re-recruitment is something that is best prevented by giving real opportunities to children once they've left an armed group," says Ironside. "Opportunities could entail going back to school, learning a trade, or having a small income-generating project or business because children really need to regain their hope for the future and visualize what else they may be able to become, aside from being part of an armed group."

In a small cement building in the city of Bukavu, 300 former child soldiers have just completed a six-month training course in sewing and tailoring with the Dutch-based nongovernmental organization War Child. At the graduation ceremony, students and parents sing songs, bang drums, and dance. Then, they stand up and give testimony to their newly learned skills.

"With this experience I will never go back to armed forces," says 19-year-old Papi Bijeri. "My weapon now is what I learned; that is how I will survive." Bijeri, who was orphaned at a young age, says he joined a rebel group "to earn some money and survive."

While fighting, Bijeri participated in gang-rape and killing, and eventually earned the position of bodyguard to a high-ranking commander, a job that earned him about $9 a month plus a bar of soap and food.

The War Child program takes children directly from drop-off centers, where they are left by armed rebel groups taking the steps required to integrate into the national army. During their six-month training, most of the children live with relatives or friends in the town. When the course is completed, they receive a small tool kit, including a prized sewing machine. It's a model that is repeated, with some variation, in programs across the region.

When Basic Needs Go Unmet

There are between 200,000 and 300,000 child soldiers worldwide. Many are abducted and forced into armed groups. Others "volunteer." Stating that young people require special protection because of their physical and mental immaturity, however, the U.N. Convention on the Rights of the Child prohibits military recruitment—voluntary or not—of children under 18.

Most child soldiers come from nations that have dissolved into civil war. Child soldiers are a symptom that states which lack the capacity to meet their citizens' most basic needs. "Poverty and its link to the crisis of child soldiers around the globe is inextricably linked to other antecedent factors," says Eddie Mandhry of the New York-based group Global Kids. "These factors include the deterioration of social infrastructures prior to or during times of war and the economic and political marginalization and disaffection of youth."

Just as poverty can motivate the struggle over resources that is often at the root of war, war itself amplifies poverty and the problems that often accompany it—problems like corruption, lawlessness, and limited education. Families collapse, schools stop running, work opportunities disappear, and food becomes scarce. Looking to bolster their ranks, warlords lure physically vulnerable and economically desperate children, many without families, into armed groups. Most end up being forced to do terrible things. Many former child soldiers in Congo report being forced to rape and kill villagers. Ronaldo says he was forced to work on the frontlines, walking for days on end without food.

"Children are quite easily manipulated," Ironside says. "And it doesn't take a whole lot for them to perhaps become motivated to do something, given their extreme poverty and the fact that they might not consider the consequences of a particular action."

As violent instability and war have ravaged Congo, per-capita annual income (adjusted for inflation) fell from $380 in 1960 to $100 in 2004, according to the IMF. The vast majority of households in eastern Congo have no running water or electricity, and few of the children attend school. Women report that armed groups regularly steal crops from their fields, leaving their families hungry.

Across the African great lakes region, where violent unrest spills across borders between Uganda, Burundi, Rwanda, and Congo, the vast majority of households live on less than a dollar a day. Not surprisingly, potential child soldiers are in large supply.

A Generation of Soldiers

But demobilization programs are taking hold in eastern Congo. Most of the income-generating and skill-building programs run by UNICEF and its partners here are coupled with counseling and group play-therapy, where children learn to cope with the atrocities they have seen or carried out.

In towns like Bukavu in the South Kivu province of eastern Congo where UNICEF programs work one-on-one with children to teach them job skills, most children are able to resist re-recruitment.

But farther north in the villages of North Kivu, where ethnic fighting between Hutu militants and the Congolese army continues to play out, the situation is worse. UNICEF officials estimate that hundreds of former child soldiers have been re-recruited in North Kivu in recent months. "About three-quarters of children who were demobilized have been re-recruited because of a lack of jobs," says Namegabe.

The head of U.N. humanitarian efforts in North Kivu, Patrick Lavand'Homme, says he fears the United Nations will be unable to meet the huge demand for basic supplies like food and water if the fighting continues. And the Congolese government has shown little interest in providing humanitarian help. As needs become more desperate, Ironside says, more than 5,000 more children in North Kivu are at risk of being re-recruited.

There are many reasons for the child soldier crisis, but until real economic needs are met here, children will continue to be attracted to the promises of food, money, and shelter offered by armed groups.

The conflict in this region has been called Africa's World War. Asked why his homeland has seen so much war, 16-year-old Ronaldo does not pause to think. As he picks up his saw and resumes his woodwork, he gives a simple answer.

"There are no jobs here. People want to work but there is no work to do. If everyone had a job that had a decent salary, there would be peace in the country." ❏

Resources: UNICEF, "Displaced children especially vulnerable to illness and military re-recruitment in North Kivu," 2007; Child Rights Information Network, crin.org; Human Rights Watch Child Soldiers Campaign, hrw.org/campaigns/crp; Amnesty International, "Democratic Republic of Congo: Children at War," 2003.

Article 10.6

THE ECONOMICS AND POLITICS OF DEPROPRIATION IN THE OTHER COLOMBIA

BY PATRICIA M. RODRIGUEZ
November/December 2010

It has rained for days, and the swampy ocean waters that surround this community of displaced fishermen in northern Colombia rise at their own whim, flooding people's houses and making life even harder than usual. Yet most of the families living in this tiny makeshift encampment in Boca de Aracataca in the Magdalena province of Colombia have gathered under a tarp to eloquently tell a group of activists from Witness for Peace, a Washington-based social justice organization, about their problems. "[The foreign companies] kicked us out of our land. We do not have water, electricity, food, nor any help from the government... we need to be respected, we need to be treated as people, and not as animals," says Alicia Camargo, who has been displaced three times already, once very violently, along with family and neighbors.

As it turns out, the source of the problems in this community—and others nearby—is the presence of multinational corporations. In this particular case, it involves a new port expansion project along the Caribbean coast near the otherwise-idyllic city of Santa Marta. The construction of this mega-port has been funded by foreign coal companies that have operated practically unrestrictedly in Colombia for nearly 15 years. When it is finished in 2013, the port will allow U.S.-based company Drummond and Swiss-based Glencore to ship an extra 30 to 60 million tons of coal per year to global markets, in addition to the nearly 69 million tons they already export. The Colombian government allegedly receives a royalty of 10% of this total export profit, but only a handful of people see this money. A large portion of the money is never transferred to the communities that are most impoverished and environmentally affected by corporate presence. Still, foreign direct investment is embraced wholeheartedly by Colombian elites who equate corporate ventures in the agricultural, mineral, and industrial sectors with growth and prosperity.

It is not uncommon to hear about how corporations bring investment to developing countries and even their "willingness" to address problem areas such as environmental contamination and child labor practices. It is sometimes said that corporations' business practices are completely socially responsible and that corporations give back to the communities in which they operate. The media give much less attention to stories about how corporations destroy local lives, directly and indirectly. Yet it happens, and in some cases it leaves a trail of unimaginable destruction and violence. In this Caribbean region of Colombia, to talk of *displacement* of communities by corporations does not do justice to the reality; rather, locals speak of *depropriation*, or the takeover of property and livelihoods with complete impunity. In this corner of the world, multinational corporations in the coal industry like Drummond and Glencore, and in the banana sector, like Dole and Chiquita Brands (among others), are not just operating on the basis of government-granted licenses to exploit natural resources. Through alliances with authorities, legal and otherwise, these companies have crafted what amounts to an informal ownership of the region. They own a large part of the railroads, highways, ports, and mines, and they have little concern for how communities feel about their presence there.

But what is it about the nature of these enterprises and the context in which they operate that make for such dominance, and what facilitates their exploitation of workers and communities? How have local people resisted these infractions, and to what degree, considering the widespread corruption of their political representatives? To answer both these questions, it helps to understand more about the region. Whether due to its strategic location, its natural resources, or its distance from the centers of power in the capital city, Bogotá, this region is often referred to as "the other Colombia." It is an allusion both to its potential and to its stigma as something of a no man's land.

Free Reign in the "Other Colombia"

Multinational companies began to arrive in the Magdalena and Cesar provinces in large part because the location offers such natural advantages. Surrounded in the east by the Sierra Nevada mountains, several municipalities in Magdalena province have direct access to the rivers that originate in these slopes. This makes the land well suited for banana plantations and other kinds of large-scale agriculture, and therefore for elite and corporate interests. It comes as no surprise that one of the U.S.-based companies with most presence throughout Latin America, the United Fruit Company (UFCO), operated in Magdalena since the beginning of the 20th century. As with its operations elsewhere, UFCO labor practices in Colombia were exploitative and repressive. During a strike by UFCO banana workers on December 6, 1928, in which they asked for better treatment and working conditions, an indefinite number of workers were massacred by company and police security forces in Ciénaga. The Nobel Prize-winning Colombian writer Gabriel García Márquez wrote a fictional account of this massacre in *One Hundred Years of Solitude*. Though UFCO left the Magdalena region in 1950s and moved to other regions of Colombia, it continued subcontracting with local growers.

In the mid to late 1980s, Chiquita Brands (formerly UFCO) and Dole rediscovered the *Zona Bananera*, or the Caribbean Banana Zone, at a time when local landowners had already been paying a "security fee" to rebel guerrilla groups that operated from the largely uninhabited Sierra Nevada, like the National Liberation Army (ELN). Noticing the potential for exclusive control of land and/or lucrative contracts with local large-scale banana growers, Chiquita and Dole officials negotiated economic deals with the landowners and security deals with the guerrillas. Their aim was to guarantee the companies' unrestricted access to highways and railroads leading to the coastal ports. In just a few years, however, small private security gangs began brutal confrontations with guerrillas in the mountains and the cities. Aware of their stronger firepower, the companies began to pay these small groups for protection instead of the guerrillas. By the late 1990s, these gang-style private security groups multiplied and fought each other for control of the territory (and for the substantial payments from landowners and multinational companies). A handful of gang leaders emerged victorious, and soon formed more structured paramilitary organizations like the powerful United Self-Defense Forces of Colombia (AUC). AUC and other paramilitary groups are known to have solid ties to drug lords as well as to military and high-level state authorities.

One of the AUC leaders in the Caribbean region is Rodrigo Tovar, popularly known as Jorge 40. He was a former army official and comes from one of a handful of powerful traditional families in the region. In the mid 1990s, Jorge 40 began to work under the command of the Castaño family, who founded the AUC when the patriarch Jesús Castaño was kidnapped and assassinated in the mid 1990s by another guerrilla group, the Revolutionary Armed Forces of Colombia (FARC). To garner control, Jorge 40 was known to carry out "cleansings" of local communities in Magdalena and Cesar provinces, targeting anyone suspected of ties to ELN or FARC. In 2000, after a guerrilla attack on a group of business and mafia leaders in the town of Nueva Venezia, Jorge 40 ordered the massacre of 70 people from this community. According to witnesses, the armed paramilitaries then played soccer with victims' severed heads to show the community that they were in complete control. There are several others like Jorge 40 who have ties to the different landowning families and to different companies. In 2007, Chiquita Brands admitted in federal court that it paid nearly $2 million to paramilitary death squads over a period of seven years. On its end, Drummond is currently being sued in a United States court under the Alien Tort Claims Act for having contracted paramilitary forces to kill three union leaders. The violence in the region is widespread, and largely tied to corporate interest in acquiring lands and controlling the regions' vast resources. Between 1997 and 2007, 4,000 people died and at least 500 were disappeared. Moreover, during the height of the violence in between 2003 and 2006, 43,300 families from the region suffered forced displacement from their communities.

On their end, the companies suffered no major consequences from the bloodbath, other than occasionally having to rearrange their deals with different paramilitary leaders. As long as they kept scheduled payments, the companies enjoyed complete control over vast lands. By 2002 Chiquita and Dole decided to divvy up the 10,000 hectares of land in the *Zona Bananera*: the medium-to-large farms that grew bananas for Dole had their main houses painted red and white, and those that grew bananas for Chiquita were painted blue and white. They also happily shared the railroad. On the other hand, small farms that for one or another reason do not have contracts with these companies have hardly survived. Many peasants have agreed to sell their lands, only to lose most of their money to criminal and paramilitary gangs that extorted them shortly after the sale. Others, out of fear, have simply never returned after their violent displacement by paramilary groups. In the near future, these corporations are likely to continue to buy lands in the region, especially with the impending passage of the free trade agreement (FTA) between the United States and Colombia. While former president Alvaro Uribe championed the push for the FTA deal with the United States, current president Juan Manuel Santos, a former defense minister and a millionaire who has solid ties to many traditional elite Colombian families, is likely to deepen the open-borders approach.

The free reign of foreign coal companies reflects a similar history. The mountainous terrain in neighboring Cesar province contains some of the biggest coal mines in Latin America. Drummond, Prodeco (a subsidiary of Glencore), and now Brazilian-owned Vale, have capitalized on this by buying part of the national railroad company FENOCO, so as to have unrestricted access to the approximately 300 miles of railroad line between the mines and the port of Ciénaga, near Santa Marta. The port installations now cover four kilometers (of a total twelve kilometers) of the coastal shores in Magdalena, but the mega-port currently under construction would extend them by another two kilometers. When the project got under way in 2008, several communities living in the swamps, or *ciénaga*, near the port were forcibly displaced by armed gunmen, and many ended in the encampment in Boca de Aracataca. The port expansion work has prevented the fishermen from being able to access close-by waters and they now have to fish in far away waters, if their boats are solid enough to make it there. The damage extends far beyond access. For years, the companies have been dumping millions of tons of coal onto communities where the railroad crosses, and into coastal waters. This is due to negligence, as residuals "accidentally" fall out when the coal is carried uncovered or dumped into the shipping containers. This has resulted in severe erosion and environmental contamination of local flora and fish. As if that did not suffice, Drummond was recently conceded the rights to Rio Toribio, including control over the station that supplies clean water to local communities. According to the fishermen, Drummond uses the water to wet down the coal so that it does not ignite in the containers on the way to global markets. This has generated the contamination of river water with coal dust, and has caused a variety of skin and respiratory diseases among the local population.

State Complicity

This depropriation and destruction occurs under the protective eye of the Colombian state. Though laws exist which delimit any alterations to the agro-ecological balance in much of the coastal area, the government blatantly disregards the laws. In December 2007 the national Ministry of Transportation declared that the entire municipality was a public interest zone for purposes of national development, paving the way for the expansion of the port. Though Drummond and Prodeco appear to have followed all the legal steps to begin the expansion project, the process has certainly faltered in many aspects. According to a report prepared by local community leaders, the companies and municipal authorities did not adequately consult local community groups about worrisome environmental and socio-economic effects. Though the royalties for mining concessions and banana profits by law should remain in the communities for social and infrastructural investment, a majority of this money is simply distributed privately to national and municipal authorities. As a community leader from Ciénaga states, "what we have here is a case of mafia triangulation, with companies, the central government, and local authorities keeping the municipal funds for themselves, and thereby diffusing any responsibility that they should have towards communities."

The foreign companies do as they please, with impunity. When unionized coal workers organize to demand respect for their labor rights, or to ask for appropriate paid sick time for work injuries, the companies fire them. Such is the case of Moisés Padilla, a former Drummond employee who belongs to the SINTRAMINERGÉTICA (National Union of Industry and Energy Workers) union. He worked for 50 years as a welder (25 at Drummond), and is now incapacitated due to severe respiratory and heart conditions. The company has successfully resisted any outside intervention, despite legal efforts of the union. In a letter to Moisés Padilla, a company representative stated that it was not company policy to consent to third-party involvement, in this case a committee of independent and state officials that could evaluate his injury claims. Union workers have less and less job security, especially since the company has recently created its own union, SINTRADRUMMOND. Although the practice was previously prohibited, a recent judicial decision has opened a loophole for companies to begin organizing their own unions. Anibal Perez, another injured worker from SINTRAMINERGÉTICA, affirms that "for us to belong to our union is considered by the state practically a crime…the state does not give us the tools and protections to make our voices heard, and the result is that we have communities full of widows, orphans, and sick workers." The union has had five of its leaders killed since 2001, and several others now live in exile after being threatened by paramilitaries.

The companies are also quick to hold on to the façade of being socially and environmentally responsible. One example: Drummond trains a certain number of people from the community to be mine workers, but rarely hires local trainees. Some think this is because it is cheaper for the company to hire migrants from other regions. Similarly, national companies like AUGURA (Association of Banana Workers of Colombia) organize some of their own workers in seemingly beneficial cooperatives. Though independent on paper, AUGURA does business strictly with Dole, and prices are arranged between top level managers from AUGURA and Dole. So even if cooperative workers would truly get a fair trade price for their bananas, the lack of liberty to make autonomous decisions within the company-run cooperatives is problematic at best.

Not that state intervention would do any good. For one thing, much of the state funding for social programs for local communities is channeled to the companies themselves, such as the AUGURA-run cooperatives. So while the state has funds that it invests in social programs, these are mostly captured by the companies. Secondly, other state-funded social programs deliver subsidies as if community members were clients. The community at large, whether they belong to the category of low-income families, displaced families, or relatives and victims of violence, barely has access to a program that distributes about $40 every two months; most do not have enough of a connection with municipal authorities to receive even this small benefit. Thirdly, though the laws exist on paper to make the state more responsible and responsive, implementation is a problem. For instance, Colombia has had a Labor Statute since 1991, but the mechanisms for its implementation have not yet been discussed in Congress. Besides, corruption pervades the state. In 2009, a national scandal erupted over a government program aimed at helping struggling farmers, the Agro Ingreso Seguro (AIS) program. The funding (partly from the U.S. Agency for International Development) began in 2006 as part of an effort to ease concern over a potential negative impact of an impending FTA with the United States, but small farmers were not the ones benefiting; the bulk of

AIS' $630 million per year was discovered to be going to rich landowners, narco-traffickers, and mobsters.

Organizing an Effective Resistance

Considering the pervasiveness of corporate interests, violence, and state complicity, what *can* the handful of community leaders, human rights defenders, and union workers do to organize effective resistance? The truth is that they cannot organize freely; their lives are threatened constantly. Despite the threats, is not so hard to understand why those who are still alive publicly denounce the companies, the Colombian government, and the United States for trampling on their dignity. "Our denunciations make us very public personas, and since we do not have money to pay for private security guards, speaking out publicly and internationally ironically gives us some sense of security," says Edgardo Alemán, a local human rights defender.

And so they *do* challenge, collectively when possible. One of the small victories of the SINTRAMIENERGÉTICA union and other allied groups has been the Collective Labor Agreement signed between the union and Drummond, for the years 2010-2013. Even at quick glance, it is easy to find the voice of the workers, and their concern for community. Article 7 states that when a job opens at Drummond, the company will give preference to skilled members of the local community; upon the death of a worker, the company commits to hiring a family member of the victim. Union leaders concur that the agreement feels more like "our list of demands" than an actual commitment by Drummond representatives. Yet many insist that a more effective interaction between the communities and the companies is the only solution. "We need to guarantee a way to capture the resources, to have a social development policy that favors our communities. If we go through the politicians, we will get nothing," says local activist and economist, Luís Eduardo Rendón.

If the state's lack of responsiveness is any indication, negotiating with the companies might in fact be a viable approach. But the success of that strategy does not depend on the amount of pressure Colombian workers and community leaders exert. In this sense, the context (and place) in which they operate limits their impact. For their voice to mean anything in a system dominated by elite power in Bogotá and abroad, it will take the U.S. government and global citizens en masse to press the companies (American companies!) and the Colombian state to be honest, and to practice their activities legally, with true social responsibility. Perhaps then there can begin to be justice for these communities in the other Colombia. ❑

Sources: Luis E. Barranco, "Como el gobierno nacional convirtió una zona agroecológica en zona de interés público para fines portuarios," EDUMAG, Ciénaga, Colombia, 2010; Marcelo Bucheli, *Bananas and Business: The United Fruit Company in Colombia, 1899-2000.* New York: New York University Press, 2005; Peter Chapman, *Bananas: How the United Fruit Company Shaped the World,* New York: Canongate, 2007; Aviva Chomsky, Garry Leech, and Steve Striffler, *Bajo el manto del carbón: Pueblos y multinacionales en las minas de El Cerrejón, Colombia,* Colombia: Casa Editorial Pisando Callos, 2007.

Article 10.7

CAN MILITARY SPENDING SOLVE THE JOBS CRISIS?

Why war is not a sustainable strategy for economic recovery.

BY HEIDI GARRETT-PELTIER

March/April 2010

The United States is currently preparing to send 30,000 additional troops to Afghanistan by summer 2010. Military contractors, deeply integrated into the U.S. economy, will continue to prosper and profit from increased military spending resulting from this surge of troops. At a time when unemployment in the domestic economy remains near 10%, it may seem convenient to fall back on the principle of military Keynesianism: War is good for the economy.

John Maynard Keynes, the British economist whose work has once again become popular in the wake of this most recent economic crisis, advocated increased government spending to lift an economy out of recession or depression. When consumers and businesses slow their spending, the government can step in to increase demand for goods and services so that businesses can continue to produce and people can remain employed. This fiscal stimulus could take the form of infrastructure projects, healthcare, education, or other productive endeavors. By this logic, military spending can lift an economy out of recession by creating demand for goods and services provided by military contractors, such as the production of tanks and ammunition or the provision of security services. Advocates of this strategy point not only to the widespread employment created by military spending, but also claim that military spending creates well-paying, stable jobs.

It is true that military spending creates jobs throughout the economy, and that many of those jobs are well-paying. But at a time when our jobless rate is high, infrastructure is crumbling, and global climate change is becoming an increasingly urgent matter, we must ask whether military spending is truly a solution to our economic woes or whether we might be able to create more jobs in productive areas that also help us meet longer-term goals.

In a recent paper that I co-authored with Robert Pollin, we show that dollar per dollar, more jobs are created through spending on clean energy, health care, and education than on the military. Further, we show that more middle-income and well-paying jobs are created in all of these areas. For each $1 billion of spending, over 17,000 jobs would be created in clean energy, close to 20,000 in health care, and over 29,000 in education. That same $1 billion would create only 11,600 jobs as a result of military spending. If we look at well-paying jobs, those that pay over $64,000 per year, these alternative domestic spending areas also outperform military spending. The same $1 billion would create 1,500 well-paying jobs in clean energy and just over 1,000 in the military—clean energy creates 50% *more* good jobs than military spending. Education, which is labor-intensive and creates many well-paying jobs per dollar of expenditure, creates close to 2,500 jobs paying over $64,000—that's 2.5 times as many as the military.

According to the National Priorities Project, military spending on the Iraq and Afghanistan wars has reached approximately $1 trillion since 2001, not including the cost of the surge of 30,000 troops. In fiscal year 2009, federal government outlays on the military were 17% of all outlays. Meanwhile, energy, resource conservation, and the environment accounted for only 1% of federal outlays, while education, training, and social services made up only 2%. Military spending is therefore *eight to seventeen times* as high as federal education- and energy-related spending.

The Obama administration is facing increased pressure to reduce the size of the fiscal deficit and the national debt, both of which have grown partly as a result of military spending. At the same time, there is an urgent need to put people back to work and to move the country toward a low-carbon future. While military Keynesianism offers one strategy for recovering from the recession, it is by no means the most effective, even putting aside the other reasons for objecting to a war economy. By reducing military spending, we can channel some of those savings to clean energy, healthcare, education, and other matters of national and global importance. ❑

Sources: "The U.S. Employment Effects of Military and Domestic Spending Priorities: An Updated Analysis," by Robert Pollin and Heidi Garrett-Peltier, available at www.peri.umass.edu; National Priorities Project, www.nationalpriorities.org.

CONTRIBUTORS

Sylvia Allegretto is an economist and deputy chair of the Center on Wage and Employment Dynamics at the Institute for Research on Labor and Employment, University of California, Berkeley.

David Bacon is a journalist and photographer covering labor, immigration, and the impact of the global economy on workers.

Joel Beinin is a professor of Middle Eastern history at Stanford University.

Dan Bell is the international program coordinator at the Ohio Employee Ownership Center at Kent State University, where he has worked since the center opened in 1987.

Herman Benson is a leader in the movement for labor union leadership reform and rank-and-file participation in the United States and founder and current secretary of the Association for Union Democracy.

Kim Bobo, founder and executive director of Interfaith Worker Justice. She is author of *Wage Theft in America: Why Millions of Working Americans Are Not Getting Paid—And What We Can Do About It.*

Patrick Bond is director of the University of KwaZulu-Natal Centre for Civil Society in Durban, South Africa.

Betsy Bowman is on the editorial collective of *Grassroots Economic Organizing*. She is among the cofounders of the bilingual Center for Global Justice in San Miguel de Allende, Mexico, where she serves as a research associate.

Roger Bybee is the former editor of the union weekly *Racine Labor* and is now a consultant and freelance writer whose work has appeared in *Z Magazine, The Progressive, Extra!, The Progressive Populist, In These Times,* and other national publications and websites.

Esther Cervantes is the former business manager of *Dollars & Sense.*

Aviva Chomsky is a professor of history at Salem State College, teaching Latin American history. She is author of *"They Take Our Jobs!" and 20 Other Myths about*

Immigration and *West Indian Workers and the United Fruit Company in Costa Rica, 1870-1940.*

Felicitas Contreras is an activist with Center for Workers and Communities in Nuevo Laredo, Mexico.

James M. Cypher is a research professor in the Doctoral Program in Development Studies at the Autonomous University in Zacatecas, Mexico. He is the co-author of *Mexico's Economic Dilemma* (2010) and *The Process of Economic Development* (2009).

Anisha Desai is executive director of the Women of Color Resource Center, a movement-building organization, focused on the leadership development, well-being, and human rights of women of color across the United States.

Elissa Dennis is a consultant to nonprofit affordable housing developers with Community Economics, Inc. in Oakland, Calif.

Dan DiMaggio an independent writer, temp worker, and member of Socialist Alternative in Minneapolis, Minn. He has an MA in history from Tufts University and was an activist with the Harvard Living Wage Campaign.

Steve Early has been active in the labor movement since 1972 as a lawyer, journalist, organizer, and union representative. He worked for the Communications Workers of America for 27 years.

Mike-Frank Epitropoulos teaches sociology at the University of Pittsburgh. He spent three years teaching in both private- and public-sector higher education in Greece before returning to the United States in 2007.

Anne Fischel teaches media and community studies at Evergreen State College in Olympia, Wash.

Bill Fletcher, Jr. is a long-time labor and international activist and writer. He currently serves as president of the Washington, D.C.-based organizing and educational center TransAfrica Forum.

Harris Freeman is a long-term visiting professor at the Labor Relations and Research Center, University of Massachusetts at Amherst, and an assistant professor of Legal Research and Writing at Western New England College School of Law.

Heidi Garrett-Peltier is a research associate at the Political Economy Research Institute in Amherst, Mass.

Amy Gluckman is co-editor of *Dollars & Sense.*

Will Goldberg is a former policy analyst at the Prison Policy Initiative.

Elise Gould is a staff economist at the Economic Policy Initiative.

Lena Graber is a former *Dollars & Sense intern.*

Daniel Gross began working for the Starbucks Coffee Co. in 2003. He helped organize the IWW Starbucks Workers Union, founded on May 17, 2004.

Shawn Hattingh is a researcher and educator for the International Labour Research Information Group in South Africa. He is a frequent commentator on labor activism in South Africa and has written on the country's role across the African continent.

Julie Herlihy is a former *Dollars & Sense* intern

Marianne Hill, Ph.D., has published articles in the *Journal of Human Development, Feminist Economics,* and other economics journals. She also writes for the American Forum and the Mississippi Forum.

Marie Kennedy is professor emerita of Community Planning at University of Massachusetts Boston and visiting professor in Urban Planning at UCLA. She is a member of the board of directors of Grassroots International.

Dan La Botz teaches history and Latin American studies at Miami University in Oxford, Ohio, and works with *Labor Notes,* the labor education and organizing center in Detroit. He is the author of books on the United States, Mexico, and Indonesia.

Rob Larson is an assistant professor of economics at Ivy Tech Community College in Bloomington, Indiana.

Kari Lydersen is the Midwest correspondent for the *Washington Post.* She is a co-author of *Shoot an Iraqi: Art Life and Resistance Under the Gun.*

Staughton Lynd is a veteran activist, historian, and legal-aid attorney who has devoted much of his writing to solidarity unionism and worker self-organization. His most recent book is *Lucasville: The Untold Story of a Prison Uprising.*

Arthur MacEwan is professor emeritus of economics at UMass-Boston and is a *Dollars & Sense* Associate.

Nina Martin is a researcher at the Center for Urban Economic Development.

Siobhán McGrath is a policy research associate with the Economic Justice Project at the Brennan Center for Justice.

John Miller is a member of the *Dollars & Sense* collective and teaches economics at Wheaton College.

William Moseley is an assistant professor of geography and former coordinator of the African Studies program at Macalester College in Saint Paul, Minnesota. He is author of *African Environment and Development: Rhetoric, Programs, Realities*.

Saladin Muhammad is a member of Black Workers for Justice, based in Raleigh, North Carolina, and of the Black Workers League, based in Rocky Mount, North Carolina.

Lin Nelson teaches environmental and community studies at the Evergreen State College in Olympia, Wash.

Immanuel Ness (co-editor of this volume) is professor of political science at Brooklyn College-City University of New York. He is author of *Immigrants, Unions, and the New U.S. Labor Market* and editor of *WorkingUSA: The Journal of Labor and Society*.

Amy Offner (co-editor of this volume) is a graduate student in history at Columbia University, former organizer with SEIU, and former book editor at *Dollars & Sense*.

Martha Ojeda, a former *maquiladora* worker, is the Executive Director of the Coalition for Justice in the Maquiladoras.

Thomas I. Palley is an economist, who has held positions at the AFL-CIO, Open Society Institute, and the U.S.-China Economic and Security Review Commission.

Carlos Pérez de Alejo is a volunteer with the Workers Defense Project and a collective member of Monkey Wrench Books, an all-volunteer, collectively run bookstore. His writings have appeared in *YES!* and *Z Magazine*.

Steven Pitts a labor policy specialist at the University of California Berkeley Center for Labor Research and Education.

Frances Fox Piven is an internationally known author and activist whose work in social theory and political sociology has focused on the role of social movements in democratic social change. She is a professor in political science and sociology at the Graduate Center of City University of New York.

Ethan Pollack is a policy analyst at the Economic Policy Institute.

Robert Pollin teaches economics and is co-director of the Political Economy Research Institute at the University of Massachusetts-Amherst. He is also a *Dollars & Sense Associate*.

Paddy Quick teaches economics at St. Francis College, Brooklyn.

Peter Rachleff teaches U.S. history at Macalester College in St. Paul, Minnesota. For the past eight years, he has been the chair of the Meeting the Challenge Committee. He is the author of *Hard-Pressed in the Heartland: The Hormel Strike and the Future of the Labor Movement*.

Dan Read is a freelance journalist and editor based in the U.K.

Alejandro Reuss, an economist and historian, is a former editor of *Dollars & Sense* and a current member of the *D&S collective*.

Maryam Roberts is the peace and solidarity program director of the Women of Color Resource Center.

Patricia M. Rodriguez an assistant professor of politics at Ithaca College.

Adria Scharf is director of the Richmond Peace Education Center in Richmond, Virginia, and a former co-editor of *Dollars & Sense*.

Jane Slaughter was a staff writer for *Labor Notes* for many years. She is the author of *Concessions and How To Beat Them* and co-author with Mike Parker, of *Choosing Sides: Unions and the Team Concept* and *Working Smart: A Union Guide to Participation Programs and Reengineering*.

Bob Stone is on the editorial collective of *Grassroots Economic Organizing*. He is among the cofounders of the bilingual Center for Global Justice in San Miguel de Allende, Mexico, where he serves as a research associate.

Andrew Strom has been a union lawyer for ten years. He is currently on the staff of Service Employees International Union, Local 32BJ, which represents over 70,000 building service workers in New York, New Jersey, and Connecticut.

Chris Sturr (co-editor of this volume) is co-editor of *Dollars & Sense*.

Anna Sussman is a freelance print and radio reporter.

Jeffrey Thompson is an assistant research professor at the Political Economy Research Institute at the University of Massachusetts-Amherst.

Chris Tilly is a former *Dollars & Sense* collective member and currently the director of of UCLA's Institute for Research on Labor and Employment and professor in the Urban Planning Department.

James Tracy is a San Francisco-based economic justice organizer and writer.

Yolanda Treviño is a former Sony *maquiladora* worker whose testimony against NAFTA is included in the book *NAFTA from Below*.

Marie Trigona is an independent journalist based in Buenos Aires. She is also a member of Grupo Alavío, a direct action and video collective.

Alan Tuckman is a senior lecturer in human resource management at Nottingham Trent University.

Rodney Ward is a longtime labor and peace activist, laid-off flight attendant, and former staff member at *Dollars & Sense,*. Rodney writes extensively about the experience of workers in the airline industry and is also working to form a Flight Attendants for Peace Network.

Jeannette Wicks-Lim is an assistant research professor at the Political Economy Research Institute, UMass-Amherst. The authors thank Alejandro Reuss and Amy Gluckman for their contributions to this article.

Timothy A. Wise, a former editor at *Dollars & Sense*, is deputy director of Tufts University's Global Development and Environment Institute.

"Short Run" authors not listed above:

Carrie Battan, Sudeep Bhatia, Rolande Johndro, Allison MacDonald, Larry Peterson, Michael Rebne, Jason Son, Barbara Sternal, Alissa Thuotte, and **Karina Wagnerman** are former *Dollars & Sense* interns.

Liv Gold and **Tyler Hauck** are former members of the *D&S* collective.

Arthur Conquest is the former *D&S* development director.

Linda Pinkow is the *D&S* development and promotions coordinator.

Editorial assistance with this volume:

Maureen Kellett and Anna Morris are *D&S* interns;

Kate Davies, Amy Gluckman, John Miller, Linda Pinkow, Alejandro Reuss, and **Bryan Snyder** are members of the *D&S* collective.

UNIVERSITY OF MASSACHUSETTS
LABOR
RESOURCE CENTER

The mission of the **Labor Resource Center** (LRC) is to advance the interests of workers and their organizations through education and research. Our work centers on the belief that the labor movement, representing both organized and unorganized workers, is an essential force for economic and social justice.

Through our education and training programs, grounded in the proven principles of **popular education and participatory research**, workers enhance their skills and knowledge as leaders, activists, and citizens. In our participatory action research, we partner with labor, community and government to build collaborative knowledge in the service of change.

The LRC programs include a B.A. and Minor in **Labor Studies** and professional Certificate in **Labor Studies and Leadership**; the **Future of Work Research Initiative**, which conducts and disseminates labor research on economic and workforce development; and the **Labor Extension** program providing non-credit community based worker education.

For more information on the University of Massachusetts Labor Resource Center, visit: www.lrc.umb.edu.